Attitudes towards Sexuality in Judaism and Christianity in the Hellenistic Greco-Roman Era

Enoch, Levi, and Jubilees on Sexuality

ENOCH, LEVI, *and* JUBILEES
on
SEXUALITY

Attitudes towards Sexuality in
the Early Enoch Literature,
the Aramaic Levi Document,
and the Book of Jubilees

William Loader

WILLIAM B. EERDMANS PUBLISHING COMPANY
GRAND RAPIDS, MICHIGAN / CAMBRIDGE, U.K.

Published 2007 by

Wm. B. Eerdmans Publishing Co.

2140 Oak Industrial Drive N.E., Grand Rapids, Michigan 49505 /

P.O. Box 163, Cambridge CB3 9PU U.K.

Printed in the United States of America

11 10 09 08 07   7 6 5 4 3 2 1

ISBN 978-0-8028-2583-4

www.eerdmans.com

Contents

CONTENTS

Acknowledgments

This book marks a first stage in my ongoing research on attitudes towards sexuality in Judaism and Christianity of the Hellenistic era. My initial work on Jubilees was aided by a grant from the Murdoch University Research Excellence Grant Scheme in 2004. The major work represented in the present studies has been undertaken as part of a project funded by the Australian Research Council, who for this purpose granted me a five year Professorial Fellowship, which I commenced mid 2005.

Murdoch University has provided invaluable infrastructure support, not least through the electronic inter-library loan scheme which has found obscure literature for me from all over the world. I have also benefited greatly from my annual pilgrimage to the Theologicum library in Tübingen University, where I have always received a warm welcome and support from the Institut für antikes Judentum und hellenistische Religionsgeschichte under the leadership of Professor Hermann Lichtenberger.

I am especially grateful to those who read and commented on earlier drafts of the main sections of book: George Nickelsburg and Marie-Theres Wacker on the Early Enoch literature; Henryk Drawnel on the *Aramaic Levi Document*, and James VanderKam on *Jubilees*. When it had all come together as one, Mary J. Marshall carefully read the whole and helped me see what author's eyes so seldom see; and for this I am most thankful.

Finally, I express my appreciation to William B. Eerdmans Jr for his support and encouragement, and for his willingness to publish the fruits of this research.

Introduction

The following studies form part of a larger undertaking which plans to examine attitudes towards sexuality in Judaism and Christianity in the Hellenistic Greco-Roman era. Within the time frame of approximately the 3rd century B.C.E. to the end of the 1st century C.E. the works considered here belong to some of the earliest and most influential. This is especially so of what came to be called, *1 Enoch*, a corpus of writings directly or indirectly associated with Enoch, at least one of which reaches back into the 4th century B.C.E. Within that corpus the *Book of the Watchers* (*1 Enoch* 1 – 36) is of particular relevance for understanding attitudes towards sexuality. It influenced later works within the corpus, especially the *Book of Dream Visions* (*1 Enoch* 83 – 90), the *Epistle of Enoch* (*1 Enoch* 92 – 105) and the *Birth of Noah* (*1 Enoch* 106 – 107), as well as the later work, the *Book of Parables* (*1 Enoch* 37 – 71), to which we shall return in a future study. That influence extended also to the *Book of Giants*, which we consider briefly here, and the *Book of Jubilees*. The latter combines Enochic tradition with a rewriting of Genesis and the early chapters of Exodus in producing a work in which sexuality is a major theme which informs both its warnings and its depiction of the blessings of human life. The other work considered here, the *Aramaic Levi Document*, is a fragmentary but fascinating set of priestly instructions, among which we find concern expressed about appropriate marriage and, like *Jubilees* and, to a lesser degree, some of the Enochic writings, about the dangers of intermarriage.

These writings are worthy of detailed study in their own right. The attempt in what follows is to examine each in its own integrity, on the basis that to any broader study of sexuality in the literature of the period belongs first a detailed analysis of each surviving text. At the same time, the investigation of each text cannot be conducted in a vacuum, but needs to take into account the contexts represented by other writings of the time, both those which are contemporary and

1

those which precede or follow. There is a sense in which the investigation of any one writing cannot be complete until the analysis of all is complete. On the other hand, such research must proceed in stages and gradually build towards the larger picture by careful and detailed analysis of each part. This study comprises such detailed analysis. It takes into account, as far as possible, the broad contemporary context of each work and engages the detailed research of others. It necessarily also raises further questions which only a wider study can adequately address, to which this work belongs as only one component.

I have deliberately formulated the focus of the study as "attitudes toward sexuality". In doing so, I am mindful that the word, "sexuality", is sometimes used in a very defined sense to describe study of gender preference or orientation and its formation. I use it here in a much broader sense to describe what others mean by the monosyllabic word, "sex". I have avoided it, in turn, because it, too, is often understood in a narrow way, to refer to sexual intercourse. By "sexuality" I mean, then, behaviours, thoughts and feelings, which people have identified as pertaining to sexual desire and its expression. I throw the net widely to include attitudes towards marriage as one of the contexts in which sexuality plays a role and towards men and women as sexual beings, generally. By using the word "attitudes" I seek to respect the nature of the material before us. We have no direct access to the sexual sensations of the ancient world or their sexuality in that sense, but our texts do provide us with a reflection of attitudes. Whether they corresponded to reality or not, the texts embody attitudes, intended or otherwise, which we can detect and which we can compare with others from the context in order to build a profile which includes a range of aspects.

Our texts sometimes contain explicit warnings relating to sexual behaviour or to actions pertinent to sexual behaviour, such as those about intermarriage in *Jubilees*. The same writing also produces a rewritten account of the creation of man and woman in a manner that gives very positive value to sexual intercourse and sexual intimacy. Occasionally, we are left wondering about the import of stories which depict what the author clearly assumes is forbidden and abominable, such as the Watchers' having sexual relations with women. Does it imply an inauguration of evils marked by similar sexual immorality or is the shocking beginning designed to explain how all kinds of other evil arose, without a particular concern with sexual wrongdoing? Does it also function as an analogy for sexual wrongdoing in the author's time or do the author's interests lie elsewhere. Sometimes there are answers found in the text themselves. Sometimes we are left with hypothetical possibilities.

The matter is all the more complex because, while such authored texts invite our speculation about an author's intentions, the texts, themselves, have a life of their own and, to some extent, also have had, in many cases, a past life, so that our weighing possible attitudes needs to take into account both how a work might have been heard and later interpreted and what assumptions it embodies through its traditions, whether or not these remain central for the author. These issues arise, in particular, with the *Book of the Watchers*, which is widely recognised both as having older component parts which have been through a process of editing and revision and as exercising major influence on subsequent generations.

The studies below seek to interpret the works from within themselves, taking into account literary form, context, and sequence, as well as tradition and redaction, so far as that is discernible (even if discerned, but without resolution). They consider passages and their contexts exegetically, rather than seeking too quickly to produce an abstract of themes or attitudes. They also work closely with the text in translation and with the underlying versions and, where available, the preserved fragments of the works in their original language. In doing so, they reflect the benefit of others' research, as will be evident both in citation of their works and in my engagement and dialogue with their findings.

Part One deals with the early Enoch Literature relevant to the theme. This includes all of so-called *1 Enoch* except the Book of Parables (37 – 71) and the final chapter (108). In treating the *Book of the Watchers* (1 – 36), I deal with it in sequence, beginning with 1 – 5, but giving particular attention to 6 – 11 and to 12 – 16 and then to comparing them, before returning to the consideration of 17 – 19 and 20 – 36 and concluding comments about the work as a whole. Examination of the *Book of Dream Visions* (83 – 90) follows, which has separate discussions of the first vision (83 – 84) and the second vision, the so-called *Animal Apocalypse* (85 – 90). Thereafter come the treatments of the *Epistle of Enoch* (92 – 105) and the *Birth of Noah* (106 – 107), which includes a comparison with similar material in the *Genesis Apocryphon*. Finally, I have included a brief discussion of the *Book of Giants*, not as a one-time component of the Enoch corpus as some have suggested, but because of its related themes.

Part Two deals with the fragmentary *Aramaic Levi Document* as a whole. Part Three, by far the longest, contains the discussion of *Jubilees*. It includes an introductory chapter which identifies the importance of the theme within the overall structure of the work. Chapter Two then deals with various elements within *Jubilees* which deal with sexual wrongdoing, including 3.2.1, "the Watchers" (also a comparison with *1 Enoch*); 3.2.2, Ham and nakedness; 3.2.3, stories of Abraham, including Abram, Sarai and Pharaoh; circumcision, Sodom, and Lot; 3.2.4, issues of intermarriage, including the rape of Dinah (and comparison with *Aramaic Levi Document*); 3.2.5, Reuben and Bilhah; 3.2.6, Joseph and adultery; 3.2.7, the speeches of key figures (Noah, Abraham, Rebecca, Isaac); and 3.2.8, the language of sexual wrongdoing. While focusing on particular passages, each section necessarily draws together material from across the writing, some of which is the focus of detailed attention elsewhere. This is particularly the case in the discussion of intermarriage, but also of some of the discussion in Chapter Three, which deals with the positive aspects in *Jubilees'* attitude towards sexuality. 3.3.1 discusses *Jubilees'* version of the creation of man and woman. 3.3.2 explores the positive image of the patriarchs and their wives (Abraham and Sarah, Isaac and Rebecca, Jacob, Leah and Rachel). Finally 3.3.3 returns to the creation story and the garden, in particular, as part of a treatment of the importance for *Jubilees* of sacred time and space in relation to sexuality. Chapter four, then, draws the findings together.

The conclusion to all three parts, "Concluding Observations", does not seek to repeat or summarise the conclusions of each of the three main parts, but rather to identify common threads and issues arising, which will be pursued in subsequent investigations.

Unless otherwise indicated English translation of biblical passages is based on the New Revised Standard Version.

PART ONE

Attitudes towards Sexuality in the
Early Enoch Literature

The book, *1 Enoch*,[1] preserved in full in translation as part of the canon of the Ethiopian church, consists of five major parts. These are each separate writings originally composed in Aramaic, so that it is appropriate to speak of a corpus of works. In this chapter we are concerned with the earlier works in the collection, among which those relevant to our theme are: *The Book of the Watchers* (*1 Enoch* 1-36, mid- to late third century B.C.E.); *The Book of Dream Visions* (*1 Enoch* 83-90, 164-160 B.C.E. or, possibly in an earlier form, around 200 B.C.E.),[2] *The*

---

[1] See the comprehensive treatment in the ground-breaking first major commentary on *1 Enoch* by George W. E. Nickelsburg, *1 Enoch 1: A Commentary on the Book of 1 Enoch Chapters 1-36, 81-108* (Hermeneia; Minneapolis: Fortress, 2001).

[2] On the various elements of *1 Enoch* see Nickelsburg, *1 Enoch 1*, 7-8 and 21-26, where he discusses the development of the corpus. Its earliest materials are the *Book of the Luminaries* and the two myths about Enoch's ascent and the angelic rebellion contained within *1 Enoch* 6-11. *1 Enoch* 12-16 reworks the Shemihazah myth, having Enoch ascend to heaven and be commissioned to indict the Watchers (25). *1 Enoch* 17-19 then combines the ascent motif with acquisition of cosmological and astronomical knowledge, and this is duplicated in a journey in reverse direction in *1 Enoch* 20-36. *1 Enoch* 1-5 may have beenadded as an introduction to something like the present *Book of the Watchers*, but which may also have included some of the material in 81:5 – 82:3; 91, 94, 104 – 105 (25). It was then expanded at some stage to include the *Book of Dream Visions* ("at least, chaps. 85-90"), and then all of *1 Enoch* 92-105 and 106 – 107, thus producing the compilation attested in 4QEn[c] (25-26). Subsequently an abbreviated form of the *Book of the Luminaries* was inserted after *1 Enoch* 36, a process which led to some relocation of other texts (namely to 81:1 – 82:4) and finally the *Book of Parables* was inserted after *1 Enoch* 36. My discussion

Epistle of Enoch (*1 Enoch* 91-105, second century B.C.E.) and *The Birth of Noah* (*1 Enoch* 106-107, composed before the mid first century B.C.E.). The earliest of all, the *Book of the Luminaries* (*1 Enoch* 72-82, third century B.C.E. or possibly earlier) deals with matters outside our theme. We also append a brief discussion of the *Book of Giants* (late third or early second century B.C.E.). *The Book of the Parables* (*1 Enoch* 37-71) belongs to a later period (possibly mid- to late first century B.C.E. or later) as does *A Final Book by Enoch* (*1 Enoch* 108), which appears to have been added after the incorporation of the *Book of the Parables* into the corpus. We shall deal with these in a later context.

1.1   The Book of the Watchers (1 Enoch 1 – 36)

1.1.1   *1 Enoch 1 – 5*

The opening five chapters of the *Book of the Watchers*, announce the coming judgement, which will bring peace for the righteous and curse and destruction for the wicked.[3] Nowhere within them do we find wickedness related to sexual wrongdoing, although, as Nickelsburg notes, "it is difficult to pinpoint certain sins or kinds of sinners as their primary target".[4] The major comment about wickedness comes in 2:1 – 5:4, which develops the theme of change. The works of the heavens "do not transgress their own appointed order" (2:1).[5] Similarly "nothing on earth

---

will take this reconstruction into account, since I am concerned with exploring the material for its information about attitudes at various stages of their development. See also the discussion in Eibert J. C. Tigchelaar, *Prophets of Old and the Day of the End: Zechariah, the Book of the Watchers and Apocalyptic* (OTS 35; Leiden: Brill, 1996) 134-51, and Annette Yoshiko Reed, *Fallen Angels and the History of Judaism and Christianity: The Reception of Enochic Literature* (New York: Cambridge University Press, 2005), who calls into question Nickelsburg's understanding of the development of the corpus and argues that, for instance, the separate attestation of the *Epistle of Enoch* in Greek witnesses and the substance of this and the other works suggest a collection of discrete documents beyond the *Book of the Watchers* (19-20).

[3] On the function of *1 Enoch* 1 – 5 as introduction to the *Book of the Watchers* with or without 6 – 11 and perhaps with 81, see Nickelsburg, *1 Enoch 1*, 132.

[4] Nickelsburg, *1 Enoch 1*, 133.

[5] Unless otherwise indicated, the English translation is that of George W. E. Nickelsburg, and James C. VanderKam, *1 Enoch: A New Translation* (Minneapolis: Fortress, 2004). For another contemporary translation see Daniel C. Olson in consultation with Melkesedek Workeneh, *Enoch: A New Translation; The Ethiopic Book of Enoch, or 1 Enoch, Translated with Annotations and Cross-References* (North Richland Hills, Tex.: BIBAL Press, 2004).

changes" (2:2). God's "works take place from year to year, and they all carry out their works for him, and their works do not alter, but they all carry out his word" (5:1). By contrast, people "have not stood firm nor acted according to his commandments" (5:4). Beyond that, the indictment adds: "you have turned aside, you have spoken proud and hard words with your unclean mouth against his majesty. Hard of heart! There will be no peace for you!" (5:4). These recall 1:9, which speaks of judgement on humanity "for all the wicked deeds that they have done, and the proud and hard words that wicked sinners spoke against him" (similarly 27:2, "who utter with their mouth an improper word against the Lord and speak hard things against his glory"; 101:3, "Why do you speak with your mouth proud and hard things against his majesty? You will have no peace").

We are left wondering what might be meant by the allusion to speaking "proud and hard words". One might assume that these are words spoken by people who in the mind of the author matter, so that the accusation is probably against people in power or who exercise some power. Nickelsburg notes: "This may refer to blasphemy, strictly speaking, to idolatry and the eating of idolatrous food, or to the consumption of blood and/or food forbidden by divine law".[6]

Equally interesting is the emphasis on order and change. This may be nothing more than an elaborate way of saying one should obey commandments as creation does. It could, however, suggest more than this, namely that some in such disobedience are actually acting contrary to the order of creation.[7] This background may well be borne in mind as hearers go on to listen to the story of the fall of the Watchers, who were disobedient by abandoning their ordered place and engaging in sexual intercourse with human women. The words, "There will be no peace for you!", in 5:4 find their echo in the words which Enoch was instructed to say to the rebellious Watchers: "You will have no peace!" (16:4). The formulation stands under the influence of Isa 48:22 ("There is no peace, says the LORD, for the wicked").[8] As the Watchers are condemned, so these people are condemned, an important structural analogy for interpreting 6 – 11 and 12 – 16, but nothing at this point suggests the sins are the same. In *1 Enoch* 98:9 – 99:10, which contains parallel material (and note the direct parallel in 101:3 cited above), the concern is calendar and this may already be the case in *1 Enoch* 1-5.[9]

On the positive side, the promises to the righteous are heavily influenced by Isaiah 65 and reflect hope of a long life on a renewed earth, not one in a heavenly

---

[6] Nickelsburg, *1 Enoch 1*, 47. He suggests the link with food may be intimated by the reference to impure mouths in 5:4, as in *Joseph and Asenath* 8:6; 11:9-9; 12:5 (158). "Thus the words of 5:4b could be directed against idolatrous teaching of a revisionist torah" (158).

[7] Nickelsburg, *1 Enoch 1*, notes the motif of nature's obedience in Jer 5:20-29; Sir 16:24-30; 1QS 3.15 – 4.26; *T. Naph.* 3:2 – 4:1; 1Q34^{bis} 3.1-4; *Pss. Sol.* 18:10-12 (153-54).

[8] So Olson, *Enoch*, 31.

[9] Nickelsburg, *1 Enoch 1*, 134, 158.

realm nor expressed as everlasting (5:7-9).[10] It is, therefore, not envisaged as a place where there is no need for procreation – and therefore, if one followed the reasoning of 15:6-7, sexual relations. The emphasis in *1 Enoch* 2:1 – 5:4 on order has the potential to be used in relation to sexual issues in a number of ways. This does not appear to happen in *1 Enoch* 1 – 5. On the other hand, as part of the introduction to the *Book of the Watchers*, it does provide a significant background for the breach of order in relation to sexual relations which is recounted in the chapters which follow. In addition, the intratextual link between 5:4 and 16:4, condemning perpetrators to having no peace, reinforces the connection.

1.1.2   *1 Enoch 6 – 11*

1 Enoch 1 – 36 brings the account of the rebellion of the Watchers in *1 Enoch* 6 – 8 and the response to it in 9 – 11. I shall first consider this material as it now stands and then turn to possible traditions which lie behind it. While it now stands as central in *1 Enoch* 1 – 36, it makes no mention of Enoch and must be seen as material which the author of the *Book of the Watchers* has taken up into his work. Coming immediately after the introductory chapters, it presents itself for the hearer in the light of concern with order and change and relates this explicitly to sexual wrongdoing. The account of the rebellion is an elaboration of Gen 6:1-4.[11]

1 Enoch 6	Genesis 6
1 When the sons of men had multiplied, in those days, beautiful and comely daughters were born to them. 2 And the Watchers, the sons of heaven, saw them and desired them. And they said to one another, "Come, let us	1 When people began to multiply on the face of the ground, and daughters were born to them, 2 the sons of God saw that they were fair; and they took wives for themselves of all that they chose.

---

[10] Nickelsburg, *1 Enoch 1*, points to the parallel idea in 25:6 and *Jub.* 23:27, suggesting 5:9 "may indicate a life as long as the prediluvian patriarchs" (164). See also George W. E. Nickelsburg, "Where is the Place of Eschatological Blessing?" in *Things Revealed: Studies in Early Jewish and Christian Literature in Honor of Michael E. Stone* (ed. Esther G. Chazon, David Satran, and Ruth A. Clements; JSJSup 89; Leiden: Brill, 2004) 53-71, 54.

[11] Devorah Dimant, "*1 Enoch* 6-11: A Fragment of a Parabiblical Work.," *JJS* 53 (2002) 223-37, notes the author's citation of Genesis, followed by a pattern of biblical and non-biblical expansions, in a manner unparalleled in the rest of the corpus of *1 Enoch* (225): biblical quotation in 6:1-2, then expansion in 6:2-8; biblical quotation (7:1ab) then non-biblical expansion in 7:1c; biblical expansion in 7:2ab, 7:3-6; non-biblical expansion partially based on biblical texts in 8:1-4; expansion based on biblical text (9:1); non-biblical expansion in 9:2-11; biblical expansion in 10:1-3; non-biblical expansion in 10:4 – 11:2 (226-28). For further discussion of the relation of *1 Enoch* 6 – 11 to Genesis and other ancient near eastern traditions see the review below, following the treatment of 6 – 11 and 12 – 16.

choose for ourselves wives from the daughters of men, and let us beget children for ourselves."	

Whereas Genesis[12] simply reports that the women *were fair*, *1 Enoch* has "beautiful and comely".[13] "The sons of God" become "the Watchers, the sons of heaven", an interpretation consistent with the usage of "the sons of God" elsewhere to refer to angels.[14] *1 Enoch* 1:2 had already referred to "the Watchers and holy ones" (also 1:5).[15] For "saw" (Gen 6:2) *1 Enoch* expands: "saw them and desired (ἐπεθύμησαν) them". Similarly *1 Enoch* elaborates "and they took wives for themselves of all that they chose" (Gen 6:2) by reporting conversation: "Come, let us choose for ourselves wives from the daughters of men, and let us beget children for ourselves." The effect is to emphasise desire as lust. It also reflects the assumption that angels do not normally beget, because they have no such need. The desire to beget children represents a corruption of what they were created to be, eternal beings. This reflects, in turn, the assumption that they are all male and that sexual activity has no place in their order of being. We shall return to this below because it becomes a topic of reflection in 15:4-7. Their choice to have

---

[12] See the recent review of research on Gen 6:1-4 in Archie T. Wright, *The Origin of Evil Spirits: The Reception of Genesis 6.1-4 in Early Jewish Literature*. (WUNT 2.198; Tübingen: Mohr Siebeck, 2005) 51-95.

[13] This assumes the Aramaic contained both adjectives. On this see the discussion in Siam Bhayro, *The Shemihazah and Asael Narrative of 1 Enoch 6-11: Introduction, Text, Translation and Commentary with Reference to Ancient Near Eastern and Biblical Antecedents* (AOAT 322; Münster: Ugarit, 2005), who notes that this is far from secure (119).

[14] "Sons of God" are a known category of heavenly beings reflected in Deut 32:8; Ps 29:1; 89:6-7; 82:6-7 (only here negative); Job 1:6; 2:1; and 38:7, and are the equivalent of "the host of heaven" as in Deut 4:19; Psalm 82; Josh 5:14-15 ; Judg 5:20; and 1 Kgs 22:19. On this see Ronald Hendel, "The Nephilim were on the Earth: Genesis 6:1-4 and its Ancient Near Eastern Context," in *The Fall of the Angels* (ed. Christoph Auffarth and Loren T. Stuckenbruck; Themes in Biblical Narrative 6; Leiden: Brill, 2004) 11-34, 19-20; and see Wright, *Evil Spirits*, 61-75, 101-102. He draws attention to a possible allusion to the watcher myth in Ps 82:5, "They do not know nor understand, in darkness they go about; all the foundations of the earth are shaken" (68-69).

[15] Bhayro, *Shemihazah and Asael Narrative*, sees the original use of "Watchers" in 6:2 as a parody on diviners and divination which an author is attacking (228-32). He sees in it an allusion to Babylonian diviners (Akkadian *barû* means a Babylonian diviner and is related to the verb to watch) (22-24). See also Nickelsburg, *1 Enoch 1*, who notes: "Although the Greek and Ethiopic translations frequently use the term 'angel' (ἄγγελος, *mal'ak*), its Aramaic equivalent מלאכא does not occur in the preserved Qumran fragments, which use עיר where the translations employ ἄγγελος and *mal'ak*" (44). See also his excursus: "the Watchers and the Holy Ones", 140-41.

sexual intercourse with human women is now also a corruption and abandonment of their order of being. It is a forbidden mixing of kinds (cf. Deut 22:9-11; Lev 18:22-23).[16] Thus what appears in Gen 6:1-2 without evaluative commentary[17] becomes in *1 Enoch* 6:1-2 an account of rebellion in which three changes put the emphasis on sexual wrongdoing: the enhanced description of the women, the addition of "lust" and the desire to beget.[18] The detail about choice which *1 Enoch* reproduces from Genesis in the form, "Let us choose for ourselves", now carries negative connotations, probably implying indiscriminate sexual relations, which might be without regard to marital status (adultery).[19]

Assuming hearers would not listen to the *Book of the Watchers* or even 6 – 11 just a single time, we may suspect that their hearing will also have been informed by 8:1, according to which the women played more than a passive role. Their beauty and comeliness was in part the fruit of their fathers' producing cosmetics with the skills they had learned from Asael on an apparently earlier angelic descent. Thus the women contributed to the Watchers' going astray.

6:3-7 does not follow smoothly after 6:2, which has portrayed the Watchers as encouraging each other to act. For it focuses on Shemihazah[20] and his fear that they might not join him and that he would be left to act alone and alone bear the guilt (6:3). They respond with an oath and "bound one another with a curse" (6:5), which enhances the deliberateness of their act.[21] *1 Enoch* numbers them at two

---

[16] On this see Ida Fröhlich, "'*Mamzer*' in Qumran Texts – The Problem of Mixed Marriages from Ezra's Time: Law, Literature and Practice," *Transeuphratène* 29 (2005) 103-15, who traces the history of the prohibition of mixing of kinds and *mamzērut* from Deuteronomy to Qumran.

[17] Nickelsburg, *1 Enoch 1*, 176; Wright, *Evil Spirits*, 6, 89.

[18] So James C. VanderKam, "Biblical Interpretation in *1 Enoch* and *Jubilees*," in *From Revelation to Canon: Studies in Hebrew Bible and Second Temple Literature* (JSJSup 62. Leiden: Brill, 2000) 276-304, 285; Dimant, "*1 Enoch* 6 – 11," 229-30. She also notes that the emphasis on begetting reflects a reading of Gen 6:4 which vocalises ילד not as *qal*, so that women beget, but as *hophal*, reflected also in *Sam. Pent.*: יוליד and probably in the LXX rendering ἐγεννῶσαν (231), thus more intentional.

[19] Dimant, "*1 Enoch* 6 – 11," suggests the author may have in mind betrothed and married women. She notes the designation of the offspring in 10:9 as *Mamzerim* (231). On the possibility that it includes lack of regard to menstrual cycles (defilement), as some interpretations of 10:11 ("in their uncleanness") and later of 15:4 ("with the blood of women") suppose, see the discussion on 7:1 below.

[20] On the name, Shemihazah, see Bhayro, *Shemihazah and Asael Narrative*, who suggests it originates in the association between a deity, Shem, and Mount Hazzi (Mt Hermon), but came to be interpreted in the context of divination, but taking Hazah as deriving from the verb חזא "to see" (233-35).

[21] So VanderKam, "Biblical Interpretation," 285.

hundred and names their chiefs.[22] Bhayro draws attention to the influence of the story of Absalom and the two hundred with him who rebelled against David and forsook Jerusalem for Hebron (2 Sam 15:7-12), which he notes has some verbal similarity to Hermon.[23] Absalom's having sexual intercourse with his father's concubines (2 Sam 16:20-22) may have helped make the connection. The Watchers descend in the days of Jared on Mt Hermon. At its base was a shrine of Pan, notorious for sexual adventure.[24] The author employs a Hebrew word play between Jared and "descend" and Hermon and "curse".[25] In terms of the severity of their wrongdoing, this is underlined in these verses in two ways: the oath and the words of Shemihazah which speak of it as "a great sin" (6:3), a term used to describe gross sexual wrongdoing in Gen 20:9 and later in *T. Reub.* 1:10 and *T. Jud.* 14:3, 4.[26]

7:1 then elaborates:

> These and all the others with them took for themselves wives from among them such as they chose. And they began to go into them, and to defile themselves through them,

---

[22] On the etymology of the names, which mainly reflect astronomical, meteorological and geographical phenomena, see the table and discussion in Marianne Dacy, "Paradise Lost: The Fallen Angels in the Book of Enoch," *Australian Journal of Jewish Studies* 17 (2003) 51-65, 54-59; and Olson, *Enoch*, 32.

[23] See Bhayro, *Shemihazah and Asael Narrative*, 237-38. He cites 1 Sam 15:23, which equates rebellion with witchcraft to account for its use (238). Bhayro claims a discrepancy between 6:6 and 6:7-8 on the basis that whereas the former uses the figure 200, the latter speaks of 10 groups of 20 led by a further 20 (240). This may be demanding too much precision.

[24] Nickelsburg, *1 Enoch 1*, notes: "Pan's association with the female spirits and his other amorous episodes raise an interesting question. Is it coincidental that the story of the Watchers and the women is set in a geographical location that is also connected with a god known for his sexual misadventures?" (245). On the sacred geography of the region in *1 Enoch* 6 – 16, see pp. 238-47, and also David W. Suter, "Mapping the First Book of Enoch: Geographical Issues in George Nickelsburg's Commentary," in *George W.E. Nickelsburg in Perspective: An Ongoing Dialogue of Learning* (2 vols; ed. Jacob Neusner and Alan J. Avery-Peck; JSJSup 80; Leiden: Brill, 2003) 2. 387-94.

[25] On this see Dimant, "*1 Enoch* 6 – 11," who argues that the author has used Hebrew sources, which include the names of Watchers and giants, but also puns relating those names to the functions of each (235). She also notes echoes of Hebrew prayers in 9:4-11 (235). On this see, however, Bhayro, *Shemihazah and Asael Narrative*, who argues that Hebrew puns in *1 Enoch* 6 – 11 "would have been readily understandable to its readers" (237). See also his critique of Dimant's appeal (238) to the possibly related Hebrew texts in 1Q19 and 1Q20, which he sees as too fragmentary (5).

[26] So Nickelsburg, *1 Enoch 1*, 176, who also points to its use in relation to other wrongdoing: idolatry (Exod 32:21, 30, 31; 2 Kgs 17:21; *1 Enoch* 104:9) and possibly murder (*T. Gad* 6:2-5).

and to teach them sorcery and charms, and to reveal to them the cutting of roots and plants.

The words, "took for themselves wives from among them such as they chose",[27] is a second reference to Gen 6:2, "they took wives for themselves of all that they chose" and has the effect of underlining what appears to be indiscriminate choice noted above in relation to *1 Enoch* 6:2. Again the author brings out the nature of the "great sin": "they began to go into them", referring to the act of sexual intercourse. The addition of "began to" implies not a single act, but a continuing activity, and its result: they began "to defile themselves through them".[28] The emphasis lies not on taking wives in the sense of setting up households, but on illicit sexual relations. Within that context *1 Enoch* also reports evil influence by way of imparting forbidden knowledge, so that the issue is more than sexual relations, though that is the primary concern.[29] The focus is initially on the impact, not on the women, but on the Watchers: defilement.[30]

One who has heard the first five chapters would doubtless relate this, their defilement, to the transgression of boundaries of order. This is also to be assumed in 6 – 11, taken on its own. A transgression of a forbidden boundary has taken place and the result is contamination for the Watchers. Later in 14:23; 15:3; and

---

[27] On the textual variations see Nickelsburg, *1 Enoch 1*, 182. The detail of "choice" is attested in 4QEn^a. See also Bhayro, *Shemihazah and Asael Narrative*, who prefers the translation of the Ethiopic as "everyone chose for himself a few" (138).

[28] The Ethiopic in 7:1 has "were promiscuous with" (from *dammara* "to insert, mix in, join together, unite, mix"; related to the word for marriage, *tedmert*), whereas the Palipolitanus Greek codex has μιαίνεσθαι "to defile" (similar to μείγνεσθαι "to mix"). Michael A. Knibb, *The Ethiopic Book of Enoch: A New Edition in the Light of the Aramaic Dead Sea Fragments: In Consultation with Edward Ullendorf* (2 vols; Oxford: Clarendon, 1978), suggests the difference reflects confusion between the Aramaic verbs טמא "to defile" and טמע "to mix" (2. 77). See also Bhayro, *Shemihazah and Asael Narrative*, 138-39.

[29] Wright, *Evil Spirits*, argues that the formulation in Gen 6:2 (and so in *1 Enoch* 6:2 and 7:1) does not suggest marriage, when one would expect the verb לקח to be followed by לאשה or לנשים (132-36), but to taking women. While I agree that a primary focus is the illicit sexual intercourse – and the allusion to Absalom implied in the 200 in 6:6 confirms this – 7:1 delineates the taking from the entering in a way that makes sense of speaking of their taking wives, and so I retain "wives" in the translation, where he argues for "women".

[30] See Nickelsburg, *1 Enoch 1*, who rightly insists that the defilement here and in 9:8 and 10:11 is not about the earth, but about the Watchers, and is incidental to the author's major theme, which is the violence wrought by the deeds of the Watchers (184). Cf. David Winston Suter, "Fallen Angel, Fallen Priest: The Problem of Family Purity in *1 Enoch*," *HUCA* 50 (1979) 115-35, 115-19; Corrie Molenberg, "A Study of the Roles of Shemihaza and Asael in *1 Enoch* 6-11," *JJS* 35 (1984) 136-46, 139.

12:4 we find the notion that the Watchers belonged to the realms of the holy and presumably some of them might have exercised a priestly function. Something like this may perhaps be assumed here. *1 Enoch.* 9:1 appears to speak of Michael, Sariel, Raphael and Gabriel looking down from "the sanctuary of heaven".[31] Michael is to exercise a high priestly function of purifying the earth in 10:20-22.[32] This does not however allow us to conclude that the author of *1 Enoch* 6 – 11 sees all the sinning Watchers as priests. It does nevertheless support the notion that this is more than simply the mixing of kinds, as though the same might equally be said in reverse of the women. Rather these are special, heavenly beings, whose act has defiled what otherwise would have remained undefiled and holy.

There are two further references to defilement in *1 Enoch* 6 – 11: 9:8, which, like 7:1, offers no elaboration and 10:11, which speaks of the Watchers mating with the daughters of men, "so that they were defiled by them in their uncleanness". This is commonly understood as a reference to women when they are in a state of uncleanness during menstruation (Lev 15:19-24).[33] The reference in 12 – 16 to the Watchers defiling themselves with the blood of women in 15:4 might also point in this direction. Sexual intercourse with menstruating women is cited as one of the instances of sexual wrongdoing in CD 5.6-7; *Pss. Sol.* 8:12.[34] But it would be strikingly specific here in 10:11, and also rather surprising, since it would mean that hearers were supposed to make that specific association already in 7:1 and 9:8, where no such indication is to hand.[35] Surely the author means us to imagine that they specifically sought out menstruating women. This interpretation is also problematic, as Wright observes, because menstruation rules out the possibility of conception, which is central to the myth.[36] None of the other accounts of the Watchers myth makes this specific charge. It would also be difficult to imagine that only this aspect defiled, that is, only when the Watchers engaged in sexual intercourse with menstruating women. The apparent emphasis on indiscriminate choice, which we have noted above as implied in the words,

---

[31] On the uncertainty surrounding "sanctuary" here, see the discussion on 9:1 below.

[32] So Nickelsburg, *1 Enoch 1*, who notes: "at least some of them serve as priests in the heavenly sanctuary (15:3); thus Michael, one of the chief among their number, can serve as the eschatological high priest, who purifies the defiled earth (10:20-22)" (44).

[33] See also Dimant, "*1 Enoch* 6 – 11," who identifies the defilement as either because of mixing of kinds or different kind or because of menstruating women, referring to 15:4 and Lev 15:19-24 (232). See also Nickelsburg, *1 Enoch 1*, who draws attention to the use of ἀκαρθαρσία to refer a woman's period of menstruation in 2 Sam 11:4 (225).

[34] Nickelsburg, *1 Enoch 1*, 271-72.

[35] Nickelsburg, *1 Enoch 1*, observes: "Here and in 9:8, different from 10:11, the uncleanness is due simply to sexual contact and not contact with women's blood. Cf. 12:4 and 15:3 over against 15:4" (184).

[36] Wright, *Evil Spirits*, 130.

"Let us choose for ourselves" (6:2), picking up "they took wives for themselves of all that they chose" from Gen 6:2, might lend some support to this understanding (i.e. they did not care if a woman was menstruating), but the problems remain.

Kvanvig has proposed that the defilement relates to the role women's blood was understood to have in conception and so is referring here to another aspect of the forbidden act of procreation. He cites Wis 7:1-2,

> I also am mortal, like everyone else, a descendant of the first-formed child of earth; and in the womb of a mother I was moulded into flesh, within the period of ten months, compacted with blood, from the seed of a man and the pleasure of marriage,

and explains that this understanding is attested in Aristotle and in later rabbinic literature. "When the male semen meets the female blood, the foetus begins to form, the female blood is fixed by the semen of the male."[37] In this process the Watchers defiled themselves with female blood. This has the advantage of applying potentially to all women and giving emphasis also to their intention to beget.

Himmelfarb, noting the reference to blood in 15:4, has suggested that it refers to the blood shed at first intercourse.[38] That assumes the Watchers sought out only virgins. Support for this view comes from the author of the *Animal Apocalypse* who portrays the women as calves *ṭaʿwā*. (86:3-4). The reference to daughters in 6:1 and 8:1 further reinforces this. In addition, one may suspect that the author would understand the Watchers to have espoused the common values of the day which put a high premium on virginity and would have sought for themselves accordingly only the best, namely virgins. This need not, however, be assumed, since *T. Reub.* 5:6 speaks of the angels appearing to women while they were having intercourse with their husbands. According to *m. Nid.* 1.3 the blood of a virgin does not make a man unclean.[39] If we assume a similar understanding on the part of the author, then a specific reference to the blood of first intercourse is unlikely or is to be taken not as a reference to blood impurity in a narrow sense, but as representative of one instance of the impurity caused through crossing the boundary and mixing with human flesh and blood.

Kvanvig and Himmelfarb are addressing the reference to blood in 15:4. Their solutions do not help to explain 10:11, if we understand by "in their uncleanness" a reference to a period of uncleanness. Menstruation might fit both, but is otherwise problematic, as we have seen, and, in any case, we cannot necessarily

---

[37] Helge S. Kvanvig, "Gen 6,3 and the Watcher Story," *Henoch* 25 (2003) 277-300, 291.

[38] Martha Himmelfarb, *The Ascent to Heaven in Jewish and Christian Apocalypses* (Oxford: Oxford University Press, 1993) 21.

[39] See Wright, *Evil Spirits*, 130.

assume that 10:11 should be read in the light of 15:4. The Aramaic of 10:11 is not preserved. Ge'ez uses *rek^ws*, a word meaning "impurity, defilement, uncleanness" and with it the verb "to be corrupted", from *māsana*; Greek (both Panopolitanus and Syncellus) uses ἀκαρθαρσία and with it the verb, "to be defiled", μιανθῆναι. In 10:11 one might read "in their uncleanness" as a reference not to time, but to the nature of women as unclean in relation to the Watchers.[40] In other words, it expressed the understanding that all human women were unclean for the Watchers as sexual partners at all times because they were of a different kind. For them, therefore, the sexual intercourse was not as innocent as the natural defilement which takes places through sexual intercourse or through touching a corpse, neither of which meets moral disapproval. For them, rather, it is a forbidden relationship, so that their defilement falls into the category of abomination.

Therefore, rather than seeing 10:11 (and so 7:1 and 9:8) as singling out particular acts of sexual intercourse by the Watchers with menstruating women, or women conceiving or virgins, it makes better sense to see it referring to defilement by having sexual intercourse with people unclean and forbidden for them. As Nickelsburg notes, we find the word, ἀκαρθαρσία *rek^ws* "impurity", used with more general application in 10:20 in relation to the uncleanness of the earth (ἀκαρθαρσία also in 10:22).[41] Their coming into contact with women's blood (as in 15:4) should not be taken as the key for understanding defilement in 7:1 and 9:8 and "uncleanness" in 10:11, nor should 10:11 (uncleanness) be taken as the basis for interpreting blood in 15:4, which is best understood as a broad allusion to mixing with human flesh and blood.

In the final section of 7:1 we then find a new aspect of the Watchers' wrongdoing: they began "to teach them sorcery and charms (Codex Panopolitanus: φαρμακείας καὶ ἐπαοιδάς; 4QEn^a preserves only חרשה), and to reveal to them the cutting of roots and plants". It is not immediately apparent that giving knowledge about "the cutting of roots and plants" is something bad (cf. *Jub.* 10:12), except that it is related here to sorcery, which *1 Enoch* assumes is forbidden. Here we see the association of women with sorcery. These women, then, are bearers of an evil tradition. Sorcery is in that sense gendered. Tigchelaar notes that "quite a number of the instructed sorceries are believed to be tied up with sexual immorality", pointing out also that חרשה φαρμακεία "can have the specific sense of 'love potions'".[42] In 8:3 we also have reference to what

---

[40] Wright, *Evil Spirits*, 131, relates the defilement to the bloodshed brought to earth by their actions, but the specific texts, 7:1; 9:8 and 10:11, focus primarily on the angels, themselves.

[41] Nickelsburg, *1 Enoch 1*, 225.

[42] Tigchelaar, *Prophets of Old*, 179. Discussing the link between women and sorcery he refers to Nah 3:4 and 2 Kgs 9:22 and the work of L. Blau, *Das altjüdische Zauberwesen* (Strasburg: Trübner, 1898) 18, 21-22, 24, 51-52. Note also Exod 22:18, which singles out

Shemihazah and his chiefs taught their wives ("cutting of plants and roots" specifically by Shemihazah; "sorcery, charms and spells" by Hermani).

Finally, 7:2 refers to their offspring: "great giants. And the giants begot Nephilim, and to the Nephilim were born Elioud".[43] This reflects interpretation of the somewhat confusing and apparently neutral statement in Gen 6:4,

> The *Nephilim* were on the earth in those days – and also afterward – when the sons of God went in to the daughters of humans, who bore children to them. These were the heroes that were of old, warriors of renown.

The mention of three categories of giants derives from Syncellus and is not attested in either the Ethiopic or the Greek of Panopolitanus and may not be original, though it is present in *Jubilees* and reflected in the three kinds of animals in the *Animal Apocalypse*.[44] It has its origins in the three different words used for the angels' offspring in Gen 6:4,[45] but plays no further role in the context.

According to *1 Enoch* 7:3-5, the beings generated by the Watchers' "great sin" outstripped the food supply, becoming carnivores, then eating human beings,

---

the sorceress for execution. Cf. Deut 18:9-14, which lists a range of such "abhorrent practices of those nations", without making them gender-specific. The example, *par excellence*, of idolatrous influence through wives is Solomon (1 Kings 11:1-8).

[43] On the identification of the three categories of giants see Nickelsburg, *1 Enoch 1*, 184-85. See also Hendel, *"Nephilim,"* who notes the reference to them in the J material in Num 13:32-33 and in Amos 2:9 (21-22). While noting the etymology of their name from *npl* "fallen" (in the flood), Num 13:32-33 suggests some survived (22). See also Loren T. Stuckenbruck, "The Origins of Evil in Jewish Apocalyptic Tradition: The Interpretation of Gen 6:1-4 in the Second and Third Centuries B.C.E.," in *The Fall of the Angels* (ed. Christoph Auffarth and Loren T. Stuckenbruck; Themes in Biblical Narrative 6; Leiden: Brill, 2004) 87-118. He notes that the description of Nimrod as a mighty man and grandson of Noah and of *Nephilim* in Num 13:33 opened the possibility either of seeing Noah as one of the giants (96) or of concluding that some giants did indeed survive the flood (91-93). The latter possibility is reflected in *Ps. Eupolemus*, who assumes there were both good and bad giants, and may also have understood Noah to have been a giant (93-98).

[44] So George Nickelsburg (personal note 14 March, 2006). See the discussion in Bhayro, *Shemihazah and Asael Narrative*, who suggests that Syncellus has imported this detail from *Jub.*7:22 (140-41). In defence of the reading above: Nickelsburg, *1 Enoch 1*, 182-83, 184; also Olson, *Enoch*, 263-65.

[45] On the names see further Tigchelaar, *Prophets of Old*, 212-13, where he discusses them in relation to the addition by Syncellus at 16:1. He writes: "I suspect Elioud is a Graecization of (ילידים) (212) which, he notes, occurs in Num 13:22, 28; Josh 15:14; 1 Chron 20:4 and 2 Sam 21:16, 18, in relation to the children of Anak, Rapha, or the Rephaim … noted for their tallness, and henceforth … also called giants" (212-13). See also Olson, *Enoch*, 34.

and finally eating each other. In doing so, they also drank blood, which *1 Enoch* and its hearers know is strictly forbidden.[46] It is interesting to note here that sexual wrongdoing plays no role in this description of the effects of the Watchers' "great sin" and the behaviour of the giants as "the lawless ones" (7:6). One might easily have expected that they would carry on the sins of the Watchers, engaging in acts of sexual wrongdoing. Rape was (is) common in warfare. Instead, they are monsters, the fruit of illicit sexual union, creating chaos, but in the description of the chaos we find no further sexual references. One might at most speculate that sinning against "birds and beasts and creeping things and fish" could entail bestiality, at least, with beasts, but nothing here or elsewhere suggests this is so.

In 8:1 we meet, somewhat unmediated, the figure of Asael, known to the hearer thus far through 6:7 as the tenth of the leaders of the 200 who accompanied Shemihazah. There is an allusion to sexual wrongdoing in the account of what he taught people, namely metalwork. For they learned not only to make weapons and armour, but also "bracelets and ornaments for women. And he showed them concerning antimony and eye paint and all manner of precious stones and dyes" (8:1b). These are not pieces of innocent information, as the sequel shows: "And the sons of men made them for themselves and for their daughters, and they transgressed and led the holy ones astray" (8:1c).[47] The latter text derives from Syncellus and is not secure. On the other hand, already the allusion to jewellery and cosmetics taught to women before the descent of Shemihazah and his accomplices opens the possibility that the women would be seen as at least complicit in the act of sexual wrongdoing, just as the instruction about weaponry

---

[46] As Molenberg, "Roles of Shemihaza and Asael," puts it, "they committed the ultimate outrage against the Levitical dietary laws" (139). Bhayro, *Shemihazah and Asael Narrative*, draws attention to the drinking of blood in later magical literature (242), but the focus in 7:6 does not seem to be magic, but rather extreme violence and abuse. See also Wright, *Evil Spirits*, 147-48.

[47] On the basis for this reading see Nickelsburg, *1 Enoch 1*, 188-89. Both the Ethiopic and the Greek of Panopolitanus include a statement which explicitly mentions sexual wrongdoing: "And there was much impiety and much fornication" (Ethiopic), "... and they committed fornication" (Greek). But see also Bhayro, *Shemihazah and Asael Narrative*, who notes that the subjects of the verbs in 8:2a are not clear (do they refer to the women or the angels?) (150) and sees the words, "led astray the holy ones", as part of Syncellus' embellishment and not as reflecting what would have been in the original (149 and 140-41). Thus he writes: "Syncellus ... would reverse the original sense of the narrative and posit the blame for the corruption of the angels with the human women" (246). 4Q202 (4QEnoch^b) 3.1 may contain a trace of 8:2 which uses the verb פחז, ("to be undisciplined, reckless"), a verb used with reference to sexual wantonness or excess in Gen 49:4 and *Aramaic Levi Document* 6:3 / 16. Only the letters פ are preserved. On this see Henryk Drawnel, *An Aramaic Wisdom Text from Qumran: A New Interpretation of the Levi Document* (JSJSup 86; Leiden: Brill, 2004) 266.

and armour implies evil consequences in their use. The effect is to supplement the comment in 6:1 that the daughters of men were "beautiful and comely". They were so in part because of cosmetics and ornamentation and these contributed to the fall of the Watchers. Supplied with such wiles by their fathers, women now appear not as victims of the Watchers' deeds, but as in part their cause. Women led them astray.[48]

This assumes that Asael commenced his teaching before the Watchers' fall. If, however, the authors of 6 – 11 saw the teaching of Asael taking place after the initial descent or part of it, then his work enhances the seductiveness of women only after the event and does not contribute to the event itself.[49] This is a possible reading, though not the way that, for instance, the author of the *Animal Apocalypse* saw it. He deduced the sequence of events as implying the prior descent of Asael, when he has first one star descend and cause lusting, and then the other stars descend and engage in sexual intercourse with the cows (86:1-4). It coheres also with the form of the myth known to *Jubilees* according to which Watchers were giving human beings instruction (indeed, their divinely commissioned role) before the sin.[50] The teaching in 8:1 was, however – different from in *Jubilees* – already sin, a fact underlined by 10:8 ("all the earth was made desolate by the deeds of the teaching of Asael, and over him write all the sins").

The detail about bracelets and cosmetics thus links the story of Asael's descent with the story of the descent of Shemihazah and his 200 by explaining what made the women additionally attractive.[51] The awkwardness in *1 Enoch* 6 – 8 is still far from resolved by this link and invites traditio-historical explanation, as many have noted, and to which we shall return. As it stands, the effect is to include women's sexuality, enhanced by cosmetics and jewellery, as a cause of the "great sin". This also coheres in that sense with the note in 7:1 that Shemihazah and his

---

[48] By implication, their fathers are also culpable, much as Hos 4:12-14 also implicates the fathers of wayward daughters. I thank Marie-Theres Wacker (personal correspondence 10 April, 2006) for this link.

[49] So Olson, *Enoch*, who notes no reference to the punishment of the women (rejecting the reading, "sirens" in 19:2) and so suggesting this sequence is "thus clearing these women of all blame" (268).

[50] See also Nickelsburg, *1 Enoch 1*, who draws attention to what appears to be evidence of an old tradition in *Ps. Clem. Hom.* 8:11-15, according to which angels descended in human form to show up sin, but then fell to human lust (196). He points also to Justin, *Apol. II* 2.5, for the idea that women were seducers to *Tg. Ps.-J.* Gen 6:2 and *T. Reub.* 5 (195). Tertullian, *De cult. fem.* 1.2, also draws on *1 Enoch* 8:1-2, citing it within its warnings against women's seductive adornment.

[51] Nickelsburg, *1 Enoch 1*, notes that were *1 Enoch* 8:1 not to refer to the seduction of the Watchers, "the passage would have to imply a polemic against sexual seduction in general – a concern that is evident nowhere else in these chapters (196).

Watchers taught women sorcery and charms, which will have been understood as including activities related to sexual behaviour.

In 8:3 we find further detail of teaching given by the Watchers. *1 Enoch* 8:1 focused on metallurgy and related ornamentation and cosmetics as Asael's contribution. In 8:3 the author returns to Shemihazah and seven other named Watchers, listing each's contribution. Shemihazah teaches spells and the cutting of roots; Hermani teaches "sorcery for the loosing of spells and magic and skill". These match the description in 7:1 ("sorcery and charms ... cutting of roots and plants"). The rest, as also their names indicate, give knowledge about astronomical (probably astrological) and meteorological signs.[52] This relates to divination and is to be distinguished from what we find in the *Book of the Luminaries*, where Enoch receives instruction from Watchers in heaven about heavenly bodies and their movements, which pertain to such matters as determining calendars. Such appropriate knowledge is presupposed in the indictment in 2:1 – 5:4.

In 8:4 the author declares: "as men were perishing, the cry went up to heaven". This appears to have little to do with the list of Watchers and their instructions, but fits closely with 7:6; "Then the earth brought accusation against the lawless ones". Perhaps mediating between the two is 8:2: "And there was much godlessness on the earth and they made their ways desolate". The latter text appears to echo the very awkward Genesis text, 6:3, and its sequel in 6:5, which makes a statement about humanity in the midst of describing the sexual intercourse of "the sons of God" with women, the presence of *Nephilim* in those days and later, and the offspring of the sexual union: the heroes of old and renowned warriors (6:2, 4): "Then the LORD said, 'My spirit shall not abide in mortals forever, for they are flesh; their days shall be one hundred twenty years'" (Gen 6:3); "The LORD saw that the wickedness of humankind was great in the earth, and that every inclination of the thoughts of their hearts was only evil continually" (Gen 6:5).

Coming immediately after the detail in 8:1, 8:2 does suggest the godlessness includes sexual wrongdoing and warrants divine punishment. On the other hand, 7:7 portrays humankind as the victims of activities of the giants, which, as we have seen, probably has no sexual allusions. *1 Enoch* 8:4 also portrays human beings as victims. The tension between these statements, 8:4 and 7:6, on the one hand, and 8:2, on the other, also underlies the following chapters where the action of the Watchers and its consequences (which include human sinfulness) are brought into relation to the flood story. The twofold allusion to the cry to heaven for help in 7:6 and 8:4 clearly signals the focus of the author on the consequences of the

---

[52] Nickelsburg, *1 Enoch 1*, 197-99; Annette Yoshiko Reed, "Heavenly Ascent, Angelic Descent, and the Transmission of Knowledge in *1 Enoch* 6–16," in *Heavenly Realms and Earthly Realities in Late Antique Religions* (ed. Ra'anan S. Boustan and Annette Yoshiko Reed; New York: Cambridge University Press, 2004) 47-66, 55-56.

Watchers' deeds, in particular that they cause devastation and death ("as men were perishing" 8:4). This is important for discerning the purpose of the author, which cannot simply be human sin, but clearly focuses here on the impact of the Watchers and the giants. It may allude to the cry of Abel's blood against the murderous act of Cain (Gen 4:10).[53]

In *1 Enoch* 9 we move to a new element of the story: another response from Watchers looking down "from the sanctuary of heaven",[54] but in contrast to the former ones, positive and appropriate. This time it is in response to the cry of humanity, not to the attractiveness of women. The Watchers are named: Michael, Sariel, Raphael and Gabriel. There follows a commissioning of the four Watchers by God in response to their intercession on behalf of humanity (*1 Enoch* 10-11). These chapters reflect the tension just noted between the idea of humanity as victim and humanity as also perpetrator. Thus 9:2 speaks of the earth as devoid of inhabitants – reflecting the devastation of the giants in 7:3 – and 9:3 has humankind draw attention to its destruction. On the other hand, the Watchers' intercession begins by referring to Asael's deeds: he "has taught all iniquity on the earth and has revealed eternal mysteries that are in heaven" (9:6), thus assuming some human responsibility, as in 8:1. Perhaps the tension is already evident in the description in 9:1 of what Michael, Sariel, Raphael and Gabriel saw, namely, "bloodshed on the earth. All the earth was filled with the godlessness and violence that had befallen it",[55] although here the primary focus is on humankind as victims.

Then the author returns to the story of Shemihazah and those with him, told in 6:1 – 7:3, repeating its substance in summary: "They have gone in to the daughters of the men of earth, and lain with them and have defiled themselves with the women" (9:8), echoing the formulation of 7:1, but enhancing further the emphasis on sexual intercourse by the addition of "and lain with them" (συνκοιμάομαι). Again it speaks of their teaching the women sorcery ("hate inducing charms" –

---

[53] So Nickelsburg, *1 Enoch 1*, 186-87.

[54] On the reading "sanctuary" (τῶν ἁγίων / קד]ש[י בן 4QEnᵃ 1 4:7), see Nickelsburg, *1 Enoch 1*, 202; also Esther Eshel and Hanan Eshel, "New Fragments from Qumran: 4QGenᶠ, 4QIsaᵇ, 4Q226, 8QGen, and XQpapEnoch," *DSD* 12 (2005) 134-57, who argue against Loren T. Stuckenbruck, "4QEnoch Giantsᵃ ar (Pls. I-II)," in *Qumran Cave 4.XXVI Cryptic Texts and Miscellanea Part I* (ed. Stephen J. Pfann et al.; DJD 36; Oxford: Clarendon, 2000) 8-41, 18, who favours "holy ones" rather than "sanctuary", that in the former one would expect מבין rather than מן (153). See also Bhayro, *Shemihazah and Asael Narrative*, 162.

[55] Bhayro, *Shemihazah and Asael Narrative*, sees in the reference to blood and violence in 9:1 an allusion to Hab 2:8, and notes that the conjunction of use of this verse with the notion of rebellion, absent from Habakkuk, occurs here and in 1QpHab, suggesting the latter stands under the influence of *1 Enoch* 9:1 (249-50).

probably against competing lovers) as in 7:1[56] and the birth of "giants, half-breeds" (9:9; cf. 7:2). The term, "half-breeds" (κίβδηλα) (9:9), highlights the disapproval of the mixing of kinds: angels and human women. The term recurs in 10:9 and 11:15. It is also used in Lev 19:19 and Deut 22:11 to translate שעטנז, to describe cloth woven from mixed substances, and in Wis 15:9 and 2:9 for alloyed metals.[57]

At the same time 9:9 states: "the whole earth is filled with iniquity". This appears to be a loose paraphrase of Gen 6:11-12 (" Now the earth was corrupt in God's sight, and the earth was filled with violence. And God saw that the earth was corrupt; for all flesh had corrupted its ways upon the earth"). Assuming a level of coherence within the narrative of *1 Enoch* 6-11 as it stands, this statement in 9:9 probably, therefore, includes reference to human iniquity beside the observation about the devastation wrought by the giants, which appears also to be the focus of the previous line as emended by Nickelsburg: "And the blood of men is shed on the earth".[58] The iniquity would include sexual wrongdoing, as practised by women in particular, as 8:1 and 7:1 suggest. But nothing in the present context indicates this specifically. 9:10 speaks of the groans not of the living, but of the slain dead, in a manner that again recalls the cry of the blood of the slain Abel, returning the focus again to violence and bloodshed.[59] While human iniquity probably includes sexual wrongdoing, nothing of the latter appears in association with the giants here or previously.

The commissioning of the archangels to act, in *1 Enoch* 10 – 11, reflects the same tension in the range of observations about the state of affairs on earth. The instruction to Sariel to inform Noah, "the righteous one", what he should do, reflects Gen 6:5-13. It obviously assumes others are unrighteous. This is consistent with the rest of *1 Enoch* 6-11 thus far, which has spoken of wickedness, which includes human wickedness, and now sets it in contrast to Noah and his seed, who are to be a new beginning for humanity. The flood will destroy wicked humanity. It is not designed to deal with the Watchers, nor with the giants who exterminate themselves (in contrast to one strand of thought in the *Animal Apocalypse* where they are destroyed by the flood, 89:6; 88:2).

In relationship to sexuality, nothing specifically identifies sexual wrongdoing as belonging to the wickedness of humanity, so that it is probably only as much present as it was in 9:9, in other words, it is not a major feature as we might have

---

[56] So Nickelsburg, *1 Enoch 1*, 213.

[57] So Nickelsburg, *1 Enoch 1*, who also draws attention to the use of the word, שעטנז, in 4QMMT for mixed marriages of priests and Levites (213 n. 38).

[58] On this see Nickelsburg, *1 Enoch 1*, 204.

[59] See Nickelsburg, *1 Enoch 1*, who points out that the prayer is more an indictment of God than an act of intercession, since it assumes God knows of the ills, but has not acted (206).

expected if an author had wanted to depict humans emulating the deeds of the Watchers. As we have seen, the author also shows no interest in portraying the giants as emulating the deeds of their parents in this regard.

The next three commissionings relate to the Watchers and their offspring. As in 9:6, Asael's sin is the first mentioned – perhaps reflecting some appreciation of the logical sequence which demands that he come first, since his teaching equips the women to seduce the Shemihazah and his accomplices. As in 8:1, his sin is not described as sexual wrongdoing, but as illicit revelation of heavenly mysteries (10:7). It is interesting that in the commissioning his teaching and that of other Watchers is merged, so that in 10:7 this is described as the action of "the Watchers" who taught their children (an echo of 8:3 according to which they taught their wives and their sons). 10:8 then returns specifically to Asael: "all the earth was made desolate by the deeds of the teaching of Asael". The final words, "over him write all the sins", probably reflects a synthesis of the ideas in *1 Enoch* 6 – 11. It traces all sin to his original initiative, which set up a sequence of events, including use of metallurgy for weapons of violence and bloodshed, and jewellery and cosmetics. This led, in turn, to the sexual wrongdoing of Shemihazah and his accomplices, with their resultant offspring, and to the teaching of the women which accompanied their deed (7:1; 8:3).

According to 10:9-10 Gabriel is to deal with the offspring. Here the author describes them not only as "half-breeds" (κίβδηλα), as in 9:9, but also as "bastards" (μαζηρέους = ממזריא) and "sons of miscegenation illicit unions" (πορνείας). As in Qumran, זנות, which is reflected in the latter phrase, refers not narrowly to prostitution, but to any illicit sexual relationship,[60] in this case to the illicit sexual relations between Watchers and women. The three designations highlight different aspects of the fruit of illicit sexual union. "Half-breeds" (κίβδηλα) emphasises the chaotic results of mixing of kinds. "Bastards" (μαζηρέους = ממזריא) emphasises birth from an illicit relationship.[61] "Sons of miscegenation illicit unions" (πορνείας) emphasises the illicit sexual union itself. This retains the strong emphasis on sexual wrongdoing, but, as we have noted before, the account does not depict the behaviour of the giants in terms of sexual wrongdoing, but rather in terms of violence and bloodshed, as one would expect from 7:3-5. The assumption is that the offspring of what are seen as illegitimate sexual relations are not innocent victims, but flawed beings, likely to cause chaos and inherently bad.

In the immediate context, that violence comes to expression only in the instruction to Gabriel that he should set them at war with one another. Already 7:5

---

[60] Nickelsburg, *1 Enoch 1*, 223.

[61] Fröhlich, "'*Mamzer*' in Qumran Times," draws attention to the reflection of this story in the designation of evil spirits in 4Q510 as "bastard spirits" רוחות ממזרים (112).

mentions that they devour one another's flesh, but Gabriel's task is to set them along a similar track, but this time to self-destruction. There are two further points of interest in this regard. First, as noted above, nothing suggests that the flood, implied in the mention of Noah in 10:1-3, plays a role in their destruction (as it does in 89:6); they bring destruction on themselves (before the flood). Secondly, the decree that they not have length of days (10:9-10) appears to reflect Gen 6:3. There it seems to apply to humanity,[62] but can be read as applying to the offspring of the Watchers.[63] Here it is applied to the giants.[64] In part their mutual self-destruction will assure this, but the text appears also to envisage a restriction independent of that: none will survive beyond five hundred years.

The instruction to Michael deals with Shemihazah and his accomplices (10:11-14) and goes beyond this to the restoration of the earth (10:15 – 11:2). The focus here is solely their illicit act of sexual union, expressed in the following terms: they "have mated with (συμμίγγνυμι, אתחברו 4QEn[b] 1 iv.9)[65] the daughters of men, so that they were defiled by them in their uncleanness (ἀκαρθαρσία)" (10:11). We discussed the expression "their uncleanness" above in the context of commenting on defilement in 7:1, where we noted that its probable reference is not to a period of uncleanness, such as menstruation, but to the fact that the women were unclean for the Watchers in a more general sense as human flesh and blood.

The author then connects their fate to that of their offspring, noting that they will witness the latter's self-destruction (10:12). In contrast to their offspring, the Watchers are to remain alive, but bound for seventy generations, after which they are to face judgement (10:12). This sequencing allows for the destruction of the

---

[62] On this see Kvanvig, "Gen 6,3 and the Watcher Story," who also notes an allusion to Gen 6:3 in the comments about longevity in 13:6, 14:4-5 and 15:4 (287-89).

[63] So VanderKam, "Biblical Interpretation," 286; Wright, *Evil Spirits*, 132, 151, and see the discussion in Kvanvig, "Gen 6,3 and the Watcher Story," who notes a similar application to the offspring of the Watchers in *Jub.* 5:8 and most likely also in Gen 6:3 LXX (ἐν τοῖς ἀνθρώποις τούτοις) (292-94).

[64] On the flood story in what he sees as the J account in Genesis and its relation to the story of the birth of the giants, see Hendel, "*Nephilim*," who notes the stylistic links between 6:1-2 and 6:5 indicating connection in J between the angels' story and evil and the flood, including the repetition of האדם, multiplying/becoming great (רב), the contrast between the sons of God seeing (6:2) and Yahweh seeing (6:5), thus setting up dramatic irony (12-13). "The verbal texture of the story's first sentence creates a series of suggestive rhetorical links between the two stories" (13). "The new presence of strange half-divine creatures – the *Nephilim* – adds to the picture of the chaotic and unstable actions of the antediluvian situation, a time of decline from the pacific days in Eden" (16-17); a sense of cosmos out of control (20).

[65] On this see Nickelsburg, *1 Enoch 1*, who draws attention to the use of the Hebrew, חבר, "associate" in a marital context (225).

giants long ago, but for the judgement of the Watchers at a later time, we must assume, a time in the near future for the author.[66] It helps set up the merging of horizons which turns the antediluvian situation into an image of the author's times. It also interesting to note that, as in the instructions to Raphael and Gabriel, no mention is made of the flood as an instrument of judgement.

In 10:15 Michael receives further instruction to "destroy all the spirits (πνεύματα *nafesāta*) of the half-breeds and the sons of the Watchers, because they have wronged men". This assumes the separate existence of the spirits (πνεύματα *nafesāta*), independent of the giants, themselves. It also highlights their activity as wronging human beings. It is not clear from the text when they have done this nor when Michael is to destroy them – presumably at the last judgement. The statement in 10:15 stands in some tension with the instruction to Gabriel who in 10:9-10 is commissioned to deal with the offspring, perhaps indicative of traditio-historical processes in which the instruction to Gabriel is a secondary expansion.[67] Gabriel initiates their mutual self-destruction, whereas here Michael is to destroy the offspring and in addition, their spirits.

The broader context would lead one to expect that the giants have been exterminated, and this would imply also the extermination of their spirits. Alternatively, "the sons of the Watchers" might be taken not to refer to the giants, but to their spirits who are also, in that sense, sons of the Watchers. Given the close connection with what follows, which assumes future renewal of the earth, we should better consider 10:15 as also part of Michael's eschatological role. Then the activity of the spirits will continue up to the final renewal of the earth. This coheres with the image presented later in 15:8-11 of the spirits surviving the giants and as still active.[68] This also helps make sense of what appears to be the author's assumption, namely that the present age continues to be beset by evil influences and not just by human sinfulness.

Nothing is said in 10:15 of the particular activity of the spirits of the half-breeds and the sons of the Watchers, beyond the fact that it is destructive. From what follows, however, we may assume it entailed actions which brought continuing contamination to the earth. While in 10:15 there is no particular link made between the spirits and sexual wrongdoing, just as that link is also not made with the activities of the giants, the description of the acts of cleansing in 10:20-22 make it likely. Michael's commission is to "destroy all perversity/malice/injustice (ἀδικία עולה 4QEn[c] 1 v.3)[69] from the face of the earth" (10:16), which relates to

---

[66] On the other hand, see Reed, *Fallen Angels*, who notes that "in the *Book of the Watchers* we find relatively little interest in history and no sharp sense of Eschaton's imminence" (62).

[67] See Nickelsburg, *1 Enoch 1*, 223.

[68] Cf. Nickelsburg, *1 Enoch 1*, 225, who sees a contrast here.

[69] So Nickelsburg, *1 Enoch 1*, 226.

the kind of violence and bloodshed brought by the giants.[70] But in 10:20 we read that he is to

> cleanse the earth from all impurity (ἀκαρθαρσία) and from all wrong and from all lawlessness and from all sin, and godlessness and all impurities (ἀκαρθαρσία) that have come upon the earth (10:20);[71]

similarly, 10:22: "And all the earth will be cleansed from all defilement and from all uncleanness (ἀκαρθαρσία)". These generic terms[72] probably include reference to sexual wrongdoing, especially given the theme of defilement in that context thus far (7:1; 9:8; 10:11), but this is not the primary focus, which would include defilement through bloodshed.

The positive image which emerges is one where there is great fertility among trees and plants, and people will beget thousands and live to an old age in peace (10:17), reflecting Isa 65:20, 22 in combination with Gen 9:1, and reversing Gen 6:3.[73] The allusion to begetting may suggest fertility extends also to human beings. This is significant in showing a vision of the future which includes sexual intercourse in the age to come, at least, for procreation, in contrast to traditions which see it as redundant or out of place. This suggests also that the author does not envisage that the righteous will live in a holy sanctuary where sexual activity would be out of place nor will live in that sense like angels, as other traditions predict (cf. Mark 12:25).

1 Enoch 6 – 11 contains a complex of material within which sexual wrongdoing plays a significant role, both on the part of Shemihazah and his Watcher companions and on the part of women, informed and equipped for seduction by their husbands as a result of the teaching of Asael and of the other Watchers who taught them sorcery and charms. It also assumes a positive role for sexual relations in a fertile world to come. The preceding chapters place the sexual wrongdoing of the Watchers in the category of their abandoning their order in creation. The author also portrays it as lusting, implicitly as responding to the attractiveness and seduction of women, and as defilement. Holy beings, who should be undefiled and remain in holy places, possibly understood in priestly terms, have transgressed. Interestingly, the resultant offspring, the series of giants,

---

[70] Nickelsburg, *1 Enoch 1*, 227.

[71] Nickelsburg, *1 Enoch 1*, notes that this is the earliest attestation of a high priestly role of atonement being attributed to Michael (228).

[72] Nickelsburg, *1 Enoch 1*, notes in relation to the early form of the testament which asserts the Enoch myth, "The testament is noteworthy for the paucity of its specific statements about the content of divine law". He continues: "The specific contents of that teaching about the law are all but taken for granted" (28).

[73] So Nickelsburg, *1 Enoch 1*, 226-27.

bring violence and bloodshed, but are not noted for any sexual wrongdoing, whereas their spirits do appear to include acts which include sexual defilement among their deeds.[74]

While there is some coherence in the statements directly or indirectly related to sexual wrongdoing, there are a number of tensions, which reflect use of different sets of ideas. Before we turn to consider the various strands within *1 Enoch* 6 – 11 and their relevance for understanding how attitudes towards sexuality are reflected in them, I want to turn to the following chapters, in which an author appears to assume *1 Enoch* 6 – 11 or at least something like it and to interpret it or at least the myth behind it. The latter applies if, as some assume,[75] 6 – 11 was added to its present context to help explain 12 – 16. That will be useful, both in informing us about the author's reading of the stories and in enabling us to compare that reading with other possible readings, including some reflected in the material itself.

1.1.3   1 Enoch 12 – 16

1 Enoch 12:1 follows awkwardly after 6 – 11. In 12:1-2 "before these things" apparently refers at least to the eschaton and probably to the flood, which is not mentioned directly in 6 – 11. "He was taken", an allusion to Gen 5:24, alludes to the end of Enoch's life. What follows in 12 – 16 focuses on Enoch, who appears nowhere in 6 – 11, but is central, earlier, in 1 – 5.[76] Here he depicted as

---

[74] James C. VanderKam, "The Interpretation of Genesis in *1 Enoch*," in *The Bible at Qumran: Text, Shape, and Interpretation* (ed. Peter W. Flint and with the assistance of Tae-Hun Kim; Studies in the Dead Sea Scrolls and Related Literature; Grand Rapids: Eerdmans, 2001) 129-48, notes that "the three offenses for which the angels are punished (shedding blood, illicit sexual intercourse, and idolatry) are part of the Noachide list" (142) pointing to the research of Devorah Dimant, *The Angels Who Sinned* (Ph. D. Diss., Jerusalem: Hebrew University, 1971) 55. See also the latter's discussion of the Noachide links in Devorah Dimant, "*1 Enoch* 6 – 11: A Methodological Perspective," in *SBLSP 1978* (ed. Paul J. Achtemeier; Missoula: Scholars, 1978) 1. 323-40, where she lists in relation to the angels: fornication, blasphemy, taking oaths, and sorcery; and in relation to the giants: robbery, murder, eating limbs from living animals and drinking blood; and in relation to Asael: murder, idolatry and fornication (328). Reed, *Fallen Angels*, questions the Noachide background, noting that *1 En.* 6–11 makes no mention of idolatry or worship of any sort; knowledge of metalworking is here used only for weapons and jewellery" (38).

[75] See Dimant, "*1 Enoch* 6-11," 224-25.

[76] On the figure of Enoch within the context of competitive histories of the time, where cultures made superior claims for their heroes and for the antiquity of their wisdom and probably in an eastern diaspora setting, see John J. Collins, *The Apocalyptic Imagination: An Introduction to Jewish Apocalyptic Literature* (2d ed.; Grand Rapids: Eerdmans, 1998) 46.

confronting the Watchers. In this material we find their deeds described and evaluated in particular ways.

In 12:4 we read that God speaks of "the Watchers of heaven, who forsook the highest heaven, the sanctuary of the(ir) eternal station, and defiled themselves with women". The descent, referred to in 6:6, also assumes they came from above, and the reference to heavenly secrets (9:6) and to chaos brought to earth, confirms that they have come from the usual abode of Watchers, the heavenly realm We saw that notions of wanting to beget and especially of defilement were to be read in the light of their being of different order and that their state should be one of purity not defilement. *1 Enoch* 12:4, however, goes beyond this in specifically emphasising their original and proper place as "the highest heaven" and as a sanctuary where they were stationed,[77] or where they belonged. Arguably, this merely spells out what hearers of *1 Enoch* 6 – 11 might have assumed, since 9:1 probably also alludes to the sanctuary of heaven, but it gives their place in the heavenly sanctuary added emphasis.

The allusion to the sanctuary in 12:4 adds a further dimension not present in 6 – 11, though arguably implied, namely that their act defiled at least some of them as priests. It continues: "As the sons of earth do, so they did and took wives for themselves. And they worked great desolation on the earth" (12:4). The wrong consisted not in what "the sons of earth do" in itself, by which is meant sexual intercourse, but in the fact that they, who were not sons of the earth, acted in this way.[78] The same expression recurs in this sense in 15:3 ("done as the sons of earth") and 15:4 ("done as they do"). At the same time, the after-effects are not lost from sight. Thus 12:4 speaks of the desolation (language used also in 10:8) produced on earth, by implication through the giants, their sons (12:6). The latter verse repeats the prediction of 10:12, that they would have to look on the self-destruction of their offspring. The focus in these verses, however, as Nickelsburg notes, is "on the defilement of the Watchers rather than on the women or the violence of the giants".[79] The twofold story of Asael, on the one hand, and of Shemihazah and his accomplices, on the other, is reflected in 13:1-2 where Enoch (not Raphael, as in 10:4-8) is sent to address Asael separately about his disclosures, which amount to "unrighteous deeds", but without further specification. Similarly 13:5 speaks in relation to all the Watchers simply of the "shame for their deeds". It is not specific, and so, without the emphasis given sexual wrongdoing in these chapters.

---

[77] But see Tigchelaar, *Prophets of Old*, who translates: "sanctuary of the Ever-enduring One", who proposes that ἡ στάσις τοῦ αἰῶνος is a misinterpretation of the divine epithet קים לעלמין, pointing to its occurrence in Dan 6:27 (190-91 n. 32). The focus remains, however, on their heavenly and holy place of origin, which they have forsaken.

[78] See also Tigchelaar, *Prophets of Old*, 193.

[79] Nickelsburg, *1 Enoch 1*, 235.

After Enoch recites to God the memorandum from the Watchers asking for clemency (13:4-7), he returns to them on God's command to reprimand them (13:8-10). The reprimand repeats the prediction that they would see the destruction of their sons (14:6; cf. 12:6; 10:12). In the account of Enoch's ascent and vision in 14:8 – 16:4 the "author is describing a tour through a heavenly *temple*" (to which 12:4 and 15:3 also allude), in which "at least some of the angels are construed as priests" engaged in approaching God.[80] This heavenly holiness forms the context in which the angel instructs Enoch about what he is to say to the Watchers (15:2-7). In this account the author draws together what he sees as the salient points in his reading of their sin in *1 Enoch* 6 – 11 or the tradition as he knew it. The result is the most detailed exposition of the deed.

Thus Enoch is to confront them in the following terms:

> Why have you forsaken the high heaven, the eternal sanctuary; and lain with women, and defiled yourselves with the daughters of men; and taken for yourselves wives, and done as the sons of earth; and begotten for yourselves sons, giants? (15:3)

This echoes 12:4, "forsook the highest heaven, the sanctuary of the(ir) eternal station, and defiled themselves with women. As the sons of earth do, so they did and took wives for themselves".

The Watchers are assumed to have been within the heavenly sanctuary, possibly fulfilling priestly functions. Their wrongdoing has a number of aspects, which the author enunciates in the following sequence. First, they have "forsaken the high heaven, the eternal sanctuary" (15:3). They should have remained faithfully serving in the heavenly temple. At the very least that indicts them for abandoning their appropriate place of work. The long and impressive description in 14:8-23 of Enoch's vision of the divine throne in the heavenly temple would enhance for the hearers the emphasis on the holiness of the heavenly sanctuary and so contribute to the emphasis here on the sin of abandoning not just their place of work, but the heavenly sanctuary.

Second, they have defiled themselves with the daughters of men (15:3).[81] Without further elaboration one might understand the defilement as sexual intercourse which renders a person temporarily unclean (Lev 15:16-18). Such impurity need not, in itself, be a sin and is normal among "the sons of earth". But it is more serious that: if they are priests in continuous service, then their defilement interrupts their service; yet still more serious, and doubtless the author's main concern: they have crossed a boundary of kind and so defiled themselves with those who are unclean for them by virtue of being human women.

---

[80] Nickelsburg, *1 Enoch 1*, 256.

[81] Nickelsburg, *1 Enoch 1*, wonders if there may be an intended contrast between the Watchers, who should remain awake, and their sleeping (κοιμάω שכב) with women (271).

The contrast between "daughters of men" and "Watchers of heaven" (15:2) reinforces this difference of kind. Their act is of the order of an abomination, such as Leviticus describes inappropriate sexual relations, namely male to male or human to animal, in 18:22-23 and 20:13-16. Two further elements enhance the seriousness of the deed. The sin was not just a single act of sexual intercourse, but continuing sexual intercourse, reflected in the charge that they had taken wives for themselves, and probably also reflected in the words: "and done as the sons of earth". Finally, their deed affected not only themselves; it produced progeny, namely the giants, an event which brought chaos to earth, though the latter is not the author's focus.

In 15:4 the author begins afresh with an explanation which further elucidates for us the author's understanding of the event:

> You were holy ones and spirits, living forever. With the blood of women you have defiled yourselves, and with the blood of flesh you have begotten, and with the blood of men you have lusted, and you have done as they do – flesh and blood, who die and perish. (15:4)

The statement combines a range of assertions. The reprimand, "with the blood of women you have defiled yourselves", recalls the statements in 6 – 11, in particular, 10:11 ("were defiled by them in their uncleanness"). We discussed the nature of the defilement in the context of the comments on 7:1 above. The allusion in 10:11 is best taken as referring not to a period of uncleanness and so to menstrual blood, an issue of importance in some later writings (CD 5.6-7; *Pss. Sol.* 8:12), but to women as unclean for the Watchers because of their different kind. It is therefore also inappropriate to assume on the basis of 10:11 that 15:4 must refer to menstrual blood. Beside the latter we considered Kvanvig's proposal that blood refers to the processes of procreation in common belief, and Himmelfarb's suggestion, that the Watchers will have chosen young virgins for themselves and that the blood refers to first intercourse, a matter attended to carefully in biblical tradition (cf. Deut 22:13-21), but not something which rendered one unclean. The reference to blood in 15:4 may belong to a rhetorical effect, where blood appears three times: in relation to women, in relation to begetting, and in relation to male lust. It appears so in Greek and Ge'ez, but according to Tigchelaar this could be based on a mistranslation of the translators, confusing דם and דמי or דמות. Accordingly he translates his retroversion into Aramaic: "And you were holy ones, eternal living spirits, yet you defiled yourselves with the blood of women, and appearing as flesh, you have begotten (children), and appearing as men you have ejected semen, to produce flesh and blood like those who die and perish".[82] In any case, it seems best not to define the reference(s) to blood too narrowly, but rather

---

[82] Tigchelaar, *Prophets of Old*, 193.

to see these statements together as understanding defilement as the result of illicit mixing in intercourse with human flesh and blood.

"With the blood of (or appearing as) flesh you have begotten", which picks up the reference to begetting in 15:3 and echoes 6:1, addresses the sin of mixing of kinds, also an emphasis in 6 – 11, and especially after the indictment in 2:1 – 5:4 about changing one's order of being. The third element, "with the blood of men you have lusted," recalls 6:1, the only other place that mentions "desire" specifically, though Tigchelaar's translation, "appearing as men you have ejected semen", puts the focus specifically on ejaculation. "Done as they do" (cf. 15:3 "done as the sons of earth"; and 12:4) is, as noted above, not disapproval of what the sons of earth do, namely engaging in sexual intercourse, but of the Watchers' doing it.

The contrast between their being "spirits, living forever" and humans who are "flesh and blood who die and perish" both frames the statement in 15:4 and forms the basis for the explanation in 15:5-7a,

> Therefore I gave them women, that they might cast seed into them, and thus beget children by them, that nothing fail them on the earth. But you originally existed as spirits, living forever, And not dying for all the generations of eternity; therefore I did not make women among you.[83]

The author is taking up the motif of begetting, given attention also in 6:1. Eternal beings have no need to beget and therefore no need for sexual activity and, by extension (on the basis that angels are male), no need for women. By implication, sexual relations are seen primarily in terms of procreation, not in terms of intimacy and companionship.[84] This differs markedly from, for instance, *Jubilees*, as we shall see.

---

[83] John J. Collins, "Before the Fall: The Earliest Interpretations of Adam and Eve," in *The Idea of Biblical Interpretation: Essays in Honor of James L. Kugel* (ed. Hindy Najman and Judith H. Newman; JSJSup 83; Leiden: Brill, 2004) 293-308, notes the implication of this for the author's understanding of the story of Adam and Eve. Human mortality was not the effect of their sin, but is the way they were created in the first place (306). Similarly David R. Jackson, *Enochic Judaism: Three Defining Exemplars* (Library of Second Temple Studies 49; London: T&T Clark, 2004) 33.

[84] Nickelsburg, *1 Enoch 1*, notes that "the view of woman, marriage, and sex expressed here is decidedly male oriented. Sex is for the purpose of procreating the man's line; woman was created for him to this end" (272). Similarly Marie-Theres Wacker, "'Rettendes Wissen' im äthiopischen Henochbuch," in *Rettendes Wissen* (ed. Karl Löning; AOAT 300; Münster: Ugarit, 2002) 115-54: "Frauen sind damit eo ipso als Sexualwesen und in Relation zum Mann definiert (und himmlische Frauen deshalb offenbar eine contradictio in adjecto)" (150) (tr. Women as such are thereby defined as sexual beings in relation to men [and

1 Enoch 15:8-11 then explains the results of the act: giants, but more importantly, their spirits, "evil spirits on earth" (similarly 16:1).[85] This appears to pick up the idea implied in 10:15, which speaks of "the spirits of the half-breeds and the sons of the Watchers", who have wronged humanity and who appear implicated in 10:16 in injustice and in 10:20-22 in a range of sins including defilement. *1 Enoch* 15:11 specifies their actions:

> The spirits of the giants <lead astray>, do violence, make desolate, and attack and wrestle and hurl upon the earth and <cause illnesses>. They eat nothing, but abstain from food and are thirsty and smite. These spirits (will) rise up against the sons of men and against the women, for they have come forth from them.

This may be an allusion to the women who sinned with the Watchers,[86] but may also reflect an echo of the suffering of women in childbirth or the curse of the serpent (cf. Gen 3:15-16).[87] It is interesting that here the focus of their actions is neither idolatry nor, as is relevant for our theme, sexual wrongdoing. "Lead astray" might suggest idolatry (as in 19:1), but the translation is uncertain and based on Nickelsburg's conjectural emendation.[88] Tigchelaar proposes a translation based on a plausible conjectural reconstruction of the Aramaic, which yields: "The spirits of the giants are Afflicters (or: lurkers), Smiters, Destroyers, Assailants, Strikers, Earth Demons, and Crushers. They do not eat anything, but hunger and thirst, hallucinate, and stumble", taking the participles as demonic

---

heavenly women are therefore a contradiction in terms]). Nickelsburg notes the absence of what he describes as the parity of Gen 1:27-28 and the partnership of Gen 2:18-24 (272).

[85] Tigchelaar, *Prophets of Old*, speculates that these verses were not originally part of the address to the Watchers, but "a secondary etiological expansion" (190). He notes that "this choice of interpretation is essential to the understanding of the sins of the Watchers" (190). It enables him to develop his theory that the concern of 12 – 16 is with priestly misbehaviour, not with accounting for the origins of sinfulness, but the received text certainly supports the latter as an important aspect, as we shall see.

[86] Nickelsburg, *1 Enoch 1*, 274.

[87] On the similarities between the Adam myth and Watchers myth, see Suter, "Fallen Angel, Fallen Priest," who notes the following: both rebel of their own free will and transcend ordered limits, seeking, respectively, special knowledge to be like God and to beget; both are tempted by a woman/women; Eve is promised knowledge and the angels impart it to women; both sets of offspring lead to chaos and bloodshed; in both the result is the blighting of earth; in both there is a cry of help to heaven; punishment entails exclusion (from the garden and from heaven) (132). "In *1 Enoch* copulation and the birth of offspring lead to exclusion from heaven; in Genesis they are the result of expulsion from the garden. Finally, the story of Adam and Eve begins in a garden, while the myth of the fallen angels ends in one (see *1 En.* 10:16-22)" (132).

[88] Nickelsburg, *1 Enoch 1*, 268, 273.

names.[89] This would put the emphasis on their role in bringing direct harm to human beings (probably envisaging all kinds of physical and mental afflictions), rather than false teaching or idolatry or sexual wrongdoing. 16:1 describes their action as making desolate (cf. 12:4; 10:8) and going unpunished (until the judgement day), "when the great age will be consummated". As Tigchelaar observes: "here we have the view that the accidents which are attributed to the evil spirits, such as, e.g., epilepsy or insanity, belong to this world, or rather, to this era, as the short reference to the 'great aeon' suggests".[90] They become, as such, the enspirited viruses, bacteria and triggers of mental illness and freak accidents of the ancient world. This defines them primarily in terms of such affliction rather than as sources of moral danger such as in the giants' violence on a grand (and probably political) scale and the Watchers' sexual wrongdoing. This kind of narrowed focus returns the emphasis to human moral action as a significant element beside and also independent of demonic afflictions.

Finally 16:3 alludes to the imparting of forbidden information to women: "the stolen mystery ... and through this mystery women and men are multiplying evils on the earth". The allusion here is to the idea expressed in 7:1; 8:3 and 9:8, which assumes women as the bearers of the tradition of sorcery.[91] The position of this warning in the final words suggests it does carry significance and weight for the author. Missing on the other hand is any reference to Asael's teaching of the skills of manufacturing cosmetics and to their use by women to lead the Watchers astray.

1.1.4   Comparing 1 Enoch 6 – 11 and 1 Enoch 12 – 16

1 Enoch 12 – 16 contains much of the detail found already in 6-11. Both sections report Watchers' sexual intercourse with women. The table below sets out the detail pertaining to sexuality in parallel columns for ease of comparison.[92]

---

[89] Tigchelaar, *Prophets of Old*, 204-207. He notes that the list of seven names matches "precisely the number of seven demons appearing so often in Mesopotamian Incantation spells" (206), which he suggests also helps explain some peculiarities in the text (206-207).

[90] Tigchelaar, *Prophets of Old*, 208.

[91] Nickelsburg, *1 Enoch 1*, notes that 15:12 may imply the culpability of women (274).

[92] On the differences between *1 Enoch* 6 – 11 and 12 – 16 more generally, see Tigchelaar, *Prophets of Old*, 155-57 and 166-67. They include absence of Enoch in the former and his exercise in the latter of functions attributed to angels in the former. Like many, he sees 12:1 as an editorial link to what may originally be independent of 6 – 11 (156).

1 Enoch 6 – 11	*1 Enoch* 12 – 16
beautiful and comely daughters (6:1)	
the Watchers, the sons of heaven (6:2)	the Watchers of heaven (12:4)
saw them and desired them (6:2)	with the blood of men you have lusted (15:4)
Let us choose for ourselves (6:2); from among them such as they chose (7:1)	
let us beget children for ourselves (6:2)	
	begotten for yourselves sons (15:3); with the blood of flesh you have begotten (15:4)
great sin (6:3)	
took wives for themselves (7:1)	
began to go in to them (7:1); they have gone in to the daughters of men (9:8)	took wives for themselves (12:4); taken for yourselves wives (15:4)
(began) to defile themselves through them (7:1); defiled themselves with the women (9:8); were defiled by them in their uncleanness (10:11)	defiled themselves with women (12:4); defiled yourselves with the daughters of men (15:3); with the blood of women you have defiled yourselves (15:4)
lain with them (9:8)	lain with women (15:3)
mated with the daughters of men (10:11)	
they (daughters) transgressed and led the holy ones astray (8:1)	
	you were the holy ones and spirits, living forever (15:4)
	forsook the highest heaven (12:4); forsaken the high heaven (15:3)
	(forsook) the sanctuary of the(ir) eternal station (12:4); (forsaken) the eternal sanctuary (15:3)
	(took wives) as the sons of earth do (12:4); "done as the sons of earth" (15:3); you have done as they (men) do (15:4)

The elements of desiring, begetting, taking wives, defiling themselves (including women's uncleanness/blood), lying with women, are in common. *1 Enoch* 12-16 does not contain the following motifs: the beauty and comeliness of the daughters, their adornment and cosmetics by which they led the holy ones astray; the choosing; the sense of continuation introduced by "began to" in 7:1; the language of going into and mating.

On the other hand *1 Enoch* 12-16 goes beyond 6 – 11 in its emphasis on forsaking the highest heaven, particularly as a sanctuary where the Watchers were stationed or belonged, and doing as the sons of earth. The latter is part of a major emphasis on the difference between mortal human beings and immortal spirits, which is used to demonstrate why Watchers do not need to beget, and therefore do not have sex and do not need women. This contrast is an extrapolation of what is probably already assumed in 6:1, the report of the clearly deviant wish on the part of the Watchers to beget. The portrayal of the Watchers as abandoning the highest heaven, understood as a temple, is an elaboration of what must also in some sense be implied in 6 – 11, at least to the extent that the hearers know that not only should the Watchers not have desired and then had intercourse with the women; they should also not have come down to do so.

1 Enoch 12 – 16 clearly goes beyond 6 – 11 in emphasising the heavenly sanctuary and its abandonment by the Watchers. Enoch's vision in the heavenly sanctuary enhances this and also helps create the impression that the Watchers (or at least some of them) functioned as priests in the heavenly sanctuary. The other notable contrast is the absence of reference to the women's attractiveness and their employment of adornment and cosmetics. At most 16:3 alludes to women being told heaven's mystery (16:2-3), picking up the idea present in 7:1; 8:3; and 9:8. Otherwise *1 Enoch* 12 – 16 mentions women as needed for procreation, as part of the order of mortals.

It is equally interesting to compare how *1 Enoch* 12 – 16 weighs various elements of the stories compared with 6 – 11. Both assume the Watchers' act of sexual intercourse with women was, as 6:3 puts it, "a great sin". Both report dire consequences, both for the Watchers and for the inhabitants of earth, but there are subtle differences. In *1 Enoch* 12 – 16 we read that the act defiled the Watchers (12:4; 15:3-4). They also "worked great desolation on the earth" (12:4). This summary statement, supplemented somewhat by the reference to their sons in 12:6 (and sons as giants in 15:3), finds a fuller explanation in 15:8 – 16:1. Here, too, we find reference to the giants (15:8, 11; 16:1), but only incidentally and without description of their deeds. At most 16:1 mentions "the day of the slaughter and destruction and death of the giants" (similarly briefly: 12:6; 14:6). Instead, the focus falls on the spirits which proceed from their dead bodies and their activities (perhaps embodied in their names) of bringing harmful afflictions to human beings, and also attacking women, in particular. The message is clear: sexual intercourse between the "holy ones and spirits who live forever" and mortal human women created, via the giants, the basis for the release of evil spirits on earth. The myth of the illicit union functions here, at least etiologically, to account for what is apparently the current experience of the author and his community, the plague of evil spirits wreaking havoc, primarily it seems at an individual level, from which they are assured the judgement will release them (16:1). There could be a reference to their leading people astray, such as to idolatry or through false teaching, but the text is too uncertain to be sure.

By contrast, *1 Enoch* 6 – 11, which also notes defilement of the Watchers, places much greater emphasis on the giants and their devastating impact, both on humanity and on all creatures – and finally on themselves: they began "to devour one another's flesh. And they drank the blood". The latter detail enhances the abhorrence of their deeds. The bloodshed, godlessness and violence are also the first things which the four angels see in response to humanity's cry (9:1). *1 Enoch* 9:9 again repeats this consequence of the illicit union, emphasising the giants. Gabriel is to initiate their self-destruction (10:9) and the Watchers are to witness this (10:12). The latter detail receives more emphasis in *1 Enoch* 12 – 16, as we have seen (12:6; 14:6). The brief statement to Gabriel that "no petition will be (granted) their fathers on their behalf" (10:10) finds significant elaboration in 12 – 16, where Enoch is petitioned by them to take this role. The only mention in 6 – 11 of the spirits who proceed from the giants, which assume such significance in 12 – 16, comes in 10:15, "Destroy the spirits of the half-breeds and the sons of the Watchers, because they have wronged men". Thus in *1 Enoch* 6 – 11 the emphasis falls not on the spirits, but on the giants. Here the focus will not be etiological, because giants have clearly deceased, but, if anything, paradigmatic.[93] Just as devastating giants were destroyed then and the earth not left to ruin, so we can expect deliverance from such devastation in our own times. The double reference to earth's appeal to heaven, connected to the suffering of devastation (7:6; 8:4), confirms this as a primary concern.

Both *1 Enoch* 6 – 11 and *1 Enoch* 12 – 16 also focus on other aspects of the story which have little or no relation to the illicit sexual union. They have to do with the imparting of knowledge. In 12 – 16 the aspect of passing on forbidden knowledge comes in the account of Enoch's commission to address Asael. There we read as the ground for the sentence against him: "because of the unrighteous deeds that you have revealed" (13:2; and as a doublet: "and because of all the godless deeds and the unrighteousness and the sin that you have revealed to humans" 13:2b). This probably alludes to the tradition in 8:1-2, but lacks its detail. *1 Enoch* 16:3 is slightly more specific in its address to the Watchers in general:

---

[93] VanderKam, "Interpretation of Genesis," notes that what he describes as the interpolation of 6:1 – 11:1 between 1 – 5 and 10:13 – 11:2 about the flood and judgement to come, makes up for the lack in Genesis of an account of so much sin as to warrant such a drastic solution as the flood – the story thus provides it (139-40). "If angels had married women and engendered giants who committed sins and ravaged the earth and humanity, they would be deserving of extraordinary punishment. Or if humanity had learned secret and forbidden arts from angels and continually performed evil deeds as a result, this too would provide a more adequate explanation for the flood" (140). It is also, however, much more than a scribal supplement to re-balance Genesis. See also Helge S. Kvanvig, "The Watcher Story and Genesis: An Intertextual Reading," *SJOT* 18 (2004) 163-83, who challenges VanderKam's explanation, noting that the account of sin in *1 Enoch* 6 – 11 relates to the Watchers and the giants, not humanity (180-81), though this overlooks human involvement in wickedness brought about through the teaching of the Watchers.

> You were in heaven, and no mystery was revealed to you; but a stolen mystery you learned; and this you made known to the women in your hardness of heart; and through this mystery the women and the men are multiplying evils on the earth.

This recalls 7:1, but, again, is much less specific. Clearly the effect is the serious spread of evils, but the text leaves us in the dark about the substance of the mystery. Read intratextually with 7:1 it probably refers to sorcery and charms. It may also explain what makes women vulnerable to the attacks of evil spirits mentioned in 15:12.

Thus in *1 Enoch* 12 – 16 there is awareness of the issue of forbidden knowledge, but the references are vague and probably at most implicate women as bearers of sorcery and charms. It is striking that most of the specific information contained in *1 Enoch* 6 – 11 is left unmentioned. There the exploits of Asael assume much greater significance, both as accounting for the metallurgy which makes for warfare and for providing the adornments and cosmetics which make women more seductive and dangerous (8:1-2). By omitting the allusion to the women's seduction of the holy ones, *1 Enoch* 12 – 16 does not have to deal with the problem of chronological sequence which presupposes first the descent of Asael, followed by the descent of Shemihazah and his accomplices. The omission is probably more the result of lack of emphasis on metallurgy and especially warfare. The battles which the author of *1 Enoch* 12 – 16 fears are battles which individuals have with evil spirits, not, apparently, the chaos caused by military warfare.[94]

The author of *1 Enoch* 6 – 11, by contrast, returns to Asael's deeds, both in the account of the angels' prayer (9:6) and in God's instruction to Raphael (10:4-8), which makes Asael the first of the Watchers to be addressed and even tells Raphael to "write over him all sins" (10:8). Paradoxically, in *1 Enoch* 12 – 16 Asael, whose specific teaching enunciated in 6 – 11 is passed over, is the only Watcher named and is singled out for separate attention (13:1-3), but his particular contribution to evil in the world is reduced to generality. The author of 12 – 16 makes no mention of the name of Shemihazah and his accomplices (apart from Asael), nor of their individual revelations (cf. 8:3). The other information about spells, cutting of roots, and sorcery (8:3) is according to 7:1 communicated to the wives of the Watchers. The author of *1 Enoch* 12 – 16 has avoided this duplication, intentionally or otherwise, but at most has some interest in portraying women as bearers of forbidden knowledge.[95]

---

[94] VanderKam, "Interpretation of Genesis," notes that the emphasis on the generation of spirits also solves another problem which a scribe might perceive in Genesis: why sin continued after the flood (141). It also does more than that.

[95] Eibert J. C. Tigchelaar, "Some Remarks on the Book of the Watchers: The Priests, Enoch, Genesis, and 4Q208," in *The Origins of Enochic Judaism: Proceedings of the First*

Annette Yoshiko Reed proposes that the contrast in attitudes towards knowledge between *1 Enoch* 6 – 11 and 12 – 16 is an indication of development away from a negative stance in the former to a more positive stance in the latter in which Enoch is established as appropriate mediator of knowledge. Thus 12 – 16 form a transition to his role as revealer of knowledge in what follows.

> The inclusion of knowledge about the sun, moon, earth, stars, lightning, and fireballs among the teachings of the fallen Watchers presents a striking contrast to the elevated status of cosmological wisdom in other parts of the *Book of the Watchers*, as well as the earlier Enochic apocalypse.[96]

She draws attention to Himmelfarb's observation, that

> knowledge of the very phenomena that are signs of faithfulness in the introduction to the *Book of the Watchers* (i.e., 1 – 5; esp. 2:1 – 5:4) and cause for praise of God in the tour to the ends of the earth (i.e., 17 – 36) here contributes to the corruption of humanity.[97]

While it is true that 6 – 11 speaks of revealed knowledge only negatively, its account is, in itself, a positive imparting of heavenly knowledge and its negativity seems mostly targeted towards particular kinds of knowledge related to divination and sorcery (with the exception of metallurgy), which continue to be treated as illicit in the rest of the *Book of the Watchers* and elsewhere in the corpus. As Tigchelaar observes, "the author does not condemn the sciences of astronomy and cosmology *tout court*, but criticizes the study or the interpretation of the נחשׁין or σημεῖα, that is, of the 'signs' and 'omens'."[98]

Enoch Seminar, University of Michigan, Sesto Fiorentino, Italy, June 19-23, 2001 (ed. G. Boccaccini; *Henoch* 24; Torino: Silvio Zamorani Editore, 2002) 143-45, notes that 12 – 16 does not deal with the teachings of the Watchers, the havoc of the giants, or the Watchers' lusting and he denies any reference to adultery or menstrual blood (143).

[96] Reed, "Heavenly Ascent ," 56. See also Reed, *Fallen Angels*, 42-43, where she also notes that "the speculative stance of the *Astronomical Book* and the majority of the *Book of the Watchers* does not look so different from the sceptical stance of Qoheleth and Ben Sira" (43). Later she observes, "it may be wise to read the range of attitudes towards cosmological speculation in *1 En.* 6–11, the redacted form of the *Book of the Watchers*, and the Wisdom of Ben Sira in terms of a lively debate about the nature and scope of religious knowledge among scribes in the pre-Maccabean period" (71).

[97] Himmelfarb, *Ascent,* 77.

[98] Tigchelaar, *Prophets of Old*, 181. On the different quality of the knowledge entailed he writes: "One should … take care to distinguish carefully between the science of 'astronomy', and the art of 'astrology'." (181). While a distinction between astrology and astronomy is probably not sustainable in the ancient world, the difference has validity, at

The apparent proscribing of metallurgy is problematic and rather extreme. One wonders whether it really implies that the author opposed smelting and espoused living without its benefits.[99] Later, for the author of the *Animal Apocalypse*, certainly, such skills would have been essential for the military pursuits of the righteous. On the other hand, nowhere do we find it explicitly affirmed in the corpus, so that one cannot reduce the objection to only the misuse of metallurgy, nor can one, by analogy, argue that the Watchers taught astrology/astronomy and meteorology of much the same kind as Enoch later learned, but that only its misuse was the issue.

Overall, then, *1 Enoch* 6 – 11 has much greater emphasis on forbidden knowledge.[100] The author must have considered this a much more significant problem in his day. It has two main aspects: learning which promotes warfare and devastation, paradigmatically portrayed in the myth of the giants, and learning which enhances what the author sees as the negative impact of women: through cosmetics and adornment enhancing their seductive power and through sorcery, charms and spells, which make them a vehicle of evil influence. One might add to this, on the basis of 8:3: forbidden learning about astronomy (better, astrology) and meteorology. This could appear as something positive or at least neutral in 6 – 11 and as foreshadowing subject matter in the rest of the *Book of the Watchers*, not to mention the *Book of Heavenly Luminaries*, but in the context of 6 – 11 the references are best taken negatively as referring to knowledge for forbidden practices. *1 Enoch* 6 – 11 thus both explains how devastation has come about, but also by implication uses the myths by analogy to warn against violence, sexual wrongdoing, sorcery and divination in his own time, with the promise nevertheless of the ultimate cleansing of the earth and restoration of righteousness for all. The universal note in 11:21 is striking: "And all the sons of men will become righteous, and all the peoples will worship (me), and all will bless me and prostrate

---

least in relation to the kind of knowledge undergirding forbidden practices. He notes that there is "plenty of evidence that in Hellenistic and Roman times Jewish groups practiced various kinds of magic and astrology" (181). See also Molenberg, "Roles of Shemihaza and Asael," 141-42 and Wacker, "'Rettendes Wissen' im äthiopischen Henochbuch," who writes: "Hier kommt es offenbar darauf an, daß das astrologische Wissen kontrolliert praktiziert wird" (127) (tr. Here the issue is clearly that in a controlled way astrological knowledge is being put into practice). See also Wright, *Evil Spirits*, 124-27.

[99] On the possibility that the motif of metallurgy derives from Gen 4:22 ("Tubal-cain, who made all kinds of bronze and iron tools"), see Wright, *Evil Spirits*, 106 and George W. E. Nickelsburg, "Apocalyptic and Myth in *1 Enoch* 6-11," *JBL* 96 (1977) 383-405, 399.

[100] On this see Tigchelaar, *Prophets of Old*, who speaks of the concern of *1 Enoch* 6 – 11 rather "with the consequences of these sins, than with the Watchers' misbehaviour as such" and identifies these results as, above all, "violence and licentiousness" (178).

themselves", a time of blessing which also includes human fertility (11:17): "they will live until they beget thousands".

1.1.5   Setting and Purpose of 1 Enoch 6 – 11 and 12 – 16

Moving beyond identifying emphases to constructing possible settings is fraught with difficulty,[101] but a task which demands attention nevertheless. In *1 Enoch* 12 – 16 we have identified an etiological role. The Watchers' story explains how it has come about that the author's community is now faced with the struggle against evil spirits, which bring harmful afflictions to human beings, attack women (who seem also to be implicated in sorcery), and possibly lead people astray to idolatry or false teaching. There is no apparent reference to suffering through warfare or foreign oppression.

The other major emphasis in 12 – 16, on the Watchers' abandoning their heavenly temple and becoming defiled by illicit and indiscriminate sexual union, will certainly reflect disapproval by the author of that happening. Is that detail, however, something more than a matter of enhancing the gravity of the offence in order to give greater credibility to the story and its effects, now being felt through the presence of evil spirits? A number of scholars have ventured the suggestion that there is more, namely that the actions of the Watchers are paradigmatic of a danger which the author sees in his own time, that is, the author sees an analogy in their actions to the sexual wrongdoing in his world.

Suter, considering 6 – 16 as a unit, proposed that for the author, just as the Watchers abandoned their role in the temple and became defiled through illicit unions, so people in the earthly sanctuary, namely priests, had been entering illicit sexual relations.[102] The issue was one of both purity and endogamy, which he then saw the author applying to priestly marriage in the light of Lev 21:1-15, where *zonah* is to be taken as referring not narrowly to a prostitute but to any inappropriate woman.[103] He points to the study of Büchler,[104] which argued, on the

---

[101] Stuckenbruck, "Origins of Evil," cautions with respect to possibilities that we find here a reaction "against trends associated with the growing influence of Hellenistic culture and/or a perceived corruption among the priesthood", that the myth "resists any wholesale reduction to a paradigmatic function" (100 n. 28). See also the review of research in Wright, *Evil Spirits*, 37-47.

[102] Suter, "Fallen Angel, Fallen Priest," restated with further argument in David Winston Suter, "Revisiting 'Fallen Angel, Fallen Priest'," in *The Origins of Enochic Judaism: Proceedings of the First Enoch Seminar, University of Michigan, Sesto Fiorentino, Italy, June 19-23, 2001* (ed. G. Boccaccini; *Henoch* 24; Torino: Silvio Zamorani Editore, 2002) 137-42.

[103] Suter, "Revisiting 'Fallen Angel, Fallen Priest'," 138-39.

basis of evidence in rabbinic material, but also Philo and Josephus, that there was a restricted circle of families (including priestly and lay) from whom priests should take wives, with the consequence that priests often married daughters of other priests or nieces, a practice expressly forbidden in CD.[105] Suter notes that bigamy and marriage of a niece feature in the third century B.C.E. Tobiad romance in a family allied to the Oniads (Josephus, *A.J.* 12.160-236) and that the issues of marrying nieces is also addressed in 4QMMT, which he reads as requiring that priests marry only daughters of priests.[106] He finds further corroboration for his views in the use of "most holy" to distinguish sons of Aaron in 4QMMT and 1QS, but also to designate angels in 1QS, which enhances the likelihood of the author using heavenly "holy ones" to speak of earthly priests.[107]

In commenting on 12 – 16, Nickelsburg, too, sees the author using the Watchers' rebellion to attack abuse of purity laws relating to sexuality among the Jerusalem priests and its polluting effects on them and the temple.[108] He sees this as a development of the concern expressed already in Ezra 9 concerning intermarriage, including by Levites and priests. One might even see the awkwardness of an allusion to sexual intercourse with menstruating women, which many suppose behind 15:4 (but which we saw above as unlikely), as evidence that the author is driven by concrete concerns with such matters, like the authors of CD 5.6-7 and *Pss. Sol.* 8:12, to which Nickelsburg draws attention.[109] Based on

---

[104] Adolph Büchler, "Family Purity and Family Impurity in Jerusalem before the Year 70," in *Studies in Jewish History: The Adolph Büchler Memorial Volume* (ed. I. Brodie and J. Rabinowitz; London: Oxford University Press, 1956) 64-98.

[105] Suter, "Revisiting 'Fallen Angel, Fallen Priest'," 139.

[106] Suter, "Revisiting 'Fallen Angel, Fallen Priest'," 139-40. On this see also Martha Himmelfarb, "Levi, Phinehas, and the Problem of Intermarriage at the Time of the Maccabean Revolt," *JSQ* 6 (1999) 1-24, 6-12. Suter reads *1 Enoch* 6 – 16 as requiring that priests marry only daughters of priests (139-40). On this see also Martha Himmelfarb, "The Book of the Watchers and the Priests of Jerusalem," in *The Origins of Enochic Judaism: Proceedings of the First Enoch Seminar, University of Michigan, Sesto Fiorentino, Italy, June 19-23, 2001* (ed. G. Boccaccini; *Henoch* 24; Torino: Silvio Zamorani Editore, 2002) 131-35.

[107] Suter, "Revisiting 'Fallen Angel, Fallen Priest'," 139-40.

[108] Nickelsburg, *1 Enoch 1*, 230-32; similarly 51, 64, 119. He notes that "the charge is reminiscent of texts that polemicize against priestly transgressions of the codes of sexual purity. This suggests that a myth of heavenly rebellion has become, in part, an indictment of human sin, specifically, the defilement of the Jerusalem priesthood and its cult" (46). Similarly on pp. 54-55 he speaks of the author seeing the temple polluted because of the sexual impurity of the priests, but also looking forward to a day when it would be purified and a source of sustenance for the righteous.

[109] Nickelsburg, *1 Enoch 1*, 231.

allusions to 4QMMT and the *Aramaic Levi Document*, Himmelfarb argues for a more specific concern: "marriages between priests and Jewish women from non-priestly families".[110]

Tigchelaar, on the other hand, who also sees an allusion to the priesthood in 15:3 ("why have you left the high, holy, and eternal heaven") and 12:4, finds in them a possible reference to Manasseh, brother of the high priest Jaddua, who according to Josephus (*A.J.* 11), married Nikaso, daughter of the Samaritan Sanballat, and to other priests of the time, who according to Josephus did similarly.[111] He also notes parallels between *1 Enoch* 12 – 16 and *T. Levi* 2 – 7, which is clearly anti-Samaritan, and the common concern of each and also of Ezra and *Jubilees* 30, as he reads it.[112] He suggests that to "do as the sons of earth" may echo the meaning of "the people of the land" in Ezra. He notes that "no forgiveness or pardon at all" is found both in *1 Enoch* 12 and 13 and in *Jubilees* 30. In a broad conclusion he asserts that

> the text has only one major theological point to make: the Watchers, as eternal holy beings have no need of progeny, in contrast to mortal humans who need women to produce children ... the basic accusation is that the Watchers have disregarded their natural order and place.[113]

Unlike Suter and Nickelsburg, Tigchelaar, therefore, sees *1 Enoch* 12-16 directed not against the Jerusalem priests from outside, but against those who left them.[114] This matches the motif of the Watchers' abandonment of the heavenly temple more literally than other proposals.

Our assessment of possible settings and purpose in 12 – 16 needs to match the emphasis apparent in the material. In this the etiological explanation of the author's current situation, where evil spirits plague people (and perhaps lead people astray to idolatry or false teaching), makes good sense of both the focus which this detail receives and the fact that it is distinctive over against 6 – 11. Negatively, the absence of all but a very general emphasis on violence, and particularly the violence of war and bloodshed, points to this as not being the

---

[110] Himmelfarb, "Levi, Phinehas," 12; similarly "Watchers," 133. "The appearance of a cluster of roughly contemporary texts taking this position, and the absence of evidence for the position elsewhere, for example in 4QD, may suggest that priests' marriage to lay women was an issue of concern in the late third and early second centuries and then faded from discussion" (134). She sees the attack as coming from rigorists (134).

[111] Tigchelaar, "Some Remarks on the *Book of the Watchers*," 144. See Tigchelaar, *Prophets of Old*, 198-203. See also Bhayro, *Shemihazah and Asael Narrative*, 9.

[112] Tigchelaar, *Prophets of Old*, 199-203. *Jubilees* 30 need not however be read as specifically anti-Samaritan and is concerned with more than priests, as also is Ezra 9.

[113] Tigchelaar, "Some Remarks on the *Book of the Watchers*," 143.

[114] Tigchelaar, *Prophets of Old*, 203.

concern which it had been in 6 – 11. The heightening of the imagery of the
heavenly sanctuary in 12 – 16 and its abandonment by the Watchers, some of
whom may have been understood to be priests, is suggestive of the kind of
explanations relating to the priesthood noted above, but not exclusive of other
concerns, as Tigchelaar suggests.

In 16:3 the author still draws attention to forbidden knowledge, which women
bear. The position of this warning in an emphatic final position cautions us against
underplaying its significance or simply seeing it as a rhetorical foil to the
legitimate revelations of Enoch.[115] This makes the narrowing of the focus which
Himmelfarb proposes on the basis of the *Aramaic Levi Document* and 4QMMT
less likely. Given this connection in 16:3, a concern with marriage of priests (only
priests?) to women who might corrupt them through forbidden knowledge points
rather to marrying Gentile women or others who might be deemed to present such
a danger. By presenting his hearers with the prospect of priests defiling themselves
with such illicit relationships the author may be engaging only in a hypothetical
ploy in order to enhance the gravity of what the Watchers did and so help explain
the gravity of the consequences which are now experienced as the plagues of evil
spirits. Alternatively, the priestly perspective on the Watchers' sin is not a ploy but
a deliberate construction on the part of the author to make indirect comment on
actual, inappropriate sexual/marital behaviour among priests in his own time. In
espousing the view of Himmelfarb, Wright notes that, should the latter have been
the case, we might have expected a defensive response in Ben Sira, which appears
to interact with Enochic Judaism, but then concludes that it must have fallen
outside Ben Sira's interest.[116] He agrees with Himmelfarb, that the criticism would

---

[115] Cf. Carol A. Newsom, "The Development of *1 Enoch* 6 – 19: Cosmology and
Judgment," *CBQ* 42 (1980) 310-29, 313-14, 320-21. Similarly Randal A. Argall, *1 Enoch
and Sirach: A Comparative Literary and Conceptual Analysis of the Themes of Revelation,
Creation, and Judgement* (EJL 8; Atlanta: Scholars Press, 1995) 27, who notes that in 16:3
Ge'ez uses *mennuna* "worthless" (27 n 59). But this does not exhaust its function in the
narrative.

[116] Benjamin G. Wright, "*Sirach* and *1 Enoch*: Some Further Considerations," in *The
Origins of Enochic Judaism: Proceedings of the First Enoch Seminar, University of
Michigan, Sesto Fiorentino, Italy, June 19-23, 2001* (ed. G. Boccaccini; Henoch 24; Torino:
Silvio Zamorani Editore, 2002) 179-87, who notes that Ben Sira shows no awareness of the
issue, either in his references to Enoch or in mentioning Phinehas in 45:23-24, where one
might expect it (186). He concludes that his concern was elsewhere than with the issues
which concerned the *Book of the Watchers* and the *Aramaic Levi Document*, such as
performance of the cult, who were legitimate priests, proper conduct of sacrifices and
calendar (186). See also his discussion in Benjamin G. Wright, "Ben Sira and the *Book of
the Watchers* on the Legitimate Priesthood," in *Intertextual Studies in Ben Sira and Tobit*
(ed. Jeremy Corley and Vincent Skemp; CBQMS 38; Washington D.C.: Catholic Biblical
Association, 2005) 241-54.

have been directed not at all priests but only some, while others are assumed to remain faithful.[117]

The proposal that the author of 12 – 16 is making some kind of paradigmatic use of the myth of the Watchers' deed to address such issues in his own day might receive further support from *1 Enoch* 1 – 5. There we noted the intratextual link between the sins of some people in the author's world and those of the Watchers which is created through the common declaration to both that they shall have no peace (5:4; 16:4). But beyond that, we are on uncertain ground and constructions depend on assumptions of varying degrees of probability. Thus it is probable that the author would have assumed that at least some of the Watchers might have been priests in the heavenly sanctuary, but less probable that he saw all in this category. This leaves open the possibility that the concern with analogous illicit sexual relations might apply to priests in the author's day, but need not apply exclusively to priests. The concern, accordingly would have two elements: priests (and perhaps others) defiling themselves through inappropriate sexual relations/ marriages, thus crossing inappropriate boundaries (and in the case of priests, abandoning the temple or the holiness appropriate to it), and, on the other hand, exposure through such marriages to sorcery and forbidden knowledge and practices which could be passed on to them by their wives.

Thus the issue being confronted seems to be more than just a matter of going beyond certain families (*pace* Himmelfarb), though it could include that. It could relate to marriages to Samaritans and to priests leaving the Jerusalem temple, as Tigchelaar proposes, but this does not account well for the element of forbidden knowledge. It might have relevance to the Tobiad marriages, but nothing requires that. The concern with intermarriage and of the exposure it brings to forbidden practices, does, however, appear to belong to an ongoing issue, which surfaces across a range of literature, from Ezra onwards, which is related, though not

---

[117] Wright, "Ben Sira," 247; Himmelfarb, "Watchers," 133; Reed, *Fallen Angels*, 65, 69. Wright concurs also with Boccaccini: "In this sense, we have here not an anti-priestly diatribe, but rather an internal (that is, intra-priestly) family squabble" (25). Gabriele Boccaccini, *Roots of Rabbinic Judaism: An Intellectual History, from Ezekiel to Daniel* (Grand Rapids: Eerdmans, 2002), sees the *Book of the Watchers* as the result of Zadokite editing of the Torah, which made possible the link between the Watcher story and Enoch. It is "not the reaction of outsiders against the Zadokite order, but rather the cry of insiders who (after a brief period of order) had seen denied (lost) (what they claimed were) their rights within the divine order" (99). He locates this reaction, which he sees represented in the rebellion in heaven, not in the third century, which "appears as a period of stability and order", but in the fourth century, "a critical period of controversy and division within the priesthood" (101). In doing so he plays down the allusion to warfare and violence as having contemporary relevance and elevates priestly legitimacy, an aspect which the *Book of the Watchers*, however, does not address, and passes over what many see as, rather, its main issue with priests, namely illegitimate marriages.

exclusively, to priests. The conjectured concern with (possibly priestly) illicit sexual relations and marriage and the exposure it brings would be more secure if we had some specific allusions to it in the references to evils confronting the hearers (such as in 15:11 – 16:1), but there are none, although it is also true, that such material in any case is minimal in 12 – 16.[118] As we shall see, this is also the case in the later writings within the corpus which we shall be considering, which make use of the myth. It is true also of the *Aramaic Levi Document*, which addresses intermarriage, but not linked to the myth of the Watchers, and in *Jubilees*, where it becomes a major theme, for which the myth functions as an illustration only once and then plays no further role in the warnings and is not linked to priesthood, specifically.

If this concern is present, it is also not clear, whether the author is expressing it from inside or outside the priesthood or the Jerusalem community. As Olson points out, and illustrates well by his cross-referenced translation, "the authors evidence an impressive command of Old Testament scriptures", even if mostly by allusion rather than direct quotation, and "expect their readers to know what we call the Old Testament scriptures".[119] Accordingly, "the Enochians never divorced themselves fully from the religion of Israel with its framework of sacred law" nor did they propound a new Torah. He sees their writings as intended to be "an interpretive, supplemental body of writings within Judaism, not as rival Bible for a breakaway movement". Wherever they are, the authors obviously write in a context where the Enoch tradition is revered and where they can assume their work will be well received, and can draw on that tradition to bring something of relevance to his hearers.

In the case of *1 Enoch* 6 – 11, where the attention falls not on the evil spirits, but on the giants and their devastation, we most likely have both an etiological and a paradigmatic use of the myth. Thus the author uses it to address the suffering of people and all creatures from the devastating effects of war and to give assurance

---

[118] See also James C. VanderKam, "Response to George Nickelsburg, '*1 Enoch*: A Commentary on the Book of *1 Enoch*: Chapters 1-36; 81-108'," in *George W.E. Nickelsburg in Perspective: An Ongoing Dialogue of Learning* (2 vols; ed. Jacob Neusner and Alan J. Avery-Peck; JSJSup 80; Leiden: Brill, 2003) 2. 379-86, who writes: "When one reads through these chapters one uncovers no reference to priests or to sacrifice; there is reference only to the sin of the heavenly angels in marrying women who lived on earth. Purity is an issue, but it is not connected with priestly concerns specifically" (386). In reply George Nickelsburg, "Response on the Commentary on *1 Enoch*," in *George W.E. Nickelsburg in Perspective: An Ongoing Dialogue of Learning* (2 vols; ed. Jacob Neusner and Alan J. Avery-Peck; JSJSup 80; Leiden: Brill, 2003) 2. 409-23, argues that "the story describes the actions of the Watchers in language analogous to that in polemics against the priesthood" and points to the critique of the cult in the *Animal Apocalypse* and the absence of reference to the second temple in the *Apocalypse of Weeks* (412).

[119] Olson, *Enoch*, 10.

that there will be deliverance, a feature much more strongly present than in 12 – 16.[120] That implies a paradigmatic use, since the giants themselves are extinct and current suffering is caused by those acting like them. Bloodshed and the devastation of war are a major theme, as we have seen. Ezek 32:17-32 LXX makes a connection between the giants who fell of old (τῶν γιγάντων τῶν πεπτωκότων ἀπὸ αἰῶνος, 32:27; cf. also 32:21, 12) and various violent enemies of Israel who join them in Hades, including Assur (32:22), Elam (32:24), Mosoch and Thobel (32:26) and their armies.

Nickelsburg suggested that this motif in *1 Enoch* 6 – 11 may have had its origins in the ravages of war which resulted from the struggles among the giant powers which emerged in the wake of Alexander.[121] He also proposed that the illicit sexual unions served as a parody of their claims to divine origin. Whether such motifs played similar roles for the author of *1 Enoch* 6 – 11 as we have it and for those who interpolated it into the *Book of the Watchers*, is another question. The emphasis of the text, itself, on the cry for help does suggest a continuing relevance of the depiction of human suffering and this is easily imaginable within the course of the third century with the wars between the Ptolemies and Seleucids.[122] Warfare and its consequences are a concern both in the depiction of the giants and in the account of Asael's revelations which make its weaponry.[123]

Whether the illicit sexual action of the Watchers still functioned as a parody, is less sure. It certainly functions as a shocking story which helps explain the

---

[120] Maxwell J. Davidson, *Angels at Qumran: A Comparative Study of 12 Enoch 1-36, 72-108 and Sectarian Writings from Qumran* (JSPS 11; Sheffield: JSOT Press, 1992), observes: "the eventual focus is on the restoration of the devastated earth" (44). "The angels of *1 Enoch* 6-11 are not functioning in the narrative as analogues of Jewish priests" (44). He concludes: "the problem of evil defies a merely human explanation because of the scope and extent of injustice" (47). "Apparently a major force is threatening the whole race, rather than an internal conflict within the priesthood, as suggested by Suter" (48).

[121] Nickelsburg, *1 Enoch* 1, 166-71. See also his earlier article, Nickelsburg, "Apocalyptic and Myth," 383-405, 389-97.

[122] Collins, *Apocalyptic Imagination*, writes of the image of devastation and violence: "It could apply to the general conditions of Hellenistic rule in the East at any point in the third century" (50). In agreement: Andreas Bedenbender, *Der Gott der Welt tritt auf den Sinai:Entstehung, Entwicklung, und Funktionsweise der Frühjüdischen Apokalyptik* (ANTZ 8; Berlin: Institut Kirche und Judentum, 2000) 184-86; Tigchelaar, *Prophets of Old*, 172-73.

[123] John J. Collins, "Theology and Identity in the Early Enoch Literature," in *The Origins of Enochic Judaism: Proceedings of the First Enoch Seminar, University of Michigan, Sesto Fiorentino, Italy, June 19-23, 2001* (ed. G. Boccaccini; *Henoch* 24; Torino: Silvio Zamorani Editore, 2002) 57-62, sees in *1 Enoch* 8-9 an "expression of the author's reaction to the novelties of the Hellenistic age, which was marked by technological progress, on the one hand, and exposure to Greek attitudes to the human body and sexuality, on the other" (60).

awful consequences and that element of shock includes a strong sense of moral outrage. Again, we face the question whether this remains at the level of aetiology or has taken on a paradigmatic role. Inevitably it must have the latter role at one level – no one should do such things! – but at another, it might be dealing with very specific applications to the world of the author and hearer. Before exploring that possibility, we turn to other significant emphases in 6 – 11.

The author is also concerned with dangerous knowledge and sees women as its source. Both the elaboration of the Shemihazah myth and the Asael material emphasise this. It includes concern about sorcery and related skills, the "science" of meteorology and astronomy, and the use of cosmetics and adornment. It is striking that the author focuses all this on women and in addition appears to make women jointly culpable for the illicit sexual union between themselves and the Watchers. The motif occurs in both the Asael and Shemihazah stories and also serves to integrate them.[124] While the author of *1 Enoch* 12 – 16 also sees women and their possession of forbidden knowledge as dangerous (16:3), that emphasis is much stronger and detailed in *1 Enoch* 6 – 11. Given the prominence of this motif in substance and function, it is very likely that it reflects the author's concern.[125]

Under what circumstances might an author see women in this way? The answer lies almost certainly not in a formal public role of women as teachers, nor in the activity of prostitution, but in their influence as wives.[126] When we ask what kind of women might bring such forbidden knowledge, the answer seems most likely to lie in the direction of foreign wives. This raises, in turn, the possibility (though does not require it) that the author also uses the illicit union of the Watchers paradigmatically to attack marriage with Gentiles. The paradigmatic perspective may extend to the depiction of the offspring, where the author uses language usually applied to the offspring of illegitimate marriage or sexual relations: "half-breeds" (κίβδηλα), "bastards" (μαζηρέους = ממזריא) and "sons of miscegenation illicit unions" (πορνείας) (9:9, 10:9-10). Whereas in *1 Enoch* 12 – 16 the paradigmatic use of the story of illicit union may relate in particular to the marriage of priests because of the emphasis on the abandonment of the heavenly sanctuary (though it need not be only priests), in *1 Enoch* 6 – 11 the

---

[124] On the importance of the angels' teaching and its effects as central to the concerns of *1 Enoch* 6 – 11, see Molenberg, "Roles of Shemihaza and Asael," who observes: "it seems a reasonable conclusion that, to the author of this text, the angels' teaching was the principal cause of distress in the world" (137).

[125] Argall, *1 Enoch and Sirach*, notes that "the charge of practising idolatry is standard rhetoric among rival teachers or traditions" (29). In *1 Enoch* 6 – 11 and 12 – 16, however, more seems to be involved than rhetorical slander.

[126] Nickelsburg (personal note 14 March, 2006) draws attention to the link between Solomon's wives and idolatry.

concern could be more general.[127] There is certainly precedent for this concern already in Ezra 9:1-2, where the grounds also include exposure to the abominations of foreign peoples through intermarriage. *1 Enoch* 6 – 11 appears to reflect a stance closer to Ezra 9 and to *Jubilees*, than it does to those writings which focus more narrowly on the priesthood.

At this point it is also interesting to note Bhayro's thesis, that 6 – 11 is concerned primarily to attack divination.[128] As noted earlier in the discussion of 6:1 and 3, he points to a possible link between the designation "Watchers" and the Akkadian word for diviners, also derived from the verb, "to watch", and notes that the name Shemihazah was probably linked to the Aramaic verb, "to see". According to his view, the devastation of the giants serves simply to reinforce how wrong such practices of divination are. The setting is the latter third of the fourth century and the target is "the importation of Babylonian ideas and practices".[129]

It seems to me, on the one hand, that this fails to give sufficient weight to the descent, to the devastating outcome for earth which causes its inhabitants to cry out for help, and to the promise of hope. On the other hand, sorcery and divination are certainly a concern. Evidence suggests such practices existed in Jewish society of the time. Even among the texts at Qumran we find instruction about incantations, casting of spells, and the use of herbs for healing.[130] The author locates sorcery in particular, however, but possibly also divination (8:3), not

---

[127] Suter, "Revisiting 'Fallen Angel, Fallen Priest'," observes: "The concern with the revelation of secrets leads in yet another direction" (140), but does not pursue it. In his view *1 Enoch* 6 – 11 already "have priestly issues in mind". He points to the designation of the giants as *Mamzerim* (10:9); the language of defilement, the reference in the Aramaic of 9:1 to "the sanctuary of heaven", the possible connection of the "gates of heaven" in 9:2, 10 to the reference to the sanctuary in 13:7-8, echoing Genesis 28, and "the role played by the archangels, apparently as priests, interceding before the throne of God for perishing humanity" (140). He notes that most of this priestly evidence comes from *1 Enoch* 9-11, perhaps reflecting reworking of these chapters by the author who added 12 – 16 (140). None of this requires that we see in 6 – 11 an attack exclusively on priestly marriages.

[128] Bhayro, *Shemihazah and Asael Narrative*, 23-26. He argues that the reference in 7:1 to teaching belonged already to the core material which was concerned primarily to engage in a "polemic against the mantic arts" and the "positive attitude to divination in such accounts as the Joseph and Daniel narratives" (26-27). "To the core SN narrative of *1 Enoch* 6-11, all divination is condemned and blamed for the current ills of the world" (38).

[129] Bhayro, *Shemihazah and Asael Narrative*, 9. While he notes "perceived sexual pollution and mixed marriages" in affirming the position of Tigchelaar, he nowhere relates his thesis of anti-divination to marriages. Indeed, the two do not fit well together because Tigchelaar's focus is Samaritan influence, whereas Bhayro is concerned with Babylonian.

[130] See Wright, *Evil Spirits*, 124-25. He also draws attention to *Jub.*10:11-12, which reports that Raphael taught Noah about herbs and medicines to help him counter the impact of evil spirits (127).

among other teachers, whom the author is alleged to attack, but quite specifically among women. This is true also of the reference to forbidden mysteries in 12 – 16. There is, then, a concern with divination, but it is focused on dangerous information and practices present in (certain women). This points, again, to mixed marriages.

Comparing the apparent concerns of 6 – 11 and 12 – 16, the former addresses the experience of devastation through violence and bloodshed, paradigmatically portrayed in the impact of the giants, explains how this has come about and offers hope.[131] The latter focuses on the impact of the evil spirits which survived the giants and their impact largely on individuals through sickness, acts of violence, and perhaps false teaching, and promises deliverance from them. Read as a whole, 6 – 16, now addresses recurring situations[132] of devastation through warfare and affliction of individuals through the plague of evil spirits.

In addition, both certainly share a sense of abhorrence at the Watchers' sexual wrongdoing, which, whatever other specific application it might have, would help reinforce abhorrence of all acts of sexual wrongdoing in general. We saw, however, that a case can be made that the concern is more specific. In 6 – 11 women are portrayed as bearers of forbidden tradition and agents of seduction in a way that appears to be concerned with their influence, and that is most likely seen as happening through marriage. This makes it also likely that the Watchers' sin, in marrying those not of their kind, functions paradigmatically for the author as a warning for people not to enter inappropriate marriages, which he sees as defiling. There seems no reason in 6 – 11 to restrict this concern to priests or to see it in terms of limiting marriages of priests to certain, mainly (or only) priestly, families. This would not make good sense of the emphasis on dangerous religious influence through wives.

---

[131] On the role of such revelation in engendering hope see George W. E. Nickelsburg, "The Apocalyptic Construction of Reality in *1 Enoch*," in *Mysteries and Revelation: Apocalyptic Studies since the Uppsala Colloquium* (ed. John J. Collins and James H. Charlesworth; JSPS 9; Sheffield: JSOT Press, 1991) 51-64, who, referring to this feature in the various elements of the *1 Enoch* corpus, observes: "Although definitive salvation lies in the future, revelation transmitted in the present time effects a significant resolution of the book's temporal, spatial, and ontological dualism" (61). "These revelations are salvific in function because they provide a means of hope in what is, by all appearances, a hopeless world, and because they encourage the righteous to stand fast against apostasy" (62).

[132] So Collins, *Apocalyptic Imagination*, who notes applicability to recurring situations as a feature and function of myth. He sees this as applying also to issues with the Jerusalem priesthood: "the problem – whatever it was – is transposed to a mythological plane. By telling the story of the Watchers rather than that of the Diadochi or the priesthood, *1 Enoch* 1 – 36 becomes a paradigm which is not restricted to one historical situation but can be applied whenever an analogous situation arises" (51), just as crises of the Babylonian period provided a filter through which in other apocalypses, crises were viewed.

On the other hand, the stronger emphasis in 12 – 16 on the Watchers' abandoning their place in the heavenly sanctuary may throw the emphasis more on priestly mismarriage. The concern with women as bearers of forbidden knowledge, although mentioned only once (but nevertheless in an emphatic position in the final words), suggests that the focus remains foreign marriages, rather than some more narrow concern to restrict marriage to certain specific families. Taken as a whole 6 – 16 exhibits, then, some coherence in an apparent concern with the influence of women as bearers of dangerous tradition to which people are exposed by inappropriate marriages, probably thought of especially as marriage to Gentiles. If there is a shift of emphasis, it is from one where the concern is general to one where the concern focuses more particularly on priests.

1.1.6   Tradition in 1 Enoch 6 – 11 and 12 – 16

It is even more difficult to explore possible sources or strands of tradition in *1 Enoch* 6 – 11 and to identify the potential concerns of each.[133] A detailed discussion is beyond the scope of this study, so that, for the most part we shall work with Nickelsburg's reconstruction. In our consideration of *1 Enoch* 6-11 as a whole, we have noted that there are tensions within the story and within the narrative, and these invite attempts to reconstruct earlier forms of the stories.[134] Like many before him, Nickelsburg notes the unevenness created by the intrusion of material about Asael, both in 8:1-3 and in 9:6, 8 and 10:4-8.[135] He sees the earliest form of the myth as a rewriting of Genesis 6 – 9 to address a situation where the author and his hearers understood themselves as victims of giant-like powers at war with one another and wreaking havoc on earth.[136] He makes the plausible suggestion, as noted above, that the setting which matched this image might well be the wars among Alexander's successors, 323-302 B.C.E. I have suggested that this probably still belongs to the meaning of the story for the author.

---

[133] See the review of research in Wright, *Evil Spirits*, 29-37.

[134] See the review of source critical analysis in Tigchelaar, *Prophets of Old*, 168-73. He concludes: "1 En. 6-11 is rather the product of an author who joined several traditions into a literary text than the result of the consecutive adding and interpolating of traditions. The author to whom I ascribe the literary work converted a number of traditions on the Watchers into a story with a new scope: the deliverance of the righteous from evil and the restoration of the earth" (176).

[135] Nickelsburg, *1 Enoch 1*, 165.

[136] Nickelsburg, *1 Enoch 1*, 166-71. See also his earlier article, Nickelsburg, "Apocalyptic and Myth," *JBL* 96 (1977) 383-405, 389-97. See also the proposal of Paul D. Hanson, "Rebellion in Heaven, Azazel, and Euhemeristic Heroes in *1 Enoch* 6-11," *JBL* 96 (1977) 195-233, who seeks to make connections with Azazel in Leviticus 16. On the latter see the critical discussion in Wright, *Evil Spirits*, 109-14.

Claims by a number of them to divine origin invited use of the Genesis myth as parody, exposing them not as divine, but as demonic. In this reconstruction he notes that the sexual component functions to explain the "quasi-divine nature of the giants and hence their qualitative difference from the human race", and the "helplessness" of the latter, exposed to powers beyond their "ken and control" and to their malevolence, since "their very conception was an act of rebellion". At the same time, should this be the case, one would have to observe that sexual wrongdoing is incidental to the chief concern: facing the violence of superpowers.[137]

Nickelsburg then suggests that the original myth underwent expansion, which included insertion of material about the Watchers' instruction of their wives about magic, medicine and potions to ward off rivals in love (7:1de; 9:8cd),[138] then the addition of a list of what each Watcher taught (8:3), and finally the insertion of the Asael material from an independent myth, concerned with instruction about making the weapons of war and, he suggests, "forbidden sexual relations".[139] Should 13:1-2 be a secondary interpolation into 12 – 16, then he holds that the Asael material may have been added to 6 – 11 after it was joined to 12 – 16.[140] Similarly if 16:2-4 is original to 12 – 16, then 7:1de; 8:3 and 9:8 were added prior

---

[137] On the other hand, Helge S. Kvanvig, "Origin and Identity of the Enoch Group," in *The Origins of Enochic Judaism: Proceedings of the First Enoch Seminar, University of Michigan, Sesto Fiorentino, Italy, June 19-23, 2001* (ed. G. Boccaccini; *Henoch* 24; Torino: Silvio Zamorani Editore, 2002) 207-12, who relates the sexual motif to invading armies, taking women and producing *Mamzerim* (210, 211), notes the motif of foreigners taking Israelite women in the Dinah episode in *Jubilees* 30 (211) and the issue of women's vulnerability to foreigners in the *Genesis Apocryphon*, *Ps. Aristeas* 12-21 and Josephus *A.J.* 13.4-6; *Ap* 1.208-11, which report that Ptolemy took 100,000 Jewish captives from Jerusalem in 319 B.C.E. (211). For him this stands beside a concern with apostate priests, which he sees reflected in *1 Enoch* 15 (211).

[138] So also James C. VanderKam, *Enoch and the Growth of an Apocalyptic Tradition* (CBQMS 16; Washington: CBA, 1984) 124, reacting against the earlier view of Nickelsburg which he expressed in "Apocalyptic and Myth". By contrast, Bhayro, *Shemihazah and Asael Narrative*, argues that the reference to teaching belongs to the core Shemihazah narrative along with 8:3 but without 6:7 (12, 18). This then enables him to argue that the primary concern of the core narrative is an attack on divination.

[139] Nickelsburg, *1 Enoch 1*, 171; 190-93.

[140] Nickelsburg, *1 Enoch 1*, 191. This is the proposal of Newsom, "The Development of *1 Enoch* 6 – 19," 310-29. But see Bhayro, *Shemihazah and Asael Narrative*, who counters Newsom's reconstruction, pointing out that had the Ariel material been added after the core of *1 Enoch* 6 – 11 had been incorporated into the *Book of the Watchers*, we should expect some reference in it to Enoch (29). The argument is, however, inconclusive. Nothing would require a reference to Enoch.

to the joining of the two blocks.[141] He notes that the interpolator in effect makes Asael (later Azazel) the primary cause of evil. I think that in this process one also needs to see the instruction by the Watchers of the women in 7:1, and then in the detailed list in 8:3, and in part also the instruction of Asael, as addressing an emerging problem with foreign wives, leading to the twofold concern, as I see it, currently expressed in the material.

More complex still and fascinating is the question of the degree to which the myth draws not only on Genesis, but also on ancient near eastern sources and on developed forms of the myth which perhaps existed alongside and some have argued independently of the Genesis account.[142] These lie beyond the scope of this study.

---

[141] Nickelsburg, *1 Enoch 1*, 191. See also Dimant, "*1 Enoch* 6 – 11," who argues that 6 – 11 should be seen as a parabiblical text, comparable with similar such texts present at Qumran, such as the *Genesis Apocryphon*, and drawing on sources written originally in Hebrew, which have been interpolated secondarily into the Enoch corpus (224-25). On this basis she rejects the suggestion of Suter, "Fallen Angels, Fallen Priests," and others that 12 – 16 is a commentary on 6 – 11. On the other hand, clearly the author of 12 – 16 knows some version of the myth present in 6 – 11 and reflects many of its motifs, including some which no longer play as significant a role, as we have shown. Dimant notes earlier speculation that 6 – 11 may be dependent on the lost Book of Noah, and cites similar material in 1Q19 which is related to *1 Enoch* 106-107. She concludes: "the author of the Aramaic *Book of the Watchers* extracted chapters 6 – 11 from a Hebrew narrative source (237). On the case for the existence of a lost Book of Noah, see F. García Martínez, *Qumran and Apocalyptic: Studies on the Aramaic Texts from Qumran* (Leiden: Brill, 1992) 24-44, 38 and Kvanvig, "Gen 6,3 and the Watcher Story," 295-96. On this see however Bhayro, *Shemihazah and Asael Narrative*, who notes that the possibly related Hebrew texts in 1Q19 and 1Q20 are too fragmentary to be any weight of argument in support of Dimant's thesis (5).

[142] Recent important studies include: Jan K. Bremmer, "Remember the Titans!" in *The Fall of the Angels* (ed. Christoph Auffarth and Loren T. Stuckenbruck; Themes in Biblical Narrative 6; Leiden: Brill, 2004) 35-61; Helge S. Kvanvig, "The Watchers Story, Genesis and Atra-hasis: A Triangular Reading," in *The Origins of Enochic Judaism: Proceedings of the First Enoch Seminar, University of Michigan, Sesto Fiorentino, Italy, June 19-23, 2001* (ed. G. Boccaccini; *Henoch* 24; Torino: Silvio Zamorani Editore, 2002) 17-21, and Helge S. Kvanvig, *Roots of Apocalyptic: The Mesopotamian Background of the Enoch Figure and the Son of Man* (WMANT 61; Neukirchen-Vluyn: Neukirchener Verlag, 1988); Andreas Bedenbender, "Traces of Enochic Judaism within the Hebrew Bible," in *The Origins of Enochic Judaism: Proceedings of the First Enoch Seminar, University of Michigan, Sesto Fiorentino, Italy, June 19-23, 2001* (ed. G. Boccaccini; *Henoch* 24; Torino: Silvio Zamorani Editore, 2002) 39-48; Bedenbender, *Gott der Welt*; Hendel, "*Nephilim*"; Stuckenbruck, "Origins of Evil"; Nickelsburg, *1 Enoch 1*, 57-62; 191-93; and earlier VanderKam, *Enoch and the Growth of an Apocalyptic Tradition*.

The setting for the writing is almost by definition a scribal one, since they were the small elite who could pen such works.[143] Enoch, too, is pictured as a scribe. Some evidence suggests an awareness of Mt Hermon and its regions, which may mean we have to do with a writer associated with northern Galilee, whether located there or not.[144] It goes beyond the evidence to claim the author is a priest, though he demonstrates concern about the priesthood.[145]

---

[143] A point made well by Richard A. Horsley, "Social Relations and Social Conflict in the *Epistle of Enoch*," in *For a Later Generation: The Transformation of Tradition in Israel, Early Judaism, and Early Christianity* (ed. Randal A. Argall, Beverly A. Bow, and Rodney A. Werline; Harrisburg: Trinity Press International, 2000) 100-15.

[144] See also Nickelsburg, *1 Enoch 1*, who estimates that these chapters stem from the mid 3rd century from northern Galilee (Dan and Mt Hermon) (230-32) and earlier George W. E. Nickelsburg, "Enoch, Levi, and Peter: Recipients of Revelation in Upper Galilee," *JBL* 100 (1981) 575-600, 585-86. See also Suter, "Mapping the First Book of Enoch," who sees the geographical reference as important and reflecting the "perceptual geography" (a term reflecting "the mental maps which people create") of a Judean scribe (393). On the difficulty of determining provenance see Esther Eshel, and Hanan Eshel, "Typonymic Midrash in 1 Enoch and in Other Second Temple Jewish Literature," in *The Origins of Enochic Judaism: Proceedings of the First Enoch Seminar, University of Michigan, Sesto Fiorentino, Italy, June 19-23, 2001* (ed. G. Boccaccini; *Henoch* 24; Torino: Silvio Zamorani Editore, 2002) 115-130, who note that familiarity with centres widely held to be sacred need not imply the writing has its origin there. See also Hanan Eshel, and Esther Eshel, "Separating Levi from Enoch: Response to 'Enoch, Levi, and Peter: Recipients of Revelation in Upper Galilee'," in *George W.E. Nickelsburg in Perspective: An Ongoing Dialogue of Learning* (2 vols; ed. Jacob Neusner and Alan J. Avery-Peck; JSJSup 80; Leiden: Brill, 2003) 2. 458-68 and, in reply, George W. E. Nickelsburg, "Response to Hanen Eshel and Esther Eshel," in *George W.E. Nickelsburg in Perspective: An Ongoing Dialogue of Learning* (2 vols; ed. Jacob Neusner and Alan J. Avery-Peck; JSJSup 80; Leiden: Brill, 2003) 2. 469-71. There he clarifies "that the core of tradition in chapters 6 – 11 and its elaboration in 12 – 16 likely emanated from circles in the region around Hermon. ... I doubt that a Judean would place the origin of the Enochic tradition at the location of the ancient rival shrine of Jeroboam" (470). See also Pieter. M. Venter, "Spatiality in Enoch's Journeys (*1 Enoch* 12-36)," in *Wisdom and Apocalypticism in the Dead Sea Scrolls and in the Biblical Tradition* (ed. Florentino García Martínez; BETL 168; Leuven: Leuven University Press and Peeters, 2003) 211-30, who reviews recent research on the setting of the *Book of the Watchers*, concluding that "the problem addressed in the *Book of the Watchers* is the notion of evil in terms of priestly concerns" (228). He then notes that "the differences are mainly linked to the matter of locality". This could mean conflict either between priests in Jerusalem and priests in the north living at the sanctuary of Dan, or between priests now all in Jerusalem, but some of whom have come from Dan or have Danite, perhaps Korahite, traditions (228). "While *1 Enoch* 8,1-9,1 refers to the results of the transgression of the fallen Watchers in terms of warfare, sorcery and astronomy, 1 Enoch 7,1-15 [*sic*; perhaps 7; 10-15?] refers to improper sexual conduct. Linking Enoch's journeys (1 Enoch 12-36) to this previous section on the fallen Watchers (1 Enoch 6-11), it

The motif of sexual wrongdoing is important in the myth, which functions both as an explanation of why the consequences are so chaotic and as a warning against intermarriage and the dangerous influences to which one is thereby exposed. It is also implicit in the portrayal of women as seductive. In 6 – 16 sexual relations are treated as either dangerous and illicit or as necessary for procreation. There is no hint that they might play any other role. Without the need for procreation, the need for sexual relations, indeed even for women, would disappear. Nevertheless, given these emphases, it is surprising that where one might expect to see references to sexual wrongdoing, they are absent or, at most, only implied. Thus the giants do not, as one might have expected, engage in rape and other sexual wrongdoing. Nor is sexual wrongdoing a feature of the activity of evil spirits. One has to conclude, paradoxically, that, while sexual abhorrence is now fundamental to the myth, it is not fundamental to discourse about the author's present, where the only apparent concern we can deduce in this regard relates to inappropriate marriages and the dangers posed by women's seductiveness and by the forbidden traditions some of them bear.

1.1.7   1 Enoch 17 – 19

The punishment of the fallen Watchers appears in the context of Enoch's journey to the northwest (*1 Enoch* 17 – 19)[146] in 19:1, where, again, we have a reference to their sin: "the angels who mingled (μίγνυμι as 10:11) with the women", another way of alluding to sexual intercourse and probably also to the mixing of kinds. As Nickelsburg observes, the emphasis falls here not on illicit revelations, but on sexual wrongdoing.[147] But here we have for the first time reference to the activity of the evil spirits in terms of idolatry: these spirits "bring destruction on men and

---

is interesting that Enoch discovers the allocated places of evildoers rather than places where specific evil practices are performed. The focus fall on places not practices" (230). Bhayro, *Shemihazah and Asael Narrative*, draws attention to the practice of smelting at Dan and favours an upper Galilee provenance for *1 Enoch* 6 – 11 (42).

[145] Suter, "Revisiting 'Fallen Angel, Fallen Priest'," speaks of the conflict as "one taking place at the centre of third century Jewish society between the central institutional system, focused upon the high priest who wields political power, and elements of the cultural system, comprised of the scribes who tell the myths that keep the priests in power" (141). He leaves open whether the latter were also priests. Collins, "Theology and Identity," notes that Enoch is portrayed as a "righteous scribe" (12:4), not a priest (60).

[146] On this section see Nickelsburg, *1 Enoch 1*, who suggests it is a tradition originally independent of *1 Enoch* 12 – 16 originating from mid to late 3rd century, but now incorporated into the *Book of the Watchers* after *1 Enoch* 12 – 16 was added and before   20 – 36 (279).

[147] So Nickelsburg, *1 Enoch 1*, 287.

lead them astray to sacrifice to demons as to gods until the day of the great judgement" (19:1). Thus this is the first explicit link between the Watchers (and their offspring) and idolatry.[148] Leading astray, if textually secure, may refer to this in 15:11, but there we find no specific reference to idolatry. The link between evil spirits and idolatry is widely attested and comes to expression dramatically in *Jubilees*, where it accounts for the idolatry in the household of Abram's father (11:4-5; 12:20).

1 Enoch 19:2 then singles out the women partners of the Watchers: "And the women of the transgressing angels will become sirens".[149] This image of women as sirens, drawn from Greek mythology, reflects the emphasis in 6 – 11 on the danger of women's sexuality (6:1), enhanced by Asael's teaching (8:1), but also by knowledge about sorcery and charms learned from Shemihazah and his accomplices (7:1; 16:3), although 19:1-2 offers no specific detail.

As Enoch continues his heavenly journey,[150] he is also shown the abode of punishment for the stars who "transgressed the command of the Lord in the beginning of their rising, for they did not come out in their appointed times" (18:15; similarly 21:5). This recalls the fundamental theme stated in 2:1 – 5:4 about changing from the divinely appointed order and probably originally represents an alternative account of the sins of the Watchers, who are portrayed as stars in 86:1-3,[151] but may have its origins in disputes in the realm of astronomy related to the *Book of the Heavenly Luminaries* (72 – 82).

---

[148] Jackson, *Enochic Judaism*, notes the allusion to Ps 106:37 and Deut 32:17, and the connection with the image of adultery used to describe Israel's relation with Yahweh in Hosea 1 – 3; Jer 2:23 – 3:25; and Ezekiel 16 (35).

[149] This follows the reading of Panopolitanus: εἰς σειρῆνας rather the Ethiopic *kama salamāwiyāt* "will become peaceful", which has read ὡς εἰρηναῖαι. See Nickelsburg, *1 Enoch 1*, 277. Cf. Olson, *Enoch*, who argues that the authors assume the women are blameless and that another reference to having no peace fits the context better (268-69). Our discussion of 8:1-2, above, makes the case that the authors do not see the women as blameless.

[150] On the similarities between the motif of the heavenly journey to the realms of the dead and Greek traditions see Nickelsburg, *1 Enoch 1*, 279-81.

[151] So Nickelsburg, *1 Enoch 1*, 288.

1.1.8   1 Enoch 20 – 36

In *1 Enoch* 20 – 36, "a rewritten and reversed version of the account of Enoch's journey to the west (chaps. 17 – 19)",[152] we encounter brief references to the Watchers' sin (21:6; cf. 21:10), but without elaboration, and a new focus, which deals with eschatology as it affects human beings. Imagery of the garden of Eden appears in 24:2 – 25:7, which describe the tree of life in the west (23:1) and in 28:1 – 32:6, which describe the paradise of righteousness in the east.[153] In the former the author locates a fragrant tree (24:4-5). The allusion is to "the tree of life" from which Adam and Eve did not eat and which the cherubim now guard (Gen 3:22-24), but no mention is made of Adam and Eve. As Collins notes, the focus is the future, not the past.[154] Accordingly, Michael tells Enoch that "no flesh has the right to touch it until the great judgement" (25:4). The tree, originally among those surrounding the seventh mountain (24:3-4), where God will conduct the last judgement (25:3), will be transplanted to Jerusalem beside the house of God,[155] so that its fragrance will be in their bones as they enter the sanctuary (25:5-6). There its fruit will nourish the chosen (25:4). The promise is not everlasting life, but long life, like that of the people before the flood (25:6; cf. also 10:17).[156] This suggests that the author is not envisaging life without procreation and sexual activity, such as 15:5-7 assumes for the eternal Watchers.

Eden imagery returns in 32:3, which speaks of "the paradise of righteousness" and of "the tree of wisdom, whose fruit the holy ones eat and learn great wisdom", also most fragrant (32:4). The angel explains:

---

[152] Nickelsburg, *1 Enoch 1*, 290, who sees this material as emanating from the late 3rd century B.C.E. (293).

[153] On the two locations see Eibert J. C. Tigchelaar, "Eden and Paradise: The Garden Motif in Some Early Jewish Texts (*1 Enoch* and Other Texts Found at Qumran)," in *Paradise Interpreted: Representations of Biblical Paradise in Judaism and Christianity* (Themes in Biblical Narrative 2; ed. Gerard P. Luttikhuizen; Leiden: Brill, 1999) 37-62, who notes that, strictly speaking, *1 Enoch* 24 – 25 is not described as a paradise (43-44). He suggests that the author may have accessed a tradition about the Garden of Eden into which the tree of life had not yet been added (45-46).

[154] Collins, "Before the Fall," 303. He takes Nickelsburg to task for using the past tense with reference to the transplantation of the tree: "God has transplanted it" (Nickelsburg, *1 Enoch 1*, 314). The latter's translation certainly uses a future: "it will be transplanted" (312). Collins notes that the account in *1 Enoch* 24 – 25 "recalls Ezekiel 28 rather than Genesis. In Ezekiel … Eden was located 'on the mountain of God' and was associated with precious stones" (304).

[155] Nickelsburg, *1 Enoch 1*, rightly cautions that this does not provide a "clue to the author's attitude towards the present state of Jerusalem and its sanctuary" (315).

[156] See Nickelsburg, *1 Enoch 1*, 315.

> This is the tree of wisdom from which your father of old and your mother of old, who were before you, ate and learned wisdom. And their eyes were opened, and they knew that they were naked, and they were driven from the garden. (32:6)[157]

The allusion is to Gen 2:16-17 ("And the LORD God commanded the man, 'You may freely eat of every tree of the garden; but of the tree of the knowledge of good and evil you shall not eat, for in the day that you eat of it you shall die'."), Gen 3:6 ("that the tree was to be desired to make one wise") and Gen 3:22 ("the man has become like one of us, knowing good and evil"), but apparently also to the other form of the myth preserved in Ezekiel 28 and 31, which appears to assume that not all wisdom gained was evil.[158]

For the author, this was an appropriate resource for "the holy ones" (32:4), but apparently not for the first parents.[159] On this reading, the act which taught them wisdom was sinful, because the wisdom was, like the mysteries wrongly imparted by the Watchers, not for them to possess (32:6).[160] The author implies that awareness of nakedness belonged in the category of inappropriate wisdom, but takes us no further, except to note the expulsion. Nothing casts light on the implications for attitudes towards sexuality. Nothing is said of the curse of the serpent and judgement on the woman and man and its consequences.

1.1.9   Conclusion

In conclusion, therefore, while the author or editor responsible for the *Book of the Watchers* is aware of the sin of Adam and Eve in taking the fruit of the tree of wisdom, their resultant awareness of nakedness and their expulsion from the garden, his primary locus for the genesis of evil in the world is the action of the Watchers. In its synthesis of what appear to be different strands of tradition, the *Book of the Watchers* traces this "great sin" to two sources: the lust of Watchers

---

[157] Argall, *1 Enoch and Sirach*, notes the parallel between Adam and Eve's receiving sexual awareness and Enoch receiving knowledge. "Through the interpreting role of angels, Enoch's eyes too are opened, as were the eyes of Adam and Eve (cf. *1 En* 1:5; 32:6)" (34).

[158] See the discussion in Nickelsburg, *1 Enoch 1*, 327-28.

[159] See, however, Collins, "Before the Fall," who notes that the Ethiopic lacks reference to "the holy ones" (see Nickelsburg, *1 Enoch 1*, 322, who reads an uncertain ἅγιοι), so that those who "eat and know great wisdom" appears to refer to the first human parents and without any sense that acquiring wisdom was a bad thing (305). Collins addresses the wrongdoing which occasioned their expulsion: "perhaps they had been forbidden to eat from this tree as a test" (305). Collins makes no reference in this context to the detail that "their eyes were opened, and they knew they were naked".

[160] Cf. Nickelsburg, *1 Enoch 1*, who asks whether the author might be suggesting "that Adam and Eve were given access to a kind of wisdom that Enoch learned by other means" (328).

for human women and the appearance and behaviour of the women, themselves, and the knowledge they received.

With regard to the women, Asael taught men about metalwork and they, in turn, provided jewellery and cosmetics for their daughters and with these they led the angels astray (8:1). By implication in 6:1 women were not simply beautiful and comely in an innocent way. Thus at one level Asael begins the process through his teaching (9:6; 10:7-8), but blameworthy action is continued by others and further implicates women. Shemihazah and his accomplices teach women sorcery and related arts (7:1; 8:3). These probably include wiles to enhance sexual pursuits. They become bearers of forbidden knowledge (16:2-3). The women who led the Watchers astray are to become sirens (19:2), but that coheres with what appears to be a concern potentially with all women and relates to the danger posed by their sexuality and their knowledge.

With regard to the Watchers, the focus of blame is chiefly upon them. In the *Book of the Watchers* seen as a whole, their wrongdoing is twofold: illicit sexual union with women and imparting forbidden knowledge.[161] The former act produced the giants, resulting in the devastation of war, and the evil spirits which continue to wreak havoc in the author's time in afflicting human beings (perhaps also leading them astray to idols or false teaching). The giants are also designated as half-breeds and *mamzerim*, in other words, people who should be rotted out from the community.

The Watchers' action is variously described as going into (7:1; 9:8), lying with (9:8; 15:3), miscegenation (10:9), mingling with (19:1), defiling themselves with (7:1; 9:8; 10:11; 12:4; 15:3, 4), mating with (10:11), doing as the sons of earth (15:3), and marrying (6:2; 12:4; 15:3), always with the focus on sexual intercourse. The *Book of the Watchers* portrays the action itself as sexual wrongdoing on a number of grounds. It crossed boundaries of species, was motivated by lust and by illegitimate and inappropriate desire to produce progeny, entailed holy ones both abandoning the heavenly sanctuary, where some at least will have had priestly roles, and becoming defiled, including through women's blood (probably understood in a broad sense), and was not one-off, but ongoing. Their departure from the order of their being sets their sin in the context of those who change God's created order, against which the indictment of 2:1 – 5:4 rails and which is reflected also in the sin of stars which did not arise as they should have (18:15; 21:5). In the context of deploring the act in 15:4-7 the *Book of the Watchers* also reveals, conversely, an attitude which sees sexual intercourse as

---

[161] Nickelsburg, *1 Enoch 1*, observes that the results of the rebellion of the Watchers "are violence and bloodshed, sexual misconduct, and wrong religious practice (i.e., magic, prognostication by means of the created elements, and a polluted temple cult)" (46).

existing solely for the purpose of procreation, so that among those who are immortal there is no need for sexual relations nor for women.

The imparting of forbidden knowledge in the first place, in chronological sequence, by Asael (8:1; see also 9:6; 10:8; 13:1-2) and then by Shemihazah and his accomplices (7:1; 8:3; 9:8; 10:7; 16:3), appears to have two main consequences: equipping men for war and equipping women for seduction and sorcery. The *Book of the Watchers* does not depict the giants as teaching, but may attribute a related role to their spirits when it speaks of them leading people astray to idolatry in 19:1 (and possibly in 15:11, should we accept the emended reading).

I have discussed the possible relevance of this material for an author and his community, in particular, in relation to *1 Enoch* 6 – 11 and 12 – 16 and to both in comparison. Having now surveyed the remainder of the *Book of the Watchers*, where there is only limited material of relevance, I shall confine myself to some summary comments. An etiological perspective informs the detail about evil spirits. It enables the *Book of the Watchers* to describe where they came from, but also to assure hearers that one day they will be overcome. It is interesting that the *Book of the Watchers* nowhere depicts their activity in relation to sexuality, which one might have expected given their origins. This is also true in relation to the giants. Mostly the giants' deeds are depicted as savagery, drinking blood and consuming one another (7:3-5). An etiological perspective also appears to play a role in relation to the giants, although it is complicated by the fact that, unlike the evil spirits, they are deceased. The aetiology works therefore by analogy: war and violence which the hearers of the *Book of the Watchers* might continue to see in their day are the result of evil powers, whether or not they might perceive in the story a parody of claims to divine parentage which probably first informed it – although such claims continued to be made. This aetiology seems more relevant in *1 Enoch* 6 – 11 than elsewhere in the *Book of the Watchers*.

By contrast, there appears to be some consistency in the *Book of the Watchers* in concern about both women's sexuality and their dangerous knowledge. That entails some thought about relations between men and women and marriage in particular. The Watchers' action is at least paradigmatic of what is abhorrent, but some aspects of their action may have been held to be more relevant than others. The description of their offspring as *mamzerim* and half-breeds functions paradigmatically: one should not do things which produce such offspring. On the other hand, nothing suggests a focus on bestiality, for instance, for which it also provided an analogy. The motif of women's forbidden knowledge, combined with the motif of the Watchers' mixing of kinds, suggests marriage to the wrong kind of women is a concern. Marriages to Gentiles might be seen both as defiling and as exposing one to dangerous influences, including sorcery and idolatry (apparent in the later level of the *Book of the Watchers*), not to speak of their dangerous sexuality, enhanced by cosmetics and jewellery. Possibly a concern with priests' marriages now shapes 12 – 16, based on the analogy of Watchers with priests. Taken as a whole, the *Book of the Watchers* identifies the danger which women pose not primarily in terms of their parentage (their families), but in terms of what influences they bring.

Where one might expect a possible allusion to sexuality, such as in the use of imagery of the garden of Eden (24:3 – 25:6 and 32:3-6), none occurs. At most one could conclude that the vision of a future, rich in fertility, including the begetting of thousands, reflects a positive approach to sexual activity, at least for procreation in the age to come (10:17), unlike traditions elsewhere which appear to assume that in the age to come no sexual intercourse takes place or is necessary or appropriate and that the righteous will live with angels and like angels in the heavenly sanctuary.[162] The book includes generic references to sin,[163] concentrated in particular in 10:20 (impurity, wrong, lawlessness, sin, godlessness, impurities; also 10:22, defilement, uncleanness; 10:16 perversity). Its reference to impurity and defilement probably includes an allusion to sexual wrongdoing.

There is thus a somewhat paradoxical outcome when we consider what appear to be the concerns of the *Book of the Watchers*. At its heart is an action of sexual wrongdoing. Much of its impact, however, is not described in terms of further actions of sexual wrongdoing, either by the offspring or by their evil spirits. On the other hand, the abhorrence which serves to explain chaos and devastation of different kinds, appears also to have been used paradigmatically in combination with a myth about the dangers of women to warn against inappropriate marriages and so to enhance the gravamen of such warnings. In the *Book of the Watchers* this combination serves now to warn against falling to women's enhanced seductive charms and so to exposure to idolatry and false or forbidden religion. Where it speaks positively of women, the *Book of the Watchers* defines women's roles

---

[162] Nickelsburg, *1 Enoch 1*, notes that "only the last part of the Epistle indicates a heavenly setting for eternal life" citing 103:1-4 and 104:1-6 (49); otherwise "most of the major sections of *1 Enoch* – drawing on Isaiah 65-66 for their inspiration – envision a renewed earth and a restored Jerusalem as the setting for the long life that the righteous will enjoy after the judgment" (49).

[163] As Nickelsburg, *1 Enoch 1*, notes, there is also little or no reference to the Mosaic law, for instance, relating to "issues like Sabbath observance, the honoring of one's parents, the rite of circumcision, and the full range of cultic laws" (51). Beyond a few references (1:4, and later: 93:6; 99:2) "*1 Enoch* is remarkably silent on the Mosaic covenant and Torah" (50). "The repeated identification of wisdom with the figure of Enoch, its transmitter, is the reverse side of *1 Enoch*'s paucity of references to the Mosaic Torah. Although it is not likely that the authors disregarded the content of the pentateuchal laws, they have leapfrogged Moses and identified Enoch as the primordial recipient of all heavenly wisdom" (52). He goes on to note how in 1:1-9 and later in 91-93 the author puts Mosaic material from Deuteronomy 30-33 into the mouth of Enoch.

narrowly in terms of procreation and sexuality, and as limited to that end. Women are otherwise redundant.

1.2   The Book of Dream Visions (1 Enoch 83 – 90)

1.2.1   The First Vision   (1 Enoch 83 – 84)

This writing begins with the account of Enoch's frightening dream from which his grandfather, Mahalalel, woke him and about which he advised him to pray to God (83:1-9). The substance of the dream had been about the collapse of heaven and the swallowing up of earth, a preview of judgement.[164] Enoch's prayer extols God, then identifies the chief concern: "And now the angels of your heavens are doing wrong" (84:4). This will refer to the sin of the Watchers which forms the central concern on *1 Enoch* 1-36, but here there is no detail. It is joined to concern about human sin. As Nickelsburg notes, no longer are human beings victims of angelic sin, a development already present in the motif of revelation and the figure of Asael in *1 Enoch* 6-11, and reflected in 106:13-15.[165] Detail follows in the second vision.

1.2.2   The Animal Vision   (1 Enoch 85:1 – 90:42)

The second vision (85:1 – 90:42)[166] is the so-called *Animal Apocalypse* which reviews history up to the author's time and beyond.[167] It begins with Adam and Eve appearing as a bull and a heifer, but nothing pertaining to sexuality in the garden story appears.[168] We simply read that a white bull came forth "and after it a

---

[164] On the likelihood that the first vision is a supplement to the second and composed after it, see Nickelsburg, *1 Enoch 1*, 346-47.

[165] Nickelsburg, *1 Enoch 1*, 353.

[166] Nickelsburg, *1 Enoch 1*, mentions the suggestion of Milik that Enoch's seeing the vision on his bed before his marriage may allude to a period of pre-marital continence (370), but it could just as easily simply be an allusion to time. Cf. Józef T. Milik, *The Books of Enoch: Aramaic Fragments of Qumran Cave 4* (Oxford: Clarendon, 1976) 231.

[167] On its likely provenance around 200 B.C.E., but in its present form around 165-163 B.C.E., see Nickelsburg, *1 Enoch 1*, 361.

[168] See, however, Nickelsburg, *1 Enoch 1*, who speculates, on the basis of later legends, that Cain's colour, black, may indicate he is begotten by Satan (371).

young heifer came forth. And with her two bull calves came forth" (85:3). The first sin it mentions is Cain's murder of Abel (85:4).[169]

On the other hand, there is reference to the sin of the Watchers, clearly in two stages. First we read that "a star fell from heaven, and it arose and was eating and pasturing among those cattle" (86:1; similarly 90:21). Then in 86:3 we read that Enoch saw "many stars descend and cast themselves down from heaven to that first star". This reflects a synthesis of the Shemihazah and Asael forms of the myth as present in *1 Enoch* 6 – 11, and refers first to Asael (so 88:1) and then to Shemihazah and his accomplices (88:3).[170] The author describes the effects of these descents differently. Of the first, it begins by noting that the star "was eating and pasturing among those cattle" (86:1). This matches the initial description of the second descending group, except that the latter says the stars became bulls and pastured among calves *ṭa'wā* (86:3), not cattle *'alhemt* (86:1).[171]

The effect of the first star's descent is a disturbance of order: "Then I saw those large and black cattle, and look, all of them exchanged their pens and their pastures and their calves, and they began to moan, one after the other" (86:2). The "black cattle" are the sons of Cain (85:5). The "large cattle" may refer to Seth's line. Both aspects require some explanation. Exchanging pens, pastures, and calves suggests something chaotic. It probably alludes to intermarriage.[172] The notion of

---

[169] Nickelsburg, *1 Enoch 1*, notes that in Gen 4:3-7 the other sin of Cain is cultic irregularity, which the allusion here may foreshadow (371). However nothing in the immediate context suggests this.

[170] So also Nickelsburg, *1 Enoch 1*, 372, who notes that 10:8 portrays Asael as responsible for all sins. Cf. Patrick A. Tiller, *A Commentary on the Animal Apocalypse of 1 Enoch* (SBLEJL 4; Atlanta: Scholars, 1993), who misreads the role of Asael in the *Book of the Watchers* as "simply one of the two hundred Watchers, although at 8:1 and 9:6 he is singled out as the chief offender and revealer of heavenly secrets" (87). Rather the author of the *Animal Apocalypse* has read the synthesis in *1 Enoch* 6 – 11 remarkably well and his depiction of the distortions which follow could well reproduce the results of Asael's revelations, particularly those which then evoke sexual activity through the women. But see also his discussion on pp. 89-96, which offers a more differentiated assessment of the relation to the Asael legend and its development. There are, as Tiller points out, differences in relation to both Asael and Shemihazah; in particular, the absence of reference to secrets and the different handling of conflict (86-87). Similarly Reed, *Fallen Angels*, 75.

[171] See Tiller, *Animal Apocalypse*, who offers a table of equivalences in Aramaic, Greek, and Ge'ez for bovids in the apocalypse (227).

[172] So Nickelsburg, *1 Enoch 1*: "The Sethites have been corrupted by their intermarriage with the Cainites" (373). So also Jackson, *Enochic Judaism*: "In the way this allegory is structured the paradigm exemplar of the fall of the Watchers is replicated – the sexual transgression occurring where interbreeding is seen to happen which necessarily occurs at the beginning of this cycle and is thus committed by Ham's and Japheth's lines" (38); similarly Reed, *Fallen Angels*, 76. Cf. Tiller, *Animal Apocalypse*, who sees only one group of large, black cattle (237). On the other hand, he observes: "They changed their

changing from established order is central to the understanding of sin in *1 Enoch* 2:1 – 5:4. Moaning (*'awyawa*) after one another may well reflect desire and sexual lust[173] which leads to intermarriage.

The effect of the descent of the rest of the stars (86:3-4) is clearly sexual. They become bulls pasturing among calves *ṭa'wā*. That we read of calves, in contrast to cattle in relation to the first descent, may indicate the different kinds of relationship reflected in the accounts of the descent of Asael and the descent of Shemihazah and his group. The depiction of the victims of the latter as calves is probably intended to enhance the sense of abuse of power. Tiller notes that "the allegorical use of the word, 'calf', is not entirely consistent in the *An. Apoc.* It sometimes refers to children and sometimes to women. When it refers to women, it may imply virgins or young women".[174] The latter is the case here and very probably implies virgins.

Nothing suggests the calves bear responsibility, in contrast to the suggestion in *1 Enoch* 8:1, that the women also contribute to leading the Watchers astray through the seductive use of jewellery and cosmetics. Certainly the second group of stars engages in sexual activity. This is graphically portrayed in 86:4, where the author uses the dramatic image of stallions and their visually striking penises. Here, then, the sexual wrongdoing of the Watchers comes to vivid expression. They are associated with horses, unclean animals.[175] The subsequent birth of elephants, camels and asses (86:4), also unclean animals, which terrify the bulls and savage them, matches the myth of the giants (85:5-6), including their three different forms (cf. 7:3 and the discussion on it above). This extends to the detail of the violence and bloodshed which ensues (86:6; cf. 7:3-5).[176]

The sequel then explains how four white, human-like beings, representing the four archangels, descend in response to the cry of the earth (87:1-2). Three rescue Enoch (87:3-4). The fourth binds the first star and throws it into the abyss (88:1). Another gives swords to the offspring, the wild animals, by which "they began to

---

stables, pastures, and calves. This probably refers to a general perversion of their former way of life and sexual sin" (94).

[173] So Siegbert Uhlig, *Das äthiopische Henochbuch* (JSHRZ 5/6; Gütersloh: Mohn, 1984) 680, who identifies it as "leidenschaftlich rufen" in a sexual sense. See also Nickelsburg, *1 Enoch 1*, 367; cf. Tiller, *Animal Apocalypse*, 238-39.

[174] Tiller, *Animal Apocalypse*, 94 n. 19.

[175] They also, therefore, contravene the law about mixing of kinds according to Lev 19:19. See Jackson, *Enochic Judaism*, 37.

[176] As Tiller, *Animal Apocalypse*, observes, there are some differences: in the *Animal Apocalypse* "no mention is made of the giants' consuming all human produce, all animals, and each other. ... the cattle are eating each other, while in the *Book of the Watchers* only the giants eat each other" (87).

strike one another" (88:2), echoing 10:9-10, but not, as there, to the point of extermination, for 89:6 indicates that they drowned in the flood. Another threw stones from heaven at the other stars and also threw them into the abyss (88:3). It is interesting that in this description only these latter are described as having "organs ... like the organs of horses" (88:3). This, too, supports the notion that only they were involved in sexual wrongdoing.

As in the account in the *Book of the Watchers*, the act of sexual wrongdoing appears primarily in association with the Watchers. Thus it is focussed on the second group of stars, rather than on the first. On the other hand, the effect of Asael appears to have been sexual lusting among the cattle, thus inappropriate sexual relations, reflecting a concern with intermarriage. Otherwise the effects of the action of the stars are expressed not in terms of sexual wrongdoing, but in terms of savagery and violence. This matches the description in the *Book of the Watchers*. There is a further implicit allusion to the effect of Watchers' sin in the detail of 89:10-12, that after Noah the bulls began to beget new species of wild and dangerous animals (also unclean animals), a motif inspired by Ezek 39:17-18.[177] This represents an expansion of the myth, analogous to the expansion in the *Book of the Watchers*, which depicts evil spirits now active in bringing harm to humans, but here the outcome is different. The new wild animals represent Gentile nations.

It is characteristic of the rest of the *Animal Apocalypse*, as it is of the *Book of the Watchers*, that sinful activity carried out by the Watchers' offspring is described not in terms of sexual wrongdoing, but as violence (again using the image of wild animals, 89:10), wolves that oppress (89:15, 19), sheep that become blind and go astray (89:32-33, 41, 51), dogs, wild boars and foxes devouring the sheep (89:41, 46), a ram forsaking the path (89:44), sheep killing other sheep and betraying God's place (89:51, 54), lions, leopards, wolves, hyenas, foxes and others treating them as fodder (89:55-58) and burning the tower and house (89:66), oppressive shepherds (angels; 89:59-65), wild boars hindering the re-builders (89:72), polluting bread on the table before the tower (89:73), blind sheep and shepherds (89:74), eagles, vultures, kites, ravens, dogs devouring the sheep (90:2-4, 7, 11-12), and sheep not listening to lambs (90:6). We hear nothing of the sexual wrongdoing of David or Solomon or anyone else. The reference in 89:75 to the sheep being scattered over the field and mixing with the wild beasts is probably another allusion to mixed marriages with Gentiles,[178] recalling the allusion to the mixing of the Sethites and Cainites (86:2).

---

[177] On this see Tiller, *Animal Apocalypse*, 271.

[178] Nickelsburg, *1 Enoch 1*, notes: "The reference to being mixed with the nations could refer to intermarriage in dispersion" (395). Similarly, Tiller, *Animal Apocalypse*, who notes that Ge'ez, *tadammarra* can mean "mixed, be united, be joined, have intercourse, or be married" (341).

When we reach the depiction of the final judgement, we find again a distinction between the first star and the others, where the stars are summoned, "beginning with the first star that had preceded those stars whose organs were like the organs of horses" (90:21). The other sinners, including the seventy shepherds who exceeded their role in killing the sheep,[179] are described in the judgement, as in the account which precedes, with no reference to sexual wrongdoing (90:22-27), even though these shepherds are also angelic beings.[180]

The image of hope in 90:28-29 depicts the Lord of the sheep bringing "a new house, larger and higher than that first one … and all the sheep were within it" (similarly 90:33-36 which describes the house as "large and broad and very full"). Already 89:36 speaks of a "house for the Lord of the sheep" before entry into the land and 89:40 identifies it as set up "in the midst of the pleasant land". Solomon's contribution is described in 89:50,

> And that house became large and broad. And a large and high tower was built upon that house for the Lord of the sheep. That house was low, but the tower was raised up and high. And the Lord of the sheep stood on that tower, and they spread a full table before him.

Already 87:3 uses the image of "tower" of the sanctuary of heaven to which Enoch ascended. 89:51 speaks of abandonment of "that house of theirs" and 89:54 of abandonment of "the house of the Lord and his tower" (similarly 89:56). Both house and tower are demolished by the Babylonians (89:66-67), but the rebuilt house and tower ("called the high tower") had before it a table on which the bread "was polluted and not pure" (89:73). There is, therefore, some debate about whether the "new house" in 90:28-29, 33-36 refers to the temple or simply to Jerusalem. Should it refer to the temple and imply the presence of all the people in the temple, we might see implications for sexuality and sexual engagement, which would be out of place in such a context. The focus seems rather to be the new Jerusalem.[181] Significantly no mention is made of a "tower", the term used

---

[179] Nickelsburg, "Apocalyptic Construction of Reality," notes that this constitutes continuing angelic sin (54).

[180] On the shepherds as angelic figures see Nickelsburg, *1 Enoch 1*, 390, and on the biblical sources, particularly Ezekiel 34 and Zechariah 11, and the chronology, pp. 391-93.

[181] So Nickelsburg, *1 Enoch 1*, 404-405, who notes that in 89:36 "house" appears to mean the camp of the people, so that house later refers to Jerusalem and "tower" to the temple. See the extensive treatment grounding this view in Tiller, *Animal Apocalypse*, 36-51. But see Loren T. Stuckenbruck, "'Reading the Present' in the Animal Apocalypse (*1 Enoch* 85-90)," in *Reading the Present in the Qumran Library: The Perception of the Contemporary by Means of Scriptural Interpretations* (ed. Kristin De Troyer and Armin Lange; SBLSymS 30; Atlanta: Scholars, 2005) 91-102, who argues that, while the house

previously for the sanctuary, and so may imply a future without a temple (thus in tension with 25:5), but be a precursor for the similar notion in Rev 21:22.

The fulfilment certainly implies the replacement of the post-exilic temple polluted by impurity (89:73), which probably included sexual impurity and intermarriage. The final image of all humanity being transformed to become white bulls (90:37-38) recalls the original creation (85:3).[182] It also implies the reversal of the result of mixed marriages alluded to in 86:2 and 89:75 and is strikingly universal in its inclusivity and as such recalls 11:21.

The book of Enoch's *Dream Visions* seems primarily concerned with the future of Israel, in particular, its deliverance from the dangers which beset it. These are of three kinds. These are, firstly, the dangers from foreign powers, depicted as savage animals[183] and both etiologically and paradigmatically related to the sexual wrongdoing of the second group of Watchers by extension of the myth. This element builds on the emphasis on violence found in *1 Enoch* 6 – 11, which is hardly present in 12 – 16. Sexual wrongdoing is the primary focus of the angels' wrongdoing mentioned in 84:4, but is expanded in the *Animal Apocalypse* where the image of horses with their protruding penises features three times in the description of the angels who descend second (86:4; 88:3; 90:21). The fact that they mount calves may also enhance the sense of abuse.

The second danger is clearly from blind sheep within and those who lead their fellow sheep astray. They appear to be related to the temple establishment and explain why the author depicts the bread of its table as polluted and impure. The third danger is paradigmatically present in the Watchers' sexual deeds with

---

imagery refers to the old and new Jerusalems, it should not be so precisely interpreted that it excludes the temple or cult (98 n. 11).

[182] So Nickelsburg, *1 Enoch 1*, 406-407.

[183] On this see Patrick A. Tiller, "Israel at the Mercy of Demonic Powers: An Enochic Interpretation of Postexilic Imperialism," in *Conflicted Boundaries in Wisdom and Apocalypticism* (ed. Benjamin G. Wright III and Lawrence M. Wills; SBLSymS 35; Atlanta: SBL, 2005) 113-21. "In the Book of the Watchers, contemporary events are compared to the ancient myth of the giants. The reader understands that like the ancient giants, Alexander's heirs are consuming and destroying the earth. The Animal Apocalypse goes even further. The allegory of the shepherds declares that the current status of Judea under the domination of foreign powers is the direct result of disobedience to God" (119). Similarly, Richard A. Horsley, "The Politics of Cultural Production in Second Temple Judea: Historical Context and Political-Religious Relations of the Scribes Who Produced *1 Enoch*, Sirach, and Daniel," in *Conflicted Boundaries in Wisdom and Apocalypticism* (ed. Kristin De Troyer and Armin Lange; SBLSymS 30; Atlanta: Scholars, 2005) 123-45, 138. Tiller writes: "The story carefully identifies the shepherds with the stars in order to demonstrate that the ancient ante-diluvian events described in the *Book of the Watchers* correspond to the contemporary situation, and not only by analogy" (119).

women, but also apparently instigated by the descent of the first star, namely
sexual relations outside of one's approved group, illustrated by the intermarriage
of Sethites and Cainites (86:2), and the "mixing" of the scattered sheep with other
animals (89:75). This may be an aspect of the teaching and behaviour of those who
lead other sheep astray and pollute the temple and could, in that context, relate
particularly to priests, but the emphasis is allusive.

Aside from this, there is no evidence of a particular concern with sexual
wrongdoing in general, and little that is positive. At most we may note reference to
Enoch's taking a wife (83:2; 85:2), which at least assumes marriage within
appropriate circles to be unproblematic, but also that his visions take place
beforehand, perhaps reflecting an assumption about holiness and celibacy.[184]

1.3   Other early Enoch material in 1 Enoch

We find almost nothing pertaining to attitudes towards sexuality in the *Book of the
Luminaries* (*1 Enoch* 72 – 82). At most one may point to the description of sin as
changing one's set order, which we find in 80:6, "Many heads of the stars will
stray from the command and will change their ways and actions". The *Book of the
Watchers* describes their punishment (21:1-5). This illustrates the sin of change,
enunciated in 2:1 – 5:4, which also applies to the change of order which
constituted the Watchers' sin; but that is not in focus here. The complaint about
people is that they will err by treating stars as gods (80:7) and will err regarding
the calculation of the calendar (82:5).

1.3.1   The Epistle of Enoch (1 Enoch 92 – 105)

While the *Narrative Bridge* of *1 Enoch* 91:1-9, 18-19) describes sin in fairly
general terms (those of a double heart, 4; iniquity, 5, 6, 7, 8, 19; blasphemy, 7;
violence, 6, 7, 18, 19; perversity, 7; sin, 6, 7; uncleanness, 7; deceit, 8; idolatry,
9),[185] the *Epistle of Enoch* (*1 Enoch* 92 – 105)[186] is much more detailed and

---

[184] So Annette Steudel, "Ehelosigkeit bei den Essenern," in *Qumran Kontrovers:
Beiträge zu den Textfunden vom Toten Meer* (ed. Jörg Frey and Hartmut Stegemann with
the collaboration of Michael Becker and Alexander Maurer; Einblicke 6, Paderborn:
Bonifatius, 2003) 115-24, 120. She points also to Jeremiah (Jer 16:2).

[185] The delineation of this section as *Narrative Bridge* is not without controversy. See
the recent attempt to demonstrate that it forms a whole with the *Apocalypse of Weeks* in
Martin Leuenberger, "Die 10-Siebent-Apokalypse im Henochbuch; ihre Stellung im
material rekonstruierten Manuskript 4QEn(g) und Implikationen für die Redaktions- und
Kompositionsgeschichte der Traumvisionen (83-91) und des paränetischen Briefs (92-105);
Teil 1," *BN* 124 (2005) 57-102.

specific about human wrongdoing. It begins with the so-called *Apocalypse of Weeks* (93:3-10; 91:11-17).[187] Enoch's opening statement there reads: "I was born the seventh in the first week, and until my time righteousness endured". This is striking, since it apparently does not consider either the sin of Eve and Adam or the deed of Cain as sufficient to count against the claim. Its account of the second week, which covers the period of the Watchers' sin, is also a simple summary: "a second week, in which deceit and violence will spring up" (93:4).[188] Descriptions of sin remain generic (deceit, violence, iniquity, 4; becoming blind and straying, 8; perversity, 9; violence, deceit, 91:11; wickedness, 91:12, 14). Nothing suggests sexual wrongdoing is an issue.[189] The focus is violence and false teaching (becoming blind, leading astray and perversity), with the latter prominent in weeks six and seven, in which the author makes a claim for his group as the chosen, as witnesses of righteousness and wise (93:10). It mentions also the judgement of the Watchers in the tenth week: "everlasting judgement ... will be executed on the Watchers of the eternal heaven, <and a fixed time of the great judgement will be rendered among the holy ones>" (91:15), but its focus is human responsibility. This coheres with the rest of the work, in which we find the statement, "lawlessness was not sent upon the earth; but men created it by themselves"

---

[186] On the dating and provenance of the core of the Epistle, which he understands as 94:6 – 104:8, see Nickelsburg, *1 Enoch 1*, who notes that it uses the *Book of the Watchers* (1 – 36) and the testamentary narrative (81 – 92), but was not known by *Jubilees*, thus placing it later than ca 160 B.C.E. and probably during the Hasmonean period (426-29).

[187] Nickelsburg, *1 Enoch 1*, dates the *Apocalypse of Weeks* to the first third of the second century B.C.E. (440).

[188] Nickelsburg, *1 Enoch 1*, notes that "deceit and violence" recur in the description of the seventh week (91:11), the time of the author, and also reflect the two major themes of the Epistle (443). Reed, *Fallen Angels*, interprets the absence of reference to the angels' descent, except their punishment, as an indication that the author downplays their "role in engendering human sin and suffering" (78).

[189] By contrast 1QS 3.13 – 4.26, which reflects a similar world view and also provides a detailed list of sins, includes "impudent enthusiasm for appalling acts performed in a lustful passion, filthy paths in the service of impurity" (4:10). On the similarities between the two texts see Klaus Koch, "History as a Battlefield of Two Antagonistic Powers in the Apocalypse of Weeks and in the Rule of the Community," in *Enoch and Qumran Origins: New Light on a Forgotten Connection* (ed. Gabriele Boccaccini; Grand Rapids: Eerdmans, 2005) 185-99, and, affirming and expanding upon the similarities, George W. E. Nickelsburg, "Response: Context, Text, and Social Setting of the Apocalypse of Weeks," in *Enoch and Qumran Origins: New Light on a Forgotten Connection* (ed. Gabriele Boccaccini; Grand Rapids: Eerdmans, 2005) 234-41, 234-35.

(98:4), perhaps even formulated to undermine the significance given in the *Book of the Watchers* to the myth of heavenly origins.[190]

The remainder of the Epistle is more specific and helps flesh out the concerns expressed in the *Apocalypse of Weeks*. It develops the contrast between the two ways (94:1-5), describing the path of iniquity primarily as the way of violence. Here we find a fleeting reference to the female figure of wisdom: "sinners will tempt people to do harm to wisdom; and no place will be found for her" (94:5), a notion articulated in the later *Parables of Enoch* at 42:1-2, but already here probably a parody on the claims being made in Ben Sira 24 for the Jerusalem priesthood, with whom or with some of whom the author here, as often elsewhere in the Enoch material, seems to be in conflict. In what follows, there are then quite specific woes addressed to those who gain riches by violence, commit blasphemy, and practice hatred and evil (94:6 – 95:2). The book continues with warnings against those who swear false oaths, repay their neighbours with evil, bear false witness, use false weights, and persecute the righteous (95:4-7), and especially against the rich, who accumulate wealth and abuse their power at the expense of the righteous (96:4-8; 97:7-10; 99:11-16; 103:5-6).[191]

In 98:1-2 the author attacks men "who will put on adornments as women, and fair colours more than virgins, in kingship and majesty and power". This might refer to transvestite behaviour, but is more likely an attack on court apparel and its extravagance.[192] This explains the reference to kingship. The writer challenges slavery: "it was not ordained <for a man> to be a slave, nor was <a decree> given for a woman to be a handmaid, but it happened because of oppression" (98:4). In this context the author also asserts: "Likewise, neither is a woman created barren, but because of the works of her hands she is disgraced with childlessness" (98:5).

---

[190] See Tiller, *Animal Apocalypse*, 96; Reed, *Fallen Angels*, 78; Olson, *Enoch*, 17.

[191] See Horsley, "Social Relations," who argues that the scribe who wrote the Epistle addressed a similar situation to the scribe who wrote Ben Sira, a situation of economic oppression, and that both wrote not as representatives of sects or groups, but from different perspectives within a common social context. Many of the *Epistle*'s concerns reflect prophetic oracles against exploitation (e.g.: possibly Amos 6:4-6 in *1 Enoch* 96:5-6; Micah 2:1-2 in 100:8; Amos 2:6 in 95:6; and situations reflected in Neh 5:1-12 and 1 Kings 12) (112-13). On the possible influence of the Epistle, and its attack on abuse of wealth, on Luke, see George W. E. Nickelsburg, "Riches, the Rich, and God's Judgment in *1 Enoch* 92-105 and the Gospel according to Luke," *NTS* 25 (1979) 324-44, reproduced in *George W.E. Nickelsburg in Perspective: An Ongoing Dialogue of Learning* (2 vols; ed. Jacob Neusner and Alan J. Avery-Peck; JSJSup 80; Leiden: Brill, 2003) 522-46; and "Revisiting the Rich and the Poor in *1 Enoch* 92-105 and the Gospel according to Luke," SBLSP 37 (Atlanta: Scholars, 1998) 2. 579-605, reproduced in *George W.E. Nickelsburg in Perspective: An Ongoing Dialogue of Learning* (2 vols; ed. Jacob Neusner and Alan J. Avery-Peck; JSJSup 80; Leiden: Brill, 2003) 2. 547-71.

[192] Nickelsburg, *1 Enoch 1*, speaks of "the extravagant behavior of the rich" (475).

This is an interesting judgement, which thus blames women for their own infertility, a striking contrast to the use of infertility in the patriarchal narratives as a prelude and sign for divine intervention and special developments.[193]

Wrongdoing is a constant theme. Fools are condemned (98:9). The "stiff-necked and hard of heart ... do evil and consume blood" (98:11). The author pronounces woes on people who "annul the words of the righteous ... write lying words and words of error; ... write and lead many astray with their lies ... alter true words and pervert the everlasting covenant" (98:14 – 99:2). Similar concerns appear in the conclusion about the book itself: "this mystery that sinners will alter and copy the words of truth, and pervert many and lie and invent great fabrications, and write books in their own names" (104:10; see also 104:11). These will have been the focus of the brief comments about perversity in the seventh week in the *Apocalypse of Weeks* (91:9-10) and probably is the allusion to wisdom's not finding a place (94:5). In 101:3 the author confronts people with the words, "Why do you speak with your mouth proud and hard things against his majesty", echoing the accusation found in 1:9 and 5:4 ("you have spoken proud and hard words with your unclean mouth against his majesty"). This might allude to blasphemy of some kind (cf. 94:9; 96:7; – but in relation to the wealthy). Unfortunately we have no indication of the substance of the false teaching.

In 99:4-5 the author goes on to describe the result of the petitions of the righteous: it will bring judgement and destruction. The author describes the consequences for families:

> At that very time, those who are giving birth will bring forth, and they will <sell> and abandon their young infant; and those who are with child will <abort>;[194] and those who are nursing will cast off their children, and they will not return to their infants or to their sucklings nor will they spare their beloved ones. (99:5)

These phenomena are not the focus of moral instruction, but serve (perhaps as standard)[195] examples of what the distress will drive people to do, including to do

---

[193] Nickelsburg, *1 Enoch 1*, notes the tension between this statement and its usual rejection of Deuteronomic argument, citing 102:4 – 104:8, and suggests "the author is evidently using a common topos to illustrate and undergird the point he has just made – that God punishes sin. Different from the cases cited in 103:9-15, here barrenness does not involve a human agent; it is a direct divine intervention" (476). Nevertheless one wonders what the author might mean by "because of the works of her hands". Might it refer to some sexual wrongdoing which would render the woman barren, like some form of abortion?

[194] This might mean spontaneous abortion because of fear or deliberately induced abortion to avoid the burden of pregnancy in the time of distress. So Nickelsburg, *1 Enoch 1*, 491.

[195] So Nickelsburg, *1 Enoch 1*, who points to similar motifs in Deut 28:53-57; Isa 49:15 and Josephus (490). See Josephus, *B.J.* 5.429-33 and 6.201-13.

such sins. Possibly the author had alluded to abortion in the statement about the causes of barrenness in 98:5, but here the focus seems solely on the desperate measures to which distress will drive mothers. In 100:1-2 the author similarly portrays family chaos, describing murder among father, brothers and sons.[196]

The attack on idolatry in 99:6-9, the only place where it is addressed in the epistle, is noteworthy for attacking the medium of visions, which the author also uses, and for using the language of blindness and leading astray, employed elsewhere in relation to the author's intramural Jewish competitors. Perhaps it attacks the idolatry of the imperial patrons to whom the ruling elite look.[197] Murder and exploitation will not escape judgement (99:11 – 100:4). The writer assures the righteous that the angels intercede for them when they see their suffering at the hands of oppressive rulers (103:9 – 104:6) and warns the sinners that their deeds are noted (104:7-8).

In this wide array of warnings of an ethical nature it is striking that we find not a single instance where the concern is sexual wrongdoing, either at an individual level or in relation to appropriate or inappropriate marriage, which, as we have seen, feature in the *Book of the Watchers* and the *Book of Dream Visions*.[198] Issues relating to sexuality appear at most in 98:5, which blames women for their infertility, and in the description of the day when "the nations will be thrown into confusion, and the families of the nations will be unsettled, on the day of the destruction of iniquity" when some will resort to abortion (99:4-5). Even in the *Apocalypse of Weeks*, where we find an allusion to the judgement of the Watchers and holy ones, nothing is mentioned of their sexual wrongdoing.

---

[196] Nickelsburg, *1 Enoch 1*, 490.

[197] So Horsley, "Social Relations," who notes the clearer differentiation in the Greek version than in the Ethiopic between the idolaters addressed in 96:7 and those mentioned at the end of this verse and in 99:6, who look to them for help (114).

[198] Gabriele Boccaccini, *Beyond the Essene Hypothesis: The Parting of the Ways between Qumran and Enochic Judaism* (Grand Rapids: Eerdmans, 1998), argues that the Epistle shares in common with *Jubilees* a focus on the elect, the motif of the heavenly tablets as the basis for authority which provides a basis for appropriating the Mosaic Torah and a comprehensive historical determinism (106-107). It is then surprising that it does not share the concern with intermarriage and sexual wrongdoing, which features so prominently in *Jubilees*.

1.3.2   The Birth of Noah (1 Enoch 106-107)

In the *Birth of Noah* (*1 Enoch* 106-107) the myth of the Watchers informs Lamech's anxiety about his child, born with a "body whiter than snow and redder than a rose" with hair "all white and like white wool and curly", and eyes that made the house shine like the sun, standing up and praising God already in the hands of the midwife (106:2-3).[199] He declares: "I think he is not from me, but from the angels" (106:6). Methuselah repeats the anxiety to Enoch his father in much the same terms (106:9-12). For people familiar with the rest of Enoch, let alone the biblical story, this narrative is surely playful in its irony and designed by the author to help people celebrate hope. It alludes to the lustful Watchers.

Enoch's response signals that the child is Lamech's own and that he is to be called, Noah, "for he will be your remnant, from whom you will find rest"(106:18).[200] The response also returns to the Watcher story, which has already informed the drama:

> In the generation of Jared, my father, they transgressed the word of the Lord/the covenant of heaven, and look, they went on sinning and transgressing the custom. With women they were mingling, and with them they were sinning. They married some of them and they went on begetting (children), not like spirits, but of flesh. (106:13-14)[201]

This version does not have two descents, but speaks simply of "they" (the precedent is "angels") and of their transgression. It notes the transgression in a way that reflects the understanding that they departed from the order in which they belonged. There is emphasis on a continuing action. The sin is sexual (mingling, marrying, begetting). Nothing is said about their giving teaching. Their offspring are mentioned only briefly: "they went on begetting (children), not like spirits, but of flesh". Noah's strange appearance and miraculous capacity at birth is sufficient for Lamech to contemplate that Noah, too, may be one of them. The word, "giant", is not used.

The prediction of judgement in 106:15 may assume the destruction of the Watchers and their offspring in the flood, but mentions only that "there will be great wrath upon earth and a flood". According to 106:17 Noah "will cleanse the earth from the corruption that is on it", which might allude to the flood, but comes

---

[199] On the parallel material in 1QapGen, see our discussion below and Nickelsburg, *1 Enoch 1*, who sees *1 Enoch* 106-107 as prior (541-42) and proposes a date "after the incorporation of the Epistle into the corpus in the first half of the second century B.C.E. ... and before the copying of 4QEn^c in the last third of the first century B.C.E." (542).

[200] On the complex issues of translation in determining the various etymologies at play for Noah's name, see Nickelsburg, *1 Enoch 1*, 547-49.

[201] On the numerous textual problems see Nickelsburg, *1 Enoch 1*, 546.

after the account of their deliverance from the flood in 106:16. The description of this corruption remains general. Further on in 106:18 the author repeats the prediction: "He and his sons will be saved from the corruption of the earth, and from all sins and from all iniquities that are consummated on the earth in his days" (106:18).[202] The "corruption" is not specified beyond "all sins and from all iniquities". While nothing suggests sexual wrongdoing is a particular interest or concern, it is noteworthy that the Watchers' sin in the first place is portrayed primarily as sexual wrongdoing.

The prediction of worse sin to come after Noah (106:19) remains general. It is possible that this also includes sexual wrongdoing, given the strong emphasis on this element in portraying the Watchers' sin, but one cannot be certain. When 107:1, however, speaks of relief from evil at the time when the "generations of righteousness" arise (presumably in the time of the author and his community), sin is portrayed as "evil and wickedness" and "violence", not primarily as sexual wrongdoing. At most one could say that the *Birth of Noah* (*1 Enoch* 106-107) retains the abhorrence of the Watchers' act of sexual wrongdoing, with particular emphasis on their transgressing boundaries and its consequences, and uses it in dramatic irony to celebrate Noah's significance. Beyond that, reference to corruption and sin remains general, once mentioning violence, but nowhere mentioning sexual wrongdoing.

The so-called *Genesis Apocryphon* (1QapGen), which will be included in a future study, contains a striking parallel to *1 Enoch* 106-107 in columns 1-5, of which columns 1, 3-4 are very fragmentary.[203] In it Lamech, himself, speaks of his

---

[202] Nickelsburg, *1 Enoch 1*, suggests that the author may see the flood as a washing of purification from the pollution resulting from sexual defilement (cf. 10:20-22), if one follows the Geʻez reading (548).

[203] See the discussion of the two accounts in Nickelsburg, *1 Enoch 1*, 541-42, who also draws attention to *1 Enoch* 83-84 and *1 Enoch* 65-67, which both report an appeal to Enoch about a fearful vision and Enoch's response. See also his detailed discussion of *1 Enoch* 106-107 and *Genesis Apocryphon* in George W. E. Nickelsburg, "Patriarchs Who Worry about Their Wives: A Haggadic Tendency in the *Genesis Apocryphon*," in *Biblical Perspectives: Early Use and Interpretation of the Bible in Light of the Dead Sea Scrolls: Proceedings of the First International Symposium of the Orion Center for the Study of the Dead Sea Scrolls and Associated Literature, 12-14 May 1996* (ed. Michael E. Stone and Esther G. Chazon; STDJ 28; Leiden: Brill, 1998) 137-58, 138-47. He calculates that the account in *Genesis Apocryphon* is 3.74 times longer than *1 Enoch* 106-107 (139). But see Eileen Schuller, "Response to 'Patriarchs Who Worry about their Wives: A Haggadic Tendency in the *Genesis Apocryphon*," in *George W.E. Nickelsburg in Perspective: An Ongoing Dialogue of Learning* (2 vols; ed. Jacob Neusner and Alan J. Avery-Peck; JSJSup 80; Leiden: Brill, 2003) 1. 200-12, who provides evidence that the "initial section with the description of the extraordinary child might have been somewhat longer in the *Genesis Apocryphon* than in *1 Enoch*" (205) and shows that this is also the case in the description

anxiety "that the conception was from the Watchers or that the seed was from Holy Ones, or (belonged) to Nephil[im]" (2:1).[204] This recalls Lamech's fear in *1 Enoch* 106:6, expressed to Methuselah, his father. We may suspect that column 1 contained a description something like *1 Enoch* 106:2-3 about Noah's appearance and behaviour.[205] 1QapGen 5.12-13 report words of Enoch about the child, that "his eyes shone like the su[n]" and that "this child (is) a flame," perhaps recalling the lost description (cf. *1 Enoch* 106:2, "When he opened his eyes, the house shone like the sun"; 106:5, "His eyes are like the rays of the sun"; similarly 106:10).[206] 1QapGen 2.1 identifies the feared connection with the Watchers as something Lamech pondered directly in himself ("I thought to myself"), whereas *1 Enoch* has the fear expressed by Lamech to Methuselah: "that he is not from me, but from the angels" (106:6). *1 Enoch* has an additional component to the fear: "And I fear him, lest something happen in his days upon earth" (indeed it does!).

1QapGen contains an exchange between Lamech and his wife, Bitenosh, in which she reassures Lamech and reminds him of the erotic pleasure of their encounter: "recall my pleasure .[   ] [in the hea]t of the time, and my breath in the

---

given Methuselah (205), in contrast to Nickelsburg, who argues that they were of approximately the same length.

[204] As Nickelsburg, "Patriarchs Who Worry about Their Wives," observes, we find a similar anxiety on the part of Joseph expressed in the Matthean infancy narrative (145-46). The response to both is the giving of a name to the child which via popular etymology indicates the future saving role of the child, but in both Matthew and Luke the divinely induced conception is affirmed, not denied. See also Nickelsburg, *1 Enoch 1*, 540.

[205] So Joseph A. Fitzmyer, *The Genesis Apocryphon of Qumran Cave 1 (1Q20): A Commentary* (3d ed.; BibOr 18/B; Roma: Pontificio istituto biblico, 2004) 122; similarly, Nickelsburg, "Patriarchs Who Worry about Their Wives," 138. The preceding columns also appear to have contained a version of the Watcher myth, which would have informed the hearer of the Lamech story (142). See also Moshe J. Bernstein, "From the Watchers to the Flood: Story and Exegesis in the Early Columns of the *Genesis Apocryphon*," in *Reworking the Bible: Apocryphal and Related Texts at Qumran: Proceedings of a Joint Symposium by the Orion Center for the Study of the Dead Sea Scrolls and Associated Literature and the Hebrew University Institute for Advanced Studies Research Group on Qumran, 15-17 January, 2002* (ed. Esther G. Chazon, Devorah Dimant, and Ruth A. Clements; STDJ 58; Leiden: Brill, 2005) 39-63, who nevertheless notes that "from the standpoint of the narrative, it is significant that there is not a great deal of space within which Lamech could be introduced (unless he was mentioned in the fragmentary portions of column 0, 1, or earlier, lost material), and for the birth and marvelous nature of the child to be described" (46).

[206] Cf. 1Q19 3.5, "[illuminated] the rooms of the house like rays of the sun". Fitzmyer, *Genesis Apocryphon*, writes that 1Q19 "seems to belong to a Hebrew version of *Enoch* that is slightly different from Ethiopic *1 Enoch*" (258). He also draws attention to 4Q535 3.3, which gives the baby's weight as "three hundred and fif[ty] shekels" (123).

midst of the sheath" (2.9-10)[207] and again: "recall my pleasure" ... "that this seed is from you; from you is this conception, and from you the planting of [this] fruit [   ], and not from any stranger, or from any of the Watchers, or from any of the sons of hea[ven" (2.13-16).[208] The erotic elaboration appears to reflect the view of conception resulting from especially highly intense and pleasurable sexual intercourse. *1 Enoch* 106-107 appears not to know of such an exchange, which has the hallmarks of novelistic embellishment of the story. Nickelsburg notes that it "is paralleled in the additions to the story of Abram and Sarai in Egypt and by other references to the characters' emotions" suggesting that it "seems to indicate an authorial tendency" in 1QapGen. [209]

The two accounts then coincide in 106:4 and 2.19 in the report that Lamech went to his father, Methuselah. Here *1 Enoch* has an account in which Lamech repeats detail of his wonderful appearance and, as noted, gives first expression to his fear. Both portray the visit as intended to persuade Methuselah to visit Enoch, his father, whose dwelling "is with the angels" (106:7; probably also in 1QapGen 2.20). *1 Enoch* 106:8-12 then gives an account of Methuselah's report to Enoch, which repeats the wondrous description of the child, using elements from 106:2-3 and 5, and Lamech's fear from 106:6. The text preserved in 1QapGen contains an account of Methuselah's approach to Enoch, but not the report. Column 3 preserves only a few words, but enough for us to recognise that it, too, includes in Enoch's reply a reference to the days of his father, Jared. The words, "evil" (4.3) and "justice" (4.11) and "on/against them" (4.14), probably belong to an explanation of the deeds of the Watchers, the evil they and their offspring wrought, and their judgement, and probably also to Noah's role. The better preserved column 5 then contains reassurance, as in *1 Enoch* 106:18, that the child is Lamech's, and includes reference by Enoch to the child's eyes shining like the sun and to him as a flame (details not included at this point in *1 Enoch* 106). Like the latter, it may have contained some reference to Noah's role (also his name?).

Given that 1QapGen appears to have been composed mid-first century C.E., as Fitzmyer argues, especially in the light of its language, but also of a number of

---

[207] Fitzmyer, *Genesis Apocryphon*, comments: "The body is understood to be a sheath, and the panting breath is like a sword moving back and forth within it. It is thus an expressive figure for emotional panting during intercourse" (131). He refers to use of sheath for the body in Dan 7:15 and *b. Sanh.* 108a.

[208] This may explain the obscurity noted by Nickelsburg, "Patriarchs Who Worry about Their Wives,": "She denies the allegation by reminding him of her sexual pleasure when they made love. The point is a bit obscure. The issue is not whether Lamech and his wife have been to bed together, but whether this child was conceived under other circumstances" (143).

[209] Nickelsburg, "Patriarchs Who Worry about Their Wives," 158.

other aspects which seem to corroborate this conclusion,[210] it is unlikely that *1 Enoch* 106-107 is dependent on 1QapGen. The reverse is more likely or both draw on a similar source for the story. The words, "[A copy of] the book of the words of Noah" (5.29], is suggestive of an unknown Book of Noah, but this remains problematic.[211] Nickelsburg points rather to the author of 1QapGen using and expanding *1 Enoch* 106-107.[212] The exchange with Bitenosh, he argues, is typical of the author's emotional embellishments; the first person narration by Lamech reflects the author's technique elsewhere, the reference to the words of

---

[210] See the discussion in Fitzmyer, *Genesis Apocryphon*, 26-28.

[211] Fitzmyer, *Genesis Apocryphon*, observes that the accounts of the wondrous child in columns 2 – 5 and in *1 Enoch* 106-107 (and 1Q19 3.4) "must have been part of a 'Book of Noah,' which is even mentioned in a Greek version related to the Aramaic Levi Document as ἡ βίβλος τοῦ Νῶε" (122). But see also his caution: "Even if such references seem to argue for a *Book of Noah*, they are not certain" (22) and "in any case, cols 2-6, which deal with the birth of the wondrous child Noah, depended on some other source, on something like *1 Enoch* 106, which most likely was not composed by the author of the rest of *1 Enoch*" (21). In his recent review of the issue, Michael E. Stone, "The Books Attributed to Noah," *DSD* 13 (2006) 4-23, noting the gap between 1QapGen columns 2–5 and the difference in the person of the narrator between the account of Noah's birth here (also in *1 Enoch* 106 – 107) and what follows after the reference to the Book of Noah, concludes that the opening columns of 1QapGen are "most probably not drawn from the same source as that which starts with the title '[copy of] the Book of the Words of Noah' at the bottom of column 5 of that scroll" (6). The title introduces a new literary source. On the allusive Book of Noah, referred to here, in the *Aramaic Levi Document*, and in *Jubilees* 10, and surmised by many as a source of material in the *Book of the Watchers*, the various accounts, including also 1Q19, and later rabbinic and Samaritan traditions, and *Jubilees*, see Stone's discussion. He concludes: "It seems to us more than likely that a Book or Books of Noah existed in the third century BCE or earlier. Some material drawn from this document is preserved in ALD, *Jubilees*, and the Genesis Apocryphon" (18). See also the early discussion in García Martínez, *Qumran and Apocalyptic*, 38 and Cana Werman, "Qumran and the book of Noah," in *Pseudepigraphic Perspectives: The Apocrypha and Pseudepigrapha in Light of the Dead Sea Scrolls: Proceedings of the [Second] International Symposium of the Orion Center for the Study of the Dead Sea Scrolls and Associated Literature, 12-14 January 1997* (ed. Esther G. Chazon and Michael E. Stone; STDJ 31; Leiden: Brill, 1999) 171-81; Michael E. Stone, "The Axis of History at Qumran," in *Pseudepigraphic Perspectives: The Apocrypha and Pseudepigrapha in Light of the Dead Sea Scrolls: Proceedings of the [Second] International Symposium of the Orion Center for the Study of the Dead Sea Scrolls and Associated Literature, 12-14 January 1997* (ed. Esther G. Chazon and Michael E. Stone; STDJ 31; Leiden: Brill, 1999) 133-49, 136-41.

[212] Nickelsburg, "Patriarchs Who Worry about Their Wives," 158. See also Nickelsburg, *1 Enoch 1*, 542.

Noah applies to what follows, not what precedes,[213] and the prominence of Enoch suggests a source in Enoch rather than Noah literature. He also notes the presence in 1QapGen of terms typical of *1 Enoch* 6 – 16.[214] Nickelsburg also argues a coherence between the story of Lamech and that of Abram in 1QapGen, on the one hand, and *1 Enoch* 6 – 11, namely the "triangulation in the plot", where the issue is: women having illicit relationships with forbidden others. He concludes that "the author of the *Apocryphon* is concerned about some kind of miscegenation. The sexuality of Israelite women is seen to constitute a danger".[215] The difficulty with that link is that *1 Enoch* 6 – 11 does not single out Israelite women, but, if anything, when speaking of women as bearers of sorcery and illicit knowledge is probably thinking of foreign women. We shall return to 1QapGen at a later point in our discussion of attitudes towards sexuality. Its interests, fears and affirmations, about sexuality go beyond what we have in *1 Enoch* 106 – 107, where it is not at all clear that the story reflects an author's more general concern with illicit sexual relations of some kind.

This story which *1 Enoch* 106 – 107 and 1QapGen share uses only one aspect of the myth, namely the illicit sexual activity of the Watchers. It plays with the notion that one of them might have had sought intercourse with Lamech's wife. It makes no reference to illicit teachings.[216] It also shows no indication that it seeks to address sexual issues, as wrongdoing or otherwise. Its concern is with enhancing Noah's significance and might possibly be with countering traditions which saw Noah as belonging to the category of giants.[217] In the case of the latter

---

[213] Similarly Fitzmyer, *Genesis Apocryphon*, who points out that "this is perhaps to be taken as the title of the following columns in the *Genesis Apocryphon*. These words follow a blank in the text, which thus marks the beginning of a new section of it" (144).

[214] Nickelsburg, "Patriarchs Who Worry about Their Wives," 141-42.

[215] Nickelsburg, "Patriarchs Who Worry about Their Wives," 152, and see pp. 150-54. Eileen Schuller, "Response to 'Patriarchs Who Worry about their Wives: A Haggadic Tendency in the Genesis Apocryphon," in *George W.E. Nickelsburg in Perspective: An Ongoing Dialogue of Learning* (2 vols; ed. Jacob Neusner and Alan J. Avery-Peck; JSJSup 80; Leiden: Brill, 2003) 1. 200-12, 208, affirms Nickelsburg's tentativeness in his suggestions about the social situation and draws attention to the observation of James C. VanderKam, "The Granddaughters and Grandsons of Noah," *RQ* 16 (1994) 457-61, that in naming an equal number of daughters to match Noah's sons, the author ensures the purity of the line, by ensuring no need to marry beyond the family.

[216] This is not to suggest that these may not be referred to earlier in 1QapGen, where what remains is so fragmentary, but includes the words, "secret" or "mystery" (1.2, 3); "medicines, magicians, and sooth[sayers   ]". See Bernstein, "From the Watchers to the Flood," 44-45.

[217] On this see Stuckenbruck, "Origins of Evil," who draws attention to *Ps. Eupolemus*, who appears to have assumed that there were both good and bad giants, the former including Noah (93-98). He notes the description in Gen 10:8-9 of Noah's grandson,

it concedes the wondrousness which such traditions might attribute to Noah, only to claim its origin has nothing at all to do with such beings, but, on the contrary, signals his special role to counter them and the consequences of their works.

1.4 Review

This summary will not repeat the detailed evaluations of 6 – 11 and 12 – 16, but name only the salient points related to attitudes towards sexuality. The action of the Watchers is treated as abhorrent sexual wrongdoing in which the Watchers abandon their proper order of being (6 – 11) and their station in the heavenly sanctuary (especially 12 – 16) and engage in intercourse with human women. Already the opening chapters, 1 – 5, with their focus on order in creation and their attack on people who abandon it, prepare the way for the abhorrence of the Watchers' deed. Not only should such action or anything of its kind never happen again; the abhorrent action helps 12 – 16 account for the presence of evil spirits which plague people in the world, by explaining how it produced evil giants, from whose bodies the spirits came. It also helps 6 – 11 account for bloodshed and violence, in this instance, more by analogy and merging of horizons, than by direct derivation.

Both 6 – 11 and 12 – 16 also appear to employ the myth paradigmatically in more specific ways, the former, to warn against wrong marital connections among human beings, and the latter, to focus within that concern particularly on priests who forge such marriages and so abandon their priestly integrity. In both, though more strongly in the former, the danger is associated with an understanding of women as bearers of forbidden knowledge and arts (such as sorcery). This pointed to intermarriage with foreigners. In addition, the account in 6 – 11 actually implies that women, by enhancing their beauty with ornaments and cosmetics, given as a result of Asael's teaching, were complicit in seducing the Watchers. The skills taught by the latter enhanced their seductive skills. This made women doubly dangerous: as sources of seduction and as sources of forbidden knowledge and arts. While 12 – 16 does not mention the element of seduction, it continues to assume the danger women pose as bearers of forbidden mysteries. Indeed, for the author of 12 – 16 women would be superfluous, as would sexual relations, but for the fact that human beings are mortal and must reproduce.

Nimrod, as a "mighty man" (גבר γίγας; cf. Gen 6:4). See also his discussion in Loren Stuckenbruck, *The Book of Giants from Qumran: Text, Translation, and Commentary* (TSAJ 63; Tübingen: Mohr Siebeck, 1997) 32-39.

The myth of the Watchers' abhorrent sexual wrongdoing also informs the account of Enoch's journeys in 17 – 19 and 20 – 36, where the Watchers' actions are described in general terms such as transgression (18:15; 21:5, 10). The exception is 19:1-2, which remains general, but speaks of mingling with women and develops the link between the spirit and idolatry. It also continues the image of women as dangerous, picturing them as sirens.

The myth appears again in the *Book of Dream Visions*, briefly in 84:4 ("the angels of your heaven are doing wrong") and then more extensively in the *Animal Apocalypse*, where we can still see the synthesis of the Asael and Shemihazah myths. As in 6 – 11, the Asael myth is linked to the evocation of inappropriate sexual activity, but here it appears to be expressed in terms of lust and intermarriage between Sethites and Cainites and is not focused on women's seduction. The first star, like Asael in 6 – 11, does not engage in intercourse with the calves/cows (representing human women); this occurs only with the many stars, as with Shemihazah and his accomplices in 6 – 11.

Nothing in the *Animal Apocalypse* reflects the imparting of forbidden knowledge or arts, although that may have been too difficult to represent allegorically. It could be read into what the first star might have been doing. The emphasis falls on the abhorrent mixing of kinds and the disastrous consequences (86:5-6; 87:1), and subsequently on the punishment of the first star and then the rest (87:2 – 88:3). As in 6 – 11, and more than in 12 – 16, the emphasis falls also on the violence of the Gentiles in the account which follows, composed from the perspectives of the victims, but also with allusions to others within Israel who lead the people astray. Leading astray may already feature in 15:11, if we accept the emended reading, where it would be the work of evil spirits and no longer just women. In 19:1 it is the spirits, rather the women, who lead astray. In the *Animal Apocalypse* it has become other members of the community. This is, at most, present in the *Book of the Watchers* in 1 – 5, with the allusion to those who speak proud and hard words against God's majesty (5:4; 1:9).

The punishment aspect of the myth reappears in the image of the judgement in 90:21, although greater emphasis falls on the seventy angels of later history who overstepped their mandate, and the blinded sheep (90:22-27). In relation to the myth it is interesting that only one of the consequences which the Watchers' deeds evoked relates to sexual wrongdoing: lusting between the large and the black cattle, which represent a forbidden relationship which will undermine the Sethite line of white cattle. There is probably an echo of concern with intermarriage with Gentiles in 89:75. The polluted temple of the post-exilic period may relate to sexual wrongdoing among priests (89:73), perhaps to intermarriage, but if so, the author has not made it explicit. Otherwise the *Book of Dream Visions* does not give attention to sexual wrongdoing in a way that indicates it is a contemporary concern for the author. It assumes marriage is normal, but placing Enoch's visions before his marriage may reflect notions of a distinctive state of holiness.

The situation is similar in the *Epistle* (92 – 105). The myth goes without explicit mention in the *Apocalypse of Weeks*, but is implied in 93:3-4, where Enoch declares that "righteousness endured" until his time and then "deceit and violence" would spring up. The rest of the *Epistle* demonstrates no particular concern with sexual wrongdoing or with anything positive about sexuality.

The next major reference to the myth comes in the *Birth of Noah*, where it is the basis for the dramatic irony, as Lamech fears Noah is the product of a sexual liaison between his wife and a Watcher, but Enoch reassures Lamech's father, Methusaleh. This brief account of the myth highlights the abhorrent act of sexual mixing by holy heavenly beings and the begetting of children. The focus appears to be the contamination of earth from which it will apparently be cleansed by the flood, but it also includes a broader emphasis on wickedness and violence beyond the flood (107:1).

Overall, given the myth's depiction of what was abominable sexual wrongdoing, intercourse between different species and defilement of the holy (perhaps priestly) angels, one might have expected some exploitation of this aspect to warn against analogous behaviour among human beings. This is not what we find. At most there is an implied concern with intermarriage in 6 – 11 and 12 – 15 and in the *Animal Apocalypse*, where it must be deduced. We also find a disparagement of women as a seductive danger (6 – 11; 19:2). Otherwise the focus falls on warfare and its destructive effects on people (6 – 11), on women as a source of forbidden knowledge and arts (6 – 16) (perhaps connected with concern with intermarriage), on the individual destructiveness of evil spirits (12 – 16), on their leading people to idolatry (19:1) and on the evils of those who lead the people astray by false teaching, a particular feature of 1 – 5 (especially 1:9; 5:1, 4; cf. 27:2), the *Animal Apocalypse* (89:32-33, 41, 51, 54, 73-74; 90:7, 27), the *Apocalypse of Weeks* (93:8-9) and the *Epistle* (94:9; 96:7; 99:8; 104:10-11). That such teaching might include permissiveness towards behaviour that pollutes the temple and defiles the priesthood is possible, but is not expressed specifically.

This is similarly the case with that element of the myth which receives less attention: the teaching given by the Watchers. Where it relates to sexuality, it is offered as the explanation for the dangers of women's sexuality through adornment and through secret wiles and sorcery and, most dramatically, in depicting the women of the Watchers as sirens. But this, too, does not become a theme for instruction at any point. One may see further blaming of women in 98:5 where they are made responsible for their own infertility because of the works of their hands and in 99:5 where they abort and abandon their children, although the latter functions to depict a situation of despair rather than to impart moral instruction. Women's sexuality, indeed their existence, is defined by the author of

15:5-7 solely in terms procreation. But there, too, the author shows no real interest in women, but is arguing why Watchers have no need for sexual activity, since they are not saddled with mortality like humans.

While statements relating to sexuality are largely related to the myth, there is one further area where one might expect it to be addressed, namely statements about eschatology and protology. With regard to the latter, issues of sexuality, so important for the Genesis account of the garden of Eden, do not feature, beyond mention of nakedness in 32:6, in relation to the expulsion from the garden. While within the corpus, the sin of the garden and of Cain is known, the major source of evil in the world is the deed of the Watchers, not those former sins, and certainly not in any sexual sense.

Similarly, the images of the future do not include sexuality as a theme, although some statements imply it. The abundant fruitfulness to which 10:17-19 looks forward, when Michael rejuvenates the earth, will include that people "will live and beget thousands and all the days of their youth and their old age will be completed in peace" (10:17). This means the author does not envisage that human beings will live like undying angels, without further need for procreation, nor that they will be in the kind of holy context where sexual activity would be out of place. According to 25:3-6 they will live a long life beside the sanctuary and with the fragrance of the tree of life in their bones. *1 Enoch* 90:29, 34-36 speaks of them dwelling in a new house, referring to the new Jerusalem, though makes no mention of the tower which in 89:72-73 represents the temple. This coheres with the image reflected in most of the corpus, according to which future fulfilment is seen to take place on earth after the model of Isa 65:17-23.[218]

If the abhorrence of the Watchers' act has any application in relation to sexuality, it seems only to be in relation to mixed marriages and dangers to which they expose a person (particularly a priest), though even this has to be deduced from the text by analogy. The multiple other possible applications, including those of crossing boundaries of kind, like bestiality or homosexuality, and others which defile or are an abomination, like incest, remarrying a divorced wife, prostitution, rape, adultery, do not appear to have warranted attention. Nor is any interest evident in positive aspects of sexual relations, such as we find in *Jubilees*. Given the sexual potency of the myth, this is remarkable.

---

[218] Nickelsburg, *1 Enoch 1*, notes 103:1-4 and 104:1-6, which apparently envisage the life of souls after death in the heavenly realm (49).

1.5   *The Book of Giants*

Józef T. Milik, who first identified the *Book of Giants* among the Qumran scrolls, conjectured that it must have once stood where now we find the *Similitudes* in the Ethiopic *1 Enoch*, namely, 37-71, and so formed an original Pentateuch of the Enochic corpus.[219] This hypothesis has not withstood the critical analysis of other scholars.[220] Rather the work, while presupposing the *Book of the Watchers*, has its own distinctive emphases and a different focus.[221] Its proximity, however, to *1 Enoch* and to the *Book of the Watchers*, in particular, makes it appropriate to include it at this point in our study.

In the most comprehensive analysis thus far Loren Stuckenbruck[222] identifies five Qumran manuscripts which he is virtually certain belong to an Aramaic document which has been designated the *Book of Giants* (1Q23; 6Q8; 4Q203; 4Q530; 4Q531), a further two which he considers probably belong (2Q26; 4Q532), three for whom it is plausible (1Q24; 4Q556; 4Q206 2 and 3), in addition to others where it is possible, but telling evidence is missing.[223] The material is very fragmentary often yielding no more than a few words, if that. The similarity to material present in the Manichean *Book of Giants*, is sufficient to indicate that

---

[219] Milik, *Books of Enoch*, 58, 77-78, 183-84.

[220] See the refutation by Jonas C. Greenfield, and Michael E. Stone, "The Enochic Pentateuch and the Date of the Similitudes," in *'Al Kanfei Yonah: Collected Studies of Jonas C. Greenfield on Semitic Philology* (ed. Shalom M. Paul, Michael E. Stone, and Avital Pinnick; Leiden: Brill, 2001) 2.595-609, and Devorah Dimant, "The Biography of Enoch and the Books of Enoch", *VT* 33 (1983) 14-29. See also Nickelsburg, *1 Enoch 1*, 172-73.

[221] Loren Stuckenbruck, "Giant Mythology and Demonology: From the Ancient Near East to the Dead Sea Scrolls," in *Die Dämonen / Demons: The Demonology of Israelite-Jewish and Early Christian Literature in Context of their Environment* (ed. Armin Lange, Hermann Lichtenberger, and K. F. Diethard Romheld, Tübingen: Mohr Siebeck, 2003) 318-38, writes: "This shift of the spotlight is reflected, in particular, by an extensive elaboration of the giants' exploits before the great deluge (e. g., in 1Q23 9+14+15; 4Q206a 1; 4Q532—533), their ominous visions of judgment (esp. 4Q530 col. ii), and their worries as they come to terms with God's wrath against them" (320). Nevertheless see the caution of James C. Vanderkam, "Response to George Nickelsburg," who notes Milik's conclusion "that 4QGiants^a was part of the manuscript 4QEn^c, and ... that 4QEn^e contained the Book of Giants," and observes: "When a student of manuscripts so skilled as Milik sets forth such a hypothesis, it must be taken very seriously" (383-84).

[222] Stuckenbruck, *Book of Giants*. See also Stuckenbruck, "Giant Mythology," 318-38.

[223] Stuckenbruck, *Book of Giants*, 41.

its third century C.E. author must have known the Aramaic *Book of Giants* or something like it.[224]

Relating fragments and then manuscripts together is a very complex task, but some indications of sequence (especially in 4Q203 and 4Q530) make it possible to conjecture the shape of at least some of the writing.[225] It is beyond our scope, and not pertinent to our task, to discuss these complexities, since the few references relevant to our study stand unaffected by the wider sequence. There is, however, sufficient coherence within the material to enable us to identify that it assumes the myth of *1 Enoch* 6 – 11 and 12 – 16, which describes the sexual wrongdoing of the Watchers and the birth of the giants as the result of their deed. Compared with the account in the *Book of the Watchers*, the *Book of Giants* is "more elaborate, especially where the unhindered atrocities of the giants are concerned" and is concerned above all with their fate. The *Book of Giants* reflects this greater interest in its identification of giants by name with specific roles (e.g., Mahaway as mediary; 'Ohyah and Hahyah as recipients of dream visions; and Gilgamesh as deceptively optimistic).[226] It mentions Enoch, who is cast more in the role of interpreter of the giants' visions which foretell their punishment. Influence of Babylonian mythology is present in the names Gilgamesh and Ḥobabish.[227]

The dependence on the *Book of the Watchers* and the absence of any reference to the Maccabean crisis make the conclusion espoused by Stuckenbruck plausible, that the work was written "sometime between the late 3rd century and 164 B.C.E."[228] He suggests that the writing appears, on the one hand, to counter a view that appears to have given giants positive roles as beings which survived the flood, especially as mediators of information to Abraham, and through Abraham to Phoenicia and Egypt, as expressed in *Ps. Eupolemus* and related fragments.[229] It shares this negative approach with the early Enoch literature. As noted above, notions that perhaps Noah, himself, was a giant, may be in the background of *1 Enoch* 106-107, which is at pains to explain Noah's wondrous being otherwise. *1 Enoch* 106-107 also shares with the *Book of Giants* the motif of traveling to find Enoch to seek his interpretation of troubling visions (4Q530 3) and the emphasis on the flood as the means of judgement.[230] Stuckenbruck sees the *Book of Giants*

---

[224] Stuckenbruck, *Book of Giants*, who also draws attention to the *Midrash of Shemhazai and 'Aza'el*, a further work which may have known the *Book of Giants* (2).

[225] Stuckenbruck, *Book of Giants*, 11.

[226] See the discussion of names in Stuckenbruck, "Giant Mythology," 320-32.

[227] Stuckenbruck, *Book of Giants*, 31-32.

[228] Stuckenbruck, *Book of Giants*, 31.

[229] Stuckenbruck, *Book of Giants*, 32-39.

[230] According to Stuckenbruck, *Book of Giants*, the flood destroyed the bodies of the giants (40). *1 Enoch* 106:15 may also imply that the flood destroyed the giants (as did *1 Enoch* 89:6; cf. 10:9, 12).

using the demise of the giants also to comfort hearers that the woes of their time engendered by evil spirits will also come to a certain end with divine judgement.[231] This assumes that the authors shared the view of *1 Enoch* 15:8-11 that evil spirits emerged from the corpses of the slain giants. In the *Book of Giants*, however, the disembodiment receives further reflection and is apparently seen as loss: "what they lose after death is the human part of their 'form' (cf. 4Q531 14). In effect, they thus become 'de-humanised' beings".[232] "Because of their reprehensible nature, the giants' punishment will involve a reconfiguration of their mode of being."[233]

The plausible notion that the account of the giants serves, at least in part, to console those who face terrors and dangers in their own day that the outcome will not be hopeless, provides a framework within which to evaluate possible references to sexuality. One might expect that times of sexual wrongdoing in primordial times might be seen as prefiguring times of sexual wrongdoing in the hearers' world. Just as in the Enoch literature (except by analogy in relation to intermarriage), it is not, however, what we find. In what survives of the *Book of Giants*, as in the *Book of the Watchers*, the activities which characterise the giants' wrongdoing do not appear to include sexual wrongdoing, even though that was the sin of the Watchers as a result of which the giants came into being.

We have specific reference to the myth of the Watchers in 4Q203 8. It reads in part:

3 A copy of the s[ec]ond tablet of the letter
4 in a document (written by) the hand of Enoch, the scribe of interpretation [... the
5 and Holy One to Shemihazah and all [his] co[mpanions ...:
6 "Let it be known to you th[at   ]
7 your activity and that of [your] wives and of your children and of
8 those [giants and their]son[s and] the [w]ives o[f all of them
9   through your fornication (בזנותכי‍ן) on the earth, for it (the earth) has [risen up [ag]ainst y[ou ... and crying out]
10 and raising accusation against you [and ag]ainst the activity of your sons[
11 the corruption which you have committed on it (חבלא די חבלתון) *vacat*[

---

[231] Stuckenbruck, *Book of Giants*: "If a continued spirit-existence of the giants following the deluge formed part of the mythological framework for the author(s), then BG's repeated reference to the giants' culpability would have reflected their belief that these spirit powers, though active in the world, are essentially *defeated powers*" (39-40). It thus shares the qualified optimism of *Jubilees*, which expresses this with its distinctive notion that only ten percent of the spirits are let loose (*Jub.*10:9).

[232] Stuckenbruck, "Giant Mythology," 337. I have corrected 19 to 14, in accordance with *Book of Giants*, 160.

[233] Stuckenbruck, "Giant Mythology," 335; see also *Book of Giants*, 159-60.

On the basis of the *Book of the Watchers* we recognise Shemihazah as the leader of the Watchers. We also note the expression, "through your fornication" (בזנותכין), which will refer to the Watchers having sexual intercourse with women, since they are the ones addressed. It does not appear to include their offspring in the "your". The double reference to corruption in *l.* 11 is also addressed primarily to the Watchers. The letter does, however, speak of others beside the Watchers. It speaks of the women, reflecting the assumption, present in the *Book of the Watchers*, that the women were in some sense complicit in the act, but probably also reflecting their role in bearing illicit knowledge. It also speaks of the giants, their sons and the wives of all of them, without further specifying their wrongdoing, although in the context of the document the reference is to their violence. Before turning to such material elsewhere in the document, we should also note the reference to a complaint. As in *1 Enoch* 9:2-3, the complaint brought by earth's inhabitants and on their behalf by the angels encompasses the Watchers' sexual wrongdoing as well as the action of their offspring.

4Q530 6 i and ii contain a further reference to the complaint: "[the souls of those kil]led are complaining against their murderers and crying out for help" (*l.* 4). 4Q531 1 appears to report the effects of the giants' activity on the world of nature (animals, trees, crops, birds) as well as humanity and makes reference to burning. 4Q532 2 mentions "great injustice (חבל) they inflicted on [the] ear[th" (probably a reference to the giants),[234] but it could refer to "corruption" as in the double reference above in 4Q203 8, in which case it would be referring to the action of the Watchers mentioned two lines earlier. 4Q531 seems also to refer to the Watchers' sexual wrongdoing. Among the few surviving words, "they defiled themselves", refers to their action; "giants and *nephilim*", to the fruit, and the remaining words appear to reflect the bloodshed and violence of their insatiability and its effects on earth. These motifs reflect the content and sequence in *1 Enoch* 7:1-5.[235] Bloodshed appears also in 4Q556 6 and 4Q206 3. Killing appears in 1Q23 9+14+15, where parallels with *1 Enoch* 7:3-5 and the Manichean *Book of Giants* suggest it is the action of giants,[236] and in 4Q203 3 and 4Q203 5, where similarly the giants are in view.[237] There appears to be a reference to birth in 4Q531 43 (of giants?; cf. 1Q23 20 "children of") and 4Q531 46 gives us the words, "came forth from the *nephilim*" (another reference to birth of giants or perhaps to the evil spirits?).

The fragmentary texts yield little for our investigation. They do appear to extrapolate from the myth in *1 Enoch* 6 – 11 and 12 – 16. Thus they share the

---

[234] Stuckenbruck, *Book of Giants*, 182.
[235] Stuckenbruck, *Book of Giants*, 151, but he seems not to give this sufficient weight.
[236] Stuckenbruck, *Book of Giants*, 59.
[237] Stuckenbruck, *Book of Giants*, 72, 77.

belief that the Watchers committed sexual wrongdoing by having sexual relations with women and by doing so, defiled themselves. They also assume some guilt on the part of the women, though this is not specified, but is probably informed by the notion that women used seduction and that they were bearers of illicit knowledge, which included matters related to sexuality. But, as in *1 Enoch*, the deeds of the giants are not portrayed in sexual terms or as sexual wrongdoing, except that it is assumed that they and their sons marry. At least within the surviving fragments we do not find an indication that this was something from which the judgement would free their community, in comparison with the violence which the giants symbolise.

PART TWO

Attitudes towards Sexuality in the
Aramaic Levi Document

The *Aramaic Levi Document* appears to have been written in the third century B.C.E., perhaps even slightly earlier or later.[238] It has come to us through various sources and in fragmentary form. These sources include seven fragmentary copies in Aramaic from Qumran, two sets of vellum leaves in Aramaic from the Cairo Geniza, extracts of a Greek translation preserved within a manuscript of the *Testaments of the Twelve Patriarchs*, a further two possible Greek citations from a fourth century monastic writer, Ammonas, and a small fragment in Syriac.[239] These have been collated, ordered, edited independently and published simultaneously in 2004 by both Greenfield, Stone and Eshel,[240] on the one hand, and Drawnel,[241] on the other, in a form which enables us to read as one the sum of

---

[238] So Jonas C. Greenfield, Michael E. Stone and Esther Eshel, *The Aramaic Levi Document: Edition, Translation, Commentary* (SVTP 19; Leiden: Brill, 2004), who also mention the possibility of the early second century (19). See also Henryk Drawnel, *An Aramaic Wisdom Text from Qumran: A New Interpretation of* the Levi Document (JSJSup 86; Leiden: Brill, 2004), who argues for late fourth or early third century B.C.E. (71). See also the discussion in the conclusion of our treatment.

[239] See the detailed discussions in Greenfield, Stone, Eshel, *Aramaic Levi Document*, 1-6, and Drawnel, *Aramaic Wisdom Text*, 21-32.

[240] Greenfield, Stone, Eshel, *Aramaic Levi Document*.

[241] Drawnel, *Aramaic Wisdom Text*. Overall Drawnel's edition is more comprehensive. On p. 7 Greenfield, Stone, and Eshel do not see their purpose as presenting an edition, despite their subtitle, and do not publish all witnesses. See the extensive critique in Henryk Drawnel, "Review: Jonas C. Greenfield, Michael E. Stone, Esther Eshel, *The Aramaic Levi Document: Edition, Translation, Commentary*," *RB* 113 (2006) 127-31.

the preserved material. Unfortunately the two editions use different versification, Greenfield, Stone and Eshel introducing a new system, and differ slightly in order[242] and extent.[243] The following discussion follows the order and versification used in Greenfield, Stone and Eshel (hereafter GSE), but identifies also Drawnel's equivalent after the "/" and where relevant draws attention to differences in order.

2.1   Levi and the Shechem Incident (1:1-3 / 1c 2)

The beginning of the document is missing. Its earliest surviving section according to GSE preserves sentences which relate to the story of Dinah, particularly Gen 34:13-16, but which appear to be "independent of biblical phraseology".[244] Drawnel, who has Levi's Prayer as the earliest section, notes with regard to the Shechem incident that "the Cairo Geniza manuscript evidence suggests that the story was well elaborated and probably occupied about four columns of the manuscript".[245] The table sets the two translations side by side:

| . . you / she defiled the s[ons of (?) ac-] cording to the manner of all people [\ to do according to the law (*or:* to do so) in all [... *took counsel with*] Jacob my father and Reu[ben my brother ...] (1:1). GSE | Since she defiled the so[ns *of Jacob with her harlotry,*] therefore every m[an *will take a wife for himself*] in order to act according to the law in the whole [*country. I consulted*] Jacob my father and Re[*uben my bro*ther *on (this?) matter*] (1c) Drawnel |

Drawnel, like Puech,[246] reads דטמאת at the beginning (hence "since"), whereas GSE read only טמאת. In the story in Gen 34:1-3, 5, 13 the act of defilement is

---

[242] The main difference concerns the location of Levi's prayer, which Drawnel, *Aramaic Wisdom Text*, brings at the beginning, and Greenfield, Stone and Eshel bring after the accounts of Levi's deeds at Shechem and of the selling of Joseph. Drawnel also locates 4Q213a (4QLevi[b]) 2 11-18, the account of the beginning of a vision, before the account of Levi's deeds at Shechem. It is beyond the scope of our theme to treat the issue of order and it does not bear on our theme. See the detailed discussions in Greenfield, Stone, Eshel, *Aramaic Levi Document*, 11-19, and Drawnel, *Aramaic Wisdom Text*, 32-55.

[243] Drawnel, *Aramaic Wisdom Text*, places 4Q213a 3-4, about a woman who desecrates her name, after the Selling of Joseph, whereas Greenfield, Stone and Eshel list it among fragments that cannot be placed in the sequence of the *Aramaic Levi Document* (219-22).

[244] Greenfield, Stone, Eshel, *Aramaic Levi Document*, 110.

[245] Drawnel, *Aramaic Wisdom Text*, 228.

[246] E. Puech, "Le Testament de Lévi en araméen de la geniza du Caire," *RevQ* 20 (2002) 511-56.

done to Dinah. Both GSE and Drawnel follow Puech in reading an uncertain ב
after the ב and so conjecture that the text spoke of "sons" as the object of טמאת
("defiled"), though GSE note that "numerous words can start with a *bet* and
perhaps a *nun*".[247] Having examined the photograph with text enhancement, I think
there is a case for reading not only a *nun* but also a *yôd*, and so טמאת לבני. It
seems likely that here, not Dinah, but others are being mentioned as the object of
the act of defilement, and these are probably to be identified as "sons", namely
Jacob's sons. Thus in all probability we are meeting an understanding of Genesis
34 which see the defilement as affecting not only Dinah, but also the family of
Jacob.

The problem remains of the person of the verb at the beginning. If it is second
person singular masculine ("you defiled"), then it is addressed to Shechem. This
coheres with the statements in Gen 34:5 in relation to Jacob and his sons that
Shechem "had defiled (טמא) his daughter, Dinah" and 34:13 "had defiled (טמא)
their sister, Dinah". If it is third person singular feminine, then it probably refers to
Dinah, herself, and would appear to imply that she was complicit in an act which
brought defilement to her people. Drawnel clearly reads דטמאת as a feminine
singular, translating: "Since she defiled" and then shows by his conjectures
(represented in italics) that he understands the author to be laying blame on her:
"Since she defiled the so[ns *of Jacob with her harlotry*,]". We shall return to this
possibility below.

The remainder of the verse is also fragmentary and beset with difficulties.

ac-] cording to the manner of all people [\ to do according to the law (*or*: to do so) in all [GSE	therefore every m[an *will take a wife for himself*] in order to act according to the law in the whole [*country*. Drawnel

Drawnel thus supplies conjectures which refer to every man taking a wife for
himself. The reference to "the law" דין (or "judgement") may be a pun on דינה,
though the name is not preserved in the fragmentary text. There seems at least to
be some reference to law or custom and this will most probably relate to marriage
law. It could allude to the requirement in Deut 22:28-29 that the rapist must marry
the violated woman or it may simply refer to some other marriage custom. Gen
34:8-12 reports Hamor and Shechem's attempt to negotiate a settlement.[248] The
remainder of 1:1 / 1c appears to have mentioned consultation with Jacob and

---

[247] Greenfield, Stone, Eshel, *Aramaic Levi Document*, 111.

[248] Greenfield, Stone, Eshel, *Aramaic Levi Document*, 111. They also refer to *Tg. Neof.*
Gen 34:12, "Make very great for me the dowry and the marriage contract and I will give
just as you say to me".

Reuben and 1:2-3 / 1c 2 then reports a response to the men of Shechem,[249] probably by Levi and Simeon, proposing they be circumcised.[250] The element of consultation is absent from the Genesis story, but reflected later in *T. Levi* 6:3, where Levi reports: "I advised my father and Reuben my brother that he would tell the sons of Hamor to be circumcised, because I was zealous because of the abomination which they had wrought in Israel" (ἐγὼ συνβούλευσα τῷ πατρί μου ʽΡουβὴμ τῷ ἀδελφῷ μου, ἵνα εἴπῃ τοῖς υἱοῖς ʽΕμμὼρ τοῦ περιτμηθῆναι αὐτούς, ὅτι ἐζήλωσα διὰ τὸ βδέλυγμα ὃ ἐποίησαν ἐν ʼΙσραήλ). This will be a reflection of use of the *Aramaic Levi Document* by the author of the testament.[251]

The conclusions thus far must be tentative. If Dinah is the subject of the verb, then the *Aramaic Levi Document* implicates her and not only Shechem in the defilement. It would represent an instance of blaming the victim and echo the way in which the *Book of the Watchers* makes women complicit in the angels' sexual wrongdoing (*1 Enoch* 8:1-2). In any case, even if Shechem is the subject, the effect is on others beside Dinah, namely, on the people as a whole, that is, in the context, the family of Jacob. In comparison with the account in *Jubilees* 30 which

---

[249] Drawnel, *Aramaic Wisdom Text*, notes the change to the plural in "they desired", reflecting also the sense of collective responsibility in Gen 34:27, that not only Shechem but his people defiled (טמאו) Dinah (229).

[250] On the unusual expression, "the foreskin of your flesh" (עורלת בשרכון), see Greenfield, Stone, Eshel, *Aramaic Levi Document*, who identify a similar formulation in Ezek 44:6-9, which speaks of the uncircumcised of flesh and spirit (113-14). The contrast between "you will look like us" (1:3) and "you will become like us" (Gen 34:15) may reflect the author's view that the Shechemites would not really have true circumcision (114-15). On the other hand, see Drawnel, *Aramaic Wisdom Text*, who notes that "the lexeme בשר is to be understood as an [*sic*] euphemism for the male pudenda", the penis, a meaning attested in Syriac (229).

[251] On the use of the *Aramaic Levi Document* by the author of the *Testament of Levi* see the discussion in Marinus de Jonge, "Levi in *Aramaic Levi* and in the *Testament of Levi*," in *Pseudepigraphic Perspectives: The Apocrypha and Pseudepigrapha in Light of the Dead Sea Scrolls: Proceedings of the [Second] International Symposium of the Orion Center for the Study of the Dead Sea Scrolls and Associated Literature, 12-14 January 1997* (ed. Esther G. Chazon and Michael E. Stone;. STDJ 31; Leiden: Brill, 1999) 71-89, who rejects the hypothesis of an intermediate work as the source of the latter, as proposed by Robert A. Kugler, *From Patriarch to Priest: The Levi-Priestly Tradition from* Aramaic Levi *to* Testament of Levi (SBLEJL 9; Atlanta: Scholars, 1996). See also Michael E. Stone, "ʻLevi Aramaic' Document and the Greek Testament of Levi," in *Emanuel: Studies in Hebrew Bible, Septuagint and Dead Sea Scrolls in Honor of Emanuel Tov* (ed. Shalom M. Paul, Robert A. Kraft, Lawrence H. Schiffman and Weston W. Fields; Leiden: Brill, 2003) 429-37.

appears to be dependent on the *Aramaic Levi Document* or on its source,[252] it is to be noted that the *Aramaic Levi Document* includes the circumcision ruse, whereas *Jubilees* suppresses it[253] and the *Aramaic Levi Document* goes beyond the account in *Jubilees* also, in apparently providing the rationale from the law (or custom) for proceeding to marriage. Missing in both is any indication of disapproval of Levi's action reflected in Gen 34:30-31, and especially in Gen 49:5-7, in which Jacob curses them for their anger. On the contrary, both the *Aramaic Levi Document* and *Jubilees* reflect a positive view of Levi's action. In the *Aramaic Levi Document* this is reflected in 12:6 / 78 where Levi mentions: "I killed Shechem and destroyed the workers of violence." Levi's act is seen in a positive light. In addition, Levi speaks only of himself without mentioning Simeon. His action is now celebrated and he is its chief focus.

The story probably functions as part of the foundational myth for Levi and the Levitical priesthood as the author understands it, especially in its role of warning people not to marry foreigners and punishing those who do. One might object that the defilement may have nothing to do with intermarriage, but rather with the act of rape. This objection would hold only if we understood Shechem as the subject of the verb, "defiled", but even then, it is much more likely that the focus is on the intermarriage. The issues of foreignness, reflected also in the circumcision motif, are much more strongly to the fore. This concern continues as a theme in the *Aramaic Levi Document* and will be applied specifically to Levi himself and, through him, as a model to Levitical priests.

2.2   Women who bring desecration (4Q213a [4QLevi[b] ar] 3-4 / 3a)

It might be possible to go further in relation to the Dinah passage if we take 4Q213a 3-4 into account, whose place in the *Aramaic Levi Document* is not

---

[252] So Kugler, *From Patriarch to Priest*, who argues that both the *Aramaic Levi Document* and later, *Jubilees*, independently drew on a Levi Apocryphon generated by this tradition (117, 130-31). Similarly James C. VanderKam, "Isaac's Blessing of Levi and His Descendants in *Jubilees* 31," in *The Provo International Conference on* the *Dead Sea Scrolls: Technological Innovations, New Texts, and Reformulated Issues* (ed. Donald W. Parry and Eugene C. Ulrich; STDJ 30; Leiden: Brill, 1999) 497-519, 510-18. See Kugler's list and discussion of significant similarities and differences between *Jub.* 30:1 – 32:9 and *Aramaic Levi Document* (146-55). Among the major differences he lists the discrepancies in dating of events in Levi's life and the absence in part or in full from *Jubilees* of significant elements of *Aramaic Levi Document*, including Levi's prayer, Isaac's instruction, family history, the wisdom speech and Levi's final warnings.

[253] *Jubilees* clearly knows it and alludes to it by referring to the "painful way" of execution (30:4, 17; cf. also 30:12).

located at all by GSE,[254] but which Drawnel locates after the selling of Joseph. Even without that connection it contributes significantly to our theme. The table sets the translations side by side.

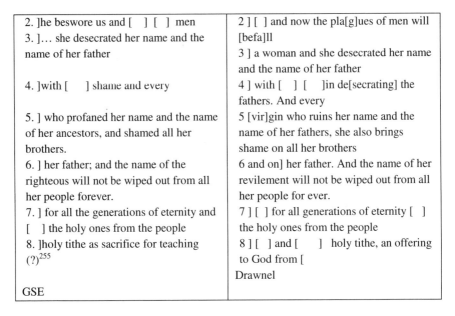

| 2.]he beswore us and [   ] [   ] men
3.]… she desecrated her name and the name of her father

4.]with [   ] shame and every

5.] who profaned her name and the name of her ancestors, and shamed all her brothers.
6.] her father; and the name of the righteous will not be wiped out from all her people forever.
7.] for all the generations of eternity and [   ] the holy ones from the people
8.]holy tithe as sacrifice for teaching (?)[255]

GSE | 2] [   ] and now the pla[g]ues of men will [befa]ll
3] a woman and she desecrated her name and the name of her father
4] with [   ] [   ]in de[secrating] the fathers. And every
5 [vir]gin who ruins her name and the name of her fathers, she also brings shame on all her brothers
6 and on] her father. And the name of her revilement will not be wiped out from all her people for ever.
7] [   ] for all generations of eternity [   ] the holy ones from the people
8] [   ] and [   ] holy tithe, an offering to God from [
Drawnel |

The description of a woman who has "desecrated (תחלל) her name and the name of her father" would certainly fit Dinah, especially if we translate טמאת in 1:1 / 1c as "she has defiled". Shaming her father and all her brothers would certainly fit Genesis 34. There is no way, however, of securing that a reference to Dinah is intended. The passage seems, in any case, at least from *l.* 4 on, to have a broader focus, namely on any woman who acts so as to bring such shame. This most likely continues into *l.* 6, where Drawnel points out that the reading is not חסיה, which GSE translate, "righteous", but הסדה, "revilement", commenting: "The leather is shrunk but the head of a *dālet* excludes the *yŏd/wāw* reading".[256] "The Aramaic

---

[254] Greenfield, Stone, Eshel, *Aramaic Levi Document*, note that the fragments "appear to vary somewhat, both in layout and perhaps in script" and may be "from a different manuscript altogether" (220). See also their discussion on pp. 17-18. Kugler, *From Patriarch to Priest*, sees it as belonging to angelic instruction of Levi in the context of a vision (78-85).

[255] "'Teaching (?)' is an error "resulting from the mistaken reading that dates back to the Qumran preliminary concordance" (Drawnel, personal note, 8 March, 2006).

[256] Drawnel, *Aramaic Wisdom Text*, 109.

חסד 'shame, revilement' fits the context of the preceding lines that speak about the shame and ruin a virgin brings on her family".[257]

It is interesting, however, that *Jubilees*, which appears dependent on the *Aramaic Levi Document* or its source, does append to its account of Dinah an excursus which deals generally with intermarriage with foreigners and uses similar language to what we find in these fragments of the *Aramaic Levi Document*. Thus *Jub.* 30:7 condemns the father or brother, who gives away daughter or sister in marriage to a foreigner, to stoning, and also condemns the daughter, herself, – to be burned. The same applies in reverse in 30:11 to sons marrying foreign women. While expanding the horizons to wider concerns, which include blaming the woman, *Jubilees* does not, however, condemn Dinah, herself, as complicit, as seems to be implied in *Aramaic Levi Document* 1:1 / 1c, if we read, "she has defiled" and possibly in *l.* 3 in the fragments we are considering. In these the focus is solely on the woman or women, but otherwise they also share much in common with the angelic discourse in *Jubilees* 30. Both use Lev 21:9 ("When the daughter of a priest profanes/desecrates [תחל] herself through prostitution [זנות], she profanes/desecrates [מחללת] her father; she shall be burned to death").[258] In his discussion Kugler also notes further common elements: the lasting shameful effect (*Jub.* 30:14); the word "shame, disgrace" (*xafrat Jub.* 30:5, 7); the reference to "plagues" or blows" (*Jub.* 30:7, 15; see also 23:13 in the context of sexual wrongdoing);[259] and the reference to tithe and offering (*Jub.* 30:16, declaring offerings of exogamous people unacceptable).[260] In its use of Lev 21:9 in 30:7 and its context, *Jubilees* applies זנות not narrowly to prostitution, but to marriages to foreigners. It also addresses it not only to the daughters of priests, but to all Israelites, which is consistent with its extrapolation from the incident concerning Dinah, who was not a priest's daughter.

The extent of similarity with *Jubilees* 30 raises a number of questions pertinent to our understanding of these fragments of the *Aramaic Levi Document*. It is possible, as Baumgartner has suggested, that here in the *Aramaic Levi Document* the focus remains narrowly on prostitution and on priests' daughters, and that the fragments have no link with the Dinah story at all.[261] With regard to

---

[257] Drawnel, *Aramaic Wisdom Text*, 236.

[258] See Greenfield, Stone, Eshel, *Aramaic Levi Document*, 221.

[259] I read "pla[g]ues" וכען, with Drawnel, *Aramaic Wisdom Text*, 109, rather than אשבען, which underlies GSE's "he beswore".

[260] Kugler, *From Patriarch to Priest*, 83-84. See Drawnel, *Aramaic Wisdom Text*, who also sees a probable allusion to the Dinah episode and notes that "although very fragmentary, lines 1 – 6 are close in their contents to the chastisement of exogamic marriages in the book of *Jubilees*" (235).

[261] Joseph M. Baumgarten, "Some 'Qumranic' Observations on the *Aramaic Levi Document*," in *Sefer Moshe: The Moshe Weinfeld Jubilee Volume* (ed. C. Cohen, A. Hurvitz

זנות (lit. "prostitution"), however, the passage in 6:3-4 / 16-17, which we shall address below, assumes a wider application of the term, such as we know also from other later texts like CD. It appears at least to include marriage to foreigners as one element in what are assumed to be inappropriate sexual relations. In 6:3-4 / 16-17 Isaac addresses Levi, so that the primary focus, assuming Levi as a model, is with the marriage of priests or perhaps even high priests. We shall return to that issue below.

With regard to the focus of concern, priests' daughters or any daughter, the *Aramaic Levi Document* fragments may be concerned with the marriage of priests' daughters. The allusion in lines 7-8 to priests[262] and to Lev 21:9, which belongs to instructions for priests, may also indicate this. The marriage of priests, themselves, to foreign women is a theme reflected elsewhere in the *Aramaic Levi Document* (6:4 / 17; 12:1 / 73), and also in *Jubilees* 30, where it comes in the context of extrapolations from the Dinah episode and in the context of statements with application to all Israelites. If Drawnel is right in reading "every virgin" in *l.* 5, then the concern, here, may also be wider than the priesthood and come very close to the position of *Jubilees*.[263] He contrasts the "shame and ruin a virgin brings on her family", with the image of Jochabed, in 11:10 / 71; 12:3 / 75, who as the daughter of a priest (namely, Levi, himself), marries appropriately within the family.[264]

If we take the parallels with *Jubilees* 30 cited above as sufficient evidence to indicate that the *Aramaic Levi Document* had similarly used the Dinah episode as a basis for wider extrapolations, then that would be another reason not to narrow the focus to priests' daughters. In any case, at least in the Dinah episode in the *Aramaic Levi Document*, the assumption is a rejection of all foreign marriages. Then the fragments either repeat the same concern or apply it to the instance of priests' daughters. In 6:3-4 / 16-17 it is specifically directed to priests, themselves (or possibly high priests), but within the overall framework of a rejection of foreign marriages for all. If the *Aramaic Levi Document* has similarly extrapolated from the Dinah episode to mixed marriages and this is reflected in the fragments, then it may well be, in the light of 1:1, that, in contrast to *Jubilees*. It also saw Dinah as an accomplice.

---

and S. M. Paul; Winona Lake: Eisenbrauns, 2003) 393-401, 400-401. See also Greenfield, Stone, Eshel, *Aramaic Levi Document*, 220.

[262] On this see the discussion in Drawnel, *Aramaic Wisdom Text*, who draws attention to the likelihood that the giving of the tithe, a tithe of holiness, formed part of the ordination (237-39).

[263] See Drawnel, *Aramaic Wisdom Text*, 235-36.

[264] Drawnel, *Aramaic Wisdom Text*, 236.

2.3   The Prayer of Levi (3:1-18 / 1a:1-19)

Levi's prayer, partially preserved in 3:1-18 / 1a:1-19 includes a brief reference to sexual wrongdoing in 3:5 / 1a:7, "Make far from me, my Lord, the unrighteous spirit, and evil thought and fornication (וזנותא πορνείαν)." This gives prominence to sexual wrongdoing, since no other evils are mentioned, except in general terms. It coheres with *Aramaic Levi Document*'s concern about defilement in 1:1-3 / 1c 2 and its use of the Dinah episode, and also with its emphases in the fragments of 4Q213a 3-4 / 3a which we have considered. It makes it likely that the reference in 3:13 / 1a:14 to impurity (ἀκαθαρσία) would include connotations of sexual wrongdoing. As Drawnel notes, "what is to be understood by the 'impurity' ἀκαθαρσία is best explained by Isaac's speech". He observes that uncleanness is paralleled there in 6:1 / 14 with sin (חטא) and then in 6:3 / 16 with fornication (פחז) and harlotry (זנות).[265]

2.4   Isaac Instructs Levi on Sexual Wrongdoing and Marriage (6:1-5 / 14-18)

The priestly teaching on purity given by Isaac in 6:1-5 / 14-18, after he had blessed Levi (5:1-8 / 8-13), is thus important confirmation of the significance of the theme of sexual wrongdoing in the *Aramaic Levi Document*. The passage is well attested, with two witnesses overlapping in 6:1-5 / 14-18, and a third in 6:1 / 14. It belongs to the largest block of continuous material among the witnesses to *Aramaic Levi Document*, 5:1 – 10: 14 / 11-61, which Drawnel describes as "wisdom instruction" or "wisdom instruction concerning priestly knowledge and craftsmanship".[266] In it Isaac addresses Levi as son and child, reflecting sapiential teaching style. Much of the teaching concerns sacrifice and weights and measures, including arithmetical material, which, Drawnel suggests, depends on Babylonian scribal tradition.[267] It exhibits a formal similarity to the *Book of the Luminaries* (*1 Enoch* 72 – 82), which also draws on Babylonian tradition.[268] Our concern is with the initial

---

[265] Drawnel, *Aramaic Wisdom Text*, 219. He notes also the closeness of 3:5 / 1a 13-14 to *1 Enoch* 10:20 (καὶ σὺ καθάρισον τὴν γῆν ἀπὸ πάσης τὰς ἀκαθαρσίας καὶ πάσης ἀδικίας καὶ πάσης ἁμαρτίας καὶ ἀσεβείας, καὶ πάσας τὰς ἀκαθαρσίας τὰς γινομένας ἐπὶ τῆς γῆς ἐξάλειψον; "and cleanse the earth from all impurity and from all wrong and from all lawlessness and from all sin, and godlessness and all impurities that have come upon the earth").

[266] Drawnel, *Aramaic Wisdom Text*, 254, 255.

[267] Drawnel, *Aramaic Wisdom Text*, 63, 91-94, 282-87, 292-93.

[268] Drawnel, *Aramaic Wisdom Text*, 91.

instructions. Their position as Isaac's opening words already gives their theme prominence. That theme concerns sexuality.

6:1 And he said to me, Levi my son, beware of all uncleanliness (טומאה ἀκαθαρσίας) and of all sin, your judgment is greater than that of all flesh. 6:2 And now, my son, I will show you the true law and I will not hide anything from you, to teach you the law of the priesthood. 6:3 First of all, be<wa>re my son of all fornication (פחז συνουσιασμοῦ) and impurity (טומאה ἀκαθαρσίας) and of all harlotry (זנות πορνείας) 6:4 And marry (סב λάβε) a woman from my family and do not defile (חלל βεβηλώσῃς) your seed with harlots (זניאן πόρνων), since you are holy seed, and sanctify your seed like the holy place since you are called a holy priest for all the seed of Abraham. 6:5 You are near to God and near to all his holy ones. Now, be pure in your flesh from every impurity (טומאה ἀκαθαρσίας) of man. GSE	14 Levi, beware, my son, of every impurity (טומאה ἀκαθαρσίας) and of every sin; your judgement is greater than all flesh. 15 And now, my son, the law of truth I will show you, and I will not conceal from you anything to teach you the law of the priesthood. 16 First of all, beware, my son, of every fornication (פחז συνουσιασμοῦ) and impurity (טומאה ἀκαθαρσίας) and of every harlotry (זנות πορνείας) 17 And you, take (סב λάβε) for yourself a wife from my family so that you may not defile (חלל βεβηλώσῃς) your seed with harlots (זניאן πόρνων), because you are a holy seed. And holy is your seed like the Holy One, for a holy priest you are called for all the seed of Abraham. 18 You are close to God and close to all his holy ones, now be pure in your flesh from, every impurity (טומאה ἀκαθαρσίας) of any man. Drawnel

The immediately preceding verse, 5:8 / 13, sets the following account of Isaac's instruction in the context of law about the priesthood: "And when he learned that I was priest of the Most High God, the Lord of heaven, he began to instruct me and to teach me the law of the priesthood". Isaac, in turn, learned it from his father, Abraham (7:4 / 22; 10:3, 10 / 50, 57), who, in turn, learned it from the book of Noah (10:10 / 57).[269] A similar appeal to Noah (but then further back, to Enoch,

---

[269] Drawnel, *Aramaic Wisdom Text*, writes: "Isaac's teaching of the sapiential order can be seen as a counterpart to the Watchers' fall and corruption. When the Watchers descended to earth, they committed fornication and starting revealing and teaching their wives illicit knowledge" (261). *Aramaic Levi Document*, however, shows no direct engagement with the myth.

unlike in the *Aramaic Levi Document*) is to be found in *Jubilees*, including concerning instruction about sexuality (7:20-21; 21:10).[270]

As Drawnel notes, the section which we are considering "is marked off with an *inclusio* of "מן כל טומאה", (6:1 and 6:5 / 14 and 18).[271] Thus "from all impurity" frames the passage, whose centrepiece is the warning in 6:3-4 / 16-17, clearly concerned with sexual wrongdoing. This will be also be the primary focus of the word, "impurity" (טומאה ἀκαθαρσίας) in the framing expression. The reference in 6:2 / 15 to "the law of the priesthood", immediately before the centrepiece, recalls 5:8 / 13, and so shows 6:3 / 16 to be a recapitulation of the statement in 6:1 / 15, but in expanded form. The passage has thus been carefully composed to highlight the theme. Drawnel notes that the warning matches Levi's prayer in 3:13 / 1a:14, that his heart be purified from all impurity.[272] In our discussion above we noted the link with 3:5 / 1a:7, which specifically mentions fornication. The words, *your judgment is greater than that of all flesh* (6:1 / 14) are best taken as a statement about Levi's greater authority to exercise judgement (as he does in relation to the Shechemites) than as a warning about greater judgement which he would have to suffer for any misdeed.[273] So to be able to judge impurity, Levi himself must be pure.[274] This also reinforces the image of Levi and the Levitical priesthood in relation to warning against and punishing sexual wrongdoing, for which the Dinah episode functions as a foundational myth.

6:3 / 16 uses three related concepts: "fornication" (פחז συνουσιασμοῦ), "impurity" (טומאה ἀκαθαρσίας) and "harlotry" (זנות πορνείας). פחז occurs in Judg 9:4 and Zeph 3:4 with the meaning, "undisciplined, reckless", not necessarily

---

[270] On the allusive Book of Noah see the discussion above in relation to the account of the birth of Noah in *1 Enoch* 106-107 (1.3.2).

[271] Drawnel, *Aramaic Wisdom Text*, 262. While he rightly observes that in 6:1 / 14 the warning is general, the self-conscious structuring reflected in the passage justifies seeing an allusion to sexual wrongdoing as already implied. It was already present by association in 3:5 /1a:7 and 3:13 / 1a:14. Drawnel also emphasises the importance of interpreting the passage in the light of what precedes, including the Shechem episode (263).

[272] Drawnel, *Aramaic Wisdom Text*, 262.

[273] So Drawnel, *Aramaic Wisdom Text*, 263-64; and Greenfield, Stone, Eshel, *Aramaic Levi Document*, 157-58. The role of Levi and the priesthood in exercising judgement could be reflected in 4:9 / 4, in which an angelic voice speaks in a vision to Levi of "the kingdom of the sword". So Marinus de Jonge and Johannes Trompf, "Jacob's Son Levi in the Old Testament Pseudepigrapha and Related Literature," in *Biblical Figures outside* the *Bible* (ed. Michael E. Stone and Theodore A. Bergren; Harrisburg: Trinity Press International, 1998) 203-36, 215-16, but *Aramaic Levi Document* seems rather to be making a contrast, as already implied in 4:7 / 3c, between the kingdom of the priesthood and another dominion which brings chaos and violence. So Drawnel, 240-47.

[274] So Drawnel, *Aramaic Wisdom Text*, 264, who also draws attention to the judicial role of priests reflected in Deut 17:9.

in a sexual context, but here it has such a context. Gen 49:4 appears to use it with
the image of water to describe Reuben's sexual sin as the result of excessive
passion.[275] 4Q202 3.1 (*1 Enoch* 8:2) preserves only the letters פכ, but they come in
a sexual context and may also reflect use of פחז in this sense.[276] The Greek,
συνουσιασμός, can simply mean "sexual intercourse", but here, as in Sir 23:6, it
refers to illicit sexual intercourse. This latter meaning preserves some of the sense
of excess implied in פחז.

GSE note the list of three things which caused the flood according to *Jub.*
7:21, fornication, illicit sexual intercourse and uncleanness, and Drawnel notes
that in *Jubilees* "impurity" and "harlotry" frequently occur together.[277] Our
discussion of *Jubilees*, below, shows how "impurity" (*rekʷs*) regularly has
connotations of sexual wrongdoing in *Jubilees* and *zemmut*, which Drawnel
translates as "harlotry" has much wider connotations. GSE note that in the LXX
ἀκαθαρσία mainly translates טומאה, but can sometimes translate נדה (Lev 20:21;
Ezek 7:20; 2 Chron 29:5).[278] Here in our passage the meaning is clearly sexual
impurity which defiles. We noted above the word טמאת ("defiled") in relation to
the Dinah episode.

The translation of זנות πορνεία by "harlotry" in both GSE and Drawnel,
rather than sexual immorality or wrongdoing, receives some support from the
reference in 6:4 / 17 to *harlots* (זניאן πόρνων). On the other hand, the warning
there, *and marry* (סב λάβε) *a woman from my family and do not defile* (חלל
βεβηλώσῃς) *your seed with harlots* (זניאן πόρνων), may be equating exogamy
with harlotry, as we shall see. Drawnel also draws attention to the correspondence

---

[275] See also Drawnel, *Aramaic Wisdom Text*, 266.

[276] Florentino García Martínez and Eibert J. C. Tigchelaar, eds, *The Dead Sea Scrolls:
Study Edition* (2 vols; Leiden: Brill, 1997), read פחז]ין (1. 406).

[277] Drawnel, *Aramaic Wisdom Text*, 266. Drawnel continues to point to the Enoch
myth of illicit sexual intercourse between the Watchers and the women (*1 Enoch* 15:3-4)
and to note the warnings based on their misdeeds in *Jubilees* (266). It is, however,
interesting that *Aramaic Levi Document* does not demonstrate connection with this
tradition. This contrasts with its use of Genesis 34, which it shares with *Jubilees*, as
Drawnel rightly notes (266).

[278] Greenfield, Stone, Eshel, *Aramaic Levi Document*, 159. They point also to *1 Enoch*
10:11 in this context. On this see our discussion of *Jubilees*. See also Lawrence H.
Schiffman, "Sacrificial Halakhah in the Fragments of the *Aramaic Levi Document* from
Qumran, the Cairo Genizah, and Mt. Athos Monastery," in *Reworking the Bible:
Apocryphal and Related Texts at Qumran: Proceedings of a Joint Symposium by the Orion
Center for the Study of the Dead Sea Scrolls and Associated Literature and* the *Hebrew
University Institute for Advanced Studies Research Group on Qumran, 15-17 January, 2002*
(ed. Esther G. Chazon, Devorah Dimant, and Ruth A. Clements; STDJ 58; Leiden: Brill,
2005) 177-202. He writes: "Ritual impurity clearly refers to defiling the sanctuary" (178).

between Isaac's warnings to Levi to flee fornication (פחז), impurity (טמאה) and harlotry (זנות) in 6:3 / 16 and the themes of defilement (טמא) and harlotry (זונה) in the Genesis account of the Dinah episode (34:5, 13, 27; and 34:31),[279] where already we see the beginnings of a broader use of the motif of harlotry.

In 6:4 / 17 Isaac addresses the issue of marriage:

ואנת אנחתא מן משפחתי סב לך ולא תהל זרעך עם זניאן
ארי זרע קדיש אנת וקדיש זרעך דיך קודשא
ארו כהין קדיש אנת מחקרי לכל זרע אברהם

σὺ <πρῶτος> ἀπὸ τοῦ σπέρματός <μου> λάβε καὶ μὴ βεβηλώσῃς τὸ σπέρμα σου μετὰ <πόρνων>.
'Εκ σπέρματος γὰρ ἁγίου εἶ, καὶ σπέρμα σου ἁγίασον καὶ τὸ σπέρμα τοῦ ἁγιασμοῦ σου ἐστίν.
'Ιερεὺς κληθήσεται τῷ σπέρματι 'Αβραάμ.

And marry a woman from my family and do not defile your seed with harlots,	And you, take for yourself a wife from my family so that you may not defile your seed with harlots,
since you are holy seed,	because you are a holy seed. And holy is
and sanctify your seed like the holy place	your seed like the Holy One,
since you are called a holy priest for all the seed of Abraham.	for a holy priest you are called for all the seed of Abraham.
GSE	Drawnel

Drawnel's translation brings out more strongly the connection between the two instructions, avoiding harlotry/illicit marriage and appropriate marriage. Here we note a different word for defile, חלל, which we also found above in 4Q213a 3-4, used concerning the women. It is the language of Lev 21:9, "When the daughter of a priest profanes/desecrates (חלל) herself through prostitution (זנות), she profanes/desecrates (חלל) her father; she shall be burned to death". We noted above the broader application of Lev 21:9 in *Jub.* 30:7, which applies it to the prohibition against any woman marrying a Gentile.[280] As we have seen, 4Q213a 3-4 also alludes to this passage, apparently in this broader sense. In relation to 6:4 / 17 Drawnel[281] draws attention to Lev 21:14 which stipulates that a high priest may not marry, among others, a polluted prostitute, which would pollute his seed.

---

[279] Drawnel, *Aramaic Wisdom Text*, 229.

[280] So Kugler, *From Patriarch to Priest*: "The admonition that Levi marry within the community, seems to imply that a woman's non-Israelite parentage would qualify her for the label זנה, 'harlot'" (103).

[281] Drawnel, *Aramaic Wisdom Text*, 267.

The passage needs to be read in its wider context:

13 He shall marry only a woman who is a virgin.
14 A widow, or a divorced woman, or a woman who has been defiled, a prostitute
(וחללה זנה), these he shall not marry.
He shall marry a virgin of his own kin (מעמיו),
15 that he may not profane his offspring among his kin (ולא יחלל זרעו בעמיו);
for I am the LORD; I sanctify him.
(Lev 21:13 15)

The author of the *Aramaic Levi Document* may be doing nothing more than tailoring the instruction in Lev 21:13-15 to Levi as the first high priest. The instruction would then, of course, be taken as applying to all high priests who succeeded him, as Schiffman observes.[282] But it is also to be noted that the instruction not to marry a prostitute is applied in Lev 21:7 to all priests: "They shall not marry a prostitute or a woman who has been defiled; neither shall they marry a woman divorced from her husband. For they are holy to their God". Lev 21:8 speaks of God as holy, another connection with our passage in *Aramaic Levi Document*. Further, if there is a connection between the concerns expressed here in 6:4 / 17 and Levi's action in Genesis 34, then limiting the focus to the high priest seems unlikely. There, as in Num 25:6-13, the concern is with any Israelite. Here, the context puts the focus on priests. The allusions to Lev 21:14, and possibly 21:7, which come from a chapter concerned with priests, also suggest a priestly focus, as Schiffman observes.[283]

It would seem then that the exhortation to marry within the family is closely associated with the instruction not to defile one's seed with "harlots", and that, as in *Jubilees*, זנות is being taken in a much broader sense than prostitution and now includes inappropriate marriage/sexual relations (*Jub.* 30:15; 23:21), in particular, taking wives from outside the family. As noted above, Drawnel captures this meaning well in his translation: "And you, take for yourself a wife from my family so that you may not defile your seed with harlots". Similarly, the author of the *Damascus Document*, in expounding the three nets of Belial and in citing Levi as

---

[282] Schiffman, "Sacrificial Halakhah," notes that "it is not clear whether this and similar laws in *Aramaic Levi* refer to all priests or only to the High Priest" (179), pointing out that Levi is ancestor not only of all priests, but also of all high priests. He applies this to both 6:3 /16 and 6:4 / 17. He notes, however, the possibility that *Aramaic Levi Document* concurs with Ezek 44:15-31 which requires that all priests be Zadokite and that they conform to the requirements which Leviticus lays only on high priests (179).

[283] Schiffman, "Sacrificial Halakhah," 178-79. He notes one of the views expressed in Tannaitic halakhah (which was later accepted as Talmudic law), that priests not marry converts and sees *Aramaic Levi Document* as totally in agreement with it (180).

an authority (CD 4.19), perhaps even in dependence on the *Aramaic Levi Document*, applies זנות more broadly, using it to address bigamy, sexual intercourse with a menstruating woman and marriage of nieces (CD 4.15 – 5.12).[284] The author may also have been aware that his image of Isaac warning Levi to marry one of his own, recalls Isaac's instruction to Jacob, not to marry a Canaanite (Gen 28:1)[285] and that the consequence of both instructions is the same: marriage within the extended family (in both cases, with Laban's family).

If, as seems likely, the instruction to Levi is understood to apply to all priests what is also enjoined of all Israelites, there remains a further question: whether that instruction intends something even more specific, such as may well be intended in 4QMMT,[286] namely that priests should marry only virgins from Levi's seed, as Himmelfarb suggests.[287] Following Kugler[288] she understands משפחתי ("my family") not as a reference to Isaac's family, but as something to be read in the context of any priest passing on instruction to his family. She associates it with מעמיו "of his own peoples" in Lev 21:14, which she also reads narrowly to mean "of his own kind" in relation to the high priest: he is to marry only within his clan, as the word appears to be used in Lev 21:1, 4 and 15. In favour of such a reading is also the emphasis in 6:4 / 17 on the holiness of Levi's seed: "since you are holy seed, and sanctify your seed like the holy place, since you are called a holy priest for all the seed of Abraham". Accordingly *Aramaic Levi Document* would be requiring of priests that they marry only within the priestly clan. The problem is that this reading does not appear to do justice to the context.

---

[284] See Jonas C. Greenfield, "The Words of Levi Son of Jacob in Damascus Document IV, 15-19," *RQ* 13 (1988) 319-22, arguing that assuming an emendation, this line from *Aramaic Levi Document* is cited in CD 4.15-19. See also Drawnel, *Aramaic Wisdom Text*, 19, 214, who concludes the dependence is difficult to establish.

[285] So Kugler, *From Patriarch to Priest*, 103. Cf. Schiffman, "Sacrificial Halakhah," who, while noting it, argues that it "seems to be of little relevance to our passage" (180).

[286] See Robert A. Kugler, "Halakic Interpretive Strategies at Qumran: A Case Study," in *Legal Texts and Legal Issues: Proceedings of the Second Meeting of the International Organization for Qumran Studies, Cambridge, 1995: Published in Honour of Joseph M. Baumgarten* (ed. Moshe J. Bernstein, Florentino García Martínez, and John Kampen, STDJ 23. Leiden: Brill, 1997) 131-40, 135-36.

[287] Himmelfarb, "Levi, Phinehas," 4, 3-6; similarly see Martha Himmelfarb, "Earthly Sacrifice and Heavenly Incense: The Law of the Priesthood in *Aramaic Levi* and *Jubilees*," in *Heavenly Realms and Earthly Realities in Late Antique Religions* (ed. Ra'anan S. Boustan and Annette Yoshiko Reed; New York: Cambridge University Press, 2004) 103-22, 105-106; and following her, Christine E. Hayes, *Gentile Impurities and Jewish Identities: Intermarriage and Conversion from the Bible to the Talmud* (Oxford: OUP, 2002) 72.

[288] Kugler, "Halakic Interpretive Strategies," 133-35.

In the instruction, "And marry a woman from my family (מָשָׁפַחתִי)," what does מַשָׁפַחתִי ("my family") mean? The most immediate and obvious reference in the case of Levi is to the family of Isaac. *Aramaic Levi Document* reports Levi's conformity with this instruction in 11:1 / 62: "And when four weeks in the years of my life were completed for me, in the twenty-eighth year I took a wife for myself from the family of Abraham my father, Milka (= Melka, Melcha), daughter of Bethuel, son of Laban, my mother's brother". Clearly "family" has to mean not the "family" descended from Isaac, but the "family" to which Isaac also belongs. There are connections by marriage: Laban, Milka's grandfather is the brother of Rebecca, Isaac's wife; and by descent: through Laban this Milka traces her lineage back to Bathuel and to Nahor, brother of Abraham. This Nahor also married a Milka, his niece, the daughter of Haran, Abraham's other brother (Gen 11:29; 22:23; 24:15, 24, 47).[289] In effect, as we have noted above, this means that the instruction to Levi has some similarities with Isaac's instructions to Jacob. Both are fulfilled in relation to the line of Laban and both understand "family" in that broader sense, which includes those connected to Abraham and his line through marriage of his brothers' descendants. Hearers familiar with Isaac's instructions in Genesis 28 would most likely make these connections.

If the Aramaic which the Greek translator used had read זַרעִי ("my seed") and not the attested reading מַשָׁפַחתִי ("my family"),[290] this would have explained the resultant scattering of no less than six uses of σπέρμα ("seed") in 6:4 / 17, and would narrow the focus (yet still not as narrow as Levi's seed), but Levi's actual marriage makes this unlikely and the Greek translation is probably based on error.[291] *T. Levi* 9:10 is probably right in its interpretive addition, when it formulates the instructions as: "Take, therefore, for yourself a wife, while you are still young, one who has no blemish and has not been defiled and is not of a race of strangers or Gentiles". It conforms not only with what Levi did for himself, but also with what he did for his sons and grandsons, and matches the instruction of Isaac to Jacob in Genesis 28 and its outcome. Thus it is unlikely that *Aramaic Levi Document* is here imposing something much more restrictive, as Himmelfarb suggests.

Within the seed of Isaac and Abraham, nevertheless, the seed of Levi is holy seed, as the second part of 6:4 / 17 emphasises. *Aramaic Levi Document*, Ezra and *Jubilees* are all concerned with people marrying foreigners, and particularly concerned when priests do so. The same may also be true of the *Book of the Watchers* in 1 Enoch, as we have seen. In Ezra the concern is expressed in terms of the abominations associated with the foreign peoples: "The people of Israel, the

---

[289] On the complications see Drawnel, *Aramaic Wisdom Text*, 304-305.

[290] So Greenfield, Stone, Eshel, *Aramaic Levi Document*, 160.

[291] See the discussion in Drawnel, *Aramaic Wisdom Text*, 123.

priests and Levites have not separated themselves from the peoples of the lands with their abominations ... Thus the holy seed has mixed itself with the peoples of the lands" (9:1a; see also 9:1b-2, 11-14). The abominations are probably mainly associated with idolatry. *Jubilees* identifies the whole people as the holy priestly seed and warns against the abominations of the peoples, primarily in terms of their sexual wrongdoing (16:15-19; 33:2). Priests who transgress in this way defile the temple (23:21-23; 30:15-16).

In the *Aramaic Levi Document* the primary focus is on the holy seed of Levi as the priestly seed, as 6:4 / 17 shows. Part of the text is ambiguous. With GSE we may read קודשא as a reference to the temple. Alternatively, it refers to "the Holy One". Drawnel draws attention to the mention of God's holiness in Lev 21:7-8, which makes the reading, "Holy One", preferable.[292] That thought continues in 6:5 / 18: "You are near to God and near to all his holy ones. Now, be pure in your flesh from every impurity (טומאה ἀκαθαρσίας) of man". The closeness to the holy ones, the angels, reinforces the exhortation to observe sexual purity.[293] It does not, however, imply denial of sexuality altogether. Priests are assumed to marry, but this must be to a woman of Israel's seed and then, for engagement in their duties, they must also cleanse themselves of all ritual impurity, as the next section amply illustrates (7:1; 8:2; 10:6-7 / 19, 26, 53-54).

2.5 Levi's Marriage and Family (10:1 – 12:9 / 62-81)

After the stern exhortations with which Isaac's instruction began, this section, which follows immediately after that instruction, makes a point of reporting that Levi followed Isaac's command to the letter. It has Levi state:

> And when four weeks in the years of my life were completed for me, in the twenty-eighth year I took a wife for myself from the family of Abraham my father, Milka, daughter of Bethuel, son of Laban, my mother's brother. (11:1 / 62)

---

[292] Drawnel, *Aramaic Wisdom Text*, 268, 123.

[293] Drawnel, *Aramaic Wisdom Text*, notes parallels in 1QSa 2.8-9 and 1QM 7.6, which also appeal to the presence of angels as grounds for requiring purity (269). He also draws attention to the *Testament of Qahat*, where Qahat addresses his sons with the words והוא קד[י]שין ודכין מן כול [ער]ברוב (4Q542 1 i.8-9; "and be holy and pure from all mingling"), where "mingling" alludes to exogamy (269).

A week of years is seven years.[294] In 12:7 / 79 Levi repeats that he was 28 when he married. The *Testament of Levi* will later confirm that this reflects marrying at a young age, slightly earlier than the norm of 30 years of age (*T. Levi* 9:10).[295] The genealogy through Bethuel to Laban is peculiar to the *Aramaic Levi Document*, but serves its purpose to show that Levi married with the extended family of Isaac, as we noted in the previous section, and to reinforce the intertextual link with Isaac's instructions to Jacob and its outcome. *Jub.* 34:20 similarly identifies Levi's wife as Melcha (= Milka/Melka) and as "one of the daughters of Aram – one of the descendants of Terah's sons".

Once the appropriate marriage partner from within the family of Abraham is found, marital and sexual relations are assumed to be normal and unproblematic. 11:2-11 / 68-72 describes the birth of the children. Predictions based on etymology serve to confirm the priestly line of Levi flowing through Kohath and not through Gershom or Merari.[296] The birth of Jochabed (יוכבד) signals "glory for Israel" (לכבוד לישראל) (11:10 / 71). The author apparently has no problem in reporting that Amram, son of Kohath, Levi's son, married Jochabed, who was thus Amram's aunt (12:3 / 75), though this is a forbidden relationship according to Lev 18:12

---

[294] Use of weeks of years is attested also in Daniel 9, *1 Enoch, Jubilees* and some Qumran writings, and reflects use by *Aramaic Levi Document* of a solar calendar, according to Drawnel, *Aramaic Wisdom Text*, 304.

[295] On thirty as an appropriate age see *Visions of Amram* 4Q545 1 i.5-6; *T. Iss.* 3:5; Gen 41:45-46; Michael L. Satlow, *Jewish Marriage in Antiquity* (Princeton: Princeton University Press, 2001) 132.

[296] The prediction connected with Kohath, "and his seed will be the beginning of kings, a priesthood for [all Is]rael", indicates that *Aramaic Levi Document* has applied Gen 49:10, originally about Judah, to Kohath. The author interprets Kohath (קהת) through the expression, "and the obedience of the peoples is his" (לו יקהת עמים). Through this link the author then applies the rest of the promise to Levi: "The scepter shall not depart from Judah, nor the ruler's staff from between his feet, until tribute comes to him and the obedience of the peoples is his". On this development see Greenfield, Stone, Eshel, *Aramaic Levi Document*, who argue that these words, preserved only in the Greek, go back to the Aramaic original, though they are missing from the Geniza manuscript (186-88). "Thus, the *Aramaic Levi Document* takes an extreme and unusual position in this matter and tends to attribute to Levi language drawn from the royal context" (188). See earlier Jonas C. Greenfield and Michael E. Stone, "Remarks on the Aramaic Testament of Levi from the Geniza," *RB* 86 (1979) 216-30, 223; also Stone, "Axis of History," 134-36; Michael E. Stone, "Aramaic Levi in its Contexts," *JSQ* 9 (2002) 307-26, 325; Drawnel, *Aramaic Wisdom Text*, 307-309. He notes also the reference to royal priesthood in 4:7 / 3c (308). See also the references to priesthood and kingship in the final verses of the *Aramaic Levi Document* (99, 100). On Ben Sira's attribution of royal features to Aaron (45:6-11), Phinehas (45:23-24) and Simon (50:1-24), see Himmelfarb, "Book of the Watchers," 134, and Wright, "Ben Sira and the *Book of the Watchers*," 252-53.

(see also 11QT^a 46.14-15). It is assumed in Exod 6:20 and Num 26:59.[297] The focus (via etymology) is rather on the role of Amram (עמרם). The text of 12:4 / 76 has a lacuna and signs of a scribal correction, but the original of *l.* 12 appears to have included ירים עמא ("exalt/raise up the people") and a reference to Egypt, and *l.* 13, another reference to exalting or lifting up (ראמא), probably preceded by "people" (עמא).[298] The achievement of raising the people up from Egypt will be through their son, Moses.[299] The author is careful in 12:1 / 73 to point out that Levi took wives for his sons from the daughters of his brothers (thus cousins), and so, by implication, underlines his obedience to Isaac's command about intermarriage by not marrying them to Egyptians.

In 12:6-9 / 78-81 *Aramaic Levi Document* has Levi give a brief *curriculum vitae*. Then (as now) the choice of detail is significant. At eighteen years of age Levi entered Canaan[300] and at the same age, he reports, "I killed Shechem and destroyed the workers of violence". This recalls the account found early in the document, of which only traces survive. It assumes no guilt or shame on Levi's part, such as a reading of Gen 49:5-7 and 34:30 might lead one to expect.[301] Already what survives in 1:1 / 1c suggests that, as in *Jub.* 30:23, the deed had Jacob's support or was at least heroic. No mention is made of Simeon; the focus is solely on Levi. The translation "workers of violence" throws the emphasis onto the violence of the deed of the Shechemites, rather than onto Levi's violence as in Gen 49:5, and highlights violence rather than the aspect of defilement which 1:1 / 1c mentions. On the other hand, in the Hebrew Bible "חמס has a broad range of meaning", as Drawnel notes, pointing out that "it may also denote an infringement of marital law (cf. Gen 16:5)".[302] Thus it may express an understanding of the act as one of violence which includes also violation and defilement. We have noted that 4Q213a 3-4 may relate its concerns with intermarriage also to this event. By

---

[297] See also *Visions of Amram* 4Q545 1 i.5-6, according to which Uzziel, the younger brother of Amram, married Amram's daughter Miriam, his niece.

[298] See the discussion in Drawnel, *Aramaic Wisdom Text*, 151-52.

[299] Greenfield, Stone, Eshel, *Aramaic Levi Document*, mention that similarly 11:6 / 67 claims that Kohath will receive the high priesthood, whereas in Exodus it is Aaron (198).

[300] For the discrepancy with the Genesis story see Drawnel, *Aramaic Wisdom Text*, 314.

[301] Idealisation of Levi is also reflected in what appears to be a retelling of the account of the selling of Joseph in Genesis 37. *Aramaic Levi Document* appears to disassociate Levi and Simeon from the act by linking them with Reuben (2:1 / 3). On this see Drawnel, *Aramaic Wisdom Text*, 82, 230-33. Similarly Levi is never included among the brothers who accuse themselves of this act in the later *Testaments of the Twelve Patriarchs* (*T. Sim.* 2:6-14; 4:2; *T. Zeb.* 1:5; 2:1; 2:1-33; 4; *T. Dan* 1:4-9; *T. Gad* 1:9; 3:3). So Drawnel, *Aramaic Wisdom Text*, 233.

[302] Drawnel, *Aramaic Wisdom Text*, 315.

mentioning the episode here in 12:6 / 78 the author evokes its significance. Levi
stood for enforcement of marital purity and punishment of its transgression,[303] just
as his later behaviour portrays him as model of marital purity, as he carries out the
instructions about sexual purity which he received from Isaac. The other points of
the résumé are ordination, marriage, entry to Egypt and death (the latter directly
reported by Levi!). Indirectly, the mention of marriage again reinforces the issues
surrounding appropriate marriage in the document thus far.[304]

2.6   Wisdom Poem 13:1-16 / 82-98 and Future Predictions (4Q213 [4QLeviᵃ ar] 1 ii.12-19; 2 9-16; 3, 4, 5 and 4Q214 [4QLeviᵈ ar] 3 / 99-104)

The penultimate section of *Aramaic Levi Document* which has survived, consists
of wisdom teaching (13:1-15 / 82-98). Its significance for our research is its
silence about the major themes in the rest of the document. It says nothing about
intermarriage or sexual wrongdoing and offers also no positive comments
pertaining to sexuality. It mentions Joseph as a model, but says nothing of his
sexual virtue. At most the section may use feminine imagery in depicting wisdom
(13:9-14 / 94-97), but this is uncertain.[305]

The final segment contains predictions about the future, but is very
fragmentary (4Q213 [4QLeviᵃ ar] 1 ii.12-19; 2 9-16; 3, 4, 5 and 4Q214 [4QLeviᵈ
ar] 3 / 99-104). In GSE they are among the unplaced fragments.[306] Already 13:16 /
99, at the end of the previous section, mentions "kings and priests". Then 100 has
"kingdom" and "glory", apparently in the context of a positive prediction. In 101

---

[303] Drawnel, *Aramaic Wisdom Text*, sees behind the exoneration of Levi a reaction
against the negative view of priestly failing reflected in such texts as Ezek 22:26 and Zeph
3:4 (316). Earlier he notes how in 4Q175 the reference to the two figures of violence in Gen
49:5 is applied to the enemies of Israel, not to the coming eschatological figures it portrays
(315). "The reinterpretation of the tradition concerning Levi became a way to create a priest
who eliminates 'violence' and does not perpetrate it, who is ritually clean and cares for the
cleanness of the community by eliminating those who cause its uncleanness" (316). Such a
stance then portrays the violence of Levi and later of Phinehas as heroic.

[304] Noting the apparent closure at 12:9 / 81 and the abrupt transition to what follows,
Kugler, *From Patriarch to Priest*, speculates that 11:1 – 12:9 / 62-81 might reflect the
conclusion to an independent source unknown to the author of *Jubilees* (117).

[305] See Greenfield, Stone, Eshel, *Aramaic Levi Document*, 204, 213;   Drawnel,
Aramaic Wisdom Text, 339-41.

[306] Greenfield, Stone, Eshel, *Aramaic Levi Document*, 216-19; 223. They also note that
1Q21 30 appears to contains the word זנות ("fornication"), but without decipherable context
(229).

we find "nations" and references to heavenly bodies, but it is too fragmentary to determine its direction. In 102 there is prediction of disobedience: "the pa]ths of righteousness you will abandon, and all the ways of [   ] you will neglect and you will walk in the darkness of satan[ ] da[r]kness will come upon you" and a hint of conflict, present also in 103: "those who h]ate you. Then he will aris[e] against you [".[307] The final verse contains the words "more glorious than the women" and may refer to Dinah or judgement, but is too fragmentary for us to ascertain its significance.

2.7   Conclusion

In conclusion, *Aramaic Levi Document* shows concern with sexual wrongdoing. This emerges despite the fragmentary nature of the text, which must bring a degree of tentativeness to all interpretations. Our discussion has made it probable that a minimal interpretation, which limits *Aramaic Levi Document*'s concerns to warnings against prostitution by daughters of priests and to instructions to Levi as the first high priest, does not adequately account for the concern with sexual wrongdoing. Rather it appears much more likely that this concern focuses primarily on marriage of Israelites to foreigners and makes a special point of enjoining this on Levi and so, by implication, on the priesthood. Their task is, accordingly, also to warn against its dangers and to execute punishment where this provision is flouted, as did Levi, their patriarch. His and their responsibility to execute judgement is greater than that of any other (6:1 / 14), and so his and their own credentials must be impeccable. *Aramaic Levi Document* consists, accordingly, of priestly instruction and embodies such warnings. In doing so, it makes Levi the sole hero of the Dinah episode and the model for executing judgement.

Kugler has made it probable that the author draws on a tradition which has combined Genesis 34, Exod 32:25-29 (the executions by Levites following the golden calf episode, which elevates them to the priesthood), Num 25:6-13 (the violent action of Phinehas against the perpetrators of exogamy) and Deut 33:8-11

---

[307] Milik, *Books of Enoch,* speculates that verse 102 alludes to Enoch's complaint against the Watchers (*1 Enoch* 13 – 16) and links corruption of humanity to the corruption of the angels and priests (24), and Drawnel, *Aramaic Wisdom Text*, entertains the possibility that *Aramaic Levi Document* aims "at equaling [*sic* – read: equating] the Watchers' responsibility for the corruption of humankind with the Levitical priestly responsibility for failing to uphold the divine order inscribed in the creation and reflected in the liturgy" (346), but the text is too fragmentary to bear such a construction. See also Greenfield, Stone, Eshel, *Aramaic Levi Document*, who note Milik's speculative reading of Enoch at the end of *l.* 2 and in *l.* 3 of 4Q213 4.

(the blessing of Levi), to develop the notion of Levi as the first priest. This tradition is already reflected in the use of these texts in Mal 2:4-7 to elevate Levi's priesthood.[308] It is not insignificant that two of the three texts which report action, Genesis 34 and Num 25:6-13, relate to sexual wrongdoing, the second in close association with idolatry which is the theme of the third (Exod 32:25-29). The focus on forbidding marriage to foreigners will have been strongly influenced by developments in the postexilic period when Ezra returned from Babylon (Ezra 9 – 10), reinforced by Nehemiah (Neh 10:29-31; 13:1-3, 23-30). There, as in Num 25:6-13, a primary concern is that intermarriage brings exposure to idolatry, an element absent from what has survived of *Aramaic Levi Document*.[309]

The *Aramaic Levi Document* reflects thus a development in which Levi is seen as the executor of God's judgement against those who engage in intermarriage with foreigners. It entails a positive reading of Levi's actions in Genesis 34 and will have been reinforced by association with the texts noted above concerning the zeal of Phinehas about marriage to foreigners. The concern of Ezra and the Levi tradition reflected in Genesis 34 and Num 25:6-13 is with marriage of any Israelite with foreigners, as also in *Jubilees*, and probably already in the *Book of the Watchers* in *1 Enoch* 6 – 11 and then, with an apparent focus especially on priests, in 12 – 16.

Aramaic Levi Document reflects both the general concern and the concern with priests, in particular. It probably reflects the general prohibition both in its handling of the Dinah episode and in the material presented in 4Q213a 3-4 / 3a. It appears also to evoke it in the intertextual play between Isaac's instructions to Levi and his marriage to a descendant of Laban, on the one hand, and, Isaac's instruction in Genesis 28 to Jacob, not to marry a Canaanite woman, and Jacob's subsequent marriage to Laban's daughters, on the other. Jochabed also marries within the family. Beside this, a primary emphasis falls on Levi and his descendants and the purity of the priestly seed. *Aramaic Levi Document* portrays Levi as a model for all priests. Accordingly, he marries within Isaac's extended family and ensures appropriate choices for his sons and grandsons. *Aramaic Levi Document* shows no concern that Levi's daughter Jochabed marries her nephew, contrary to Lev 18:12. The primary focus in *Aramaic Levi Document* is rejection of exogamous marriage.

On the other hand, it would be wrong to see *Aramaic Levi Document*'s concerns as limited solely to exogamous marriage. In Levi's prayer the petition to

---

[308] Kugler, *From Patriarch to Priest*, 9-22.

[309] On the widespread concern with exogamy see also Greenfield, Stone, Eshel, *Aramaic Levi Document*, who note its importance in Tob 4:12, 4QNaph and the *Visions of Amram* 4Q545 1 i.5-6 (160). See also Drawnel, *Aramaic Wisdom Text*, who, while noting that Tobit appeals to the practice of Noah, observes that Genesis gives no detail about his wife, but that we find her genealogy in *Jub.* 4:33, which supports Tobit's assumption (267).

be kept from sexual wrongdoing is given prominence as one of few specific requests in the prayer. Similarly in the careful composition of 6:1-5 / 14-18, the warning against sexual wrongdoing also receives prominence. It frames the passage in 6:1 / 14 and 6:5 / 18, and becomes the theme of the centre piece in 6:3-4 / 16-17, where it is elaborated. While the primary focus there is exogamous marriage, the warnings against sexual wrongdoing are doubtless broader and include, at least implicitly, prostitution. Levi is thus the champion of sexual morality and he and his descendants are both to model appropriate sexual behaviour and to stamp out sexual wrongdoing.

If the opening word of what has survived of the Dinah episode is to be read "she defiled", then the author appears also to have implicated Dinah in sexual wrongdoing. The blame attached to the women in 4Q213a 3-4 / 3a probably also relates to exogamy and may even be an extrapolation from the Dinah story, although that is not secure. Both there, and in the instructions to Isaac we also noted the application of Lev 21:9 (and in the latter, also 21:14 and 21:7) in a way that broadens their reference, in the one case, from prostitution to any illicit sexual relationship, especially exogamy, and in the other, to all priests.

As Drawnel notes,[310] the depiction of Ezra's leadership as a priest and scribe appears also to have shaped the image of Levi as priest and scribe. In that capacity Levi is portrayed in the *Aramaic Levi Document* as a bearer of traditions of wisdom and Babylonian scribal metrology. *Aramaic Levi Document* "ascribes to the Levitical priesthood a prominent social position by claiming for them judicial, priestly, and royal authority".[311] Drawnel, too, sees this prominence reflected already in Mal 2:4-7 and draws attention to the importance of the teaching role ascribed to Levi.[312] It is in this context that the author understands the role of the Levitical priesthood, which includes a major concern with sexual purity.

The combination of priestly and royal functions has led some to speculate whether *Aramaic Levi Document* may originate from Hasmonean times, when both roles were fused,[313] but both the antiquity of the earliest fragments (second

---

[310] Drawnel, *Aramaic Wisdom Text*, 67-71.

[311] Drawnel, *Aramaic Wisdom Text*, 70. "Through the divine election and Isaac's instruction Levi is the founder of a royal priesthood responsible for upholding just order (*A.L.D.* 1a v. 18; 3a-7; 14-50)" (14). On Babylonian tradition he writes: "The author of Levi's composition was well acquainted with Babylonian school tradition, imitated Babylonian metrological exercises, and adopted the Babylonian practice of metro-arithmetical education in the context of wisdom literature. He must have received his own scribal education in a Babylonian school or was trained in a Levitical didactic system modelled on the Babylonian scribal education" (63).

[312] Drawnel, *Aramaic Wisdom Text*, 71.

[313] So Pierre Grelot, "Notes sur le Testament araméen de Lévi (Fragment de la Bodleian Library, colonne a)," *RB* 63 (1956) 391-406, 396, 406; similarly Klaus Beyer, *Die*

half of the second century B.C.E.) and the dependence of *Jubilees* on *Aramaic Levi Document* or on a common source make that improbable. Nothing in the *Aramaic Levi Document* suggests conflict with Hellenism[314] nor does the Aramaic reflect Greek influence.[315] The relatively mild treatment of dissent, compared with documents which belonged to the critical period of the early second century B.C.E. and later,[316] and its uncontroversial use of a solar calendar, also suggest that *Aramaic Levi Document* belongs back in the third century or possibly earlier,[317] where it reflects similarities in its use of Babylonian scribal tradition to the *Book of the Luminaries* in *1 Enoch*.[318] The combination of royal and priestly motifs in the depiction of Levi and his line reflects that they were the ones who effectively exercised the key roles of governance in this period.[319] The final segments of *Aramaic Levi Document* do indicate tensions and dissent among Levi's descendants, but *Aramaic Levi Document* does not read as a *Kampfschrift*, designed to counter opponents.[320] Rather, it presents an ideal Levi, who both

---

aramäischen Texte vom Toten Meer samt den Inschriften aus Palästina, dem Testament Levis aus der Kairoer Genisa, der Fastenrolle und den alten talmudischen Zitaten: Ergänzungsband (Göttingen: Vandenhoeck & Ruprecht, 1984) 188-89.

[314] Drawnel, *Aramaic Wisdom Text*, 65. Cf. Anders Hultgård, *L'Eschatologie des Testaments des Deuze Patriarches: 1. Interpretation des Textes* (Acta Universitatis Upsalienses: Historia Religionum 6; Stockholm: Almqvist & Wiksell, 1977) 41-45; Anders Hultgård, "The Ideal 'Levite', the Davidic Messiah and the Saviour Priest in the Testaments of the Twelve Patriarchs," in *Ideal Figures in Ancient Judaism: Profiles and Paradigms* (ed. John J. Collins and George W. E. Nickelsburg; SBLSCS 12; Chico: Scholars, 1980) 93-110, who locates the *Aramaic Levi Document* in the pre-Maccabean conflicts in the context of anti-Hellenistic movements (94-95).

[315] Drawnel, *Aramaic Wisdom Text*, 65, 74.

[316] On this see Schiffman, "Sacrificial Halakhah," who argues that the issues in *Aramaic Levi Document* "are more oriented toward sacrificial procedure, toward filling the gaps in the biblical text and describing the manner in which rites are to be performed" and that the details "are as close to rabbinic laws as they are to sectarian ones" (202). It does not fit the mould of legal materials known from Qumran like 4QMMT, the *Temple Scroll*, CD and the minor legal texts. Cf. Kugler, *From Patriarch to Priest*, who sees the author espousing a notion of priesthood with requirements that "differ … from the norms required by the Torah" and add "the exercise of wisdom and scribal skills" (136).

[317] So Kugler, *From Patriarch to Priest*, 135.

[318] See Drawnel, *Aramaic Wisdom Text*, 91.

[319] Drawnel, *Aramaic Wisdom Text*, cites the late fourth century historian Hecataeus of Abdera who writes of Judea as a place where not kings but priests rule (71-72).

[320] So rightly Drawnel, *Aramaic Wisdom Text*: "Nothing in the text warrants Kugler's assumption that liturgical divergences from the torah prescriptions connote polemical overtones within the priestly class" (84). Cf. Kugler, *From Patriarch to Priest*: "Altogether the themes and the narrative pattern suggests that the author is engaged in a constructive

models appropriate behaviour and instructs his descendants – at greatest length about cultic procedures.[321]

It is within this context that it also shows a major concern with sexual wrongdoing in general, but, when specified, focuses on intermarriage with foreigners and in particular, though not exclusively, among priests. It is quite likely that failure to observe such requirements is among the sins of those in the priesthood who are deemed to have abandoned the paths of righteousness (4Q213 4 / 102), but nothing suggests a major group or movement espousing such behaviour. This then makes it difficult to be more specific about *Aramaic Levi Document*'s historical situation, including suggestions that it addresses the departure of priests to Samaria, as Drawnel proposes.[322] It does not read as a crisis document responding to an emergency. The dangers of intermarriage and sexual wrongdoing will have existed throughout all periods, especially when the Jews were living in relatively stable relations with their neighbours. On the positive side, *Aramaic Levi Document* reports marriage within the prescribed boundaries as normal and unproblematic, including for Levi and the priesthood, without any indication that sexual relations within the appropriate context are anything other than good.

---

polemic against some form of the priesthood" (136). See also Schiffman, "Sacrificial Halakhah," 202.

[321] Drawnel, *Aramaic Wisdom Text*, writes: "The Document's composition was caused by educational concerns nurtured by priestly instructors responsible for the preparation of a professional class of priestly administrators and rulers" (79).

[322] Drawnel, *Aramaic Wisdom Text*, points to the account in Josephus about the marriage between Nikaso, daughter of Sanballat governor of Samaria and Manasseh, brother of the Jewish high priest Jaddua (Josephus *A.J.* 11.302-47), when other priests also married exogamously 309-12 (72-73). "The author of this priestly composition tried to reinstate the endogamic principle for the Levitical priesthood in opposition to those priests who might have defected from the Jerusalem sanctuary on account of their exogamous marriages, as related by Josephus" (74). On Milik's speculative claim of Samaritan authorship, see Drawnel's discussion (66, 75). Cf. Milik, *Books of Enoch*, 24 and also Kugler, *From Patriarch to Priest*, 137-38.

PART THREE

Attitudes towards Sexuality in the Book of Jubilees

3.1   Introduction

Jubilees is a substantial document emanating from the first half of the second century B.C.E. Originally written in Hebrew, it is most fully preserved in Ethiopic, which appears to have been a translation from a Greek version.[323] There are also sections of it preserved in Latin (also translated from the Greek) and Syriac (translated probably from the Hebrew).[324] Most significantly, the caves of the

---

[323] In what follows I base myself on the text, James C. VanderKam, *The Book of Jubilees: A Critical Text* (CSCO 510; Louvain: Peeters, 1989), and for the English translation use James C. VanderKam, *The Book of Jubilees: Translated* (CSCO 511; Louvain: Peeters, 1989).

[324] See the overview of research in James C. VanderKam, *The Book of Jubilees* (Sheffield: Sheffield Academic Press, 2001) 13-17, and in detail concerning the versions: VanderKam, *Jubilees Translated*, v-xxxiv. See also his discussion in "Jubilees and Hebrew Texts of Genesis-Exodus," in *From Revelation to Canon: Studies in Hebrew Bible and Second Temple Literature* (JSJSup 62; Leiden: Brill, 2000) 448-61, where he notes the value of the versions for establishing the Hebrew text of *Jubilees* and its likely use of a distinctive Hebrew text of Genesis and Exodus, which agrees more often with LXX and the Samaritan Pentateuch than with MT, but is different in other respects from all three. On possible influence on the Ethiopic of *Jubilees* from the Ethiopic Pentateuch he writes: "a high percentage of the 80 readings in Ethiopic Jub which agree with the Ethiopic Pentateuch alone among the versions is also supported by the Latin manuscripts of Jub – and the Latin translation of Jub was hardly influenced by the Ethiopic Bible" (456-57). See also his earlier extended discussion, which his article updates: James C. VanderKam, *Textual and*

Dead Sea have given up fragments from, it appears, at least 14 different copies of *Jubilees* in Hebrew, earlier by far than the other witnesses and reflecting the original language.[325] This complex attestation creates difficulties, particularly in the fact that for most of *Jubilees* we are dealing with a translation of a translation, from which it is not always easy to ascertain the likely shape of the Hebrew text. There is some solace in the fact that where we do have Hebrew texts, these confirm the general reliability of the translations. From his extensive analysis VanderKam concludes that Ethiopic *Jubilees* "is an extraordinarily precise reflection of the original Hebrew text".[326]

While this means that arguments based on exact wording will be difficult for much of *Jubilees*, there is nevertheless a substantial amount of text. Within it there is a considerable focus on issues relating to sexuality. This is to be expected in so far as *Jubilees* retells much of Genesis, which contains a number of narratives relevant to the theme. These include the creation narratives, the Eden story, the misdeeds of the angels with the women, Ham's uncovering his father's nakedness, the sexual immorality of Sodom, Lot's daughters' act of incest, the rape of Dinah, Esau's marriage to a Canaanite woman (and Judah and Simeon's), Reuben's intercourse with his father's concubine, Onan's spilling his semen on the ground, Judah's incest with his daughter in law, and the attempt to seduce Joseph.

These stories not only reappear in the narrative in *Jubilees*, but sometimes with extensive elaboration (most notably, Reuben's sin) and are frequently used as the foundation for specific commands and elaborations. Those relating to sexuality make up five of the twelve instances where the angel of the Lord addresses Moses directly during his dictation with the words, "Now, you, command ...", (listed in 3.2. below). This evidence for a strong interest in *Jubilees* on right sexual behaviour receives further confirmation in those sections which have no parallel in Genesis, but present extensive warnings in the form of speeches of key figures about the dangers of sin. In these, the warnings about wrongdoing in relation to matters of sexual behaviour assume a central role. Such wrongdoing not only characterises times of sin in history, but also apparently poses a major threat in the author's own time.

Historical Studies in the Book of Jubilees (HMS 14; Missoula, Mont.: Scholars Press, 1977) 103-206.

[325] See James C. VanderKam, "Jubilees, the Book of," in *Encyclopedia of the Dead Sea Scrolls* (2 vols; ed. Lawrence H. Schiffman, and James C. VanderKam; Oxford: Oxford University Press, 2000) 1. 434-38, 435; James C. VanderKam and J. T. Milik, "*Jubilees*," in *Qumran Cave 4.VIII Parabiblical Texts Part I* (ed. Harold Attridge et al.; DJD 13; Oxford: Clarendon, 1994) 1-185.

[326] VanderKam, *Textual and Historical Studies*, 287.

Jubilees also allows us to recognise underlying assumptions which inform some of its attitudes towards sexuality. These relate in particular to the understanding of the apportionment of sacred space and sacred time, which is of fundamental importance for the writing. Part of its understanding of appropriate sexual behaviour is knowing where and when sexual behaviour and nakedness are appropriate or inappropriate. For instance, sexual intercourse was out of place in the Garden of Eden, which *Jubilees* sees as a Holy of Holies and is out of place on the holy day of the sabbath. In a similar way, the boundary between the holy seed of the people of God and Gentiles assumes major importance: to cross it by intermarriage constitutes a breach of divine order.

In approaching the issue in *Jubilees* I shall proceed by considering the writing largely by following its statements in sequence in order to seek as far as possible to discern the balance and emphasis it brings for the hearer. At the same time I shall assume that statements need to be read in the light of the whole, both what precedes and what follows. For those who copied and used *Jubilees*, this book provided "testimony" (to use its own self designation), which was a basis for teaching and reflection, and was to be heard more than once. The aim of this analysis will not be simply to list or describe all relevant references, but rather to see them in the perspective of the whole and to uncover, where possible, the attitudes they represent.

The analysis has three main parts. In the first, I consider statements which frame the work as a whole. These include the prologue and introduction (1:1-29), on the one hand, where Yahweh, himself, speaks, and the final chapter, on the other hand, where the angel returns to key concerns. In this part I also consider the angel's final speech in the conclusion of the first half of the book, clearly marked as such by the conclusion of *Jubilees* 23: "Now you, Moses, write down these words because this is how it is written and entered in the testimony of the heavenly tablets for the history of eternity" (23:32; cf. 1:5, 7, 26, 27; 2:1).

I then turn to *Jubilees'* presentation of sexual wrongdoing, which it mostly develops in association with particular events, but also in major speeches. The section concludes with a consideration of the abstract terms which appear in these contexts, which in turn interpret them. Finally, a third section considers other attitudes to sexuality in the broadest sense, including positive appreciation of sexuality and concerns about its place in space and time. The conclusion then synthesises the findings from all three sections.

3.1.1   *The Prologue and Introduction (1:1-29)*

The Prologue announces that the book has as its focus: "the divisions of the times of the law and of the testimony, of the events of the years, of the weeks of their jubilees". This might give the impression that it is concerned primarily with right timing, in particular, calendar and chronology.[327] The summary of what Yahweh gave to Moses, whom he had summoned to Mt Sinai's heights, makes it clear that there is a twofold emphasis: (i) "the Lord showed him what (had happened) beforehand as well as what was to come" and (ii) "he related to him the divisions of all the time – both of the law and of the testimony" (1:4). This finds it echo in the closing segment of the introduction:

> Now you write all these words which I tell you on this mountain: what is first and what is last and what is to come during all the divisions of time which are in the law and which are in the testimony and in the weeks of their jubilees until eternity – until the time when I descend and live with them throughout all the ages of eternity (1:26).[328]

The emphasis is not just on timing and chronology, which assume great importance throughout *Jubilees*, but on events and, within them, on behaviour.[329]

---

[327] James C. VanderKam, "Studies in the Chronology of the Book of *Jubilees*," in *From Revelation to Canon: Studies in Hebrew Bible and Second Temple Literature*, 276-304. JSJSup 62; Leiden: Brill, 2000) 522-44, observes: "The calendar remains more in the background of the book and does not play a highly visible or prominent role in it. ... the writer attached much greater significance to the chronological system within which he has chosen to frame his presentation" (522). On pp. 528-32 he sets out the chronology of *Jubilees* in tabular form. Part of its concern with chronology was also to show that what the Pentateuch brings as laws from Mosaic times belonged already as divine law to earlier times. On this see also *Book of Jubilees*, 2001, p. 100.

[328] On the issue of the authority which *Jubilees* claims and its relation to the authority of the Law see Hindy Najman, *Seconding Sinai: The Development of Mosaic Discourse in Second Temple Judaism* (JSJSup 77; Leiden: Brill, 2003) 41-69, who concludes that for *Jubilees* the Torah of Moses remained a central authority (67). Cf. Ben Zion Wacholder, "*Jubilees* as the Super Canon: Torah-Admonition versus Torah-Commandment," in *Legal Texts and Legal Issues: Proceedings of the Second Meeting of the International Organization for Qumran Studies, Cambridge, 1995: Published in Honour of Joseph M. Baumgarten* (ed. Moshe J. Bernstein, Florentino García Martínez, and John Kampen, STDJ 23; Leiden: Brill, 1997) 195-211, who argues that *Jubilees* set itself above canonical Genesis as supercanonical. See also the discussion in Martha Himmelfarb, "Torah, Testimony, and Heavenly Tablets: The Claim to Authority of the *Book of Jubilees*," in *A Multiform Heritage: Studies on Early Judaism and Christianity in Honor of Robert A. Kraft* (ed. Benjamin G. Wright; Homage Series 24; Atlanta: Scholars, 1999) 19-29 and James C. VanderKam, "Studies on the Prologue and *Jubilees* 1," in *For a Later Generation: The Transformation of Tradition in Israel, Early Judaism, and Early Christianity* (ed. Randal A. Argall, Beverly A. Bow, and Rodney A. Werline; Harrisburg: Trinity Press International, 2000) 266-79. See also Liora Ravid, "Purity and Impurity in the Book of Jubilees," *JSP* 13 (2002) 61-86, who points out that there are notable absences in *Jubilees* of Pentateuchal laws, including, above all, ritual impurity and rites of purification.

[329] This is also true of 1 Enoch according to *Jub.* 4:19: "While he slept he saw in a vision what had happened and what will occur – how things will happen for mankind during

This is immediately apparent in Yahweh's opening words in 1:5-6. These speak of "the evil they have done in straying from the covenant".[330] They contrast Yahweh's faithfulness with the people's faithfulness (" I have been more faithful than they"), perhaps alluding to the traditional marriage metaphor (e.g. Hosea 1-3). *Jub.* 1:7 then speaks of their "stubbornness and defiance" (cf. Deut 31:27).[331] We then hear specific comment about the nature of the unfaithfulness. "They will turn to foreign gods" (1:8) and "they will forget all my commandments – everything that I command them – and will follow the nations, their impurities (*rek^{w}s*)[332], and their shame (*xasār*)" (1:9). The Hebrew may have read "their disgrace (כלמתם) and their shame (חרפתם)" or "their idols (גלוליהם) and their abominations (תועובתם)".[333] Clearly, idolatry is in view, as the words which immediately follow confirm: "They will serve their gods, and (this) will prove an obstacle for them – an affliction, a pain, and a trap" (1:9).[334] However, in addition, the reference to forgetting the commandments and to following "the nations, their impurities, and their shame", need not be restricted to idolatry. As we shall see, concern with

---

their history until the day of judgement. he saw everything and understood. He wrote a testimony for himself and placed it upon the earth against all mankind and for their history". For a comprehensive discussion of timing in *Jubilees* see James M. Scott, *On Earth as in Heaven: The Restoration of Sacred Time and Sacred Space in the Book of Jubilees* (JSJSupp 99; Leiden: Brill, 2005) 19-158. He demonstrates that *Jubilees* has an elaborate symmetrical system of chronology based on sabbaths and jubilees, but also less explicit, on the cultic cycles of the *Mishmarot* (the priestly courses of 6 years) and the "*Otot*" (49 mishmarot, i.e. 294 years). *Jubilees* envisages a World Era of 5880 years/120 jubilees/840 weeks from creation to new creation, divided into three parts, from Adam to the death of Moses; from entry into the land until the end of the exile and from the return to the culmination of the new creation and the building of the eschatological temple on Zion (150-53).

[330] On the translation, "straying", whereas the Ethiopic has a causative verb, see VanderKam, *Jubilees Translated*, 2 n. 1:5.

[331] On the influence of Deuteronomy 31 and Isaiah 8 in the terminology of *Jub.* 1:7-11 see George J. Brooke, "Exegetical Strategies in Jubilees 1-2: New Light from 4QJubilees^a," in *Studies in the Book of Jubilees* (ed. Matthias Albani, Jörg Frey, and Armin Lange; TSAJ 65; Tübingen: Mohr Siebeck, 1997) 39-57, 50-53.

[332] Ge'ez words are given in brackets in their lexical form throughout (e.g. nom. sing. masc. for nouns, etc.).

[333] On the differing reconstructions of the Hebrew of *Jub.* 1:9 see the discussion in 3.2.8 below.

[334] The words, "an obstacle for them – an affliction, a pain, and a trap (ול]מוקש [ולצור ול[עני]) [לנגף] ", appear to be drawn from Isa 8:14: "a stone to strike against, a rock one stumbles over ... a trap and a snare (מכשול...לפח ולמוקש ולצור ולאבן נגף)". On this see Brooke, "Exegetical Strategies," 51.

sexual wrongdoing becomes a major element in such statements elsewhere, and would be likely to be heard as implied here also.

The speech then continues with the other major theme in a first reference to captivity: calendar.

> They will be captured and will fall into the enemy's control because they have abandoned my statutes, my commandments, my covenantal festivals, my sabbaths, my holy things which I have hallowed for myself among them, my tabernacle and my temple which I sanctified for myself in the middle of the land so that I could set my name on it and that I could live (there). (1:10)

It then returns to the charge of idolatry, now specifically:

> They made for themselves high places, (sacred) groves, and carved images; each of them prostrated himself before his own in order to go astray. They will sacrifice their children to demons and to every product (conceived by) their erring minds. (1:11)[335]

The second reference to captivity is fuller:

> Then I will hide my face from them. I will deliver them into the control of the nations for captivity, for booty, and for being devoured. I will remove them from the land and disperse them among the nations. (1:13)

Before it we read of rejection of God's messengers:

> I will send witnesses to them so that I may testify to them, but they will not listen and will kill the witnesses. They will persecute those studying the law diligently. They will abrogate everything and will begin to do evil in my presence. (1:12)

The disobedience is persistent: "They will forget all my law, all my commandments, all my verdicts. They will err regarding the beginning of the month, the sabbath, the festival, the jubilee, and the decree" (1:14). Again we recognise the two elements: calendar and commandments. The two captivities might refer to the fall of Israel and then of Judah. Alternatively, the second may allude to events of the author's own time. It is clear that the author's present and future must be in focus in 1:15-18, which speak of return from among the nations,

---

[335] On the link between demons and idolatry in *Jubilees*, see James C. VanderKam, "The Demons in the *Book of Jubilees*," in *Die Dämonen / Demons: The Demonology of Israelite-Jewish and Early Christian Literature in Context of their Environment* (ed. Armin Lange, Hermann Lichtenberger, and K. F. Diethard Romheld; Tübingen: Mohr Siebeck, 2003) 339-64, 240-41.

in particular, turning to God "with all their minds, and all their souls, and all their strength", peace and a rebuilt temple.

Yahweh's opening speech in 1:5-18 thus serves as an introduction and overview of history seen from the perspective of judgement and hope. There are specific references to forms of idolatry and neglect of particular commandments. While there are no specific references to sexual wrongdoing, the reference in 1:9 to following "the nations, their impurities (*rek^{w}s*), and their shame" and to flouting the law in 1:12 and 14 would, as we shall see, most likely include sexual wrongdoing, since it emerges as an important element of what *Jubilees* understands by the sins of the nations and by "impurities".

The introduction continues with Moses' intercession (1:19-21), modelled on his appeal in Exod 33:12-16, but here he seeks not to avert God's judgement of destruction, but to avert his people's falling into "the control of the nations". That concern is with sin: "Lord my God, do not allow your people and your heritage to go along in the error of their minds, and do not deliver them into the control of the nations with the result that they rule over them lest they make them sin against you" (1:19). That the nations might lead them to sexual wrongdoing is a common feature in *Jubilees*, as we shall see. For *Jubilees*' hearers, Moses' intercession is less likely to refer to the far off past than to their contemporary situation, in which they are to recognise the influence of foreign nations under whose control they live. The concern is with Belial's rule (1:20) and traps (1:20 and 21; echoing 1:9 and the language of Isa 8:14).[336] The hope is for people to have changed minds, using language which echoes Psalm 51 (1:21; note that people understood this psalm as a confession by David for a sexual sin).

Yahweh's response in 1:23-25 reiterates the hope expressed in 1:15-18. It includes another reference to stubbornness (1:23; cf. 1:7), but holds out the hope that there will be confession of sins. Using the imagery of circumcised minds, this hope foresees obedience to the commandments on the basis of inner renewal and a sense of community with God as loving father and with the angels. In 50:5 this blessed future is associated with a time when "Israel is pure *(nasha)* of every sexual evil (lit. sin [*'abbasā* of sexual immorality [*zemmut*]), impurity (*rek^{w}s*), contamination (*gemmanē*), sin (*xaṭi'at*), and error".

With that, Yahweh returns to the twofold focus of the testimony: events, past, present, and future, and the right divisions of time, telling Moses to write *Jubilees*

---

[336] On the link between the nations and the spirits of Beliar see Jackson, *Enochic Judaism*, 42. "The reference to 'snare', particularly in this context, is a direct allusion to Exod. 23.33; 34.12; Deut. 7.16 where God and Moses warn Israel about the seductive role (the term מוקש refers to the bait or lure in a trap) that the Gentiles and specifically their gods will play in Israel's history once they have entered the promised land" (42). He notes a similar linking of Gentiles and "sons of Beliar" in 15:33 concerning neglect of circumcision.

and instructing the angel of the presence to dictate it (1:26-28).[337] As angels mediated the Law, so the angel of the presence takes the tablets of the testimony and begins the instruction. The summary includes another strong vision of a renewed creation, with Yahweh's kingdom based in Zion and its temple, and health and blessing for the elect (1:28, 29).

One might expect the testimony to contain a complete survey of events, past, present, and future. What follows covers only the events up until the time of Sinai, substantially, Genesis, and rather more briefly, Exodus 1 – 14. One could be led to believe that other volumes are to follow, but there is no indication of this. On the other hand, the recounting of these stories provides a setting in which to give instruction which applies right up until the author's time, and especially to his time, frequently underlined by the affirmation that a law or commandment "has no temporal limit" (30:10; 32:10) and in one instance using the striking image that the law is not to be "circumcised": "There is no circumcising of days, nor omitting any day of the eight days because it is an eternal ordinance ordained and written on the heavenly tablet" (15:25).

The introduction is strikingly positive about the future.[338] But this hope stands in sharp contrast to its opposite: minds in error, neglecting true worship (and its times) and following the ways of the nations in idolatry and possibly their impurity. The warning about sin forms a key element within this frame of thought. Impurity associated with the nations, as we shall see, has sexual wrongdoing as a key component.

---

[337] On the problem created in the Ethiopic and Latin versions, that sometimes Moses is instructed to write and sometimes the angel is instructed to write, see James C. VanderKam, "The Putative Author of the Book of Jubilees," in *From Revelation to Canon: Studies in Hebrew Bible and Second Temple Literature* (JSJSup 62; Leiden: Brill, 2000) 439-47, originally *JSS* 26 (2000) 209-17, who argues plausibly that references to the angel writing, as in 1:27 represent a misreading of the Hebrew *hiphil* as a *qal* form, so that behind "write" is the Hebrew word meaning, "cause to write, dictate", a problem which would have gone back to the Greek translator and reflecting a relatively common error, evidenced in the LXX. The Hebrew fragment 4Q216 4.6 appears to confirm this (see VanderKam, *Book of Jubilees*, 2001, p. 18). See also Brooke, "Exegetical Strategies," 42.

[338] See, for instance, Klaus Berger, *Das Buch der Jubiläen* (JSHRZ II.3; Gütersloh: Gerd Mohn, 1981), who highlights the positive aspects of *Jubilees'* hope and its understanding of the sabbath-based solar calendar: "In keiner anderen jüdischen Schrift dieser Zeit ist so oft von Freude die Rede wie in Jub, nirgendwo sonst wird der Wein so positiv bewertet, und der Sabbat ist nach Jub unter anderen dazu da, zu essen und zu trinken und sich zu freuen (daher auch das Verbot des Sabbatfastens in L 12)" (283) (tr. In no other Jewish writing of the period is there such frequent reference to joy as in *Jubilees*; nowhere else is wine valued so positively [hence also the prohibition of fasting on the sabbath in 50:12]).

3.1.2 *Warnings about Sexual Wrongdoing in Jubilees 23 and 50*

The speech of Yahweh (1:5-18), Moses' reply (1:19-21) and Yahweh's response (1:22-28), all draw attention to sin, variously described as doing evil, straying from the covenant, being unfaithful, defiant and stubborn, forgetting the commandments, being trapped by Belial in sin, having minds of error and contrary natures. Specifically, this shows itself in espousing idolatry, following the ways of the nations, neglecting God's commandments, giving up right observance of the sacred calendar and rejecting God's witnesses and those who study the law. We noted the likelihood that the concern about following "the nations, their impurities, and their shame" includes a reference to sexual wrongdoing. This is also likely in the reference to the danger posed by the nations which reappears in Moses' intercession. This finds some confirmation in the discourses of the angel which conclude part one (*Jubilees* 23) and part two of the book (concluding the book as a whole in *Jubilees* 50).

The final instructions given by the angel to Moses concern the sabbath (50:6-13), match the first exposition of an observance in *Jubilees*, namely, also the observance of the sabbath (2:19-33).[339] Its introduction speaks also of the sabbaths of the land and the jubilees, and then returns to statements of hope, doubtless intended for the author's contemporaries, and recalling the promissory statements of Yahweh at the book's beginning:

> The jubilees will pass by until Israel is pure (*nasha*) of every sexual evil (lit. sin [*'abbasā*] of sexual immorality [*zemmut*]), impurity (*rek*^w*s*), contamination (*gemmanē*),

---

[339] Helge S. Kvanvig, "Jubilees – Read as a Narrative," in *Enoch and Qumran Origins: New Light on a Forgotten Connection* (ed. Gabriele Boccaccini; Grand Rapids: Eerdmans, 2005) 75-83, notes Aristotle's view in the *Poetics* that a story needs a beginning, a middle, and an end, and sees this, in particular, in the importance of the sabbath in *Jub.* 2:16-33 and 50:1-13 (76). He then notes that the story of the Watchers comes at the 25th of 50 jubilees and expounds its importance for the work (77). My analysis sees the structural mid point in *Jubilees* 23, which shares a common eschatological vision with the beginning and end, but Kvanvig rightly emphasises the centrality of the Watchers and sexual wrongdoing in *Jubilees*. See also the expanded form of the article: Helge S. Kvanvig, "*Jubilees* – Between Enoch and Moses: A Narrative reading," *JSJ* 35 (2004) 243-61. See also Lutz Doering, "The Concept of the Sabbath in the Book of Jubilees," in *Studies in the Book of Jubilees* (ed. Matthias Albani, Jörg Frey, and Armin Lange; TSAJ 65; Tübingen: Mohr Siebeck, 1997) 179-205, who points out that another reason why the sabbath frames *Jubilees* is that *Jub.* 50:1 recalls Exod 16:1, alluding to the occurrence of the sabbath in the manna story (Exod 16:5, 22-30) (180).

sin (*xaṭi'at*), and error. They will no longer have any satan or any evil person. The land will be pure from that time until eternity. (50:5)[340]

Sexual wrongdoing is named explicitly.

Sexual wrongdoing also features at the conclusion of the first half of the book, namely *Jubilees* 23, which, like Yahweh's speech and the final chapter, refers to the climax of the jubilees, and in which most recognise allusions to the time of the author. After recounting the burial of Abraham the angel addresses the matter of his age, 175 years, noting that there had been a decrease from the ancients (before the flood) who lived 19 jubilees to the time of Abraham. People aged more quickly "because of the wickedness (*'ekay*) of their ways – with the exception of Abraham" (23:9).[341] The angel then turns to the future, noting an increase in the rate of aging and loss of knowledge (23:11-12). In addition, times of great stress will come, described as

> blow upon blow, wound upon wound, distress upon distress, bad news upon bad news, disease upon disease, and every (kind of) punishment like this, one with the other: disease and stomach pains; snow, hail, and frost; fever, cold, and numbness; famine, death, sword, captivity, and every (sort of) blow and difficulty. (23:12b-13)

The angel then gives the cause: "All of this will happen to the evil generation which makes the earth commit sin (*'abbasa*) through pollution (*rek*[w]*s*), sexual impurity (*zemmut*),[342] contamination (*gemmānē*), and their detestable actions (*saqorār*)" (23:14). Again, sexual wrongdoing is clearly in focus. The explanation continues with further description of the evil generation, noting that "children will find fault with their fathers and elders because of sin (*xaṭi'at*) and injustice, because of what they say and the great evils (*'ekay*) they commit", and because of their abandoning the covenant (23:16).[343] "They all have acted wickedly (*'akya*)", speaking "what is sinful (*'abbasa*)". "Everything that they do is impure (*rekus*) and something detestable (*saqorār*); all their ways are (characterized by) contamination (*gemmānē*), and pollution (*rek*[w]*s* – omitted by VanderKam in

---

[340] See also Scott, *On Earth as in Heaven*, who underlines the importance of the end corresponding to the beginning in *Jubilees* (81-82). Scott also notes several parallels between the restoration expectation in *Jub.* 23:29-31 and Isa 61:1-3 (139).

[341] On the awkwardness of including Abraham's reduced age among the consequences of wickedness, while asserting Abraham had no part in wickedness, see John C. Endres, *Biblical Interpretation in the Book of Jubilees* (CBQMS 18; Washington DC: Catholic Biblical Association of America, 1987) 53.

[342] VanderKam, *Jubilees Translated*, combines "pollution" (*rek*[w]*s*), "sexual impurity" (*zemmut*) in the one expression, "sexual impurity" (143).

[343] Berger, *Jubiläen*, rightly sees in the reference to children not family disobedience, but evidence of a younger group critical of the abuses of older leaders (299).

translation[344]) and corruption (*musenā*)" (23:17). Given the explicit reference in 23:14, we should assume sexual wrongdoing is part of what is being attacked.

Jub. 23:19 turns to divisions among groups, already hinted at in 23:17, over the law and the covenant, doubtless referring to divisions in the author's time. The predictions of Yahweh in 1:10 about abandoning commandment, covenantal festivals, sabbaths, holy things and the temple, find their echo in 23:19b: "For they have forgotten commandment, covenant, festival, month. sabbath, jubilee, and every verdict". 23:21 notes: "They will defile *(rak^wsa)* the holy of holies with the impure *(rek^ws)* corruption (*musenā*) of their contamination (*gemmānē*)". Here we have an apparent reference to corrupt priestly leadership, including the high priest, who alone could enter the holy of holies.[345] The speech has used such language in 23:14 with an explicit reference to sexual wrongdoing. What defiles the holy of holies probably includes such wrongdoing, along with other violations of the law. *Jub.* 23:21 mentions specifically those who, having escaped punishment at the hands of the faithful group, "will not turn from their wickedness to the right way because all of them will elevate themselves (for the purpose of) cheating and through wealth so that one takes everything that belongs to another. They will mention the great name but neither truly nor rightly".[346]

Then God will arouse "sinful nations" against them and a situation of hopelessness ensues. Human lifespan is reduced to the years of childhood (23:24-25) until the time of restoration: "The children will begin to study the laws, to seek out the commands, and to return to the right way" (23:26). The result is a return towards lifetimes of 1000 years and more:

> Then there will be no old man, nor anyone who has lived out his lifetime, because all of them will be infants and children. They will complete and live their entire lifetimes peacefully and joyfully. There will be neither a satan nor any evil one who will destroy. For their entire lifetimes will be times of blessing and healing. (23:28-29)[347]

---

[344] VanderKam, *Jubilees Translated*, 144.

[345] So VanderKam, *Book of Jubilees*, 2001, p. 58, 134; Ravid, "Purity and Impurity," 82.

[346] On the issue of the contemporary allusions in *Jubilees* 23 see Robert H. Charles, *The Book of Jubilees or the Little Genesis: Translated from the Editor's Ethiopic Text* (London: A&C Black, 1902), 147-48; Endres, *Biblical Interpretation*, 56; Berger, *Jubiläen*, 298-300; the extensive review in VanderKam, *Textual and Historical Studies*, 207-54; and more recently James C. VanderKam, "The Origins and Purposes of the Book of Jubilees," in *Studies in the Book of Jubilees* (ed. Matthias Albani, Jörg Frey, and Armin Lange; TSAJ 65; Tübingen: Mohr Siebeck, 1997) 3-24, and George W. E. Nickelsburg, *Jewish Literature between the Bible and the Mishnah* (2d ed.; Minneapolis: Fortress, 2005) 71-74. We return to the issue in the conclusion below.

[347] On the influence of Isa 65:17-25 on *Jubilees* 23, here Isa 65:20 on 23:28, see Scott, *On Earth as in Heaven*, 121-25.

This echoes 50:5, "The jubilees will pass by until Israel is pure of every sexual evil, impurity, contamination, sin, and error. They will no longer have any satan or any evil person. The land will be pure from that time until eternity". The two passages share the specific terminology of "satan nor any evil one/person" (cf. also the idealisation of Pharaoh's realm in Joseph's time: "The pharaoh's rule was just, and there was no satan or any evil one"; 40:9).

We shall have cause to return to some of the detail of this passage, not least the notion of all being infants and children, which may suggest the possibility of a sex free society, but, for the present, we note that this passage is an expansion of the notions we find in Yahweh's speech and in the closing chapter of *Jubilees*, and that beside other abuses, sexual wrongdoing assumes great significance. *Jub.* 23:14 is specific, referring to "sin through sexual impurity, contamination, and their detestable actions". This, in turn, informs the meaning of "wickedness (*'ekay*)" in 23:9 and 10, and should be understood as included in the references in 23:15-17 to evil, wickedness, and doing what "is impure (*rekus*) and something detestable (*saqorār*)" and producing "contamination (*gemmānē*), pollution (*rek^{w}s*) and corruption (*musenā*)". The context does not allow us to conclude that the designation, "sinful nations" (23:23, 24), includes a reference to their sexual sins, although this is likely, given the descriptions of the nations elsewhere in *Jubilees*, as we shall see.

Like 23:21, the future vision reflected in Yahweh's speech also links destruction, subjection to enemies, and neglect of the temple:

> Many will be destroyed. They will be captured and will fall into the enemy's control because they have abandoned my statutes, my commandments, my covenantal festivals, my sabbaths, my holy things which I have hallowed for myself among them, my tabernacle and my temple which I sanctified for myself in the middle of the land so that I could set my name on it and that I could live (there). (1:10)

It promises a rebuilt temple: "I will build my temple among them and will live with them; I will become their God and they will become my true and righteous people" (1:17), echoed in the author's narrative in 1:29, "the temple of the Lord will be created in Jerusalem on Mt Zion". Interestingly, we find the same vision in 4:26, which speaks of four holy places on earth: "For there are four places on earth that belong to the Lord: the Garden of Eden, the mountain of the east, this mountain on which you are today – Mt Sinai – and Mt. Zion (which) will be sanctified in the new creation for the sanctification of the earth. For this reason the earth will be sanctified from all its sins (*'abbasā*) and from its uncleanness (*rek^{w}s*) into the history of eternity". These "sins" and "uncleanness" doubtless include the sins of sexual wrongdoing.

It is appropriate to read the statements about the future in the introduction, the conclusion and the centre (or conclusion to the first half of *Jubilees*) in the light of each other. When one does so, it becomes clear that sexual wrongdoing belongs to the writer's major concerns. We need, however, to expand this observation by exploring what precisely is meant and how it relates to other concerns. In Yahweh's speech it is closely associated with idolatry, but also, as in *Jubilees* 23, with neglect of calendar laws and with the nations. There it may also characterise the sins of leading priests. *Jubilees* 23 and 50 both mention "satan or any evil person". *Jubilees* 1 speaks of entrapment by Belial.

Key words which feature in these passages include: "sexual impurity" (*zemmut*), "impurity/impure, defile" (*rek^{w}s, rak^{w}sa*), "contamination" (*gemmānē*), "corruption" (*musenā*), "detestable actions" (*saqorār*), "wickedness, acting wickedly" (*'ekay, 'akya*), "sin" (*'abbasā*), "sin" (*xaṭi'at*), and "shame" (*xasār*). Rather than investigate each of these at this stage, I discuss them in detail below in 3.2.8 together with their Hebrew and Latin counterparts and within their groupings, which are already evident in 23:24 and 17. I want first to turn to the other key passages in *Jubilees*. The narratives help inform the meaning of these words. They also significantly expand our understanding of the author's concerns about sexual wrongdoing.

3.2   Warnings about Sexual Wrongdoing

Acts of sexual wrongdoing receive major attention in *Jubilees*. They become the basis for excurses by the angel in which he lays down strict and permanent laws. Of the twelve occasions, when the angel addresses Moses directly with the instruction, "Now you command ...",[348] five relate to warnings about sexual wrongdoing. The list below provides an overview:

2:26 sabbath
6:13 blood
6:20 festival of weeks
6:32 364 day year and the festivals
15:28 circumcision
28:7 first marrying the eldest daughter
30:11 no intermarriage with foreigners
33:13 incest with father's wife (1)
33:18 incest with father's wife (2)
41:26 incest with daughter-in-law or mother-in-law
49:15 passover (1)
49:22 passover (2)

---

[348] There are minor variations: "Now you command the Israelites" (2:26; 6:13, 20, 34; 15:28; 28:7; 41:26; 49:15). 30:11, 33:13 and 49:22 add the name, "Moses". 33:18 has "Now you, Moses, write for Israel ..."

The emphasis on sexual wrongdoing has the angel declare directly:

> No sin is greater than the sexual impurity (*zemmut*) which they commit on the earth because Israel is a holy people for the Lord its God. It is the nation which he possesses; it is a priestly nation; it is a priestly kingdom; it is what he owns. No such impurity (*rek^ws*) will be seen among the holy people. (33:20)

Sexual wrongdoing is a regular theme. In what follows we turn to the key passages related to major motifs in the sequence in which they occur in the book.

3.2.1   The Watchers

The first passage which addresses sexual wrongdoing is the account of the Watchers (5:1-12). They are already mentioned in 4:15 in explaining the meaning of Jared's name and in 4:22 in relation to Enoch's testimony against them. Up to this point the angel has retold the creation story (2:1-33), which climaxes in the instruction to keep the sabbath. He has recounted the making of woman and the joining of man and woman (3:1-7), to which we shall return in section 3.3 below. In what follows he gives instructions about purification after childbirth, related to the entry of Adam and then Eve to the Garden of Eden (3:8-14); recounts their sin there and its consequences, also significant for our theme, but not in the context of sexual wrongdoing (3:15-34); reports the murder of Abel, an occasion to prohibit malicious assaults (4:1-6); and outlines the generations since Adam (4:7-33). The latter includes an excursus on Enoch (4:17-19, 21-26), who also received instruction about the sacred calendar (4:18) and was informed "in a vision what had happened and what will occur – how things will happen for mankind during their history until the day of judgement" (4:19) and so was the first to write a testimony (4:18a).

The account of the Watchers' sin is based on Genesis 6:1-8.[349] Both accounts are set out below.

Jubilees	Genesis
5:1 When mankind began to multiply on the surface of the entire earth and	6:1 When people began to multiply on the face of the

---

[349] See the detailed discussion in James C. VanderKam, "The Angel Story in the Book of *Jubilees*," in *Pseudepigraphic Perspectives: The Apocrypha and Pseudepigrapha in Light of the Dead Sea Scrolls: Proceedings of the [Second] International Symposium of the Orion Center for the Study of the Dead Sea Scrolls and Associated Literature, 12-14 January 1997* (ed. Esther G. Chazon and Michael E. Stone; STDJ 31; Leiden: Brill, 1999) 151-70, and J. T. A. G. M. van Ruiten, *Primaeval History Interpreted: The Rewriting of Genesis 1-11 in the Book of Jubilees* (JSJSup 66; Leiden: Brill, 2000), 181-97.

daughters were born to them,
the angels of the Lord — in a certain (year) of this jubilee
— saw that they were beautiful to look at.
So they married of them whomever they chose.
They gave birth to children for them and they were giants.
5:2 Wickedness (*'ammaḏā*) increased on the earth. All
animate beings corrupted their way — (everyone of them)
from people to cattle, animals, birds, and everything that
moves about on the ground. All of them corrupted their
way and their prescribed course. They began to devour one
another, and wickedness increased on the earth. Every
thought of all mankind's knowledge was evil like this all
the time.
5:3 The Lord saw that the earth was corrupt, (that) all
animate beings had corrupted their prescribed course, and
(that) all of them — everyone that was on the earth – had
acted wickedly before his eyes.
5:4 He said that he would obliterate people and all animate
beings that were on the surface of the earth which he had
created.
5:5 He was pleased with Noah alone.
5:6 Against his angels whom he had sent to the earth he
was angry enough to uproot them from all their (positions
of) authority. He told us to tie them up in the depths of the
earth; now they are tied within them and are alone.
5:7 Regarding their children there went out from his
presence an order to strike them with the sword and to
remove them from beneath the sky.
5:8 He said: 'My spirit will not remain on people forever
for they are flesh. Their lifespan is to be 120 years'.
5:9 He sent his sword among them so that they would kill
one another. They began to kill each other until all of them
fell by the sword and were obliterated from the earth.
5:10 Now their fathers were watching, but afterwards they
were tied up in the depths of the earth until the great day of
judgment when there will be condemnation on all who
have corrupted their ways and their actions before the
Lord.
5: 11 He obliterated all from their places; there remained
no one of them whom he did not judge for all their
wickedness.
5:12 He made a new and righteous nature for all his
creatures so that they would not sin with their whole nature
until eternity. Everyone will be righteous — each
according to his kind — for all time.

ground, and
daughters were born to
them,
2 the sons of God
saw that they were fair;
and they took wives for
themselves of all that they
chose.
3 Then the LORD said,
"My spirit shall not abide
in mortals forever, for they
are flesh; their days shall
be one hundred twenty
years."
4 The Nephilim were on
the earth in those days –
and also afterward – when
the sons of God went in to
the daughters of humans,
who bore children to them.
These were the heroes that
were of old, warriors of
renown.
5 The LORD saw that the
wickedness of humankind
was great in the earth, and
that every inclination of
the thoughts of their hearts
was only evil continually.
6 And the LORD was
sorry that he had made
humankind on the earth,
and it grieved him to his
heart.
7 So the LORD said, "I
will blot out from the earth
the human beings I have
created – people together
with animals and creeping
things and birds of the air,
for I am sorry that I have
made them."
8 But Noah found favor in
the sight of the LORD

Perhaps the Hebrew of *Jubilees* read, as Genesis, בני אלהים, "sons of God". The Ethiopic may either reflect an interpretation of בני אלהים, "sons of God" to mean angels or stand under the influence of a LXX variant reading which had already done so, reading οἱ ἄγγελοι τοῦ θεοῦ.[350] *Jubilees* adds a reference to the year of jubilee, a constant concern in the book, but otherwise follows Genesis closely. The dating, indicated in 4:33, shows that it is the twenty-fifth jubilee.[351] As VanderKam notes,

> the twenty-fifth one would be the last jubilee in the first half of the history, since the book covers 50 jubilee periods (50:4). The meaning may be that the first half of the narrated history concluded with the ominous event of the angelic desire for women which led to an illicit mixing of beings from different orders and eventually to the evil that had to be punished by the flood.[352]

He goes on to conclude that "perhaps this is one reason why the writer is so insistent that the Israelites not intermarry with the peoples of Canaan after they enter the land in the fiftieth jubilee." As we shall see, such focus on sexual wrongdoing, expressed structurally by this dating, is, indeed, a central concern of the book.

The translation, "married", interprets the literal statement, "took wives for themselves", which reflects the Hebrew:

Gen 6:2 וַיִּקְחוּ לָהֶם נָשִׁים מִכֹּל אֲשֶׁר בָּחָרוּ
and they took women/wives for themselves from any they chose.

The language of marriage should not lead us to think that some kind of ceremony took place. Nothing indicates that the offence was elopement or rape, such as in

---

[350] See John William Wevers, *Septuaginta: Vetus Testamentum Graecum I: Genesis* (Göttingen: Vandenhoeck und Ruprecht, 1974) 108; and John William Wevers, *Notes on the Greek Text of Genesis* (SBLSCS 35; Atlanta: Scholars, 1993) 75-76. Erik W. Larson, "The LXX and Enoch: Influence and Interpretation in Early Jewish Literature," in *Enoch and Qumran Origins: New Light on a Forgotten Connection* (ed. Gabriele Boccaccini; Grand Rapids: Eerdmans, 2005) 84-89, argues that in both *Jub.* 4:15 and here in 5:1 the Ethiopic has used a text which read "angels" in place of "sons", under the influence of the Old Greek of Genesis (86). On the background to "sons of God" here in Genesis, see our discussion of *1 Enoch* 6:1, above.

[351] See the discussion in Van Ruiten, *Primaeval History Interpreted*, on the two possible datings of the vague temporal reference, the first year of either the twenty-fifth jubilee or the twenty-sixth, the former implying that the giants would have completed their 120 years ten years before the flood which would not be seen as designed to destroy them, or later, in which case it was (193).

[352] VanderKam, "Angel Story," 158.

the instance of Dinah, but an act of sexual intercourse is assumed,[353] resulting in pregnancy and the birth of the giants.[354]

This depiction stands in contrast to the account in *1 Enoch* which portrays the Watchers as rebelling against God in heaven and there lusting after women of earth (*1 Enoch* 6:2; 8:1; 15:7; cf. also *T. Reub.* 5:6).[355] By contrast, in *Jubilees* they have been commissioned by God (5:6; 7:21) and "came down" to earth, as the play on the name Jared reminds us in 4:15, "to teach humankind and to do what is just and upright on the earth."[356]

The nature of the offence is already hinted at in 5:1 in what immediately follows: "They gave birth to children for them and they were giants". They were the products of a mixing of two different kinds: angel and human. This receives confirmation from the earlier reference to their wrongdoing in the account about Enoch: "He testified to the Watchers who had sinned (*'abbasa*) with the daughters of men because these had begun to mix with (*dammara*) earthly women so that they became defiled (*rakʷsa*)" (4:22). The literal translation may bring this out more clearly: "mix so that they became defiled with earthly women".[357] The word, *dammara*, can allude to sexual intercourse and joining in marriage and may not here necessarily express the sin of "mixing" of kinds. Later, however, in 5:2-3 we see that the sin did consist in the Watchers' transgressing their boundaries and corrupting their way, thus setting off a chain reaction among created beings.

In rewriting Genesis 6, *Jubilees* transfers the somewhat unmediated and ambiguous statement in Gen 6:3, "The LORD said, 'My spirit shall not abide in mortals forever, for they are flesh; their days shall be one hundred twenty years'" (6:3), to *Jub.* 5:8, where it makes better sense after the account of corruption on earth, including among humankind, but must refer here no longer to humans but to the giants.[358] This is also the reading assumed in *1 Enoch*, as we have seen (see *1*

---

[353] Wright, *Evil Spirits*, suggests that the formulation in Gen 6:2 (and so in *1 Enoch* 6:2 and 7:1) refers not to marriage, when one would expect the verb לקח to be followed by לאשה or לנשים, but to taking women (132-36). Certainly the focus in *Jubilees* is sexual intercourse rather than the continuing relationship, but in *1 Enoch* 6 – 11 the latter is assumed as the context for imparting forbidden information.

[354] On the background to the identification of the *Nephilim* as giants, including Num 13:33, and their negative portrayal in *Jubilees* see Van Ruiten, *Primaeval History Interpreted*, 189-90.

[355] On the different interpretations see Stuckenbruck, "Origins of Evil," 111-15.

[356] So Betsy Halpern-Amaru, *The Empowerment of Women in the Book of Jubilees* (JSJSup 60; Leiden: Brill, 1999) 159-60; Stuckenbruck, "Origins of Evil," 114-15; VanderKam, "Angel Story": "It protects the reputation of heaven by distancing it from evil" (155).

[357] So VanderKam, *Jubilees Translated*, 27 n. 4:22.

[358] So VanderKam, "Angel Story," 160. He notes this ensures that the giants die before the flood and that the flood is seen as judgement on human wickedness. Similarly

Enoch 10:9-10). *Jubilees* also simplifies the complicated statement in Gen 6:4, which first mentions the *Nephilim*, and then afterwards the fact that the sons of God had intercourse with the women, who then bore heroes and warriors. *Jubilees* simply states: "They gave birth to children for them and they were giants" (5:1). It will later reflect knowledge of tradition about three kinds of giants (7:22).

Then in 5:2 *Jubilees* takes up Gen 6:5, which describes "wickedness" (רעה; *Jub.* 5:2, *'ammaḍā*) among humankind, but connects it with what precedes by using words which imply that the offence committed by the Watchers was repeated among human beings and all the animal world (thus warranting their destruction – the destruction also of animals clearly a matter of concern to some even then). Thus it writes, they "corrupted (*māsana*) their way (*fenot*)". The expression occurs twice in 5:2, and is repeated in 5:3 and 10. It appears to be drawn from Gen 6:12, "And God saw that the earth was corrupt; for all flesh had corrupted its way (השחית דרכו κατέφθειρεν ... τὴν ὁδὸν αὐτοῦ) upon the earth". Once in 5:2, and also in 5:3, it comes in the fuller form: "corrupted (*māsana*) their way (*fenot*) and their prescribed course (*šerʿat*)". 5:10 has: "corrupted (*māsana*) their ways (*fenot*) and their actions (*megbār*)". This notion persists in the verses which follow: 5:13 "transgress (*ʿadawa*) from the way (*fenot*) it was ordained (*šarʾa*) for them to go"; 5:17 "corrupted (*māsana*) their ways (*fenot*) and their plans (*mekr*)"; 5:19 "transgress (*ʿadawa*) from anything that had been ordained (*šarʾa*)". Interestingly, this language may also be applied to the prescribed pattern of the sacred calendar – so 6:33 "transgress (*ʿadawa*) the prescribed pattern (*šerʿat*)"; also 6:34.[359] Here, too, the notion is one of order and disorder. 6:35-36 says it will lead to their forgetting the right way and walking in the festivals of the nations and following a lunar calendar.[360]

Stuckenbruck, "Origins of Evil," 112, who notes that *Jubilees* fuses the Genesis tradition of the flood as judgement against human wickedness and the Enochic tradition of the flood as judgement against the Watchers, so that "the deluge is God's response to the sins of humanity which, in turn, have been fuelled by the activities of the wayward angels" (111). He observes: "The persistence of at least some giants in the form of spirits beyond the flood is retained in *Jubilees*," since they had already "assumed their disembodied state prior to the flood (5:8-9)" (112).

[359] On the language of following one's prescribed pattern, see Jacques T. A. G. M. van Ruiten, "The Covenant of Noah in *Jubilees* 6.1-38," in *The Concept of the Covenant in the Second Temple Period* (ed. Stanley E. Porter and Jacqueline C. R. de Roo; Leiden: Brill, 2003) 167-90, where he notes it expresses "the permanent character of the natural order" (176).

[360] See also Robert Hayward, "The Sanctification of Time in the Second Temple Period: Case Studies in the Septuagint and *Jubilees*," in *Holiness Past and Present* (ed. Stephen C. Barton; London: T&T Clark, 2003) 141-67, who argues that a possible background to this warning lies in the linking of the *Pesah* festival with the Greek *Dionysia*,

By analogy the Watchers "corrupted their way" when they chose sexual intercourse with other than their own kind (and with their own kind sexual intercourse was in any case not an option nor necessary, as elsewhere, *1 Enoch* 15:5-7 explains). They corrupted/perverted (*māsana*) and transgressed (*'adawa*) their way (*fenot*), prescribed course, pattern or order (*šer'at*; *mekr*), and actions (*megbār*). Their sexual wrongdoing assumes major significance in *Jubilees* and becomes paradigmatic for all sexual wrongdoing. In what did it consist? One explanation remains at a formal level: they departed from their prescribed path in the simple sense that they were disobedient to prescribed commandments. But this, while true, is insufficient. There is an assumed content which implies that their actions went contrary to their order of being as angels. They should not have responded to the beauty of human women and "married of them whomever they chose" (5:1) or "mixed with earthly women" and thus become "defiled" (4:22). Such behaviour would also be reprehensible among human beings, but the element which makes this, their sin, so distinctive is the mixing of kinds. It was not that it would be sanctioned had they been guided to be more careful in their selection of human women.

How might the author have seen this sin applying to human beings – and animals, when they, too, corrupted their way? Two major possibilities might be bestiality and homosexual acts. *T. Naph.* 3:1-5 and 4:1 links the Watchers and Sodom in what appears to be an attack on Gentiles for changing the order of their nature, resulting in both idolatry and, it seems, homosexual acts, in a manner reminiscent of Paul in Rom 1:24-28. But nowhere else in *Jubilees* do we find expressions of concern with homosexual behaviour. It should not be ruled out here, but, at most, the analogy appears to apply to inappropriate sexual mixing and for *Jubilees*, as we shall see, that is a key element in the case against intermarriage. Thus Abraham warns his descendants in language reminiscent of the sins of the Watchers: "They are not to commit sexual offences (by) following their eyes and their hearts so that they take wives for themselves from the Canaanite women" (20:4b). That also represents an illicit crossing of boundaries, a transgression of the order set by God who established Israel as holy.

It is interesting, nevertheless, that *Jubilees* does not, here, make the analogy explicit between Watchers engaging in illicit sexual intercourse and people (or priests) doing so, though it surely presupposes it, and will use the analogy in 7:20-21. This recalls our finding in the *Book of the Watchers* where we similarly find no explicit analogy, but there must presume it would have been made, even though explicit prohibition of intermarriage by people or priests is never expressed – in

---

which according to 2 Macc 6:7 Antiochus imposed on all Jews, but which, Hayward suggests, may already have been associated by some with *Pesah* celebrations (166).

contrast to the repeated prohibitions in *Jubilees* and the likely allusions in the *Aramaic Levi Document*.

The only other place where we find the language of corrupting (*māsana*) one's way (*fenot*) and which comes closest to an application of the implied analogy is in Jacob's reassurances to Rebecca in 25:7 and 10. Jacob assures Rebecca: "I have kept myself from sinning (*'abbasa*) and from becoming corrupted (*māsana*) in any ways during my entire lifetime because father Abraham gave me many orders about lewdness (*mer'āt*) and sexual impurity (*zemmut*)" (25:7); "I will behave rightly and will never conduct myself corruptly (from *māsana*) (lit. corrupt my way)". 4Q222 preserves for us the words behind "conduct myself corruptly (lit. corrupt my way)": אשחית דרכי. There the primary focus appears to be marrying a Canaanite, although the context suggests that this language is being used not so much with a view to the marrying as to corrupt behaviour, such as that into which Canaanite women might lead him:

> with all the impure things (*rek^ws*) that they do because everything that they do (consists of) sexual impurity (*zemmut*) and lewdness (*mer'āt*). They have no decency [lit. there is no righteousness with them (*masc.*)] because (what they do) is evil. [lit. it/he is bad] (25:1).

Such sexual wrongdoing may well include acts deemed as contrary to one's nature.[361]

The context of 5:2 offers no elaboration. Within 5:3 we simply have the assertion: "The Lord saw that the earth was corrupt (*māsana*), and all of them — everyone that was on the earth – had acted wickedly (*'akya*) before his eyes". Neither bestiality nor homosexual acts is mentioned in the wider context. 5:4 talks of obliterating people and all animate beings and introduces Noah as alone finding grace in God's sight. 5:6 reports instructions for the angel and his peers to bind the Watchers in the depth. 5:7 reports the decree to kill the giants with the sword. 5:9 depicts the giants as killing themselves. 5:10-11 reports the Watchers seeing this and all standing under judgement. If such giants might have recalled ancient Greek cultural myths, they are quickly despatched – perhaps with a hint of ridicule.

---

[361] Jackson, *Enochic Judaism*, referring to the sin as depicted in 4:22, writes: "The emphasis here seems to be more one involving cultic uncleanness akin to mixed marriages and the priesthood" (42), but, as we shall see, even there, such language carries strong moral overtones. Interestingly, and in some tension with this, he interprets the corrupting effects of the Watchers as something affecting creation, so that, he argues, the language of 5:12 concerning the effects of the flood "implies the restoration of biological purity to each species/kind (cf. *Jub.* 5.13)" (43). "The Enochic paradigm that all change is deviance is, in *Jubilees*, developed to its logical conclusions across a range of particularly cultic issues" (102).

The focus on nature returns in 5:12 with an extraordinary promise of hope:

> He made a new and righteous nature (*fetrat* – nature, character) for all his creatures so that they would not sin with their whole nature (*fetrat*) until eternity. Everyone will be righteous — each according to his kind — for all time.

It is typical of *Jubilees* to follow predictions of judgement by promises of hope. See already 1:23 "I will cut away the foreskins of their minds and the foreskins of their descendants' minds. I will create a holy spirit for them and will purify them in order that they may not turn away from me from that time forever". This one in 5:12 appears to take its shape from the previous story. A new nature replaces the old.[362] The old had corrupted its way.[363] The focus again on kind ("each according to his kind"), an echo of the created order in Genesis 1, suggests that the nature of the sin focuses, in particular, on improper sexual relations, that is, mixing of kinds.

Jubilees does however offer more about the sins and wickedness of humankind before the flood to supplement the curt description in 5:3, but it comes in the story of the flood, itself. 5:13-16 emphasises the fairness of God's judgement against those who "transgress (*'adawa*) from the way (*fenot*) it was ordained (*šar'a*) for them to go" (5:13). *Jub.* 5:17-19 mentions the possibility of forgiveness for people turning from their wickedness, sins, and errors. Noah is the ideal, who "did not transgress (*'adawa*) from anything that had been ordained (*šar'a*) for him" (5:19).

Further light is shed on the Watchers and their sin and the subsequent wickedness of humankind in Noah's advice to his descendants in the light of the

---

[362] Hermann Lichtenberger, "Zu Vorkommen und Bedeutung von *yetser* im Jubilaenbuch," *JSJ* 14 (1983) 1-10, notes the occurrence of יצר in *Jub.* 35:9 and, in relation to our context, in 5:2 and 7:24, both dependent on Gen 6:5 (5-7) and in 1:22, influenced by Deut 31:21 (8). He concludes that here "Der 'Trieb' sei er 'gute' oder 'böse', agiert nicht im Herzen des Menschen, sondern יצר ist gutes oder böses Denken oder Planen des Menschen selbst, das im Herzen geschieht" (10) (tr. The "drive", whether "good" or "evil", does not operate independently in human hearts, rather יצר is a good or evil manner of thinking or planning on the part of human beings, themselves, which happens in the heart).

[363] VanderKam, "Demons," notes that already Genesis 9 intimates a new beginning (356) and sees *Jubilees* developing this in ways that suggest that people thereafter, such as the people of the tower, "did not sin with their entire nature and God did not obliterate them" (362, similarly 358). He sees in this also the explanation for the ninety percent reduction in the number of evil spirits, so that "in contrast with the prediluvian sinners who apparently did sin with their whole nature and thus brought on the flood, those afterward would be differently constituted so that sin would be more controlled and punishment could be postponed until the day of judgment" (358).

judgement of the flood.[364] He advises them to "keep themselves from fornication (*zemmut*), uncleanness (*rek^ws*), and from all injustice". (7:20). Clearly sexual sin is in mind, but its focus is the action of the Watchers, as the following verses explain: 7:21 "For it was on account of these three things that the flood was on the earth, since (it was) due to fornication (*zemmut*) that the Watchers had illicit intercourse (*zammawa*) — apart from the mandate (*te'zāz* command, order; edict, law, commandment) of their authority (*kwennanē*, authority, charge) — with women. When they married of them whomever they chose they committed the first (acts) of uncleanness (*rek^ws*)". The words about mandated authority reflect the view that they had come to earth with a divine commission, but instead had transgressed the limits set for them and their kind by having sex with human women. This might imply nothing more than disobeying orders, as we noted above, but the wider context, especially the language about corrupting or perverting their ways, suggests the particular aspect of transgressing the limits of their kind through intercourse.[365]

It is hard to distinguish the first two of these "three things, fornication (*zemmut*) and uncleanness (*rek^ws*)" of which Noah speaks here in 7:20, except that the latter, "uncleanness" (*rek^ws*), is to be seen as the result of their actions of "fornication" (*zemmut*). The alternative is to try to distinguish two acts of wrongdoing: sexual intercourse with married women, i.e. adultery, or outside marriage, and sexual intercourse within a forbidden relationship (not incest, but the wrong kind). Nothing suggests the former. The expression, "take as wives", need not in itself suggest adultery. The sequence: fornication – uncleanness, corresponds to 4:22, "mix so that they became defiled (*rak^wsa*) with earthly women".

The sexual element in the wickedness of the Watchers and their descendants is clearly present also in the allusion to the giants in Abraham's speech to his sons and their children in 20:5:

> He told them about the punishment of the giants and the punishment of Sodom — how they were condemned because of their wickedness; because of the sexual impurity (*zemmut*), uncleanness (*rek^ws*), and corruption (*musenā*) among themselves they died in (their) sexual impurity (*zemmut*).

---

[364] On the connection between the sins of the angels and the flood, not made in Genesis, but important in *Jubilees* and reflecting earlier tradition, such as *1 Enoch* 10, see van Ruiten, *Primaeval History Interpreted*, 195-97.

[365] VanderKam, "Angel Story," draws attention to the connections in Lev 18:26-28 about defiling the land with what immediately precedes it in Leviticus 18, namely, warning against sexual wrongdoing (166).

Accordingly, Abraham continues with the warning: Now you keep yourselves from all sexual impurity (*zemmut*) and uncleanness (*rek^w s*) and from all the contamination (*gemmānē*) of sin (*xaṭi'at*)" (20:6).

The third of the *three things* for which according to 7:21 the flood came was "injustice". *Jub.* 7:22 takes this up in referring to the birth of the *Nephilim*: "They fathered (as their) sons the Nephilim". Here, unlike in 5:1, the author takes up the reference in Gen 6:4 to the *Nephilim* and, using tradition from *1 Enoch*, expounds their wrongdoing primarily as bloodshed, involving also humans: "They were all dissimilar (from one another) and would devour one another: the giant killed the Naphil; the Naphil killed the Elyo; the Elyo mankind; and people their fellows". Injustice and bloodshed then encompass both the human and animal world (7:23-24).

Jub. 7:24 retains the focus on attitude of mind: "All the thoughts and wishes of mankind were (devoted to) thinking up what was useless and wicked all the time". This contrasts with the renewed minds promised to the repentant in 5:13 (and 1:23). 7:25 repeats the reference to the judgement of the flood: "Then the Lord obliterated all from the surface of the earth because of their actions and because of the blood which they had shed in the earth". The words, "because of their actions and because of the blood which they had shed", will encompass both sexual wrongdoing and injustice, understood primarily as violence and bloodshed.

Jubilees returns frequently to the Watchers and the giants. Thus beside sinning with human women, some left behind "an inscription which the ancients had incised in a rock", which Kainan later read and copied "and sinned on the basis of what was in it, since in it was the Watchers' teaching by which they used to observe the omens of the sun, moon, and stars and every heavenly sign" (8:3-4).[366]

The Watchers have very great significance because they, or ten per cent of them, become the demons which assault humankind. Noah will plead successfully for help against these "impure (*rekus*) demons" who were misleading his grandchildren and making them act foolishly, and allude to the evils of the Watchers in his own time (10:1-7).[367] It should not surprise us if the demons

---

[366] Van Ruiten, *Primaeval History Interpreted*, speculates that the failure to mention the sexual sin of the Watchers in this context may reflect the fact that according to *Jubilees* Kainan did not marry outside his family (318 n. 21). Cf. however, Reed, *Fallen Angels*, who argues that Jubilees wants to show that "his corruption by the Watchers' teaching is tied to a propensity for exogamy, akin to the paradigmatic 'intermarriage' between 'the sons of God' and 'daughters of men'" (93).

[367] Ida Fröhlich, "Enoch and *Jubilees*," *Enoch and Qumran Origins: New Light on a Forgotten Connection* (ed. Gabriele Boccaccini; Grand Rapids: Eerdmans, 2005) 141-47, writes of *Jubilees'* integrating three different sources of material concerning demons: the

continue their interest in sexual wrongdoing. That is one aspect of their activity according to the previous verse, 9:15, where Noah's grandchildren face judgement: "because of all the evil impurity (*rek*ʷ*s*) of their errors by which they have filled the earth with wickedness (*'ekay*), impurity (*rek*ʷ*s*), fornication (*zemmut*), and sin (*xaṭi'at*)".

Sexual sins continue in their repertoire as they persuade Noah's sons to sin:

> They began to make statues, images, and unclean things (*rek*ʷ*s*); the spirits of the savage ones (*dawwāg*) were helping and misleading (them) so that they would commit sins (*'abbasa*), impurities (*rek*ʷ*s*), and transgression (*'abbasā*). Prince Mastema was exerting his power in effecting all these actions and, by means of the spirits, he was sending to those who were placed under his control (the ability) to commit every (kind of) error and sin (*xaṭi'at*) (and every (kind of) transgression (*'abbasā*); to corrupt (*māsana*), to destroy, and to shed blood on the earth. (11:4-5)

Their activity is related to the situation which Abram confronted according to 11:16-17,where "everyone was going astray after the statues and after impurity (*rek*ʷ*s*)".[368] "He began to pray to the creator of all that he would save him from the errors of mankind and that it might not fall to his share to go astray after impurity (*rek*ʷ*s*) and wickedness (*mennānē*)". He prays similarly in 12:20, "Save me from the power of the evil spirits who rule the thoughts of people's minds" (see also 19:28: "May the spirits of Mastema not rule over you"). According to 15:31-32, God alone rules over Abraham's seed, whereas the spirits rule over other peoples:

> He sanctified them and gathered (them) from all mankind. For there are many nations and many peoples and all belong to him. He made spirits rule over all in order to lead them astray from following him. But over Israel he made no angel or spirit rule because he alone is their ruler.

Part of the spirits' role, in continuing the evil work of the Watchers, is to incite to sexual wrongdoing as well as leading people astray to commit bloodshed and idolatry. The story that Abram was able to keep the birds at bay from destroying the crops (11:18-22; cf. Gen 15:11 and *Jub.* 14:12) may well function at a symbolic level – he held the demons at bay. The text identifies the birds as agents of Mastema (cf. also the birds in a similar role in the sower parable and its

---

Enochic story of the Watchers, the childbed demons of folk belief (as here), and the Satan figure of Job as in the sacrifice of Isaac (145).

[368] On the reading, *impurity*, whereas Syriac has *molten images*, see VanderKam, *Jubilees Translated,* 67 n. 11:16, who argues in favour of the former, more difficult reading.

interpretation in Mark 4:15).[369] Neither the assurance in 15:31-32 that God, and not the demons, rule over Abraham's seed, nor the gift of "a new and righteous nature for all his creatures so that they would not sin with their whole nature until eternity" (5:13), a gift to all, guaranteed sinlessness. At most, they appear to assume that people now have greater capacity to resist sin, especially Abraham's seed, which begins in the right realm; and repentance and change is possible.[370]

Jubilees returns once more to the giants in the context of speaking of the inhabitants of Gilead (29:9-11). Here these giants are called *Rafaim*.

> The Lord destroyed them because of the evil things they did (*'akya*), for they were very wicked (*dawwāg* lit. savage). The Amorites – evil and sinful – lived in their place. Today there is no nation that has matched all their sins. They no longer have length of life on earth. (29:11)

The evil deeds probably include sexual wrongdoing, but the focus is probably more on savagery.

In this section we have looked at the story of the Watchers and their impact on humankind before the flood. Their wrongdoing, described as "fornication", lay, in particular, in having sexual intercourse with other than their own kind. The initial application to human beings also attacks doing what is not in accordance with their

---

[369] See also *Apoc. Abr.* 13:3-8, which identifies Azazel acting through an unclean bird. Berger, *Jubiläen*, 388, notes a possible background for the story of the ravens in the Let Jer 53-55: "For [idols] cannot set up a king over a country or give rain to people. They cannot judge their own cause or deliver one who is wronged for they have no power. They are like crows (κορῶναι) between heaven and earth. When fire breaks out in a temple of wooden gods overlaid with gold or silver, their priests will flee and escape, but they will be burned up like timbers". This antedates *Jubilees* and is also a likely source for the Syriac accounts to which Sebastian P. Brock, "Abraham and the Ravens: A Syriac Counterpart to *Jubilees* 11-12 and its Implications," *JSJ* 9 (1978) 139-52, alludes: the *Catena Severi* and the *Letter of James of Edessa to John of Litarba*. These know a variant of the story according to which God sends the ravens, Terah sends Abraham to drive them away, Abraham asks God to take them away, and Abraham persuades his father to abandon idols whose house he then burns before fleeing. Cf. also Cory D. Crawford, "On the Exegetical Function of the Abraham/Ravens Tradition in Jubilees 11," *HTR* 97 (2004) 91-97, who speculates that *Jubilees* read "seed" in the promise of Gen 15:8 as referring not to progeny, where its fulfilment is questionable, but literally to agricultural seed (64). *Jubilees* may also see in Abram's alleged invention of the seed plough a fulfilment of the promise in Gen 12:3 that he would be a blessing to the nations.

[370] On this see James C. VanderKam, "Anthropological Gleanings from the Book of Jubilees," in *Der Mensch vor Gott: Forschungen zum Menschenbild in Bibel, antikem Judentum und Koran: Festschrift für Hermann Lichtenberger zum 60. Geburtstag* (ed. Ulrike Mittmann-Richert, Friedrich Avemarie, and Gerbern S. Oegema; Neukirchen: Neukirchener Verlag, 2003) 117-31, 127-29.

nature or prescribed course. This would most naturally refer to bestiality or homosexual behaviour or both. If *Jubilees* is written against the backdrop of the dangers inherent in Hellenistic culture, the latter is more likely to be in view. One might also see in the debacle of the giants a disparagement of its myths. It is interesting that the Watchers play other roles. Some are indeed good and remain good.

Beyond that, references to the wickedness of the generation before the flood include sexual wrongdoing, but these are in general terms such as we found in the material considered earlier, and without specific detail. This is also true of the spirits of the Watchers, the demons of Mastema, and their activity after the flood among Noah's sons. Promoting sexual wrongdoing belongs to their repertoire. The story of the Watchers thus plays a key role within Jubilees in accounting for a causal sequence of events. This is so even though there are few direct references to the event in the chapters which follow. [371] As Kvanvig observes, "This incident functions in two ways in the narrative, both as a paradigm of evil and as the ultimate cause of evil".[372] Their deed is paradigmatic of three evils, fornication, uncleanness and injustice (7:20). He writes:

> To avoid these sins it was necessary for the Israelites and their ancestors to separate from Gentiles and above all not to mix with them sexually. This theme is repeated throughout the book, particularly in the great speeches (20:1-10; 22:10-24; 25:1-23). It is also the main plot in the story of Jacob and Esau. (26:1-29)[373]

Such wickedness is described as "fornication (*zemmut*), uncleanness (*rek^{w}s*), ... injustice" (7:20); "evil impurity (*rek^{w}s*) ...wickedness (*'ekay*), impurity (*rek^{w}s*), fornication (*zemmut*), and sin (*xaṭi'at*) ... impure (*rekus*) demons" (9:15 – 10:1); "unclean things (*rek^{w}s*)... sins (*'abbasa*), impurities (*rek^{w}s*), and transgression (*'abbasā*) ... sin (*xaṭi'at*), transgression (*'abbasā*); corrupt (*māsana*)" (11:4); "impurity (*rek^{w}s*)" (11:17); "impurity (*rek^{w}s*) and wickedness (*mennānē*)" (11:18). These terms occur relatively frequently in *Jubilees*. We shall return to them once we have completed our treatment of the narratives significant for our theme.

---

[371] So Kvanvig, "*Jubilees* – Between Enoch and Moses," 248-52.

[372] Kvanvig, "*Jubilees* – Between Enoch and Moses," 249.

[373] Kvanvig, "*Jubilees* – Read as Narrative", 77. He goes on to argue that the story of the Watchers "is not only the paradigm for sin and evil, but also constitutes the root cause for the evil that haunts men" since it gave rise to the demons (78). In contrast to VanderKam, who suggests it plays a modest role in *Jubilees* as a whole, he argues that beneath the surface "both the episodic and the logical structure of the narrative draw heavily on it. ... The basic theme of the Jacob story and the Watcher story is the same, sexual impurity" (78). Cf. VanderKam, "Angel Story," 154.

Jubilees' account of the Watchers and their progeny reflects not only Genesis 6, but also traditions in *1 Enoch*. The following section discusses this relationship.

Jubilees and 1 Enoch

Elements of the story in *Jubilees* clearly go beyond what we find in Genesis. These include the elaboration of Gen 6:12 about people corrupting their way and its extension to all animate beings, manifesting itself in their devouring one another in 5:2-3. Similarly the detail about uprooting the angels and binding them in the depths of the earth till the day of judgement (5:6, 10) and having their offspring selfdestruct through war while their fathers looked on (5:7-10) goes beyond Genesis. It matches some of the detail in the *Book of the Watchers* and the *Animal Apocalypse* of *1 Enoch*, which also interprets the account of the angels and of their offspring in starkly negative terms. There we read of instructions to Gabriel to "bind Asael hand and foot, and cast him into the darkness" in a deep place in the wilderness until the judgement (10:4-6; see also 88:1). Michael is similarly to bind Shemihazah and his accomplices to be confined in the valleys of the earth till the judgment (10:11-12; see also 88:3), once they have first witnessed their offspring in a war of self-destruction (10:12; 12:6; 14:6; see also 88:2), which is unleashed, in turn, by an instruction to Gabriel to bring about their death (10:9). The reference in *Jub.* 4:22 to the Watchers' defilement also appears dependent on the Enoch story, which highlights this motif (7:1; 9:8; 10:11).[374]

If, as seems likely in the light of these details, the author knows the myth of the Watchers from *1 Enoch*, he has handled it with a degree of autonomy or

---

[374] On the dependence of *Jubilees* on *1 Enoch* see James C. VanderKam, "Enoch Traditions in *Jubilees* and Other Second-Century Sources," in *From Revelation to Canon: Studies in Hebrew Bible and Second Temple Literature* (JSJSup 62; Leiden: Brill, 2000) 305-31. He argues for dependence on the *Book of the Watchers* (*1 Enoch* 1-36), the *Book of the Luminaries* (*1 Enoch* 72-82), the *Book of Dream Visions* (*1 Enoch* 83-90) and the *Epistle of Enoch* (*1 Enoch* 92 – 105) (309-26). See also VanderKam, *Book of Jubilees*, 2001, p. 137. See also Michael A. Knibb, "Which Parts of *1 Enoch* Were Known to *Jubilees*? A Note on the Interpretation of *Jubilees* 4.16-25," in *Reading from Right to Left: Essays on the Hebrew Bible in Honour of David J.A. Clines* (ed. J. Cheryl Exum and Hugh G. M. Williamson; JSOTSup 373; London: Sheffield Academic Press, 2003) 254-62, who questions dependence on the *Epistle* and the *Apocalypse of Weeks*. See also Jacques van Ruiten, "A Literary Dependency of Jubilees on 1 Enoch," in *Enoch and Qumran Origins: New Light on a Forgotten Connection* (ed. Gabriele Boccaccini; Grand Rapids: Eerdmans, 2005) 90-93, who argues the lack of textual evidence for dependence, such as exact wording of the kind evident in *Jubilees'* use of Genesis, and so also questions dependence on the *Book of Dream Visions*, including the use of such dependence for dating *Jubilees* (93). See also Jacques van Ruiten, "A Literary Dependency of Jubilees on 1 Enoch: A Reassessment of a Thesis of J. C. VanderKam," *Henoch* 26 (2004) 205-209.

perhaps also drawn on other sources.[375] His account of violence among humans and in the animal kingdom and of their beginning to devour one another (5:2-3) is distinctive in its emphasis on corruption in humankind and the animal kingdom. While this should be seen as an effect of the Watchers' deeds, this is not explicit here,[376] and differs from the effects depicted in *Book of the Watchers*. There the Watchers produce giants, who devour all the produce (*1 Enoch* 7:3) and commit violence against humankind and against animals (*1 Enoch* 7:4-5; similarly in the *Animal Apocalypse* 86:6; 87:1). Warfare among humans is at most implied as the effect of Asael's teaching the skills to make weapons (*1 Enoch* 8:1). On the other hand, the *Animal Apocalypse* reports that the bulls (human beings) attack one another (86:6; 87:1). *Jubilees* is also closer to the *Animal Apocalypse*, in identifying human wickedness as coming into existence before the deed of the Watchers (*1 Enoch* 85:4, a reference to Cain's slaying Abel, but nothing about Adam's sin; cf. *1 Enoch* 32:6).[377]

With regard to the giants' violence, *Jub.* 5:7-9 does not speak of the giants' violence against humankind and against animals. Stuckenbruck notes that in the *Jubilees* account "the motif of intramural violence ... is restricted to the giants themselves".[378] The more elaborate description in 7:22, however, which includes the names of three kinds of giants similar to *1 Enoch* 7:2 (so Syncellus, but not the same), does indicate that the Elyo killed human beings and that violence and bloodshed subsequently spread to humankind and the animal kingdom (7:23-24) and so supports a reading of 5:2-3 as something effected by the Watchers' act. According to 1 Enoch 7:5 they also drink blood (*1 Enoch* 7:5). Drinking blood becomes a major theme in *Jub.* 6:18, 38 and 7:29-33, but not as an act attributed to the giants.

While the giants selfdestruct, as in *1 Enoch*, the fate of the Watchers, who must face judgement, becomes for the author of *Jubilees* a paradigm for any who transgress their nature without discrimination (5:13-16).[379] As Stuckenbruck notes, "What the angels have done *inter alia* through both their sexual union with women and their teaching serves, by way of negative example, as a warning for anyone

---

[375] So van Ruiten, *Primaeval History Interpreted*, 197; see also the discussion in Kvanvig, "Gen 6,3 and the Watcher Story," who sees the reference in *Jub.* 4:17-26 to Enoch's writings as evidence that he must have known them (295).

[376] As Reed, *Fallen Angels*, observes, "the causal link between the Watchers' sexual misdeeds and the proliferation of human wickedness is no clearer than in Gen 6" (91). But see our discussion above, where it is, at least, implied.

[377] See VanderKam, "Enoch Traditions," 328.

[378] Stuckenbruck, "Origins of Evil," 111.

[379] According to VanderKam, "Enoch Traditions," "The tale of the Watchers performs ... the function, not of accounting for the origin of evil, but of explaining its escalation just before the flood" (329). *Jub.* 5:13-16 indicate that it does more than that.

who would behave in the same way".[380] This is implied in the *Book of the Watchers*, but never made explicit.[381] There the focus is on defilement of holy beings, who, according to 12 – 16, have abandoned their heavenly station, and are perhaps even thought of as priests in the heavenly sanctuary. This has then led some to suspect that their sexual wrongdoing a warning to priests, in particular, but it may be wider than just to priests, as our discussion above has shown. In *Jubilees*' account, the motif of defilement occurs in 4:22, and becomes a major emphasis elsewhere, as we shall see, where it applies, in particular, to intermarriage of both any Israelite and of priests. The suspected analogy in the *Book of the Watchers* is brought to full application in *Jubilees*, but never in quite as explicit a manner as saying: as the Watchers defiled themselves by taking human wives, so you must not defile yourselves by taking wives from beyond your kind, namely from beyond the holy people, Israel, though it comes close to it. The author cites the Watchers as a negative example of sexual wrongdoing in *Jub.* 7:21, but beyond that, the myth plays no further role in the many exhortations concerning intermarriage. This would be surprising if the author, at least, of *1 Enoch* 12 – 16, had intended people to hear an allusion to illicit marriages of priests. The author of *Jubilees* has not heard it that way. At most, the myth finds an echo later in Jacob's assertion that he has not "corrupted his way" (25:7), an echo of the exposition of the consequences of the Watchers' deeds in 5:2-4, but, as in the *Aramaic Levi Document*, what inspires the concern with intermarriage lies elsewhere.

The repeated motif in *Jubilees* 5 of transgressing one's nature derives from Gen 6:12, as we have seen, but it might also stand indirectly under the influence of *1 Enoch* 2:1 – 5:4, where wisdom instruction appeals to natural order to warn against flouting what God has ordained. *Jubilees* appears also to share with *1 Enoch* 6 – 11 the view that the giants selfdestructed before the flood and that the Watchers were bound (cf. *1 Enoch* 89:6 which has the giants die in the flood). *Jub.* 7:21-25 indicates a causal connection between the Watchers' sexual wrongdoing and the flood, but in a manner that suggests a sequence of causation resulting in the human wickedness which was dealt with in the flood.

Jubilees differs somewhat from *1 Enoch* in its explanation of evil spirits, though it shares the same terminology.[382] In both, they survived the flood. While *1 Enoch* 15 has them emerge from the corpses of the giants and so survive the flood, *Jubilees* simply derives them from the Watchers, whom it describes as "the fathers

---

[380] Stuckenbruck, "The Origins of Evil," 115.

[381] As Reed, *Fallen Angels*, observes, "at the root of evils that led to the Flood lies the impurity caused by the improper choice of marriage partners. The typological interpretation of angelic sin thus echoes the implicit critique of impure priests in 1 En. 12 – 16" (92).

[382] So VanderKam, "Demons," 350.

of these spirits" (10:5).[383] In this, *Jubilees* is closer to the formulation in *1 Enoch* 10:15, which can be read as referring to the spirits as the sons of the Watchers. *Jubilees*, however, differs from *1 Enoch* in massively qualifying the extent of their presence, reporting that they, too, were bound (10:1-7) and then only ten per cent of their number were released (10:8-14). It also identifies their leader, Mastema (משטמה), from the same root as "satan" (שטן),[384] meaning : "enemy or adversary", and so merges the Watcher myth, with its spirits let loose, with the more controlled tradition, reflected in Job 2 and Zechariah 3, of a "satan" participating in the divine court and negotiating with Yahweh. In 17:16, for instance, Mastema negotiates the testing of Abraham. As Reed notes, *Jubilees* also portrays their activity, such as enticement to idolatry, not as "an extension of the Watchers' corrupting teaching but part of Mastema's activity as divinely sanctioned *satan*".[385] Another contrast is *Jubilees*' account of their allotment to rule the nations, while God rules Israel (15:31-32),[386] an element of *Jubilees*' major concern with demarcation of the holy from the unholy. The somewhat narrow compass of the activity suggested by *1 Enoch* 15:11, especially if we accept the reconstruction of Tigchelaar,[387] finds an echo in *Jubilees*' note that Noah was taught antidotes to their plagues (largely understood as the afflictions of various forms of illness):

> We told Noah all the medicines for their diseases with their deceptions so that he could cure (them) by means of the earth's plants. Noah wrote down in a book everything (just) as we had taught him regarding all the kinds of medicine. (10:12-13)

Jubilees, however, goes beyond this in attributing to them much greater roles, such as their leadership of the nations, and their inspiration to idolatry and sexual wrongdoing, though primarily the responsibility for such actions lies with human beings, themselves, not with the spirits. As Reed notes, this part of the change in focus towards human culpability characteristic both of *Jubilees* and of the *Animal*

---

[383] VanderKam, "Demons," notes that "fathers" here could mean "ancestors" (349). He notes that *1 Enoch* 19:1 refers to the spirits of the angels who mingled with women (350).

[384] See the discussion of the names, "Mastema", "Satan", and "Belial/Beliar" in Wright, *Evil Spirits*, 157-60.

[385] Reed, *Fallen Angels*, 94. She adds: "*Jubilees* even stresses that there would be no need for him and his demons to torment humankind, if it were not for one fact: 'The evil of humankind is great'" (94).

[386] On the background to this notion, including Deuteronomy 32, see VanderKam, "Demons," who also draws attention to Psalm 106:35-37 and Psalm 95:5 LXX, which identifies the gods of the nations as δαιμόνια (352-53).

[387] Tigchelaar, *Prophets of Old*, 204-207, and on this, see the discussion of *1 Enoch* 15:11 above.

Apocalypse and the *Epistle of Enoch,* [388] which declares, "Lawlessness was not sent upon the earth; but men created it by themselves" (98:4).

In relation to sexuality, *Jubilees* shares with *1 Enoch* the depiction of the giants' activity primarily in terms of violence and bloodshed, but, unlike *1 Enoch*, may also allude to sexual wrongdoing on their part:

> He told them about the punishment of the giants and the punishment of Sodom — how they were condemned because of their wickedness; because of the sexual impurity, uncleanness, and corruption among themselves they died in (their) sexual impurity. (*Jub.* 20:5)

The reference to sexual wrongdoing probably applies only to Sodom, as the following verse indicates. Thus the depiction of the giants in *Jubilees* appears to echo that of the *Book of the Watchers* in not portraying the giants as emulating the actions of their fathers in this regard, somewhat contrary to what one might otherwise expect, both given the focus on the Watchers' wrongdoing and given the frequency with which sexual violence accompanies warfare and bloodshed (then and now).

The demons ply a wider repertoire than the giants, which, as in *1 Enoch* 15:11-12, includes bringing harm and illness to individuals, against which the angels teach Noah herbal antidotes (10:10, 12-14). In *Jubilees* their repertoire appears more extensive. The major concern in Noah's speech is that demons (like the giants before them) will lead Noah's sons to bloodshed (7:27-28; similarly 10:1-6 and in Mastema's role description in 10:10) and consumption of blood (7:29-33). Both elements are associated more with giants in the *Book of the Watchers*. Elsewhere *Jubilees* shows the range as including also idolatry (11:2-5; 12:3, 5, 20) and enticement to sexual wrongdoing (22:16-22), closely connected with separation from Gentiles. *1 Enoch* 6 – 16 does not link it explicitly to the role of demons, though such separation matters, particularly where sexual enticement and exposure through foreign women to sorcery and divination is assumed.

In *Jubilees*, unlike in both the *Book of the Watchers* and the *Animal Apocalypse*, we do not have reference to two descents, that of Asael (the first star), and that of Shemihazah and his associates (the other stars). As in the *Birth of Noah* (*1 Enoch* 106:13-14), there is a single descent. There is no reference to the teaching of metallurgy by Asael and, associated with it, the enhanced seduction of women through cosmetics and jewellery. The guilt lies squarely on the Watchers. As also in the *Animal Apocalypse*, nothing in *Jubilees'* version of the myth suggests women were to blame in seducing the Watchers. Within most allusions to the myth in *Jubilees* the focus is on the Watchers' sexual intercourse with human women, as in the *Animal Apocalypse* and the *Birth of Noah*. This may simply be

---

[388] Reed, *Fallen Angels*, 95.

the result of reworking the story, particularly to suit the author's emphasis on sexual wrongdoing.

While in some respects *Jubilees* may be acting rather autonomously in using *1 Enoch*, it probably also knows a form of the myth, which is independent both of Genesis and the accounts in *1 Enoch*. A major difference is its portrayal of the background for sending the Watchers. In 4:15 it reports that during Jared's "lifetime the angels of the Lord who were called Watchers descended to earth to teach mankind and to do what is just and upright on the earth". It depicts their descent not as the result of lusting for attractive women, whom they see from on high, which leads them to rebel and abandon their heavenly sanctuary (cf. *1 Enoch* 6:1-7; 12:4; 15:3), but as the result of a divine commission ("his angels whom he had sent to the earth" 5:6). They had a "divine mandate" (7:21). Their image is, in that sense, closer to Asael, who taught metallurgy, but *1 Enoch* sees that as inappropriate knowledge which led to making weapons of war and the adornments and cosmetics which women used to meet the eyes of Shemihazah and his companions with seduction (*1 Enoch* 8:1-2; see also the sequence of the first star and the many stars in 86:1-6). Their having a divine mandate does not serve to ameliorate their guilt, as Reed suggests, who see *Jubilees* thereby characterising these angels not as evil so much as weak and thus disobedient".[389] Rather, if anything, their having mandate enhances their guilt. This comes to the fore especially in 7:21-25.

The list of teaching brought by Shemihazah and his companions in *1 Enoch* 8:3 begins with sorcery and spells (recalling 7:1), but ends with information about the signs of the sun, moon, stars, shooting stars, and the earth, not so distant from what Enoch learns in the *Book of the Luminaries* (*1 Enoch* 72-82), and is hailed as a model of order in *1 Enoch* 2:1 – 5:4. One might even argue that the task of these Watchers might well have been to give such licit information, although, as *Jubilees* notes, primarily with a focus on what is "just and upright" (4:15). Such is now the kind of instruction given Moses from heavenly sources. According to 4:21 angels instruct Enoch concerning "everything on earth and in the heavens – the dominion of the sun – and he wrote down everything". Elsewhere *Ps-Eupolemus* has angels give instruction to Enoch, and giants who survived the flood are probably to be seen as bearers of this learning to Abraham.[390] Teaching does not in fact feature as a negative aspect in *Jubilees*' portrait of the Watchers wrongdoing, although 8:1-4 shows that the author knows of illicit teaching stemming from the Watchers about omens and heavenly signs.[391] Later angels taught Noah herbal medicine (10:10, 13). This recalls the negative image in *1 Enoch* 7:1 about

---

[389] Reed, *Fallen Angels*, 90.

[390] Stuckenbruck, "Origins of Evil," 93-98, 113.

[391] So VanderKam, "Enoch Traditions," 328.

Shemihazah and his companions teaching such things as the cutting of roots (see also 8:3).[392] There is, at least some ambiguity about what constitutes appropriate knowledge, although, as we have seen, the *Book of the Watchers* appears to target certain kinds of information and practices, related to sorcery and divination. This, then, finds an echo in what *Jubilees* considers to be the illicit knowledge discovered by Kainan and in what Yahweh tells Abraham, who begins to observe the stars, is redundant and superfluous, because "everything is under his control" (12:16-18). It is significant, as Reed notes, that

> of all the teachings attributed to the fallen angels in the *Book of the Watchers* – metalworking cosmetics, sorcery, pharmacology, spell-binding, celestial divination, and generally "all manner of sins" – *Jubilees* includes only one. In effect, the author has transformed the motif of illicit angelic instruction from an etiology of sin into an etiology of divination.[393]

Significantly, also, such knowledge is not gendered as in 1 Enoch, where it forms part of what makes women dangerous.

Jubilees has thus either drawn on other traditions, or more likely, creatively reworked the ones at its disposal. The best case for dependence lies with *Jubilees'* use of the *Book of the Watchers*, where most of the specific parallels occur. It may have known the version in the *Animal Apocalypse*, though, with the *Book of the Watchers*, it differs from it in relation to the demise of the giants, who, according to *Jubilees*, selfdestruct before the flood, but shares with it other distinctive features. These include perhaps the notion that human beings fought among themselves, the belief that wrongdoing was in the world before the Watchers' deed, and the view, however differently expressed, that the nations are to be seen as under demonic leadership (wild animals). It does not share with either the *Book of the Watchers* or with the *Animal Apocalypse* the twofold visitation of first Asael, and then, Shemihazah and his associates, nor that the Watchers' descent (a single descent) was an act of lust or rebellion. The latter motif cannot be derived from the Enochic sources which we have nor from Genesis, and probably indicates the author also used sources for the myth unknown to us.

Beyond the initial act of sexual wrongdoing, the Watchers' having sexual intercourse with human women, the account of their influence deals with sexual wrongdoing as an important theme, but, as in much of *Jubilees*, without much specific detail. There are, however, specific acts. One occurs among Noah's sons and to this we turn.

---

[392] Stuckenbruck, "Origins of Evil," writes: "Just as in the Enochic traditions, *Jubilees* derives good and bad knowledge, respectively, from good and bad angels. However, just what it is that distinguishes the good from the bad is different" (114).

[393] Reed, *Fallen Angels*, 93.

3.2.2   Ham Uncovers his Father's Nakedness (7:7-25)

The narrative is based on Gen 9:20-27. Both accounts are set out below.

Jubilees 7	Genesis 9
(1-5 Noah plants a vineyard and celebrates the feast of the grape harvest)	20 Noah, a man of the soil, was the first to plant a vineyard.
6 He was very happy and he and his sons happily drank some of this wine.	21 He drank some of the wine and
7 When evening came, he went into his tent. He lay down drunk and fell asleep.	became drunk,
He was uncovered in his tent as he slept.	and he lay uncovered in his tent.
8 Ham	22 And Ham, the father of Canaan,
saw his father Noah naked and went out	saw the nakedness of his father,
and told his two brothers outside	and told his two brothers outside.
9 Then Shem took some clothes, rose — he and Japheth	23 Then Shem and Japheth took a garment,
and they put the clothes on their shoulders	laid it on both their shoulders,
as they were facing backwards.	and walked backward
They covered their father's shame	and covered the nakedness of their father;
as they were facing backwards.	their faces were turned away, and they did not see their father's nakedness.
10 When Noah awakened from his sleep,	24 When Noah awoke from his wine
he realized everything his youngest son had done to him.	and knew what his youngest son had done to him,
He cursed his son and said: "Cursed be Canaan. May he become an abject slave to his brothers".	25 he said, "Cursed be Canaan; lowest of slaves shall he be to his brothers."
11 Then he blessed Shem and said:	26 He also said,
"May the Lord, the God of Shem, be blessed.	"Blessed by the LORD my God be Shem;
May Canaan become his slave.	and let Canaan be his slave.
12 May the Lord enlarge Japheth,	27 May God make space for Japheth,
and may the Lord live	and let him live
in the place where Shem resides.	in the tents of Shem;
May Canaan become their slave'.	and let Canaan be his slave."

The differences are minor.[394] They come mainly in 7:11-12, which deal with what appears to be the main interest of the passage, the cursing of Canaan. Canaan and the Canaanites are to become the slaves of Shem and his sons. Later, *Jubilees* will explain that the Canaanites should never even have been in the land called after them in the first place, because it was not allotted to them (10:29), but here the

---

[394] See the detailed discussion in van Ruiten, *Primaeval History Interpreted*, 282-87.

curse is motivated by Ham's misdeed. In *Jubilees*, Noah blesses the God of Shem, not Shem, and declares that God will live in the place where Shem resides, not that Japheth will do so. This reinforces the holiness of the land. The curse of Canaan required a serious warrant. In both accounts that warrant lies in the alleged sexual wrongdoing of Canaan's father, Ham. The story assumes that the judgement of the father's sin may rightly fall on the son.

The act of sexual wrongdoing consisted in Ham's looking at the naked body of his father. The concern is that he saw his father's genitals. The brothers go to great lengths to cover their father's genitals without seeing them – by facing backwards. Noah realises in the morning "everything his youngest son had done to him". Had he done more than look? He had not uncovered his father, for Noah had gone to bed in that drunken state and lay uncovered, as the narratives, without the slightest disapproval of such behaviour, tell us. The narrative does not suggest that Ham did more than look. Correspondingly, the brothers make every effort not to look.

Nakedness had been a theme already in the context of the story of the garden, to which we shall return below. Here in relation to it we note only the issues of nakedness. *Jubilees'* idealised image of Adam in the garden portrays his nakedness as unproblematic: "While he was working (it) he was naked but did not realize (it) nor was he ashamed" (3:16). This reflects Gen 2:25, "And the man and his wife were both naked, and were not ashamed". It contains a play on words between naked ערום and the serpent being crafty ערום, which *Jubilees* does not seek to replicate. While *Jubilees* speaks only of Adam, it assumes both were naked. They had already had sexual intercourse at the point of the women's creation (*Jub.* 3:6-7). They do not have sexual intercourse in the garden, but they are sexual beings and have no shame about their nakedness. It may be that *Jubilees* speaks only of Adam and not "the man and his wife" in order to avoid the suggestion that Adam looked on the nakedness of his wife,[395] although this somewhat strains credibility, given the account of her creation. Yet *Jubilees* clearly assumes sexual continence throughout their stay in the garden and only after the expulsion mentions sexual intercourse, which leads to the birth of children (3:33; 4:1). Both accounts of the eating of the fruit are set out below.

Jubilees 3	Genesis 3
20 … So she took some of it and ate (it).	6 … she took of its fruit and ate; and she
21 She first covered her shame with fig	also gave some to her husband, who was
leaves and then gave it to Adam.	with her,
He ate (it),	and he ate.
his eyes were opened,	7 Then the eyes of both were opened,
and he saw that he was naked.	and they knew that they were naked;

---

[395] So van Ruiten, *Primaeval History Interpreted*, 90.

22 He took fig leaves and sewed (them); (thus) he made himself an apron and covered his shame.	and they sewed fig leaves together and made loincloths for themselves

Jubilees follows Genesis in identifying the moment of eating the fruit as the point where awareness of nakedness and the need to cover one's sexual parts begin. It enhances the story by reporting the actions of each rather than of both together. The woman covers her shame before she approaches Adam to offer him the fruit.[396] Perhaps this, too, seeks to avoid the suggestion that Adam looked on her nakedness in the garden with eyes awakened to shame.[397]

Jubilees also follows Genesis in reporting that God made skins for them for clothing (Gen 3:21; *Jub.* 3:26), but moves immediately to their dismissal from the garden and to Adam's action: "while he was leaving: he burned incense as a pleasing fragrance" (3:27). This fits the image of Eden as the Holy of Holies before which incense was offered.[398] In this context *Jubilees* again refers to nakedness: Adam made a morning offering of incense – "in the early morning when the sun rose at the time when he covered his shame".[399] This was appropriate for a priest officiating in the holy place (Exod 20:26; 28:40-43). Then 3:30-31 notes:

> But of all the animals and cattle he permitted Adam alone to cover his shame. For this reason it has been commanded in the tablets regarding all those who know the judgment of the law that they cover their shame and not uncover themselves as the nations uncover themselves.

In part, this reflects learned interest in dealing with the question why only human beings wear garments, but, more significantly, it underlines the requirement to clothe oneself as a divine commandment, and at the same time sets it in contrast to the behaviour of the nations.[400] It is likely that the very different attitude towards nakedness in Hellenistic culture lies behind this comment. This would cohere with what we have already noted in discussing the Watchers and also with the references, later, to abandoning circumcision, which would have exposed Jewish

---

[396] See Halpern-Amaru, *Empowerment*, who sees the setting of the man and the woman in parallel as resulting in "a greater awareness of the woman as a character and a more sympathetic view of her" (13).

[397] So van Ruiten, *Primaeval History Interpreted*, 96.

[398] So van Ruiten, *Primaeval History Interpreted*, 88.

[399] On the dual reference in *Jubilees*, as in Genesis, to Adam's covering himself, see van Ruiten, *Primaeval History Interpreted*, 106-107 n. 100.

[400] Scott, *On Earth as in Heaven*, observes that *Jubilees* emphasises the expulsion from the garden in order to establish a parallel with the exile of Israel from the Land. "In a similar way, the text is concerned that Israel in exile will act like the nations" (135).

men to potential embarrassment in naked sports.[401] Part of the problem with nakedness at the Hellenistic gymnasium was its proximity to the temple and that priests might attend. Male nakedness in the holy space was an offence to God.[402] Strictly speaking, nakedness was acceptable in the Holy of Holies which was the garden of Eden, as long as the first couple were unaware, although sexual intercourse was not. Once they became aware of their nakedness, it became and remained unacceptable. Now it is assumed that in all public places nakedness is to be covered.

The command to cover one's nakedness features also in Noah's speech.

> Noah began to prescribe for his grandsons the ordinances and the commandments — every statute which he knew. He testified to his sons that they should do what is right, cover the shame of their bodies, bless the one who had created them, honor father and mother, love one another, and keep themselves from fornication, uncleanness, and from all injustice (7:20-21).

If the formulations are designed to reflect the account of Ham's misdeed, then we might recognise its influence not only in "cover the shame of their bodies", but also in "bless the one who had created them" (Noah blesses the God of Shem), and "honor father and mother" (Ham dishonoured Noah).

The specific sexual wrongdoing in the Ham story is thus a son's seeing the genitals of his father. It is a special case of a more general prohibition of not uncovering one's sexual parts which we find associated with the account of the garden of Eden. *Jubilees* characterises this as typical of the nations and this may well reflect reaction to practices in Hellenistic culture of naked sports. This may well also lie behind *Jubilees'* treatment of the account of Abraham and of the command concerning circumcision, to which we turn.

---

[401] On this see VanderKam, *Book of Jubilees*, 2001, p. 21, and our discussion in the conclusion.

[402] So Michael L. Satlow, "Jewish Constructions of Nakedness in Late Antiquity," *JBL* 116 (1997) 429-54, 449-51.

3.2.3   Stories of Abraham

3.2.3.1   Abram, Sarai and Pharaoh (13:11-15)

Jubilees recounts the sojourn of Abram in Egypt during which the Pharaoh took Sarai.

Jubilees 13	Genesis 12
11 So Abram went to Egypt in the third year of the week. He lived in Egypt for five years before his wife was taken from him by force. 12 Egyptian Tanais was built at that time – seven years after Hebron. 13 When the pharaoh took Abram's wife by force for himself, the Lord punished the pharaoh and his household very severely [lit. punished with great punishments] because of Abram's wife Sarai. 14 Now Abram had an extremely large amount of property: sheep, cattle, donkeys, horses, camels, male and female servants, silver, and very (much) gold. Lot — his brother's son — also had property. 15 The pharaoh returned Abram's wife Sarai and expelled him from the land of Egypt. He went to the place where he had first pitched his tent — at the location of the altar, with Ai on the east and Bethel on the west. He blessed the Lord his God who had brought him back safely.	10 Now there was a famine in the land. So Abram went down to Egypt to reside there as an alien, for the famine was severe in the land. 11 When he was about to enter Egypt, he said to his wife Sarai, "I know well that you are a woman beautiful in appearance; 12 and when the Egyptians see you, they will say, 'This is his wife'; then they will kill me, but they will let you live. 13 Say you are my sister, so that it may go well with me because of you, and that my life may be spared on your account." 14 When Abram entered Egypt the Egyptians saw that the woman was very beautiful. 15 When the officials of Pharaoh saw her, they praised her to Pharaoh. And the woman was taken into Pharaoh's house. 16 And for her sake he dealt well with Abram; and he had sheep, oxen, male donkeys, male and female slaves, female donkeys, and camels. 17 But the LORD afflicted Pharaoh and his house with great plagues because of Sarai, Abram's wife. 18 So Pharaoh called Abram, and said, "What is this you have done to me? Why did you not tell me that she was your wife? 19 Why did you say, 'She is my sister,' so that I took her for my wife? Now then, here is your wife, take her, and be gone." 20 And Pharaoh gave his men orders concerning him; and they set on the way, with his wife and all that he had.

Jubilees makes significant changes. It omits Abram's strategy of connivance in calling Sarai his sister. Instead, it reports curtly in 13:11 that "his wife was taken from him by force" and repeats this in 13:13. Accordingly, Pharaoh is punished (13:13). The sexual wrongdoing is clear. Pharaoh took what belonged to Abram and did so "by force". This might amount to adultery by force and so, rape. Against this conclusion Halpern-Amaru argues that, with frequent shifts of subject and scene, the rapid narrative generates the perception that the divine intervention 'because of Abram's wife Sarai' comes immediately and that there has been no time for violation of her purity.[403]

The argument, however, is not strong. The "frequent shifts of subject and scene" and "rapid narrative" need not imply this at all. Halpern-Amaru points out that *Jubilees* omits reference to Sarai's beauty, Abram's ruse, and reverses Abram's good fortune so that it becomes a fruit of God's providence, not a reward from Pharaoh for his enjoyment of Sarai.[404] Nevertheless *Jubilees* uses the word, *hyd*, which expresses an act of force, so that at least in the Ethiopic some violence is done to Sarai in that act and the conclusion that sexual violence followed lies close at hand. On the other hand, one should imagine that within the author's value system, had Sarai had sexual intercourse with Pharaoh, she, like Bilhah, later, would have become unclean for her husband (33:7). It would also have implied contamination of the line. Interestingly, *Genesis Apocryphon*'s richly elaborated account (19.10 – 20.33) also speaks of Sarai being taken "by force" (20.11), but then makes very clear that Sarai remained untouched. *Jubilees* probably agrees.[405]

The focus seems, however, to be less on what happened to Sarai, and more on portraying Abram as victim and as beyond reproof by deleting his deceit. Consistent with this, *Jubilees* deletes altogether the second similar story about Abraham's connivance about Sarah because of Abimelech during his stay in Gerar (see Gen 20:1-18). He also omits the similar story about Isaac (see Gen 26:6-11). At most, one finds hints of the Genesis story concerning Rebecca in the warning attributed to Abimelech: "Any man who touches him or anything that belongs to him is to die" (*Jub.* 24:13), where "touch", in relation to Rebecca, will have sexual connotations. The author may well want to protect the image of Rebecca, who plays a key role in his accounts.

The focus on Abraham's experience with Pharaoh reappears in the discussion between God and Mastema, who proposes that Abraham be tested (17:15-18). The angel notes that God was aware that Abraham had already been extensively tested (eventually ten times – so 19:8), including when his wife was taken away forcibly (17:17). Pharaoh represents the world of foreign nations who practise sexual wrongdoing, in this case, if we assume intentions were fulfilled, both adultery and rape.

Much more significant is the commandment about circumcision.

---

[403] Cf. Halpern-Amaru, *Empowerment*, 49.

[404] Halpern-Amaru, *Empowerment*, 48-49.

[405] See also the rewriting of the episode of Abram and Pharaoh in Josephus *B.J.* 5.381; *Gen. Rabb.* 41.2; *Lev. Rabb.* 32.5. All indicate Sarai remained unviolated.

3.2.3.2 Abraham and Circumcision (15:11-34)

Jub. 15:11-14 closely matches the account in Gen 17:10-14 of the commandment to Abraham to circumcise all his males. The same is true of *Jubilees'* account of the circumcision of Isaac, Abraham himself, and his male household in 15:23-24 (cf. Gen 17:23-27). Then *Jubilees* adds a further exhortation: 15:25-34. It underlines the permanence of the law, warns against, as it puts it, using the image of circumcision, "circumcising of days" (15:25), that is, cutting them short. It reinforces the command with further threats of judgement in having the angel of the presence declare: "this is what the nature of all the angels of the presence and all the angels of holiness was like from the day of their creation" (15:27). That is not only exemplary, but also a ground for circumcision, because, as 15:28 states, "in front of the angels of the presence and the angels of holiness he sanctified Israel to be with him and his holy angels". This is an important assumption, as we shall see. Circumcision is a sign of belonging; for angels, with continence.

Jub. 15:28 again emphasises the command by issuing Moses with the direct instruction: "Now you command..." In 15:33-34 we then find a striking prediction, which in all probability reflects the author's time:

> The Israelites will prove false to this ordinance. They will not circumcise their sons in accord with this entire law because they will leave some of the flesh of their circumcision when they circumcise their sons. All the people of Belial will leave their sons uncircumcised just as they were born. (15:33)

The wrongdoing appears to be of two kinds: incomplete circumcision (leaving some of the flesh) and neglect of circumcision altogether by "the people of Belial". The likely reference is to Jews in the early second century who were known to have been concerned about their circumcision (1 Macc 1:14-15).[406] Already *Jub.* 1:20 mentions Belial in the context of influence from "the nations" and of people being trapped from following the proper path, where Moses prays that the people may not be destroyed.

This relates closely to the concerns about nakedness, noted earlier. As 15:34 puts it, "For they have made themselves like the nations". It is also highly probable that the judgement to which 15:34 then refers relates to the events of the period:

> Then there will be great anger from the Lord against the Israelites because they neglected his covenant, departed from his word, provoked, and blasphemed in that they did not perform the ordinance of this sign. For they have made themselves like the nations so as to be removed and uprooted from the earth. They will no longer have

---

[406] See the discussion in the previous section and the discussion of research in VanderKam, "*Origins and Purposes,*" 20.

forgiveness or pardon so that they should be pardoned and forgiven for every sin, for (their) violation of this eternal (ordinance).

The next major section deals with those who came to symbolise the sinful nations, Sodom and Gomorrah.

3.2.3.3   *The Destruction of Sodom (16:5-9) and the Sin of Lot (16:8)*

Genesis begins its story of Sodom and Gomorrah by recounting the appearance of Yahweh to Abraham (18:1), which becomes the appearance of three men, who promise that Sarah will have a son, and by relating Sarah's response (18:2-15). *Jubilees* reduces this episode to a mere 4 verses. Genesis then portrays these men as setting out for Sodom and Gomorrah and relates a conversation between Abraham and Yahweh in which Abraham persuades Yahweh to spare Lot (18:16-33). There follows in Genesis 19 the account of the visit of two angels to Lot, the gathering of the mob of men who want to male-rape the two angels, and the awful story of Lot offering up his daughters in their place (19:1-14). Lot then receives instructions to flee, which he does successfully, though on the way losing his wife, who looked back (19:15-29).

Jubilees reduces all this to only two verses (16:5 and 7). This is surprising given the importance of Sodom's wickedness elsewhere in *Jubilees* (e.g. 20:5). One suspects that, had male rape been an issue in the author's day, he would have exploited the Genesis story. This is not the case. Perhaps the issue was not irrelevance, but the offensiveness of Lot's offer of his daughter, which goes unmentioned with so much else. The first verse, 16:5, describes the event of judgement and its cause:

> During this month the Lord executed the judgment of Sodom and Gomorrah, Zeboim and all the environs of the Jordan. He burned them with fire and brimstone and annihilated them until the present in accord with what I have now told you (about) all their actions — that they were savage (*dawwāg*) and very sinful (*xaṭi'at*), (that) they would defile themselves (*rakʷsa*), commit sexual sins (*zemmut*) in their flesh, and do what was impure (*rekʷs*) on the earth.

The second verse, 16:7, records how the angel of the presence was involved in Lot's escape: "But we went about rescuing Lot because the Lord remembered Abraham. So he brought him out from the overthrow (of Sodom)" (16:7).

The detail of the cities' wrongdoing remains general. *Jubilees* may have assumed that its hearers would be familiar with the story. "Savage" captures something of the violence of the mob's attempt at male-rape. The rest remains general and indicates behaviour of a kind that extends beyond what is reported. It is typical of *Jubilees* to remain very general in its descriptions. How were they "very sinful (*xaṭi'at*)" and how would they "defile themselves (*rak*^{w}*sa*), commit sexual sins (*zemmut*) in their flesh, and do what was impure (*rek*^{w}*s*)"? Sexual wrongdoing is clearly a significant element. We may assume that the hearers of *Jubilees* would recall the story of attempted male-rape and would probably also imagine that they engaged in male homosexual acts generally, although this is not expressed. Gen 18:20 is also general: "Then the LORD said, 'How great is the outcry against Sodom and Gomorrah and how very grave their sin!'" (similarly 13:13 "Now the people of Sodom were wicked, great sinners against the Lord").

Within *Jubilees*, however, we find a number of references to Sodom and its fate in warnings. We see this use coming already in 16:6, which stands between the report of the judgement and that of the rescue: "The Lord will execute judgment in the same way in the places where people commit the same sort of impure actions (*rek*^{w}*s*) as Sodom — just like the judgment on Sodom". These "impure actions (*rek*^{w}*s*)" are primarily sexual. The first such instance follows immediately in the account of Lot and his daughters. "He and his daughters committed a sin on the earth which had not occurred on the earth from the time of Adam until his time because the man lay with his daughter" (16:8). The comment follows: "It has now been commanded and engraved on the heavenly tablets regarding all the descendants that he is to remove them, uproot them, execute judgment on them like the judgment of Sodom" (16:9). Compared with the account in Gen 19:30-38, *Jubilees'* very brief report now includes Lot as equally guilty along with his daughters. As in the story of Ham, *Jubilees* also espouses the political focus which the story has in Genesis to disparage the people of Moab and Ammon.[407]

The negative example of Sodom reappears in Abraham's speech to his sons and their children in 20:5, again, with the emphasis on sexual wrongdoing:

> He told them about the punishment of the giants and the punishment of Sodom — how they were condemned because of their wickedness (*'ekay*), because of their sexual impurity (*zemmut*), uncleanness (*rek*^{w}*s*), and corruption (*musenā*) among themselves they died in (their) sexual impurity (*zemmut*).

We note the link between the wickedness of the giants and the wickedness of Sodom, but the focus on sexual wrongdoing probably belongs to the latter, as the following verse indicates. That focus continues in 20:6

> Now you keep yourselves from all sexual impurity (*zemmut*) and uncleanness (*rek*^{w}*s*) and from all the contamination (*gemmānē*) of sin (*xaṭi'at*) so that you do not make our

---

[407] Halpern-Amaru, *Empowerment*, notes that the contamination also belongs to Lot's ancestry, since Haran died trying to save his father's idols and his mother is listed without pedigree (126).

name into a curse, your entire lives into a (reason for) hissing and all your children into something that is destroyed by the sword. Then you will be accursed like Sodom, and all who remain of you like the people of Gomorrah.

Sometimes the focus is directly on the severity of the judgement as in 22:22 ("As the people of Sodom were taken from the earth, so all who worship idols will be taken"; similarly 36:10), but even here the immediate context keeps the focus also on sexual wrongdoing: "for through Ham's sin Canaan erred. All of his descendants and all of his (people) who remain will be destroyed from the earth" (22:21).

In this section we have reference to the sin of incest, in which according to *Jubilees* Lot willingly colludes. The theme of incest will reappear below in relation to Reuben and to Tamar. We are left, however, only to imagine the gross wickedness of Sodom. The reference to savagery evokes the Genesis story of the mob's attempt at male-rape, but beyond that, we have more generic assertions of sexual wrongdoing: savage (*ḍawwāg*) and very sinful (*xaṭi'at*), ... defile themselves (*rakʷsa*), commit sexual sins (*zemmut*) in their flesh, and do what was impure (*rekʷs*) (16:5); impure actions (*rekʷs*) (16:6); wickedness (*'ekay*), ... sexual impurity (*zemmut*), uncleanness (*rekʷs*), and corruption (*musenā*) among themselves they died in (their) sexual impurity (*zemmut*) (20:5); sexual impurity (*zemmut*) and uncleanness (*rekʷs*) and contamination (*gemmānē*) of sin (*xaṭi'at*) (20:6). The author of *Jubilees* will have assumed his hearers could work out for themselves what these meant, but helped by other material within the book.

One of the major themes in *Jubilees*' account of the patriarchs returns to the people of Ham, the descendants of Canaan, in particular. It is the matter of intermarriage with Canaanites and Gentiles generally. It relates closely to the way *Jubilees* depicts the episode of the rape of Dinah. We therefore consider both together.

3.2.4 *Issues of Intermarriage and the Rape of Dinah*

3.2.4.1 *Warnings about Intermarriage*

Jubilees has already alluded to the "sinful nations" and their ways (1:9; 3:31; 6:35). Sodom and Gomorrah are the prime examples. Sometimes there have been references to the nations without further specification, but in others the issue is sexual wrongdoing. Thus they do not cover their sexual parts (3:31). Those who reject circumcision emulate them (15:34). The account of Ham introduced the accursed people of Canaan (7:7-12). They come into focus in particular in relation to the marriages of Isaac and his sons, Jacob and Esau. The issue of intermarriage with Canaanites becomes a major theme closely associated with concerns about sexual wrongdoing. Its roots lie even further back in *Jubilees'* understanding of creation, where God set Israel aside as a special people (2:19-20).[408]

The first hints of the issue of intermarriage come already in the genealogy of Adam's descendants. Seth marries not a daughter of Cain, as one might be led to conclude from Genesis, but his sister, Azura (4:11). This in part avoids marriage to a niece, a forbidden relationship for *Jubilees*, but it also avoids marrying into an evil line. *Jubilees* is concerned with such corrupting influences. Marrying outside the extended family or to corrupt families brings evil. So when Arpachsad marries his niece, this sets off the sinful act of Kainan, their son.[409] Similarly, following the marriage of Eber and then Peleg to wives of uncertain lineage, the offspring is called Reu, "evil", an aetiology to which *Jub.* 10:18 draws attention and which it links to the building of the tower of Babel: "He named him Ragew,[410] for he said: 'Mankind has now become evil through the perverse plan to build themselves a city and a tower in the land of Shinar'". Finally, Nahor's marriage outside the family, to "Iyaseka, the daughter of Nestag of the Chaldeans" (11:10), appears to be seen by *Jubilees* as the source of the idolatry which Abram must later confront.

The issue of appropriate and inappropriate marriage reappears in *Jubilees'* depiction of Sarai as Abraham's sister. In a similar way to Seth's marriage, this achieves two purposes. It avoids portraying Abraham as marrying his niece, a forbidden relationship, and it also avoids marriage to the daughter of Haran, whom it paints as an idolater.[411] Concern with choosing appropriate mates also accounts for the deletion of the scenes where first, Abraham's servant chances to meet Rebecca, and then Jacob chances to meet Rachel.[412] Choosing a spouse must be

---

[408] So, rightly, Eberhard Schwarz, *Identität durch Abgrenzung: Abgrenzungsprozesse in Israel im 2. vorchristlichen Jahrhundert und ihre traditionsgeschichtlichen Voraussetzungen: Zugleich ein Beitrag zur Erforschung des Jubiläenbuches* (Europäische Hochschulschriften 162; Frankfurt: Peter Lang, 1982): "Der Satz von der Aussonderung Israels aus den Völkern durch Gott selbst ist der ideologische Hintergrund für die Abgrenzungsforderung" (22) (tr. The statement about Israel's separation from the nations through God is the ideological background for the demand that they remain apart). See also VanderKam, "Anthropological Gleanings," 118-22.

[409] So VanderKam, *Book of Jubilees*, 2001: "The concern that drove the recording of such information was to prove the purity of the chosen line and to show that when a person did marry a woman from outside approved limits evil resulted" (115). But see Halpern-Amaru, *Empowerment*, who argues that Arpachsad married not his niece, but his grand niece (23, 30).

[410] On the name Ragew (MT Gen 11:18 רעו; LXX 'Ραγαύ) see VanderKam, *Jubilees Translated*, 61, 10:18 and John Rook, "The Names of the Wives from Adam to Abraham in the Book of *Jubilees*," *JSP* 7 (1990) 105-17, 115.

[411] On this see Halpern-Amaru, *Empowerment*, 34-36, and the discussion in the section on Abraham and Sarah below.

[412] See Halpern-Amaru, *Empowerment*, 38, 41-42.

undertaken much more seriously if dangers are to be avoided. So when *Jubilees* states tersely that Abraham took a wife for his son, Isaac (19:10), the issue is more than abbreviation. Similarly, *Jubilees* removes the almost casual response of Laban's to Jacob in Gen 29:19, "It is better that I give her to you than that I should give her to any other man".[413] Marriage, for *Jubilees*, is a good deal more serious than such a comment might indicate.

Already in his first address to his children (20:1-10) Abraham warns about sexual wrongdoing in the context of intermarriage. The speech shifts in 20:3 from being a report in the third person, to being one in the first person plural, perhaps reflecting close identification of the author with its relevance for his own time. Thus it reports Abraham's instruction "that we should keep ourselves from all sexual impurity (*zemmut*) and uncleanness (*rek^{w}s*); and that we should dismiss all uncleanness (*rek^{w}s*) and sexual impurity (*zemmut*) from among us" (20:3). The speech continues with specific instruction concerning women: "If any woman or girl among you commits a sexual offence, burn her in fire" (20:4a). It then returns to men:

> They are not to commit sexual offences (by) following their eyes and their hearts so that they take wives for themselves from the Canaanite women, because the descendants of Canaan will be uprooted from the earth (20:4b).[414]

The embedding of the warning about intermarriage within other concerns about sexual wrongdoing makes sense in the light of the author's reports later, which imply that such women are a source of sexual wrongdoing. That men might be "following their eyes and their hearts so that they take wives for themselves from the Canaanite women" recalls the sins of the Watchers with women in that they "saw that they were beautiful to look at. So they married of them whomever they chose" (5:1).

The exhortation is then reinforced with reference to the giants and Sodom in a manner typical of *Jubilees*, which depends heavily on intratextuality for building its case against sexual wrongdoing, and so fills its abstract terms with meaning:

> He told them about the punishment of the giants and the punishment of Sodom — how they were condemned because of their wickedness (*'ekay*), because of the sexual

---

[413] So Halpern-Amaru, *Empowerment*, 42.

[414] On the change to masculine plural see VanderKam, *Jubilees Translated*, 116 n. 20:4. See also Schwarz, *Identität*, who draws attention to the surprising motivation for forbidding intermarriage here in 20:4 and 22:20: because Canaan's seed is to be destroyed (33). He notes also that 22:21 relates this not primarily to Canaan's sin in taking the land, but to Ham's sexual wrongdoing against his father (34).

impurity (*zemmut*), uncleanness (*rek*^{w}*s*), and corruption (*musenā*) among themselves they died in (their) sexual impurity (*zemmut*). (20:5)

The connection is repeated in the following verse:

> Now you keep yourselves from all sexual impurity (*zemmut*) and uncleanness (*rek*^{w}*s*) and from all the contamination (*gemmānē*) of sin (*xaṭi'at*) so that you do not make our name into a curse, your entire lives into a (reason for) hissing and all your children into something that is destroyed by the sword. Then you will be accursed like Sodom, and all who remain of you like the people of Gomorrah. (20:6)

Then in 20:7 the speech continues with reference to idolatry, showing the implied close connection between sexual wrongdoing and idolatry among the Canaanites: "Do not follow their idols and their uncleanness (*rek*^{w}*s*)". The issue is thus not intermarriage *per se*, as though the sole concern is racial purity, but the influence to which according to *Jubilees* this exposes one, including both idolatry and sexual wrongdoing.

We shall return to this speech below, but for the present we note the prohibition of intermarriage with the Canaanites in the context of warnings about sexual wrongdoing. These begin with the general statement about "sexual impurity" (*zemmut*) and uncleanness (*rek*^{w}*s*)" and then move to the more specific: a woman or a girl who commits a sexual offence, who is to be burned with fire (20:4). In 30:7 a woman is to be burned who has been offered by her father to a Canaanite man: "burned because she has defiled (*rak*^{w}*sa*) the reputation of her father's house; she is to be uprooted from Israel". Jacob had earlier refused to give Dinah in marriage to Shechem in response to his father's request (30:3). Here in 20:3-5, the motif of fire recurs in the allusion to Sodom. Later, Judah's judgement on his daughter-in-law for prostitution assumes judgement by fire (41:17 = Gen 38:24). Incest carries a similar penalty: "Anyone who acts in this way — anyone who lies with his mother-in-law — is to be burned in fire so that he burns in it because impurity (*rek*^{w}*s*) and contamination (*gemmānē*) have come on them. They are to be burned" (41:25).[415] The sexual wrongdoing of the woman or girl in 20:4a might be prostitution, but it could equally be incest or being married to a Canaanite, especially in the light of the prohibition of men being drawn to go after Canaanite wives, which follows immediately in 20:4b. As we shall see in discussing the case of Dinah below, this penalty has its origins in laws against the

---

[415] On the motif of fire in relation to sexual wrongdoing as impurity, see Jacob Milgrom, "The Concept of Impurity in *Jubilees* and the *Temple Scroll*," *RevQ* 16 (1993) 277-84, 281. See also C. Albeck, *Das Buch der Jubiläen und die Halacha* (Berlin: Scholem, 1930) 26-29.

daughters of priests engaging in prostitution, which *Jubilees* now applies to the whole nation on the basis that the whole people is holy to God.

The warnings about the wickedness of humankind 21:21-23 in Abraham's instruction to Isaac, make no specific mention of sexual wrongdoing or of intermarriage in particular, but, reading them within the broader concerns of the *Jubilees*, we should see them as including those concerns, since these represent major dangers posed by the nations. The nations are characterised by "sin (*xaṭi'at*) and wickedness (*'ekay*) and all their deeds of impurity (*rek*ʷ*s*), worthlessness (*mennānē*) and contamination (*gemmānē*)" (21:21). The warning in 21:22 to avoid sins punishable by death might well allude to sexual wrongdoing, where capital punishment applies. Avoiding the nations includes also not marrying such foreigners. This is implied in the exhortation: "Depart from all their actions and from all their impurity (*rek*ʷ*s*)" (21:23).

At his celebration of the feast of Weeks with his sons (22:1-6) Abraham returns to the theme. He blesses God (22:7-9), then summons Jacob, his grandson, and declares before him what he had prayed that God would do for him. His statements include: "May he purify (*nasha*) you from all filthy pollution (*reshat rek*ʷ*s*) so that you may be pardoned for all your sin (*'abbasā*) and error through ignorance" (22:14). Given the wider concern in the context with sexual wrongdoing, this should be assumed to belong to what is meant by "all filthy pollution (*reshat rek*ʷ*s*)". In 22:16 he then addresses Jacob directly warning him about the nations:

> Separate from the nations, and do not eat with them. Do not act as they do, and do not become their companion, for their actions are something that is impure (*rek*ʷ*s*),and all their ways are defiled (*gammana*) and something abominable (*mennānē*) and detestable (*saqorār*).

The new element here is the command not to eat with them or to become their companions. While this may mean little more than having to do with the nations at all, it is likely that the author is deliberately singling out meals. If elsewhere Hellenistic practices are in view, we might see here a reference to *symposia*, although it could also refer to pagan cultic meals in general.[416] The focus could be the food eaten (which might be unclean or contain blood),[417] but the author speaks

---

[416] On the extent of influence of the Hellenistic banquet among Jews see Sandra R. Shimoff, "Banquets: The Limits of Hellenization," *JSJ* 27 (1996) 440-52, who traces its early influence in *Aristeas*, Ben Sira 31:12-19; 32:1-13 (445), and also, in part, at Qumran (seating by rank and mixing of wine) (450).

[417] On this, see Schwarz, *Identität*, who notes the importance of the food laws in Leviticus 11 and Deuteronomy 14, and especially the prohibition of eating blood, which *Jubilees* emphasises (7:6-7, 10-14; 7:28-33; 21:6, 18; cf. Gen 9:4) (24). He considers it

of actions, so that we should probably take his statements to include acts of sexual wrongdoing frequently associated with such meals, especially *symposia*. Other actions would be likely to include veneration of false gods. This is made more likely by 22:17 which seems to have in mind funeral cults: "They offer sacrifices to the dead, and they worship demons".[418] "They eat in tombs". There corpse impurity would also be a major concern.[419]

The speech continues, repeating the concern about impurity. "May he remove you from their impurity (*rek^{w}s*) and from all their error" (22:19). The association with sexual wrongdoing is apparent through what immediately follows, namely, the warning about marrying a Canaanite: "Be careful, my son Jacob, not to marry a woman from all the descendants of Canaan's daughters, because all of his descendants are (meant) for being uprooted from the earth" (22:20).[420] Again *Jubilees* links this with sexual wrongdoing elsewhere: "For through Ham's sin Canaan erred. All of his descendants and all of his (people) who remain will be destroyed from the earth". Here both the act and the people of the Canaanites are relevant. *Jub.* 22:22 then draws the parallel with Sodom: "As the people of Sodom were taken from the earth, so all who worship idols will be taken". Marrying a Canaanite woman goes one step further than eating with such people and becoming their companions. The dangers are idolatry and sexual wrongdoing, as in 20:7. The latter will becomes even clearer as we consider similar speeches below. Abraham's speech ends: "May the most high God keep you from

---

likely that the reference in 22:16 is to pagan cultic meals. He interprets "do not become their companions" on the assumption that its Hebrew original intended to prohibit making political alliances, an issue he sees reflected in 1 Macc 1:11 ("Let us go and make a covenant with the Gentiles around us") (29). Were an allusion to clean and unclean animals to be assumed, this would be unusual, since, as Ravid, "Purity and Impurity," argues, this does not feature elsewhere among *Jubilees*' concerns (65).

[418] On this see Adolphe Büchler, "Traces des idées et des coutumes hellénistiques dans le Livre des Jubilés," *REJ* 89 (1930) 321-48, who draws attention to *Sib. Or.* 3:547 as part of argument for links between *Jubilees* and the Hellenistic world of Egypt (324).

[419] Milgrom, "Concept of Impurity," notes that while the primary concern would appear to be corpse pollution, it also alludes to the possibility of intermarriage (282). See also Endres, *Biblical Interpretation*, 44. If the allusion is to corpse impurity, this would be striking since elsewhere *Jubilees* pays no attention to it. On this see Ravid, "Purity and Impurity," 66.

[420] Endres, *Biblical Interpretation*, commenting on the warnings in 22 about intermarriage beside those against idolatry, which he places in the context of Seleucid hellenization, writes: "In addition to these forbidden practices, marriage with non-Jews made it almost impossible to root out the pollution from the land, once the Gentile sinners had married into the Jewish community" (44).

corruption (*musenā*); and from every erroneous (*seḥtat*) way may he rescue you" (22:23).

Following this we have the account of Abraham's death (23:1-7) and the discourse of the angel of the presence which brings to a climax the first half of the book (23:8-32). The many references in this speech to wrongdoing are to be read in the light of what we have considered in the book so far, where it is clear that an important part of such action is sexual wrongdoing. This informs the reading of such references as pollution (*rekᵂs*), sexual impurity (*zemmut*), contamination (*gemmānē*) detestable actions (*saqorār*) (23:14). Everything that they do is impure (*rekus*) and something detestable (*saqorār*); all their ways are (characterized by) contamination (*gemmānē*), and pollution (*rekᵂs*) and corruption (*musenā*) (23:17); They will defile (*rakᵂsa*) the holy of holies with the impure (*rekᵂs*) corruption (*musenā*) of their contamination (*gemmānē*) (23:21). In the second half of the book these concerns are related in particular to the issue of intermarriage.

We have noted above that *Jubilees* does not report the story of Isaac, Rebecca and Abimelech (Gen 26:1-11). Of the three stories in Genesis, two involving Abraham, only the first mentions the taking of the wife and then makes no mention of Abraham's conniving strategy. In the account of Isaac there is an echo of the story in Abimelech's declaration that people are not to touch what is Isaac's, although there, too, *Jubilees* appears to have deliberately removed any possible allusion to Rebecca being violated by deleting reference to Isaac's wife: "Any man who touches him or anything that belongs to him is to die" (24:13); cf. Gen 26:11 "Whoever touches this man or his wife shall be put to death". *Jubilees* does, however, mention the conflict over the wells, which leads to the cursing of the Philistines (24:24-30), who will fall into the hands of the sinful nations and the Kittim. *Jubilees* names the Kittim separately not because they do not deserve the appellation, "sinful", but because of their distinctive role in its own time. The allusion is probably to the influential coastal cities of Phoenicia and Philistia who were important conduits of Hellenistic culture in the region and who were also vulnerable to Seleucid (and earlier Ptolemaic) expansion.[421] While in this context the association of sinful nations and the Kittim has no particular reference to sexual wrongdoing, the dangers of Hellenism which takes this form are an important backdrop for what follows, where the Canaanites represent their influence. As Endres notes, *Jubilees* does not miss the opportunity in 24:26 to

---

[421] See most recently again Jeff S. Anderson, "Denouncement Speech in *Jubilees* and Other Enochic Literature," in *Enoch and Qumran Origins: New Light on a Forgotten Connection* (ed. Gabriele Boccaccini; Grand Rapids: Eerdmans, 2005) 132-36, 134, taking up a proposal by Charles, *Jubilees*, 154-56. Endres, *Biblical Interpretation*, believes that *Jubilees* "interpreted the tension between Isaac and Abimelech as a type of the struggle between faithful Jews and Seleucid collaborators and invaders of his own day" (66).

attribute Isaac's failure to find water (its reading of Gen 26:32 in a form matching the LXX) to his "unjustified pact with Gentiles".[422]

We return to the theme of intermarriage with Canaanites in 25:1-3, where, like Abraham before her, Rebecca instructs Jacob not to marry a Canaanite:

> My son, do not marry any of the Canaanite women like your brother Esau who has married two wives from the descendants of Canaan. They have embittered my life with all the impure things (*rekʷs*) that they do because everything that they do (consists of) sexual impurity (*zemmut*) and lewdness (*merʿāt*). They have no decency [lit. there is no righteousness with them (masc.)] because (what they do) is evil (*ʾekuy*) [lit. it/he is bad]".[423] (25:1)

Genesis reports Esau's marriage to two Hittites and the bitterness it caused his parents: "When Esau was forty years old, he married Judith daughter of Beeri the Hittite, and Basemath daughter of Elon the Hittite; and they made life bitter for Isaac and Rebekah" (26:34-35).[424] Perhaps under the influence of the second reference in Genesis to this situation (Gen 27:46, "Rebekah said to Isaac, 'I am weary of my life because of the Hittite women'"), *Jubilees* speaks of the bitterness in relation only to Rebecca. It paints Esau, therefore, as the prime negative example, returning to it again in 27:8 and 35:15, although it is aware that Esau finally marries appropriately when he marries Mahalath a daughter of Ishmael (29:13), but mentions it only incidentally. It even presents Esau as deliberately tempting Jacob to marry one of the sisters of his Canaanite wives (25:8).

More important, Rebecca's instruction gives the reason why such intermarriage is inappropriate and so explicates the prohibitions of 21:21-23 and 22:16-22, where sexual wrongdoing seemed to be implicit. Here it is explicit:

> They have embittered my life with all the impure things (*rekʷs*) that they do because everything that they do (consists of) sexual impurity (*zemmut*) and lewdness (*merʿāt*). They have no decency [lit. there is no righteousness with them (masc.)] because (what they do) is evil (*ʾekuy*).[lit. it/he is bad]".

The "impure things (*rekʷs*)" relate to "sexual impurity (*zemmut*) and lewdness (*merʿāt*)". The masculine form of the pronoun "them" indicates a broadening of perspective to speak of the Canaanite people as a whole, not just of their women. The Canaanites are thus described as lacking "decency (lit. righteousness)" and

---

[422] Endres, *Biblical Interpretation*, 69.

[423] On the literal translation see VanderKam, *Jubilees Translated*, 159 n. 25:1.

[424] Endres, *Biblical Interpretation*, interprets *Jubilees*' omission of the names of the wives as "the height of insult", and its subordination of the Genesis account (Gen 26:34) within Rebecca's speech as expressing the author's disdain (75). On *Jubilees*' equation of Hittite with Canaanite, Endres notes a similar shift in Josephus *A. J.* 1.265 (76).

doing "evil (*'ekuy*)". The explication of "impure things (*rek^ws*)" in terms of "sexual impurity (*zemmut*) and lewdness (*mer'āt*)" is important for other contexts which speak of "impurity" or "impure things", where such connotations also lie close at hand. Even so, "sexual impurity and lewdness" remain undefined. Clearly, here, as earlier, the issue is not intermarriage *per se*, but what according to *Jubilees*, it inevitably brings, in particular, sexual wrongdoing.

The prohibition of intermarriage with the Canaanites continues to receive major emphasis in Rebecca's repetition of her instruction in 25:3, "Do not marry any of the women of this land but (someone) from my father's house and from my father's clan. Marry someone from my father's house", and in the remainder of the verse, where the motif of "righteousness" recurs: "The most high God will bless you; your family will become a righteous family and your descendants (will be) holy" (cf. "there is no righteousness with them" 25:1). It then portrays Jacob in ideal terms as fully committed to compliance: "nor have I even considered marrying any women of all the descendants of Canaan's daughters" (25:4). He has not even considered it! He also recalls Abraham's instruction: "For I recall, mother, what our father Abraham ordered me — that I should not marry anyone from all the descendants of Canaan's house" (25:5; cf. 20:4), cites his brother's frequent temptation to him to do so (25:8), and swears an oath that he will not commit such an offence (25:9).

This ideal response of Jacob also offers more insight into what *Jubilees* see as sexual wrongdoing. Thus it probably includes sexual intercourse before marriage: "Mother, I am now nine weeks of years [63 years] and have known no woman. I have neither touched (one) nor become engaged (to one)" (25:4). He repeats these claims in 25:7, where he cites his commitment to marry within the family:

> For this reason I have kept myself from sinning (*'abbasa*) and from becoming corrupted (*māsana*) in any ways during my entire lifetime because father Abraham gave me many orders about lewdness (*mer'āt*) and sexual impurity (*zemmut*).

We are being pointed by the author to earlier speeches, thus confirming what we deduced was their implied focus on sexual wrongdoing. The terms, "lewdness (*mer'āt*) and sexual impurity (*zemmut*)", had been used of the Canaanite people earlier (25:1). In 25:4 and 7 they focus on pre-marital engagement in sexual activity (knowing and even touching). It need not have this focus in 25:1, but may have been understood to include such behaviour. Other language of significance is the use of the words, "righteous" in 25:10 ("I will behave rightly"; cf. 25:1, 3) and "corrupt (*māsana*)" in 25:7 and 25:10: "will never conduct myself corruptly (lit. corrupt my way)" (*māsana fenot*; אשחית דרכי)". The latter recalls the special language used to describe the Watchers' sexual sin and its emulation among human beings and animals (5:2-3). Here, as there, it comes in the context of sexual behaviour, after Jacob has committed himself by oath in Rebecca's presence not to marry any of the descendants of Canaan's daughters nor do as his brother had done (25:9). As Milgrom observes, the issue also relates to the notion of Jacob and his descendants as "holy" (Deut 7:6; 14:2, 21; 26:19; 28:9), noting that in her instruction to Jacob about intermarriage Rebecca refers three times to Jacob as "holy seed" (25:3, 12, 18), hence the use of purity language.[425] For *Jubilees*, the contamination derives especially from ethical wrongdoing, an emphasis which, as Milgrom notes, has its background in the prophetic literature (Hos 6:8-10; Ezek 22:11-15) and in the notion that any transgression of God's commandments brings pollution (Num 15:22-23; Lev 4:2).[426]

Jubilees returns to the issue of intermarriage in 27:8-10, again taking as its starting point a passage in Genesis which speaks of Esau's wives.

Jubilees 27	Genesis 27
8 Rebecca went in and said to Isaac: "I despise my life because of the two Hittite women whom Esau has married. If Jacob marries one of the women of the land who are like them, why should I remain alive any longer, because the Canaanite women are evil?"	46 Then Rebekah said to Isaac, "I am weary of my life because of the Hittite women. If Jacob marries one of the Hittite women such as these, one of the women of the land, what good will my life be to me?"
9 So Isaac summoned his son Jacob, blessed and instructed him, and said to him: 10 "Do not marry any of the Canaanite women. Set out and go to Mesopotamia, to the house of Bethuel, your mother's father. From there take a wife from the daughters of Laban, your mother's brother."	28:1 Then Isaac called Jacob and blessed him, and charged him, "You shall not marry one of the Canaanite women. 2 Go at once to Paddan-aram to the house of Bethuel, your mother's father; and take as wife from there one of the daughters of Laban, your mother's brother."

In comparison with Genesis, *Jubilees* mentions Esau again explicitly by adding "whom Esau has married", replaces "one of the Hittite women" with "one of the women of the land", to enhance the generalising focus, and adds a reason: "because the Canaanite women are evil (*'ekuy*)". We might expect the hearer to bring to the latter the information implied in 25:1-10. They are evil in particular in relation to sexual wrongdoing, which characterises their people. Elsewhere *Jubilees* speaks of "the sinful nations" (23:23, 24, 27). Isaac responds to Rebecca's request and, as in Genesis, instructs Jacob not to marry a Canaanite: "Do not marry any of the Canaanite women". It comes here for the first time in Genesis; this is already its third occurrence in *Jubilees* where it has already been expressed by

---

[425] Milgrom, "Concept of Impurity," 281-82.
[426] Milgrom, "Concept of Impurity," 280.

Abraham and then Rebecca. In Genesis it appears almost as a ploy on Rebecca's part to enable Jacob to leave home without dishonouring his father. In *Jubilees* the initiative is far from a ploy. It is an imperative: Jacob must not marry a Canaanite and so must seek a wife from the kin elsewhere.

We shall return below to the special treatment in *Jubilees* of Laban's arrangement that Jacob first marry Leah, when we discuss the figure of Jacob. Jacob's flight from Laban takes him to Gilead, where finally Laban and Jacob reconcile. There *Jubilees* inserts an excursus on the former inhabitants of Gilead which coheres with the negative image of the nations. It returns to the subject matter of Genesis 6 and again mentions the giants, called *Rafaim*.

> The Lord destroyed them because of the evil things they did (*'akya*), for they were very wicked (*dawwāg* lit. savage). The Amorites – evil (*'ekuy*) and sinful (*xate'*) – lived in their place. Today there is no nation that has matched all their sins (*xaṭi'at*). They no longer have length of life on earth. (29:11)

As we have seen earlier, "the evil things they did" will have included sexual wrongdoing (cf. 20:5). This is probably also true of the Amorites. Their limited length of life recalls *Jubilees'* statement about the effects of wickedness in *Jubilees* 23, which, again, included sexual wrongdoing. The apparent digression keeps the focus on the sinfulness of the nations.

In the context of describing the resettlement of Jacob, Esau and Isaac, *Jubilees* mentions in the briefest possible terms Esau's marriage to Mahalath, Ishmael's daughter (29:8-9). Genesis brought this detail immediately after Isaac's instruction to Jacob not to marry a Canaanite (28:1-5). Esau had been so impressed by Isaac's instruction and by the pain he had caused Isaac that he now took an additional wife (Gen 28:6-9). *Jubilees* appears intent on sustaining the negative image of Esau and so omits reference to his change of heart.

3.2.4.2 *The Rape of Dinah*

The concern with the sinful nations returns with the account of Dinah and the Shechemites (30:1-4), based on Genesis 34:1-31.[427]

---

[427] See the extensive treatment in Endres, *Biblical Interpretation*, 120-54. See also Cana Werman, "*Jubilees* 30: Building a Paradigm for the Ban on Intermarriage," *HTR* 90 (1997) 1-22; Halpern-Amaru, *Empowerment*, 128-32; Himmelfarb, "Levi, Phinehas," 12-16; Christine E. Hayes, "Intermarriage and Impurity in Ancient Jewish Sources," *HTR* 92 (1999) 3-36, 15-25; Hayes, *Gentile Impurities*, 73-81; David Rothstein, "Sexual Union and Sexual Offences in *Jubilees*," *JSJ* 35 (2004) 363-84, 382-84.

Jubilees 30	Genesis 34
2 There Jacob's daughter Dinah was taken by force [lit. Eth and L: they took by force] to the house of Shechem, the son of Hamor the Hivite [LXX has Horite], the ruler of the land. He lay with her and defiled (rak^{w}sa) her. [lit. he defiled (rak^{w}sa) her since he slept with her] Now she was a small girl, twelve years of age.	1 Now Dinah the daughter of Leah, whom she had borne to Jacob, went out to visit the women of the region. 2 When Shechem son of Hamor the Hivite, prince of the region, saw her, he seized her and lay with her by force.

There are differences between the two accounts.[428] They agree on the detail that the act was one of force: taking her by force and lying with her (*Jub.* 30:2) or taking her and lying with her by force (Gen 34:2). *Jubilees* omits the detail that Dinah visited the women of the region, possibly because this might suggest she had put herself thereby in danger and that she should not have been mixing with the people of the land. Whereas Genesis makes Shechem directly responsible for the seizure, *Jubilees* indicates that more than one person was involved: *they took by force*. This may be intended to reflect on the people as a whole and not just on Shechem. *Jubilees* also adds: "he defiled (*rak^{w}sa*) her" and so reads: "he defiled (*rak^{w}sa*) her since he slept with her". It is preferable to retain the literal order,[429] since the one act results in the state of defilement. The motif of defilement comes later in Genesis (34:5, 13, 27). Finally, *Jubilees* emphasises that she "was a small girl, twelve years of age". This enhances the crime, because it means that Dinah had just reached marriageable age.[430] Her smallness enhances it still further – she had even less chance of resisting because of her size. *Jubilees* is recounting an isolated incident, but one which it wants the hearers to recognise as typical of the impurity of the nations expressed in this act of sexual violation. *Jubilees* clearly sees Dinah as a victim, unlike the apparent reading in *Aramaic Levi Document* which makes her share the blame in defiling her family (1:1 / 1c).

In what follows in 30:3-4 *Jubilees* abbreviates the Genesis story drastically, omitting most of Gen 34:3-31. Gone is the reference to Shechem's love (Gen 34:3,

---

[428] They begin already with 30:1, which has Jacob come to Salem near Shechem, whereas Genesis has him erect an altar near Shechem.

[429] On the translation see VanderKam, *Jubilees Translated*, 191 n. 30:2.

[430] On the complexities of Dinah's age in 30:2 which appears to conflict with information elsewhere in *Jubilees*, see Endres, *Biblical Interpretation*, 125-27, who concludes: "It seems to me simply to point out the heinous nature of the crime, the abduction and rape of so young a girl" (127).

8). Gone is Jacob's response to the proposal of marriage and the agreement[431] on the basis of the Shechemites' being circumcised (34:8-24). This would have accorded with the provision in Deut 22:28 that following rape an obligation for marriage followed. All references to the circumcision ruse have disappeared. It appears that *Jubilees* cannot even tolerate intermarriage with a Gentile who submits to circumcision and converts.[432] The motif of circumcision appears in 30:12, but in the context of prohibiting any such marriage. All that remains is the outrage of Jacob and his sons. *Jubilees* expresses this in terms of defilement: "Jacob and his sons were angry with the Shechemites because they had defiled (*rak^w sa*) their sister Dinah" (30:3), matching the addition of "defile (*rak^w sa*)" in 30:2 above.

The motif of deception remains. "They spoke deceptively [lit. with evil] with them,[433] acted in a crafty way toward them, and deceived them". But we hear nothing of the nature of that deception. Similarly we hear of the vengeance of Levi and Simeon "in a painful way" (30:4), but nothing about why it was so painful. Gone is Jacob's discontent with the actions of Levi and Simeon and their response: "Should our sister be treated like a whore?" (Gen 34:31).[434] One could read *Jubilees* to imply that Jacob lived up to his name and was also involved in the deception, but *Jubilees* is more concerned to justify their action and make it a model for all the descendants of Levi and to hail him a "friend and a just man" before God (30:17-20, 23).

The initial narrative of the event concludes with a third reference to the nature of the wrongdoing: "they had violated (*xafra*) their sister Dinah" (30:4). The angel of the presence then embarks on an extended discourse in which the incident becomes the basis for wider extrapolation:

> Nothing like this is to be done anymore from now on — to defile an Israelite woman. For the punishment had been decreed against them in heaven that they were to annihilate all the Shechemites with the sword, since they had done something shameful in Israel" (30:5).[435]

---

[431] As Endres, *Biblical Interpretation*, notes, for the author "negotiations with Gentiles would have horrified him and his community, for that would constitute a participation in Gentile uncleanness" (129).

[432] See Hayes, *Gentile Impurities*, 77.

[433] On the secondary addition of Levi and Simeon at this point in the Latin see VanderKam, *Jubilees Translated*, 191 n. 30:3-4.

[434] As Endres, *Biblical Interpretation*, notes, gone also in *Jubilees* is the criticism of Simeon and Levi which Genesis brings in 49:5-7 (148-49).

[435] Halpern-Amaru, *Empowerment*, notes the sudden shift to explicit biblical citation and the offer of a rationale for including the Dinah material which is without parallel in other accounts in *Jubilees*. It leads her to the conclusion that "it would appear that the author remained less than satisfied with his own interpretive use of the tale" (132). The

It takes as its basis the comment in Genesis: "he had committed an outrage in Israel by lying with Jacob's daughter, for such a thing ought not to be done" (Gen 34:7). Attention then falls on a number of acts of sexual wrongdoing. The defilement of Dinah consisted in making her unclean for another man (as in 33:7). "They [Genesis has the singular but all are deemed to be guilty] had done something shameful (*gabru xafrata*) in Israel" (similarly 30:7). "Something shameful (*gabru xafrata*)" evokes עֵרוַת דָּבָר in Deut 23:15; 24:1). Here in *Jubilees* the issue is not remarriage of women divorced by their first husband and then divorced again or widowed (as Deut 24:1), but rendering a virgin unclean. "There should not again be something like this within Israel — defiling (*rak^wsa*) an Israelite virgin" (30:6).

While the rape of a virgin stands as a prohibition in its own right, independent of involvement of "the nations", for *Jubilees* they are a source of such sin. In what follows the focus then falls not on the act of abduction and rape, but on the marriage of an Israelite woman with a Gentile. The transition is somewhat artificial, since the author must deal with an incomplete analogy, which will attack both parties, whereas in the original story Dinah is not portrayed as guilty. Thus he continues:

> If there is a man in Israel who wishes to give his daughter or his sister to any foreigner [lit. who is of the seed of the nations], he is to die. He is to be stoned because he has done something sinful and shameful within Israel. The woman is to be burned because she has defiled (*rak^wsa*) the reputation of her father's house; she is to be uprooted from Israel. (30:7)

Again we have the expression, "something ... shameful (*gabru xafrata*)". Giving one's daughter or sister to a foreigner are shameful acts worthy of death – to be visited on both the father or brother and the daughter.

A combination of texts informs the exposition. Burning the woman goes far beyond Torah in strictness. It matches the penalty which Judah wants to apply when he hears of Tamar's alleged prostitution in 41:17. This implies that *Jubilees* is equating intermarriage with prostitution. Perhaps the objection of the brothers found in Gen 34:31 but not in *Jubilees* ("Should our sister be treated like a whore?"), helped establish the connection, but, in addition, *Jubilees* has taken Lev 21:9 "When the daughter of a priest profanes herself through prostitution, she profanes her father; she shall be burned to death" and applied it to all Israel. *Aramaic Levi Document* appears also to applies this text to intermarriage (4Q213a 3-4 / 3a). It is not that *Jubilees* is argumentatively linking prostitution and

---

metaphoric reading imported to make the connection between the narrative and the discourse entails a break in style.

intermarriage in some speculative way which equates the two. Rather, he is reflecting a use of the word, זנות, for a wider range of sexual wrongdoing than prostitution.[436] We see this later in CD 4.15 – 5.12, and, as noted, it is assumed also in *Aramaic Levi Document*, upon which or upon whose common sources *Jubilees* depends.

Beside the broader use of זנות, the other major change is the application now to all Israel. The rationale for such an application lies in the author's belief that all Israel is holy, not just the priesthood, and that only Israel is holy.[437] *Jub.* 16:15-19 had already drawn on the language of Exod 19:6 to identify Jacob's seed as "a kingdom, a priesthood, and a holy people". The same image recurs in 33:20 ("It is the nation which he possesses; it is a priestly nation; it is a priestly kingdom; it is what he owns. No such impurity will be seen among the holy people").

Israel's holiness is explicitly stated in 30:8, where the author broadens the perspective further to include the prohibition of adultery.

No adulterer (*zamma*) or impure person (*rekus*) is to be found [masc.][438] within Israel throughout all the time of the earth's history, for Israel is holy to the Lord. Any man who has defiled (*rak^wsa*) (it) [L. *eum*; missing in Eth] is to die; he is to be stoned. [lit. they are to stone him].

While "adulterer" is clear, "impure person" remains without further definition, but, given the context, will have sexual connotations. These are not digressions, but typical of the sexual wrongdoing of the nations which holy Israel must avoid. The reference to stoning reflects the particular application of this principle to intermarriage, which receives further exposition in 30:9-10.

Here we find another text being taken up to serve the argument. Lev 18:21 forbids the practice of passing one's seed (offspring) to Molech, addressing child

---

[436] On the equation of intermarriage with harlotry see Endres, *Biblical Interpretation*, 137, 139. An analogous expansion takes place also in Greek with the word, πορνεία. See the discussion in Joseph Jensen, "Does Porneia Mean Fornication?" *NovT* 20 (1978) 161-84; F. Hauck, S. Schulz, "πόρνη," *TDNT* 6 (1968) 579-95; S. Erlandsson, "זָנָה," *TDOT* 4 (1981) 99-104.

[437] Cana Werman, "The Concept of Holiness and the Requirements of Purity in Second Temple and Tannaitic Literature," in *Purity and Holiness: The Heritage of Leviticus* (ed. M. J. H. M. Poorthuis and J. Schwartz; Jewish and Christian Perspectives Series 2; Leiden: Brill, 2000) 163-79, writes: "Although the Book of *Jubilees* expands the Biblical prohibitions to apply to the entire world, it restricts holiness. According to *Jubilees*, holiness is ascribed only to the People of Israel. It is not a goal to be sought but an absolute, a description of Israel's condition. The author of *Jubilees* used the term bestowed by Ezra – 'holy seed/descendants' – to refer to the People of Israel (16:26)" (172-73).

[438] See VanderKam, *Jubilees Translated*, 191 n. 30:8.

sacrifice ("You shall not pass any of your offspring over to Molech)".[439] *Jubilees* applies it to the situation where a man gives his daughter in marriage to a Gentile. Molech now represents not idolatry, but Gentiles.[440]

> There is no remission or any forgiveness; but rather the man who has defiled (*rak*^w*sa*) his daughter within all of Israel is to be eradicated because he has given one of his descendants to Molech and has sinned (*'abbasa*) by defiling (*rak*^w*sa*) them. (30:10)

Such a man is to be stoned (30:8), as Lev 20:2 requires: "Any of the people of Israel, or of the aliens who reside in Israel, who give any of their offspring to Molech shall be put to death; the people of the land shall stone them to death".

The different texts explain the different modes of execution between the man (stoning; Lev 18:21; 20:2) and the woman (burning; Lev 21:9) in 30:7. The man has "done something sinful and shameful within Israel". The woman has "defiled (*rak*^w*sa*) the reputation of her father's house". In such a case the guilt would appear to lie with the father, but even the woman's compliance and her refusal to resist is apparently sufficient ground for her burning. An underlying assumption running through the passage is that such sins bring defilement not only to the person, but also to Israel, which is holy: "for Israel is holy to the Lord" (30:8).[441]

The theme of intermarriage continues in the next section, where the angel underlines its importance by one of the twelve direct addresses to Moses, in the form: "Now you, Moses, order the Israelites ..." (30:11). The command is "that they are not to give any of their daughters to foreigners and that they are not to marry [lit. to take] any foreign women because it is despicable (*mennun*) before the Lord". Notice that this now comes back to include men marrying foreigners, which has thus far been the primary focus in *Jubilees*. The focus had been on women marrying foreigners as the author extrapolated from the case of Dinah.

---

[439] See the discussion in Jacob Milgrom, *Leviticus: A New Translation with Introduction and Commentary* (3 vols; AB 3; New York: Doubleday, 1991, 2000, 2001) 2. 1551-55.

[440] See Milgrom, "Concept of Impurity," 283; Werman, "*Jubilees* 30"; Himmelfarb, "Sexual Relations," 29-30; also Himmelfarb, "Levi, Phinehas," 13. She notes this interpretation also in Targum Pseudo-Jonathan, referring to Geza Vermes, "Leviticus 18:21 in Ancient Jewish Bible Exegesis," in *Studies in Aggadah: Targum and Jewish Liturgy in Memory of Joseph Heinemann* (ed. J. J. Petuchowski and E. Fleischer; Jerusalem: Magnes Pr. and Hebrew Union College, 1981) 108-24. See also Rothstein, "Sexual Union," who finds the application of Lev 18:21 as further evidence that for *Jubilees* marriage is effected by sexual intercourse and that *Jubilees* proscribes all sexual relations with gentiles (382-83). See also Hayes, *Gentile Impurities*, 74.

[441] See also Milgrom, "Concept of Impurity," 282; Endres, *Biblical Interpretation*, noting the application of Lev 19:1 with its call to all people to be holy (139-41).

We then read in 30:12 that this is the real import of the story of Dinah's rape for *Jubilees*: while it illustrates the sinfulness of the nations, "the real crime" addressed by *Jubilees* is intermarriage, not rape:[442]

> For this reason I have written for you in the words of the law everything that the Shechemites did [lit. all their works] to Dinah and how Jacob's sons said: "We will not give our daughter to a man who has a foreskin because for us that would be a disgraceful thing (*ṣe'lat*)".

Again, *Jubilees* grounds the prohibition in Israel's holiness and expands it beyond the instance of the Dinah story to include both men and women: "It is a disgraceful thing (*ṣe'lat*) for the Israelites who give or take (in marriage) one of the foreign women because it is too impure (*rekus*) and despicable (*mennun*) for Israel" (30:13). In 30:14 *Jubilees* then allows us to see its concern with Israel of its own time: "Israel will not become clean (*neṣuḥ*) from this impurity (*rekʷs*) while it has one of the foreign women or if anyone has given one of his daughters to any foreign man". This somewhat "ups the stakes", because it not only attacks intermarriage, but also targets all existing marriages in which one partner is non Israelite. Intermarriage is taking place in his own day, probably in the context of the impact of Hellenisation. We shall return to discussion of the possible contemporary context of this prohibition below at the conclusion of this section.

The warning of judgement, which follows in 30:15, is remarkably similar to that of *Jubilees* 23, which also addresses contemporary concerns. *Jub.* 30:15 reads:

> For it is blow upon blow and curse upon curse. Every punishment, blow, and curse will come. If one does this [Heb probably would have been רבד] or shuts his eyes to those who do impure things (*rekʷs*) and who defile (*rakʷsa*) the Lord's sanctuary and to those who profane his holy name [as Lev 20:3], then the entire nation will be condemned together because of all this impurity (*rekʷs*) and this contamination (*gemmānē*) [L. only *abominationis*].

This recalls the language of 23:13-14:

> But the greater part of his time will be (characterised by difficulties, toil, and distress without peace, because (there will be) blow upon blow, wound upon wound, distress upon distress, bad news upon bad news, disease upon disease, and every (kind of) punishment like this, one with the other: disease and stomach pains; snow, hail, and frost; fever, cold, and numbness; famine, death, sword, captivity, and every (sort of) blow and difficulty. All of this will happen to the evil generation which makes the earth commit sin (*'abbasa*) through pollution (*rekʷs*; omitted by VanderKam), sexual impurity (*zemmut*), contamination (*gemmānē*), and their detestable actions (*saqorār*).

---

[442] So Endres, *Biblical Interpretation*, 133-35.

Both have in common the distinctive rhetorical form in describing the judgement, "blow upon blow" and other terms joined by "upon", but also the focus on sexual wrongdoing as the ground for judgement.

As 23:21-23 go on to speak of such behaviour defiling the temple and of misusing the holy name, so 30:15-16 speak of defiling the temple, again suggesting that some of the abuses are among contemporaries of the author who have leadership roles in the priesthood.[443] The author sees judgement falling on the nation for such abuse:

> then the entire nation will be condemned together because of all this impurity (*rek^{w}s*) and this contamination (*gemmānē*). There will be no favoritism nor partiality; there will be no receiving from him of fruit, sacrifices, offerings, fat, or the aroma of a pleasing fragrance so that he should accept it. (So) is any man or woman in Israel to be who defiles (*rak^{w}sa*) his sanctuary. (30:15-16)

Conversely 30:18-19 speak of the role of Levi's descendants, "chosen for the priesthood and as levites to serve before the Lord as we (do) for all time ... to carry out justice, punishment, and revenge on all who rise against Israel". The issue of intermarriage appears to be one of the matters of dispute between the author and his group, who include priests, and others, who also include priests, who defile the temple through sexual wrongdoing and have brought God's judgement on the people. The contemporary reference probably explains the heavy emphasis on forbidding intermarriage.

The Levites are to punish such breaches among both priests and people. They are blessed as successors of Levi whom the heavenly tablets record "as a friend and a just man" (30:20). In 30:21-22 the angel informs Moses that he has "written this entire message" in order that Moses might "tell the Israelites not to sin or transgress the statutes or violate the covenant which was established for them so that they should perform it and be recorded as friends". Typical of *Jubilees*, which identifies the special role of Levitical priests, we find the privilege of being a "friend" of God extended beyond Levi and his descendants to all Israel. Those who transgress the statutes in these ways are "enemies". Finally, in 23:23 the angel reports the heavenly record according to which the deed of Jacob's sons, the killing of the people of Shechem, was "right, justice, and revenge against the sinners" and "recorded as a blessing". This sweeps aside Jacob's disapproval in Gen 49:5-7 and 34:30 and matches the similarly heroic portrait of Levi and his deeds in *Aramaic Levi Document* (12:6 / 78). It also justifies taking up arms in the author's time to prevent the defilement of Israel and of the temple through sexual wrongdoing of this kind. Drawing attention to the conjunction between Abraham

---

[443] As Jackson, *Enochic Judaism*, puts it well: "The priestly concern of the author here breaks through the veil of the narrative to address his own contemporary agenda" (48-49).

and Phinehas, both reckoned as just (Gen 15:6; Ps 106:31) and Levi, and to the fact that both Abraham and Levi are declared friends of God (*Jub.* 19:9; 30:20), Hayes observes: "Thus there is a direct line from Abraham, to Shimeon and Levi, to Phinehas – all of whom are accounted righteous for their opposition to miscegenation".[444] Endres also notes that the author's view reflects the positive depiction of Levi in Deut 33:8-11 and coheres with the violent image of the zeal of Phinehas in Num 25:6-13, alluded to in 1 Macc 2:24-25, 54, which reflects the probable setting of the author.[445]

The prominence of Levi and the omission of Jacob's disapproval recorded in the Genesis account (Gen 34:30) and, worse still, his curse in Gen 49:5-7, is striking, but all the more so because only certain of Levi's descendants, namely those who were Aaronic or of Zadokite line exercised priesthood, whereas others performed menial and service roles. *Jubilees* makes no mention of either Zadok or, more significantly as a figure from the time which it covers: Aaron.[446] Indeed, Liora Ravid sees the author attacking Zadokite priests, even the high priest, including on the issue of intermarriage, and intentionally diminishing the latter's role on the Day of Atonement. Citing instances of forgiveness in 1:15-17 and 23-24; 5:17-18 (atonement day); 23:18-25 in last days; 41:23-24 (Judah) she argues: "in contrast to the Torah and Qumran literature, these examples indicate that a person wishing to be absolved from sin is not commanded to bathe in water, but to pray".[447] *Jubilees* depicts the patriarchs as priests, but notably without any concern for natural impurities and the rites to deal with them, even corpse impurity, as the account of the death of Abraham shows.[448] VanderKam counters that the absence of reference to purification rites and to atonement day ritual is to be explained more simply by the fact that the author is aware of writing about a period before the temple existed.[449] But this may not be an adequate explanation,

---

[444] Hayes, *Gentile Impurities*, 79-80.

[445] Endres, *Biblical Interpretation*, 150-51.

[446] Ravid, "Purity and Impurity," 83. On the development of Zadokite and Aaronic priesthood and the marginalisation of other Levitical families, see Boccaccini, *Roots of Rabbinic Judaism*, 43-111.

[447] Ravid, "Purity and Impurity," 74. Himmelfarb, "Sexual Relations," notes the contrast between *Jubilees* and the Temple Scroll which "brings ordinary Jews closer to priests by making the purity laws more elaborate and thus heightening their impact on both priests and lay people" (22).

[448] Ravid, "Purity and Impurity," 66.

[449] VanderKam, "Anthropological Gleanings," 129 n. 29. On the Day of Atonement, see VanderKam's observations on *Jubilees'* treatment of the treachery against Joseph, which takes place on the tenth day of the seventh month (34:10), the day on which Bilhah died (34:15-16). It is also the day later designated as the Day of Atonement, which also entailed the killing of a goat. See his note about sadness and annual purification in relation to the killing of the goat (34:18-19; see also 5:17-19) (130).

given that many later rites are retrojected in *Jubilees* into the time of the patriarchs. In the case of corpse impurity, for instance, one might have expected some indication that this was problematic, as Ravid suggests. She argues, however, *Jubilees* is not anti-priestly; it affirms cultic activity: patriarchs "brought sin-offerings (6.2; 16.22), were careful to cover the blood of the sacrifice (7.30-31)",[450] prepare themselves for holy places, and are concerned with calendar and defiling of the sabbath,[451] but their focus is above all what Ravid calls, "metaphysical impurity".[452]

Jubilees appears therefore to reflect priestly interests from beyond the acknowledged priestly circles and at the same time to affirm the holiness and priestliness of the nation as a whole. This is the context of its strictures against intermarriage. It has used the Dinah episode as the basis for extrapolations designed to counter sexual wrongdoing. While it includes rape and also adultery, its primary focus is marriage to foreigners. Nothing indicates that it is directed particularly against marriage with the people later associated with Shechem, namely Samaritans. Rather, its focus is on anyone who does not belong to the holy seed of Israel and applies equally to both foreign men and foreign women. It achieves its severity by expanding the application of key texts from Leviticus, so that what applied to the daughters of priests plying prostitution now applies to all women and to illicit sexual relations and marriage, and so that what applied to priests now applies to all Israelites.

We have noted at a number of points the possible relationship with the *Aramaic Levi Document,* where we have a fragmentary of its account of the Dinah episode in 1:1-3 / 1c 2 and material concerning intermarriage, which has much in common with our passage, in 4Q213a 3-4 / 3a. They are not sequential, so that allusions in the latter to the Dinah episode must be treated with caution, but are not thereby rendered improbable. Like *Jubilees, Aramaic Levi Document* appears also to make Levi a hero and so probably also suppressed Jacob's negative comments. Levi's heroism relates to his killing the Shechemites. Both *Aramaic Levi Document* and *Jubilees* attribute to Levi and his descendants a responsibility to execute judgement against those who flout the prohibition of intermarriage with Gentiles. *Aramaic Levi Document* appears to have applied the warning against daughters of priests who ply prostitution, Lev 21:9, in a similar way to *Jubilees,* both with regard to the meaning of זנות and to the application beyond priestly families. *Aramaic Levi Document* also uses Lev 21:14 and 21:7 to enhance its argument, particularly in relation to priests. The former, addressing the restrictions on whom a high priest may marry, does not appear to be used in Jubilees, but the

[450] Ravid, "Purity and Impurity," 86.
[451] Ravid, "Purity and Impurity," 75.
[452] Ravid, "Purity and Impurity," 71.

latter, which speaks of similar restrictions applying to priests, may well do, particularly, its final statement, "For they are holy to their God", which finds an echo in Jub. 30:8, "For Israel is holy to the Lord". As noted in our discussion of *Aramaic Levi Document* above, Kugler points to other common elements between 4Q213a 3-4 / 3a and *Jubilees*: the lasting shameful effect (*Jub.* 30:14); the word "shame, disgrace" (*xafrat Jub.* 30:5, 7); the reference to "plagues" or "blows" (*Jub.* 30:7, 15; see also 23:13 in the context of sexual wrongdoing); and the reference to tithe and offering (*Jub.* 30:16 declaring offerings of exogamous people unacceptable).[453]

If *ALD* 4Q213a 3-4 / 3a begins with an allusion to the Dinah episode, as the singular suggests, then we may assume that it shares with *Jubilees* the concern to proscribe intermarriage. We have shown that to be likely. On the other hand, it is also particularly concerned with priests, as the specific instructions later given to Levi show, which require that he not engage in harlotry (which, there, has come to mean, illicit sexual relations), but marry someone from his own family (6:1-5 / 14-18). *Aramaic Levi Document* does not share *Jubilees*' stance which emphasises the priestly character of all the people. *Aramaic Levi Document* does, however, link Isaac's instruction to Levi in the regard to his instruction to Jacob not to marry a Canaanite, a motif developed extensively in *Jubilees*, as we shall see below.

There are, however, some significant differences between the two accounts and their extrapolations. Jubilees seems deliberately to have portrayed Dinah as an innocent victim, whereas *Aramaic Levi Document* apparently makes her complicit in both passages. That the latter also mentions the circumcision ruse appears to assume some negotiation over marriage norms or rules.

The Dinah episode lent itself to use for reflection on marriage with Gentiles. What links *Aramaic Levi Document* and *Jubilees* is more than that. It includes particular applications of priestly law from Leviticus and a sanitised account of Levi's exploits which makes him a hero and model for his successors on the pattern of Phinehas. There are also aspects in common which are beyond our theme, in particular, the instructions about preparing sacrifices and Isaac's blessing. In *Aramaic Levi Document* roles attributed to Judah have been assimilated to the priesthood of Levi, whereas in *Jubilees* they remain distinct though nevertheless subordinate. Yet the disparity in the evaluation of Dinah and the different foci, primarily on priests in *Aramaic Levi Document* and on people in *Jubilees*, implies either a critical reworking by *Jubilees* of *Aramaic Levi Document* or use of a common source.[454]

---

[453] Kugler, *From Patriarch to Priest*, 83-84.

[454] On the relationship between *Jubilees* and *Aramaic Levi Document* see James C. VanderKam, "Isaac's Blessing of Levi and His Descendants in *Jubilees* 31," in *The Provo International Conference on the Dead Sea Scrolls: Technological Innovations, New Texts, and Reformulated Issues* (ed. Donald W. Parry and Eugene C. Ulrich; STDJ 30; Leiden:

3.2.4.3   Intermarriage in the Rest of Jubilees

Concern with the issue of intermarriage continues to echo in the later chapters of *Jubilees*. They include much without parallel in Genesis, but within a framework which uses the Genesis material in a slightly different order. In particular, *Jubilees* brings the account of Joseph's successful resistance against sexual temptation before the account of Judah and Tamar. The details are set out in the table below.

Jubilees	Genesis
34:10-19 Joseph sold into Egypt	36-37 Joseph sold into Egypt
34:20-21 the wives of Jacob's sons	38 Judah and Tamar
35 Rebecca settles the relationship between Jacob and Esau	39 Joseph's success then fall after the attempted seduction
36 Isaac's farewell to his sons	
37-38 Esau reneges; he and his sons are defeated	
39-40 Joseph's success then fall after the attempted seduction and his rise to power in Egypt	
41 Judah and Tamar	

Jubilees brings the account of Joseph's being sold to the Egyptians in 34:10-19. We shall return to discuss its portrayal of Joseph in greater detail below, but, for the present context, it should be noted that the introduction of this material so early, five chapters before its sequel, means that, for the hearer, the story of Joseph sits in the background of what follows. It is relevant to the theme of this section in that it entails a relationship, albeit by force, with a foreign nation.

The issue of intermarriage returns directly in 34:20-21, which lists the wives of Jacob's sons. Here it is interesting to note that Simeon married a Canaanite (Gen 46:10), but later changed his mind and married a woman from Mesopotamia, like his brothers. This somewhat retrieves his sin. Judah married Betasuel a Canaanite (Gen 38:2), which will become the source of more sexual wrongdoing, as we shall discuss in more detail below. Its relevance in this section is that it

---

Brill, 1999) 497-519, 511-18, who sees the relationship best explained by both using a common source. He does not rule out the possibility of some contact especially since many of the motifs in Isaac's blessing of Levi are to be found scattered through the *Aramaic Levi Document* (516-18). He notes the rise of non-pentateuchal traditions which give prominence to Levi, reflected already in Mal 2:4-7, and derived in part from the belief reflected in 1 Sam 2:27-36, that Levi was chosen as priest already in Egypt (519).

serves as one more illustration of the wickedness of Canaanite women.[455] It is interesting that the information that Joseph married an Egyptian, Asenath, appears unproblematic. To this, too, we shall return.

Levi's wife receives the most detailed pedigree: Melcha (as in *ALD* 11:1 / 62, "Melcha, daughter of Bethuel, the son of Laban"), a daughter of Aram descended from Terah, reflecting Levi's prominence which outshines that of Judah whose lineage is traced through Tamar.[456] Beside Levi, the next greatest detail attaches, surprisingly, to Naphtali. This may well reflect the prominence of the Tobiad family and its history of links with the priesthood. Tobit furnishes the family with a pedigree from Naphtali.[457] It also helps explain the favourable treatment of Bilhah, Naphtali's mother, analogous to the favourable treatment of Levi's mother, Leah, as our discussion below in 3.3.2.3 shows.

In 35:9-12 *Jubilees* continues the theme of disparaging Esau and his marriage to foreign wives in the words of Rebecca to Isaac. Esau has been "malicious since his youth, … devoid of virtue … has wholeheartedly abandoned" his parents, treated them badly, stolen their possessions, patronised them, behaving bitterly towards Jacob who is "perfect and true", and has shown himself a loyal and supportive son. Isaac concurs, noting his change of mind from preferring Esau, and declares:

> Now my mind is disturbed about his actions. Neither he nor his descendants are to be saved because they will be destroyed from the earth and be uprooted from beneath the sky. He has abandoned the God of Abraham and has gone after his wives, after impurity (*rek^{w}s*), and after their errors (*sehtat*) – he and his sons. (35:14)

As elsewhere in the context of intermarriage, "impurity" will carry connotations of sexual wrongdoing.

---

[455] Werman, "*Jubilees* 30," observes: "*Jubilees* tries to erase intermarriage in the patriarchs' families. It grants Aramean women the status of honorary Jewishness and reports the marriages of Jacob's sons to Aramean women" (1). But for *Jubilees* the issue is not "honorary Jewishness", but approved descent for which *Jubilees* is consistent in approving descendants of Terah.

[456] See also Halpern-Amaru, *Empowerment*, 118.

[457] Boccaccini, *Roots of Rabbinic Judaism*, writes of Tobit: "The book of Tobit overturned the verdict of the tradition of Ezra and marked the recognition of the genealogy 'of the descendants of Tobiah' as an exiled family from the tribe of Naphtali" (125). For discussions of the Naphtali tradition see Halpern-Amaru, *Empowerment*, 118-19; Betsy Halpern-Amaru, "Bilhah and Naphtali in *Jubilees*: A Note on 4QTNaphtali," *DSD* 6 (1999) 1-10 and Vered Hillel, "Why not Naphtali?" in *Things Revealed: Studies in Early Jewish and Christian Literature in Honor of Michael E. Stone* (ed. Esther G. Chazon, David Satran, and Ruth A. Clements; JSJSup 89; Leiden: Brill, 2004) 279-88, on his significance in the testament tradition.

Esau's reputation goes from bad to worse in the accounts which follow, where he reneges on his commitment to peaceful coexistence with Jacob, takes up arms with his sons, and must accept defeat and subjection at the hands of Jacob's sons (38:1-14) under the leadership of Judah (38:5). Judah thus fulfils the role given him in Isaac's blessing as Israel's enthroned prince (31:18-20) beside the priesthood blessed in Levi (31:13-17).

When *Jubilees* then returns to the Joseph story in 39:1 – 40:13, one might have expected that it would further develop the theme of sexual wrongdoing and the evils of intermarriage with the wicked nations. Instead, one finds only the former. Joseph resists the temptation from Potiphar's wife to lead him to commit adultery.

> But he did not surrender himself. He remembered the Lord and what [lit. the words] his father Jacob would read to him from the words of Abraham — that no one is to commit adultery with a woman who has husband; that there is a death penalty which has been ordained for him in heaven before the most high Lord. The sin will be entered [will ascend] regarding him in the eternal books forever before the Lord. (39:6)

Surprisingly, *Jubilees* offers no further elaboration. It does not make Potiphar's wife a symbol of the wicked nations, although her deeds are clearly wicked. More surprisingly, it reports that Joseph accepted an Egyptian wife: "The king named Joseph Sefantifanes and gave Joseph as a wife the daughter of Potiphar, the daughter of the priest of Heliopolis", the Greek name of the city On (40:10; cf. Gen 41:45-46). Intermarriage with an Egyptian is apparently not a problem. This is extraordinary, given the lumping together of the Canaanites and the Egyptians as sources of sexual wrongdoing in Lev 18:3 ("You shall not do as they do in the land of Egypt, where you lived, and you shall not do as they do in the land of Canaan, to which I am bringing you"). We shall return to this in the summary evaluation of this section below.

Jubilees does not portray Joseph as guilty of the sin of intermarriage. Rather, as *Jubilees* has idealised Jacob, so it has also idealised Joseph. The basis for this was already well supplied in Genesis. Joseph emerges as the ideal ruler who knew how to resist sexual wrongdoing. By contrast Judah, the patriarch from whom Israel's rulers are to descend, is flawed. He has committed two wrongs: he has married a Canaanite and he then engages in sexual wrongdoing with Tamar. Judah's marriage of a Canaanite is of foundational significance. That information was provided already in 34:20. Given the emphasis on this as a serious sin, a hearer might well have wondered at that point what this might mean for Judah. This is especially the case since *Jubilees* has made a special point of singling Judah out beside (and in second place to) Levi in the blessing by Isaac in 31:18-20. He and his sons are to rule Israel and send fear into the nations, to bring peace to Israel and blessing or curse to those who bless or curse them. Judah then demonstrates partial fulfilment of the blessing in defeating Esau and his sons. There the author brings us up to his own day ("until today"; 38:15) with detail about the kings of Edom (38:15-24).

The promise, however, stands in tension with Judah's flawed marriage. It enhances the sense that not only Judah, but also his successors, are problematic, and that one aspect of this is sexual wrongdoing. Hearers of *Jubilees* might have thought of David's sexual wrongdoing and marriage to foreign wives, but also of the successive failure of Judah' and Israel's kings, with few exceptions. By the third century B.C.E., their role has effectively been taken up within priestly rule.

Jubilees achieves the contrast between Joseph as the ideal ruler and Judah the failed one, on the one hand, by building up expectations about Judah and then, on the other, by isolating the incident of Joseph's personal fortunes in Egypt and placing it before his account of Judah's failure.[458] In this, it builds on a contrast already implied in Genesis. The language describing Joseph's rule matches that of *Jubilees'* vision of the future and echoes the promise to Judah about his descendants. Under Joseph's influence "the pharaoh's rule was just, and there was no satan or any evil one" (40:9).[459] The marks of satan and the impure spirits are above all sexual wrongdoing, as had been the marks of the Watchers from whom they sprang. Pharaoh's rule matches *Jubilees'* vision for the future expressed in 23:28-29, "There will be neither a satan nor any evil one who will destroy. For their entire lifetimes will be times of blessing and healing", and in 50:5,

> The jubilees will pass by until Israel is pure (*naṣha*) of every sin (*'abbasā*) of sexual immorality (*zemmut*) [VanderKam has "sexual evil"], impurity (*rekʷs*), contamination (*gemmānē*), sin (*xaṭi'at*), and error (*gēgāy*). They will no longer have any satan or any evil person. the land will be pure from that time until eternity.

This vision finds its echo in the promise to Judah's sons: "At the time when you sit on the honourable throne that is rightly yours, there will be great peace for all the descendants of the beloved's sons" (31:20). Joseph and Judah (with his successors)

---

[458] Cf. Halpern-Amaru, *Empowerment*, who argues that "the accounts are pointedly constructed such that there are no allusions to invite Judah/Joseph comparison" (112), noting the deletion of Judah's role in the sale of Joseph, the interruption of the Joseph story by the account of Judah and Tamar not when Joseph is still suffering, but when he is already elevated, in the substitution of Reuben for Judah as the perpetrator of wrongdoing reflected in the intratextual links, and in Bilhah's mortal grief at the death of Joseph (112-13).

[459] Berger, *Jubiläen*, notes: "Insbesondere die Zeit der Regentschaft Josephs in Ägypten hat den Charakter einer quasimessianischen Heilsperiode; sie erhält dieselben Attribute wie die erwartete zukünftige Heilszeit" (282) (tr. In particular the period of Joseph's rule in Egypt has the character of a quasi-messianic salvific era; it is given the same attributes as the expected future time of salvation).

stand in stark contrast, all the more poignant because *Jubilees* has elevated Judah's role to one of great importance for Israel beside (and beneath) that of Levi.

Thus the story of Judah and Tamar contributes further to theme of the evil of intermarriage and the sexual impurity of the Canaanites. *Jubilees* uses it also to address matters of incest to which we shall return in the next section in discussing Reuben and Bilhah. Implicit in the story of Judah and Tamar is the sexually corrupting influence of Canaanite women and the disastrous consequences of intermarriage for the people and also for its rulers.

The account of Judah and Tamar in 41:1-21 follows Gen 38:1-30 closely. The details of Judah's marriage to Shua, a Canaanite (Gen 38:1-4), had been briefly mentioned in *Jub.* 34:20, where she is called Betasuel. *Jubilees* begins with the account of Judah taking Tamar as a wife for Er, his firstborn, matching the information in Genesis, but it goes beyond it in emphasising that she was "one of the Aramean women" (41:1). This qualified her as an acceptable candidate for marriage. Judah had to this point done the right thing, not repeating his own mistake of taking for Er a Canaanite woman.[460] Gen 38:7 simply states: "But Er, Judah's firstborn, was wicked in the sight of the LORD, and the LORD put him to death" (38:7). *Jubilees*, on the other hand, explains his wickedness:

> He hated (her) and did not lie with her because his mother was a Canaanite woman and he wanted to marry someone from his mother's tribe. But his father Judah did not allow him. That Er, Judah's first-born, was evil, and the Lord killed him (41:2-3).

For *Jubilees*, here is one more piece of evidence of the wickedness of the Canaanites, especially in relationship to sexual wrongdoing, and so of the danger of marrying a Canaanite. 41:4-6 then recounts Judah's instruction to Onan that he perform his levirate duty with Tamar. He refuses, spills his semen on the ground, and suffers the judgement of death. The story of Onan closely matches the Genesis account in 38:8-10, but now stands under the shadow of his Canaanite mother and is slightly modified. 41:5 reads, "so he entered the house of his brother's wife and poured out the semen on the ground" in contrast to Gen 38:9, "he spilled his semen on the ground whenever he went in to his brother's wife". As Rothstein[461] observes, the addition of the words, "the house of" removes the implication that

---

[460] So Halpern-Amaru, *Empowerment*, 113-14. See also the discussion in Michael Segal, "The Relationship between the Legal and Narrative Passages in *Jubilees*," in *Reworking the Bible: Apocryphal and Related Texts at Qumran: Proceedings of a Joint Symposium by the Orion Center for the Study of the Dead Sea Scrolls and Associated Literature and the Hebrew University Institute for Advanced Studies Research Group on Qumran, 15-17 January, 2002* (ed. Esther G. Chazon, Devorah Dimant, and Ruth A. Clements; STDJ 58; Leiden: Brill, 2005) 203-28.

[461] Rothstein, "Sexual Union," 364.

intercourse took place. It probably implies masturbation, though *Jubilees* never addresses the latter as an issue. Both Er and Onan have committed acts of sexual wrongdoing by avoiding intercourse. *Jubilees* adds no further comment. Thus Tamar remains a virgin, as the angels later report: "We told Judah that his two sons had not lain with her. For this reason his descendants were established for another generation and would not be uprooted" (41:27).[462] We return to this below.

There then follows the infamous story of Judah thinking that Tamar was a prostitute and being shamed at the point when he was about to execute judgement on her. The story in *Jubilees* follows Genesis closely, but, again, there are some changes reflecting the major theme of the evil of Canaanite women. Both mention Judah's instruction that Tamar was to remain in her father's house until *Shelah* (Genesis; *Selom* in *Jubilees*), the youngest son, grew up. Genesis mentions Judah's anxiety about losing his third son in a similar way (38:11), but *Jubilees* does not mention this fear. Instead, it once more introduces the figure of Bedsuel (as she is now called), his Canaanite wife: "He grew up, but Judah's wife Bedsuel did not allow her son Selom to marry (her)" (41:7). His Canaanite wife is again to blame.

Jubilees then returns to the Genesis account, noting the death of Judah's notorious wife and reporting his trip to shear sheep in Timnah (41:7-8; Gen 38:12). *Jubilees* omits reference to Judah's mourning for her, by simply reporting that he went to Timnah not after a period of mourning, but in the next year. For *Jubilees*, Judah knew not to mourn for a Canaanite wife! There are only minor differences about the way the accounts describe Tamar's dress. Genesis continues with the notion that Judah was doing Tamar an injustice because of his fear, mentioned in (38:11), by noting "She saw that Shelah was grown up, yet she had not been given to him in marriage" (38:14). *Jubilees* omits this detail. The security which Judah leaves behind, according to *Jubilees*, is: "the ring on my finger, my neck chain, and my staff which is in my hand" (41:11). Genesis has: "Your signet and your cord, and the staff that is in your hand" (38:18).[463] As Halpern-Amaru notes, *Jubilees* has subtly changed the sequence, so that the request for surety comes not before, but only after the act of sexual intercourse, thus at one level, separating the act from the negotiation.[464]

The search for "the prostitute" is similarly described, although Gen 38:21 uses the word meaning "temple prostitute", which has no equivalent in *Jubilees*.

---

[462] Thus "house" is not likely here to be used in a euphemistic sense, as in Prov 2:18, for female sexual organs. Cf. Cecilia Wassen, "The Story of Judah and Tamar in the Eyes of the Earliest Interpreters," *Literature and Theology* 8 (1994) 354-66, 360.

[463] Halpern-Amara, *Empowerment*, comments that these in *Jubilees* are "personal objects, not symbols" (115).

[464] Halpern-Amaru, *Empowerment*, 115. "In that single act of intercourse, Tamar conceives Perez, the ancestor of King David. The creative reworking separates conception of the progenitor of the Davidic line from even the pretence of prostitution" (115).

Concerned to protect Judah, it would not want to portray him as potentially engaging with pagan temples. *Jubilees* reinforces Tamar's alleged sexual wrongdoing by adding to the statement, "Bring her out and let her be burned" (41:17 = Gen 38:24), the words: "because she has done something impure (*rek*ʷ*s*) in Israel" (41:17), language which it commonly uses to allude to sexual wrongdoing. The judgement reflects the instruction of Abraham in 20:4 that "If any woman or girl among you commits a sexual offence, burn her in fire", a generalising expansion of the prohibition in Lev 21:9 against the daughters of priests engaging in prostitution under threat of burning (here applied more widely, as usual in *Jubilees*). In 41:28 the author alludes directly to Abraham's instruction in declaring that in this case it should not apply.

Genesis concludes: "Then Judah acknowledged them and said, 'She is more in the right than I, since I did not give her to my son Shelah.' And he did not lie with her again" (38:26). *Jubilees* has revised and expanded this to read: "'Tamar has been more just than I; therefore, do not burn her'. For this reason she was not given to Selom, and he did not approach her again" (41:19). This may be the only hint that his going to a prostitute was wrongdoing. The words, "for this reason", might allude to Judah's confession as in Genesis and reflect on his injustice in not giving Selom to Tamar, but that detail has been deleted from the story in *Jubilees*. It more likely refers to Tamar's having become unclean for Selom by having had sexual intercourse with another man and, even worse for him, his father (Lev 18:8; 20:11). The comment in both *Jubilees* and Genesis that Judah did not approach Tamar could be understood against the background that in some sense he might have had that right, having "married" her, but, from another perspective, 41:23 would see that as continuing to commit a sin of incest in contravention of Lev 18:15 and 20:12. Finally, *Jub.* 41:21 notes the birth of Perez and Zerah, dated to the time when the plenteous years in Egypt turned to famine (so 41:28!), so probably to be understood as a symbol of judgement on Judah's act.[465]

The focus on laws of incest is central in what follows, where the angel explains the implications of what took place.

> Judah knew that what he had done was evil because he had lain [Syriac: slept] with his daughter-in-law. In his own view he considered it evil, and he knew that he had done wrong and erred, for he had uncovered his son's covering. (41:23)

The reference is to Lev 18:15 ("You shall not uncover the nakedness of your daughter-in-law: she is your son's wife; you shall not uncover her nakedness") and 20:12 ("If a man lies with his daughter-in-law, both of them shall be put to death; they have committed perversion, their blood is upon them"). *Jubilees* then goes on to rehabilitate poor Judah, who, the hearer senses, is also, in some sense, a victim:

---

[465] So Berger, *Jubiläen,* 520.

He began to lament and plead before the Lord because of his sin. We told him in a dream that it would be forgiven for him because he had pleaded very much and because he had lamented and did not do (it) again. He had forgiveness because he turned from his sin and from his ignorance, for the sin was a great one before our God (41:23-25).

Whether the sympathy which the rewritten narrative evokes for Judah also plays a role in his rehabilitation is not explicit. The sin remains a sin.

In what follows, *Jubilees* has the angel shift to loosely analogous situations, but in which no such mercy is to be shown. It begins, not as one might expect with relations between fathers and daughters-in-law, but, in reverse direction, with relations between men and mothers-in-law: "Anyone who acts in this way — anyone who lies with his mother-in-law — is to be burned in fire so that he burns in it because impurity and contamination have come on them. They are to be burned" (41:25). The reference to burning here makes it likely that the author also has Lev 20:14 in mind, which addresses that situation and prescribes that penalty: "If a man takes a wife and her mother also, it is depravity; they shall be burned to death, both he and they, that there may be no depravity among you". While this refers to sleeping with one's mother-in-law (the mother of one's wife), the author also assumes that it applies conversely, namely, to women sleeping with their fathers-in-law, as with Tamar and Judah.[466] Thus 41:26 goes on to address both situations: "Now you order the Israelites that there is to be no impurity among them, for anyone who lies with his daughter-in-law or his mother-in-law has done something that is impure. They are to burn the man who lay with her and the woman." The reciprocal extension of prohibitions is evident later in the extension of the prohibition of marrying nephews to apply also to marrying nieces in CD 5.1-11 and 11QT[a] 66.15-17, a view also presupposed in *Jubilees*.[467]

As noted above, *Jubilees* takes great care to rework the story of Judah and Tamar so as to sustain its continuing concern with sexual wrongdoing, but also to explain why neither Judah nor Tamar was executed (as Lev 18:29 requires), and how their progeny retained their status as God's holy people and were not

---

[466] Rothstein, "Sexual Union," observes that in applying the penalty of burning to incest, *Jubilees* reads Lev 20:14 not as simultaneous marriage of mother and daughter, but as sexual relations with one, then the other, and then returning to the first (380-81). Applying the principle of reciprocal application, this helps explain why *Jubilees* applies the penalty of burning to a situation where a woman has sexual relations with both a father and son. Rothstein notes also that *Jubilees* appears to treat אשר יקח (which can mean "whoever takes in marriage") and אשר ישכב ("whoever has sexual intercourse with" as Deut 27:23 and Lev 20:12) as interchangeable (382).

[467] So Rothstein, "Sexual Union," 379-80; Segal, "Relationship," 224. See also Endres, *Biblical Interpretation*, 187; Jackson, *Enochic Judaism*, 49.

annihilated like the descendants of Lot (16:7-9). Rothstein[468] reviews the issues as follows. The addition of "the house of" in 41:5 helps secure the affirmation by the angels in 41:27 that Tamar remained a virgin. "We told Judah that his two sons had not lain with her. For this reason his descendants were established for another generation and would not be uprooted" (41:27). This could mean that Judah's unwitting act would not be incest in the sense of intercourse with his married daughter, because the marriage had not been consummated through sexual intercourse, even though *Jub.* 21:23 clearly speaks of her as Judah's daughter-in-law. But, as Rothstein points out, this would still leave problems, with regard to both Judah and Tamar. Deut 22:23-37 forbids intercourse with a woman betrothed to another man. The situation is, at most, somewhat ameliorated by the fact that she was in a state of "hold", waiting for Shelah. *Jubilees* does seem to have made a point of emphasising her virginity as a mitigating factor in determining the extent of guilt.

Having already intimated Judah's forgiveness in 41:24-25, the author has the angel return to it in 41:28: "For in his integrity he had gone and demanded punishment because Judah had wanted to burn her on the basis of the law which Abraham had commanded his children". The reference is to *Jub.* 20:4, but the penalty of burning had already been addressed in 41:25. Here the focus is on Judah demanding just punishment,[469] not, as there, for incest but for having engaged in prostitution (as the author's reading of Lev 21:9 required). It is interesting that nothing more is said about Tamar's act of prostitution as sin. This is probably because prostitution was not the intent, but rather the cover for gaining a legitimate husband, and, in any case, in 41:28 the angel seems intent again on mitigating the severity of Judah's guilt.

After the event it became apparent that Tamar had also committed a sin of incest by sleeping with her father-in-law, so that the judgement by fire, based on the reciprocal extension of Lev 20:14 in 41:25, also applied to her. While the mention of Tamar's virginity in 41:27 serves primarily to ameliorate – but not cancel – Judah's guilt, it probably also plays a role by association in explaining Tamar's survival. Rothstein suggest two further elements which helped *Jubilees* explain Tamar's survival.[470] Tamar would not have known the prohibition of

---

[468] Rothstein, "Sexual Union," 364-71.

[469] Rothstein, "Sexual Union," 368-69 n. 17, challenges the view of Halpern-Amaru, *Empowerment*, that 41:28 helps explain why the progeny was not annihilated (117), arguing that its purpose is to explain how Judah knew the appropriate punishment or to deflect criticism about its harshness, but this overlooks the emphasis on Judah's righteousness in 41:28, which enhances the case already supported by his contrition and by the angel's reassurance about Tamar's virginity, which *Jubilees* uses to ameliorate (but not excuse) the sin.

[470] Rothstein, "Sexual Union," 369.

which Judah was aware, because it was not yet revealed, and possibly *Jubilees* may mean us to read her action against the background that a father-in-law might legitimately fulfil levirate obligations.[471] The first suggestion is speculative, although it appears as an explanation for the more lenient treatment of Reuben in 33:16. The second must also be read into the text. It is an option which hearers might bring to the text, given that it played a role in the account of Onan. If it plays a role – and I do not consider this to be established – then the result is a dilemma, where to fulfil one obligation (though that was not his intent) Judah contravened another. It seems more likely that the author is intent on portraying Judah as a tragic figure, who began with a wrong choice, marrying a Canaanite wife, and then was trapped by circumstances largely beyond his control into a sin of incest, for which, given the ameliorating circumstances, but also his acknowledgement of wrongdoing, he was forgiven – and with him, Tamar.

Assuming coherent authorship in *Jubilees* 41, a twofold concern emerges. The author uses the sin of Jacob and Tamar as the starting point for warnings against incest, and at the same time must account for failure to apply the full penalty in the story. While the exposition in 21:23-28 does the former, the latter is addressed in both the telling of the story and the explanation, not least in the emphasis on Tamar's virginity. She was, indeed, Judah's daughter-in-law, but not in the same sense as had she already consummated her marriage with her husbands. This aspect, carefully articulated in both narrative and application, combines with the reference to Judah's repentance and subsequent conformity to the Law, helps to account for Judah and Tamar's survival and above all for the continuance of Judah's line.[472] *Jubilees* may, in fact, be less interested in seeking to ameliorate the sin, than to ameliorate its implications for the progeny. It did this by showing that the unwitting nature of the sin and Judah's contrition, combined with Tamar's virginity, were enough to obviate any lasting contamination on Judah's

---

[471] Rothstein, "Sexual Union," 368-69; similarly Segal, "Relationship," 219.

[472] Segal, "Relationship," identifies discrepancies between the narrative and the legal section. The narrative seeks to ameliorate the sin against the background of levirate marriage, which it interprets as allowing a father to fulfil the obligation where brothers cannot, whereas the legal section has no hesitation in declaring Judah's act a sin of incest. The narrative describes Tamar's apparent guilt by applying to her Lev 21:9, which had already been extended beyond priests' daughters to all women in Abraham's instruction in *Jub.* 20:4, whereas the legal section cites the penalty of fire on the basis of extending Lev 20:14 from sexual intercourse with a woman and her mother (so mother-in-law) to its converse (222-27). He then raises the issue whether the discrepancy should be seen as either the result of the author's using rewritten Genesis material as a source or of seeing the legal sections as additions to an existing work (227-28). But, as we have seen, the emphasis on virginity is common to both sections, the application of the levirate principle to Judah doubtful, and the differences over what constitutes Tamar's guilt derive from whether one is speaking before or after the event has been seen for what it was.

descendants, whose holiness is of importance to the author.[473] As VanderKam puts
it, "The royal line was thus saved from a heavy infusion of Canaanite impurity,
although in a morally dubious way".[474] At the same time, though not
contaminated, this beginning to the royal line is far from auspicious, and probably
reflects the author's awareness of what was to become a royal succession marked
by a high level of inadequacy, including sexual wrongdoing, and properly seen as
inferior to the line of Levi.

We shall return to the concern with incest in the next section where it is also a
theme in the story of Reuben and Bilhah. For the present we may note that the
problem arose in the first place because of the influence of the Canaanite woman
whom Judah should not have taken as wife.

Moses' foreign wife would also have been an embarrassment for *Jubilees*,
which solves the problem by passing over it in silence. Zipporah and her father
Jethro, never appear in the text.[475] *Jubilees* also rewrites the story of Moses'
beginnings to remove the impression that he was exposed in formative years to
Egyptian culture. Thus it portrays Jochabed as a nurturing mother, who, rather
than abandoning her son, tends him by night, as his sister, Miriam, tends him by
day (47:4). Moses then spends his first twenty-one years being nurtured by his
parents (47:9). He learned the art of writing from his father.[476] He is thus not
shaped in his formative years by a foreign culture, but by a faithful family of
Israel.[477]

3.2.4.4   Review

Intermarriage with Canaanites, with uncircumcised foreigners (30:13), is clearly a
major concern in *Jubilees*. It comes on the lips of Abraham (20:4; 22:21), Rebecca
(25:1, 3) and Isaac (27:10), whereas Genesis has only the latter express it (28:1). It
also lies behind the accounts of the marriages of generations before the flood in
Jubilees 4, which emphasises that people married within the family. It includes
concern "not to contaminate the holy line", as VanderKam suggests,[478] but it is

---

[473] So Halpern-Amaru, *Empowerment*, 116-17.

[474] VanderKam, *Book of Jubilees*, 2001, p. 79

[475] See Halpern-Amaru, *Empowerment*, 124-25. See also Jacques T. A. G. M. van
Ruiten, "The Birth of Moses in Egypt according to *The Book of Jubilees* (*Jub* 47.1-9)," in
*The Wisdom of Egypt: Jewish, Early Christian, and Gnostic Essays in Honour of Gerard P.
Luttikhuizen* (ed. Anthony Hilhorst and George H. van Kooten; AJEC 59; Leiden: Brill,
2005) 43-65, 58.

[476] On the importance of this motif in *Jubilees*, see van Ruiten, "Birth of Moses," 63.

[477] On this see Halpern-Amaru, *Empowerment*, 124.

[478] VanderKam, "Origins and Purposes," 18-19; similarly VanderKam, *Book of
Jubilees*, 2001, p. 125.

clearly about more than that. For *Jubilees*, the problem of intermarriage is inseparable from the anxiety about the contaminating effects, especially of sexual wrongdoing. As VanderKam notes: "Impurity is also associated with improper marriages and illicit sexual relations".[479]

As Hayes shows convincingly, the issue is not ritual impurity, as though intermarriage produced contamination by physical touch, but moral impurity, which takes place in the act of illicit sexual relations, described as *zenut*.[480]

> For *Jubilees*, intermarriage is Pentateuchally prohibited *zenut*, an immoral act of sexual union with one of the nonholy seed, generating a moral impurity that defiles the holy seed of Israel. *Jubilees* does not assume, as some have argued, a Gentile ritual impurity that defiles the Israelite.[481]

Jonathan Klawans notes that a supposed inherent ritual impurity of Gentiles, were it present, would pose a problem for *Jubilees* which assumes Gentile slaves in Jewish households (15:12-13, 24).[482] He also notes that *Jubilees* refers to ritual purity in only a few passages, like the childbirth purity laws in 3:8-14, and the impurity of the second tithe after a year (32:13).[483] Similarly Ravid notes the lack of interest both in purity laws and in provisions for purification in *Jubilees*, but also that it is "not concerned with impurity arising from the human body, forbidden foods or unclean animals".[484] She argues that even where purification is an issue, such as before entering the Garden of Eden or before approaching other holy sites, purification "is invariably intended not to eradicate impurity, but to enhance the sanctity of the 'holy seed'".[485] Of intermarriage Hayes writes: "it is in itself a violation of Torah law. Intermarriage is prohibited in Lev 18 and 20 as one of the heinous sins which can generate severe moral impurity. That impurity defiles the line of descendants of an interethnic union".[486] In this sense she argues it can also be described as "a genealogical impurity."[487]

For *Jubilees*, however, the issue is not just the marriage, the illicit act of sexual intercourse. It is also the moral influence which *Jubilees* sees as inevitable

---

[479] VanderKam, *Book of Jubilees*, 2001, p. 132.

[480] See also Ravid, "Purity and Impurity," who speaks of "metaphysical impurity" (71).

[481] Hayes, *Gentile Impurities*, 76. She sets her view in contrast to Endres, *Biblical Interpretation*, 75 n. 49, 145 and Werman, "*Jubilees* 30," 11, 14-15. See also her discussion on pp. 73-81 and in Hayes, "Intermarriage and Impurity,"15-25.

[482] Jonathan Klawans, *Impurity and Sin in Ancient Judaism* (Oxford: Oxford University Press, 2000) 180 n. 36.

[483] Klawans, *Impurity*, 47.

[484] Ravid, "Purity and Impurity," 75.

[485] Ravid, "Purity and Impurity," 74, similarly 75, 76.

[486] Hayes, *Gentile Impurities*, 81.

[487] Hayes, *Gentile Impurities*, 80.

through such unions, especially focussed on sexual wrongdoing. In relation to moral impurity Ravid argues:

> According to the book of *Jubilees*, there is no impurity in Israel's nature; only the Gentile nations are inherently impure. The Israelites are pure by their very nature; but they may be defiled by sexual contact with the Gentiles, or by adopting the latter's customs and way of life. As long as they refrain from falling into such offenses, their pure nature will remain unsullied.[488]

Speaking of such relationships Klawans writes: "The concern here is not that Gentile persons are ritually defiling, but that Gentile behavior is morally abominable, because Gentiles practice idolatry (22:17-22) and perform sexual transgression (20:3-7)."[489]

Sometimes *Jubilees* simply speaks of impurity, where we could consider that the sole focus is idolatry. But in most instances sexual impurity is to the fore. As Halpern-Amaru notes, concern with cultural influence, i.e. idolatry, seems limited to "the less particularistic contexts of the antediluvian genealogy and in Abraham's testament to all his children".[490] Thus one of the major reasons for the prohibition of marriages with Canaanites is that they will lead Israelite men into sexual wrongdoing. Canaanite women are "evil" (27:8). "Everything that they do (consists of) sexual impurity and lewdness" (25:1). "*Jubilees* consistently associates Canaanite women with 'sexual impurity, uncleanness,' 'lewdness,' 'evil' (20:3-4; 25:1; 27:8) and likens unions with such women to the sins of the Watchers and Sodomites (20:5)".[491]

---

[488] Ravid, "Purity and Impurity," 70. See also Himmelfarb, "Sexual Relations," who observes: "At the center of *Jubilees*' interest in sexual behaviour are not the purity laws, ... but rather the laws of forbidden sexual relations" (25).

[489] Klawans, *Impurity and Sin*, 48. He speaks thus of the defiling effect of sins, including murder, idolatry and sexual wrongdoing (seen also as the sin of Sodom and Gomorrah) (179 n. 27). Hayes, *Gentile Impurities*, questions whether Gentiles are inherently morally impure in either Ezra or *Jubilees*, as Klawans earlier implies, since both acknowledge their right to be present in the community as resident aliens (81). Cf. Klawans: "As in Ezra and Nehemiah, the moral impurity of Gentiles is deemed to be inherent, and therefore intermarriage is prohibited (30:7)" (48). But Klawans continues: "Indeed, not only is intermarriage prohibited, but it appears to have become a source of moral defilement in its own right, presumably because of the fear that it leads to idolatry (30:8-9, 13-14)" (48).

[490] Halpern-Amaru, *Empowerment*, 154.

[491] Halpern-Amaru, *Empowerment*, 121. Cf. Endres, *Biblical Interpretation*, who speaks of : "The recurring prohibition of exogamy ... retrojected into the pre-Mosaic period, not only in the speeches (e.g., *Jub.* 22:20a), but also in the narrative" (213). But we need to see it is not just exogamy, but, associated with it, sexual wrongdoing in particular. It is not racial purity, nor even idolatry, primarily. "Exogamous marriage presented the most acute transgression, since it exposed the Israelite spouse and the children to the dangers of

Hayes sees *Jubilees* standing in continuum with Ezra in making the holy seed the rationale for forbidding intermarriage:

> While Ezra emphasizes the profanation and sacrilege that result from intermarriage, *Jubilees* places emphasis on intermarriage as an act of *zenut* (sexual immorality) that not only profanes but also defiles the holy seed of Israel, in addition to profaning God's holy name, defiling the sanctuary, and threatening the entire community.[492]

She notes the development of the ban on intermarriage from the initial prohibition with the seven Canaanite nations (Deut 7:3-4 and Exod 34:15) "based on the fear that intimate contact with Canaanites will lead Israelites to imitate their idolatrous and immoral ways"[493] to the ban in Deut 23:2-9 based on ethnic enmity, to Ezra's ban based on the identification of Israel as holy seed (Ezra 9:1-2; Mal 2:11-12), based on P notions of sacrilege.[494] Intermarriage can be tolerated where holiness is focused on the priesthood as in P, but H and D portray all Israel as holy and so the line followed in Ezra and *Jubilees* forbids all from sexual mingling with Gentiles.[495] The pollution created by intermarriage clearly extends to the people as holy and also to the temple. As Himmelfarb observes, "If the Holiness Code extends some of the status P reserves for priests to all Israel by emphasising the holiness of the people, *Jubilees* goes even further".[496]

> Failure to observe the ban on intermarriage results in defilement of the Temple. Even ordinary Jews are thus given a sort of priestly power. Only if they observe God's commandments regarding sexual relations will sacrifices, the priestly work *par excellence*, be acceptable.[497]

Everyone should be zealous like Levi. She relates this, in turn, to *Jubilees'*

---

idolatry, which the Gentile partner always represented" (233). He goes on to say: "In *Jubilees*, the author combined a concern for sexual impurity with the rejection of idolatry; the main characters witness to this stance" (233). It is indeed even stronger than that: the primary concern is sexual wrongdoing.

[492] Hayes, *Gentile Impurities,* 80.

[493] Hayes, "Intermarriage and Impurity," 6.

[494] Hayes, "Intermarriage and Impurity," 11. See also her expansive analysis in *Gentile Impurities,* 19-72.

[495] Hayes, *Gentile Impurities,* 81. Similarly Halpern-Amaru, *Empowerment*: "On every occasion when the polemic appears in the context of Israel, the argument stresses defilement and pollution." This explains also, she argues, the concern with genealogy, which is so vital for the priesthood. *Jubilees* makes all people "adjuncts to the priestly class" (154).

[496] Himmelfarb, "Sexual Relations," 30.

[497] Himmelfarb, "Sexual Relations," 30-31.

little interest in purity laws related to sexual relations, but it claims that forbidden sexual relations defile the sanctuary; when Jews engage in sexual relations, they are taking on priestly responsibilities for guaranteeing the purity of the sanctuary.[498]

In relation to holiness in *Jubilees*, Halpern-Amaru argues that it does not include the land,[499] unlike H.[500] *Jubilees*

> manifests a particular interest precisely in those matters of purity, intermarriage and idolatry that are linked to the retention of the Land in Torah legislation. However, when he inserts the legal material into his rewriting, he makes a point on not connecting them with acquisition and/or retention of the Promised Land.[501]

She cites Noah's instructions, and the stories of Dinah, Bilhah and Tamar:

> In each instance *Jubilees* … shifts the point of emphasis from defilement of the Land to defilement of the people of Israel, God's holy nation, "his own possession", the nation that "he owns". (33:11)[502]

This coheres with what she sees as *Jubilees*' displacement of the exile-restoration motif from the centre by one of "spiritual return and regeneration",[503] but, as Scott

---

[498] Himmelfarb, "Sexual Relations," 13-14. See also her comments in Martha Himmelfarb, "*Jubilees* and Sectarianism," in *Enoch and Qumran Origins: New Light on a Forgotten Connection* (ed. Gabriele Boccaccini; Grand Rapids: Eerdmans, 2005) 129-31, where she argues that *Jubilees* differed from the Qumran sectarians in seeing ancestry as constituting Israel as the holy people (130). Cf. Jackson, *Enochic Judaism*, who places *Jubilees* among writings which have as their focus not all of Israel, but an elite (214).

[499] Betsy Halpern-Amaru, "Exile and Return in *Jubilees*," in *Exile: Old Testament, Jewish, and Christian Conceptions* (ed. James H. Scott; JSJSup 56; Leiden: Brill, 1997) 127-44; similarly Milgrom, "Concept of Purity," 279, who notes that *Jubilees* avoids speaking of the land's defilement (186-87 n. 66).

[500] So Himmelfarb, "Sexual Relations," who notes that in *Jubilees* the fear is defiling the sanctuary as P, not the land as H. "Thus *Jubilees* follows H in extending the category of impurity to forbidden sexual relations, but it follows P in limiting the geographical extent of susceptibility to impurity to the Temple" (31).

[501] Halpern-Amaru, "Exile and Return," 138.

[502] Halpern-Amaru, "Exile and Return," 138.

[503] Halpern-Amaru, "Exile and Return," 141. The focus, she argues, moves from exile and restoration to an eschatology of return to paradise and to full age (142). "It appears that at the cosmic level of his eschaton the author has totally disengaged exile and return from the historical context of the Land. However in *Jubilees* cosmic and covenant history intersect. The garden of the first human is not the usual paradise. It is God's dwelling place, the site of the holy of holies" (142). "From the postexilic perspective of the author, restoration of a lost purity, not exile and return to the Land, is the signature of the imminent eschaton" (143).

has shown, place, including the temple, Zion, and the land remain of importance in *Jubilees*, especially for its eschatological vision.[504]

> From *Jubilees'* perspective, sacred space and sacred time will be brought into conformity with the foreordained divine will. When Israel finally repents of its sinful ways, not least with respect to the calendar, the period of the restoration will commence with the return of the exiles to the Land, as 'year zero' in the countdown to the culmination of the restoration 2450 years later at the second jubilee of jubilees.[505]

Noting the centrality of the temple and Zion he also sets this perspective within the land, citing 50:5, "Then they will live confidently in the entire land. They will no longer have any satan or any evil person. The land will be pure from that time until eternity" (186).[506] Scott is surely correct in noting the role land plays within the overall eschatological vision of *Jubilees*, but it remains the case that *Jubilees* never speaks of defilement of the land in the context of the sin of sexual wrongdoing.

Jubilees employs the language of contamination and pollution. It is probably best not to press the alternatives, as though it assumes either ritual impurity or only moral influence. The objection to intermarriage is, in fact, complex. It does include the fear that exposure through marriage to Gentiles will bring exposure to immoral influences (and idolatrous influence, although this is not as strong). But, on these grounds, the act of marrying anyone might be potentially objectionable. The concern with genealogies appears to assume continuing morally and religiously corrupting influence conveyed through a family line. But the absolute prohibition of intermarriage, even in the face of conversion and circumcision, suggests an ontology which goes beyond potential moral influence to the assumption that the act of marrying a Gentile is polluting. That pollution is more than potential or real

---

[504] Scott, *On Earth as in Heaven*, who notes the importance of restoration in *Jubilees'* eschatology (135) and the implied seriousness of the fall: "*Jubilees* regards the first sin to have had an all-important and harrowing effect on the whole subsequent human history. Moreover, *Jubilees* envisions a corresponding increase in human longevity which results from direct divine intervention as a consequence of Israel's repentance of sin, an acknowledgement of 'their sins and the sins of their ancestors' (*Jub.* 1:22)" (137). On the importance of Zion and the land in the hope of restoration see his major section on the land of Israel (161-209). He argues that it belongs to the structure of reversal based on liberation from slavery informed by Leviticus 25 and is part of the hope of the new creation (165-66). He also reinforces this view by citing *Jubilees'* statements about Israel as the new Adam ruling the whole earth, including all nations (a reversal of her history) (166-72), showing the importance for *Jubilees* of defining the extent of the land (183-86, 188-206) and portraying it in Edenic terms (187-88).

[505] Scott, *On Earth as in Heaven*, 206.

[506] Scott, *On Earth as in Heaven*, 186.

immoral influence on the person involved. It affects also the nation and the temple. This clearly takes it beyond only immoral influence.

There is also a further implicit assumption: that immoral influence will always be present among Gentiles. This latter assumption is what makes the act of intermarriage a sin and so a pollutant. It is an embracing of moral pollution. As a result already the act of intermarriage constitutes a breach and a pollutant, but for *Jubilees* this is always seen in connection also with what grounds that assumption of pollution in the first place, namely, abhorrent actions, including idolatry but especially sexual wrongdoing. Thus the rationale apparent in Deut 7:3-4 and Exod 34:15 concerning the idolatry and immorality among the nations continues to operate in *Jubilees*. Even in the story of Dinah, where in the application all the focus turns to the issue of intermarriage, we see what grounds the judgement that such intermarriage is pollutant, namely, in the abhorrent behaviour which the author enhances by highlighting Dinah's vulnerability and innocence. That the nations are "too impure (*rekus*) and despicable (*mennun*)" (30:13) is related also to their sexual wrongdoing. The ontology of pollution among Gentiles will strongly relate to the belief expressed in *Jub.* 15:31-32 that the evil spirits rule them, whereas God rules over Israel.

A further question sometimes arises about the extent of the prohibition, both with regard to whom one might marry and with regard to who is doing the marrying. Werman, for instance. suggests that *Jub.* 7:13 limits the prohibition of intermarriage to only the cursed Canaan and his descendants (cf. Gen 10:6).[507] The presence of Hagar, an Egyptian, within Abraham's household and, above all, Joseph's wife, Asenath, an Egyptian, not only counts against assuming Gentiles to be inherently pollutant, but also against assuming that intermarriage with all Gentiles is polluting. In this regard, Halpern-Amaru identifies four levels of acceptance of wives: 1. women "of appropriate consanguinity (i.e., the woman is neither aunt nor niece of her spouse) and descended from the line of Terah"; 2. "secondary wives ... , who descend from the line of Aram, son of Shem and brother of Arpachshad"; 3. "Egyptian women"; and 4. "Women who originate from the Canaanite peoples".[508]

The fourth category may be too sharply drawn, although it is one way of explaining why to marry into the line of one of Ham's sons is acceptable, namely

---

[507] Werman, "*Jubilees* 30," notes: "Joseph is the only son of Jacob who marries an illicit foreigner (an Egyptian). The author must, therefore, present a more favorable portrayal of the Egyptians than those in the Bible, in order to render the action of a member of Jacob's family less unacceptable. The curse against Canaan applies solely to him and not to the entire family of Ham, as in the Bible; Egypt has no share in Canaan's act. Egypt objects to Canaan's settlement in the land of Shem's sons" (3). Similarly Halpern-Amaru, *Empowerment*, 104.

[508] Halpern-Amaru, *Empowerment*, 130.

Mizraim, rather than into the line of the cursed Canaan. But what about other Gentiles, for instance, from the descendants of Japheth? In 25:1 Rebecca appears not simply to be instructing Jacob not to marry a Canaanite, but more positively to marry within his own broad clan. Are the sins of the nations only those of Canaan? This would not make sense of the warning about circumcision and nakedness in the early chapters, especially if they refer to Hellenistic practices and perhaps to the influence of the Kittim. Clearly *Jubilees* disapproves of Nahor's marrying a Chaldean in 11:9 and the same applies to the marriages of Eber (8:7), Peleg (10:18), and Ragew (11:1). The answer may lie elsewhere than in distinguishing between the sons of Ham. *Jubilees* appears to be distinctly positive in its attitude towards Egyptians, contrary to its pentateuchal sources, and its acceptance of Asenath flows from there, rather than from an approval of all Gentile intermarriage outside of the Canaanite nations.

Egyptians practised a form of circumcision, but then so did most Canaanites. The marriage coheres with what appears to be a positive stance towards Egypt in *Jubilees*. Thus according to *Jubilees* the ruler who oppresses Israel in Egypt is not an Egyptian, but a Canaanite who had invaded the land ("The king of Canaan conquered the king of Egypt and closed the gates of Egypt. He conceived an evil plan against the Israelites in order to make them suffer." 46:11-12). This may allude to the evil of the Seleucids in the author's day and sympathies with the Ptolemaic regime. Docherty also notes that *Jubilees* omits "the embarrassing references in Genesis to the fact that to eat with the Hebrews or to follow the Hebrews' occupation of shepherding were an abomination to the Egyptians (Gen 43:32; 46:31-34; cf. *Jos. Asen.* 7.1)."[509] Halpern-Amaru points out that Mizraim even tries to dissuade Canaan from taking land belonging to Shem (10:29-33).[510] We shall return to the special place of Egyptians in *Jubilees* in the conclusion.

Halpern-Amaru asks why the polemic against intermarriage is "so heavily focussed on foreign wives", rather than foreign men.[511] She notes that the process of integration of foreigners was more rapid if a Jewish male married a foreign wife, because of the complexities of property rights. "The offspring of the foreign woman who adopted the residence and the national culture of her Israelite husband

---

[509] Susan Docherty, "Joseph the Patriarch: Representations of Joseph in Early Post-biblical Literature," in *Borders, Boundaries and the Bible* (ed. Martin O'Kane; JSOTSup 313; London; New York: Sheffield Academic Press, 2002) 194-216, 210.

[510] Halpern-Amaru, *Empowerment*, 104. See also her discussion on pp. 121-22, where she notes that Joseph's wife has the same Egyptian origin as Hagar, but that *Jubilees* has, in addition, identified her as daughter of Potiphar, thus, like *T. Jos.* 18:3; *Gen. Rab.* 85:2; 86:3; 89:2, merging the identity of Pharaoh's chief cook, who first purchased Joseph, and the father of Asenath.

[511] Halpern-Amaru, *Empowerment*, 151.

could potentially be absorbed within a generation."[512] *Jubilees* takes a conservative approach to such integration and to the kind of conversion entailed, for instance, in the case of Achior in Judith. Its strict line is in accord with CD 14.3-6 and 4QpNah 3-4, which treat proselytes as a separate category, and 4QFlor 1.3-4, which declares that in future "an Ammonite, a Moabite, and a bastard and an alien and a proselyte" shall never enter the temple. She notes that the Temple Scroll forbids entry to proselytes into the temple for up to three or four generations. She also suggests that *Jub.* 50:7 may reflect a deliberate change of status of the resident alien to the total outsider, replacing גֵּר of Exod 20:10 by נכרי.[513] This would fit the deletion of circumcision from the Dinah story. "*Jubilees* is opposed to any mode of entry into the holy community other than by birth."[514]

> With its genealogical system, its minimal expression of concern with the cultural impact of intermarriage in contrast with its obsessive concern with generic purity, and its ascription of a priest-like status to all Israelites, *Jubilees* clearly manifests an apprehension that is more concerned with being the assimilator than with becoming assimilated.[515]

Intermarriage is a major concern for the author. Himmelfarb, however, questions this, noting "The vehemence of *Jubilees'* rhetoric is not necessarily an indication of the prominence of the practice that elicits it", citing incest between father and daughter as an instance of this, where widespread practice, she argues, is surely not assumed.[516] The latter is, of course, an argument from silence, but the difference between the two is that intermarriage receives such extensive treatment in *Jubilees* and is brought into connection with clear allusions to the author's world. We shall return to this below, but it is at least likely that such emphasis reflects the author's concern and that this emphasis has to do with how the author sees contemporary dangers. It is significant that in both Jubilees 23 and 30 intermarriage (of both men and women) is brought into relationship to defilement of the temple and to national disaster. Whatever the setting, the concern is clearly both with intermarriage and the influences which it brings, in particular, in relation to sexual wrongdoing

The most dramatic examples are the rape of Dinah by the Shechemites and the sin of Judah. In the first *Jubilees* heightens the severity of the crime by painting Dinah as a small girl only 12 years old (30:2) and sharpens the contrast between Jacob and his sons and the Shechemites who together seized Dinah (30:2, 3).

---

[512] Halpern-Amaru, *Empowerment*, 155.

[513] Halpern-Amaru, *Empowerment*, 157.

[514] Halpern-Amaru, *Empowerment*, 157; similarly Hayes, *Gentile Impurities*, 85.

[515] Halpern-Amaru, *Empowerment*, 159.

[516] Himmelfarb, "Levi, Phinehas," 16.

Although the application focuses on the sin of marrying a Canaanite or giving one's daughter in marriage to Canaanites (30:7,10-11), the act of wrongdoing remains in the background as characteristic of the sins of the nations. Even in the explanation which follows other sins beside the sin of intermarriage remain in view, including rape of virgins (30:5-6) and adultery (30:8).

Similarly the account of Judah and Tamar and the sins which precede it find their origin in the influence of Judah's Canaanite wife, emphasised by *Jubilees* (41:2). *Jubilees* heightens the contrast emphasising that Tamar was an Aramean (41:1). These sins include failure to consummate marriage through sexual intercourse (41:2-3) and rejecting levirate duty and spilling semen (41:4-6). But Bedsuel's influence (41:12; not Judah's fear as in Gen 38:11,14), also contributes to sins within Israel, such as Tamar's act of prostitution, which also entailed breaching the laws concerning incest (41:7), of which Judah, too, is guilty (41:23). *Jubilees'* mention of Judah's Canaanite wife in 34:20 comes long before the events that ensued in 41:1-21. Given Judah's special position, blessed by Isaac (31:18-20) along with Levi (31:13-17), the hearer expects the worst and for those who knew the notorious outcome this enhances the drama. But *Jubilees* uses the intervening chapter to depict Judah in the military role in the context between Esau and Jacob, foreshadowing the conflict between Israel and Edom right through to the author's own day. *Jubilees* also juxtaposes Judah and Joseph in a way that the latter provides the model of the idea ruler, who resists sexual wrongdoing, and the former is flawed by marrying a Canaanite with disastrous consequences of entanglement of sexual wrongdoing.

Jubilees also develops a stronger contrast between Jacob and Esau as model examples of opposite responses to the instruction not to marry a Canaanite (25:5, 8-9). That Esau finally marries correctly is noted, but only incidentally (29:13), unlike the account in Genesis which suggests change of heart (28:1-5). Jacob had kept himself celibate, indeed, not touched a woman before his move to seek a wife from the household of Laban (25:4,7). Rebecca issues instructions and ensures success for Jacob throughout as the son whom she loves. In this context *Jubilees* introduces the law about always taking in marriage the elder daughter before the younger (29:26).

The sexual sinfulness of the Canaanites does not however stand alone. *Jubilees* draws it into relation with the sins of Sodom (22:22), the generation of the giants and their successors in the land, the Amorites, whose sexual wickedness shortens their lives (29:11), as it did from the time of Abraham (23:8-11) and the sin of Ham, their forefather (22:22). It also appears to address its own contemporary situation, perhaps in the allusion to the Kittim (24:24-30), but in particular in the continuing emphasis on the prohibition of intermarriage (30:14), the danger of priests defiling the temple through sexual wrongdoing (30:15-17), and in Abraham's instruction to separate from the nations and not to eat with them, a possible allusion to the dangers of symposia (22:16). The warnings of judgement for sin, including sexual wrongdoing, in *Jubilees* 23, the passage most widely recognised as addressing the author's situation, find a parallel in *Jubilees* 30:14 (cf. 23:13-14). Levi's descendants are apparently to exercise similar justice in the author's world (30:18-19) and so show themselves God's friends and not enemies (30:20-23). This fits the blessing of Levi in 31:13-17, which looks to future times. The blessing of Judah in 31:18-20 also brings contemporary princely power into view in the author's own time. Thus intermarriage has to be seen as a constant theme, sufficiently so, that it doubtless had direct relevance to the author's time.

3.2.5   Reuben and Bilhah

While we have already given considerable attention to the story of Judah and Tamar in the context of discussing the sexual evil of the Canaanites, we also noted that the angel of the presence applies it in particular to the prohibition of incest between father-in-law and daughter-in-law. Earlier, the account of Reuben and Bilhah, a single verse in Gen 35:22, becomes a narrative of 8 verses in our text of *Jubilees* (33:2-9) and the basis for teaching which extends to 33:20, also concerned with incest.

Gen 35:22 reads: "While Israel lived in that land, Reuben went and lay with Bilhah his father's concubine; and Israel heard of it". The deed also receives attention in Jacob's farewell speech in Genesis 49 in his words to Reuben which include: "Unstable as water, you shall no longer excel because you went up onto your father's bed; then you defiled it – you {Gk Syr Tg: Heb [he] } went up onto my couch!" (49:5; cf. also 1 Chron 5:1). To Genesis' brief account Jubilees adds that Reuben "saw Bilhah ... bathing in water in a private place". As Kugel has noted, the allusion to bathing may reflect an early interpretation of פחז כמים as meaning not "unstable as water", but "wanton in water".[517] There are intertextual echoes in 35:22 with the story of David and Bathsheba (2 Sam 11:2), although Bathsheba was not bathing "in a private place". The assumption is that Reuben saw Bilhah naked. The enticement through the eyes is a regular motif in stories of seduction (see already 20:4). *Jubilees* expresses the result: "he loved her". Thus Reuben finds her attractive and "falls in love" with her. The words can be neutral, but here they describe a process which according to *Jubilees* ought not to have occurred. *Jubilees* then imagines what happens next: "At night he hid.[518] He entered Bilhah's house at night and found her lying alone in her bed and sleeping

---

[517] James L. Kugel, "Reuben's Sin with Bilhah in the *Testament of Reuben*," in *Pomegranates and Golden Bells: Studies in Biblical, Jewish, and Near Eastern Ritual, Law, and Literature in Honor of Jacob Milgrom* (Winona Lake: Eisenbrauns, 1995) 525-54, 530.

[518] Only Ethiopic refers to night; cf. Latin and Syriac. On this see VanderKam, *Jubilees Translated*, 218 n. 33.3.

in her tent. After he had lain with her, she awakened and saw that Reuben was lying with her in the bed" (33:3-4). The account is not without its problems. How could he have sexual intercourse with her while she apparently remained asleep? The account in the *Testament of Reuben* "solves" this problem by assuming she was so drunk she did not notice (3:14). Perhaps *Jubilees* assumes the hearer will supply such detail from the story of Ham and Noah, where Noah lay drunk on his bed. Then the sexual wrongdoing would also include rape, but nothing in what follows addresses that.[519]

There are also intratextual links with the story of Joseph.[520] There Potiphar's wife calls out unjustly. Here Bilhah calls out justly (reflecting Deut 22:25-27). "She uncovered the edge of her (clothing),[521] took hold of him, shouted out, and realized that it was Reuben". It is interesting that *Jubilees* attends to such detail as that Bilhah does not simply cry out, but uncovers the edge of her clothing. The assumption is that this will show that she has been undressed by someone else and will remove any suspicion that she was compliant. Only after taking hold of him and shouting out does she realise it is Reuben. The identification added a new dimension to what had happened. "She was ashamed because of him".[522] "Once she had released her grip [lit. her hands] on him, he ran away. She grieved terribly [lit. very much] about this matter and told no one at all" (33:5-6). This was now not only rape (which must be assumed), but contravention of the laws of incest. The emphasis clearly falls on the latter, both in the narrative and in the exposition which follows. It will also account for Bilhah's letting Reuben go. He is not an intruder, but part of the household. She must not shame him in a public way. She is also victim to Reuben's lust, but behaves (according to the values of the time) appropriately.[523] Her actions might recall the actions of Joseph in reverse.[524] She then again acts appropriately, in informing Jacob[525] and grieving greatly. He, too,

---

[519] See the discussion in Segal, "Relationship," 206-208, who points to the tension between the narrative, which excuses Bilhah as innocent, and the legal interpretation that follows which withholds punishment from both on the grounds that the law was not yet known to all (210-14), suggesting to him "two different interpreters" (210-14).

[520] So also Halpern-Amaru, *Empowerment*, 110.

[521] Latin has *sagum* = garment כנף in Hebrew. On this see VanderKam, *Jubilees Translated*, 219 n. 33:4.

[522] Agreeing with the Syriac. Latin reverses the genders. On this see VanderKam, *Jubilees Translated*, 219 n. 33:5.

[523] So Halpern-Amaru, *Empowerment*, who notes "her regard for peaceful family relationships implied in her remaining silent (33:6)" (110).

[524] So also Halpern-Amaru, *Empowerment*, 110.

[525] Halpern-Amaru, *Empowerment*, speaks of her "pious concern that brings her to break that silence in order to prevent Jacob from engaging in sexual relationships with a contaminated woman (33:7)" (110).

acted appropriately in recognising she had become unclean for him and so in no longer having sexual relations with her.

In the sequel, which describes Bilhah's response to Jacob, we see some fundamental assumptions. By having had sexual intercourse with Reuben (however against her will), Bilhah has become unclean for Jacob. In the narrative she expresses it thus: "I am not pure (*naṣḥa*) for you because I am contaminated (*gamana*) for you,[526] since Reuben defiled (*rak^wsa*) me and lay with me at night. I was sleeping and did not realize (it) until he uncovered the edge of my (garment) and lay with me" (33:7). We find this principle reflected for instance in Deut 24:1-4. *Jub.* 33:9 makes this explicit: "Jacob did not approach[527] her again because Reuben had defiled (*rak^wsa*) her".[528]

Jacob's anger at Reuben, according to 33:8, is that "he had uncovered the covering of his father". This is the language of incest legislation (Lev 18:7 "You shall not uncover the nakedness of your father ערות אביו גלה, which is the nakedness of your mother; she is your mother, you shall not uncover her nakedness"; Deut 27:30 "Cursed be anyone who lies with his father's wife, because he has uncovered his father's skirt (גלה כנף אביו)". Nothing is said about rape, although both Bilhah's precautionary action and her explanation emphasise that she was not a willing partner.

The angel of the presence then focuses on the event as a case of incest. "As for any man who uncovers the covering of his father — his act is indeed very bad (*'ekuy*) and it is indeed despicable (*mennun*) before the Lord" (33:9). The incest laws of Lev 18:6-18 do not make mention of concubines, but clearly they are subsumed under the category of wives. Sexual intercourse with one's father's wife (and by implication, concubine) is prohibited in a number of places in the Law (Lev 18:8; 20:11; Deut 22:30; 27:30). *Jub.* 33:10-11 repeat the prohibition, identifying its source:

---

[526] VanderKam, *Jubilees Translated*, treats it as a comparative, thus, *too contaminated,* but this does not take into account the fact that she was rendered unclean, not too unclean (2. 220 n. 33:7).

[527] On the different readings where Latin and Syriac read "know" and Ethiopic, "approach", see VanderKam, *Jubilees Translated*, 220 n. 33:9. In any case it refers to sexual engagement.

[528] See also Rothstein, "Sexual Union," 371-75, who also points to David's setting aside his former concubines who had been defiled by Absalom (2 Sam 20:3). The defilement is "a notion which *Jubilees* understood as reflecting ontological reality" (376). He rightly questions the interpretation of Kugel, "Reuben's Sin with Bilhah," who proposes that not having further sexual relations with Bilhah is a matter of restricting the progeny to just the twelve sons (538-40). This would then have to apply to all his wives, including Leah and Zilpah, as Rothstein notes (374-75).

For this reason it is written and ordained on the heavenly tablets that a man is not to lie with his father's wife and that he is not to uncover the covering of his father because it is impure (*rekus*). They are certainly to die together the man who lies with his father's wife and the woman too – because they have done something impure (*rekus*) on the earth. There is to be nothing impure (*rek^{w}s*) before our God within the nation that he has chosen as his own possession.

The prohibition, accompanied by the penalty, is to be found in Lev 20:11, "The man who lies with his father's wife has uncovered his father's nakedness; both of them shall be put to death; their blood is upon them". The angel then cites a second occurrence, creatively modified: "Again it is written a second time: 'Let the one who lies with his father's wife be cursed because he has uncovered his father's shame'. All of the Lord's holy ones said: 'So be it, so be it'" (33:12). This modifies Deut 27:30 which reads: "Cursed be anyone who lies with his father's wife, because he has uncovered his father's skirt. All the people shall say, 'Amen!'" The citation is loose. The response now comes from "the Lord's holy ones", meaning his angels. The discourse continues with one of the twelve emphatic addresses to Moses which elevate the importance of the instruction: "Now you, Moses, order the Israelites..." (33:13). Such incest is a

capital offence [lit. judgement of death, Heb מות משפט]^{529} ... an impure thing (*rek^{w}s*) ... for which there is no expiation ... the man who has done this ... is to be put to death, to be killed, and to be stoned and uprooted from among the people of our God ... not to be allowed to live a single day on the earth because he is despicable (*mennun*) and impure (*rekus*). (33:13-14)

Jubilees must then explain why Reuben did not suffer this fate (33:15-16):

They are not to say: 'Reuben was allowed to live and (have) forgiveness after he had lain with the concubine-wife of his father while she had a husband and her husband his father Jacob — was alive.' For the statute, the punishment, and the law had not been completely revealed to all but (only) in your time as a law of its particular time and as an eternal law for the history of eternity.

From the time of Moses onwards, however, it is fully revealed (33:17).^{530} The emphasis on incest continues: "For all who commit it on the earth before the Lord

---

^{529} So VanderKam, *Jubilees Translated*, 222 n. 33:13. Note 21:22 also speaks of a mortal sin in Abraham's instruction to Isaac in the light of the people of Sodom and sinfulness of humankind – probably with sexual wrongdoing in mind.

^{530} On the problem that Reuben must at least have known about the sin of adultery, Rothstein, "Sexual Union," suggests that perhaps *Jubilees* means us to see Reuben believing that this did not apply to someone who was not a full wife (378-79).

are impure (*rekus*), something detestable (*saqorār*), a blemish (*nekafat*), and something contaminated (*gemmānē*)" (33:19). "No sin is greater than the sexual impurity (*zemmut*) which they commit on the earth. ... No such impurity (*rek^{w}s*) will be seen among the holy people" (33:20; cf. Exod 19:6; *Jub.* 16:18). We note the language used here in the context of sexual wrongdoing which we find elsewhere: "impure" (*rekus*), "detestable" (*saqorār*), "a blemish" (*nekafat*), "contaminated" (*gemmānē*), "sexual impurity" (*zemmut*).

The major emphasis on the prohibition of incest with one's father's wife is striking. It is also noteworthy that there is silence about what must also be assumed: that this was an act of rape. Incest returns as a major theme in the story of Judah and Tamar, as we have seen. There, too, we have the direct address to Moses: "Now you, Moses, order the Israelites ..." (41:26), which signals its importance, and there, too, there is need to explain why the perpetrators survived (in this instance: repentance, though with no explanation for Tamar). It had earlier occurred between Lot and his daughters. There *Jubilees* passes over the event very briefly, only modifying it from the Genesis account to the extent that it treats Lot as guilty along with his daughters (16:8). *Jub.* 16:9 then declares the judgement:

> It has been commanded and engraved on the heavenly tablets regarding all his descendants that he is to remove them, uproot them, execute judgement on them like the judgement of Sodom, and not to leave him any human descendants on the earth on the day of judgement.

33:20 confirms the emphasis on sexual wrongdoing reflected throughout *Jubilees*: "No sin is greater than the sexual impurity (*zemmut*) which they commit on the earth".

3.2.6   Joseph and Adultery

Jubilees has already made reference to adultery within the warnings which follow the account of the rape of Dinah:

> No adulterer (*zamma*) or impure person (*rekus*) is to be found [masc.] within Israel throughout all the time of the earth's history, for Israel is holy to the Lord. Any man who has defiled (*rak^{w}sa*) (it) [L. *eum*; missing in Eth.] is to die; he is to be stoned [lit. they are to stone him]. For this is the way it has been ordained and written on the heavenly tablets regarding any descendant of Israel who defiles (*rak^{w}sa*) (it): "He is to die; he is to be stoned". This law has no temporal limit. (30:8-10)

It could be assumed in the story of Abram and Sarai in Egypt: "his wife was taken from him by force" (13:11, 13), but this is unlikely.

In addition, *Jubilees* brings the specific example of attempted seduction to adultery in the story of Joseph (39:5-11). As in Genesis, the Joseph saga takes up a substantial portion of the book.[531] Nevertheless, *Jubilees* has chosen to tell the story of Joseph in three parts. The scene of the attempted seduction in *Jub.* 39:5-11 shares much with its source, Gen 39:6-20. Both emphasise Joseph's attractiveness and the effect of looking on such beauty, a motif which occurs in the account of the seduction by the Watchers of the human women and in the story of Reuben and Bilhah. As in the latter story, *Jubilees* adds that the Egyptian woman "loved him" (39:5; cf. 33:2). The next step in both stories is the attempt to have sexual intercourse. *Jubilees* does not disparage beauty in a sexual context (see its account of both Leah and Rachel, 28:5), but is clear about appropriate and inappropriate responses, depending on contexts. Reuben committed an act of sexual wrongdoing. Joseph resisted. Jacob fulfilled divine will.

Jubilees states simply: "But he did not surrender himself" (39:6). It does not repeat Joseph's explanation in Genesis that Joseph respects his master. Instead, the Joseph of *Jubilees*:

> remembered the Lord and what [lit. the words] his father Jacob would read to him from the words of Abraham — that no one is to commit adultery with a woman who has a husband; that there is a death penalty which has been ordained for him in heaven before the most high Lord. The sin will be entered [will ascend] regarding him in the eternal books forever before the Lord. (39:7)

Through the angel's explanation the author underlines the prohibition of adultery and reinforces it with the threat of the death penalty.[532] *Jubilees* offers no such teaching on the lips of Abraham, but it is to be understood as one of those "mortal sins" like incest (33:13) of which he spoke in 21:22 without specifying adultery, in particular, and is to be assumed also under his other warnings about impurity.

In 39:7 *Jubilees* brings us back from the digression, by repeating the detail of Joseph's remembering: "Joseph remembered what he had said". Accordingly, he "refused to lie with her". *Jubilees* then heightens the persistence of the temptation by replacing the "day after day" of Gen 39:10 with: "She pleaded with him for one year and a second, but he refused to listen to her" (39:8). The final act matches Genesis for detail except that *Jubilees* reports that she locked the door and that

---

[531] Docherty, "Joseph the Patriarch," observes: "As the story unfolds, the focus is on Joseph to such an extent that the other characters familiar from Genesis almost disappear from the scene" (209).

[532] So also Docherty, "Joseph the Patriarch," 211, who also notes the implied allusion to Joseph's rejection of adultery in the speech of Mattathias to his sons in 1 Macc 2:53, "Joseph in the time of his distress kept the commandment, and became lord of Egypt" (196).

Joseph had to break it down to flee (39:9)! Such was the strength of his commitment to keeping the Law. *Jubilees* trims the rest of the story so that the Egyptian woman no longer informs the household, but only her master, who saw not only the clothes but the broken door (39:10-11). While there is no softening of the prohibition of adultery, the story has a change of tone, as Halpern-Amaru notes.[533] Thus the woman's "attempts at seduction are more poignant and less coarse". She pleads rather than demands, does not humiliate her husband by announcing the deed before his household, but waits to tell him directly, and Potiphar emerges with greater dignity, doubtless to honour Joseph's lineage.

The account of Joseph's imprisonment, and subsequent rise, follows, including, in its climax, the information that Joseph received the daughter of one, Potiphar, as his wife, and at age 30 took up his position with the pharaoh (40:10-11; cf. Gen 41:45-46). Joseph is both a model Israelite and the model ruler.[534] The model man marries at the age when apparently most good men marry. Like Jacob, he has remained celibate before marriage. He has successfully negotiated the temptation to commit adultery. This stands in contrast to Judah, whose sin could potentially also be interpreted as adultery,[535] and, probably more important for the author of *Jubilees*, in contrast to his successors. As noted above in 3.2.4 in discussing intermarriage, *Jubilees* enhances the contrast between Joseph, the model ruler, and Judah, whose fortunes are beset by evil because of intermarriage with a Canaanite.

At the same time, as Halpern-Amaru observes, *Jubilees* makes Levi, rather than Joseph, the key figure of his generation in the line succession in the family.[536]

---

[533] Halpern-Amaru, *Empowerment*, 122.

[534] Docherty, "Joseph the Patriarch," notes what she sees as the entirely positive portrait of Joseph in *Jubilees*, achieved by omitting such details as the bad report he gave about his brothers (Gen 37:2), his special coat given him as his father's favourite, which engendered resentment from his brothers (37:3-4), his grandiose dreams (Gen 37:5-11), but also Joseph's use of his cup for divination (cf. Gen 43:2, 10) and the embarrassing feature (for friends of Egypt) that eating with Hebrews and being shepherds like Hebrews was abominable (Gen 43:32; 46:31-34) (208-12). But see the discussion below, in the light of which omission of the grandiose dreams may also reflect a changed assessment of Joseph's importance. On the omission of dreams see also Armin Lange, "Dream Visions and Apocalyptic Milieu," in *Enoch and Qumran Origins: New Light on a Forgotten Connection* (ed. Gabriele Boccaccini; Grand Rapids: Eerdmans, 2005) 27-34, who observes that *Jubilees* consistently either deletes dreams or avoids (or even loses) their allegoric character, a feature which reflects deliberate differentiation from the apocalyptic milieu of Danielic and Enochic groups and a more priestly background (33).

[535] One reading speaks of Tamar's sin as adultery (41:16).

[536] So Betsy Halpern-Amaru, "Burying the Fathers: Exegetical Strategies and Source Traditions in *Jubilees* 46," in *Reworking the Bible: Apocryphal and Related Texts at Qumran: Proceedings of a Joint Symposium by the Orion Center for the Study of the Dead*

Joseph is not the mediator of the patriarchal covenant. Accordingly, *Jubilees* reworks the brief transitional material in Exod 1:1-8, so that

> the death of Joseph is neither a turning point in the narrative nor of major significance in Israelite history. Other historical circumstances precede and precipitate the enslavement of Jacob's descendents in Egypt.[537]

While *Jubilees* retains Joseph's significance in the public sphere, it reduces his significance in the sphere of the family, where he is treated just as one of the sons among whom the privileged one is not Joseph (*Jubilees* had also earlier omitted his dreams to that effect), but Levi, to whom Jacob gave his books and those of his father (45:16).[538] "Jacob's designation of Levi as heir to the patriarchal books (*Jub.* 45:16) replaces his final testament to Joseph (Gen 47:29-31)."[539] Referring to *Jub.* 46:10, Halpern-Amaru writes: "By placing Amram at the patriarchal homestead, i.e., 'on the mountain of Hebron,' *Jubilees* assigns to him the precise role that its exegesis had so deliberately taken away from the biblical Joseph".[540]

Sea Scrolls and Associated Literature and the Hebrew University Institute for Advanced Studies Research Group on Qumran, 15-17 January, 2002 (ed. Esther G. Chazon, Devorah Dimant, and Ruth A. Clements; STDJ 58; Leiden: Brill, 2005) 135-53. See also Halpern-Amaru, "Midrash," 345-47.

[537] Halpern-Amaru, "Burying the Fathers", 136.

[538] Halpern-Amaru, "Burying the Fathers", 138-40.

[539] Halpern-Amaru, "Burying the Fathers", 145. She sees *Jubilees* achieving this, in part by drawing on traditions also present in 4QVisions of Amram/4Q543-4Q547 (145-49). "Diminution of Joseph's significance and elevation of Levi and his line are the chief interests that drive the exegesis in *Jubilees* 46" (152).

[540] Halpern-Amaru, "Burying the Fathers", 144-45.

3.2.7   The Speeches of Noah and the Patriarchs

Among the major additions which *Jubilees* makes to the narrative of Genesis are farewell speeches or instructions, sometimes associated with responses or conversations. As such they have an important role in indicating primary concerns of the author.[541] These include the following:

7:20-39 Noah instructs his sons and grandsons

19:15-31 Abraham blesses Jacob (1)
20:1-13 Abraham instructs his sons and their families
21:1-26 Abraham instructs Isaac
22:10-24 Abraham blesses Jacob (2)
22:27-30 Abraham blesses Jacob (3)

25:1-3 Rebecca warns Jacob about Canaanite women
(25:4-10 Jacob responds)
25:11-14 Rebecca gives thanks for Jacob
25:15-23 Rebecca blesses Jacob

31:11-17 Isaac blesses Levi
31:18-20 Isaac blesses Judah

35:1-8 Rebecca and Jacob converse on Jacob's goodness and Rebecca's burial
35:9-17 Rebecca talks to Isaac about Jacob and Esau
35:18-27 Rebecca seeks to reconcile Jacob and Esau
36:1-17 Isaac's farewell speech to Jacob and Esau

Surprisingly, *Jubilees* omits the only major farewell speeches in Genesis, those of Jacob for Joseph's sons (48:1-22) and for his own sons (49:1-28), noting them only in summary (45:14). The blessings of Levi and Judah by Isaac reflect a special interest in the two roles which belong to their tribes, the future priesthood and the future ruler. The other speeches include both blessing and instruction, and apply to both the immediate descendants and to successive descendants. It is especially noteworthy that the key figures giving such instruction include not only Noah, Abraham and Isaac, but also Rebecca, who, while taking her gendered place in subordination to Isaac, shows herself superior in wisdom and perception.

---

[541] So also Schwarz, *Identität*, 18.

I return to her role below in discussing the way figures within the narrative function. In this section I want to concentrate on the substance of these speeches of instruction, in particular, in relation to sexuality, a theme, as we have seen, also implied in Yahweh's opening speech and explicit in the angel's excurses. Thus far we have noted aspects of the speeches in relation to particular motifs. This discussion will look at the speeches in themselves and so consider their statements about sexual wrongdoing within that context.

3.2.7.1 *Noah Instructs his Sons and Grandsons (7:20-39)*

Noah's instruction is reported indirectly in 7:20. "During the twenty-eighth jubilee Noah began to prescribe for his grandsons the ordinances and the commandments — every statute which he knew". The angel's report then highlights motifs which have featured in the narrative thus far.[542]

> He testified to his sons that they should do what is right, cover the shame of their bodies, bless the one who had created them, honor father and mother, love one another, and keep themselves from fornication (*zemmut*), uncleanness (*rek^{w}s*), and from all injustice (7:20).

The angel then provides the interpretation of some of these references, in particular in relation to the generation of the giants.

> For it was on account of these three things that the flood was on the earth, since (it was) due to fornication (*zemmut*) that the Watchers had illicit intercourse (*zammawa*) – apart from the mandate (*te'zāz*) of their authority (*kwennanē*) – with women. When they married of them whomever they chose they committed the first (acts) of uncleanness (*rek^{w}s*). (7:21)

As noted above, the uncleanness (*rek^{w}s*) is the result of the illicit intercourse (*zemmut*). The two ideas belong together as cause and result. The focus is not simply on transgressing commandments, but transgressing boundaries between angels and human, illegitimate mixing. The third thing, injustice, expressed itself in killings, as 7:22-24a explains. Giants killed giants and the killing spread to human beings and even to animals. *Jubilees* explains that this was more than a series of wicked actions; it included thoughts and attitudes: "All the thoughts and wishes of mankind were (devoted to) thinking up what was useless and wicked all the time" (7:24b). The brief passage concludes by drawing together all three things in the summary of evil which warranted God's judgement in the flood: "Then the

---

[542] See also David Lambert, "Last Testament in the Book of Jubilees," *DSD* 11 (2004) 82-107, 99.

Lord obliterated all from the surface of the earth because of their actions and because of the blood which they had shed in the earth" (7:25). We should also note the allusions in 7:20. The instruction that they should "cover the shame of their bodies" derives from the story of the garden of Eden (3:30-31). Honouring parents probably alludes to Ham's dishonouring his father (7:7-8). Loving one another will partly allude to the story of Cain and Abel (4:2-4).

Noah's direct instruction comes in 7:26-39, introduced without transition with "We", as though Noah had already been speaking in 7:20-25.[543] The address begins with concerns that Noah's sons will fight each other, under the influence of the demons, and risk a similar obliteration to that executed on Noah's generation (7:26-27). 7:28 then juxtaposes two elements somewhat artificially (as already in Gen 9:3-6) on the basis of the word, blood: "For everyone who sheds human blood and everyone who consumes the blood of any animate being will all be obliterated from the earth". There follows instruction about not consuming blood (7:29-33). A similar juxtaposition concludes the instruction:

> Do not eat the life with the meat so that your blood, your life, may not be required from every person who sheds (blood) on the earth. For the earth will not be purified of the blood which has been shed on it; but by the blood of the one who shed it will the earth be purified in all its generations. (7:32-33)

In 7:36-39 Noah gives instruction about the offering of the first fruits of what is planted. It begins with a similar artificial word play.

> Do what is just and right so that you may be rightly planted on the surface of the entire earth. Then your honor will be raised before my God who saved me from the flood waters. You will now go and build yourselves cities, and in them you will plant every (kind of) plant that is on the earth as well as every (kind of) fruit tree. (7:34-35)

The author uses the motif of righteous planting elsewhere. Here the focus is on a particular observance. Such instruction we are told derives from Enoch.

In relation to themes of sexuality the important detail is in the indirect speech, in particular, 7:20-21. At the same time, we should note that the author assumes a nexus between sexual wrongdoing and other wrongdoing, exemplified in this speech by the story of the Watchers, whose sexual wrongdoing produced giants who brought bloodshed and injustice. Similar concern comes to expression in the multiple speeches of Abraham.

---

[543] According to Charles, *Jubilees*, 1902, 7:20-39 was a fragment of the lost *Book of Noah* (61 n. 20); similarly García Martínez, *Qumran and Apocalyptic*, 36.

3.2.7.2 *The Speeches of Abraham*

These are the most substantial speeches and include no less than three blessings of Jacob. This reflects some radical rewriting of Genesis. Gen 25:19-28 brings the account of Rebecca's barrenness, her subsequent conception, the struggle of Esau and Jacob in her womb, the Lord's prediction that the people of one child would serve the other, the appearance of the children at birth, and Jacob's grasping of Esau's heel. *Jubilees* trims this to a simple account of Rebecca giving birth to Jacob and Esau, noting that Jacob was perfect and upright, while Esau was a harsh, rustic, and hairy man (19:13).

Jubilees 19	Genesis 25
13 … Jacob was perfect and upright, while Esau was a harsh, rustic, and hairy man. Jacob used to live in tents.	
14 When the boys grew up, Jacob learned (the art of) writing,	27 When the boys grew up,
but Esau did not learn (it) because he was a rustic man and a hunter.	Esau was a skilful hunter, a man of the field,
He learned the art of warfare, and everything he did was harsh.	while Jacob was a quiet man, living in tents.
15 Abraham loved Jacob but Isaac (loved) Esau.	28 Isaac loved Esau, because he was fond of game; but Rebekah loved Jacob.

The distinctive features of *Jubilees*' idealised portrait of Jacob will concern us below. The key aspect to note here is that Jacob's birth comes in *Jubilees* before Abraham's death, not after it, as in Genesis. As a result, *Jubilees* can depict Abraham's attitude towards Jacob, including blessings and instructions. Accordingly, here in 19:15 initially not Rebecca, but Abraham loves Jacob in contrast to Isaac, although the author will retain and enhance the motif of Rebecca's special love for Jacob. That already begins to happen as he depicts Abraham instructing Rebecca to take special care of him (19:17), becomes explicit in 19:19, and reaches its full enhancement in 19:31 ("Rebecca loved Jacob with her entire heart and her entire being very much more than Esau; but Isaac loved Esau much more than Jacob"). Abraham's words to Rebecca include prediction of the special role of the people of Israel (19:17-25), climaxing in the wish: "May they serve (the purpose of) laying heaven's foundations, making the earth firm, and renewing all the luminaries which are above the firmament". Israel's renewal is inseparable from the renewal of all creation, including the stars which went astray (cf. *1 Enoch* 18:15).

3.2.7.2.1   Abraham Blesses Jacob (1) (19:15-31)

Abraham offers a first blessing to Jacob explicitly in 19:26-29. The implications for the story of Jacob are that his status as the blessed one was not the result of deceit, but given by no lesser authority than Abraham, himself. It includes also a warning about the spirits of Mastema: "May the spirits of Mastema not rule over you and your descendants to remove you from following the Lord" (19:28). The hearer is left to fill out the meaning of this warning. 15:31-32 had already spoken of the nations as ruled by spirits to lead them astray from God and the need to guard Israel, God's own people. Part of that meaning will be to avoid the sins of sexual wrongdoing which are rooted in the origins of these spirits, namely the sins of the Watchers.

3.2.7.2.2   Abraham Instructs his Sons and their Families (20:1-13)

This focus on sexuality finds its confirmation in the account of Abraham's address to his sons and their families (20:2-10).[544] As with Noah's speech, the angel reports the instruction in indirect speech. Its themes are similar, as the table below shows:

Abraham's Instruction, *Jubilees* 20	Noah's Instruction, *Jubilees* 7
2 He ordered them to keep the way of the Lord so that they would do what is right and they should love one another; that they should be like this every war so that they could go against each other (who was) against them; and do what is just and right on the earth; 3 that they should circumcise their sons in the covenant which he had made with them; that they should not deviate to the right or left from all the ways which the Lord commanded us; that we should keep ourselves from all sexual impurity (*zemmut*) and uncleanness (*rek^{w}s*); and that we should dismiss all uncleanness (*rek^{w}s*) and sexual impurity (*zemmut*) from among us.	20 He testified to his sons that they should do what is right, cover the shame of their bodies, bless the one who had created them, honor father and mother, love one another, and keep themselves from fornication, uncleanness, and from all injustice.

---

[544] On the significance of the speeches and their biblical background see Lambert, "Last Testament". He argues that Gen 18:19 plays a significant role in the development of Abraham's speech in *Jub.* 20:1-10, which takes from there the emphasis on what is right and what is just (85-94). Other biblical sources for his testament include Gen 28:1-4, the advice against exogamy (96).

The emphasis falls on brotherly love, including cooperation in the face of a common enemy, observance of circumcision (newly given to Abraham in 15:11-14), and, as in the instruction of Noah: keeping from sexual wrongdoing. The latter receives the major emphasis. We meet the familiar terms: "sexual impurity (*zemmut*)" and "uncleanness (*rek*ʷ*s*)". There is a slip of person in 20:3 from indirect speech about what "they" (Abrahams' children should do) to "we", in particular, in relation to the warning about sexual wrongdoing, perhaps highlighting its contemporary relevance for the author. This emphasis continues with the specific reference to women committing sexual offences, and then to men, where the seduction of the eyes and the heart might lead them to take Canaanite wives.

> If any woman or girl among you commits a sexual offence (*zammawa*), burn her in fire; they are not to commit sexual offences (*zammawa*) (by) following their eyes and their hearts so that they take wives for themselves from the Canaanite women, because the descendants of Canaan will be uprooted from the earth (20:4).

As in Noah's speech, the warning is buttressed by reference to the punishment of the giants, but also of Sodom:

> He told them about the punishment of the giants and the punishment of Sodom — how they were condemned because of their wickedness (*'ekay*), because of the sexual impurity (*zemmut*), uncleanness (*rek*ʷ*s*), and corruption (*musenā*) among themselves they died in (their) sexual impurity (*zemmut*). Now you keep yourselves from all sexual impurity (*zemmut*) and uncleanness (*rek*ʷ*s*) and from all the contamination (*gemmānē*) of sin (*xati'at*) so that you do not make our name into a curse, your entire lives into a (reason for) hissing and all your children into something that is destroyed by the sword. Then you will be accursed like Sodom, and all who remain of you like the people of Gomorrah. (20:5-6)

The speech then concludes in 20:7 with a warning against idols: "I testify to you my sons: love the God of heaven and hold fast to all his commandments. Do not follow their idols and their uncleanness (*rek*ʷ*s*)". Here "uncleanness (*rek*ʷ*s*)" probably continues the reference to sexual wrongdoing from the previous verses, but in close association with idolatry, the focus of 20:8. The speech concludes with a promise that worshipping the most high God would bring blessing through them to all peoples (20:9-10).

3.2.7.2.3 *Abraham Instructs Isaac (21:1-26)*

In 21:1 Abraham turns specifically to Isaac, alone. Abraham's instruction is extensive (21:2-25). It begins with Abraham referring to his own example of rejecting idols (21:2-4). 21:5 states the conclusion: "Now you, my son, keep his commands, ordinances, and verdicts. Do not pursue unclean things ($rek^w s$), statues, or molten images". "Unclean things ($rek^w s$)" probably refers primarily to idolatry, as the preceding context suggests, although we note the frequent use of the word in relation to sexual impurity. 21:6 then repeats the instruction given already by Noah about consuming blood: "Do not eat any blood of an animal, cattle, or of any bird that flies in the sky". There follow instructions about how to offer sacrifices and consume them (21:7-11), based on instructions received from Noah and Enoch, which wood is to be used in sacrifices (21:12-15), washing, removal of blood, avoidance of eating blood, or receiving bribes about bloodshed (21:16-20). Apart from the possible allusion in 21:5, the speech does not address sexual wrongdoing to this point. Much of it has a parallel in *Aramaic Levi Document* in Isaac's instruction to Levi (7:1 – 9:18 / 19-47), which makes reference to previous instruction by Abraham (10:3 / 50).

In 21:21-24, however, the attention turns from cultic concerns to moral wickedness. "I see, my son, that all the actions of mankind (consist of) sin (*xaṭi'at*) and wickedness (*'ekay*) and all their deeds of impurity ($rek^w s$), worthlessness (*mennānē*) and contamination (*gemmānē*)" (21:21).[545] In the context of *Jubilees* this will include sexual wrongdoing, which has featured so strongly. *Jub.* 21:22 warns about sin worthy of death: "Be careful not to walk in their ways or to tread in their paths so that you may not commit a mortal sin before the most high God". It will include those sins of sexual wrongdoing whose punishment is death, to which *Jubilees* has already referred (20:4) and to which it returns (33:13, 18). The language which follows also suggests this context of meaning.

> Then he will hide his face from you and will hand you over to the power of your offenses. He will uproot you from the earth and your descendants from beneath heaven. Your name and descendants will be destroyed from the entire earth. (21:22b)

Accordingly, 21:23 warns against impurity: "Depart from all their actions and from all their impurity ($rek^w s$)". Finally, Abraham holds before Isaac the image of a righteous plant, already alluded to by Noah (21:24). The speech concludes with a blessing for the future (21:25).

3.2.7.2.4   Abraham Blesses Jacob (2) (22:10-24) and Abraham Blesses Jacob (3) (22:27-30)

Abraham's second blessing of Jacob (22:10-24) follows his own prayer of thanksgiving (22:7-9). It begins with a reference to doing what is right: "My son,

---

[545] Note the focus on sexual wrongdoing at the beginning of Isaac's instruction to Levi in *Aramaic Levi Document* 6:1-5 / 14-18.

Jacob, may the God of all bless and strengthen you to do before him what is right and what he wants". Beyond the positive, we also find concern about sin: "May he purify (*nasha*) you from all filthy pollution (*reshat rek^ws*) so that you may be pardoned for all your sin (*'abbasā*) and error (*sehtat*) through ignorance" (22:14). "Filthy pollution (*reshat rek^ws*)" probably includes reference to sexual wrongdoing. Given the emphasis thus far, this is likely. It is, however, even more likely to lie behind the warnings which follow.

> Separate from the nations, and do not eat with them. Do not act as they do ,and do not become their companion, for their actions are something that is impure (*rek^ws*), and all their ways are defiled (*gammana*) and something abominable (*mennānē*) and detestable (*saqorār*). (22:16)

We have discussed them in the context of mixing with the nations. The nations worship idols and, above all, they practice sexual wrongdoing. The allusion to mixing in meals suggests sexual wrongdoing in the context of *symposia* and similar feasts, and probably reflects the author's concern with the impact of Hellenisation in his time.

The focus on sexual wrongdoing is also present in what follows. 22:19 repeats the concern about impurity: "May he remove you from their impurity (*rek^ws*) and from all their error (*sehtat*)". The following verses also suggest this focus: "Be careful, my son Jacob, not to marry a woman from all the descendants of Canaan's daughters, because all of his descendants are (meant) for being uprooted from the earth" (22:20). The same associations continue in the reference to Ham's sin in 22:21. Idolatry is the focus of 22:22, where idolaters are threatened with the same fate as the people of Sodom. Abraham's prayer, in conclusion, is that Jacob will be kept from all such sin: "May the most high God keep you from corruption (*musenā*); and from every erroneous (*sehtat*) way may he rescue you" (22:23).

The final and third blessing of Jacob (22:27-30) is very brief and lacks further specific instruction.

3.2.7.3 *Rebecca's Instructions, Blessings and Advice*

3.2.7.3.1 *Rebecca Warns Jacob about Canaanite Women (25:1-3) and Jacob Responds (25:4-10)*

The third block of material includes instruction by Rebecca of Jacob and includes also Jacob's ideal response, which has the effect of reinforcing the message of the instruction. It is also striking that Rebecca is the spokesperson. This reflects her special role, which we discuss below. In 25:1-3 Rebecca warns Jacob about Canaanite women and bemoans Esau's decision to reject such advice. "My son, do not marry any of the Canaanite women like your brother Esau who has married two wives from the descendants of Canaan" (25:1). In *Jubilees*, Abraham had already advised against doing so (20:4). This makes Esau's act, one of disobedience. Genesis had mentioned no such instruction on the part of Abraham, but in Gen 26:24-25, after reporting Esau's Hittite wives, it adds the negative comment that "they made life bitter for Isaac and Rebekah". Gen 27:46 limits the embitterment to Rebecca:

> Then Rebekah said to Isaac, "I am weary of my life because of the Hittite women. If Jacob marries one of the Hittite women such as these, one of the women of the land, what good will my life be to me?"

Jubilees picks up the latter. Thus she states: "They have embittered my life", but then *Jubilees* supplies an explanation of how they did so:

> with all the impure things (*rek*^{w}*s*) that they do because everything that they do (consists of) sexual impurity (*zemmut*) and lewdness (*mer'āt*). They have no decency [lit. there is no righteousness with them (*masc.*)] because (what they do) is evil [lit. it/he is bad]. (25:1)

The issue is sexual wrongdoing.

Rebecca's report of being embittered by Esau's wives in Gen 27:46 is part of her ploy to persuade Isaac to send Jacob to Laban to seek a wife from his household and so enable Jacob to escape from Esau. When *Jubilees* repeats that story, the report of embitterment is far from a ploy. It expresses a central concern:

> Rebecca went in and said to Isaac: "I despise my life because of the two Hittite women whom Esau has married. If Jacob marries one of the women of the land who are like them, why should I remain alive any longer, because the Canaanite women are evil ('*ekuy*)"? (27:8)

Jubilees is thus using the tradition twice, the first time to introduce her special instruction to Jacob in 25:1, and then here in 27:8. The explanation, "because the Canaanite women are evil ('*ekuy*)", receives its content from the words of her instruction which follow 25:1, which identify their evil as "sexual impurity (*zemmut*) and lewdness (*mer'āt*)".

Returning to her words to Jacob in 25:1-3, she repeats her instruction of 25:1 in 25:3: "Now, my son, listen to me. Do as your mother wishes. Do not marry any of the women of this land but (someone) from my father's house and from my father's clan. Marry someone from my father's house". Jacob's positive response has the effect of reinforcing the theme of the instruction and expands it. Jacob has refrained from committing intercourse before marriage, indeed, more than that, has not even touched a woman, and certainly has not even considered marrying a woman of Canaan:

> Then Jacob spoke with his mother Rebecca and said to her: "Mother, I am now nine weeks of years [63 years] and have known no woman. I have neither touched (one) nor become engaged (to one), nor have I even considered marrying any women of all the descendants of Canaan's daughters". (25:4)

Thus according to *Jubilees*, he has obeyed Abraham's instruction, unlike Esau:

> For I recall, mother, what our father Abraham ordered me — that I should not marry anyone from all the descendants of Canaan's house. For I will marry (someone) from the descendants of my father's house and from my family. (25:5)

Again, we find reference to the underlying concern with sexual wrongdoing expressed in similar terms to those of Rebecca's instruction:

> For this reason I have kept myself from sinning (*'abbasa*) and from becoming corrupted (*māsana*) in any ways during my entire lifetime because father Abraham gave me many orders about lewdness (*mer'āt*) and sexual impurity (*zemmut*). (25:7)

The author then continues the negative portrait of Esau as he has Jacob report Esau's pressure to get Jacob to be disobedient:

> Despite everything he ordered me, my brother has been quarreling with me for the last 22 years and has often said to me: "My brother, marry one of the sisters of my two wives". But I have not been willing to do as he did. (25:8)

Jacob's response is ideal and he seals it with an oath:

> I swear in your presence, mother, that during my entire lifetime I will not marry any of the descendants of Canaan's daughters nor will I do what is wrong as my brother has done. Do not be afraid, mother. Be assured that I will do as you wish. I will behave rightly and will never conduct myself corruptly (דרכי אשחית *māsana fenot*). (25:9-10)

3.2.7.3.2 *Rebecca Gives Thanks for Jacob (25:11-14) and Blesses him (25:15-23)*

In response to Jacob's reply, Rebecca gives thanks to God for Jacob and asks to be able to give Jacob a righteous blessing (25:11-13). Accordingly a spirit of righteousness descended into her mouth (25:14) and she spoke a blessing (25:15-23). It is expressed in positive terms. It begins by speaking to God: "Blessed are you, righteous Lord, God of the ages" (25:15a), and from there transfers to Jacob: "and may he bless you more than all the human race" (25:15b). The content does not include instruction and warning. The blessing contains a very personal expression of Rebecca's affection in terms of birth and suckling:

> As you have given rest to your mother's spirit during her lifetime, so may the womb of the one who gave birth to you bless you. My affection and my breasts bless you; my mouth and my tongue praise you greatly. (25:19)

3.2.7.4   The Blessing of Levi and of Judah by Isaac

We pass over Isaac's blessings of Levi (31:11-17) and Judah (31:18-20) briefly, because they bear only indirectly on the issue of attitudes towards sexuality. In contrast to Jacob's blessing of his twelve sons in Gen 49:1-28, which *Jubilees* covers with a single verse (45:14), the writer gives great prominence to Levi and Judah. Levi's sons are to serve in the temple "like the angels of the presence and like the holy ones" (31:14). Strikingly, their roles include being "princes, judges, and leaders of all the descendants of Jacob's sons" (31:15). Judah's descendants will have to find their significant place in subordination to these roles. Levi's authority will express itself above all in teaching, declaring the word of the Lord justly and exercising judgement (31:15). The blessing honours Leah for rightly naming Levi and promises the benefits of sharing the Lord's table (31:16). It concludes, like the following blessing of Judah, with a blessing for those who bless his descendants and a curse for those who do not (31:17). *Jubilees* itself illustrates the teaching role. As we have seen, the story of Dinah has been rewritten to portray the actions of Levi (and Simeon) as appropriate to Levi's role, thus assuming for the priesthood the task of prosecuting above all sexual wrongdoing with justice. The author's concern with sexual wrongdoing reflects this role in action.[546] According to 45:16 Jacob "gave all his books and the books of his fathers to his son Levi so that he could preserve them and renew them for his sons until today". While at one level this narrowing of the succession makes a better transition to the next great figure in covenantal history, Moses,[547] it is surely much more than this, and reflects the continuing significance of priestly leadership, though defined as Levitical, limited neither to the line of Zadok nor to that of Aaron, whom Jubilees passes over in silence.

---

[546] De Jonge and Tromp, "Jacob's son Levi," 203-36, observe: "The image of Levi in Isaac's blessing is essentially a laudatory description of actual functions in the Hellenistic period, when Jerusalem priests were in fact the rulers, teachers, and judges" (213). They also note that *Jubilees* is surprisingly silent about the role of atoning for the people (212).

[547] So Schwarz, *Identität*, 20.

The blessing of Judah in 31:18-20 assumes a military role for his descendants, through which Israel's safety and peace is secured. Judah will fulfil this role at the head of the army of his brothers against Esau and his sons. Unlike with Levi, whose deeds conform to divine will, *Jubilees'* account of Judah has an element of the tragic. His marrying a Canaanite dogs his story despite his best efforts, which *Jubilees* is careful to record. Again, the issue of sexual wrongdoing is a major focus, but the blessing offers no hints of this. Instead, it functions as a foil of positive expectation, over against which Judah's failure, in sexual wrongdoing, comes into stark relief.

3.2.7.5 Rebecca speaks of Jacob and Esau with Isaac

We return to Rebecca in 35:1-27. First she speaks to Jacob about honouring his father and brother during their lifetime (35:1) and Jacob responds, affirming his continuing compliance (35:2-5). Rebecca confirms Jacob's goodness, then tells Jacob that she will die (35:6), which Jacob does not accept (35:7-8). Rebecca then speaks to Isaac about her two sons (35:9-12). It amounts to another depiction of Esau's evil thoughts and deeds. Isaac then acknowledges his change of heart towards Jacob from Esau (35:13-17), not least because Esau has followed after his foreign wives.

> Now my mind is disturbed about his actions. Neither he nor his descendants are to be saved because they will be destroyed from the earth and be uprooted from beneath the sky. He has abandoned the God of Abraham and has gone after his wives, after impurity (*rek^{w}s*) , and after their errors (*sehtat*) – he and his sons (35:14).

Going after "his wives, after impurity (*rek^{w}s*), and after their errors (*sehtat*)" will include the charge of sexual wrongdoing which characterises these wives and their ways. Rebecca then summons Esau and bids him bury her and love his brother, with which Esau willingly complies (35:18-24). She makes a similar request of Jacob with which he complies (35:25-26). Both then buried her that year (35:27).

After these interchanges Isaac summons both sons, also speaks of burial, urges brotherly love, and swears them to a covenant in those terms on the name of God that they will continue to worship God and live together in peace (36:1-17). Here we find no reference to sexual wrongdoing, although the example of Sodom is cited as a warning (36:10). Here it is a threat against whoever breaches the covenant.

Sexual wrongdoing is thus a major theme in most of the speeches. Beside the blessings of Levi and Judah, only Isaac's speech (36:1-17) is an exception. The speeches in *Jubilees* represent major additions to the material found in Genesis and are placed on the lips of major authorities (who include Rebecca). They underline the importance of the theme for the author.

3.2.8   The Language of Sexual Wrongdoing

We are now in a position to examine some of the common terms used in relation to sexual wrongdoing in *Jubilees*. Taken in isolation, some of these remain abstract, but when we read them within their contexts and within the context of *Jubilees* as a whole, we are able to identify their particular connotations.

One of the problems faced by any discussion of key terms is the nature of our primary sources. In many cases we have only the Ge'ez text, but in some instances we have parallels in Syriac and Latin, and in a few, we have fragments of the Hebrew text, the language of the original. These are helpful in enabling us to reconstruct what might have been the Hebrew behind the terms, especially given the frequency with which a limited number of particular Ge'ez words occur, and assuming the likelihood that in each case they translate the same Hebrew word, though this can never be certain. In the citing of Ge'ez below, I follow the practice of citing the lexical entry, namely the primary form of the noun, verb or adjective, rather than the inflected forms. In the transcription I follow Lambdin.[548]

The following discussion begins with those instances relevant to our theme where we have a Hebrew text and can compare the variants. It then considers instances where we have both Latin and Ge'ez, before turning to instances where only the Ge'ez survives. The Syriac does not contribute anything significant for this purpose. The purpose is to seek to identify key words used in the context of sexuality and their associations.

One of the most common words comes already in 1:9, "For they will forget all my commandments – everything that I command them – and will follow the nations, their impurities (*rek^{w}s*), and their shame (*xasār*)". It is the word, *rek^{w}s*, in the expression translated by VanderKam: "their impurities (*rek^{w}s*) and their shame (*xasār*)".[549] Wintermute translates: "their defilement and shame".[550] In 4Q216 2.6 we have the Hebrew, of which very little is preserved, but which was initially reconstructed as follows:

ו[אחר כ]ל[מתם ואחר חרפה]   and [after their dis]gr[ace and after] their [shame].[551]

---

[548] Thomas O. Lambdin, *Introduction to Classical Ethiopic (Ge'ez)* (HSS 24; Missoula: Scholars, 1978) 8-9.

[549] VanderKam, *Jubilees Translated*, 3.

[550] O. S. Wintermute, "*Jubilees*," in *The Old Testament Pseudepigrapha* (2 vols; ed. James H. Charlesworth; New York: Doubleday, 1983, 1985) 2. 35–142, 52.

[551] So VanderKam and Milik, DJD 13, 8. Unless otherwise indicated I follow the translation of García Martínez and Tigchelaar, eds, *Dead Sea Scrolls: Study Edition*.

The combination, כלמה and חרפה, is not uncommon in the Hebrew Bible, often also with בשת (e.g.: Isa 30:3-5; Pss 44:14, 16; 71:13; Jer 51:51). It is used of personal shame and disgrace (e.g.: Pss 69:8; 109:25) or the shame and disgrace it wishes on others (Pss 71:13; 109:29; Jer 20:11). Ezekiel uses it of Israel's shame and disgrace (16:52-54, 63). In *Jubilees* it refers to the "disgrace" and "shame" of the nations. However, this reconstruction of 4Q216 has now been thrown into doubt by the identification of fragments belonging to 1Q22 which appear to closely match the content of *Jub.* 1:9.

Tigchelaar reconstructs the relevant portions of 1Q22 and 4Q216 (4QJubilees) as follows, [552] for which I offer a literal English translation:

[ויל]כו א[חר] שקצי ה[ג]ו[י]ם [ו]הו[עובותם [ואחר גל]ולי]הם
[and they will go af]ter [the abominations/detestable things of the] nat[ions] [and their abo]minations [and after id]ols. (1Q22.7)

ויל[כו אחר הג]וים ו]אחר ג[לו]לי]הם ואחר תעבת[ם
and they will go after the nations and [after their i]d[ols and after] their abominations]. (4Q216 2.5-6 = *Jub.* 1:9bc)

Tigchelaar notes that whereas the Ge'ez words, *rekʷs* and *xasār*, "generally mean 'impurity' and 'disgrace', these also are the two words most commonly used to translate Greek βδέλυγμα, which in turn is the common rendering of both Hebrew שקץ, שקוץ and תעבה and in the LXX once for גלול in 1 Kgs 21:26".[553] In *Jub.* 21:5 a form of *rekʷs* stands where the Hebrew, preserved in 4Q220, has גלול and in *Jub.* 21:23 it stands where Hebrew has תועבה in 21:23 (attested in both 4Q219 and partially in 4Q221). While the reconstruction has had to work with very fragmentary texts, its strength is that the few lines of the 1Q22 fragment also match some of the content of *Jub.* 1:14, including a reference to *Jubilees*. The common phrases, not always in the same order, do not reflect citation of one by the other, though of the two, Tigchelaar proposes that the simpler text of 1Q22, which elsewhere shows no indication of familiarity with *Jubilees* 1, is the older.[554]

Our author may, therefore have been adopting traditional phraseology. The combination, *rekʷs/xasār*, גלול/תועבה or חרפה/כלמה occurs only here. In substance, however, the Ge'ez translation, perhaps aided by what lay before it in the Greek, has employed the word, "impurity/impurities (*rekʷs*)", here, which is very common in *Jubilees*, and carries with it the connotations it has in the rest of the book. In other words, the translator will have understood the primary concern,

---

[552] Eibert Tigchelaar, "A Cave 4 Fragment of Divre Mosheh (4QDM) and the Text of 1Q22 1:7-10 and Jubilees 1:9, 14," *DSD* 12 (2005) 303-12, 303-307.

[553] Tigchelaar, "Cave 4 Fragment," 307.

[554] Tigchelaar, "Cave 4 Fragment," 307-308.

even in the opening statement about abominations, as having to do, not only with idolatry but also the sexual wrongdoing which characterised the nations. The focus is on what the nations do. For those who heard *Jubilees* more than once in the context of teaching, for the author, and very probably for the translator in Ge'ez, this aspect is likely to have been present. For those hearing the Ethiopic it would begin already in 1:9 with the first occurrence of *rek^w s*.

The next instance where we can compare the Ge'ez and Hebrew in relation to key terms is at 21:21, "I see, my son, that all the actions of mankind (consist of) sin (*xaṭi'at*) and wickedness (*'ekay*) and all their deeds of impurity (*rek^w s*), worthlessness (*mennānē*) and contamination (*gemmānē*)". 4Q219 preserves only a little of the Hebrew which may be reconstructed:

ונאצ[ה ותבל ...], [their works are uncleanness, abominatio]n and filth.

Both occurrences of תבל in the Hebrew Bible relate to sexual wrongdoing (sexual relations with an animal, Lev 18:23, and incest with a daughter-in-law, Lev 20:12). נאצה usually means "contempt" or "blasphemy" and is translated in the LXX by βλασφημία. The Ge'ez word, *mennānē*, includes "repudiation, rejection" within its range of meaning, as well as: "worthlessness, wickedness". In this instance, the sinfulness of humankind is characterised by impurity/defilement/pollution (which may have various associations and as we have seen these include sexual impurity), rejection/repudiation (by implication of God and God's laws) and behaviour which is abominable/filthy (possibly, though not necessarily, with allusion to sexual wrongdoing).

There is one further instance where we are helped by having a Hebrew text: "They will defile (*rak^w sa*) the holy of holies with the impure (*rek^w s*) corruption (*musenā*) of their contamination (*gemmānē*)" (Wintermute: "with their pollution and with the corruption of their contamination") (23:21). The reconstruction of the Hebrew text reads as follows:

[ויטמאו את קודש הקודשים בטמ[א בח]בל תועבותיהמה]
[they will defile the Holy of Holies with impu]rity, and with the cor [ruption of their contaminations].

Behind the words for "defile" and "impurity" appear to be the Hebrew stem טמא, which in the Pi'el form of the verb means "to make unclean". We note that this means that behind the Ge'ez, *rek^w s*, would lie two different words in Hebrew in 1:9 and 23:21. Behind the third word, *musenā*, meaning "corruption", appears to lie the word חבל, which can mean "destruction" or "corruption". The final word, תועבה, is commonly translated, "abomination". Ge'ez uses the same word here (*gemmānē*) as it does to translate תבל in 21:21, where we saw that it also means "something abominable or filthy". We also have a Latin translation which renders these words:

poluent in abominationibus ueritatis et inmunditiis.
they will defile the sanctuary with abominations of the truth and impurities.[555]

The surprising *ueritatis*[556] appears to be an explanatory addition. *Abominationibus* corresponds to *rek^w s*; *inmunditiis,* (impure, dirty, unclean) to *gemmānē*. The table below sets out the occurrences of key words related to our theme and their equivalents in the Hebrew, Ge'ez, and Latin.

Hebrew texts exist for some further passages related to these terms, but unfortunately in most the Hebrew of the terms themselves is missing. In 25:10, "Do not be afraid, mother. Be assured that I will do as you wish. I will behave rightly and will never conduct myself corruptly (*māsana*)", 4Q222 preserves for us the words behind "conduct myself corruptly": אשחית דרכי. 4Q221 contains some of 33:12-15, including possibly the word, ו[נאצ]ה translated "disgrace" in 33:13, which Ge'ez renders by *rek^w s*, its word for impurity. 4Q219 preserves part of 21:23, including the words: ומכול תועבותיהמה which are preserved also in 4Q221, ומכול חו[ן]עבחם], translated, "from all their abominations". For this, Ge'ez uses *rek^w s*: "from all their impurity". 4Q223-224 does not preserve the word behind "impurity" in 35:14, but preserves תעות for "errors (*seḥtat*)".

The versional evidence adds little to our review of key terms. The Syriac of 11:16 is incomplete, lacking the reference to impurity, and 11:17 is missing altogether. In 33:7 it has no equivalent of "because I am too contaminated for you", which VanderKam suggests, is as a result of abbreviation or parablepsis.[557]

Latin has 16:5, where, for "defile themselves (*rak^w sa*), commit sexual sins (*zemmut*) in their flesh, and do what was impure (*rek^w s*) on the earth", it has: ... *inmundi spurcitias exercentes in carnibus suis et facientes abominationes super terram* ("... impure people would commit filthy acts in their flesh, and do abominable things on the earth"). Latin often has *abominatio* where the Ge'ez has *rek^w s* (as also in 16:6 and see the Table below). *Spurcitia*, "filthy", has as its equivalent: *zemmut*, "sexual impurity". The sense in the context is clearly sexual. For "where people commit the same sort of impure actions (rek^w s) as Sodom" in 16:6, Latin has: *ubicumque fecerint abominationis sodomum.*

Latin also preserves a version of 20:5, "because of their wickedness (*'ekay*), because of the sexual impurity (*zemmut*), uncleanness (*rek^w s*), and corruption

---

[555] Unless otherwise indicated I cite the translation of the Latin in VanderKam, *Jubilees Translated.*

[556] On this see VanderKam, *Jubilees Translated*, 146 n. 23:21.

[557] VanderKam, *Jubilees Translated*, 220 n. 33:7.

(*musenā*) among themselves they died in (their) sexual impurity", which it renders, *propter malitiam ipsorum quod conmisscebant se cum fornicariis et inmunditiam exercebant et omnem abominationem faciebant* ("because they commingled with prostitutes, engaged in unclean acts, did every [kind of] abominable act").[558] For *conmisscebant se cum fornicariis* Ge'ez has *zemmut* "sexual impurity"; for *inmunditiam*, *rek^{w}s* ("uncleanness"; elsewhere "impurity") and for *abominationem*, *musenā*, "corruption". Latin lacks the concluding section of 20:5, "they died in (their) sexual impurity (*zemmut*)" and also the opening of 20:6, "Now you keep yourselves from all sexual impurity (*zemmut*) and uncleanness (*rek^{w}s*) and from all the contamination (*gemmānē*) of sin (*xaṭi'at*)",[559] but in 20:7, for "Do not follow their idols and their uncleanness (*rek^{w}s*)", it reads, *nolite ire post omnes abominationes ipsorum et post omnes inmunditias* ("do not follow all their abominations and all their uncleanness"). For "idols" Latin has *abominationes*, for "uncleanness (*rek^{w}s*)", *inmunditias*. In addition Latin adds "all" (*omnes*) before each.

For 22:14,

> May he purify (*nasha*) you from all filthy pollution (*reshat rek^{w}s*) so that you may be pardoned for all your sin (*'abbasā*) and error (*sehtat*) through ignorance,

Latin reads:

> *mundabit* [fut. Indic.] *te ab omni inquinamento et iniustitia ut propritius sit omnibus iniustitiis tuis et neglegentiae tuae.*
> He will purify you from all filth and unjustice so that he may forgive all your unjust acts and your sins of negligence.

Thus for "filthy pollution (*reshat rek^{w}s*)" Latin has *inquinamento et iniustitia* and for "sin (*'abbasā*)", *iniustititia*.

For 22:16,

> for their actions are something that is impure (*rek^{w}s*),and all their ways are defiled (*gammana*) and something abominable (*mennānē*) and detestable (*saqorār*),

Latin reads:

---

[558] On the divergent Latin and Ethiopic texts see VanderKam, *Jubilees Translated*, 116-17 n. 20:5.

[559] On this see VanderKam, *Jubilees Translated*, 117 n. 20:6.

quoniam opera ipsorum pollutio et omnis uia ipsorum inmunditia et abominatio et spurcitia.

for their actions are something that is impure, and their entire way is something impure, abominable, and filthy.

Thus for *pollutio* Ge'ez has the $rek^w s$ stem ("impure"), for *inmunditia*, *gammana*, "defiled", for *abominatio*, *mennānē* ("worthlessness") and for *spurcitia*, *saqorār* ("detestable"). In 22:19, "May he remove you from their impurity ($rek^w s$) and from all their error (*seḥtat*)", for "from their impurity ($rek^w s$)" Latin has: *abominationibus.*

For 23:14,

All of this will happen to the evil generation which makes the earth commit sin (*'abbasa*) through pollution ($rek^w s$),[560] sexual impurity (*zemmut*), contamination (*gemmānē*), and their detestable actions (*saqorār*),

Latin reads:

et omnia haec superuenit superuenient super generationem quae est iniqua quae iniquitatem facit in terra et inmunditia et fornicationes et pollutiones abominationes operum ipsorum.[561]
And all these will happen to the generation which is evil, which commits sin on the earth along with impurity, sexual wrongs, contamination, their detestable actions.

Thus for "sin (*'abbasa*)" Latin has *iniqua*, for "pollution ($rek^w s$)", *inmunditia*; for "sexual impurity (*zemmut*)", *fornicationes*; for "contamination (*gemmānē*)", *pollutiones*, and for "detestable actions (*saqorār*)", *abominationes operum ipsorum.*

For 23:17,

Everything that they do is impure (*rekus*) and something detestable (*saqorār*); all their ways are (characterized by) contamination (*gemmānē*), and pollution ($rek^w s$)[562] and corruption (*musenā*),

Latin has:

---

[560] Omitted in translation by VanderKam, *Jubilees Translated*, 143.

[561] On the different syntax between Ethiopic and Latin see VanderKam, *Jubilees Translated*, 143 n. 23:14.

[562] Omitted by VanderKam, *Jubilees Translated*, in translation (144).

omnes operationes eorum inmunditia et odium et universae uiae eorum pollution.. et exterminium.

Everything that they do is impure and something hateful; all their ways are (characterized by) contamination ... abomination, and destruction.

Thus for "impure (*rek^w s*)" Latin has *inmunditia*, for "something detestable (*saqorār*)", *odium* ("hatred", but can also mean "annoyance, disgust, offence"), for "contamination (*gemmānē*)", *pollution..* (should be *pollutiones*); for "pollution (*rek^w s*)" Latin has no equivalent, and for "corruption (*musenā*)" Latin has *exterminium*.

The word, *defile* (causative from *rak^w sa*), occurs in the Dinah story at 30:2, 3, 7, 8, 10 (2x), 15 and 16, Latin, in each instance, using the verb *poluo*, except 30:7, where it uses *contaminare*, and 30:10, where in the second instance it uses *intaminare*. 30:4 uses *xafra* (in the causative, "to shame") in "because they had violated their sister Dinah". Latin uses the verb *poluo*: *quod polluerant dinam sororem suam* (cf. Gen 34:5 and 13 Hebrew טמא; LXX: 34:5 ἐμίανεν; 13 ἐμίαναν). "Something shameful (*gabru xafrata*)" in both 30:5 and 7 is in Latin *ignominiam*. In 30:8, "No adulterer (*zamma*) or impure person (*rekus*)" reads in Latin *fornicaria et abominatio*. "Any man who has defiled (*rak^w sa*) (it) [missing in Eth.]" reads in Latin: *et omnis homo quicumque polluerit eum.*

For 30:13-14,

It is a disgraceful thing (*se'lat* – also used in 30:12) for the Israelites who give or take (in marriage) one of the foreign women because it is too impure (*rek^w s*) and despicable (*mennun*) for Israel. Israel will not become clean (*neṣuh*) from this impurity (*rek^w s*) while it has one of the foreign women or if anyone has given one of his daughters to any foreign man,

Latin has:

et obprobrium istrahel qui dant siue accipiunt a filiabus gentium propter quod abominatio est et inmunditia in omni istrahel et non mundabitur istrahel ab abominatione ista si fuerit illi mulier de gentibus et non mundabimus [?] de filiabus nostris omnibus gentibus.

It is a disgraceful thing for the Israelites who give or take (in marriage) one of the foreign women because it is a despicable thing and an impure thing in all Israel. Israel will not become clean from that despicable thing if it has one of the foreign women, and we will not become clean (?) one of our daughters to all foreigners.

Thus for "disgraceful thing (*se'lat*)" in 30:13 Latin reads: *obprobrium*; for "impure (*rek^w s*)", *abomination*; for "despicable (*mennun*)", *inmunditia*; and in 30:14 for "clean (*neṣuḥ*) from this impurity (*rekʷs*)", *mundabitur ... ab abominatione.* For 30:15,

> If one does this or shuts his eyes to those who do impure things (*rekʷs*) and who defile (*rakʷsa*)the Lord's sanctuary and to those who profane his holy name, then the entire nation will be condemned together because of all this impurity (*rekʷs*) and this contamination (*gemmānē*),

Latin reads:

> *si praeterierit et despexerit faciens abominationis et polluerit sanctificationem dei et qui polluunt nomen sanctum eius iudicabitur tota plebs simul de omnibus abominationibus huius.*
> And if the one does the despicable thing disregards (it) and looks away and defiles God's sanctuary and those who defile his holy name, then the entire nation will be condemned together because of all the despicable (acts) of this one.

Thus for both occurrences of "impure things (*rekʷs*)" Latin uses *abominatio*, but has no equivalent of "contamination (*gemmānē*)" after the second.

For 30:16 "(So) is any man or woman in Israel to be who defiles (*rakʷsa*) his sanctuary" Latin reads *et erit in istrahel omnis homo siue mulier polluens sanctificationes* ("So is any man or woman in Israel to be who defiles the holy things"). For 30:22, "But if they transgress (*'adawa*) and behave in any impure ways (*rekʷs*), then they will be recorded on the heavenly tablets as enemies", Latin reads: *si autem transgressi fuerint testamentum et fecerint ex omnibus uiis abominationem quae*cumque [sic] *scripta in tabulis caeli inimici dei erunt* ("But if they transgress the covenant and do what is despicable in any of the ways which have been recorded on the heavenly tablets"). Again for "impure ways (*rekʷs*)" Latin uses *abominatio*.

For 33:7 "I am not pure (*nasha*) for you because I am contaminated (*gamana*) for you [Syriac omits],[563] since Reuben defiled (*rakʷsa*) me", Latin reads *non sum tibi munda quoniam polluta sum abs te quoniam polluit me ruben.* Thus for "I am contaminated (*gamana*)" Latin uses *munda*; for "defiled (*rakʷsa*)", *poluo.*

For 33:19-20,

> For all who commit it on the earth before the Lord are impure (*rekus*), something detestable (*saqorār*), a blemish (*nekafat*), and something contaminated (*gemmānē*). No sin is greater than the sexual impurity (*zemmut*) which they commit on the earth. ... No such impurity (*rekʷs*) will be seen among the holy people,

---

[563] VanderKam, *Jubilees Translated*, translates as a comparative, "I am too contaminated" (220).

Latin has:

> *propter quod inmunditia et abominatio et odium et pollutio omni [omnes] qui faciunt*
> *ea super terra in conspectu dei nostri. Et est peccatum magnum super terram ... non*
> *est inmunditia in medio populi sancti.*
>
> For all who commit them on the earth before our God are something impure,
> something detestable, an offence, and something contaminated. It is a great sin on the
> earth ... no impurity is among the holy people.

Latin has no negative at the beginning of 33:20 and no reference to sexual
impurity. It may be implied, but could have dropped out because of parablepsis.[564]
In 33:19, for "impure (*rekus*)" Latin has *inmunditia*; for "something detestable
(*saqorār*)", *abomination*; for "a blemish (*nekafat*), *odium*; for "something
contaminated (*gemmānē*)", *pollutio*. In 33:20 for impurity (*rek^w s*) it has
inmunditia.

Throughout *Jubilees* we find many of the above terms recurring, often in
combination. In addition to the combinations noted above in the parallel Hebrew
and Latin texts, these include the following:

4:22 He testified to the Watchers who had sinned (*'abbasa*) with the daughters of
      men because these had begun to mix with earthly women so that they became
      defiled (*rak^w sa*). Enoch testified against all of them.

4:26 For this reason the earth will be sanctified from all its sins (*'abbasā*) and from
      its uncleanness (*rek^w s*) into the history of eternity.

5:2   Wickedness (*'ammaḍā*) increased on the earth. All animate beings corrupted
      (*māsana*) their way — (everyone of them) from people to cattle, animals, birds,
      and everything that moves about on the ground. All of them corrupted
      (*māsana*) their way and their prescribed course (*šer'at*). They began to devour
      one another, and wickedness (*'ammaḍā*) increased on the earth. Every thought
      of all mankind's knowledge was evil (*'ekuy*) like this all the time.

5:3   The Lord saw that the earth was corrupt (*māsana*), (that) all animate beings had
      corrupted (*māsana*) their prescribed course (*šer'at*).

5:10-11 ... there will be condemnation on all who have corrupted (*māsana*) their ways
      ... for all their wickedness (*'ammaḍā*).

5:19 ... all who corrupted (*māsana*) their ways and their plans (*mekr*).

7:20 ... and keep themselves from fornication (*zemmut*), uncleanness (*rek^w s*), and
      from all injustice.

7:21 For it was on account of these three things that the flood was on the earth, since
      (it was) due to fornication (*zemmut*) that the Watchers had illicit
      intercourse (*zammawa*) – apart from the mandate (*te'zāz*) of their authority
      (*k^w ennanē*) – with women. When they married of them whomever they chose
      they committed the first (acts) of uncleanness (*rek^w s*).

---

[564] So VanderKam, *Jubilees Translated*, 223 n. 33:20.

9:15   All of them said: "So be it for them and their children until eternity during their generations until the day of judgement on which the Lord God will punish them with the sword and fire because of all the evil impurity (*rekʷs*) of their errors (*gēgāy*) by which they have filled the earth with wickedness (*'ekay*), impurity (*rekʷs*), fornication (*zemmut*), and sin (*xati'at*)."

11:4   They began to make statues, images, and unclean things (*rekʷs*); the spirits of the savage ones (*dawwāg*) were helping and misleading (them) so that they would commit sins (*'abbasa*), impurities (*rekʷs*), and transgression (*'abbasā*).

11:5   ... to commit every (kind of) error (*gēgāy*) and sin (*xati'at*) and every (kind of) transgression (*'abbasā*); to corrupt (*māsana*), to destroy, and to shed blood on the earth.

11:16   Abram ... began to realise the errors (*sehtat*) of the earth – that everyone was going astray after the statues and after impurity (*rekʷs*).

11:17   He began to pray to the creator of all that he would save him from the errors (*sehtat*) of mankind and that it might not fall to his share to go astray after impurity (*rekʷs*) and wickedness (*mennānē*).

20:3-4 that we should keep ourselves from all sexual impurity (*zemmut*) and uncleanness (*rekʷs*); and that we should dismiss all uncleanness (*rekʷs*) and sexual impurity (*zemmut*) from among us. If any woman or girl among you commits a sexual offence (*zammawa*), burn her in fire; they are not to commit sexual offences (*zammawa*) (by) following their eyes and their hearts so that they take wives for themselves from the Canaanite women.

25:1   They have embittered my life with all the impure things (*rekʷs*) that they do because everything that they do (consists of) sexual impurity (*zemmut*) and lewdness (*mer'āt*). They have no decency [lit. there is no righteousness with them (*masc.*)] because (what they do) is evil [lit. it/he is bad].

25:7   For this reason I have kept myself from sinning (*'abbasa*) and from becoming corrupted (*māsana*) in any ways during my entire lifetime because father Abraham gave me many orders about lewdness (*mer'āt*) and sexual impurity (*zemmut*).

35:14   He has abandoned the God of Abraham and has gone after his wives, after impurity (*rekʷs*) , and after their errors (*sehtat*) – he and his sons.

39:6   But he did not surrender himself. He remembered the Lord and what [lit. the words] his father Jacob would read to him from the words of Abraham — that no one is to commit adultery (*zammawa*) with a woman who has a husband; that there is a death penalty which has been ordained for him in heaven before the most high Lord. The sin (*xati'at*) will be entered [will ascend] regarding him in the eternal books forever before the Lord.

41:17   because she has done something impure (*rekʷs*) in Israel.

41:25   He had forgiveness because he turned from his sin (*xati'at*) and from his ignorance, for the sin (*'abbasā*) was a great one before our God. Anyone who acts in this way — anyone who lies with his mother-in-law — is to be burned in fire so that he burns in it because impurity (*rekʷs*) and contamination (*gemmānē*) have come on them. They are to be burned.

41:26 Now you order the Israelites that there is to be no impurity (*rek^w s*) among them, for anyone who lies with his daughter-in-law or his mother-in-law has done something that is impure (*rek^w s*).

50:5   The jubilees will pass by until Israel is pure (*naṣḥa*) of every sin (*'abbasā*) of sexual immorality (*zemmut*) [VanderKam has sexual evil], impurity (*rek^w s*), contamination (*gemmānē*), sin (*xaṭi'at*), and error (*gēgāy*).

A number of terms occur which relate to the issue of sexual wrongdoing in *Jubilees*. The material considered above shows that in some instances we can trace the probable Hebrew terms, in some we must depend on the versions. Among these we sometimes have both a Latin and Ge'ez translation; in others we are dependent solely on the Ge'ez text. The consistency with which *Jubilees* uses these terms and combines them makes it possible to build a profile of their meaning. Even more so, the contexts in which the terms occur enable us to recognise their connotations intratextually within the book.

The following chart identifies the key terms in three groups: Hebrew words and their parallels; Latin words and their parallels; Ge'ez words with and without parallels. A second chart follows which lists those passages where these terms occur together. An evaluation follows.

Key Terms Relating to Sexuality in *Jubilees*		
(references without parallel are in italics)		
Hebrew	Ge'ez	Latin
Hebrew and the versions		
גלול (/ כלמה) 1:9	rek^w s	
חֶבֶל 23:21	musenā	(veritas)
תועבה (/ חרפה) 1:9	xasār	
טמא 23:21	rek^w s	abominatio
כלמה (/ גלול) 1:9	rek^w s	
נאצה 21:21	mennānē	
33:13	rek^w s	
שחת 25:10	māsana	
חבל 21:21	gemmānē	
תועבה (/ חרפה) 1:9	xasār	
23:21	gemmānē	inmunditia
21:23	rek^w s	
תעות 35:14	sehtat	
Latin compared with Ge'ez and Hebrew		
	rek^w s	abominatio 16:5, 6; 22:19; 30:14, 15, 22
	rekus	30:8, 13

טמא		23:21
	musenā	20:5
	mennānē	22:16
	saqorār	23:14; 33:19
	rak^{w}sa	contaminare 30:7
	musenā	exterminium 23:17
	zemmut	fornicariis 20:5
	zemmut	fornicatio 23:14
	zamma	fornicaria 30:8
	gabru xafrat	ignominia 30:5, 7
	'abbasa	iniqua 23:14
		iniustitia
	rek^{w}s	20:14
	'abbasā	20:14
	rak^{w}sa "defile themselves"	inmundi "impure people" 16:5
		inmunditia
	rek^{w}s	20:5,7; 23:14, 17; 33:20
תבל	rekus	33:19
	gammana	20:16
	gemmānē	23:21
	mennun	30:13
	seḥtat	inquinamentum 22:14
	rak^{w}sa	intaminare 30:10
	'ekay	malitia 20:5
	ṣe'lat	obprobrium 30:12
		odium
	nekafat	33:19
	saqorār	23:17
		pollutio
	gemmānē	23:14, 17; 33:19
	rek^{w}s	22:16
	gamana	pollutus 33:7
	rak^{w}sa	poluo 23:21, 30:8, 16, 33:7
	xafra	30:4
		spurcitia
	zemmut	16:5
	saqorār	22:16
Ge'ez compared with Hebrew and Latin		
	'abbasā 20:14 *4:26; 50:5* 'abbasa	iniustitia

	23:14	iniqua
	4:22; 11:4; 25:7	
	'ekuy *5:2*	
	'ekay *9:15; 21:21*	
	20:5	malitia
	'ammadā *5:2 (2x); 5:11*	
	gēgāy	
	9:15; 11:5; 50:5	
תבל	gemmānē	
תועבה	21:21	
	23:21	inmunditia
	23:14, 17; 33:19	pollutio
	41:25	
	gammana	
	22:16	inmunditia
	33:7	pollutus
	50:8	
נאצה	mennānē	
	21:21	
	22:16	abominatio
	mennun 30:13	inmunditia
	mer'āt	
	25:1, 7	
חֶבֶל	musenā	
	23:21	(veritas)
	20:5	abominatio
	23:17	exterminium
אשחית	māsana 25:10	
	5:2 (2x), 3 (2x), 10, 19	
	neṣuḥ 33:7	mundus
	naṣha *50:5*	
גלול / כלמה	rek^ws	
נאצה	1:9	
טמא	33:13	
תועבה	23:21	abominatio
	21:23	
	20:5, 7; 23:14, 17; 33:19, 20	inmunditia
	16:5, 6; 22:19; 23:21; 30:14, 15, 22	abominatio
	22:14	iniustitia
	22:16	pollutio
	4:26; 7:20, 21; 9:15 (2x); 11:4, 16, 17; 16:6; 20:3 (2x), 6; 21:21; 22:19; 25:1;	

	33:11, 13, 20; 35:14; *41:17, 25, 26; 50:5*	
	rekus 30:8, 13	abominatio
	23:17; 33:10 (2x), 14, 19	
	rak^wsa 23:21, 30:2, 3, 8, 10 (1), 15, 16; 33:7	poluo
	16:5	inmundi (nn)
	30:7	contaminare
	30:10 (2)	intaminare
	4:22	
תעות	sehtat 35:14	
	22:14	inquinamentum
	11:16, 17; 22:19	
	saqorār 23:14; 33:19	abominatio
	22:16	spurcitia
	23:17	odium
	xafra 30:4	poluo
	xati'at *9:15; 11:5; 20:6; 39:6;* *50:5*	
	zemmut 16:5	spurcitia
	20:5	(fornicariis)
	23:14	fornicatio
	7:20, 21; 9:15; 20:3 (2x) 5, 6; 25:1, 7; 33:20; 50:5	
	zamma 30:8	fornicaria
	zammawa *7:21; 20:4 (2x)*	

Word Strings Concerning Sin in *Jubilees*
God to Moses 1:9 will follow the nations, their disgrace/idols (גלול / כלמה) / impurities (rek^ws), and their abominations (תועבה) / shame (חרפה / xasār)
The Angel in the context of Enoch and holy places 4:26 For this reason the earth will be sanctified from all its sins ('abbasā) and from its uncleanness (rek^ws) into the history of eternity.
Concerning the time of the Watchers 5:2 Wickedness ('ammaḍā) increased on the earth. All animate beings corrupted (māsana) their way ... All of them corrupted (māsana) their way and their prescribed course (šer'at). They began to devour one another, and wickedness ('ammaḍā) increased

on the earth. Every thought of all mankind's knowledge was evil (*'ekuy*) like this all the time. 5:3 ...the earth was corrupt (*māsana*), (that) all animate beings had corrupted (*māsana*) their prescribed course (*šer'at*)... all who have corrupted (*māsana*) their ways ... 5:11 for all their wickedness (*'ammaḍā*) ...5:19 ... all who corrupted (*māsana*) their ways and their plans (*mekr*).

Noah's instructions
7:20 and keep themselves from fornication (*zemmut*), uncleanness (*rekʷs*), and from all injustice.
7:21 For it was on account of these three things that the flood was on the earth,
since (it was) due to fornication (*zemmut*) that the Watchers had illicit intercourse (*zammawa*) — apart from the mandate (*te'zāz*) of their authority (*kʷennanē*) — with women. When they married of them whomever they chose they committed the first (acts) of uncleanness (*rekʷs*).

Noah's sons about future judgement
9:15 because of all the evil impurity (*rekʷs*) of their errors (*gēgāy*) by which they have filled the earth with wickedness (*'ekay*), impurity (*rekʷs*), fornication (*zemmut*), and sin (*xaṭi'at*).

Mastema's influence among Chaldeans
11:4 so that they would commit sins (*'abbasa*), impurities (*rekʷs*), and transgression (*'abbasā*). 11:5 ... to commit every error (*gēgāy*) and sin (*xaṭi'at*) transgression (*'abbasā*); to corrupt (*māsana*), to destroy, and to shed blood on the earth.

Abram about his society
11:16 ... began to realise the errors (*seḥtat*) of the earth – that everyone was going astray after the statues and after impurity (*rekʷs*). 11:17 He began to pray to the creator of all that he would save him from the errors (*seḥtat*) of mankind and that it might not fall to his share to go astray after impurity (*rekʷs*) and wickedness (*mennānē*).

Angel about Sodom
16:5 defile themselves (*rakʷsa*), commit sexual sins (*zemmut*) in their flesh, and do what was impure (*rekʷs*) on the earth ... 16:6 ... where people commit the same sort of impure actions (*rekʷs*) as Sodom.

Abraham to his children
20:3 keep ourselves from all sexual impurity (*zemmut*) and uncleanness (*rekʷs*); and that we should dismiss all uncleanness (*rekʷs*) and sexual impurity (*zemmut*) from among us.

Abraham to his children
20:4 If any woman or girl among you commits a sexual offence (*zammawa*), burn her in fire; they are not to commit sexual offences (*zammawa*) (by) following their eyes and their hearts so that they take wives for themselves from the Canaanite women.
20:5 .. because of their wickedness (*'ekay*), because of the sexual impurity (*zemmut*), uncleanness (*rekʷs*), and corruption (*musenā*) among themselves they died in (their) sexual impurity (*zemmut*).
20:6 Now you keep yourselves from all sexual impurity (*zemmut*) and uncleanness (*rekʷs*) and from all the contamination (*gemmānē*) of sin (*xaṭi'at*).

Abraham to Isaac
21:21 sin (*xaṭi'at*) and wickedness (*'ekay*) and all their deeds of impurity (*rekʷs*), worthlessness (*mennānē*) and contamination(*gemmānē*).

Abraham to Jacob 22:16 for their actions are something that is impure (*rek^ws*), and all their ways are defiled (*gammana*) and something abominable (*mennāne*) and detestable (*saqorār*).
Angel about the future 23:14 pollution (*rek^ws*), sexual impurity (*zemmut*), contamination (*gemmāne*) detestable actions (*saqorār*).
Angel about the future 23:17 Everything that they do is impure (*rekus*) and something detestable (*saqorār*); all their ways are (characterized by) contamination (*gemmāne*), and pollution (*rek^ws*) and corruption (*musenā*).
Angel about the future 23:21 They will defile (*rak^wsa*) the holy of holies with the impure (*rek^ws*) corruption (*musenā*) of their contamination (*gemmāne*).
Rebecca about Esau's wives 25:1 They have embittered my life with all the impure things (*rek^ws*) that they do because everything that they do (consists of) sexual impurity (*zemmut*) and lewdness (*mer'āt*).
Jacob to Rebecca 25:7 For this reason I have kept myself from sinning (*'abbasa*) and from becoming corrupted (*māsana*) in any ways during my entire lifetime because father Abraham gave me many orders about lewdness (*mer'āt*) and sexual impurity (*zemmut*).
Angel expounding Rape of Dinah 30:13 It is a disgraceful thing (*ṣe'lat*) for the Israelites who give or take (in marriage) one of the foreign women because it is too impure (*rekus*) and despicable (*mennun*) for Israel. 30:14 Israel will not become clean (*neṣuḥ*) from this impurity (*rek^ws*) while it has one of the foreign women or if anyone has given one of his daughters to any foreign man. 30:15 ... then the entire nation will be condemned together because of all this impurity (*rek^ws*) and this contamination (*gemmāne*).
Angel about Reuben 33:19 ... all who commit it on the earth before the Lord are impure (*rekus*), something detestable (*saqorār*), a blemish (*nekafat*) , and something contaminated (*gemmāne*). 33:20 No sin is greater than the sexual impurity (*zemmut*) which they commit on the earth. ... No such impurity (*rek^ws*) will be seen among the holy people.
Angel about Judah and Tamar 41:17 because she has done something impure (*rek^ws*) in Israel ... 41:25 He had forgiveness because he turned from his sin (*xaṭi'at*) and from his ignorance, for the sin (*'abbasā*) was a great one before our God. Anyone who acts in this way — anyone who lies with his mother-in-law — is to be burned in fire so that he burns in it because impurity (*rek^ws*) and contamination (*gemmāne*) have come on them. They are to be burned. 41:26 Now you order the Israelites that there is to be no impurity (*rek^ws*) among them, for anyone who lies with his daughter-in-law or his mother-in-law has done something that is impure (*rek^ws*).
Angel about the future 50:5 The jubilees will pass by until Israel is pure (*nasha*) of every sin (*'abbasā*) of sexual immorality (*zemmut*)[VanderKam has sexual evil], impurity (*rek^ws*), contamination (*gemmane*), sin (*xaṭi'at*), and error (*gēgāy*) .

The word, *zemmut*, and the related words, *zammawa* and *zamma*, deal specifically with sexual wrongdoing. Leslau, whose lexicon informs the ranges of meanings for the words discussed below, gives their meanings as *zammawa* "fornicate, commit adultery; commit whoredom, have illicit intercourse"; *zemmut* "fornication, adultery, whoredom, harlotry, unchasteness"; *zamma* "harlot, prostitute, adulteress".[565] The most common in *Jubilees* is *zemmut*. In Latin we find words from the stem *fornicare*, but once, in 16:5, *spurcitia*, which it also uses for *saqorār*. No Hebrew equivalent in *Jubilees* survives. *Zemmut* is used in Noah's warning to his sons about the sexual wrongdoing of his generation and of the Watchers and giants (7:20, 21); in his sons' warning about the focus of future judgement (9:15); in relation to Sodom (16:5); in Abraham's instructions to his children in relation to Sodom and to Canaanite women (20:3-6); in the angel's prediction of the future (23:14); in Rebecca's words about Canaanite women (25:1) and Jacob's assurance (25:7); in the angel's exposition of Reuben's sin (33:20); and the angel's final words about the future (50:5). These contexts define its particular meanings. It is clearly a word which encompasses a wide range.

Another word which has directly sexual connotations is *mer'āt*, which appears twice only, once on the lips of Rebecca warning Jacob against the evils of Canaanite women (25:1) and once in Jacob's reassuring response (25:7). In both instances it occurs in combination with *zemmut*. Leslau lists its meaning as follows: "debauch (*sic* – probably debauchery), lasciviousness, indecency, lust, wantonness, immodesty, luxury".

More importantly, *zemmut*, frequently occurs in association with words which have a wider range of meaning, but which, through this association and their contextual setting, also include reference to sexual wrongdoing. One of these is *rek^w s*. Leslau gives the meaning as "filth, impurity, defilement, uncleanness, pollution, abomination, anything unclean or vile". From the same stem we have *rekus* "unclean, polluted, impure, defiled, profane, abominable, corrupt, foul"; with the verbal form: *rak^w sa* "be unclean, be impure, be polluted, be contaminated; be defiled, be profaned"; causative *'ark^w asa* "defile, contaminate, pollute, defame, profane, declare, unclean". It is the most common of the words noted in our texts.[566] The Hebrew apparently had כלמה or גלול at 1:9, נאצה in 33:13, טמא in 23:21 and תועבה in 21:23.[567] The Latin, too, has a range of equivalents: mostly

---

[565] Wolf Leslau, *Comparative Dictionary of Ge'ez (Classical Ethiopic: Ge'ez–English / English–Ge'ez with an Index of the Semitic Roots* (Wiesbaden: Otto Harrassowitz, 1987).

[566] Halpern-Amaru, *Empowerment*, expressing a preference for "impurity" as a translation rather than "uncleanness", states incorrectly that VanderKam translates the term throughout as "uncleanness" (22 n. 40). VanderKam also sometimes uses the translation, "impurity", e.g.: 1:9; 9:15 (2x); 11:16, 17; 21:21, 23; 22:16, 19.

[567] Milgrom, "Concept of Impurity," notes what he calls a confusion between desecration חלל (applicable to time) and pollution טמא (applicable to space) in both

abominatio, but also *inmunditia* and *pollutio*. All of these words have a wide range of meaning, so that their particular reference largely depends on the context and on intratextual associations. These can be tested most effectively where we have the full text, namely Ge'ez, but at least the implications of the contexts and the association of words will apply just as much to the Latin and Hebrew words.[568]

Rek^{w}s occurs in combination with *zemmut* and in contexts where it refers to sexual wrongdoing in 7:20-21 (Noah on sexual wrongdoing and the Watchers); 16:5-6 (about Sodom); 20:3-6 (Abraham's warning about sexual wrongdoing); 25:1 (Rebecca on Canaanite wives); and 33:19 (about Reuben). A reference to sexual wrongdoing is also implied in the combination with *zemmut* in: 9:15 (Noah's sons on future judgement); and probably in 23:14 (the angel on future sin) and 50:5 (the angel again on future sin). On its own or in other combinations, *rek^{w}s* refers to sexual wrongdoing/impurity in 4:26 (about Enoch and the Watchers); 30:13, 14, 15 (expounding the rape of Dinah and intermarriage); 41:17, 25, 26 (Judah and Tamar and its exposition). In other instances *rek^{w}s* alludes to idolatry, but often also in association with sexual wrongdoing. This is the case in the description of Mastema and his spirits which precedes Abraham's confrontation of idolatry. They continue the sins of the giants and the Watchers, which were characterised by sexual wrongdoing (11:4-5). Especially given his later instructions in 20:3-6, this is to be seen as also among Abram's concerns in 11:16, 17. It is likely also to be implied in Abraham's instruction about impurity to Isaac (21:21), where we find the string of terms, "sin (*xaṭi'at*) and wickedness(*'ekay*) and all their deeds of impurity (*rek^{w}s*), worthlessness (*mennānē*) and contamination (*gemmānē*)". Abraham's instruction to Jacob warns of *rek^{w}s* in another string of words in a context which links Gentiles with both idolatry and sexual wrongdoing (22:16-22): "impure (*rek^{w}s*), and all their ways are defiled (*gammana*) and something abominable (*mennānē*) and detestable (*saqorār*)" (22:16). The same concerns are reflected in the angel's warnings in 23:14-21, which use *rek^{w}s* in similar string (23:17, 21). The common association of *rek^{w}s* in settings concerned with sexual wrongdoing and in association with terms concerned with sexual wrongdoing makes it likely that in contexts where no

---

Jubilees and the Temple Scroll (279), but argues that the trend is already evident in Ezekiel (Ezek 20:39; 36:20 cf. Lev 20:3; 22:2, 32) and that the distinction had broken down already by the time of Ezekiel (279-80).

[568] Himmelfarb, "Sexual Relations," notes that "the repeated use of the language of impurity reflects the influence of the Holiness Code, particularly Lev. 18:24-30, which repeats the verb טמא six times in the course of its sermon on the defiling effect on the land of forbidden sexual relations" (29). She notes the use of purity language in 1QS 4.10-11 in a moral sense in דרכי נדה בעבודות טמאה, a stance close to that of *Jubilees* (35).

specific reference is found, the word carries such connotations. This is very likely for instance in 1:9.

The same applies more generally to other words. Many have fairly broad meanings but by association and through context they frequently carry connotations of sexual wrongdoing and its shamefulness in *Jubilees*. These include:

> *māsana* "decay, be spoiled, be corrupt, deteriorate, become rotten, be made desolate, be laid waster, be ruined, be abolished, be destroyed, perish"; causative: *'amāsana* "spoil, ruin, corrupt, pervert, subvert, deteriorate, demolish, destroy, lay waste, devastate, make desolate, wipe out" / *musenā* "rotting, corruption, perdition, ruin, desolation, devastation, destruction, depravity, perversion".
>
> *mennānē* "rejection; disdain, vileness, repudiation, renunciation, worthlessness, wickedness" / *mennun* "rejected, despised; reprobate, renounced, repudiated, despicable, abominable, ignoble, contemptible, revulsive, vile, worthless".
>
> *gammana* "pollute, defile, profane, sully, soil, stain, contaminate, violate" / *gemmānē* "profanation, pollution, defiling, contamination".
>
> *saqorār* "horror, abomination, disgust".

The following general words for sin also gain their specific meaning by association within their contexts:

> *xaṭi'at* "sin"; *'abbasā* "sin"; *'ammaḏā* "wickedness"; *'ekay* "wickedness"; *seḥtat* "error, sin"; *gēgāy* "error, sin". Other words occurring infrequently include: *xafrat* "shameful"; *nekafat* "blemish"; *xasār* "wretchedness, poverty, ignominy"; *ṣe'lat* "cursing, reviling, disgrace".

While for the most part we are dependent on the Ge'ez text, with some help from the Latin, both of which are translations of the non-extant Greek, and, for our purposes, little from the Syriac, and just a few fragments of the Hebrew, nevertheless the study of key words makes some contribution to our analysis. At least, as VanderKam observes, the Ge'ez text appears to be a careful translation, measured by what we have of the Hebrew. Even then it is striking that behind the most common Ge'ez word in our field, *rek^{w}s*, the few Hebrew texts which we have attest at least four different words. On the other hand, *Jubilees* makes regular use of abstract words expressing what is abhorrent and does so frequently in combinations. This provides opportunity to explore the association of terms and ideas, on the one hand, and to examine them in their contexts, on the other, with the result that we can uncover what those who heard and studied *Jubilees* would be likely to have understood by the abstract terms and how the author probably intended them to be understood. Their use in combination with terms referring to sexual wrongdoing and in contexts where that is their referent, builds a network of meaning in which these terms can be said to carry strong connotations of sexual wrongdoing.

The study of language coheres then with other important indicators in identifying sexual wrongdoing as a major theme in *Jubilees*. These other indicators include the focus of patriarchal speeches; that five of the twelve special commands to Moses to instruct Israel relate to sexual themes; the prominence of the removal of sexual wrongdoing in eschatological speeches and at key structural points in the narrative (especially the conclusion to the first half and to the work as a whole); and the pivotal significance if the Watchers' sexual wrongdoing and the abiding consequences it unleashed both before and after the flood. These cohere, in turn, with the major emphasis given the theme of sexual wrongdoing in such key episodes as the sins of Sodom, the rape of Dinah, the sin of Reuben, the tragedy of Judah, and the virtue of Joseph. The sin of intermarriage is a persistent theme. It is grounded in belief that God's holy people will be polluted especially through the sexual wrongdoing of the nations, represented in the evil of the Canaanite women.

These negative conclusions need, however, to be evaluated in the light of other, mostly positive statements which *Jubilees* makes about sexuality, and to these we turn.

3.3   Other Aspects related to Sexuality in *Jubilees*

3.3.1   *Creation and Marriage*

The account of the creation in *Jubilees*[569] begins with a summary instruction of the angel to Moses: "Write all the words about the creation – how in six days the Lord God completed all his works, everything that he had created, and kept sabbath on the seventh day. He sanctified it for all ages and set it as a sign for all his works" (2:1).[570] The emphasis falls on the sabbath. This matches the emphasis which the sabbath receives in what follows. *Jub.* 2:2-14 describe the six days of creation. *Jub.* 2:15-33 is then an extended excursus on he sabbath. The six days receive brief but distinctive treatment in which works are numbered through the days, resulting in a total of 22. The sun is prominent, reflecting the importance of the solar calendar.[571] The first day is significantly rewritten to emphasise the creation of spirits and angels and to emphasise God's mind as a resource (2:2).

By contrast the sixth day is very brief. *Jubilees* does not take up the statements about humankind being in the image or likeness of God, although it preserves the motif in 6:8 (drawn from Gen 9:6). Thus not only is Gen 1:26 missing, but so is the reference in 1:27 to "image". Similarly *Jubilees* does not reproduce Gen 5:1-2, which repeats the ideas of 1:26-27. Perhaps the author seeks to avoid potential misunderstanding along the lines of the confusion of men and gods in the invasive Hellenistic traditions.[572] With these omissions went also the

---

[569] For a detailed comparison with the Genesis account see van Ruiten, *Primaeval History Interpreted*, 9-46.

[570] As in LXX, Samaritan Pentateuch, Old Latin and Syriac, *Jubilees* will have read sixth day in Gen 2:2, not seventh as in MT: "And on the seventh day God finished the work that he had done."

[571] On this see VanderKam, "Genesis 1 in *Jubilees* 2," who notes that *Jubilees*' denial of any significance to the moon stands in contrast not only to a lunar calendar but also to the calendar affirmed by the group at Qumran and in *1 Enoch* 72 – 82, which assumes a role for both sun and moon (513). See also Mark Stratton Smith, "Reading, Writing and Interpretation: Two Notes on Jubilees and Pseudo-Jubilees," in *Hamlet on a Hill: Semitic and Greek Studies Presented to Professor T. Muraoka on the Occasion of His Sixty-Fifth Birthday* (eds. M. F. J. Baasten and W. Th. van Peursen; Leuven: Peeters, 2003) 441-47, who points to the influence of Mal 3:20 on *Jubilees*' depiction of the suns as healing (443-44).

[572] VanderKam, "Genesis 1 in *Jubilees* 2," notes the observation of J. Jervell, *Imago Dei: Gen. 1, 26f. im Spätjudentum, in der Gnosis und in den paulinischen Briefen* (FRLANT 75; Göttingen: Vandenhoeck und Ruprecht, 1960) 21, that there was a growing reluctance already in the second century B.C.E. to interpret Gen 1:26-27 in public (514).

plural, "Let us make" (Gen 1:26).[573] Instead *Jubilees* simply repeats the key words of Genesis, as the Hebrew fragments confirm:

עשה את האדם זכר ונקבה "he made humankind, male and female" (2:14; cf. Gen 1:27 אלהים את האדם בצלמו בצלם אלהים ברא אתו זכר ונקבה ברא אתם (ויברא),[574]

but uses the word עשה ("he made") rather than ברא ("he created").[575] It then retains from Gen 1:28 the command to rule over all creation, but leaves the command to be fruitful and multiply until 6:5, where it derives from Gen 9:1. Its absence here, therefore, should not be seen as disapproval. As the author recounted the creation story, it was not important enough to mention at this point. This coheres with the emphasis on companionship in the accounts of the creation of woman both in Genesis and in *Jubilees*, which make no mention of procreation.

After the long excursus on the sabbath, *Jubilees* returns to the narrative of creation, taking up the account from Genesis in 2:18. The parallels are set out in the table below.[576]

Jubilees 3	Genesis 2
1 On the sixth day of the second week	18 Then the LORD God said, "It is not good that the man should be alone; I will make him a helper as his partner."
we brought to Adam, on the Lord's orders, all animals, all cattle, all birds, everything that moves about on the earth, and everything that moves about in the water – in their various	19 So out of the ground the LORD God formed every animal of the field and every bird of the air, and brought them to the man

---

[573] VanderKam, "Genesis 1 in *Jubilees* 2," notes: "the writer does not have God consult with them about fashioning humankind" (514).

[574] Earlier VanderKam, *Jubilees Translated*, 12 n. 2:14, had noted that the use of "man" and "woman", rather than "male" and "female", counts against the notion that *Jubilees* implied androgyny; cf. Hermann Rönsch, *Das Buch der Jubiläen oder die kleine Genesis* (Amsterdam: Rodopi, 1970; Leipzig: Pues's Verlag, 1874) 261-62 n. 1. The Hebrew, however, of 2:14, now preserved in 4Q216, does not support a change from "male and female" to "man and woman". The Geʿez reading is still assumed in Betsy Halpern-Amaru, "*Jubilees*, Midrash in," in *Encyclopaedia of Midrash* (ed. Jacob Neusner and Alan J. Avery Peck; Leiden: Brill, 2005) 1. 333-50, 337.

[575] Brooke, "Exegetical Strategies," suggests Gen 1:26 may have led to the change from ברא (Gen 1:27) to עשה (41, 43).

[576] See also the detailed comparison in van Ruiten, *Primaeval History Interpreted*, 71-84.

kinds and various forms:

the animals on the first day;

the cattle on the second day;

the birds on the third day;

everything that moves about on the earth on the fourth day;

and the ones that move about in the water on the fifth day.

2 Adam named them all, each with its own name.

Whatever he called them became their name.

3 During these five days Adam was looking at all of these male and female among every kind that was on the earth.

But he himself was alone;

there was no one whom he found for himself who would be for him a helper who was like him.

4 Then the Lord said to us: "It is not good that the man should be alone.

Let us make him a helper who is like him".

5 The Lord our God imposed a sound slumber on him and he fell asleep.

Then he took one of his bones for a woman.

That rib was the origin of the woman from among his bones.

He built up the flesh in its place

and built the woman.

6 Then he awakened Adam from his sleep.

When he awoke, he got up on the sixth day.

Then he brought (him) to her.

He knew her and

said to her:

"This is now bone from my bone and flesh from my flesh.

 This one will be called my wife,

for she was taken from her husband".

7 For this reason a man and a woman are to become one,

and for this reason he leaves his father and his mother.

He associates (cling/join to, *ḍamara*) with his wife, and they become one flesh.

---

to see what he would call them; and whatever the man called every living creature, that was its name.

20 The man gave names to all cattle, and to the birds of the air, and to every animal of the field;

but for the man there was not found a helper as his partner.

21 So the LORD God caused a deep sleep to fall upon the man, and he slept;

then he took one of his ribs

and closed up its place with flesh.

22 And the rib that the LORD God had taken from the man he made into a woman

and brought her to the man.

23 Then the man said,

"This at last is bone of my bones and flesh of my flesh;

this one shall be called Woman, for out of Man this one was taken."

24 Therefore a man leaves his father and his mother

and clings to his wife,

and they become one flesh.

Jubilees reports the creation of woman in the second week on the sixth day (3:1-7). According to 3:1 the angels were instructed to bring to Adam the created animate beings: the animals on the first day, the cattle on the second, birds on the third, other earthly creatures on the fourth, and creatures of the water on the fifth. The purpose was so that Adam would name them. This represents an interesting rewriting and reinterpretation of the Genesis narrative. *Jubilees* has not taken up the account of God's creating a human being/adam/earthling from the ground (though it knows Gen 3:19b, which it rephrases in 3:25 as: "for earth you are and to earth you shall return"). It also averts the difficulty of having two accounts of creation by omitting all reference to the second, instead, taking up elements of it into its creation by days.[577] The exception is the creation of woman, based on Gen 2:21-23.

Having stated in 2:14 that on the sixth day God made humankind male and female, *Jubilees* appears to have understood the first human being as male and female, but in the sense that the male, whom it calls Adam (2:23 אדם; 3:1), incorporates the potential for the female, rather than that the first human being was androgynous and lost something at the creation of the woman.[578] This understanding may explain the addition at 3:5, "That rib was the origin of the woman from among his bones". Thus the author can recount the formation of woman as taking place in the second week without having this stand in contradiction to the statement of 2:14. In 3:8 the author makes the point explicitly: "In the first week Adam and his wife — the rib — were created, and in the second week he showed her to him". This stands in contrast to a reading of Gen 2:20-23, for instance, which would see it explicating what is already implied in summary in 1:27.

It is interesting further that *Jubilees* omits part of the original motivation for bringing the animals to Adam. They are not seen as potential companions of the man, as Gen 2:18 supposes: "Then the LORD God said, 'It is not good that the man should be alone; I will make him a helper as his partner'." Nor are they formed from the ground for this purpose as Gen 2:19a reports: "So out of the ground the LORD God formed every animal of the field and every bird of the air". Instead, only the thought of Gen 2:19b is preserved: "and brought them to the man to see what he would call them; and whatever the man called every living creature, that was its name". In *Jubilees* the angel and his fellows bring the animals to

---

[577] On this see VanderKam, "Genesis 1 in *Jubilees* 2," who notes how in 2:7 *Jubilees* includes in its depiction of the third day mention of the creation of the Garden of Eden, first introduced in Genesis in Gen 2:8, and also the term "the Lord God" from Gen 2:9 (511-12). See also Brooke, "Exegetical Strategies," 47; Halpern-Amaru, "Midrash," 335.

[578] Halpern-Amaru, *Empowerment*: "Neither the hermaphrodite human of rabbinic imagination nor the asexual earth creature of recent feminist interpretations, the original human of *Jubilees* is a male with an undeveloped female aspect" (9).

Adam (3:1). Thus according to *Jub.* 3:2, "Adam named them all, each with its own name. Whatever he called them became their name". One might speculate that the author thus sought to avoid any notion of companionship, in particular, sexual relationship between the man and the animals (cf. 5:2). This is certainly possible, but need not be so.

The focus for companionship thus falls solely on man and woman in the narrative. But in 3:3 *Jubilees* has introduced interesting new traits into the story as he found it in Gen 2:19-24. It reports the man's attentiveness to male and female among the animals: "During these five days Adam was looking at all of these male and female among every kind that was on the earth". This implies positive interest on Adam's part in the sexual differentiation among the animals and thus on the possibilities it created. Given that the outcome of the story speaks of sexual intercourse and a sexual relationship in the companionship of marriage, this comment places a positive value on sexual relations. It is interesting to have this first expressed in relation to animals and to note that it is in no way derogatory. It informs the statement which immediately follows: "But he himself was alone; there was no one whom he found for himself who would be for him a helper who was like him".[579] He wants to be with someone the way male and female animals relate to each other. This is something positive and good. At the same time, an additional perspective is preserved as *Jubilees* takes over the form of words found in Genesis which speaks of "helper": "but for the man there was not found a helper who was like him" (Gen 2:20b): "there was no one whom he found for himself who would be for him a helper who was like him" (*Jub.* 3:3).

In 3:4, *Jubilees* then returns to what in Genesis had been the starting point for forming animals and bringing them to Adam: "Then the LORD God said, 'It is not good that the man should be alone; I will make him a helper as his partner'" (Gen 2:18). Here in *Jubilees*, however, the accumulation of both passages from Genesis into *Jub.* 3:3-4 gives major emphasis to the creation of woman as the fulfilment of the man's need for relationship.[580] *Jubilees* may have read a plural in the Hebrew text rather than the singular "I will make". Certainly it now assumes it, as the angel reports involvement in the innovation: "Then the Lord said to us: 'It is not good that the man should be alone. Let us make him a helper who is like him'"

[579] Gary Anderson, "Celibacy or Consummation in the Garden: Reflections on Early Jewish and Christian Interpretations of the Garden of Eden," *HTR* 82 (1989) 121-48, speaks of God's creation of the animals as "an instructive event which informs Adam of his incompleteness and need of a mate" (128). Similarly van Ruiten, *Primaeval History Interpreted*, 80. On the active, "he found", see VanderKam, *Jubilees Translated*, 16, 3:3; Halpern-Amaru, "Midrash," 337.

[580] Similarly Anderson, "Celibacy or Consummation," 128. Similarly, van Ruiten, *Primaeval History Interpreted*, 81.

(3:4). Such involvement seems thoroughly positive, with no hint of a resultant, inferior product.[581]

There is a cumulative impact in the text of the additional material and of the way *Jubilees* has concentrated the two Genesis passages. Adam misses what he sees of sexual partnership among the animals, is alone and finds no such partner of his own kind as partner and helper. God, too, observes, that this state of affairs of man's aloneness is not good. The male needs a partner like himself. The cumulative effect is to lay greater emphasis on the creation of woman and especially the coming together of man and woman, in particular in a sexual sense, as something willed by God. In *Jubilees* the focus is thus on such companionship; it does not develop the notion of "helper".

The sexual component has received greater attention thus far, compared with the Genesis account, and receives similar attention in what follows. *Jub.* 3:5 matches Gen 2:21 in reporting that God caused a deep sleep to fall on Adam and that God took one of his bones. *Jubilees*, unlike Genesis, does not describe this specifically as a rib at first, but does so in the addition: "That rib was the origin of the woman from among his bones". Partly this achieves the effect that Adam's statement that the woman is "bone from my bone" directly echoes the description of God's action: "Then he took one of his bones for a woman" (3:5). Partly with the addition ("That rib was the origin of the woman from among his bones") the effect is also to underline that the woman was built from a bone that was part of the man, not that he was once male and female and is now less than what he was.

Jubilees' description of God's action, "he built up the flesh in its place and built the woman" (3:5) differs from Gen 2:21-22, which says that God "closed up the flesh" and "formed" the woman.[582] Perhaps *Jubilees* wants further to reinforce the notion that the man is not thereby rendered incomplete. It then provides a revised account of the rest of Gen 2:22, where the latter simply reads: "and brought her to the man". Instead, *Jubilees* states: "Then he awakened Adam from his sleep. When he awoke, he got up on the sixth day. Then he brought (him) to

---

[581] van Ruiten, *Primaeval History Interpreted*, suggests that the LXX uses the plural to put the creation of man and woman on the same level (80), but see, to the contrary, my discussion in William Loader, *The Septuagint, Sexuality and the New Testament: Case Studies on the Impact of the LXX in Philo and the New Testament* (Grand Rapids: Eerdmans, 2004), which argues that, whatever the intention, the closer link created between this passage and 1:26-27, by this and other modifications, results in a hierarchical reading, where woman is in the image of man as man is in the image of God (57-59). On the Ethiopic text see VanderKam, *Jubilees Translated*, 16 n. 3:4.

[582] Anderson, "Celibacy or Consummation," finds in *Jubilees* a precursor to later rabbinic views reflected in *Gen. Rab.* 19:3 and 18:6, which saw Gen 2:22 "as a description of the first marriage ceremony. The act of 'building' is understood as God's acting as Adam's groomsman" (124).

her". Some variants read "brought her to him", reflecting Genesis, but the case for the reading "brought (him) to her" is on balance stronger according to VanderKam.[583] *Jubilees* assumes that the initiative to build a woman began on the fifth day. On the sixth day Adam awakes. God then brings him to the woman. *Jubilees* may be influenced by the order in 2:24, where the man goes to the woman, leaving the household of his father and mother behind to begin a new household. It may well be also under the influence of 2:24 that *Jubilees* adds: "and he knew her". The act of sexual intercourse takes place here and is part, therefore, of the fulfilment of Adam's desire evoked by his observing the animals to find a partner and helper for himself.[584]

Adam's declaration in Gen 2:23, "This at last is bone of my bones and flesh of my flesh; this one shall be called Woman (אשה), for out of Man (איש) this one was taken", comes to us in *Jubilees* in a slightly different form: "This is now bone from my bone and flesh from my flesh. This one will be called my wife, for she was taken from her husband". The Ethiopic does not reproduce the pun.[585] The Hebrew of *Jubilees* may have done. The declaration as it stands in *Jubilees* includes the meaning that the woman has been formed from the man – although the narrative does not tell us that Adam has realised what has happened to him, such that we might see his statement as a deduction from such knowledge. Rather, it celebrates that now he has a sexual partner and companion, such as he saw among the animals. The "now" (with the LXX νῦν in contrast to "at long last" Hebrew: הפעם) may also suggest that this reality has been established by the fact of their coming together in sexual intercourse, but the Hebrew of *Jubilees* may have matched the Hebrew of Genesis.[586] But for the hearer, both aspects are present: he has his desire and his desire is fulfilled because one of his own bones

---

[583] See the discussion in VanderKam, *Jubilees Translated*, 16 n. 3:6, who writes that whereas "the versions at Gen 2:22 indicate that the Lord brought the woman to the man, this implies that the reversal of roles in some mss. of *Jubilees* is more likely to be original because it differs from Genesis", though he admits the possibility that the change which consists of a minor stroke in a letter may be the result of miscopying or the tendency to lengthen the a-vowel after a guttural. Van Ruiten, *Primaeval History Interpreted*, opts for the latter possibility (84).

[584] Anderson, "Celibacy or Consummation," 128; Halpern-Amaru, *Empowerment*, 10. Van Ruiten, *Primaeval History Interpreted*, cites Josephus *A.J.* 1.36 as a parallel (84 n. 360), but there we read ἐγνώρισεν ἐξ αὐτοῦ γενομένην.

[585] On the reading, "my wife", see VanderKam, *Jubilees Translated*, 16 n. 3:6, who points out that it agrees against all other versions with EthGen 2:23. See also his note on "her husband", which *Jubilees* shares with, among others, the LXX (2. 17 n. 3:6).

[586] Anderson, "Celibacy or Consummation," emphasises that the sense of "at last" relates to at long last finding a sexual mate, more directly evident in *Jubilees*, but there also as a reading of Genesis (125-28), and reflected in later rabbinic tradition.

became the source for the creation of woman. Certainly the text should be seen as a celebration of partnership and sexual union. *Jub.* 3:5 mentions this specifically and *Jubilees* appears to have reworked it, as we have seen, to match the statement of Gen 2:24, which it reproduces in 3:7.

The reproduction of Gen 2:24 in 3:7 also warrants further attention. Not only does *Jubilees* reproduce it, but it takes one element of the saying and puts it up front as an addition: "For this reason a man and a woman are to become one". Then follows the statement: "and for this reason he leaves his father and his mother. He associates with his wife, and they become one flesh". The latter matches Gen 2:24, "Therefore a man leaves his father and his mother and clings to his wife, and they become one flesh". The repetition of the final element of the saying, so that it now forms the first element as well, underlines the importance of the oneness, including sexual union.

There are a number of points where the variations may reflect the fact that the Ethiopic is a translation of the Greek, which may well have stood under the influence of the LXX. This appears not to be the case with the additions and rearrangements, but it may account for the following changes. The plural, "Let us make" in *Jub.* 3:4, in contrast to Hebrew, "I will make", may well reflect the ποιήσωμεν of the LXX. *Jub.* 3:1 appears to use the name, Adam, as does LXX in Gen 2:19, whereas the Hebrew אדם is ambiguous. The LXX uses the generic ἄνθρωπος in 2:18 in describing the man's aloneness, but *Jubilees* seems to require what was originally אדם to be understood as more distinctively male (as it is in Gen 2:20 LXX, where it is even Αδαμ). In 3:5 Jubilees preserves the notion of a "deep sleep" (Gen 2:21; cf. LXX which has ἔκστασιν). LXX influence may be seen behind 3:5, "He built up the flesh in its place", which is closer to ἀνεπλήρωσεν σάρκα ἀντ' αὐτῆς than to ויסגר בשר תחתנה lit. "he closed up flesh instead of it". It is likely in what follows: in the "now" (cf. the LXX νῦν in contrast to "at long last" Hebrew: הפעם), but also in αὕτη κληθήσεται γυνή ὅτι ἐκ τοῦ ἀνδρὸς αὐτῆς ἐλήμφθη αὕτη. This reflects the LXX's inability to reproduce the pun. *Jubilees* goes even further adding a first person possessive pronoun to woman: "This one will be called my wife, for she was taken from her husband".[587] In taking over Gen 2:24, however, *Jubilees* does not have with LXX, "the two", οἱ δύο.

Jubilees does not reproduce Gen 2:25 ("And the man and his wife were both naked, and were not ashamed") immediately. It comes later in *Jub.* 3:16. Nor is

---

[587] Halpern-Amaru, *Empowerment*, notes that "her husband" "may simply reflect the author's biblical text" or "if it reflects the hand of the exegete/author, the alteration that corrects the grammar also enhances the marriage partnership motif that is being developed in the rewritten narrative" (144-45).

there an attempt to preserve the pun between the word for naked (עָרוֹם) and the word for the craftiness of the serpent (עָרוּם), evident in Gen 2:25 and 3:1.

In its account of the creation of woman, *Jubilees* has enhanced the sense of sexual union between man and woman in the context of marriage and household as something willed by God. It does this by introducing the sexuality of the animals as something to be desired, and by revising Gen 2:22 in the light of Gen 2:24, so that the man is brought to the woman and not vice versa, has sexual intercourse with her, and then makes the declaration about her being bone of his bone and flesh of his flesh. The sexual union is further enhanced by the doubling of the single statement from Gen 2:24. At the same time, as Halpern-Amaru observes, the sexual politics of *Jubilees* assumes masculinity as "the dominant principle of the natural order ... femininity as a potential in existence from the time of the creation of humanity", and without full development of this potential "the human creature, for all its male dominance, is inadequate".[588]

Jubilees also creates a sense of harmony between the man and the woman in the garden. Thus instead of reporting instructions to Adam, as Gen 2:16-17, which it omits, *Jub.* 3:17, which has its parallel in Gen 3:1, brings that additional information in a way that emphasises that the prohibition came not just to the man but to both, reflecting the theme of partnership.[589] Thus the woman speaks of "us" in responding to the serpent:

> She said to him: "From all the fruit of the tree(s) which are in the garden the Lord told us: 'Eat'. But from the fruit of the tree which is in the middle of the garden he told us: 'Do not eat from it and do not touch it so that you may not die'". (3:18)

Similarly, whereas Gen 3:7 notes the effect on both together of taking the fruit ("Then the eyes of both were opened, and they knew that they were naked; and they sewed fig leaves together and made loincloths for themselves"), *Jubilees* separates the two events:

> So she took some of it and ate (it). She first covered her shame with fig leaves and then gave it to Adam. He ate (it), his eyes were opened, and he saw that he was naked. He took fig leaves and sewed (them); (thus) he made himself an apron and covered his shame. (3:20-22)

Jubilees then omits the account of God's entry into the garden in the evening and his conversation with the man and the woman (Gen 3:8-13). Halpern-Amaru notes

---

[588] Halpern-Amaru, *Empowerment*, 11.

[589] So Halpern-Amaru, *Empowerment*, 140.

that the omission "removes the indication of tension and alienation" created by the petty blaming which there takes place.[590]

This positive attitude towards sexual union in the context of marriage and household reverberates throughout *Jubilees*. Sexual wrongdoing appears to be seen as something inherently good but taking place primarily in the wrong context and with the wrong people or wrong kind. Men and women grow up and marry in *Jubilees*. If Jacob reflects the ideal, they do not so much as a touch a woman sexually before they approach marriage (25:4). They marry and have sexual relations. They bear children, although this is not cited as the sole reason for sexual union. Indeed, the command to multiply first occurs only where it is based on Gen 9:1, in the context of Noah's instruction after the flood: "Now you increase and multiply yourselves on the earth and become numerous upon it" (6:5).

Like Gen 4:1, *Jub.* 3:34 reports that Adam "knew" his wife, that is, they had sexual intercourse. *Jub.* 3:6 reports that he already "knew" the newly formed woman on the day of her creation. This reflects an awareness that not every act of intercourse produces children, nor need it do so. *Jub.* 4:1 then simply reports: "she gave birth to Cain". It does not report conception as a stage in the process, as does Gen 4:1, nor does it reproduce the pun in the words of Eve: "I have produced (קָנִיתִי; Cain = קַיִן) a man with the help of the Lord". *Jub.* 4:1 continues in similar terms to report the birth of Abel and of Awan, a daughter. The latter goes without mention in Genesis, although Gen 4:17 assumes Cain married a wife. *Jubilees* supplies the gap. The wife is his sister, Awan (4:9). This is an incestuous marriage according to Lev 18:9, 11, but *Jubilees*, which would have upheld prohibition of such marriages, was apparently willing to contemplate it in this exceptional situation, although, unlike elsewhere where such anomalies occur, it offers no apologetic explanation. We find a similar situation in *Jub.* 4:8, where *Jubilees* mentions Azura as daughter of Adam (and his wife). That provided a wife for Seth (4:11). This is an innovation on the part of *Jubilees*, which thus avoids the likely conclusion from Genesis that Seth would have married a daughter of Cain. That would have been bad in two respects: marrying into a bad family has serious consequences and marrying a niece is for *Jubilees* as forbidden as a woman

---

[590] Halpern-Amaru, *Empowerment*, 14. She notes that *Jubilees* refers to the couple, not just Adam, in what follows in 3:26, 29-32 and "generally softens the catastrophic tone of the biblical expulsion scene": they "are 'dismissed' (3:26) or 'leave' (3:27) the garden"; there is no tree of life and there are no cherubim set to keep them away (14-15) and *Jubilees* then portrays them as jointly grieving the death of Abel (4:7) (15; see also 140). Van Ruiten, *Primaeval History Interpreted*, notes the similar omission of the blaming in Gen 4:9-10 (97). In addition he mentions the inconsistencies within the Genesis account (that Adam was afraid because he was naked whereas he had already covered himself), the image of God as "innocent and uninformed", and the apparent concern of *Jubilees* to create a positive image of Adam (97-98).

marrying her nephew (Lev 18:13-14). We have already noted *Jubilees'* constant concern with marriage into families where there is bad influence, which is the case here with Cain, and always assumed to be the case with Canaanites and the uncircumcised. *Jubilees* also takes very seriously the prohibition of marrying nieces, as later do the writers of the sectarian documents at Qumran (CD 5.1-11 and 11QTemple 66.15-17),[591] in contrast to the later Pharisaic positive attitude towards marrying nieces.

Subsequently, for the first three generations wives are siblings, thus avoiding intermarriage with Cain and his family. Thereafter they are cousins.[592] *Jub.* 4:10 reports in the usual way that "Adam knew his wife Eve, and she gave birth to nine more children". *Jub.* 4:7 indicates a period of mourning after Abel's death before "Adam and his wife ...became happy" (*tafaśśeḥa*). Then "Adam again knew his wife, and she gave birth to a son for him". The juxtaposition of becoming happy and engaging in sexual intercourse is probably not fortuitous. It coheres with *Jubilees'* natural affirmation of sexual relations. The formulation "bore him a son (ותלד לו בן)" occurs frequently in *Jubilees* 4 (4:9, 11, 13, 14, 15, 16, 20, 28, 33). Gen 5:4 simply mentions that after Seth Adam "had other sons and daughters", an expression which then recurs in relation to Seth (5:7), Enosh (5:10); Kenan (5:13), Mahalalel (5:16), Jared (5:19), Enoch (5:22); Methuselah (5:26), and Lamech (5:30). This is part of a formulaic account which focuses solely on the male, his firstborn, his age and death. Earlier Gen 4:17-22 had listed Cain's firstborn sons, but then in the case of Lamech, also his two wives by name: Adah and Zillah, and the latter's son and his sister by name. By contrast, *Jubilees* shows interest in passing on the names of Adam's daughters, Awan and Azura, as we have seen, who then become the wives of Cain and Seth respectively, and proceeds to tell us the names of the wives of Enosh (Noam, also his sister; 4:13), Kenan (Mualelit, also his sister; 4:14), Mahalalel (Dinah, a paternal cousin; 4:15), Jared (Barakah, a paternal cousin; 4:16), Enoch (Edni, a paternal cousin; 4:20), Methuselah (Edna, a paternal cousin; 4:27),[593] Lamech (Betanosh, a paternal cousin; 4:28), and Noah (Emzara, a paternal cousin; 4:33).

While *Jubilees* differs from Genesis in omitting age, and, instead, dates the marriage and the birth of the firstborn in each instance, it shows remarkable

---

[591] So Rothstein, "Sexual Union," 379-80.

[592] So also Halpern-Amaru, *Empowerment*, 19. See also VanderKam, *Jubilees Translated*, 25 n. 4:15, on the misreading of the Ethiopic MSS. which write "sister" instead of "brother".

[593] Halpern-Amaru, *Empowerment*, notes that *Jubilees* departs from the pattern of stating that the women gave birth to the child, by reporting that Methuselah was father of a child, probably to avoid suggestion of contamination through the Watchers (21).

interest in the marriages and in the women involved, not just the men.[594] The names of the wives carry meaning through their etymologies, as Rook has shown.[595] For instance, when Cain marries his sister Awan, whose name means either "iniquity" or "wickedness", there is little prospect of any good coming from that line, and when Enoch marries Edni, whose name reflects Eden, one senses the opposite.

We find a continuing interest in the names of the women when *Jubilees* reworks the material of Genesis 10 in describing the descendants of Noah's sons, Japheth, Ham, and Shem.[596] Thus *Jub.* 7:14 mentions that Ham built a city and named it after his wife, Neelatamauk. Japheth, too, named a city after his wife, Adataneses (7:15). Shem did similarly, naming it: Sedeqatelebab (7:16). The pattern of naming wives of descendants and dating the year of marriage and of the birth of the firstborn, which we found in *Jubilees* 4, repeats itself in *Jubilees* 8, 10 and 11. Thus we read of Arpachsad and his wife, "Rasueya, the daughter of Susan, the daughter of Elam" (8:1); of Kainan[597] and his wife, "Melka, the daughter of Madai, Japheth's son" (8:5); of Shelah and his wife, "Muak, the daughter of Kesed, his father's brother" (8:6); of Eber and his wife, "Azurad, the daughter of Nebrod" (8:7); of Peleg and his wife, "Lomna, the daughter of Sunaor" (10:18); of Ragew and his wife, "Ara, the daughter of Ur, Kesed's son" (11:1); of Serug and his wife, "Melcha, the daughter of Kaber, the daughter of his father's brother" (11:7); of Nahor and his wife, "Iyaseka, the daughter of Nestag of the Chaldeans" (11:9); and of Terah and his wife, "Edna, the daughter of Abram, the daughter of his father's sister" (11:15).

Within this sequence there are problems, which the naming of the wives serves to expose. Marriage outside the chosen line invited disaster.[598] Arpachsad's marriage apparently to his niece (unless she was his grand-niece), in effect

---

[594] On the question whether *Jubilees* added the names of the women independently or drew on tradition see van Ruiten, *Primaeval History Interpreted*, who notes that some of the names also occur in the *Genesis Apocryphon* and suggests that both works probably draw on a common tradition (123).

[595] Rook, "Names of the Wives," 107-17.

[596] On the marriages from Adam to Noah and Noah to Abraham see Halpern-Amaru, *Empowerment*, 18-28. As she puts it in Halpern-Amaru, "Midrash," "The pattern is consistent throughout the genealogy; in each instance where a union involves a bride from outside the family line, no lineage credentials are offered for the woman, and the offspring from the union and/or the peers of their generation engage in some sinful activity" (342).

[597] On the additional generation of Kainan, see VanderKam, *Jubilees Translated*, 50 n. 8:1, noting that *Jubilees* shares this with LXX and OL. See also van Ruiten, *Primaeval History Interpreted*, 315-16.

[598] VanderKam, *Book of Jubilees*, 2001, p. 115.

produced the sin of Kainan their son.[599] Kainan's marriage into the house of
Japheth creates potential problems (though not exogamous), since it exposes him
to other influences, as his contact with the tradition of the Watchers shows
(8:2-4).[600] The names of the offspring of exogamous marriages express the danger:
e.g., Sereg produced Ragew (evil).[601] Nahor's marriage outside the family to
"Iyaseka, the daughter of Nestag of the Chaldeans", appears to be seen by *Jubilees*
as the beginning of the idolatrous influences which the young Abram must
challenge. Such marriages foreshadow the dangers of marrying Canaanite women.

While the concern appears to be to assert the purity of the line and to warn of
the dangers consequent on exogamous marriage and the exposure it brings to evil,
Jubilees does not achieve this at the expense of the women nor at the expense of
licit sexual relations. "Women are neither the temptresses of, nor the foils for,
men".[602] As in Eden, sin occurs when both men and women err. Neither women's
sexuality nor sexual behaviour itself is problematised. The problem is
inappropriate choices and their consequences.

The formulaic listing continues in 12:9, mentioning Abram and his wife,
Sarai, the daughter of his father, and in 12:10 with mention of his brother Haran
and his wife (unnamed) and their son, Lot, and of the marriage of the other
brother, Nahor. This brings us to the marriages of the patriarchs, which in *Jubilees*
have been developed in a new way, reflective of the theme of partnership
intimated in the creation story and having some bearing on attitudes towards
sexuality and sexual intimacy, which is integral to these marriages. To these we
now turn.

---

[599] See also Halpern-Amaru, *Empowerment*, who notes the ambiguity in 8:1 where
Arpachshad could be marrying either a niece or a grand-niece, but suggests that since
Jubilees, like the Qumranites, appears to disapprove of marrying nieces the latter is more
probable (22-23). See her discussion generally of marriages from Adam to Noah and Noah
to Abraham (18-28).

[600] On this see Halpern-Amaru, *Empowerment*, 24.

[601] See Halpern-Amaru, *Empowerment*, 26.

[602] Halpern-Amaru, *Empowerment*, 27.

3.3.2   The Patriarchs and their Wives

The aim of this section is to look at *Jubilees'* treatment of the figures of the patriarchs in the light of the question: what does it reflect about the author's attitudes towards sexuality?[603]

3.3.2.1   Abraham and Sarah[604]

The initial expansions of the Abraham story relate to idolatry. *Jubilees* probably sees this as the fruit of Nahor's having married a Chaldean (11:10). Abram's success against the ravens and invention of the seeding plough (11:18-22, 23-24) are probably to be seen as a success against the spirits of Mastema (11:11-13), as noted above in the discussion of the Watchers. His confrontation of his father about the idols (12:1-8) and his burning of the temple of idols in which Haran was burned to death (12:12-14) are exemplary of rejection of idolatry and idolaters. Nothing in this context relates to matters of sexuality except Nahor's sin in the first place. According to 12:17-18 a heavenly voice also dismisses "the studies of Chaldeans: to practice divination and to augur by the signs of the sky", which Nahor had acquired (11:8), as irrelevant, since God controls the weather. Abram rejects all this, affirming God alone and praying to be saved "from the power of the evil spirits who rule the thoughts of people's minds" (12:19-20). In the broader context of *Jubilees* such resistance includes resisting sexual impurity. Fortunately, his father, Terah, had also preserved holy traditions in Hebrew, which the angel taught Abram; he could study them "throughout the six rainy months" (12:27).

Abram does not wait to be told to leave Haran, as in Gen 12:1, but raises the issue, first, himself (12:21). Terah blesses him on his departure (12:28-29). *Jubilees* recounts Abram's marriage to Sarai in 12:9, much as in Gen 11:29, but now Sarai is clearly his sister,[605] a conclusion perhaps influenced by the account of Abraham's ruse in Gerar where he portrays her as his sister (Gen 20:12) – indeed his half-sister, the daughter of his father but not his mother.[606] But *Jubilees* omits this story and gives no indication that Sarai is a half-sister. There is, thus, no amelioration of the problem which the text poses that Abram acts contrary to Lev 18:9, "You shall not uncover the nakedness of your sister, your father's daughter or your mother's daughter," and 18:11, "You shall not uncover the nakedness of

---

[603] For the discussion of the ideal marriages which *Jubilees* creates for the patriarchs, see especially Halpern-Amaru, *Empowerment*, 33-73.

[604] I follow Genesis in using Abram and Sarai, where its context uses them.

[605] On this see Halpern-Amaru, *Empowerment*, 34-36.

[606] VanderKam, *Book of Jubilees*, 2001, p. notes that this, in effect, ensures that in Gen 20:12 Abram will not be lying when he identifies Sarai as his sister (47), but *Jubilees* omits this ruse.

your father's wife's daughter, begotten by your father, since she is your sister"
(similarly 20:17). While one might argue that Seth had little alternative: better to
marry your sibling than your niece and into a evil line, this is not the case with
Abram. *Jubilees*, which elsewhere rails against incest vehemently, shows,
however, no indication of seeing a problem in the marriage of siblings here.
Egyptians might smile knowing the pattern of the Ptolemies. *Jubilees* is silent.

Gen 20:12 might be omitted, but it cannot be controverted or explained away,
as many later sought to do and certainly not by making her Abram's niece.
Jubilees is careful to show that the generations before Abram never marry nieces,
but only sisters or cousins. Thus any suggestion based on a reading of Gen 11:29
which identified her with Iscah daughter of Haran and thus as Abram's niece,[607]
for *Jubilees* a forbidden relationship, is averted. In *Jubilees*' dating of events Sarai
marries even before Haran does and so is not associated with one whom *Jubilees*
portrays "as an irredeemable idolater", who dies trying to rescue his father's idols
from the fire.[608] In this way *Jubilees* sets her marriage in parallel to the marriage of
Seth to Azura (4:11). Seth similarly avoided marrying into an evil line and avoided
marrying his niece by marrying his sister. As Halpern-Amaru observes, "In both
instances, it is the feminine signature for the beginning of a particularly significant
line. ... Twenty one generations removed, they come as close as their era can to
the perfect union of the separated first mates."[609]

The figure of Sarai/Sarah differs subtly from her portrait in Genesis.[610] While
Genesis shows no interest in her background and provides at first only the
information that she was barren (11:30), *Jubilees* "deletes all reference to her
barrenness and creates a formal, full marriage announcement which presents Sarah
as an ideal female partner for the first patriarch" (12:9-11).[611] "Ideal genealogical
credentials, not barrenness, is the first signature of a matriarch."[612] In 13:1 Sarai
appears briefly, again along with those whom Abram took with him, much as in
Gen 12:5.

The next significant difference from Genesis in relation to matters pertaining
to sexuality in the story of Abram and Sarai comes in the account of Abram's stay
in Egypt (13:11-15; cf. Gen 12:10-20). Here we can review the details and changes
briefly because we discussed it in greater detail above in 3.2.3.1. In Gen 12:11-13
Abram connives to protect himself by instructing Sarai to declare herself his sister.

---

[607] Halpern-Amaru, *Empowerment*, points to the tradition reflected in *L.A.B.* 23:4;
Josephus *A.J.* 1.150; *Tg. Ps.-J.* Gen 11:19; *b. Meg.* 14a; *b. Sanh.* 69b; *Gen. Rab.* 38.14 (35
n. 4).

[608] Halpern-Amaru, *Empowerment*, 36.

[609] Halpern-Amaru, *Empowerment*, 37.

[610] See the discussion in Halpern-Amaru, *Empowerment*, 34-37.

[611] Halpern-Amaru, *Empowerment*, 34.

[612] Halpern-Amaru, *Empowerment*, 40.

He and his household benefited when Sarai's beauty was noticed and she was taken into Pharaoh's house (12:14-16). The ruse is exposed (12:18-19), Sarai, returned (12:19) and Abram and his household, expelled (12:19-20). *Jubilees* omits Abram's ruse, thus removing his potential espousal of adultery. It also omits reference to Sarai's beauty, which gave rise to Abram's ploy. Instead, all the guilt falls on Pharaoh, who is twice described as taking Sarai by force: "He lived in Egypt for five years before his wife was taken from him by force" (13:11); "When the pharaoh took Abram's wife by force for himself, the Lord punished the pharaoh and his household very severely [lit. punished with great punishments] because of Abram's wife Sarai" (13:13). Abram emerges totally innocent. Even had *Jubilees* included the ruse about Sarai as his sister, it would now not be a lie, since according to *Jubilees* she was, indeed, his sister.

By its emphasis on Pharaoh's taking Sarai by force *Jubilees* appears at first sight to have no hesitation about making Sarai the victim of forcible sexual wrongdoing. This stands in contrast to the kind of protection which the Genesis account of Abraham and Abimelech offers, which reports that Abimelech did not in fact have sexual relations with her, did not even touch her (Gen 20:1-18). In discussing the episode in 3.2.3.1 above, however, we noted Halpern-Amaru's counter argument that Sarai suffered no violation, but her case based on narrative flow is not strong. One might, nevertheless, have expected *Jubilees* to protect Sarai's image; rape would have rendered her unclean for Abram and thus contaminated the line. Genesis Apocryphon is explicit: nothing happened..

After the accounts of Abram's return to Bethel (13:16; cf. Gen 13:1-4), the separation from Lot (13:17-21; Gen 13:5-18), Lot's capture and rescue (13:22-25; cf. Gen 14:1-12; with the significant addition of the law of tithing: *Jub.* 13:26-27), the restoration of Sodom's booty (13:28-29; cf. Gen 14:22-24), and the covenant sacrifice (14:1-20; cf. Gen 15:1-21), *Jubilees* continues to follow Genesis in reporting the account of Sarai and Hagar (14:21-24; cf. Gen 16:1-15). First, unlike in Genesis, Abram shares the promise of descendants with his wife, Sarai (14:21). Only at this point does *Jubilees* mention Sarai's barrenness, which now becomes much more than a personal problem. It is a shared concern about fulfilment of God's promise of descendants. It leads to the proposal that Abram take Hagar (14:22). *Jubilees* has not taken up the account of Hagar's looking with contempt on Sarai nor of Sarai's harsh response (Gen 16:4b-14). Sarai does not maltreat Hagar nor is Abram therefore implicated in the action by sanctioning it. Hagar is not allowed the dignity of an encounter with the angel of the Lord and a heavenly blessing for her son. Instead, *Jubilees* simply reports that Hagar conceived and gave birth to Ishmael (14:24; cf. Gen 16:7-15). We return to *Jubilees*' account of her banishment below.

Jubilees appears to see no problem in Abram's following Sarai's advice in having sexual relations with Hagar, her Egyptian maid. This is interesting on two

counts: she was Egyptian and she was his wife's maid. The status makes her of
lesser influence and perhaps, as in the case of Joseph, Egyptians were not
forbidden. They, like the Canaanites, are descendants of Ham, but *Jub.* 7:13 makes
quite specific that the curse fell on Canaan, not on all Ham's sons (cf. Gen 10:6).
But, as we noted in discussing intermarriage in 3.2.6 above, something more
appears to be at play, since the prohibition of intermarriage is not restricted in
Jubilees only to descendants of Canaan. There appears to be an assumption that
the husband and head of the household also had a right to sexual relations with
household servants.

In *Jub.* 15:1-24 *Jubilees* takes up the account of the covenant, including the
renaming of Abram and Sarai to Abraham and Sarah, and the instruction about
circumcision from Genesis 17. Abraham's response to the announcement that he
would have a son by Sarah is more restrained. He is very happy (15:17), but does
not laugh, as in Gen 17:17. *Jubilees* adds instruction about the permanence of the
law of circumcision (15:25-34), discussed above in 3.2.3.2. *Jubilees* considerably
abbreviates the account of the angels' visit to Abraham and the announcement of
Sarah's giving birth to a son and her response of laughter (16:1-4; cf. Gen
18:1-15), as it does the account of Sodom's sin and destruction (16:5-9; cf. Gen
18:16 – 19:38). *Jubilees* then passes over the account of Abraham's ruse to pass
off Sarah as his sister (before Abimelech; Gen 20:1-18), again removing his
collusion with potential adultery, although the Genesis story suggests no sexual
intercourse took place (20:4, 6). The remaining trace of the passage is the brief
reference to Abraham's migration to the mountains of Gerar in 16:10. It would
have been a serious blemish on Abraham's character. *Jubilees* had already
rewritten the episode with Pharaoh to protect against that, as we have seen above
(13:11-15; cf. Gen 12:10-20).

The account of Isaac's birth in 16:13-14 reflects Gen 21:1-7, but without
Sarah's comments about laughter (21:6-7). *Jub.* 16:15-19 is material unique to
Jubilees, in which the angel and his colleagues visit Abraham with promises about
Isaac and Jacob. Jacob and his progeny would become God's share or lot (16:17-
18). It draws on the language of Exod 19:6 in identifying them as "a kingdom, a
priesthood, and a holy people" (cf. "It is the nation which he possesses; it is a
priestly nation; it is a priestly kingdom; it is what he owns. No such impurity will
be seen among the holy people"; 33:20). It is significant that the angels then repeat
to Sarah all that they had said to Abraham (16:19). This is the only instance where
Sarah emerges beyond the role given her in Genesis. It elevates her status, but not
nearly as much as Rebecca's to follow.

Jubilees' special interests are reflected in the addition of the feast of booths in
16:20-31. *Jub.* 17:1 reports the weaning of Isaac and the associated feast, as in
Gen 21:8. *Jub.* 17:2-14 reports the banishment of Hagar and Ishmael, closely
following Gen 21:9-21. The difference is that, unlike in Genesis, Sarah has

received separate instructions from the angels about the promise that she would conceive (16:3 and 19). Her knowledge then enables her to correct Abraham's equal favour towards Ishmael (17:4-6). The jealousy motif remains (17:4), but the effect throughout is to incorporate Sarah into an ideal partnership with Abraham.[613]

In 17:13 *Jubilees* repeats from Gen 21:21 that Hagar found a wife for Ishmael "from the Egyptian girls", apparently not seen as problematic. *Jubilees* then omits the conflict with Abimelech and subsequent covenant (Gen 21:22-34). This coheres with the omission of the episode of Sarah and Abimelech (Gen 20:1-18) and also with the later cursing of Abimelech and the Philistines. Instead, *Jubilees* brings an introduction to the testing of Abraham in a scene which resembles Satan's proposals about Job in Job 2:1-6. Here Mastema proposes that God test Abraham (17:15-18). In the passage the angel explains that Abraham had already faced tests and includes among these: "through his wife when she was taken forcibly" (17:17). The testing in relation to Isaac follows in 18:1-19 (Gen 22:1-19). *Jubilees* passes over the account of the sons of Nahor (Gen 22:20-24) and brings a much shorter account of Sarah's death and burial (19:1-7; cf. Gen 23:1-20), which it interprets as further testing of Abraham (19:8-9).

Jubilees also forgoes recounting the long narrative concerned with finding Rebecca as a wife for Isaac (Gen 24:1-67). As noted above, this removes the dangerous thought that marriage could be the result of chance encounters instead of careful planning and explains also the similar deletion later of Jacob's encounter with Rachel. Thus *Jubilees* simply mentions that Abraham took Rebecca as a son for Isaac and gives her credentials (19:10; based on Gen 25:19). She belongs to the generation after Isaac, being the daughter of his cousin Bethuel, a pattern noted above, reflecting the usual age differential. We shall see in the next segment that *Jubilees* again has to trim some detail to ensure the appropriateness of her lineage.

In 19:11-12 *Jubilees* mentions Abraham's marriage to Keturah (cf. Gen 25:1-6). *Jubilees* is careful to ensure by discrete additions that she is not a foreigner, but "one of the children of his household servants" and that Hagar had died, so Abraham was not a bigamist.[614] At that point, Genesis records the death of Abraham (25:7-11) and the descendants of Ishmael (25:12-18), but for *Jubilees*, the latter is irrelevant and the former, out of place, because its Abraham has still much to do of great significance, above all, in blessing his grandson, Jacob, as we have seen.

Jubilees trims the account of the birth of Esau and Jacob of the detail of Rebecca's being barren, of the struggle in the womb and of Jacob's grasping

---

[613] On this see Halpern-Amaru, *Empowerment*, 47-55 and 76-80.

[614] See Endres, *Biblical Interpretation*, 21. He also notes *Jubilees*' omission of the reference to Abraham's concubines in 20:11 (cf. Gen 25:6) (29).

Esau's heel (19:13-15). This belongs to the idealisation of Jacob. According to 19:16-25, Abraham already recognises Esau's deficiencies and, significantly, calls Rebecca to explain Jacob's special role. In her presence he blesses him (19:26-29). He then gives instruction to all his children (20:1-10), which, as we have seen, includes instruction relating to issues of sexuality. He instructs Isaac about sacrifices, but also about impurity, including sexual impurity (21:1-25). In 22:7-9 he gives thanks and in 22:10-24 he instructs Jacob, again with a strong emphasis on sexual wrongdoing, and blesses him once more in 22:27-30. The entire section of blessings and instruction, 19:13 – 22:30, is innovation on the part of *Jubilees* and, as we have seen, embodies key concerns. In 23:1-7 *Jubilees* returns to Gen 25:7-11, the death of Abraham, but with expansions which elevate Jacob and Rebecca, and then offers an extensive commentary on human wickedness and the future in 23:8-31, which brings the first half of *Jubilees* to a climactic exposition of its concerns.

At one level, the account of Abraham coheres with the summary accounts of the marriages which precede it in affirming marriage and sexual intercourse within marriage. There is also a strange coherence in having Abraham marry his sister, like the earlier marriages. *Jubilees* leaves this unaddressed. It also appears to see Abraham's having sexual intercourse with Hagar as unproblematic.

On the other hand, Nahor's mismarriage to a Chaldean appears to be the source of the problems of idolatry (inspired by Mastema's evil spirits and their ornithological symbols) which Abraham heroically counters. This foreshadows the connection between foreign wives and idolatry but also sexual wrongdoing in later parts of *Jubilees*. *Jubilees* presents Abraham as equipped with Hebrew to become a student of traditions which his father passed from Noah and Enoch. For the hearer of *Jubilees*, these will naturally include teaching about sexual wrongdoing which featured among their concerns. These do not come to expression until the final instructions which Abraham gives to Isaac and then to Jacob. In 39:6 Joseph recalls how Jacob read to him Abraham's words, including the prohibition of adultery.

For *Jubilees*, Abraham cannot behave contrary to these traditions and thus in a way that provokes adultery, so must be the victim of Pharaoh's adultery and rape of Sarai, or his attempt to violate her (should *Jubilees* want us to read the attempt as unsuccessful), not its cause. Similarly, in the case of Abraham and Abimelech, Abraham is saved from any such implications by silence. He also cannot be seen to sanction Sarah's injustice towards Hagar. It is surprising that *Jubilees* has Abraham make no comment about the wickedness of Sodom when facing its destruction, given the reference to it in the speeches of his last days. Sarah emerges from *Jubilees* with a higher profile than in Genesis. Her barrenness no longer serves as precursor to a special role, but is incidental, and is overcome to fulfil a promise which she shares with Abraham for whom she is an ideal wife with appropriate genealogy. *Jubilees'* account of her forcible seizure by Pharaoh protects Abraham, but strangely does nothing to avert the conclusion that he violated her, although given *Jubilees'* concern with lineage and uncleanness this is probably not intended. *Jubilees* has included Sarah as a recipient of separate angelic visits and covenant promises, and portrayed her as acting more in its interests and those of her partner, Abraham, than from personal spite, though this trace remains. Rebecca emerges from the narrative even more strongly than Sarah as a major hero, and to her partnership with Isaac we turn.[615]

3.3.2.2 Rebecca and Isaac

Rebecca emerges into prominence in Abraham's final speeches. *Jub.* 19:10 had mentioned her being chosen by Abraham to be Isaac's wife. As with Sarah, there are some potential complications about her lineage. These concern Milcah as ancestress of Rebecca (19:10). *Jubilees* names only her husband, Nahor, Abraham's brother. It omits detail about Milcah's father, who according to Gen 11:29 was her husband's brother, making her the niece of her husband. Thus Rebecca's lineage, as enunciated, is not contaminated by a forbidden uncle-niece marriage.[616] Unlike with Sarai, *Jubilees* has in this instance an unambiguous biblical text standing in the way of its beliefs, not just a potential reading. Its recourse is silence.[617]

Jub. 19:13 mentions Rebecca's giving birth to Esau and Jacob. *Jubilees* omits reference to her initial barrenness (Gen 25:20-21), as it did with Sarai. It possibly saw it as a diminishment, certainly not as a sign of miraculous great things to come, as in Genesis. Next we find Rebecca receiving Abraham's instruction about Jacob (19:16). Jacob, we have been told in 19:13, "was perfect and upright". In 19:15 *Jubilees* reshapes Gen 25:28, which reads: "Isaac loved Esau, because he was fond of game; but Rebecca loved Jacob", so that it now reads: "Abraham loved Jacob but Isaac (loved) Esau". Thus *Jubilees* omits the grounds for Isaac's preference for Esau, helping reduce it in this way to the level of ungrounded favouritism.[618] *Jub.* 19:16 then returns to the form of Genesis: Abraham "summoned Rebecca and gave her orders about Jacob because he saw that she loved Jacob much more than Esau". While the difference between Isaac's and Rebecca's love already exists in Genesis, *Jubilees* heightens it, later reporting that

---

[615] Halpern-Amaru, *Empowerment*, notes: "It is quite possible that the biblical portrait of Rebekah provides a skeletal archetype for the facilitator role of all the matriarchs in *Jubilees*" (80). On Rebecca see also VanderKam, *Book of Jubilees*, 2001, p. 116.

[616] See Halpern-Amaru, *Empowerment*, 39-40.

[617] See Halpern-Amaru, *Empowerment*, 122-23.

[618] So Endres, *Biblical Interpretation*, 26.

she loved him "with her entire heart and her entire being very much more than Esau" (19:31). This thus forms an *inclusio* with 19:15.

In *Jubilees* Jacob is not a doubtful character, as the pun on his name (supplanter) implies (though *Jubilees* brings the pun in the context of the blessing by Isaac; 26:30). Rebecca has clearly chosen the right focus for her affection and Abraham recognises this: "My son Isaac now loves Esau more than Jacob, but I see you rightly love Jacob" (19:19). Only later will Isaac get it right. She stands in the authoritative succession of Abraham (Noah and Enoch). Abraham, therefore, entrusts her with the care of Jacob, explaining: "he will occupy my place on the earth and (will prove) a blessing among mankind and the glory of all the descendants of Shem" (19:17). Abraham is also blessing Rebecca: "May your hands be strong and your mind be happy with your son Jacob, because I love him much more than all my sons" (19:20). This goes far beyond what we find in Genesis. Correspondingly, Rebecca is on hand to witness Abraham's first blessing of Jacob (19:26-29). Abraham's act of blessing defuses the difficulty of the blessing of Jacob by Isaac through deception.

Remaining with the figure Rebecca, we find she next appears in 22:4, in the context of the celebration of the feast of weeks, making bread out of fresh wheat and giving some to Jacob to bring to Abraham. Only then does Isaac send "through Jacob [his] excellent peace offering [and wine to his father] Abraham" (22:5). When Jacob finds that Abraham has died while he lay close to him, he immediately seeks out Rebecca (23:4). She then goes to Isaac. The story has no parallel in Genesis. Rebecca is again playing the key role.

Jubilees was confronted in Gen 26:6-11 with a third story about a patriarch, his attractive wife, and a local ruler, with regard to Isaac, Rebecca and Abimelech. Rather than omit it altogether, as it does with Abimelech, Sarah and Abraham (Gen 20:2-18), or turn it into (attempted) adultery and rape on the part of the ruler, as in the account of Abram, Sarai, and Pharaoh in 13:10-15 (Gen 12:10-20), *Jubilees* retains the reference to Isaac's going down to Gerar and the Philistine king in a time of famine (24:8-11; Gen 26:1-5). It then makes no mention of the initiative of Isaac to protect himself by saying Rebecca is his sister, nor of its sequel where Abimelech sees him fondling his wife. In not doing so, *Jubilees* is protecting both Isaac and, above all, Rebecca, who is thus neither sexually humiliated nor diminished by his act. One may catch a hint of the original story in 24:13, which reports Abimelech's declaration: "Any man who touches him or anything that belongs to him is to die" (as in Gen 26:11). Even without the preceding story from Genesis, the statement might still be heard as pertaining also to sexual wrongdoing, but for any who do not know that story, it reads primarily as confirmation that nothing would go wrong. It goes wrong in other ways and Isaac curses the Philistines. As a result of the omission of Gen 26:6-11, Rebecca emerges unscathed.

Rebecca reappears in 25:1, warning Jacob not to marry a Canaanite. *Jubilees* is extrapolating from material found in Gen 27:46, where Rebecca complains to Isaac about Esau's Hittite wives and expresses her anxiety should Jacob also marry Canaanites. *Jubilees* recounts that scene in 27:8, following closely the formulation of Gen 27:46, although clearly making the concern about intermarriage much more central and much less just a ploy to rescue Jacob from Esau. Gen 27:46 – 28:5 recount Isaac's response to Rebecca, his sending Jacob off to Laban. We find the same story in *Jub.* 27:8-12. *Jubilees* has, however, also used the tradition of Rebecca's complaint to develop a sequence where Rebecca instructs Jacob directly about Canaanite women (25:1-3), Jacob responds showing himself to be upright in every way (25:4-10) and Rebecca blesses God and blesses Jacob and his descendants (25:11-23). She thus stands in succession with Abraham and Noah. In her blessing she uses richly feminine images: "As you have given rest to your mother's spirit during her lifetime, so may the womb of the one who gave birth to you bless you. My affection and my breasts bless you; my mouth and my tongue praise you greatly" (25:19). This coheres with the very positive attitude towards, or, at least, interest in women found elsewhere in *Jubilees*.

Jubilees does, finally, tell the story of Isaac's blessing of Jacob (26:1-35; cf. Gen 27:1-40). Now, however, the context is different. God's blessing has already been conveyed by Abraham and Rebecca. *Jubilees* has told us that Jacob is perfect and upright in all his ways. In a sense the question is now, therefore: how is it possible to put Isaac right?[619] *Jubilees* changes little in the way Rebecca is portrayed in the story, except that now we have even greater understanding for her action. Significantly, Jacob does not say to Isaac, "I am Esau your firstborn son", a blatant lie, as in Gen 27:19, but more truthfully: "I am your son; I have done as you told me" (26:13). Only the latter part is a direct lie. *Jubilees* then explains why Isaac failed to recognise Esau after touching him and hearing his voice: "He did not recognise him because there was a turn of affairs from heaven to distract his mind" (26:18). So Jacob even has heavenly support for his act! Again, *Jubilees* seeks to save Jacob from perjuring himself in response to Isaac's question: "Are you my son Esau?" (26:19; Gen 27:24), by having him respond not, "I am" (Gen 27:24), but "I am your son" (26:19).

Rebecca retains the initiative, as in Genesis, warning Jacob of Esau's intentions and encouraging him to flee to Laban (27:1-3; Gen 27:41-45). The Genesis account ends with Rebecca's words, "Why should I lose both of you in one day?" Before these words *Jubilees* adds that Jacob might, instead, kill Esau. Losing both would mean losing one by murder and the other by execution for

---

[619] As Halpern-Amaru, *Empowerment*, observes: "What motivates the deception and moves Rebekah to action are the interests of her husband. Isaac, the patriarch, is about to make the grievous error of transmitting the patriarchal blessings to the wrong son" (88).

murder. Rebecca's initiative, as in Genesis, is to save Jacob and herself from this danger by conveniently raising the issue of intermarriage, only, for *Jubilees* this is also a significant issue in itself.

Rebecca next appears in material without parallel in Genesis, as the grieving mother (27:12-18).[620] In part, this reflects Jacob's significance, which is now underlined by another blessing by Isaac. In part, it portrays Rebecca as a truly caring mother and emphasises the positive relationship between Isaac and Rebecca despite the setbacks. Halpern-Amaru comments:

> The scene is one of multiple demonstrations of the emotional bond between husbands and wives in the ideal marriages of *Jubilees*. Albeit without creating direct dialogue, the author encourages the reader to imagine a similar kind of bond between Adam and Eve as they mourn over the murder of Abel. (4:7)[621]

Jubilees, like Genesis, emphasises that Laban is Rebecca's brother (28:1; Gen 29:10 – twice; already 27:3; Gen 27:43). In material peculiar to *Jubilees*, Rebecca next appears in 29:16, as the recipient of Jacob's affection, who also sent gifts to his father, in contrast to Esau. She appears again in 31:5-7, in the context of Jacob's return. In innovative material *Jubilees* reports how Rebecca again takes the initiative:

> Jacob went to his father Isaac and his mother Rebecca in the house of his father Abraham. He took his two sons with him – Levi and Judah. He came to his father Isaac and his mother Rebecca. Rebecca went out of the tower into the tower gates to kiss Jacob and hug him because she had revived at the time she heard (the report): "Your son Jacob has now arrived". She kissed him. (31:5-6)

Not only does she take the primary role in greeting Jacob and continue to show her affection for the one whom God had blessed through Abraham; she now also blesses the two sons who carry key leadership roles in the future people of Israel:

> When she saw his two sons, she recognised them. She said to him, "Are these your sons, my son?" She hugged them, kissed them, and blessed them as follows: "Through

---

[620] On the parallel between the account of Rebecca's grieving and Tob 5:17-21, see Endres, *Biblical Interpretation*, 95-97, a parallel suggested by A. S. Hartom, *Sefer ha-Yoblot we-Dibre – 'Iyyob. Ha-s^efarim Ha-hitsonim; Sippure-Aggadah B* (Tel-Aviv: Yabneh, 1969) 84, who also suggests that "sister" in *Jub.* 27:14, 17 and Tob 5:20 be interpreted as "my friend / my relation" or as language of affection or love (27; cited in Endres, 96-97). Similarly, see also Fitzmyer, *Genesis Apocryphon*, on the use of אח in Aramaic "as a polite form of address among Aramaic-speaking peoples from at least the fifth century B.C. on" (130).

[621] Halpern-Amaru, *Empowerment*, 60.

you Abraham's descendants will become famous. You will become a blessing on the earth". (31:7)

Isaac, too, will bless them, fulfilling the formal role of the patriarch, but Rebecca was there first.

In a further innovation *Jubilees* reports that Jacob had built an altar and would make a sacrifice before the Lord, as he had vowed. Isaac is too old to mount the donkey brought for him. His mother, Rebecca, takes his place (31:27, 30). Again, this puts Rebecca in a prominent position. She and her nurse Deborah accompany Jacob to Bethel (31:31). "She had become the primary caretaker for the blessings of Abraham."[622] Rebecca then returns to Isaac, bringing gifts from Jacob (32:31-32). Finally, Jacob and all his sons return to Isaac and Rebecca (33:21). Significantly, they bow before both Isaac and Rebecca (33:23), who, in turn, both bless them (33:23).

Rebecca is again taking the initiative in 35:1, instructing Jacob to honour both his father and his brother. In response to his asseveration of obedience, she confirms: "My son, throughout my entire lifetime I have noticed no improper act in you but only proper one(s)" (35:6). She is again placed in a position of great authority, warranting the goodness of Jacob. Innovative material continues in her announcement of her death and Jacob's response of laughter in disbelief (35:6-8). The exchange includes some ideal statements about Rebecca:

> she was sitting in front of him in possession of her strength. She had lost none of her strength because she could come and go; she could see and her teeth were strong. No sickness had touched her throughout her entire lifetime. (35:7)

For the author these are not neutral description, but evidence of goodness.

Her initiative continues in approaching Isaac about the danger of Esau to Jacob (35:9). Her words denigrate Esau in contrast to Jacob (35:10-12). In some sense this extends the motif found in Gen 27:46, where she had approached Isaac over Esau's Hittite wives. It is another innovation of *Jubilees* and again highlights Rebecca's significance. In effect, she finally persuades Isaac that he has loved the wrong son. She thus elicits from Isaac not only statements about Esau, but also about his descendants, and so the author's own time (35:13-17). But then it is Rebecca who summons Esau, instructs him about brotherly love and makes him swear to agree (35:18-24). She does the same with Jacob (35:25-26). It was her last testament before she died (35:27), all the more powerful because *Jubilees* goes on to report how Esau's sons persuaded him to abandon his agreement to peace and love (37:1-13). Again, Isaac's speech (36:1-17) follows after the account of Rebecca's, before he too died (36:18) and was buried with Rebecca (36:21).

---

[622] Halpern-Amaru, *Empowerment*, 90.

Already in Genesis Rebecca is a stronger figure than Isaac. She loves the right son and cares for him, helping him to escape his brother and initiating his marriage. But *Jubilees* takes this much further. It removes the negative traits of Jacob, picturing him as ideal. In this way Rebecca's love for him cannot be seen as whim. Her favour finds reinforcement through Abraham, himself, who virtually authorises her as bearer of the tradition. She witnesses his blessing of Jacob. She is to care for the chosen one on his authority. She elicits Jacob's declarations of sexual purity and ensures he does not marry a Canaanite like Esau. *Jubilees* thus exploits this detail to provide a platform for Rebecca's teaching on the dangers of sexual wrongdoing. Even the act of deceit in procuring Isaac's blessing for Jacob now appears much less deceitful and is blessed by heaven which manipulates Isaac's perception powers. She grieves for the fleeing Jacob. Without sacrificing the household patriarchal structure, *Jubilees* nevertheless portrays Rebecca as the initiator and leader. She is the first to make an offering in the feast of weeks, the first whom Jacob tells of Abraham's death, the first to greet Jacob when he returns with Levi and Judah and the first to bless them; she replaces Isaac at the Bethel sacrifice; she blesses the twelve sons with Isaac; she elicits and confirms Jacob's claim of uprightness, and, in the end, she persuades Isaac he has backed the wrong son and is the first to seek to reconcile her sons.

Beside all this *Jubilees* seeks to portray Rebecca in herself as an ideal woman. Possibly this explains the omission of reference to her initial barrenness. In any case, she does not need Isaac to pray for her in that regard (cf. Gen 25:21). *Jubilees* also passes over the incident with Abimelech which might have tarnished her honour. She carries the traditional roles of nurturer and is portrayed as present as a woman in her physicality, referring to her womb, her affections, her breasts, her mouth and tongue; she kisses and hugs. *Jubilees* also affirms her bodily health (eyesight, teeth) as a sign of her virtue.

Jubilees paints a remarkable picture of Rebecca and so an interesting image of what it sees as womanhood. It assumes the possibility of strong leadership and spiritual responsibility for the tradition.[623] At the same time this still appears within the traditional patriarchal structure, but Isaac, who remains head of the household, is not the real leader or real power within it. Rebecca is. This affirmation of women may relate to the phenomenon we have noticed elsewhere in *Jubilees*, where it shows an interest in naming women. It also bears relation to the theme of sexuality, because it both affirms sexual relations in the context of marriage as it does elsewhere and in consistency with the creation story, and it has

---

[623] Endres, *Biblical Interpretation*, observes that Rebecca's "position is not so surprising in an era when the real heroes of Jewish literature were Judith, Esther and the courageous mother of the seven sons in 2 Maccabees" (218).

Rebecca bear the warnings about sexual wrongdoing which had been a central element in the instructions of Noah and Abraham.

The title of this section also includes Isaac who deserves some secondary consideration beside Rebecca. Isaac was crucial to the promise to Abraham about his descendants. The angel informs Sarah that his name, Isaac, was "ordained and written on the heavenly tablets" (16:2). *Jubilees* repeats the story of the banishment of Ishmael for the sake of Isaac (17:4-14) and tells of the ordeal where Abraham was told to sacrifice Isaac (18:1-16), but in all this Isaac has a relatively passive role. Isaac's survival is crucial and thus it still matters that he gives the blessing to Jacob not Esau. But from the birth of Esau and Jacob, Isaac favours the wrong son. He is marginalised by Abraham and Rebecca and absent when they bless Jacob (19:16-30).

On the other hand, Abraham entrusts him with instruction about sacrifice and warns him about idolatry and impurity, probably including sexual wrongdoing (21:1-25). There is no such blessing and instruction about sacrifice given by Rebecca, so that, despite her high profile, the patriarchal structure of the succession remains intact. Thus Isaac conducts the sacrifice at the festival of weeks (22:3). Isaac takes his family to Philistine Gerar and curses the Philistines (24:8-33). As noted above, *Jubilees* omits the detail about Isaac representing Rebecca as his sister, thus protecting the images of both Isaac and Rebecca. Similarly, we saw how *Jubilees* expands the account in Genesis of Rebecca's initiative to suggest Jacob seek a wife from the daughters of her brother Laban, almost as a ploy to ensure his escape from Esau, and makes it into a sequence in 25:1-23 where she elicits and confirms his sexual purity and instructs him about sexual wrongdoing. The effect is to render Isaac's instruction to Jacob to go to Laban as secondary (although still carrying patriarchal authority). His instruction does not include Rebecca's "wisdom" about the dangers of sexual wrongdoing. Isaac appears to lack such insight.

As in Genesis, the ruse to secure Isaac's blessing of Jacob makes him almost a passive player, although within the structure he remains the major authority. He comforts the grieving Rebecca with the affirmation that Jacob "is just in his way. He is perfect; he is a true man" (27:17). But we must still wait, until Rebecca can finally persuade him to change his affection. Isaac blesses Levi and Judah (31:13-20) – after Rebecca has done so. He has them sleep with him on either side "and it was credited to him as something righteous" (31:23), so Isaac is certainly not a negative figure. He had favoured the wrong son and may by implication be tarnished by Esau's mismarriages. *Jubilees* omits the detail in Genesis that they also caused him disappointment. But this implication is not drawn. Rather, Isaac remains in the key patriarchal role, but lags behind Rebecca in wisdom and initiative. This is well represented in the final scenes where Isaac takes the authoritative role in having his sons foreswear to live in peace, but only after

Rebecca had cautioned him about Esau and changed the priority of his affection, and had, herself, initiated commitment to reconciliation.

There is little about Isaac which relates directly to our theme. He is like an echo of Rebecca, but from a higher station. The situation is different again with Jacob, Leah and Rachel, where Jacob is clearly dominant.

3.3.2.3   Jacob, Leah, and Rachel

Jubilees assumes the central importance of Jacob from the beginning, where it includes a vision about Jacob's children:

> The Lord will appear in the sight of all, and all who know that I am the God of Israel, the father of all Jacob's children, and the king on Mt Zion for the ages of eternity. Then Zion and Jerusalem will become holy. (1:28)

The sabbath belongs to them as descendants of Jacob:

> I have chosen the descendants of Jacob among all of those whom I have seen. I have recorded them as my first-born son and have sanctified them for myself throughout all the ages of eternity. I will tell them about the sabbath days so that they may keep sabbath from all work on them. (2:20)

Jacob is the turning point. *Jubilees* marks off 22 generations before Jacob, just as the act of creation consists of 22 acts of God before the sabbath (2:23-25). By implication Jacob and his people are part of divine order of creation from the beginning, as important as the sabbath, itself. In 16:17 the angel informs Abraham that "one of Isaac's sons would become a holy progeny and would not be numbered among the nations for he would become a share of the Most High" (cf. 15:31-32, "For there are many nations and many peoples and all belong to him. He made spirits rule over all in order to lead them astray from following him. But over Israel he made no angel or spirit rule because he alone is their ruler").

When Jacob finally appears, *Jubilees* has rewritten the Genesis account of his birth, deleting the struggle in Rebecca's womb and the detail of Jacob's coming second and grasping Esau's heel (Gen 25:23, 26). It adds its own description: "Jacob was perfect and upright" (19:13). In contrast to Esau who "was a harsh, rustic, and hairy man, Jacob used to live in tents" – no longer neutral descriptions as in Genesis, but indicative of superiority.[624] Thus *Jubilees* adds: "Jacob learned (the art of) writing, but Esau did not learn (it) because he was a rustic man and a hunter. He learned the art of warfare, and everything he did was harsh" (19:14). In

---

[624] Endres, *Biblical Interpretation*, notes targumic tradition that "tents" were academies (24).

omitting reference to struggle in the womb, *Jubilees* had also omitted God's prediction about the two nations and that the elder would serve the younger. This theme comes later in the speeches of Rebecca and Isaac (35:22-23).

Esau is negatively portrayed from the beginning, in contrast to Jacob. Already in 15:30 we find this implication: "For the Lord did not draw near to himself either Ishmael, his sons, his brothers, or Esau. He did not choose them (simply) because they were among Abraham's children, for he knew them". In 19:16 without further explanation we read that "Abraham observed Esau's behaviour". Esau is rejected because he is bad; Jacob is chosen because he is good. Abraham tells Rebecca: Jacob "will occupy my place on the earth and (will prove) a blessing among mankind and the glory of all the descendants of Shem" (19:17). Similar statements follow, climaxing in the hope: "May they serve (the purpose of) laying heaven's foundations, making the earth firm, and renewing all the luminaries which are above the firmament" (19:25). Abraham's first blessing of Jacob underlines the succession and the hope that the spirits of Mastema may not rule over Jacob and his people (19:26-29). *Jubilees* has two further speeches directed by Abraham to Jacob, as noted above (3.2.7.2), repeating the theme of future blessing and developing further the warnings about the nations, about idolatry, intermarriage with Canaanites and sexual impurity (22:7-30). Jacob sleeps beside Abraham (23:1-3), as Levi and Judah will do with Isaac, a sign of special privilege.

Genesis brings the account of Esau's selling his birthright immediately after the account of the birth of the two sons, but *Jubilees* waits until Abraham's final speeches and then his death. It adds as the conclusion: "So Jacob became the older one, but Esau was lowered from his prominent position" (24:7). Jacob's behaviour is not seen as a blemish. Jacob's goodness comes to the fore in the exchange which *Jubilees* has created between Rebecca and Jacob (25:1-23). As both Abraham and Rebecca have blessed Jacob, so both warn about marriage to Canaanites. Jacob's goodness consists then, in part, in his observance of this instruction. At its heart is the concern with sexual immorality, as we have seen above. Jacob has not even touched a woman (25:4). By contrast, Esau, in disobedience to Abraham's instruction, has pressured him to marry a Canaanite and so enter their realm of sexual wrongdoing (25:8). We see the continuing theme of denigration of Esau.

The account of Isaac's blessing of Jacob in *Jubilees* does not diminish Jacob. Heaven is on his side (26:18). Although Esau pleads deception and points to Jacob's name (26:30), the hearer knows from what precedes that Rebecca's ploy and Jacob's compliance are part of the divine plan. That included the future subservience of Esau and his descendants to Jacob and his people, as in Genesis (26:34; cf. Gen 27:40). *Jubilees* remains close to Genesis in describing Esau's anger and Rebecca's ploy to rescue Jacob (26:29-30), but within the context of *Jubilees* the issue of right marriage has assumed much greater importance, having already been a theme in both Abraham's and Rebecca's instruction.

The long narrative of Jacob's dealings with Laban reaching from Gen 29:1 to 32:1 is trimmed considerably by *Jubilees*.[625] First, it adds Rebecca's grieving (27:13-18), which further underlines Jacob's goodness as his father declares him "just in his way ... perfect ... a true man" (27:17). After Jacob's night at Bethel (27:19-25), where again he receives promises for his descendants, as in Genesis, *Jubilees* omits the story of Jacob's encounter with Rachel (cf. Gen 29:1-19). Chance encounters are no way to find a wife. Instead, it reports briefly on the arrangement with Laban for Rachel (28:1) and then on his complaint on receiving Leah, whom he recognises not the next morning as in Gen 29:25, but on the wedding night (28:4). *Jubilees* turns this into an occasion for teaching about divine law which requires that one marry the eldest first (28:2-10). At this point the image of Jacob comes closest to being tarnished, but he shows virtue again in allowing himself to be instructed by his father-in-law.

The account of Jacob's consequent sojourn with Laban in *Jubilees* is thus remarkable for its highlighting of Laban's reason for first giving Leah to Jacob before Rachel. The Genesis account simply reads: "Laban said, 'This is not done in our country – giving the younger before the firstborn'" (29:26). There is no indication of endorsement. In *Jubilees* however, Laban is expressing divine law: "Laban said to Jacob: 'It is not customary [lit. it is not like this] in our country to give the younger daughter before the older one'" (28:6). The rule is given the status of being one of the special instructions introduced by: "Now you command", and one written on the heavenly tablets:

> It is not right to do this because this is the way it is ordained and written on the heavenly tablets: that no one should give his younger daughter before his older one, but he should first give the older and after her the younger. Regarding the man who acts in this way they will enter a sin in heaven. There is no one who is just and does this because this action is evil in the Lord's presence. Now you order the Israelites not to do this. They are neither to take nor give the younger before giving precedence to the older because it is very wicked. (28:6-7)

This is extraordinary in two senses. We find nothing like it elsewhere which might have served as a precedent,[626] and, secondly, marrying two sisters is a breach of Lev 18:18 ("And you shall not take a woman as a rival to her sister, uncovering her nakedness while her sister is still alive"). This recalls *Jubilees'* willingness also to set aside the prohibition of marrying one's own sister, noted in relation to

---

[625] See the detailed discussion of changes and tendencies in Endres, *Biblical Interpretation*, 85-119, 158-71.

[626] Halpern-Amaru, *Empowerment*, observes: "There is no comparable prohibition either in the Pentateuch or in rabbinic halakha" (45) and goes on to note *Jubilees'* concern elsewhere with primogeniture.

Abram and Sarai. The author might have reasoned that Laban spoke before that Law was known,[627] but the text assumes this is abiding Law. Clearly, marrying two sisters of the same clan is preferable to exogamy,[628] but the tension remains.

In relation to this law, the hero Jacob would have been guilty, although in the narrative it does not appear to reflect negatively on Jacob. Laban emerges positively to the extent that he voices divine law, despite the fact that *Jubilees* knows he has household idols which Rachel will steal when Jacob flees.[629] *Jub.* 29:1-4 mentions the departure, but fails to mention Rachel's theft. It comes to light, however, in 31:2, where the gods are destroyed.

Jubilees even protects Laban's image from deceit over Rachel, just as it does, Jacob, in the blessing scene. Thus in *Jub.* 28:2 Laban responds to Jacob's request, "Give me my wife", with the words, "I will give you your wife", just as Jacob responds to Isaac's question, "Are you my son Esau?" with the words, "I am your son" (26:19).[630] As Halpern-Amaru notes, "There is no evidence that Laban is anything less than a caring uncle, no negotiations upon Jacob's arrival, and no indication of indentured servitude".[631] She later observes:

> The reworking clearly intends to convey a portrait of family relationships radically different from those portrayed in Genesis. All the characters are rehabilitated: Laban is not deceitful; Jacob is not cunning; and neither he nor his wives shows any impropriety toward uncle/father.[632]

We shall return to the characterisation of Rachel and Leah after discussing the remaining relevant detail about Jacob. As with Abraham and Hagar, *Jubilees* sees no problem in Jacob's having sexual intercourse with first, Bilhah, Rachel's maid, then Zilpah, Leah's maid (28:17-21). In the dividing of the flocks of Laban and Jacob, *Jubilees* removes the implication of deceit from the story as told in Gen 30:37-43. Jacob comes through morally unscathed (28:25-30).

---

[627] So Louis Ginzberg, *The Legends of the Jews* (5 vols; Philadelphia: Jewish Publication Society of America, 1925) 5. 295 .

[628] So Endres, *Biblical Interpretation*, who writes, "the legislation about marrying two sisters was of lesser importance than that which forbade marrying the younger first, or marrying Gentiles", even though the author would assume such laws antedated Sinai (104).

[629] Halpern-Amaru, *Empowerment*, notes that Laban shares with his forefather, Nahor, the involvement with idols (93). Cf. Werman, "*Jubilees* 30," who argues that the positive image of Laban results from *Jubilees'* attempt to portray Aramean women in an acceptable light (1). This overlooks the emphasis on the harmonious family and the fact that according to *Jubilees* descendants of Terah are legitimate partners.

[630] On the constructed correspondence, see Halpern-Amaru, *Empowerment*, 44-45. She also notes the element of heavenly sanction introduced into both scenes (45).

[631] Halpern-Amaru, *Empowerment*, 91.

[632] Halpern-Amaru, *Empowerment*, 92.

His departure is not under a cloud, except that he had not informed Laban of his departure (29:1-4). Laban pursues him, but then both are reconciled without the acrimony of the Genesis account. Similarly, *Jubilees* reports the reconciliation of Jacob and Esau very briefly (29:13; cf. Gen 32:2 – 33:16). Gone also is the story of Jacob's wrestling with a supernatural being, which Hayward notes, might suggest Jacob had something in common with a Greek athletic hero.[633]

Jubilees then reports Jacob's concern for his parents, showing himself a model of honouring them according to the commandment, in contrast, again, to Esau who had abandoned his father and taken his father's flocks and wives with him (29:14-20; 35:10 adds: "by force"). *Jubilees* brings here the information that Esau finally married correctly ("Esau had married Ishmael's daughter"; 29:18a), but reduces it to incidental information, stripped of the comment in Gen 28:6-9, that this was a deliberate response by Esau out of concern for his parents.

In the account of the rape of Dinah, Jacob does not baulk at his sons' actions, but supports them. Jacob and his sons together "spoke deceptively [lit. with evil] with them, acted in a crafty way toward them, and deceived them" (30:3), but all reference to circumcision has disappeared. The heavenly decree which follows justifies the deception and the violence. Again, Jacob (and his sons) come through unscathed. They are heroes in the rooting out of sexual wrongdoing. *Jubilees* introduces a number of expansions at this point, not only to underline the teaching about sexual wrongdoing, but also to empower future leaders. It reports the appointment of Levi and his descendants to a role of priesthood and discipline (30:18). Jacob brings Levi and Judah for blessing by Isaac (31:1-32). Levi's status is confirmed in a dream at Bethel and Jacob pays him a tithe and ordains him (32:1-10). Jacob receives divine instruction not to build a temple at Bethel (32:16-29).[634]

Jubilees then moves to setbacks suffered by Jacob. The first is Reuben's having sexual intercourse with Bilhah, a story much expanded in *Jubilees*. Jacob

---

[633] Hayward, "Sanctification," 161, 164. Noting the employment of Hellenistic terms drawn from the field of drama to refer to time in the LXX, he concludes: "*Jubilees* carefully avoids any hint that Jewish sacred time might bear comparison with Greek festivals, and passes over in silence any biblical suggestion that Jacob-Israel might have something in common with a Greek athletic hero" (164).

[634] On this see Esther Eshel, "*Jubilees* 32 and the Bethel Cult Traditions in Second Temple Literature," in *Things Revealed: Studies in Early Jewish and Christian Literature in Honor of Michael E. Stone* (JSJSupp 89; ed. Esther Chazon, David Satran and Ruth Clements; Leiden: Brill, 2004) 21-36. She explains the conjunction of both the positive attitudes towards Bethel and this rejection of the building of the temple as a reflection of *Jubilees*' concern to maintain the centrality of the Jerusalem temple and of the critical treatment of Bethel in Amos and Hosea. She suggest it depended on traditional material possibly preserved in 4Q527.

observes the Law in no longer having sexual relations with her because she had become unclean for him (33:2-9). More far-reaching was the apparent loss of Joseph, narrated already in *Jubilees* 34, but whose sequel, reporting Joseph's fortunes in Egypt, comes much later, in *Jubilees* 39. This sets up another contrast: between Judah and Joseph.

The contrast between Jacob and Esau dominates the interim chapters in which *Jubilees* creates new dialogues and instructions involving both Rebecca and Isaac. The first highlights again Jacob's goodness. Rebecca confirms Jacob's assertion that he has never done anything wrong (35:1-6). His laughter at Rebecca's assertion that she would die seems playful rather than a serious misdemeanour (35:6-8). *Jubilees* then has Rebecca warn Isaac about Esau (35:9-12). It denigrates Esau because he has abandoned his parents, as noted earlier in 29:14-20, but here, with the addition, that in going away he took Isaac's flocks and possessions away "by force" (35:10) and then acted patronisingly towards his parents (35:11). By contrast, Rebecca declares Jacob to have been good and generous towards his parents: "he has virtue only, no evil" (35:12). Esau "has been malicious since his youth and ... devoid of virtue" (35:9).

Isaac is thus persuaded to change his affection and adds his own analysis, returning to the ongoing theme of foreign wives and sexual wrongdoing: "He has abandoned the God of Abraham and has gone after his wives, after impurity, and after their errors – he and his sons" (35:14). The following scenes show Rebecca admonishing Esau to peace and Esau responding with affirmations of love which he will later recant. He acknowledges that Jacob will rule over him and swears an oath not to do him harm (35:18-24). More briefly *Jubilees* reports a similar commitment to love on the part of Jacob (35:25-27). This sets up the basis for the dramatic contrast which follows, where Esau's sons persuade him to abandon his oath (37:1-13). But first *Jubilees* reinforces the effect by having Isaac elicit an oath of mutual love before dividing his property between them (36:1-18).

Jubilees keeps reinforcing the positive image of Jacob. Esau and his sons attack Jacob while he is still mourning, an outrage, and the people of Hebron warn Jacob "because they loved Jacob more than Esau, since Jacob was a more generous and kind man than Esau" (37:15). Judah assumes military leadership in defence against Esau and his sons and persuades Jacob to shoot his brother in obvious self-defence (38:1-2). This, too, does not count against Jacob's virtue. When Jacob's sons have subdued the enemy, Jacob chooses to make peace on the basis of the Edomites' submission, which accords with divine plan and prediction (38:11-14).[635] Jacob has again done right.

---

[635] On the probable allusion to the conflicts of the early second century B.C.E., see Endres, *Biblical Interpretation*, 158, 182.

Jacob does not appear again directly in the narrative until the conclusion of the Joseph story, when Joseph summons his father to Egypt (43:16-24) and God assuages his anxiety about coming 44:1-10). The accounts of Jacob's arrival and settling in Egypt follow Genesis closely with little variation (45:1-15). As his last act *Jubilees* reports: "He gave all his books and the books of his fathers to his son Levi so that he could preserve them and renew them for his sons until today" (45:16). This not only echoes the detail at his birth that he had learned to read and write (19:14). It also portrays Jacob as mandating the work of preservation and renewing the holy books, authorising Levi and the priesthood to continue this role – down to the author of *Jubilees*.

The image of Jacob has been sanitised and idealised. Beside the promises concerning his descendants which are a constant feature in the narrative, Jacob's own virtue is a model. *Jubilees* achieves this by omitting Genesis material which can be read as reflecting badly on Jacob or revising it to remove offence. It also achieves this by denigrating Esau throughout. Positively, it achieves this by emphasising that Jacob adheres to what are *Jubilees*' primary concerns. These include honouring parents and brotherly love, but especially sexual purity by not marrying a Canaanite woman and not therefore participating in their evil which consists in sexual impurity. The obverse side to this is that Jacob deals with sexual wrongdoing with great severity and entrusts this task of discipline and judgement to Levi and his descendants, the priests. The dangers of sexual wrongdoing begin, however, to show among his own sons. This, in part, lies behind the contrast which *Jubilees* develops between Judah and Joseph, and also indirectly addresses issues of sexual wrongdoing among Judah's descendants.

It is interesting also to note the treatment of Rachel and Leah in *Jubilees*. The account in *Jubilees* of Jacob's marriage to Laban's daughters differs from Genesis in particular in its treatment of Laban's decision to give Leah before Rachel. Whereas in Genesis this seems like treachery and plays with the irony that Jacob the cheater is cheated, in *Jubilees* Laban, far from cheating Jacob, is upholding divine commandment, which forbids taking the younger sister first (28:6-7). The effect of his compliance with divine law is also to give the image of Leah more dignity. She is no longer a pawn. She is rightly and properly Jacob's first wife. *Jubilees* goes beyond Genesis in describing the woman: "Leah's eyes were weak, though her figure was very lovely, but Rachel's eyes were beautiful, her figure was lovely, and she was very pretty" (28:5; cf. Gen 29:17, "Leah's eyes were weak,[636] and Rachel was graceful and beautiful"). Leah, too, is beautiful. We note also that *Jubilees* shares with Genesis a positive stance towards female beauty.

---

[636] NRSV translates the uncertain word, רכות as "lovely". *Jubilees* understood it as "weak". On various interpretations of רכות, see Endres, *Biblical Interpretation*, 101-103.

There is nothing here of the dangers of sexual attraction. It coheres with *Jubilees'* approach to the creation of man and woman.

Issues of fertility dominate the accounts which follow in *Jubilees*, as they do in Genesis. Both speak of the opening of Leah's womb (*Jub.* 28:11; Gen 29:31), but *Jubilees* does not take up the explanation for this found in Genesis: "When the Lord saw that Leah was unloved" (Gen 29:31). Rather, it turns it around and applies it to Rachel: "Now Rachel's womb was closed because the Lord saw that Leah was hated but Rachel was loved" (28:12). *Jubilees* recounts the birth to Leah of her four sons, Reuben, Simeon, Levi, and Judah, whom Jacob names, but *Jubilees* does not take up the etymologies of Genesis. It returns to the etymology of Levi in the context of his blessing by Isaac (31:16). Given Levi's importance for *Jubilees* it is no surprise that we find also a significant upgrading of Leah's image.

Jubilees follows Genesis in reporting Rachel's jealousy and Jacob's angry response (28:16; cf. Gen 30:1-2), but slightly modified to the extent that Jacob implies his ongoing sexual relationship with Rachel: "Have I withheld the product of your womb from you? Have I abandoned you?" cf. Gen 30:2, "Am I in the place of God, who has withheld from you the fruit of the womb?" The effect in both is to bring Rachel down from having favoured status in Jacob's eyes.[637] *Jubilees* also follows Genesis in reporting Rachel's offer of Bilhah and the children born to him through her, Dan and Naphtali, but again without the etymologies (28:17-19; Gen 30:3-8). Similarly, *Jubilees* follows the account of Leah's envy and her offer of Zilpah, the sister of Bilhah,[638] and the children born to her, Gad and Asher, but again without the etymologies (28:20-21; Gen 30:9-11).[639] Halpern-Amaru notes that *Jubilees* assumes that Jacob continues to have sexual relations with Rachel as part of continuing marital intimacy and otherwise makes specific reference to sexual intercourse in relation to Leah, Bilhah, and Zilpah, only when they bear children. Accordingly, Rachel's "inability to conceive

---

[637] Halpern-Amaru, *Empowerment*, suggests something more than I believe the text conveys, when she writes: "Recast as a sensitive spouse, Jacob reassures Rachel of his affection by gently reminding her (and the reader) that even though she has not conceived, he has maintained, and by implication, will continue, a sexual relationship with her" (65).

[638] On *Jubilees'* addition in 28:9 that Bilhah was Zilpah's sister, see Endres, *Biblical Interpretation*, who points out that this removed any possibility of understanding Bilhah as a slave and secured her semitic descent (105).

[639] Halpern-Amaru, *Empowerment*, notes: "Jacob still loves Rachel and does not love Leah. But the contrast between the situations of the two women no longer dominates their story" (66). "The rivalry between the women remains. But no longer is Leah pursuing her husband's affections and Rachel pursuing motherhood. Both women are motivated by the same thing: the desire for children. The entire issue of Jacob's affections becomes subtext" (67).

is not related to an absence of physical intimacy; it has not lessened her husband's affection or altered their relationship".[640] One of the assumptions underlying such ideal marriages is, on the one hand, continuing physical intimacy, within which there may or may not be procreation and, on the other hand, sexual intercourse for procreation.

At this point Genesis brings the story of the mandrakes, believed to enhance fertility. Reuben brings them for his mother Leah, but Rachel intervenes, asking Leah for some, finally agreeing to allow Jacob to sleep with Leah one night in exchange for some mandrakes (30:14-16). *Jubilees* omits this detail – perhaps disapprovingly?[641] – and simply gives the detail about the resultant children, again without etymologies: Issachar, and twins Zebulun and Dinah (28:22-23; Gen 30:17-21). Only *Jubilees* identifies the latter as twins here. Finally, *Jubilees* reports the birth to Rachel of Joseph, again without etymology (28:24; Gen 30:22-24).

Jub. 29:2-3 reports Jacob's summoning of Leah and Rachel and that "he spoke tenderly to them so that they would come with him to the land of Canaan", to which they responded, "We will go with you wherever you go". Gone is resentment towards Laban (cf. Gen 31:14-16). These are model behaviours on both sides and appear to reflect Ruth's response to Naomi in Ruth 1:16.[642] In its account of the flight from Laban *Jubilees* makes no mention of Rachel's taking her father's gods and of the drama it creates when Laban seeks them and when Rachel responds by feigning to be menstruating and so not able to dismount her camel which would have revealed them (cf. Gen 31:19, 32, 34-35). *Jubilees* shows it knows the story about the idols by later referring to their destruction (31:1-2). Rachel reappears in 32:3 in the brief account of the birth of Benjamin, which is reported a second time in 32:33 including the etymology and reporting her death in childbirth (cf. Gen 35:16-20).

Leah reappears in Isaac's blessing of her son, Levi, in 31:16, where Isaac refers to Leah rather than Jacob (cf. 28:14) as the one who named him: "Your mother named you Levi, and she has given you the right name. You will become one who is joined to the Lord and a companion of all Jacob's sons". The dual naming has its origins in Gen 29:34 ("Again she conceived and bore a son, and said, 'Now this time my husband will be joined to me, because I have borne him three sons'; therefore he was named Levi").[643] This reflects *Jubilees*' concern with marriage partnership and with the central role which it sees Levi playing in Israel's

---

[640] Halpern-Amaru, *Empowerment*, 65-66.

[641] So Endres, *Biblical Interpretation*, who suggests it "probably disturbed this author's estimation of Rachel and Leah's character; this author probably judged the story both useless and offensive to his community" (106).

[642] See Halpern-Amaru, *Empowerment*, 70.

[643] See Halpern-Amaru, *Empowerment*, 68.

future, hence the redirecting of the pun on joining, from Leah's relation with Jacob to Levi's relation to God and to Jacob's seed.[644] This also coheres with a shift in emphasis in *Jubilees* from barrenness as the forerunner of something special, to lineage. "Lineage, not infertility, is the noteworthy characteristic of the wife of a patriarch."[645] "*Jubilees* breaks apart the triad of associations – infertility, maternity to primary heir, and spousal love – that diminish Leah's status as a matriarch."[646]

We find mention of Leah accompanying Jacob in returning to Isaac in 33:1, leaving Bilhah exposed to Reuben's lust (33:2-8). Leah, however, receives special mention in the context of her death: Jacob

> loved her very much from the time when her sister Rachel died because she was perfect and right in all her behaviour and honoured Jacob. In all the time that she lived with him he did not hear a harsh word from her mouth because she was gentle and possessed (the virtues of) peace, truthfulness, and honor. As he recalled all the things that she had done in her lifetime, he greatly lamented her because he loved her with all his heart and with all his person (36:23-24).

Finally, then, Leah becomes a model, and the account of Jacob's love and lamentation for her also elevates her status. It also coheres with the very positive status attributed to women in *Jubilees*, which includes affirmation of their sexuality.[647] In her case, however, we are also dealing with the attempt by the

---

[644] See Halpern-Amaru, *Empowerment*, 69, 98-99.

[645] Halpern-Amaru, *Empowerment*, 100.

[646] Halpern-Amaru, *Empowerment*, 101.

[647] See also Betsy Halpern-Amaru, "The Naming of Levi in the Book of *Jubilees*," in *Pseudepigraphic Perspectives: The Apocrypha and Pseudepigrapha in Light of the Dead Sea Scrolls: Proceedings of the [Second] International Symposium of the Orion Center for the Study of the Dead Sea Scrolls and Associated Literature, 12-14 January 1997* (ed. Esther G. Chazon and Michael E. Stone; STDJ 31; Leiden: Brill, 1999) 59-69. She notes that whereas Jacob names Levi in 28:12, the blessing of Levi in 31:16 attributes the naming to Leah: "Your mother named you Levi, and she has given you the right name. You will become one who is joined to the Lord and a companion of all Jacob's sons". She sees this reflecting a more general concern in *Jubilees* to portray matriarchs and their marriages as "ideal unions of co-partners" (62). A similar tendency is noticeable in the treatment of Sarah and Rebecca (62-63). In Jacob's marriage both Rachel and Leah now pursue motherhood. Issues of affection for Jacob are no longer prominent. Both are in partnership with him. The naming of Levi with two etymologies recalls the naming of Samuel (1 Sam 1:20, 27-28) (65). By this association *Jubilees* not only underlines Levi's future prophetic role, but also makes it clear that infertility is not a necessity prior to the birth of a distinguished heir, nor in a polygamous marriage is one's husband's affection (66), though that comes later, too late for her to assume comparable leadership roles to Rebecca and Sarah (68-69). See also her, *Empowerment*, 95, where she notes the paradox that none of Rachel's sons is significant for *Jubilees*, in contrast to Levi (95-97).

author to show her a worthy mother of Levi, who is to bear the patriarchal tradition.

It is finally of note that *Jubilees* also has a positive image of Bilhah. In part, this will reflect the positive role which *Jubilees* gives to her son, Naphtali.[648] It identifies her as Zilpah's sister (28:9) and both as born within Laban's household (28:3) and so not Canaanite.[649] On the other hand, *Jubilees* makes no mention of her becoming Jacob's wife (cf. Gen 30:4); at best she is his concubine wife (33:15).[650] She behaves virtuously despite being victim to Reuben's lust.[651] Later she appears in 34:15 grieving the apparent loss of Joseph – and dies. Jacob also grieves for Bilhah (34:16). Together with the loss of Joseph and of Dinah, these become the foundation for the Day of Atonement (34:18-19). The women matter. At the same time, as with Levi and Leah, so here with Naphtali and Bilhah, we most likely have a reflection of concern to enhance the image of one of the families of significance beside Levi in the time of the author, namely the Tobiads, whom the Book of Tobit gives a pedigree from Naphtali.[652]

This selective interest in wives of the true lineage continues to be reflected in the case of Esau, where Genesis names his Canaanite wives (26:34-35), but *Jubilees* does not do so, although their existence plays a major role. As we have seen, *Jubilees* reduces to just a few words the report in Gen 28:6-9 that Esau finally married rightly, taking Mahalath, daughter of Ishmael ("Esau had married Mahalath, Ishmael's daughter"; 29:18). Nor does *Jubilees* take over the detail of Esau's descendants from Gen 36:1-14, which again includes the names of his wives.

Jubilees does, by contrast, name the wives of Jacob's sons.

The name of Reuben's wife was Oda; the name of Simeon's wife was Adebea, the Canaanitess; the name of Levi's wife was Melcha, one of the daughters of Aram – one of the descendants of Terah's sons; the name of Judah's wife was Betasuel, the Canaanitess; the name of Issachar's wife was Hezqua; the name of Zebulun's wife was

---

[648] So Halpern-Amaru, *Empowerment*, 109.

[649] So Halpern-Amaru, *Empowerment*, 105-106, who notes that 4QTNaphtali identifies Bilhah's mother as an אמה and that *Jubilees* may be rejecting a tradition that handmaiden (שפחה) implies that both women were daughters of Laban by a concubine.

[650] On this, see Halpern-Amaru, *Empowerment*, who suggests that *Jubilees* may be aware of the tradition reflected in *T. Naph* 1:6, that Rachel deceived Jacob in offering her as wife, although *Jubilees* retains her status as concubine-wife (108). "All of this – the emphasis on Bilhah's surrogacy, the absence of a formal announcement of her marriage, her 'half way house' status as concubine-wife, and her life in seclusion after the violation – is a response to the inappropriateness of a patriarchal wife, even a secondary one, being violated and becoming sexually impure" (109).

[651] See the discussion in 3.2.5 above.

[652] On Naphtali's significance see the discussion of the passage in 3.2.4.3 p. 177 above.

[Neeman]; the name of Dan's wife was Egla; the name of Naphtali's wife was Rasu'u of Mesopotamia; the name of God's wife was Maka; the name of Asher's wife was Iyona; the name of Joseph's wife was Asenath, the Egyptian; and the name of Benjamin's wife was Iyaska. Simeon, after changing his mind, married another woman from Mesopotamia like his brothers. (34:20-21)

While *Jubilees* identifies the origin only of Naphtali's wife (as coming from Mesopotamia), 34:21 assumes that where the origin is not stated, these are not foreign wives. This leaves: Joseph, as an exception, whose marriage is apparently deemed legitimate, probably since Egyptians are special in *Jubilees* (40:10); Simeon, who repented (cf. Esau, similarly), and Judah, who reaped the consequences (41:1-22). We have discussed these exceptions elsewhere. For the present context we note the list as further evidence of interest in the wives. By contrast, the list of Jacob's sons in Gen 35:23-26 makes no reference to wives.

While Joseph's marriage to an Egyptian is exceptional, but apparently acceptable, he is otherwise a model, resisting adultery while single and marrying at 30 (40:10-11, as in Gen 41:45-46). With Jacob, Isaac, and Abraham, and their wives, however, we find that *Jubilees* has distinctive developments. They become models of marriage and family.

The final figure of relevance for considering family and sexuality in *Jubilees* is Moses. We have already noted, in 3.2.4 above, the embarrassment which Moses' foreign wife would have posed for *Jubilees*, and its solution of making no mention of Zipporah or her father. His mother, Jochabed, also posed a problem, because she was married to her nephew, Amram, son of Kohath, who, like Jochabed, was a child of Levi (Exod 6:20; Num 26:59).[653] *Jubilees* gives no notice of such detail in its text, thus saving Moses from the impurity of such a forbidden relationship according to Lev 18:12 (see also 11Q Temple 66.14-15). On the other hand, *Jubilees* is careful to portray Jochabed as a caring mother, who with her husband brings up Moses within an Israeilte household for his first twenty-one years (47:9), reducing exposure to Egyptian influence to something secondary.[654]

3.3.2.4 Conclusion

Halpern-Amaru notes that "the themes of mutual concern and spousal partnership appear in all the unions of patriarchs and matriarchs", all of which have some basis in the Genesis text, which *Jubilees* then expands, the exception being the creative depiction of Jacob and Leah during the final years of his life. Both the idealisation of Leah and Jacob's change of heart "are necessary, for in *Jubilees*, the lines of

---

[653] On this see Halpern-Amaru, *Empowerment*, 122-23. *ALD* 12:3 / 75 shows no sign that its author saw this as problematic.

[654] See Halpern-Amaru, *Empowerment*, 124-25.

Israel's priests and kings must descend not only from a perfect mother, but also from an untroubled marriage union".[655] She continues: "The focus on the marital relationships of the founding parents functions as a subtle, but essential, aspect of the *Jubilees* argument for endogamy".[656] "Unions with inappropriate women produce corrupt progeny."[657] She also notes that *Jubilees* removes any sense of an emotional bond between patriarchs and women who are not their primary wives and any special status they might appear to have in Genesis in relation to God or to their husbands.[658] Thus Hagar receives no angelic message and does not encounter God and *Jubilees* moves the focus of conflict from her and Sarah to the status of Ishmael.[659]

There is, therefore, a very positive attitude towards marriage and family and sexuality within that context in *Jubilees*. It shares with Genesis an acceptance of men having more than one wife and, where necessary, also having sexual relations with handmaids of their wives and concubines. There are, however, boundaries. Marriage must be within one's extended family except in special circumstances such as Joseph and Asenath, but not with women from uncircumcised peoples, like the Canaanites, and never between nephew and aunt or niece and uncle. As we have just seen *Jubilees* applies this prohibition both ways: against marrying a nephew, as clearly stated in Lev 18:13-14, and illustrated in the omission by *Jubilees* of information about Jochabed's marriage; and, conversely (for some, like the Pharisees later, controversially) by implication against marrying one's niece. The latter prohibition features as the sole or contributing factor to *Jubilees*' revisions in relation to Seth and Azura (4:11), Abram and Sarai (12:9; cf. Gen 11:29; 12:20); and Milcah (19:10). It is extraordinary that, at the same time, *Jubilees* apparently has no difficulty in a man marrying his sister in contravention of Lev 18:9, 11, as in the case of Abram and Sarai and the first three generations of humankind, and in Jacob's marrying two sisters in contravention of Lev 18:18, provided he marries the elder of the two first. Otherwise, *Jubilees* vigorously

---

[655] Halpern-Amaru, *Empowerment*, 72. See also her discussion of the empowerment of the matriarchs as co-partners in the implementation of the covenant (75-102).

[656] Halpern-Amaru, *Empowerment*, 72.

[657] Halpern-Amaru, *Empowerment*, 73. See also Berger, *Jubiläen*, who writes: "Die Väterüberlieferung wird mithin unter dem Gesichtspunkt der Bewährung der Familie rezipiert" (281) (tr. The tradition of the fathers is thus being appropriated from the perspective of the preservation of family). But he means something much wider and cites prohibition of mixed marriages, support for parents, prohibition of incest with father's or son's wife. "Dem Verfasser geht es dabei nicht um Familie an sich, sondern um deren religiös-kultische Integrität" (281 n. 8) (tr. The author's concern is not family as such, but its religio-cultic integrity).

[658] Halpern-Amaru, *Empowerment*, 72.

[658] Halpern-Amaru, *Empowerment*, 106-107.

[659] So Halpern-Amaru, *Empowerment*, 107-108.

upholds other laws against incest. Such are the boundaries, but within the right space *Jubilees* portrays a very positive image of marriage and sexual intimacy and rewrites Genesis accordingly.

Issues of right space and time apply not only in relation to the family but to the community as a whole and especially in relation to the holy, and to these we turn.

3.3.3   Sexuality in Sacred Space and Time: Eden and Beyond

One of the major concerns of *Jubilees* is regard for the spheres of holiness in time and space. This comes to expression already in the summons to Moses to come to the summit of Mt Sinai to meet the Lord and in the summary description in the opening words of the prologue: "These are the words regarding the divisions of the times of the law and of the testimony, of the events of the years, of the weeks of their jubilees" (similarly 1:4, 26, 29). In God's instruction to Moses about the unfaithfulness of the people *Jubilees* notes not only idolatry and sexual impurity but also failure with regard to time and space:

> They will be captured and will fall into the enemy's control because they have abandoned my statutes, my commandments, my covenantal festivals, my Sabbaths, my holy things which I have hallowed for myself among them, my tabernacle and my temple which I sanctified for myself in the middle of the land so that I could set my name on it and that I could live (there) (1:10).

The calendar is of particular concern: "They will forget all my law, all my commandments, all my verdicts. They will err regarding the beginning of the month, the Sabbath, the festival, the jubilee, and the decree" (1:14). This stands in close proximity to the statement about future disregard for those who study Torah in 1:12: "I will send witnesses to them so that I may testify to them, but they will not listen and will kill the witnesses. They will persecute those studying the law diligently". The writer will have identified with the latter.

With regard to time it becomes clear already in the retelling of creation that the sun is the determinant for the calendar (2:9). The instructions to Noah make explicit the commitment to a 364 day solar calendar (6:32-37). Correspondingly, *Jubilees* gives detailed attention to dating throughout and in particular to the dating of major feasts. The order with regard to time reaches from the weekly sabbath to the jubilee of years. The details of the sacred times cannot be our focus here, except in so far as they pertain to the broad issue of sexuality. At an abstract level, right order is so fundamental for *Jubilees* that it also embraces behaviour related to sexuality. This also expresses itself in terms of time and space.

We find this already in the exposition of the sabbath at the conclusion of the account of the days of creation. The sanctification of the sabbath and the sanctification of the people belong together. The sabbath instructions embrace the angel's account, being the focus of the first application of the creation narrative (2:26-33) and the final discourse of the book (50:1-13). It was mandatory for high angelic orders to observe the sabbath (2:17-18). The angel then reports that God informed them that he would separate a people for himself who would also observe the sabbath (2:19-22). *Jubilees* connects the 22 works of creation with the 22 leaders between Adam and Jacob, apparently to identify Jacob and Israel as also part of God's creation, for the purpose of holiness and blessing (2:23-24). Israel's identity is bound to observance of the sabbath. As the sabbath, the 23rd, is holy, so Jacob/Israel, the 23rd, is holy, and part of God's order of creation.[660] That sanctification marks them out from among the nations, who among other things are a source of sexual impurity.

The first major instruction introduced by the words, "Now you command...", tells Moses to instruct the people that they are not to do any work on the sabbath, and not to defile it: "Now you command the Israelites to observe this day so that they may sanctify it, not do any work on it, and not defile (*rak^wsa*) it for it is holier than all (other) days" (2:26); similarly 2:25, "For this reason he gave orders regarding it that anyone who would do any work on it was to die; also, the one who would defile (*rak^wsa*) it".[661] The matching instructions of the final chapter include among acts that defile the sabbath: sexual intercourse.

> Any man who desecrates (*gammana*) this day; who lies with a woman; who says anything about work on it — that he is to set out on a trip on it, or about any selling or buying; who on it draws water which he had not prepared for himself on the sixth day; or who lifts any load to bring (it) outside his tent or his house is to die. (50:8)[662]

---

[660] So VanderKam, "Anthropological Gleanings," 121. Concerning 2:19a "I will now (nāhu) separate a people for myself from among my nations", he observes: "Although Israel would come into being many centuries later, one could argue that the force of the particle nāhu, reflecting Hebrew הנה, is to stress the present character of the action – that God separated Israel from his other peoples at the beginning" (120). "Hence, the salient fact about the writer's anthropology is that there are two orders of people" (122). That separateness also includes the language of Israel, Hebrew, the language of Creation (128).

[661] 4Q218 preserves fragments of 2:26. The word for "defile" is missing, but restored as טמאו.

[662] Anderson, "Consummation or Celibacy," notes also the juxtaposition with the eschatological concept of the "holy kingdom" in 50:9, and argues that *Jubilees* assumes that the sabbath is a foretaste of the eschatological era and "raises the Sabbath to the rank of a (Temple-) festival" (130). "Sexual relations, because they are forbidden within the Temple, are also forbidden on the Sabbath. The Sabbath is a means of actualizing, in a non-Temple environment, the requirements of Temple existence" (130), in contrast to rabbinic literature which "enthusiastically enjoined marital relations on the Sabbath" (131).

Accordingly, defilement in 2:25-26 most likely also includes a reference to engagement in sexual intercourse. *Jubilees* affirms sexual intercourse, as both the account of the creation of man and woman and the remainder of the book clearly demonstrate, but at the right time, not on the sabbath.

The issue of the right place and time is also a feature of the Eden narrative. In *Jubilees'* innovative account, the man knew the woman, that is, had sexual intercourse with the woman, already at her formation on the sixth day in the second week of creation (3:6), but outside the garden. Forty days after Adam's creation, according to *Jub.* 3:8-14, God brought him into the Garden of Eden and did the same with the woman after 80 days. The woman is also deemed to exist in Adam as a rib from the sixth day of the first week. Thus *Jubilees* provides a rationale for the laws in Lev 12:2-5 about a woman's ceremonial uncleanness after birth (7 days for a male, 14 days for a female) and the period of blood purification (33 days for a male, 66 days for a female).[663] It uses the differentiation between the creation of the man after 6 days and the creation of the woman after 13 days to explain the differentiation detailed in the law. The rationalisation is somewhat contrived, since it is the man who enters Eden after 40 days, not a woman after giving birth to a male, but nevertheless *Jubilees* uses this to reinforce its high regard for the sacred order of time and to place this Law back at the beginning of time.[664] Nothing indicates that Adam and Eve were unclean at their creation nor that they were rendered unclean through sexual intercourse (Lev 15:18; 22:4-7; cf.

---

[663] For detailed discussion see van Ruiten, *Primaeval History Interpreted*, 85-89. Himmelfarb, "Sexual Relations," notes that this is somewhat exceptional in *Jubilees*: "At the center of *Jubilees'* interest in sexual behaviour are not the purity laws, ... but rather the laws of forbidden sexual relations" (25). She observes that *Jubilees* shows no tendency as does the Temple Scroll to intensify such purity laws (26-27). She notes, for instance, that *Jubilees*, which elsewhere shows great interest in blood, never discusses menstrual blood, perhaps, she suggests, because it had become too controversial (33). See also Milgrom, "Concept of Impurity," who writes: "The biblical rules of impurity are enlarged in Qumran and rabbinic literature. But the book of *Jubilees* is devoid of any innovations" (277). Even the sanctity of Eden he sees as an extrapolation from God's presence there in Gen 2:6. *Jubilees'* innovation is to shift the origins of laws back to the time of patriarchs and where possible to creation, itself. Thus the sin in Eden is sacrilege: touching a holy tree (277).

[664] 4Q265 7 ii.11-17 also knows this link. On this see Joseph M. Baumgarten, "Purification after Childbirth and the Sacred Garden in 4Q265 and *Jubilees*," in *New Qumran Texts and Studies* (Leiden: Brill, 1994) 3-10. See also the discussion of our passage in Beate Ego, "Heilige Zeit – heiliger Raum – heiliger Mensch: Beobachtungen zur Struktur der Gesetzesbegründung in der Schöpfungs- und Paradiesgeschichte des Jubiläenbuches," in *Studies in the Book of Jubilees* (ed. Matthias Albani, Jörg Frey, and Armin Lange; TSAJ 65; Tübingen: Mohr Siebeck, 1997) 207-19, 211-15. Philo also appears to link the days for purification after childbirth with the creation story (*Q.G.* 1.25).

also Exod 19:15), though the author probably assumed the latter.[665] Ravid, however, suggests that their period of waiting may have had less to do with impurity than it had to do with preparation to enter holy space by enhancing their holiness.[666] She notes that Jubilees makes no mention of a rite of purification.[667] Accordingly they needed time to be pure before entering the garden, "not because they were impure, but because in order to enter the Garden of Eden they were required to purify themselves and acquire a degree of sanctity that would permit them to enter the holiest place on earth".[668] On the other hand, the fact that they apparently do not then engage in sexual intercourse again until after leaving the garden, suggests an understanding of the holiness of this space which would make sexual intercourse inappropriate and so assume it made one unclean with regard to the holy place.

The use of Adam and Eve's entry into the garden as an aetiology for the laws of purification after childbirth is made possible by the author's assumption about the garden as holy space. *Jubilees* explains that the Garden of Eden "is the holiest in the entire earth" (3:12). Lev 12:6 speaks of the woman coming to the tent of meeting after 40 or 80 days for the ritual of purification, which was then taken as instruction to come to the temple (or at least to the priest). *Jubilees* treats the Garden of Eden as a temple.[669] Later, in the context of discussing Enoch, *Jubilees* explains:

> For there are four places on earth that belong to the Lord: the Garden of Eden, the mountain of the east [Syriac Chronicle says south], this mountain on which you are

---

[665] So Anderson, "Consummation or Celibacy," 128-29; van Ruiten, *Primaeval History Interpreted*, 86-87.

[666] So Ravid, "Purity," 76-79.

[667] Ravid, "Purity," 76.

[668] Ravid, "Purity," 80.

[669] Similarly, 4Q265 7 ii.14 alludes both to the garden and to "all its young shoots" as sacred; similarly 1QH 8.10-13. See Baumgarten, "Purification after Childbirth," 6-7. He also proposes that מקדש אדם in 4QFlor be read as "sanctuary of Adam" referring to the garden of Eden (8-9), also in his "The Qumran Sabbath Shirot and Rabbinic Merkabah Traditions," *RevQ* 15 (1988) 212-23 and similarly M. O. Wise, "4QFlorilegium and the Temple of Adam," *RevQ* 15 (1991) 123-32. See also the discussion in Jacques T. A. G. M van Ruiten, "Visions of the Temple in the Book of *Jubilees*," in *Gemeinde ohne Tempel/ Community without Temple: Zur Substituierung und Transformation des Jerusalemer Tempels und seines Kults im Alten Testament, antiken Judentum und frühen Christentum* (ed. Beate Ego, Armin Lange and Peter Pilhofer; WUNT 118; Tübingen: Mohr Siebeck, 1999) 215-27, who notes that "*Jubilees* speaks in a negative way of the actual temple", but in a positive way of former sanctuaries, including Eden and a future temple linked with Zion (224).

today – Mt Sinai – and Mt. Zion (which) will be sanctified in the new creation for the sanctification of the earth. (4:26)

Of Noah it reports:

> He knew that the Garden of Eden is the holy of holies and is the residence of the Lord; (that) Mt. Sinai is in the middle of the desert; and (that) Mt. Zion is in the middle of the navel of the earth. The three of them — the one facing the other — were created as holy (places). (8:19)

Accordingly, Enoch is reported to have performed priestly functions in Eden: "He burned the evening incense of the sanctuary which is acceptable before the Lord on the mountain of incense" (4:25). Similarly Adam performed priestly roles:

> On that day, as he was leaving the Garden of Eden, he burned incense as a pleasing fragrance – frankincense, galbanum, stacte, and aromatic spices — in the early morning when the sun rose at the time when he covered his shame (3:27).

In its revised scheme of events, *Jubilees*, therefore, has the formation of woman and the first act of sexual intercourse between the man and the woman take place before they enter the garden, not, as in Genesis, within the garden itself. In addition to identifying Eden as holy space, *Jubilees* also carefully defines the time which Adam and the woman spent there. Already there is a barrier of time to be respected regarding childbirth impurity and blood purification, as we have seen. Then, according to 3:15-16, the man and his wife worked for seven years (the first week of the first jubilee of seven weeks of years) under instruction from the angels, tending it for fruit and crops, protecting it from the animals, and storing its produce to share. This is an ideal image. *Jubilees* also mentions their nakedness with no sense of shame or embarrassment. This is also an ideal image, carrying with it the implication that naked human bodies are not evil, anymore than are acts of sexual intercourse and giving birth to children. It does, however, depend on time and place. *Jubilees* has already mentioned that the man and the woman have had sexual intercourse, so that their not having shame seems not to equate to lack of sexual awareness or desire. On the other hand, as the story proceeds, it appears that they did not engage in sexual intercourse in the Garden of Eden. The author may well have accounted for this state of affairs, in part, by the fact that they were busy working the garden, as he reports in 3:15-16 and again in 3:35 in a sexual context, thus using their sexual energies elsewhere.

Something changed, however, with the action of the serpent. Before addressing the question of what precisely changed, given that *Jubilees* assumes that they had already experienced sexual intercourse and presumably sexual desire, we need to consider the details of *Jubilees'* account both of the temptation and of its consequences. *Jubilees* dates the action very precisely: after the seven years, in the second month, on the seventeenth day. Apart from the new emphasis on partnership, noted in the discussion of creation above, the conversation between the woman and the serpent in *Jub.* 3:17-19 remains very close to the account in Gen 3:1-5. Like the LXX, *Jub.* 3:20 includes three features which make the fruit attractive: "The woman saw that the tree was delightful and pleasing to the eye and (that) its fruit was good to eat", compared with the Hebrew which we have of the Genesis account. Like the LXX, *Jubilees* also has no equivalent to the statement in Gen 3:6 that "that the tree was to be desired to make one wise".

More strongly than in Genesis, *Jubilees* emphasises that the result of taking and eating the fruit was awareness of nakedness. The former notes: "Then the eyes of both were opened, and they knew that they were naked; and they sewed fig leaves together and made loincloths for themselves" (3:7). *Jubilees* makes it into two separate events:

> So she took some of it and ate (it). She first covered her shame with fig leaves and then gave it to Adam. He ate (it), his eyes were opened, and he saw that he was naked. He took fig leaves and sewed (them); (thus) he made himself an apron and covered his shame. (3:20-22)

Jubilees then omits God's entry into the garden and the blaming that ensues (Gen 3:8-13) and also notes only that God cursed the serpent, not the content of that curse (3:23; cf. Gen 3:14-15).[670] God's words of anger to the woman and to the man are closer to the LXX than the Hebrew.

Genesis 3 LXX	Genesis 3 MT	Jubilees 3
16 καὶ τῇ γυναικὶ εἶπεν	16 אל האשה אמר	23 At the woman, too, he was angry because she had listened to the serpent and eaten. He said to her:
πληθύνων πληθυνῶ τὰς λύπας σου καὶ τὸν στεναγμόν σου ἐν λύπαις τέξῃ τέκνα καὶ πρὸς τὸν ἄνδρα σου ἡ ἀποστροφή σου καὶ αὐτός σου κυριεύσει. 17 τῷ δὲ Αδαμ εἶπεν	הרבה ארבה עצבונך והרנך בעצב תלדי בנים ואל אשך תשוקתך והוא ימשל בך 17 ולאדם אמר כי שמעה לקול אשתך	24 "I will indeed multiply your sadness and your pain. Bear children in sadness. Your place of refuge (or return) will be with your husband; he will rule over you" 25 Then he said to Adam: "Because you listened to

---

[670] Van Ruiten, *Primaeval History Interpreted*, notes that *Jubilees* does not make a connection between the serpent and Mastema or Satan (92, 100).

ὅτι ἤκουσας τῆς φωνῆς τῆς γυναικός σου καὶ ἔφαγες ἀπὸ τοῦ ξύλου οὗ ἐνετειλάμην σοι τούτου μόνου μὴ φαγεῖν ἀπ' αὐτοῦ ἐπικατάρατος ἡ γῆ ἐν τοῖς ἔργοις σου ἐν λύπαις φάγῃ αὐτὴν πάσας τὰς ἡμέρας τῆς ζωῆς σου 18 ἀκάνθας καὶ τριβόλους ἀνατελεῖ σοι καὶ φάγῃ τὸν χόρτον τοῦ ἀγροῦ 19 ἐν ἰδρῶτι τοῦ προσώπου σου φάγῃ τὸν ἄρτον σου ἕως τοῦ ἀποστρέψαι σε εἰς τὴν γῆν ἐξ ἧς ἐλήμφθης ὅτι γῆ εἶ καὶ εἰς γῆν ἀπελεύσῃ	ותאכל מן העץ אשר צויתיך לאמר לא תאכל ממנו ארורה האדמה בעבורך בעצבון תאכלנה כל ימי חייך 18 וקוץ ודרדר תצמיח לך ואכלת את עשב השדה 19 בזעת אפיך תאכל לחם עד שובך אל האדמה כי ממנה לקחת כי עפר אתה ואל עפר תשוב	your wife and ate from the tree from which I commanded you not to eat, may the ground be cursed on account of you. May it grow thorns and thistles for you. Eat your food in the sweat of your face until you return to the earth from which you were taken. For earth you are and to the earth you will return".

It is not, however, evident that *Jubilees* takes up the possible implications of the LXX texts which reflect negatively on a woman's sexual desire as a constant returning to her husband, thus to repeated pain and to subjugation to her husband in that sense. *Jubilees* lacks the other connections which the LXX version makes possible.[671] It lacks the detail of man's formation from the ground, which in the LXX is from "the earth" (γη; Gen 2:7), and so lacks its echo in speaking of his return to "the earth" (3:25; Gen 3:19 LXX γῆ; cf. Hebrew: עפר). It lacks the idea of the man made in God's image and likeness which the LXX appears to use as a basis for portraying the woman as made in the man's likeness. Accordingly, it cannot evoke, as LXX, the impression that those processes are in some sense being reversed in God's judgement, the man returning to serve his source (the earth) and the woman returning to serve hers (the man). It also lacks the detail about the serpent's trickery, which in the LXX can be read as seduction and be taken as implying flaws in the woman's character, related to her sexuality. While the Ethiopic word, *megbā'*, which can mean "place of return or refuge", preserves some degree of ambiguity like the LXX, and possibly under its influence, the absence of the connections present in the LXX make the meaning "refuge" more likely. The influence of LXX formulations may well, in any case, have come in the

---

[671] On these distinctive features of the LXX account see Loader, *Septuagint, Sexuality, and the New Testament*, 27-59.

process of translation of *Jubilees* into Greek and not reflect the Hebrew text of *Jubilees*.[672]

In substance, the account in *Jubilees* explains women's pain in childbirth, their taking refuge in their husband, and their falling under his control, as the result of the woman's transgressing the prohibition, and explains the man's toil similarly. It need not have any particular relevance for attitudes towards sexuality in *Jubilees* beyond women's pain in childbirth and the assumed framework of the patriarchal household structure which is thus established. *Jubilees* appears to make no more of it than that. The emphasis in *Jubilees'* narrative falls rather on nakedness, as already in the account of the eating and its consequences. Thus *Jubilees* moves on immediately to the report that God clothed them and dismissed them from the garden (3:26), whereas Gen 3:20 first reports Adam's naming of Eve and the name's etymology as the mother of all living. That detail must wait in *Jubilees* till 3:33. Perhaps it reflects *Jubilees'* concern to avoid suggesting there was sexual intercourse in the garden and that sexual intercourse and childbearing in itself was in any way related to the curse.[673]

There is thus greater interest in nakedness. Accordingly, *Jubilees* has the man model appropriate priestly behaviour before burning incense: he covers his nakedness at sunrise (3:27). In part, this reflects concern to portray Adam as fulfilling the function of a high priest, just as Aaron is instructed to cover all naked parts (Exod 28:40-43).[674] Priests burned incense before the Holy of Holies (Exod 30:7-8, 34-38; Num 16:39-40; 2 Chron 26:16-20). Accordingly, Adam did so "as he was leaving the Garden of Eden" (3:27), which is the holy of holies.

Jubilees then explains that animals lost their language and that they were dispersed to their ordained places (as though the events in the garden formed part

---

[672] On the rendering of Gen 3:16 in *Jub.* 3:24, see Jacques T. A. G. M. van Ruiten, "Eve's Pain in Childbearing? Interpretations of Gen 3:16a in Biblical and Early Jewish Texts," in *Eve's Children: The Biblical Stories Retold and Interpreted in Jewish and Christian Traditions* (ed. Gerard P. Luttikhuizen; Biblical Narrative 5; Leiden: Brill, 2003) 3-26, 13-14. He notes that the imperative "bear!" is paralleled elsewhere only in EthGen 3:16 (14). See also his discussion in *Primaeval History Interpreted*, 100-101, where he notes that for עצבונך והרנך ("your sadness and your childbearing") *Jubilees* has "your sadness and your pain", and LXX has "your sufferings and your signing" (τὰς λύπας σου καὶ τὸν στεναγμόν σου), both perhaps reflecting a variant Hebrew text or rendering the unusual word, ערון, freely as one expression. *Jubilees* and LXX also share the reading, "return" or "refuge", reading תשבה for תשקה ("desire") (101). On the latter see also VanderKam, *Jubilees Translated*, 19 n. 3:24, where he notes that *Jubilees* shares this reading also with Old Latin and EthGen 3:16.

[673] So van Ruiten, *Primaeval History Interpreted*, 104, 134.

[674] So Ego, "Heilige Zeit – heiliger Raum," 215; van Ruiten, *Primaeval History Interpreted*, 107.

of the original divine plan),[675] but this, too, comes in the context of concern about nakedness: "But of all the animals and cattle he permitted Adam alone to cover his shame" (3:30). In 3:31 *Jubilees* presses home the point:

> For this reason it has been commanded in the tablets regarding all those who know the judgment of the law that they cover their shame and not uncover themselves as the nations uncover themselves.

Thus the story of the Garden of Eden serves to introduce the major theme noted above: nakedness among the nations and associated sexual wrongdoing.

The account in *Jubilees* leaves open many questions. What becomes of the apparent ideal of man and woman naked with no shame, working the garden? Might it one day be reconstituted or restored? In relation to sexuality, it raises the question whether the man and the woman continued to have sexual intercourse in the garden. The answer is almost certainly in the negative. Given that *Jubilees* applies the purity laws of Leviticus to the garden as a holy place in explaining the laws of uncleanness and purification after childbirth, it is most unlikely that it would contemplate seminal emission and resultant uncleanness occurring in the garden (Lev 15:18; 22:4-7).[676] Indeed, 3:34-35 appears to support this when it reports: "They were childless throughout the first jubilee; afterwards he knew her. He himself was working the land as he had been taught in the Garden of Eden". There appears to be an assumption that his engagement in working the land somehow made not having sexual intercourse tolerable, an understanding present elsewhere (e.g. *T. Iss.* 3:5). The words, "afterwards he knew her", clearly imply that no sexual intercourse took place in Eden. This is more than an incidental detail. It reflects the understanding on the part of *Jubilees* that the Garden of Eden was a holy place where such activity was out of place. *Jubilees* is probably reflecting this assumption also when it postpones the naming of Eve with its etymology of motherhood from immediately after the curses to much later in 3:33,

---

[675] Cf. Plato's *Timaeus*, where we find a similar conjunction of failure and divine intention: Animals and other forms of life (including women!) come into being because of souls of men who fail, but this is at the same time the demiurge's means of creation (39E, 41B, 42B, 91A).

[676] Anderson, "Consummation or Celibacy," also draws attention to the requirement that the high priest remain separate from his wife for the week before Yom-Kippur (*m. Yoma* 1.1) (129). See also van Ruiten, *Primaeval History Interpreted*, who draws attention to the requirement in Exod 19:15 that men abstain from sexual intercourse for three days before approaching Sinai (86), to the *Temple Scroll* which applies apply this to entry into the city (45.11-12) and to the *Damascus Document*, which forbids sexual intercourse in the city (11.21 – 12.2). See also my discussion in William Loader, *Sexuality and the Jesus Tradition* (Grand Rapids: Eerdmans, 2005), 225-26. Van Ruiten discusses the background of sacred temple idea in Jewish literature (89).

as noted above. By this it also achieves a separation between the curse and its announcement of pain in childbirth from the actual accounts of motherhood in the following chapter.[677]

Before their awareness of their nakedness, the man and woman were nevertheless naked in the holy place, deemed offensive before God in the case of male nakedness.[678] *Jubilees* shows no signs of seeing a problem in this, although there are signs that it wants to give the impression that the man did not look on the nakedness of his wife, when it speaks in 3:16 only of Adam as naked and unashamed and not of "the man and his wife" as Gen 2:25. But that can only make sense if it is looking within the context of awareness of shame. *Jubilees* appears therefore to presume that there was once a state of being where nakedness without shame and without a sexual agenda was even acceptable in the holy place.

This notion has potential relevance where images of future hope employ the motif of a return to Eden or envisage the place of hope in cultic terms as a temple. It helps make sense of the statement attributed to Jesus in the discussion with the Sadducees that in the world to come they neither marry nor are given in marriage, referring to the act of sexual intercourse (Mark 12:25). It also coheres with *Jubilees'* prohibition of sexual intercourse in sacred time, namely the sabbath (50:8), and may be an implication of the note in 15:28 that Israel's destiny is "to be with him and his holy angels".

It may also belong with the images of the future found in the angel's exposition of age in *Jubilees* 23. There the angel explains that wickedness, including sexual wrongdoing, has reduced human lifetime from just below 1000 years to its present state and is likely to get worse. At worst "the children's heads will turn white with grey hair. A child who is three weeks of age will look old like one whose years are 100, and their condition will be destroyed through distress and pain" (23:25). By contrast, return to study and observance of the Law will bring the reverse:

> In those days the children will begin to study the laws, to seek out the commands, and to return to the right way. The days will begin to become numerous and increase, and mankind as well – generation by generation and day by day until their lifetimes approach 1000 years and to more years than the number of days (had been). (23:26-27)

More important for our theme, these people will not be adults but remain children:

---

[677] So van Ruiten, "Eve's Pain," 14.

[678] The offensiveness of male nakedness, in particular, exposure of the penis, both in holy places before God and in hierarchical contexts before one's superior, may reflect in part that the background lies in the phallus as a symbol of power over others. To cover it is to submit. On attitudes towards male nakedness, see Satlow, "Jewish Constructions of Nakedness".

Then there will be no old man, nor anyone who has lived out his lifetime, because all of them will be infants and children. They will complete and live their entire lifetimes peacefully and joyfully. There will be neither a satan nor any evil one who will destroy. For their entire lifetimes will be times of blessing and healing. (23:28-29)

If "all of them will be infants and children", then this, too, probably implies a state where no sexual relations take place. It bears some similarity to later traditions which picture the future in ideal terms where becoming like children is taken to mean being naked and unashamed and may already be reflected in statements like: "for of such is the kingdom of God" (cf. Mark 10:14).[679]

---

[679] We find this most clearly expressed in *Gos. Thom.* 22; *Gos. Eg.* in Clement *Strom.* 3.92; *2 Clem.* 12:2-6; and *Gos. Thom.* 37.

3.4   Conclusion

Jubilees has much to say which is pertinent to attitudes towards sexuality. While perhaps best known for its severe warnings, it also contains strongly affirmative attitudes towards sexuality.

In its version of the creation story (2:1-18), the statement about the creation of humankind has been radically simplified (2:14; cf. Gen 1:27b). No longer supplementary to God's intention to make humankind after his own image (cf. Gen 1:26, 27a) and no longer closely associated with the command to be fruitful and multiply (Gen 1:28), the information that God made *adam* male and female stands in its own right and takes central focus. Merging both creation stories, *Jubilees* understands this as the making of the man, Adam, who contains within himself the bone from which one week later woman would be made.

This Adam is not understood as androgynous, but as a male human being, who then observes male and female animals (3:3). It is striking that *Jubilees* employs this notion to engage Adam in the perception of his own need, whereas Genesis portrays it as a concern of God and his co-creators (cf. Gen 2:18). The most natural reading of *Jubilees* is that Adam sees the companionship among animals, in particular, between male and female animals in which sexual union plays a primary role, and longs for something similar, himself. This reflects a very positive attitude towards sexual relations and informs, in turn, the understanding of God's observation about human need. The focus is less on helper and more on companion, including sexual intimacy.

The wish finds its fulfilment in God's creation of woman from the bone/rib of the man, as in Genesis, but the joy "at last" comes to expression as God brings the man to the woman, rather than the reverse as in Genesis (3:5-6; Gen 2:22). *Jubilees* appears to have used Gen 2:24, the statement about a man leaving his parents and being joined to his wife, in order to reframe Gen 2:22. Accordingly, the man comes to the woman and their first act is sexual intercourse (3:6), thus beginning the fulfilment of the man's longing for intimate companionship.

The emphasis on companionship then reshapes the narrative of the garden of Eden in subtle ways, so that we read of both receiving instruction about the forbidden tree, not just Adam (3:18; cf. Gen 2:16-17), and of each having the experience of becoming aware of nakedness (3:20-22; cf. Gen 3:7). In addition, *Jubilees* has omitted the dialogue where each blames the other (cf. Gen 3:8-13). Adam and Eve then become paradigmatic of the marital relationship, including sexual intimacy, which will then also characterise the way *Jubilees* retells the stories of the patriarchs. It appears already to inform the imagery of Yahweh's opening speech which, following prophetic precedents, contrasts his own faithfulness to the relationship as greater than Israel's faithfulness (1:6). The wives of the patriarchs become partners with their husbands in ensuring the fulfilment of the promises. While the trait of jealousy remains (17:4), *Jubilees'* portrait of Sarah makes her primary concern the fulfilment of the promise. Her barrenness is no longer a sign of great events to come (cf. Gen 11:30), but reduced to incidental detail beside the lineal integrity and call to participate in the promises (12:9-11; 14:22). *Jubilees* simply omits Rebecca's barrenness. Sarah, like Abraham, now encounters angels in her own right (16:2-3, 12, 19). Gone is Abraham's ruse of self protection which exposes her to potential sexual abuse – and perhaps none even occurs (13:11-15; cf. Gen 12:10-20).

Jubilees exploits the already strong image of Rebecca in Genesis to make her the primary link between Abraham and Jacob (19:16-25), but she exercises that role always as Isaac's companion and support, even when that means she must engineer his conformity to God's intention and it takes her a lifetime to persuade Isaac finally to recognise God's choice (35:13-14). Jubilees portrays her as a woman in her physicality, referring to her womb, her affections, her breasts, her mouth and tongue; she kisses and hugs.

Intimate companionship, including sexual intimacy, characterises Jacob's marriage with Rachel. The sexual attractiveness of both her and her sister is not a danger but a delight as *Jubilees* portrays it (28:5). Even Laban becomes a kind family uncle. While sexual intimacy with Rachel throughout the marriage is assumed, sexual intercourse with Leah and with the handmaids receives special mention as something functional, but approved for bearing offspring (28:11-24). Tension remains, but tricks with mandrakes to enhance fertility disappear (Gen 30:14-16). Yet finally *Jubilees* retrieves Leah from being the unloved. In Jacob's final years it makes her the loving companion, indeed the ideal wife, fitting for the mother of the one who for *Jubilees* is Israel's greatest son, Levi (36:23-24).

The elevation of women and the affirmation of marital intimacy are special traits in *Jubilees*. That includes a positive attitude towards sexuality, sexual attractiveness, and sexual intercourse as an expression of intimacy as well as for procreation. Such companionship is still far from equal partnership and to be seen within overarching frameworks, including patriarchal structure. This is evident even in the marriage of Isaac and Rebecca where Isaac lags along far behind his wife in insight, but is still the one to give blessings and cultic instructions.

It is also already evident in the story of Adam and Eve. *Jubilees* retains God's declaration of judgement on the man and the woman (3:23-25; Gen 3:16-19). For the latter it will mean pain in childbirth, taking refuge with her husband and submission to him. This appears not to imply that sexual intimacy is changed or that the woman now cannot help herself wanting to have children, but simply to refer to pain and the dependence reflected in patriarchy. We see Adam also taking a distinctively male role at the conclusion of the scene, where as a priest he offers incense before the Holy of Holies, identified with Eden (3:27). This latter reflects the fact that the companionship exists also within a cultic framework of sacred space and sacred time.

The wider structural frameworks of sacred time and space and propriety have major significance for *Jubilees* and raise major questions. One emerges already in the Eden story. According to *Jubilees* the man and the woman already have an intimate relationship and have engaged in sexual intimacy before they enter the garden (3:5), yet apparently they abstain from sexual intercourse while in the garden, only develop awareness of shame concerning nakedness after eating the fruit, and resume having sexual intercourse only after they leave the garden (3:34). This reflects *Jubilees*' understanding of the garden as a temple (3:12; 4:26; 8:19), which also informs its rationale for the days of purification after childbirth of a male and a female. Sexual intercourse is not to take place in the temple nor should one be naked there, though the latter provision also applies beyond the garden. While this stands in contradiction to the fact of their acceptable nakedness before they ate the fruit, *Jubilees* probably saw no problem in this, but will have seen nakedness with the awareness which that event created as the problem. It invites speculation about whether *Jubilees* might even contemplate a return to that primal state, but there is no indication in the text. The same might be said of the fact that these two were both in what *Jubilees* declares to be the Holy of Holies.

Sacred space and time inform also *Jubilees*' concern with the solar calendar, which it employs to place events in their right order. They also play an important role in defining appropriate and inappropriate sexual behaviour. Sexual intercourse is out of place in the garden of Eden because it is a holy place. Similarly sexual intercourse is out of place on the holy sabbath according to *Jubilees* (50:8). In the right space and time, however, sexual relations are something very positive.

This brings us back to a certain tension in *Jubilees*' understanding of sexuality. On the one hand, it affirms sexuality in a manner that goes far beyond its source in Genesis and gives us an ideal, reflected in the primal parents and the patriarchs and matriarchs, of harmonious, mutually supportive, and sexually intimate marriage. On the other hand, in its most holy place there is no sexual activity and at most we imagine a nakedness in innocence without shame. This may well be reflected in the eschatological hope which *Jubilees* expresses in 23:28-29, according to which people will live for 1000 years, "all of them will be infants and children. They will complete and live their entire lifetimes peacefully and joyfully. There will be neither a satan nor any evil one who will destroy. For their entire lifetimes will be times of blessing and healing". Perhaps it sees this as mirroring the life of angels, whose circumcision relates rather to continence than to engagement (15:27). *Jubilees* does not relieve the tension by diminishing sexuality. Its exposition leaves the issue unresolved.

Jubilees also attends to boundaries other than those of time and space. One set of such boundaries relates to having sexual relations only with one's own kind.

Perhaps *Jubilees* is already warding off such dangers when it avoids formulations in the creation story which might suggest the idea that Adam could find a sexual companion among the animals (3:1-3). It is certainly the main feature in *Jubilees'* account of the Watchers, who begin, unlike in the *Book of the Watchers*, as God's commissioned educators sent to humankind (5:1-12). Repeatedly *Jubilees* designates their sin as corrupting or perverting their way. In having sexual intercourse with human women they not only potentially committed adultery and simply chose whomever they wanted; they crossed the boundary of kind. *Jubilees* not only portrays this as sin, but also reinforces its impropriety by depicting its effects: giants are born and from among the bound angels some are let loose as demons into the world. The corruption spreads to humankind and to the animal world. That may have included similar sexual transgressions, including bestiality and homosexual activity, but this is not said. The major focus in depicting the sins of the giants and of humankind before the flood is on war and bloodshed.

Later we also see that demonic influence accounts for idolatry and especially sexual wrongdoing, so that *Jubilees* holds out the hope that a day will come when there will be no satan and evil person, and Israel will free of sexual impurity and corruption (23:29; 50:5; 40:9). While the Watcher episode features later in the work only briefly, it has immense significance. Structurally, *Jubilees* gives it central significance by placing it in the 25th jubilee of 50 jubilees. This matches its substantial importance as accounting for the demonic influences which dog subsequent history. It originates in sexual wrongdoing and directly or indirectly inspires all sexual wrongdoing to come. This stands in contrast to the *Book of the Watchers*, where the relevance of the Watchers' deeds to sexual wrongdoing in the author's time must be deduced by analogy, but is never stated directly. In *Jubilees*, however, sexual wrongdoing, particularly, through crossing inappropriate boundaries of kind (holy Israel – unholy nations) features strongly.

The dualism of *Jubilees* is characterised by the holy, on one side, and the evil and contaminating influence of the Watchers and their spirits, on the other. This goes a long way towards explaining the way *Jubilees* defines what is appropriate and inappropriate in the realm of sexual behaviour. On the one hand, in the right time and space, it belongs to the good and holy, even if not in the sacral sphere. At the wrong time and in the wrong place, it is moral transgression which also contaminates and defiles the nation.

We see this framework operating already from the beginning. In the sequence of marriages to the time of Noah, *Jubilees* gives the reader the names not only of men, but of women. In part, this coheres with the greater importance it gives to women. It is also related to marriage boundaries. Those who belong to what is to become the holy line, descending from Adam through Seth to Noah and then to Abraham, must not marry inappropriately. In the first instance, what is inappropriate is defined by Cain's sinfulness. So Seth marries not a daughter of

Cain, but his sister (4:11). Negative influence is the chief concern later when Arpachsad apparently marries his niece (unless she was his grand niece) and Kainan strays (8:1-4) and when Nahor does similarly, leading to the influx of idolatry, which Abram must confront in his father (11:9, 11-24; 12:1-8). The assumption is not that some marriages outside the line are acceptable provided no evil influence is to hand, but rather that any marriage outside the approved limits inevitably produces evil influence. One could reduce this to a concern with purity of the line in almost a racial or tribal sense, but it is clearly inseparable from the presupposition that marrying outside the approved line exposes one to evil influence. Choosing a wife must be undertaken with care. Accordingly *Jubilees* cannot reproduce the stories of chance encounters which find Rebecca for Isaac and which bring Jacob and Rachel together (19:10; 28:1; cf. Gen 24:1-67; 29:1-12). There is danger and it is contaminating for more than just the individual.

This is particularly evident in the speeches of Noah, Abraham, and Rebecca, and in the stories of Judah and in the discourse which follows the story of Dinah (30:5-23). If one begins with the latter, the picture emerges of defilement of Israel, not just of the individuals concerned, when a woman marries a Canaanite. Such defilement also reaches the temple (30:16) and can pollute the Holy of Holies (23:21). *Jubilees* applies prohibitions from Leviticus which are concerned with priests' daughters who engage in prostitution, to any woman of Israel marrying a Canaanite (30:7; Lev 21:9) and applies the prohibition of giving one's seed to Molech to the act of giving away one's daughter in marriage to a Gentile (30:9-10; Lev 18:21). The suppression of the agreement about circumcision in the Dinah story in *Jubilees* probably indicates that it sees all such marriages as an abomination, whether the Gentile submits to circumcision or not (30:12-14). While the Dinah story necessarily throws the focus onto women marrying Gentile men, the discourse is equally forbidding of the converse (30:11).

The language of defilement and impurity, which *Jubilees* frequently employs, may give the impression that ritual contamination is the chief concern. The focus, however, is not ritual impurity by touch, which might even be removed with relative ease and does not carry moral overtones (ceremonial impurity is not sin, but part of life to be managed), but something more of the order of the pollution which brings defilement to the people and the temple, such as we find in Deut 7:3-4 and Ezra 9:1-2. We are still, however, in the realm of something more than corrupting moral influence. It is not the case that such marriages are forbidden only if negative moral influence is present. They are forbidden absolutely. But, again, conversely, this cannot be separated from moral influence.

The rationale appears to be: all such relationships inevitably bring the pollution of sin and so belong to the category of offence which defiles not only the individuals concerned but the nation and the temple. The concern with intermarriage cannot, therefore, be reduced to the category of ritual impurity, nor is it limited to racial purity or pollution through foreign seed. Rather, *Jubilees* regularly explains it on the basis of moral influences and especially sexual wrongdoing. While this is not to the fore in the discourse after the Dinah episode, it plays a major role elsewhere. Rebecca's instruction not to marry a Canaanite explains that Esau's wives have caused her pain because of their sexual wrongdoing, and she then generalises this with the claim that Canaanite women are to be seen as evil because of this (25:1-3). Jacob's reassurance not only affirms that he will take her advice, but also addresses the sexual agenda, reporting that his own sexual behaviour has been right and that he has not corrupted his way, words echoing the terminology used in relation to the Watchers' sexual sin (25:4-10).

While bloodshed and idolatry are the fruit of demonic work according to the early chapters of *Jubilees* and idolatry presents itself as a concern related to foreign marriages, sexual wrongdoing is really the main focus for *Jubilees*. This is so from beginning to end, as we have seen. The concern with impurity (*rek^{w}s*) is a constant feature. When expounded, it nearly always focuses on sexual wrongdoing. It belongs to a cluster of terms, which often occur in strings, which centre above all on sexual wrongdoing. Quantitatively it is by far the most frequent target of special warnings.[680] It accounts for five of the twelve major warnings where the angels uses the formula: "Now, you Moses, command" (28:7; 30:11, 13; 18; 41:26). It features strongly throughout the testamentary speeches created by the author and the author's eschatological hope looks for a day when it will cease to be (50:5). In *Jubilees* the angel generalises from the prohibition on incest to declare:

> No sin is greater than the sexual impurity (*zemmut*) which they commit on the earth because Israel is a holy people for the Lord its God. It is the nation which he possesses; it is a priestly nation; it is a priestly kingdom; it is what he owns. No such impurity (*rek^{w}s*) will be seen among the holy people. (33:20)

Intermarriage and sexual wrongdoing belong closely together. Both call for closer definition. With regard to intermarriage, before Noah all marriages outside the family line are shown to be inappropriate and to have negative consequences. This is also true down to the time of Abraham. In that time, however, and since then, *Jubilees* frequently expresses the prohibition in terms of the Canaanites, that is, the descendants of Canaan, whom God cursed because of his father's sin (7:7-12). One might then attribute their negative status in a formal way to their being cursed peoples. That is, indeed, the case in 20:4 and 22:20, where part of the motivation for the prohibition is that Canaan's seed is to be uprooted. It is certainly, however,

---

[680] Schwarz, *Identität*, notes: "die Häufigkeit und Intensität, mit der im Jubiläenbuch das Mischehenverbot eingeschärft wird" (32) (tr. The frequency and intensity with which the prohibition of mixed marriages is sharpened in the *Book of Jubilees*).

more than that, because we regularly find reference also to their sexual wrongdoing.

Some have appealed to the prohibition in relation to Canaanites to explain what appear to be anomalies, namely that Joseph marries Asenath, an Egyptian (40:10), and the presence of Hagar, an Egyptian, as Sarah's maid and with whom Abraham has sexual intercourse. This is certainly strange because Lev 18:3 introduces its warning about sexual impurity by direct reference to the Egyptians ("You shall not do as they do in the land of Egypt, where you lived, and you shall not do as they do in the land of Canaan, to which I am bringing you"). Are Egyptians now exceptions because, while descendants of Ham, they are not descendants of Canaan? This would then imply that the prohibition of intermarriage is narrowly focused on the Canaanite nations and has no relevance for other descendants of Ham nor to descendants of Japheth. This seems unlikely to be the case. *Jubilees* affirms endogamy within the chosen line. Usually that means rejecting intermarriage with Canaanites, but not always just with Canaanites. *Jubilees* disapproves of Nahor's marrying a Chaldean (11:9) and similarly of the marriages of Eber, Peleg, and Ragew (8:1-10). *Jubilees* can also speak simply of the uncircumcised (30:12). Its concern with the behaviour of the nations over whom the spirits of Mastema rule (15:31) seems to imply danger from all quarters (15:33-34). Concern with nakedness and with abandoning full circumcision may indeed target Hellenistic practices and, at least, therefore, groups other than Canaan's descendants (cf. 1 Macc 1:14-15).

Rather than being simply instances of allegedly acceptable Gentile nations not descended from Canaan, Egyptians seem in *Jubilees* to have a distinct status. *Jubilees* does not see the presence of Hagar as an Egyptian and as sexual partner for procreation in Abraham's household (14:21-24) as problematic nor does it see Joseph's marriage to Asenath as inappropriate. On the contrary, the latter belongs in a context which makes Egypt under Pharaoh of Joseph's time a veritable model of the eschaton ("The pharaoh's rule was just, and there was no satan or any evil one", 40:9; cf. 50:5, "they will no longer have any satan or any evil person. The land will be pure from that time until eternity"). This coheres with a generally positive attitude towards Egypt elsewhere in *Jubilees*. The ruler of Egypt, for instance, who oppressed Israel in Egypt was not an Egyptian but a Canaanite ("The king of Canaan conquered the king of Egypt and closed the gates of Egypt. He conceived an evil plan against the Israelites in order to make them suffer". 46:11-12). *Jubilees* is strangely silent about any evil to which Joseph might have been exposed through his marriage, even though it was, apparently, to the daughter of the woman who tried to seduce him (40:10), but even then *Jubilees* softens her image. Rather, *Jubilees* enhances Potiphar's credentials and appears to value his (albeit pagan) priesthood (40:10). It also omits mention of negative attitudes of Egyptians towards eating with Jews and toward them in their occupation as shepherds (Gen 43:32; 46:31-34), although it is careful to rewrite Moses' story so that his upbringing is Jewish not Egyptian (47:9) and has no hesitation in portraying the violent seizure of Sarai (13:11-15).

There is thus what appears to be a special sympathy for Egypt which allows *Jubilees* not to see either Hagar or Asenath as polluting. Mizraim even tries to dissuade Canaan from his unjust claims on the land which came to bear his name (10:29-33). But Egypt's special status cannot be satisfactorily explained simply on the basis that it is not Canaanite. We are left wondering. Possibly *Jubilees* made an exception for Egyptians because they practiced circumcision, but in this they were not alone (cf. Jer 9:25-26). Perhaps apparently irrelevant details such as the note in 13:12 that the building of Egyptian Tanais took place seven years after Hebron (drawn from Num 13:22) reflects some direct contact or interest. Might it explain *Jubilees*' willingness to accept sibling marriages, reflecting a level of acceptance of the practice of the Ptolemies – although the sibling marriages in *Jubilees* may simply reflect the limited options available? One is left speculating whether the author might have some connection with pro-Ptolemaic groups in Jerusalem, associated with the high priests, Onias III and IV,[681] and perhaps the Tobiads whose would-be ancestor, Naphtali, it also honours.

While *Jubilees* warns against intermarriage especially because of the sexual wrongdoing of the Gentiles, it rarely goes beyond abstract categories to describe actual behaviours. Even the sins of the Sodomites, which are described as sexual (20:5), remain vague. Assuming hearers knew the Genesis story, the brief mention of violence would have evoked the category of male rape. Perhaps the association with the Watchers, who corrupted their way, might suggest homosexual acts generally. We may, by implication, assume on the basis of the story of the Watchers, that Gentiles under their sway would also be corrupting their ways, probably through bestiality and homosexual acts (5:1-12), but this is not explicit. There is no overt condemnation of homosexual behaviour or of bestiality. *Jubilees*

---

[681] Berger, *Jubiläen*, 299 n. 2, notes but disputes the suggestion of Rönsch (*Jubiläen*, 162) concerning a possible origin of *Jubilees* in Egypt. Berger lists the arguments: the extent of material based in Egypt (*Jubilees* 39-50, except for *Jubilees* 41); the idealising of Joseph's reign; and Isaac's addressing his wife as "sister: in 27:14, 17, evidence gathered in Büchler, "Traces des idées et des coutumes hellénistiques". Rönsch does not, however, sustain this view. On pp. 524-27 he argues against an Egyptian setting, concluding: "Ebenso aussichtslos in Bezug auf Verwirklichung würde in einem anderen Lande, als in Palästina, ja in dem von allen Nationen überflutheten Aegypten geradezu thöricht und chimärisch würde das Dringen auf strengste Absonderung von den Heiden gewesen sein, welches doch durch das ganze Buch sich hindurchzieht" (525) (tr. It would also be hopeless to try to insist on a separation from the Gentiles, which runs through the book as a theme, in any other land than in Palestine, and especially stupid and absurd in Egypt which was flooded with people from all nations).

does not demonstrate concern with either. *Jubilees* shows major concern with the nations and their influence, but apparently assumes the hearers can fill in the detail about the sexual wrongdoing with which they are primarily charged. Their festivals and their feasts were known to the hearers to expose one to sexual wrongdoing, so no detail is necessary (20:16-17; 6:35-36; 1:9).

Unlike in the *Book of the Watchers*, and the *Animal Apocalypse*, *Jubilees* might include sexual wrongdoing among the exploits of the giants (20:5), although this seems unlikely. Given the occurrence of rape in the context of warfare, this is, perhaps, a surprising omission. Elsewhere *Jubilees* does speak of violation. Pharaoh takes Sarah by force, at least with the intention of adultery and rape (13:11-15). In *Jubilees* Shechem does not act alone, but his community is involved in the abduction and rape of Dinah, whose plight *Jubilees* greatly enhances by describing her as a small girl, only 12 years of age (30:2). This raises in turn a question about the author's perspectives about what he deemed important. In the case of Bilhah he not only applauds her silent collusion, but also makes nothing of the rape against her, focussing rather on the offence against Jacob (33:8-9). Similarly, *Jubilees* applies the incident with Dinah primarily to intermarriage with Gentiles (30:7-23), and mentions only briefly the issue of rape (30:5), although it is fundamental to the story.

Jubilees assumes prostitution is forbidden, at least when engaged in by a woman, whereas Judah's visiting a "prostitute" receives no specific condemnation (41:10). There is also little concern shown for Tamar, although *Jubilees* has rewritten the story to ensure she retains her virginity and that the seriousness of Judah's sin is thereby ameliorated (41:2-5, 27). The attempts at seduction by Potiphar's wife depict the will to engage in adultery (39:6). Adultery is mentioned directly in 30:8 and illustrated by Joseph's continence (39:6). Bedsuel's meddling results in the sins by Judah's sons of not engaging in intercourse with one's wife or spilling one's semen without engaging in sexual intercourse (41:2-5).

Not all of *Jubilees*' concerns relate to the danger posed by intermarriage and exposure to the sexual wrongdoing of the nations. Sometimes the focus may not be related to the issue of intermarriage. This is true of incest, in which, according to *Jubilees*, Lot colludes with his daughters (16:8), and which receives attention after both the account of Bilhah's rape (33:10-20) and the story of Judah and Tamar (41:23-28), although that situation arose through Judah's foolish marriage to a Canaanite in the first place. It is also true of prostitution, in which Tamar feigns to engage. Incest is vehemently opposed, although *Jubilees* can make an exception for Seth and Abraham, who marry their sisters, and for Jacob who marries two sisters, without any indication that such a relationship was problematic (4:11; 12:9; 28:6-10; cf. Lev 18:9, 11, 18). The prohibition of incest comes to expression a number of times in *Jubilees*' application of the prohibition of aunt–nephew marriages in Lev 18:13-14 to uncle–niece marriages, which causes the author of *Jubilees* either to rewrite or to omit material from his sources.

Jubilees also applies the principle drawn from Deut 24:1-4, that once a woman has had sexual intercourse with another man, she has become unclean for her husband and to re-engage in sexual intercourse with him would be an abomination. Thus Jacob must not engage with Bilhah (33:7) and Dinah has been defiled for others (30:2, 5). There is also the rule which Laban enunciated and which the angel declares a heavenly command, that one must always marry the eldest daughter first (28:6-7). We learn from Jacob's affirmation that not corrupting one's way means for a young man not having sexual relations with a woman before marriage or even touching one (sexually) (25:4).

Some areas remain uncertain in relation to sexual practices and sexual wrongdoing. The rule of Laban, just noted, assumes polygyny. Nothing in *Jubilees* suggests a move away from polygyny. In fact, the story of Jacob's marriage to Jacob and Leah becomes a model for managing such relationships, including where one wife is favoured. The other is then not to be discarded or neglected and might later become the key companion. The situation is more complex with those who belong to the household as slaves. *Jubilees* is not happy to have them share special intimacy with their husbands nor roles in relation to God and the promises of the covenant. Thus Hagar does not meet God (14:24; 17:2-14; cf. Gen 16:7-15; 21:8-21). But on the other hand, Bilhah exhibits what for *Jubilees* is exemplary behaviour, suffering her violation at the hands of Reuben in silent collusion and only speaking up when Jacob could have been rendered unclean (33:1-8). The enhancing of Bilhah's status recalls *Jubilees'* positive development of Leah, probably for similar reasons, with the latter to honour the line of Levi, and the former to honour the line of Naphtali.

There are also silences. We find nothing about divorce, the command to be fruitful and multiply, or concerns prohibiting sexual intercourse with a woman who is menstruating or who is pregnant. Masturbation is presumed in the case of Onan, but never addressed as an issue in itself. *Jubilees* does not mention purity issues relating to menstruation, discharges, or seminal emissions, concerns which feature in the *Temple Scroll*. There is no reference to homosexual acts or bestiality.

Some concerns are so great that they warrant the author's employment by the angel of the formula: "Now, you Moses, command…". These include the rules about marrying the eldest daughter first (28:7); about intermarriage with foreigners (30:11); about incest with one's father's wife (33:13 and 18); and incest with one's daughter-in-law or mother-in-law (41:26). To these one might add the warning about circumcision (15:28), that it not be neglected or done only partially under the influence of the nations and their espousal of nakedness. The prohibition which receives most emphasis by way of illustration and extrapolation is intermarriage associated with sexual wrongdoing, though the latter is mostly left unspecified and the author of *Jubilees* appears to assume his hearers would know to what his many allusions to sexual impurity refer.

Sexual wrongdoing, whether in the context of intermarriage with Gentiles or in the context of Israel's own life, defiles not only the person, but also the people and the temple. *Jubilees* is concerned with all Israel, not with just a select elite group of holy ones (33:2; 16:15-19, citing Exod 19:6).

One does not have the impression from *Jubilees* that sexual relations are something negative or temporary. While it operates with an understanding of evil spirits let loose in the world, this does not lead to hopelessness and denial of the possibility of goodness. *Jubilees* embraces a theism which assumes God is in control of history, but within that history there is a battle which can be won.[682] Thus the Watchers' legacy of rebellion continues to have an impact through their offspring, the evil spirits who survived the flood, but in response to Noah's plea and God's compromise with Mastema, only one tenth of the spirits are let loose, while the others remain bound. *Jubilees* differs, therefore, from what we find in *1 Enoch* 15:8-10. There, evil spirits emerge uncontrolled from the corpses of the giants. In *Jubilees* they arise from among the bound Watchers and are subject to controlled release. Furthermore, *Jubilees* portrays this in a manner much closer to the depiction of the satan of Yahweh's court in Job, to which, in *Jubilees*, Mastema has access and where he negotiates the release of the evil spirits, as, later, he negotiates the testing Abraham (17:16). The resultant dualism is thus less acute and the confidence of overcoming their wiles and of their ultimate demise, stronger.

Hope is further enhanced through the changes which God brought about in the nature of all creatures, including all human beings, after the flood. "He made a new and righteous nature for all his creatures so that they would not sin with their whole nature until eternity. Everyone will be righteous – each according to his kind – for all time" (5:12).[683] This has to be a statement of possibility rather than realisation, but it is strikingly positive and universal. It needs to be considered, however, within the context of the later statements about continuing activity of the Watchers' spirits and of the major distinction between Israel and the nations as set out in 15:31-32. There we read that all nations belong to God and that he appointed spirits to rule over them to lead them astray, except for Israel, over which he alone rules. This is decidedly pessimistic about the nations, but not about Israel whom he chose already at creation to be holy.[684] There is a twofold

---

[682] See Boccaccini, *Beyond the Essene Hypothesis*, 94-96.

[683] Boccaccini, *Beyond the Essene Hypothesis*, notes that for *Jubilees* "the cosmos is not in itself contaminated, as it was for the earlier Enoch tradition" (94).

[684] On this see VanderKam, "Anthropological Gleanings," 118-22; Boccaccini, *Beyond the Essene Hypothesis*, 93.

implication: the people have a very good chance of resisting evil and they need to do so especially because sin defiles not only themselves but the holy seed.

At the heart of the author's concerns is sexual wrongdoing. That now includes intermarriage with unholy seed, but that cannot be seen in isolation from corrupting influence, especially of a sexual kind.[685] It also includes sexual wrongdoing within Israel. *Jubilees*, however, has an understanding of creation, of creation's renewal, of limited demonic power, and of God's special relationship with Israel, which not only makes it possible to resist sexual wrongdoing, but also to lives of sexual fulfilment and intimacy in ways that reflect God's intention in creation. Unlike in the *Book of the Watchers* and the *Aramaic Levi Document*, women are neither primarily vehicles for reproduction nor necessarily sources of danger, but valued companions in partnership (which men lead). This, too, appears to be a reflection of a more positive stance towards the possibility of goodness in the author's qualified dualism.

Jubilees wrote within a context, and doubtless intended his work to have an impact, which we see that it did have, at least among those who copied the work and preserved it at Qumran. Finding the possible audience for whom the author wrote and identifying his historical setting is fraught with difficulties beyond the scope of this research to discuss in detail. Within these questions, we can, however, make some observations about where the concern with sexual issues in *Jubilees* might fit.

Many attempts to find contemporary references relate directly to the theme. Neglect or removal of the marks of circumcision and concern with nakedness, characterised as typical of the Gentiles and reflecting the mode of Hellenistic sports, connect with reports in 1 Macc 1:14-15 and 2 Macc 4:9, 12-15 about Hellenistic influence championed by "certain renegades" and Jason during the early years of the reign of Antiochus Epiphanes, prior to the Maccabean revolt in 167 B.C.E.[686] Such a background may also explain *Jubilees'* avoidance of

---

[685] See also Boccaccini, *Beyond the Essene Hypothesis*, 95. "*Jubilees* is obsessed with maintaining boundaries between the clean and the unclean, the holy and the profane" (95).

[686] See the discussion in VanderKam, *Book of Jubilees*, 2001, p. 21, 140; VanderKam, "Origins and Purposes," 19-21; VanderKam, "Genesis 1 in *Jubilees* 2," 519-21; Geza Vermes, "Genesis 1-3 in Post-biblical Hebrew and Aramaic Literature before the Mishnah," *JJS.* 43 (1992) 221-25, 222; van Ruiten, *Primaeval History Interpreted*, 88; Jackson, *Enochic Judaism*, 103; Nickelsburg, *Jewish Literature*, who finds the allusions to Hellenistic reform strong evidence favouring a date of the early 160s for the origin of *Jubilees*. He notes that Hellenistic influence continued in the Hasmonean period, as Erich S. Gruen, *Heritage and Hellenism: The Reinvention Of Jewish Tradition* (Berkeley: University of California Press, 1998), shows, 28-40, but that it was not of the kind which *Jubilees* addresses (362 n. 27). But cf. Robert Doran, "The Non-Dating of Jubilees: Jub. 34-38; 23:14-23 in Narrative Context," *JSJ* 20 (1989) 1-11, who sees the reference to nakedness in *Jub.* 3:31 "a concern for purity and maintaining proper sexual relationships in a holy

anything which might suggest confusion of gods and humans (such as the image motif in Gen 1:26-27) or inappropriate sexual relations among kinds (homosexual and bestial; as in a possible analogy between Adam's relation to the woman and his relation to animals), though this is at most an argument from silence.

More difficult is the matter of intermarriage, but not because it seems to have no contemporary relevance for the author.[687] It strains credibility to suggest that it is much like the prohibition of incest, a general warning, since it occupies too great a prominence in the writing.[688] Nor should it be considered mainly in relation to the Dinah story and its exposition, as though the chief dangers were primarily women marrying foreign men, because elsewhere in *Jubilees* the reverse is the case and *Jubilees* is clearly concerned with both, though Himmelfarb rightly notes that women might assimilate more quickly than men. Similarly, the extent of the warnings against intermarriage throughout *Jubilees* in clearly non-Samaritan contexts cautions against reading the Shechem episode as a reflection of problems of marriage with Samaritans.[689]

---

people, rather than a specific anti-gymnasion reference" (11). Other possible allusions to typically Hellenistic influence may be present in allusions to the dangers of eating with Gentiles (*symposia*?) and perhaps an intention to disparage Greek traditions, if not Hellenistic rulers, in the account of the mad slaughter among the giants (5:9), reflecting one possible earlier setting for this aspect of the myth as recounted in the *Book of the Watchers*. See also Hayward, "Sanctification," who argues that *Jubilees* deliberately avoids any suggestion that might link Jewish and Greek festivals or associate Jacob's struggle with the ideal *agon*-motif in Hellenism (161, 164).

[687] Himmelfarb, "Levi, Phinehas," 16. "*Jubilees*' condemnation of intermarriage does not indicate that it was combatting a widespread practice" (23).

[688] Cf. Himmelfarb, "Levi, Phinehas," 16.

[689] Halpern-Amaru *Empowerment*, 152-53, rejects the view that it was directed against the Samaritans, against John J. Collins, "The Epic of Theodotus and the Hellenism of the Hasmoneans," *HTR* 73 (1980) 91-104, 99, and R. J. Coggins, *Samaritans and Jews* (Oxford: Blackwell, 1975) 88-93. See also Schwarz, *Identität*, who sees this as an element of the author's concern: "Die Völker, von denen es sich abzugrenzen gilt, sind speziell die hellenistischen Seleukiden, aber auch all die derzeit um Israel herum lebenden Völker, insbesondere die Bevölkering des ehemaligen Nordreichs, die Samaritaner" (23) (tr. The peoples from whom they are to remain separate are especially the hellenistic Seleucids, but also all the people living around Israel, especially the population of the northern kingdom, the Samaritans). "Es scheint also denkbar, dass die betonte Herausstellung des Mischehenverbots im Jubiläenbuch sich einerseits gegen die assimilationsbereite Haltung bestimmter hellenistenfreundlicher Juden wendet und andererseits gezielt vor der Verbindung mit der Bevölkerung des benachbarten Samariens warnt" (111) (tr. It seems therefore thinkable that the emphasis on prohibition of mixed marriages in the *Book of Jubilees* on the one hand targets the assimilationist stance of certain Jews who were pro-

The problem is that we have no independent evidence either for the period of Hellenistic influence before the revolt or for the period immediately following, that intermarriage was an issue.[690] This does not, of course, count against such a reading, especially if other details point to that era. It would seem, however, that the dangers of intermarriage are more likely to arise during a period of relative openness rather than one where the community was on the defence and under offensive threat, such as in the time of the Maccabean revolt and the immediately ensuing years. According to Doron, "one of the emphases of the author of *Jubilees* is an insistence on group solidarity, an argument which would probably not have been necessary after 167, but more required in the preceding period".[691] Himmelfarb has raised the possibility that *Jubilees* may be addressing the assimilation likely to have taken place during the reign of John Hyrcanus (134-104), who absorbed the Idumeans into his territory and so "led neighbouring Gentiles such as the Idumeans to identify as Jews".[692] The danger can be imagined also at other times, including much earlier, especially during the period when Hellenistic influence appeared to be gaining the upper hand.[693] In favour of the

---

hellenistic and on the other warns specifically against links with the population of neighbouring Samaria).

[690] Schwarz, *Identität*, already acknowledged this lack of evidence (108), to which Himmelfarb, "Levi, Phinehas," has again drawn attention (17-23); similarly Halpern-Amaru *Empowerment*, 152-53. On earlier attempts to relate the author's concern with intermarriage to a historical context, see Halpern-Amaru, *Empowerment*, 152-53. She cites Bernhard Beer, *Das Buch der Jubiläen und sein Verhältnis zu den Midraschim* (Leipzig: Wolfgang Gerhard, 1856) 56-57; Charles, *Jubilees*, lix, lxi. See also the review in VanderKam, "Origins and Purposes," 3-24.

[691] Doran, "The Non-Dating of Jubilees," 11.

[692] Himmelfarb, "*Jubilees* and Sectarianism," 131. "This type of assimilation to Judaism, or at least to the Jewish people, helps to account for *Jubilees*' anxiety about intermarriage, a phenomenon otherwise little attested before or after the Maccabean revolt" (131). Doron Mendels, *The Land of Israel as a Political Concept in Hasmonean Literature* (Tübingen: Mohr Siebeck, 1987) also argues for the Idumean conquest as the background to *Jubilees* (80). Cf. earlier Charles, *Jubilees*, who sees the author writing in "the palmiest days of the Maccabean dominion" in the time of Hyrcanus, between 135 and 105 B.C.E., and looking forward to an alternative ruler to the Hasmonean rulers, namely a messiah from Judah's line (xiv).

[693] Endres, *Biblical Interpretation*, 236-38. Berger, *Jubiläen*, writes: "Dieses Buch ist Ausdruck eines Reformwillens und als solcher gegen eine Partei gerichtet, die sich zweifelos gleichfalls als Reformpartei verstand: gegen hellenisierende Juden" (279) (tr. The book is an expression of the will to reform and and as such directed against a party which doubtless likewise understood itself as a reforming party, namely, against hellenising Jews). The pseudonymity serves also the attempt, "auf der Basis der Autorität der Väter und des Mose noch einmal allen verschiedenen Gruppen des Volkes ein gemeinsames, historisch

earlier period is the reference to nakedness and uncircumcision which appears best explained in terms of the Hellenistic influence described in 1 and 2 Maccabees. A dating of *Jubilees* to the period of John Hyrcanus is problematic, given that 4Q216 dates from that time if not earlier[694] – unless we assume it to be the autograph or something very close to it.

The problem of intermarriage was longstanding. It was addressed in both Ezra and Nehemiah (Ezra 6:21; 9 – 10; and Neh 10:18-44)[695] and in the third century surfaced again in the marriage of the high priest's brother to the daughter of Sanballat, governor of Samaria (*A.J.* 11.306-11).[696] That crisis, Josephus reveals, reflected one dramatic instance of what was more widespread (11.312). Both the early Enoch literature and the *Aramaic Levi Document* reflect concerns about intermarriage, particularly, though not exclusively, concerning priests (see our discussion above). The pre-eminence of the line of Levi and consequent subordination of that of Judah, including in *Aramaic Levi Document* the usurpation of Judah's blessing and roles, helps explain the ambiguous image of Judah in *Jubilees*, whose future leadership is acknowledged, but whose fatal intermarriage with Bedsuel and subsequent sexual wrongdoing with Tamar foreshadow the

---

begründetes Selbstverständnis zu vermitteln. Jub ist der Versuch, die durch den Hellenismus bedrohte Identität des Volkes durch Rückgriff auf Vätertraditionen herzustellen" (298) (tr. On the basis of the authority of the patriarchs and Moses to offer a common, historically substantiated self-understanding again to all the various groups among the people. *Jubilees* is attempting to restore the identity of the people which is threatened by Hellenism through drawing on the patriarchal traditions). "Träger ist demnach eine antihellenistische priesterliche restaurative Reformgruppe, die sowohl mit den Asidäern als auch mit der kurz danach entstandenen Qumrangruppe in enger historischer Verbindung steht" (298) (tr. The bearers are accordingly an antihellenistic, priestly reform movement seeking to bring restoration, which has close historical links with both the Hasidim and the Qumran community which came into being shortly afterwards). See also Schwarz, *Identität*, 17-36; 108-11; 127-29, who notes that the problem of intermarriage fits well into the period of the Hellenizers (108). He argues that the curses in 30:15-16 seem current and relevant (109) and to relate to priests and leadership (109-10).

[694] VanderKam, *Book of Jubilees*, 2001, p. 16, 18.

[695] On the background to the prohibition of intermarriage in pre-exilic tradition forbidding covenants with the nations (which he sees echoed in 1 Macc 1:11) and in post-exilic demands of separateness, see Schwarz, *Identität*, 41-62, who points to the significance of Exod 34:10-26 and Deut 7:3 and then in the post-exilic period to Psalm 106:34-35; Ezra 6:21; 9 – 10; and Neh 10:18-44 (64-68). He notes that the separation is directly related to Israel's understanding of herself as created by God as a holy people (Lev 20:22-26 and 1 Kgs 8:53) or holy seed (Ezra 9:2; *Jub.* 2:19) (78-80).

[696] On this, see the discussion of the historical questions raised by Josephus' account and its likely basis in history, in James C. VanderKam, *From Joshua to Caiaphas: High Priests after the Exile* (Minneapolis: Fortress, 2004) 63-84.

failings of most in his line in contrast to the wisdom of Joseph. The image of a flawed Judah reflects a trend, evident already from the beginning of the third century, to subordinate the role of Judah to that of Levi, especially through the long period when the high priest was effectively both the religious and civil leader, which is clearly still the case in the decades before the Maccabean uprising.[697]

It is not difficult to imagine that the danger of illicit sexual relations with Gentiles would have been ongoing and have been likely to have arisen in all periods when there was not heightened conflict with neighbouring peoples. Endres links the danger of intermarriage with idolatry, which he sees as belonging in the context of Seleucid hellenisation: "In addition to these forbidden practices, marriage with non-Jews made it almost impossible to root out the pollution from the land, once the Gentiles sinners had married into the Jewish community".[698] Our observations about positive attitudes towards Egypt may indicate some pro-Ptolemaic sympathies.

Nickelsburg argues that absence of reflection on the crisis of 167 B.C.E., which provoked the revolt, make it likely that *Jubilees* stems from the preceding years, when there had been acts of oppression, but not to the same degree as in 167 B.C.E.[699] "The author's many prohibitions of contact with and imitation of the Gentiles suit a document stemming from this period. Among the practices interdicted are nudity and uncircumcision (3:31; 15:33-34); observance of 'the feasts of the Gentiles,' that is, the lunar calendar (6:35); intermarriage (20:4; 22:20; 25:1; 27:10; 30:1-15); idolatry (20:7-9; 22:16-18); and consuming blood (6:12-14; 7:30; 21:6)".[700]

On the other hand, some features indicate authorship after the Maccabean crisis. *Jubilees*' rule preventing war on the sabbath (50:12) may be a reaction against the compromise to which Judas and some Hasidim were driven (1 Macc

---

[697] See VanderKam, *From Joshua to Caiaphas*, who writes that already by the end of the Persian period "the high priest had attained an exalted status" and "was head of the cultic, political, and even military affairs of the nations" (84). For the early Hellenistic period up to the revolt, during which for the most part the high priest appears to have been the chief instance of power, see his discussion, 112-239.

[698] Endres, *Biblical Interpretation*, 44. See also the discussion in VanderKam, "Origins and Purposes," 20-22.

[699] Nickelsburg, *Jewish Literature*, 73. See also George W. E. Nickelsburg, "The Bible Rewritten and Expanded," in *Jewish Writings of the Second Temple Period: Apocrypha, Pseudepigrapha, Qumran Sectarian Writings, Philo, Josephus* (ed. Michael E. Stone; CRINT 2: The Literature of the Jewish People in the Period of the Second Temple and the Talmud; Assen, Netherlands: Van Gorcum; Philadelphia: Fortress, 1984) 89-156, 102-103; and Doran, "The Non-Dating of *Jubilees*," who writes: "One of the emphases of the author of *Jubilees* is an insistence on group solidarity, an argument which would probably not have been necessary after 167, but more required in the preceding period" (11).

[700] Nickelsburg, *Jewish Literature*, 73. See also Schwarz, *Identität*, 102-106.

2:32, 39-41).[701] VanderKam detects possible references to Judas' campaign in Edom in *Jubilees*' account of the wars against the Amorites (34:2-9) and Edom (37:1 – 38:14),[702] though this is far from conclusive.[703] He also points to the conflict over calendar, which underlies *Jubilees*, as reflecting the imposition of a lunar calendar by Antiochus (Dan 7:25).[704] On the calendar, however, the allusion in 1:14 to erring with regard to the calendar may not suggest a crisis evoked by external imposition through Antiochus, but internal differences arising from those who will, as it puts it, "forget all my law, all my commandments, and all my verdicts". Schwarz also draws attention to Abraham's advice to Isaac to be quiet for fear of being killed (12:7), as possibly reflecting the dangers of that crisis.[705]

The dating is complicated by the need to determine possible dependence on Enochic writings, clearly presupposed in 4:17-19. References to Enoch's teaching about heavenly bodies probably reflects knowledge of the *Book of the Luminaries*. VanderKam points to *Jubilees*' apparent dependence both on the *Epistle of Enoch* and on the *Book of Dream Visions*, which clearly assumes the revolt,[706] which means Jubilees must have been composed after 164-163 B.C.E. This is not, however, beyond dispute. Van Ruiten, for instance, argues that the parallels

---

[701] Berger, *Jubiläen*, 299. Cf. Doering, "Concept of the Sabbath," who doubts that the prohibition of war on the sabbath in *Jub.* 50:8 alludes to the decision reported in 1 Macc 2:40-41, because it is "formulated so lapidarily and non-polemically" and for similar reasons doubts that the prohibition of sexual intercourse on the sabbath has polemical overtones against the opposite trend evident in some later rabbinic traditions (*b. B. Qam.* 82a; *y. Meg.* 4.1 [75a]; *m. Ned.* 3.10; 8.6) (201). The strict prohibitions in 2:29 and 50:8 belong to traditions older than *Jubilees*, which, however, is intent on addressing proper observance against Hellenistic inroads which threatened Israel's identity (202). See also his discussion and refutation of recent attempts to identify *Jub.* 50:6-13 as a later addition to *Jubilees* 50, in Lutz Doering, "*Jub* 50:6-13 als Schlussabschnitt des *Jubiläenbuchs* – Nachtrag aus Qumran oder ursprünglicher Bestandteil des Werks?" *RevQ* 20 (2002) 359-87.

[702] VanderKam, *Textual and Historical Studies*, 214-54.

[703] See the discussion in Doran, "The Non-Dating of *Jubilees*," and Nickelsburg, *Jewish Literature*, 73. Doran argues that "Jacob does in Jub 34:2-9 what Abraham did in Genesis 14 and Jub 13:22-29. This narrative similarity marks Jacob as the true heir of Abraham, the son who follows in Abraham's footsteps" (4). Accordingly, it need have nothing to do with the Maccabean wars. He similarly challenges Berger's claim that 46:6-11 reflects the death of Ptolemy VI in 145 B.C.E. (4); cf. Berger, *Jubiläen*, 10. *Jubilees* 35 – 38:14 serve not as a reflection on Maccabean wars, but to highlight the contrast between family disunity and reconciliation, modelled, respectively by Jacob and Esau and by Joseph and his brothers (5-7). Similarly, he claims, 23:16-21 is "designed to emphasize general social collapse, not the parties and politics of the Maccabean period" (10).

[704] VanderKam, "Origins and Purposes," 22.

[705] Schwarz, *Identität*, 107.

[706] VanderKam, *Book of Jubilees*, 2001, p. 21; VanderKam, "Enoch Traditions".

adduced may indicate not dependence, but a common milieu and interest in interpreting the *Watcher* myth.[707] He notes lack of textual evidence for dependence of the kind evident in *Jubilees'* use of exact wording of Genesis. Similarly, Knibb argues that the statements in *Jub.* 4.16-25 "allude to a wider cycle of traditions concerning Enoch than those contained within 1 Enoch and cannot entirely be correlated with the book".[708] Even if one supposes, with VanderKam, dependence on the *Book of Dream Visions*, the author may have been dependent on a version not yet updated to take the Maccabean uprising into account.[709]

The author may be writing in the aftermath of the revolt, or before, but it is least likely that he writes in the midst of it. It lacks the intensity of the *Animal Apocalypse* and Daniel. As John Collins observes: "*Jubilees* is not related to a historical crisis in as obvious a manner as the Animal Apocalypse or Daniel. Yet it too is a product of the Maccabean era".[710] He believes that

> the "children" who begin to study the laws and rise up and drive out their adversaries can be plausibly identified with the Hasidim or a wing of that party, and the prohibitions against nudity, marriage with gentiles, and fighting on the Sabbath make good sense in that context.[711]

Boccaccini, who also sees the author writing in the aftermath of the revolt, argues that *Jubilees* is the product of a Jew of the Enochic tradition recognizing and incorporating Zadokite scripture within an Enochic framework by including the Mosaic law among heavenly tablets, in an attempt to provide a new foundation for a holy Israel.[712] "In the aftermath of the Maccabean revolt, the Enochians

---

[707] So van Ruiten, "Literary Dependency," 92-93.

[708] Knibb, "Which Parts of *1 Enoch* Were Known to *Jubilees*?", 255.

[709] On the complex history of the *Book of Dream Visions*, see Nickelsburg, *1 Enoch 1*, 360-61; but see also Tiller, *Animal Apocalypse*, 70-79, who would still put the original work near 165 and after Judas' initial victories over Apollonius and Seron (166 B.C.E.), represented by 90.12., 'and they wanted to remove its horn but were unable'" (78).

[710] Collins, *Apocalyptic Imagination*, 83.

[711] Collins, *Apocalyptic Imagination*, 83. "The crisis perceived in *Jubilees*, however, is not the political crisis or persecution, which dominates the book of Daniel. It is rather the crisis of piety, occasioned by the neglect of the solar calendar and disregard for the laws" (84). Berger, *Jubiläen*, sees 23:19-26 as a self portrayal of young, poor, lowly, beggars and keepers of the law (299). Nickelsburg, *Jewish Literature*, writes: "The Book of Jubilees issued from an unnamed reformist group related to those responsible for the composition of 1 Enoch 72-82, 85-90, and 93:1-10 + 91:11-17" (74).

[712] Boccaccini, *Beyond the Essene Hypothesis*, 86-98. "The genius of Jubilees is to make Moses part of the same tradition" (89). "The heavenly tablets became the center of a complex history of revelation involving several revealers (Enoch, Noah, Abraham, Jacob,

gained momentum, confidence, perhaps even popularity, to such an extent that
they attempted to speak as the most authentic voice of the entire people of
Israel".[713] Far from being an alienated group, "the audience of *Jubilees* is evidently
to be found among the nation as a whole, not among an embattled sectarian
community".[714] He then sees this as the context for the new emphasis on
forbidding intermarriage and recognizes the centrality of these concerns.[715]

Jubilees may, then reflect concerns of a teacher over a period of time,
including the pre-Maccabean days, but also the first years of the revolt.[716] As
VanderKam observes of the author, "the points he stresses and the themes of the
book seem directed precisely against the assimilation the 'renegades' of 1
Maccabees envisaged and their theory about a golden age of unity with the
nations".[717] He refers to 1 Macc 1:11-13 and possibly related ideas in Jer
44:17-18.[718] This explains "the impassioned angelic testimonies about the
importance of circumcision and sexual purity, including endogamy".[719] If *Jubilees*,
at least in its final form, follows the revolt and looks to a hopeful future, it must be
located in a rather narrow window of time between the events of Antiochus'
decree and the restoration of the temple, on the one hand, which it does not need to
relate, and the emergence of serious dissatisfaction with the Hasmonean leaders, of
which we hear nothing.[720] At most one might see the idealisation of Joseph as a
model being held before Judas or perhaps Jonathan, but otherwise we hear no hints
of dissent.

Issues of nakedness and circumcision better reflect the earlier period, but
might continue to be current in a document warning against the dangers of the
Gentile world. Intermarriage also fits better the period before the revolt, but may
have had continued relevance after the revolt, though one would imagine, less so,
as an issue facing the priesthood, than before. The issue of demarcation of holy

---

Moses)" (89). "The centrality and uniqueness of the Zadokite torah are lost in its being only
one document in a larger written tradition, including Enochic documents and *Jubilees*" (90).

[713] Boccaccini, *Beyond the Essene Hypothesis*, 98.

[714] Boccaccini, *Beyond the Essene Hypothesis*, 97.

[715] Boccaccini, *Beyond the Essene Hypothesis*, 95.

[716] This is already assumed by Charles, *Jubilees*, who, while dating the book to the
reign of Hyrcanus, locates the issue of intermarriage to 200-160 B.C.E. "when the
destructive tendencies of Hellenism on Jewish character and religion had come to a head"
(lxi) and argues similarly for the references to issues of nakedness, circumcision, and the
sabbath (lx-lxi).

[717] VanderKam, *Book of Jubilees*, 2001, p. 140.

[718] On this see Elias Bickerman, *The God of the Maccabees: Studies on the Meaning
and origin of the Maccabean Revolt* (Leiden: Brill, 1979) 27.

[719] VanderKam, *Book of Jubilees*, 2001, p. 140.

[720] VanderKam, *Book of Jubilees*, 2001, estimates between 160 and 150 B.C.E. (21).

Israel from unholy nations might belong to the nation building or nation rebuilding in the wake of the restored temple, but would equally fit the earlier period. That call to holiness would have expressed itself in stern warnings against sexual wrongdoing (such as had brought God's punishment in the immediate past), both in relation to behaviour within Israel, but especially in relation to contamination and evil moral influence from Gentiles.

Jub. 23:23 can easily be read as a reference to God's judgement at the hands of Antiochus:

> He will arouse against them the sinful nations who will have no mercy or kindness for them and who will show partiality to no one, whether old, young, or anyone at all, because they are evil and strong so that they are more evil than all mankind. They will cause chaos in Israel and sin against Jacob. Much blood will be shed on the earth, and there will be no one who gathers up (corpses) or who buries (them).

The prediction continues with reference to those who will "begin to study the laws, to seek out the commands, and to return to the right way", surely a reference to the author and his associates and reflecting the optimism found earlier in 1:15-16 and 23-24. If 23:23 alludes to the crisis, then we find ourselves beyond it in a time of renewal. Thus the call in *Jubilees* is far from a desperate warning. In *Jubilees*, it is marked by an optimism about the future for Israel as a whole, especially under the wise instruction of the author and his group. This positive image expresses itself in ideals of family in which sexual intimacy between husband and wife is valued for its own sake. But it stands in a context in which warding off the influence of the nations remains a dominant concern, particularly, the dangers of intermarriage (and of existing mixed marriages) and of associated sexual wrongdoing. This can hardly be a relic from earlier worries, given its prominence in *Jubilees*, and so is either to be explained as a matter which must have concerned the author in the late 160s or the 150s B.C.E., or to be taken as further ground for arguing that *Jubilees* seems to fit more readily into the early 160s B.C.E. Then passages such as 23:23 might refer to previous experiences.

Whatever the correct dating, *Jubilees* clearly sees issues of sexuality as of major importance, both negatively, as presenting a present danger through intermarriage with the nations, and positively, through its remarkably affirmative portrayal of sexual intimacy and its value in marital relations.

Concluding Observations

The purpose of these concluding comments is not to repeat the conclusions to parts one to three, but to identify some of the main trends. They need to be read in association with those more detailed conclusions.

It is striking that, while the early Enoch literature has at its core an overtly sexual act, the Watchers' intercourse with women, there is little evidence that the writers saw sexual wrongdoing as a major theme to be addressed. What the hearers and authors of the *Book of the Watchers* would have seen as a shocking and abominable act, somewhat in contrast to the rather neutral sounding account of Genesis, set off a sequence of events which helped them explain their contemporary world. The ills of that world appear, then, as violence and bloodshed on a global scale, represented by the giants. One might have expected rape to feature among their monstrous deeds, but this is not the case. Not even the roles of the evil spirits, who emerge from their corpses, seem to have a sexual theme. In other words, the appalling act of sexual wrongdoing committed by the Watchers serves to explain a wide range of evils which followed; but it is not there to serve as an example of major contemporary concerns with sexuality. Sexual wrongdoing probably belonged within the general concern about impurity and sin, which Michael would remove at some time in the future, but only as one aspect of sin among others. This remains the case, arguably, also in the *Animal Apocalypse*, the *Epistle of Enoch* and the *Book of Noah*. While the strength of disapproval which makes the Watchers' deed so appalling and so momentous in its impact was not matched by a continuing concern with matters sexual, that disapproval, in itself, already reflects some engagement with sexual themes and values. Nevertheless the account of the deed functions aetiologically, not as a paradigm of present concerns about sexual wrongdoing.

This general observation, however, needs some qualification. As it stands, the myth of the angels' sexual wrongdoing is juxtaposed to a myth of angelic instruction, which through Asael's initiative partly precedes it and which focuses particularly on women. As a consequence they acquire jewellery and cosmetics, which enhance their powers of seduction. From the others they acquire knowledge of sorcery, potions and spells, which do the same. While the Watchers have long since been bound and the giants have selfdestructed, women remain. The implication in the *Book of the Watchers* is that their knowledge and their enhanced seductive power continue to pose a danger. In that sense, they shared part of the blame for the Watchers' sexual wrongdoing in the first place, and they pose a danger in the present. It is not too speculative to link this to a concern about appropriate marriage partners and to see in it an allusion to the dangers, above all, of foreign women, who were the mostly likely to be seen as bearers of the forbidden sorcery.

The possible concern with intermarriage is thus a reasonable deduction, but is nowhere stated explicitly, at least, in the *Book of the Watchers*. It does make an appearance in the *Animal Apocalypse* in two places, though their interpretation is debated, and, in any case, they are hardly evidence that it was a central concern for that author. The *Book of the Watchers* may also imply concern with intermarriage, especially of priests, in the way, especially in 12 – 16, it depicts the Watchers as abandoning their heavenly sanctuary and defiling themselves with the women, a motif already present, to some degree, in 6 – 11. Then one might speculate that the author is, indeed, addressing a contemporary concern, namely, with the marriage of priests, probably to foreign women, especially if we combine it with the observations about sorcery. Such conclusions, reached by deduction, are possible, but they are nowhere stated directly as the author's concerns, nor, apart from the two disputed references in the *Animal Apocalypse*, do they feature in the early material which the myth inspired. This is also true of the expressions of concern with intermarriage in the *Aramaic Levi Document* and in *Jubilees*, where the Watchers' deed functions once, early on, as an example, but not with specific application to priests, and then falls out of view in the many other exhortations about sexual wrongdoing and intermarriage which appear in the remainder of the work.

In principle, the notion that they may be there by analogy is supported by the fact that the author appears to use the myth of the giants as an analogy. They are past history, but they symbolically reflect present realities for the author, namely, war and bloodshed and the suffering they bring. The application of the Watchers' sexual wrongdoing to putative concerns of the author with mixed marriages, especially of priests, and then the attempts to find a setting for these in known events of history, such as marriage with Samaritans or mixed marriages with the Tobiads, remain at the level of speculation, but should not be ruled out. Concern with mixed marriages had a long history and is likely to have been relevant at a number of points within the period in which the *Book of the Watchers* might have been composed. The fact remains, however, that, apart from the two possible allusions in the *Animal Apocalypse*, such concerns do not come directly to expression in the Enoch literature considered, let alone as a major concern, such as one might have expected given the foundational myth.

Aside from putative concerns, other areas pertaining to sexuality appear in the narrative as unproblematic. Enoch marries and has children, Lamech, similarly. The vision of the future, in *1 Enoch* 10, envisages abundant life, including the bearing of many children. Nothing suggests a future constrained by its holiness to restrict sexual intimacy or sexual expression, such as we find later, for instance, as a possibility in *Jubilees*. There is no suggestion of an immortality that would render sexual intercourse superfluous, such as the author of *1 Enoch* 15 supposes for the angels in the context of their rebuke. That rebuke, however, reflects a very narrow understanding of sexual intercourse, which Luke will later espouse (20:34-36), which defines it in terms only of procreation and, accordingly, depicts women as superfluous beyond the reproductive role. But the comments are incidental, though still telling, and they cohere with the rather negative portrait of women and their wiles elsewhere in the *Book of the Watchers*, which even depicts the women of the Watchers as sirens.

The *Aramaic Levi Document* does not appear to be inspired by the myth of the Watchers. Its comments about sexual wrongdoing are both general, in Levi's prayer, and specific, in Isaac's instruction, and appear to draw inspiration also from Levi's exploits against the people of Shechem in response to the rape of Dinah. The fragmentary text appears to implicate Dinah, herself, and, at least, in that sense, matches the blaming of women in the *Book of the Watchers*. There is a high level of probability that this document addresses intermarriage with foreigners directly and in doing so applies what were originally instructions about priests and high priests concerning prostitutes, to marriage with any forbidden woman. Certainly this becomes an explicit instruction to Levi (and one would assume, thereby, his successors, priests, and not only high priests). The document portrays Levi not only as model policeman and executor of God's judgement against those who ignore such instruction (without any hint of the disapproval which Genesis records concerning his acts), but also as the model Israelite and priest who marries appropriately and ensures his sons and grandsons do the same. This amounts also to an affirmation of marriage as unproblematic, even to the extent of including a report of an aunt-nephew marriage without any sign of this being problematic as a contravention of Leviticus.

Jubilees takes up proportionately the most space in this book because issues pertaining to sexuality assume very great significance in the writing. The analysis of the frequent strings of words depicting sin and wrongdoing showed that their associations were predominantly with sexual wrongdoing. This matches emphases within its structure and its rhetoric. Such sexual wrongdoing covered a range of concerns, including naked exposure (probably targeting Hellenistic sports, which will also account for the criticism of those who abandon circumcision), rape, adultery, incest, prostitution, but, above all, marriage to foreigners by men or women and including by priests and high priests. Its exposition of the latter matches *Aramaic Levi Document*, with which it shares much in common, in the exposition of the Dinah story, although with significant differences, not least, in portraying Dinah as an innocent victim and not as complicit. Thus Levi is also the hero for *Jubilees*, which, like the *Aramaic Levi Document*, passes over other claims to priestly lineage such as Aaron and Zadok, in silence. *Jubilees* also applies the instructions in Leviticus about priests and their daughters and about prostitution, to all Israel and to illicit marriages with all forbidden women, taking the application still further by equating intermarriage with giving one's children to Molech.

Jubilees, however, is more strongly interested in the whole people, rather than the priesthood, and sees all the people as holy and priestly, developing the thought of Exod 19:6. It has a highly developed sense of Israel as God's holy creation, different from the nations as the sabbath is different from the other days. At one level, warnings about intermarriage appear to reflect concern with national or racial purity. At another, they seem targeted, above all, towards the Canaanites, to the extent that some have wondered if they, alone, are the concern. Taken together, the various warnings clearly exhibit a wider concern. While Egyptians come off lightly, all nations expose Israel to danger and pollution, and intermarriage is about much more than racial purity. When *Jubilees* occasionally goes beyond prohibition to identify the particular dangers to which intermarriage to foreigners exposes the Israelite and Israel, it highlights in particular the sexual wrongdoing and perversions of the nations, much more so than, for instance, concerns with idolatry, as in Ezra, or with sorcery, as, apparently, in the *Book of the Watchers*. Such wrongdoing defiles not only the individual, but the people as a whole, and the temple.

Jubilees knows and exploits the myth of the Watchers' sexual wrongdoing, although it knows it in a form which differs in some respects from the account in the *Book of the Watchers*. This is particularly so in the fact that the Watchers are portrayed as fulfilling a divine commission on earth before they engaged with the women. *Jubilees* does not portray the women as complicit. It shares with the earlier myth the account of the giants and their deeds, and, similarly, portrays this in terms of violence and bloodshed without any allusion to sexual wrongdoing such as rape. Its account of the evil spirits, however, is much modified. They do not emerge as wild spirits from the giants' corpses, but from among the Watchers, and then only in a kind of controlled release, where just one tenth is allowed to plague humanity, and to do so, as it were, on the basis of a contract negotiated by their leader, Mastema, with Yahweh. This reflects a different stream of demonology and evil forces, which has its roots elsewhere than in the myth, namely in Job (and Zechariah).

As spirits from the Watchers, these beings receive a similarly narrow role definition to the one we find in *1 Enoch* 15:11, virtually as the enspirited viruses, bacteria and triggers of other ills, of the ancient world, against which Noah is taught medical antidotes. As there, nothing suggests a role in relation to *Jubilees'* major theme of sexual wrongdoing. *Jubilees'* concerns are not generated primarily by the myth or its application. It does, however, make connections with the myth, including allusion to the angels' misdeed as one among many examples of the sexual wrongdoing against which it warns, and uses the destruction of the giants and the binding of the Watchers as an example to warn of the severity of God's judgement. Its world is populated by such forces, often summarised in the figure, Satan. The world free of this Satan will also be free of sexual impurity. The primary responsibility, however, in the fight against sexual wrongdoing, according to *Jubilees*, lies not with evil spirits, but with human beings, the people of Israel, a fact reflected repeatedly in the major discourses of the patriarchs and matriarchs. In this it stands with the *Epistle of Enoch*, which, despite belonging to the Enoch corpus, makes little of the Watcher myth, instead declaring: "Lawlessness was not sent upon the earth; but men created it by themselves, and those who do it will come to a great curse" (98:4).

One of the remarkable features of *Jubilees* is that it concerns itself not only with sexual wrongdoing, but also with portraying sexual relations in the right context in a very positive light. This goes far beyond the incidental and unproblematic nature of appropriate marriage, such as is reflected in *Aramaic Levi Document* and the Enochic literature we have considered, and certainly way beyond the notion in the latter that sexual relations are primarily for the purpose of procreation, without which both sexual relations and women would be redundant. Women are not blamed. Dinah was not complicit. Women are significant partners, both sexually beyond procreation and in many other ways.

We find this much more positive attitude especially in the creation narrative. There, the man observes male and female among the animals, and longs for similar companionship, himself. This gives a very positive value to sexual intimacy, where most, even today, would see sexual relations in the animal kingdom as an analogy only to be used only disparagingly. The narrative then proceeds to show the man's wish reaching fulfilment in the creation of the woman and in his going to her and engaging in a first act of sexual intercourse. This is not sexual intercourse for procreation. That happens much later, after they had entered and then left the garden. Rather it is a central aspect of an intimate relationship between the first man and the first woman which the author enhances by emphasising common activity in the garden and by deleting elements of contention and blaming, present in the Genesis account. Even the judgement on their disobedience seems reduced to the woman's experience of pain in childbearing and any suggestion that somehow sexual desire itself is a curse is absent from the text.

The positive emphasis on marriage and marital intimacy, including sexual intimacy, continues in the accounts of the patriarchs and their wives. The women, while still within a patriarchal marriage system, emerge as significant bearers of the divine promise in a way that goes far beyond Genesis. Abraham's chief ally in this role is Rebecca, who far outshines her husband, even more than in Genesis. Within this much more positive portrait of the women is a matching positive value given to women's sexual attractiveness (both Rachel's and Leah's – it is not something to be feared) and to sexual relations. There, particularly in the account of Jacob and his wives and concubines, a distinction is drawn between continuing sexual intimacy, on the one hand, and sexual intercourse for procreation, on the other, in the way Jacob relates to each and does justice to each. It is Jubilees' ideal of how polygamy should work.

Such positive relations are set in contrast, therefore, to the forbidden marriages, which include those with Gentiles, but also those which transgress the laws of incest. With regard to the latter, *Jubilees*, in contrast to the *Aramaic Levi Document*, not only forbids marriages to nephews, but, equally, marriage to nieces, and reworks genealogies to make them conform, while retaining marriage to sisters where all other options would mean something worse. Within the right kind of marriage relationship *Jubilees* sees sexual relations as a valued expression of intimacy and companionship.

At the same time, we find in *Jubilees* some trends which entail complications for this positive approach. Sexual intercourse is forbidden on the sabbath. It is also forbidden in the holy place and so does not take place between Adam and Eve in the garden of Eden, which *Jubilees* describes as a temple, indeed as the holiest of holy places. There they keep busy, caring for the garden, apparently thus enabling them to live without continuing sexual engagement, which began outside the garden. This raises the question of the future of sexual relations in the author's eschatology. One of its images pictures human beings as becoming forever like children. Another imagines a future where Israel joins God's holy ones. Though it is never drawn, one implication of this line of thought is that the future will entail a return to innocence in a context where sexual relations play no role and have no place. Was this the kind of innocence which the sexually experienced Adam and Eve enjoyed in the garden before their sin and the awareness which brought shame? Unfortunately, the author offers no more than threads, without indicating that this is the fabric of expectation which they would have woven.

These works stand beside others which belong to their time and place and continue their influence in subsequent generations. The history of their ideas, the versions of their traditions, the interaction with their emphases and the ignorance of their concerns, are part of a larger picture. Not all in their time were worried about intermarriage with Gentiles. Not all saw sexual relations as something to be treasured. Some will apparently weave threads into a scheme which adds constraint to the expression of sexuality, both in this life and in the world to come. Attitudes towards sexuality continue to be a feature of some writings, while they disappear or are apparently invisible or irrelevant in others. The investigation of the theme in the Early Enoch Literature, the *Aramaic Levi Document* and *Jubilees* is the beginning of a larger task to explore this central aspect of our common humanity in other works of the period.

Bibliography

Albeck, C. *Das Buch der Jubiläen und die Halacha* (Berlin: Scholem, 1930)

Anderson, Gary. "Celibacy or Consummation in the Garden: Reflections on Early Jewish and Christian Interpretations of the Garden of Eden," *HTR* 82 (1989) 121-48

Anderson, Jeff S. "Denouncement Speech in Jubilees and Other Enochic Literature," in *Enoch and Qumran Origins: New Light on a Forgotten Connection* (ed. Gabriele Boccaccini; Grand Rapids: Eerdmans, 2005) 132-36

Argall, Randal A. *1 Enoch and Sirach: A Comparative Literary and Conceptual Analysis of the Themes of Revelation, Creation, and Judgement* (EJL 8; Atlanta: Scholars Press, 1995)

Argall, Randal A. "Competing Wisdoms: 1 Enoch and Sirach," in *The Origins of Enochic Judaism: Proceedings of the First Enoch Seminar, University of Michigan, Sesto Fiorentino, Italy, June 19-23, 2001* (ed. G. Boccaccini; *Henoch* 24; Torino: Silvio Zamorani Editore, 2002) 169-78

Baumgarten, Joseph M. "The Qumran Sabbath Shirot and Rabbinic Merkabah Traditions," *RevQ* 15 (1988) 212-23

Baumgarten, Joseph M. "Purification after Childbirth and the Sacred Garden in 4Q265 and Jubilees," in *New Qumran Texts and Studies* (Leiden: Brill, 1994) 3-10

Baumgarten, Joseph M. "Some 'Qumranic' Observations on the Aramaic Levi Document," in *Sefer Moshe: The Moshe Weinfeld Jubilee Volume* (ed. C. Cohen, A. Hurvitz and S. M. Paul; Winona Lake: Eisenbrauns, 2003) 393-401

Bedenbender, Andreas. *Der Gott der Welt tritt auf den Sinai: Entstehung, Entwicklung, und Funktionsweise der Frühjüdischen Apokalyptik* (ANTZ 8; Berlin: Institut Kirche und Judentum, 2000)

Bedenbender, Andreas. "Traces of Enochic Judaism within the Hebrew Bible," in *The Origins of Enochic Judaism: Proceedings of the First Enoch Seminar,*

University of Michigan, Sesto Fiorentino, Italy, June 19-23, 2001 (ed. G. Boccaccini; *Henoch* 24; Torino: Silvio Zamorani Editore, 2002) 39-48

Bedenbender, Andreas. "Unter Engeln und Riesen: Anmerkungen zur Stellung von Daniel, Henoch und Noah in einigen frühjüdischen Schriften," *Texte & Kontexte* 26 (2003) 35-48

Bedenbender, Andreas. "The Enochic Circles, the Hasidim, and the Qumran Community," in *Enoch and Qumran Origins: New Light on a Forgotten Connection* (ed. Gabriele Boccaccini; Grand Rapids: Eerdmans, 2005) 200-203

Beer, Bernhard. *Das Buch der Jubiläen und sein Verhältnis zu den Midraschim* (Leipzig: Wolfgang Gerhard, 1856)

Berger, Klaus. *Das Buch der Jubiläen* (JSHRZ II.3; Gütersloh: Gerd Mohn, 1981)

Bernstein, Moshe J. "'Walking in the Festivals of the Gentiles': 4QHosea a 2.15-17 and Jubilees 6.34-38," *JSP* 9 (1991) 21-34

Bernstein, Moshe J. "From the Watchers to the Flood: Story and Exegesis in the Early Columns of the *Genesis Apocryphon*," in *Reworking the Bible: Apocryphal and Related Texts at Qumran: Proceedings of a Joint Symposium by the Orion Center for the Study of the Dead Sea Scrolls and Associated Literature and the Hebrew University Institute for Advanced Studies Research Group on Qumran, 15-17 January, 2002* (ed. Esther G. Chazon, Devorah Dimant and Ruth A. Clements; STDJ 58; Leiden: Brill, 2005) 39-63

Beyer, Klaus. *Die aramäischen Texte vom Toten Meer samt den Inschriften aus Palästina, dem Testament Levis aus der Kairoer Genisa, der Fastenrolle und den alten talmudischen Zitaten: Ergänzungsband* (Göttingen: Vandenhoeck & Ruprecht, 1984)

Bhayro, Siam. *The Shemihazah and Asael Narrative of 1 Enoch 6-11: Introduction, Text, Translation and Commentary with Reference to Ancient Near Eastern and Biblical Antecedents* (AOAT 322; Münster: Ugarit, 2005)

Bickerman, Elias. *The God of the Maccabees: Studies on the Meaning and Origin of the Maccabean Revolt* (Leiden: Brill, 1979)

Blau, L. *Das altjüdische Zauberwesen* (Strasburg: Trübner, 1898)

Boccaccini, Gabriele. *Beyond the Essene Hypothesis: The Parting of the Ways between Qumran and Enochic Judaism* (Grand Rapids: Eerdmans, 1998)

Boccaccini, Gabriele. *Roots of Rabbinic Judaism: An Intellectual History, from Ezekiel to Daniel* (Grand Rapids: Eerdmans, 2002)

Boccaccini, Gabriele. "Enoch, Qumran and the Essenes: The Rediscovery of a Forgotten Connection," in *George W.E. Nickelsburg in Perspective: An Ongoing Dialogue of Learning* (2 vols; ed. Jacob Neusner and Alan J. Avery-Peck; JSJSup 80; Leiden: Brill, 2003) 1. 123-32

Bremmer, Jan K. "Remember the Titans!" in *The Fall of the Angels* (ed. Christoph Auffarth and Loren T. Stuckenbruck; Themes in Biblical Narrative 6; Leiden: Brill, 2004) 35-61

Brock, Sebastian P. "Abraham and the Ravens: A Syriac Counterpart to *Jubilees* 11-12 and its Implications," *JSJ* 9 (1978) 139-52

Brooke, George J. "Exegetical Strategies in Jubilees 1-2: New Light from 4QJubilees[a]," in *Studies in the Book of Jubilees* (ed. Matthias Albani, Jörg Frey, and Armin Lange; TSAJ 65; Tübingen: Mohr Siebeck, 1997) 39-57

Büchler, Adolphe. "Traces des idées et des coutumes hellénistiques dans le Livre des Jubilés," *REJ* 89 (1930) 321-48

Büchler, Adolphe. "Family Purity and Family Impurity in Jerusalem before the Year 70," in *Studies in Jewish History: The Adolph Büchler Memorial Volume* (ed. I. Brodie and J. Rabinowitz; London: Oxford University Press, 1956) 64-98

Carmichael, Calum M. "The Story of Joseph and the *Book of Jubilees*," in *The Dead Sea Scrolls in Their Historical Context* (ed. Timothy H. Lim et al.; Edinburgh: T&T Clark, 2000) 143-58

Charles, Robert H. *The Book of Jubilees or the Little Genesis: Translated from the Editor's Ethiopic Text* (London: A&C Black, 1902)

Charlesworth, James H. "A Rare Consensus Among Enoch Specialists: The Date of the Earliest Enoch Books," in *The Origins of Enochic Judaism: Proceedings of the First Enoch Seminar, University of Michigan, Sesto Fiorentino, Italy, June 19-23, 2001* (ed. G. Boccaccini; *Henoch* 24; Torino: Silvio Zamorani Editore, 2002) 225-34

Coggins, R. J. *Samaritans and Jews* (Oxford: Blackwell, 1975)

Collins, John J. "The Epic of Theodotus and the Hellenism of the Hasmoneans," *HTR* 73 (1980) 91-104

Collins, John J. "The Apocalyptic Technique: Setting and Function in the Book of Watchers," *CBQ* 44 (1982) 91-111

Collins, John J. *The Apocalyptic Imagination: An Introduction to Jewish Apocalyptic Literature* (2d ed.; Grand Rapids: Eerdmans, 1998)

Collins, John J. "Pseudepigraphy and Group Formation in Second Temple Judaism," in *Pseudepigraphic Perspectives: The Apocrypha and Pseudepigrapha in Light of the Dead Sea Scrolls: Proceedings of the [Second] International Symposium of the Orion Center for the Study of the Dead Sea Scrolls and Associated Literature, 12-14 January 1997* (ed. Esther G. Chazon and Michael E. Stone; STDJ 31; Leiden: Brill, 1999) 43-58

Collins, John J. "Ethos and Identity in Jewish Apocalyptic Literature," in *Ethos und Identität: Einheit und Vielfalt des Judentums in hellenistisch-römischer Zeit* (ed. Matthias Konradt and Ulrike Steinert; Paderborn: Schöningh, 2002) 51-65

Collins, John J. "Theology and Identity in the Early Enoch Literature," in *The Origins of Enochic Judaism: Proceedings of the First Enoch Seminar, University of Michigan, Sesto Fiorentino, Italy, June 19-23, 2001* (ed. G. Boccaccini; *Henoch* 24; Torino: Silvio Zamorani Editore, 2002) 57-62

Collins, John J. "Before the Fall: The Earliest Interpretations of Adam and Eve," in *The Idea of Biblical Interpretation: Essays in Honor of James L. Kugel* (ed. Hindy Najman and Judith H. Newman; JSJSup 83; Leiden: Brill, 2004) 293-308

Crawford, Cory D. "On the Exegetical Function of the Abraham/Ravens Tradition in Jubilees 11," *HTR* 97 (2004) 91-97

Dacy, Marianne. "Paradise Lost: the Fallen Angels in the Book of Enoch," *Australian Journal of Jewish Studies* 17 (2003) 51-65

Davenport, G. L. *The Eschatology of the Book of Jubilees* (SPB 20; Leiden: Brill, 1971)

Davidson, Maxwell J. *Angels at Qumran: A Comparative Study of 1 Enoch 1-36, 72-108 and Sectarian Writings from Qumran* (JSPS 11; Sheffield: JSOT Press, 1992)

Dimant, Devorah. "The Biography of Enoch and the Books of Enoch," *VT* 33 (1983) 14-29

Dimant, Devorah. "1 Enoch 6 – 11: A Methodological Perspective," in *SBLSP 1978* (ed. Paul J. Achtemeier; Missoula: Scholars, 1978) 1. 323-40

Dimant, Devorah. "1 Enoch 6–11: A Fragment of a Parabiblical Work," *JJS* 53 (2002) 223-37

Docherty, Susan. "Joseph the Patriarch: Representations of Joseph in Early Post-biblical Literature," in *Borders, Boundaries and the Bible* (ed. Martin O'Kane; JSOTSup 313; London; New York: Sheffield Academic Press, 2002) 194-216

Doering, Lutz. "Jub 2,24 nach 4QJubª VII,17 und der Aufbau von Jub 2,17-33," *BN* 84 (1996) 23-28

Doering, Lutz. "The Concept of the Sabbath in the Book of Jubilees," in *Studies in the Book of Jubilees* (ed. Matthias Albani, Jörg Frey, and Armin Lange; TSAJ 65; Tübingen: Mohr Siebeck, 1997) 179-205

Doering, Lutz. "*Jub* 50:6-13 als Schlussabschnitt des *Jubiläenbuchs* – Nachtrag aus Qumran oder ursprünglicher Bestandteil des Werks?" *RevQ* 20 (2002) 359-87

Doran, Robert. "The Non-Dating of Jubilees: Jub 34-38; 23:14-23 in Narrative Context," *JSJ* 20 (1989) 1-11

Drawnel, Henryk. *An Aramaic Wisdom Text from Qumran: A New Interpretation of the Levi Document* (JSJSup 86; Leiden: Brill, 2004)

Drawnel, Henryk. "Review: Jonas C. Greenfield, Michael E. Stone, Esther Eshel, *The Aramaic Levi Document: Edition, Translation, Commentary*," *RB* 113 (2006) 127-31

Ego, Beate. "Heilige Zeit - heiliger Raum - heiliger Mensch: Beobachtungen zur Struktur der Gesetzesbegründung in der Schöpfungs- und Paradiesgeschichte des Jubiläenbuches," in *Studies in the Book of Jubilees* (ed. Matthias Albani, Jörg Frey, and Armin Lange; TSAJ 65; Tübingen: Mohr Siebeck, 1997) 207-19

Ellens, J. H. and Florentino García Martínez, "Enochians and Zadokites," in *The Origins of Enochic Judaism: Proceedings of the First Enoch Seminar, University of Michigan, Sesto Fiorentino, Italy, June 19-23, 2001* (ed. G. Boccaccini; *Henoch* 24; Torino: Silvio Zamorani Editore, 2002) 147-53

Elliott, Mark. "Origins and Functions of the Watchers Theodicy," in *The Origins of Enochic Judaism: Proceedings of the First Enoch Seminar, University of Michigan, Sesto Fiorentino, Italy, June 19-23, 2001* (ed. G. Boccaccini; *Henoch* 24; Torino: Silvio Zamorani Editore, 2002) 63-75

Endres, John C. *Biblical Interpretation in the Book of Jubilees* (CBQMS 18; Washington, DC: Catholic Biblical Association of America, 1987)

Erlandsson, S. "זָנָה," *TDOT* 4 (1981) 99-104

Eshel, Esther. "Jubilees 32 and the Bethel Cult Traditions in Second Temple Literature," in *Things Revealed: Studies in Early Jewish and Christian Literature in Honor of Michael E. Stone* (JSJSupp 89; ed. Esther Chazon, David Satran and Ruth Clements; Leiden: Brill, 2004) 21-36

Eshel, Esther and Hanan Eshel, "Typonymic Midrash in 1 Enoch and in Other Second Temple Jewish Literature," in *The Origins of Enochic Judaism: Proceedings of the First Enoch Seminar, University of Michigan, Sesto Fiorentino, Italy, June 19-23, 2001* (ed. G. Boccaccini; *Henoch* 24; Torino: Silvio Zamorani Editore, 2002) 115-30

Eshel, Esther, and Hanan Eshel, "New Fragments from Qumran: 4QGen[f], 4QIsa[b], 4Q226, 8QGen, and XQpapEnoch," *DSD* 12 (2005) 134-57

Eshel, Hanan and Esther Eshel, "Separating Levi from Enoch: Response to 'Enoch, Levi, and Peter: Recipients of Revelation in Upper Galilee'," in *George W.E. Nickelsburg in Perspective: An Ongoing Dialogue of Learning* (2 vols; ed. Jacob Neusner and Alan J. Avery-Peck; JSJSup 80; Leiden: Brill, 2003) 2. 458-68

Fitzmyer, Joseph A. "The Aramaic Levi Document," in *The Dead Sea Scrolls and Christian Origins* (Studies in the Dead Sea Scrolls and Related Literature; Grand Rapids: Eerdmans, 2000) 237-48

Frey, Jörg. "Zum Weltbild im Jubiläenbuch," in *Studies in the Book of Jubilees* (ed. Matthias Albani, Jörg Frey, and Armin Lange; TSAJ 65; Tübingen: Mohr Siebeck, 1997) 261-92

Fröhlich, Ida. "Apocalypticism and the Religion and Ritual of the 'Pre-Sinaitic' Narratives," in *Enoch and Qumran Origins: New Light on a Forgotten Connection* (ed. Gabriele Boccaccini; Grand Rapids: Eerdmans, 2005) 148-51

Fröhlich, Ida. "Enoch and Jubilees," in *Enoch and Qumran Origins: New Light on a Forgotten Connection* (ed. Gabriele Boccaccini; Grand Rapids: Eerdmans, 2005) 141-47

Fröhlich, Ida. "'Mamzer' in Qumran Texts - The Problem of Mixed Marriages from Ezra's Time: Law, Literature and Practice," *Transeuphratène* 29 (2005) 103-15

García Martínez, Florentino. *Qumran and Apocalyptic: Studies on the Aramaic Texts from Qumran* (STDJ 9; Leiden: Brill, 1992)

García Martínez, Florentino and Eibert J. C. Tigchelaar, eds, *The Dead Sea Scrolls: Study Edition* (2 vols; Leiden: Brill, 1997)

Ginzberg, Louis. *The Legends of the Jews* (5 vols; Philadelphia: Jewish Publication Society of America, 1925)

Glasson, T. Francis. *Greek Influence in Jewish Eschatology* (London: SPCK, 1961)

Greenfield, Jonas C. "The Words of Levi Son of Jacob in Damascus Document IV, 15-19," *RevQ* 13 (1988) 319-22

Greenfield, Jonas C. and Michael E. Stone, "Remarks on the Aramaic Testament of Levi from the Geniza," *RB* 86 (1979) 216-30

Greenfield, Jonas C. and Michael E. Stone, "The Enochic Pentateuch and the Date of the Similitudes," in *'Al Kanfei Yonah: Collected Studies of Jonas C. Greenfield on Semitic Philology* (ed. Shalom M. Paul, Michael E. Stone, and Avital Pinnick; Leiden: Brill, 2001) 2.595-609

Greenfield, Jonas C., Michael E. Stone, and Esther Eshel, *The Aramaic Levi Document: Edition, Translation, Commentary* (SVTP 19; Leiden: Brill, 2004)

Grelot, Pierre "Notes sur le Testament araméen de Lévi (Fragment de la Bodleian Library, colonne a)," *RB* 63 (1956) 391-406

Gruen, Erich S. *Heritage and Hellenism: The Reinvention of Jewish Tradition* (Berkeley: University of California Press, 1998)

Gruenwald, Ithamar. "The Cultural Setting of Enoch-Apocalypticism: New Reflections," in *The Origins of Enochic Judaism: Proceedings of the First Enoch Seminar, University of Michigan, Sesto Fiorentino, Italy, June 19-23, 2001* (ed. G. Boccaccini; *Henoch* 24; Torino: Silvio Zamorani Editore, 2002) 213-23

Gruenwald, Ithamar. "Apocalypticism and the Religion and Ritual of the 'Pre-Sinaitic' Narratives," in *Enoch and Qumran Origins: New Light on a Forgotten Connection* (ed. Gabriele Boccaccini; Grand Rapids: Eerdmans, 2005) 148-51

Halpern-Amaru, Betsy. "The First Woman, Wives, and Mothers in Jubilees," *JBL* 113 (1994) 609-26

Halpern-Amaru, Betsy. "Exile and Return in Jubilees," in *Exile: Old Testament, Jewish, and Christian Conceptions* (ed. James H. Scott; JSJSup 56; Leiden: Brill, 1997) 127-44

Halpern-Amaru, Betsy. *The Empowerment of Women in the Book of Jubilees* (JSJSup 60; Leiden: Brill, 1999)

Halpern-Amaru, Betsy. "The Naming of Levi in the Book of Jubilees," in *Pseudepigraphic Perspectives: The Apocrypha and Pseudepigrapha in Light of the Dead Sea Scrolls. Proceedings of the [Second] International Symposium of the Orion Center for the Study of the Dead Sea Scrolls and Associated Literature, 12-14 January 1997* (ed. Esther G. Chazon and Michael E. Stone; STDJ 31; Leiden: Brill, 1999) 59-69

Halpern-Amaru, Betsy. "Burying the Fathers: Exegetical Strategies and Source Traditions in Jubilees 46," in *Reworking the Bible: Apocryphal and Related Texts at Qumran: Proceedings of a Joint Symposium by the Orion Center for the Study of the Dead Sea Scrolls and Associated Literature and the Hebrew University Institute for Advanced Studies Research Group on Qumran, 15-17 January, 2002* (ed. Esther G. Chazon, Devorah Dimant, and Ruth A. Clements; STDJ 58; Leiden: Brill, 2005) 135-53

Halpern-Amaru, Betsy. "Jubilees, Midrash in," in *Encyclopaedia of Midrash* (ed. Jacob Neusner and Alan J. Avery Peck; Leiden: Brill, 2005) 1. 333-50

Hanson, Paul D. "Rebellion in Heaven, Azazel, and Euhemeristic Heroes in *1 Enoch* 6-11," *JBL* 96 (1977) 195-233

Hartom, A. S. *Sefer ha-Yoblot we-Dibre – 'Iyyob. Ha-s^{e}farim Ha-hitsonim; Sippure-Aggadah B* (Tel-Aviv: Yabneh, 1969)

Hauck, F. and S. Schulz, "πόρνη," *TDNT* 6 (1968) 579-95

Hayes, Christine E. "Intermarriage and Impurity in Ancient Jewish Sources," *HTR* 92 (1999) 3-36

Hayes, Christine E. *Gentile Impurities and Jewish Identities: Intermarriage and Conversion from the Bible to the Talmud* (Oxford: OUP, 2002)

Hayward, Robert. "The Sanctification of Time in the Second Temple Period: Case Studies in the Septuagint and Jubilees," in *Holiness Past and Present* (ed. Stephen C. Barton; London: T&T Clark, 2003) 141-67

Hempel, Charlotte. "The Place of the *Book of Jubilees* at Qumran and beyond," in *The Dead Sea Scrolls in Their Historical Context* (ed. Timothy H. Lim et al.; Edinburgh: T&T Clark, 2000) 187-96

Hendel, Ronald. "The *Nephilim* were on the Earth: Genesis 6:1-4 and its Ancient Near Eastern Context," in *The Fall of the Angels* (ed. Christoph Auffarth and Loren T. Stuckenbruck; Themes in Biblical Narrative 6; Leiden: Brill, 2004) 11-34

Hillel, Vered. "Why not Naphthali?" in *Things Revealed: Studies in Early Jewish and Christian Literature in Honor of Michael E. Stone* (ed. Esther G. Chazon, David Satran, and Ruth A. Clements; JSJSup 89; Leiden: Brill, 2004) 279-88

Himmelfarb, Martha. *The Ascent to Heaven in Jewish and Christian Apocalypses* (Oxford: Oxford University Press, 1993)

Himmelfarb, Martha. "Levi, Phinehas, and the Problem of Intermarriage at the Time of the Maccabean Revolt," *JSQ* 6 (1999) 1-24

Himmelfarb, Martha. "Sexual Relations and Purity in the Temple Scroll and the Book of Jubilees," *DSD* 6 (1999) 11-36

Himmelfarb, Martha. "Torah, Testimony, and Heavenly Tablets: The Claim to Authority of the *Book of Jubilees*," in *A Multiform Heritage: Studies on Early Judaism and Christianity in Honor of Robert A. Kraft* (ed. Benjamin G. Wright; Homage Series 24; Atlanta: Scholars, 1999) 19-29

Himmelfarb, Martha. "The Book of the Watchers and the Priests of Jerusalem," in *The Origins of Enochic Judaism: Proceedings of the First Enoch Seminar, University of Michigan, Sesto Fiorentino, Italy, June 19-23, 2001* (ed. G. Boccaccini; *Henoch* 24; Torino: Silvio Zamorani Editore, 2002) 131-35

Himmelfarb, Martha. "Jubilees and Sectarianism," in *Enoch and Qumran Origins: New Light on a Forgotten Connection* (ed. Gabriele Boccaccini; Grand Rapids: Eerdmans, 2005) 129-31

Horsley, Richard A. "Social Relations and Social Conflict in the *Epistle of Enoch*," in *For a Later Generation: The Transformation of Tradition in Israel, Early Judaism, and Early Christianity* (ed. Randal A. Argall, Beverly A. Bow, and Rodney A. Werline; Harrisburg: Trinity Press International, 2000) 100-15

Horsley, Richard A. "The Politics of Cultural Production in Second Temple Judea: Historical Context and Political-Religious Relations of the Scribes Who Produced *1 Enoch*, Sirach, and Daniel," in *Conflicted Boundaries in Wisdom and Apocalypticism* (ed. Kristin De Troyer and Armin Lange; SBLSymS 30; Atlanta: Scholars, 2005) 123-45

Hultgård, Anders. *L'Eschatologie des Testaments des Deuze Patriarches: 1. Interpretation des Textes* (Acta Universitatis Upsaliensis: Historia Religionum 6; Stockholm: Almqvist & Wiksell, 1977)

Hultgård, Anders. "The Ideal 'Levite', the Davidic Messiah and the Saviour Priest in the Testaments of the Twelve Patriarchs," in *Ideal Figures in Ancient Judaism: Profiles and Paradigms* (ed. John J. Collins and George W. E. Nickelsburg; SBLSCS 12; Chico: Scholars, 1980) 93-110

Jackson, David R. *Enochic Judaism: Three Defining Exemplars* (Library of Second Temple Studies 49; London: T&T Clark, 2004)

Jensen, Joseph. "Does Porneia Mean Fornication?" *NovT* 20 (1978) 161-84

Jervell, J. *Imago Dei: Gen. 1,26f. im Spätjudentum, in der Gnosis und in den paulinischen Briefen* (FRLANT 75; Göttingen: Vandenhoeck und Ruprecht, 1960)

Jonge, Marinus de. "Levi in *Aramaic Levi* and in the *Testament of Levi*," in *Pseudepigraphic Perspectives: The Apocrypha and Pseudepigrapha in Light of the Dead Sea Scrolls: Proceedings of the [Second] International Symposium of the Orion Center for the Study of the Dead Sea Scrolls and Associated Literature, 12-14 January 1997* (ed. Esther G. Chazon and Michael E. Stone; STDJ 31; Leiden: Brill, 1999) 71-89

Jonge, Marinus de and Johannes Trompf, "Jacob's Son Levi in the Old Testament Pseudepigrapha and Related Literature," in *Biblical Figures outside the Bible* (ed. Michael E. Stone and Theodore A. Bergren; Harrisburg: Trinity Press International, 1998) 203-36

Klawans, Jonathan. *Impurity and Sin in Ancient Judaism* (Oxford: OUP, 2000)

Knibb, Michael A. *The Ethiopic Book of Enoch: A New Edition in the Light of the Aramaic Dead Sea Fragments: In Consultation with Edward Ullendorf* (2 vols; Oxford: Clarendon, 1978)

Knibb, Michael A. "Perspectives on the Apocrypha and Pseudepigrapha: The Levi Traditions," in *Perspectives in the Study of the Old Testament and Early Judaism: A Symposium in Honour of Adam S. van de Woude on the Occasion of His 70th Birthday* (ed. Florentino García Martínez and Edward Noort; VTSup 73; Leiden: Brill, 1998) 197-213

Knibb, Michael A. "Enoch Literature and Wisdom Literature," in *The Origins of Enochic Judaism: Proceedings of the First Enoch Seminar, University of Michigan, Sesto Fiorentino, Italy, June 19-23, 2001* (ed. G. Boccaccini; *Henoch* 24; Torino: Silvio Zamorani Editore, 2002) 197-203

Knibb, Michael A. "The Book of Enoch in the Light of the Qumran Wisdom Literature," in *Wisdom and Apocalypticism in the Dead Sea Scrolls and in the Biblical Tradition* (ed. Florentino García Martínez; BETL 163; Leuven: Leuven University Press, Peeters, 2003) 193-210

Knibb, Michael A. "The Use of Scripture in 1 Enoch 17-19," in *Jerusalem, Alexandria, Rome: Studies in Ancient Cultural Interaction in Honour of A. Hilhorst* (ed. Florentino García Martínez and Gerard P. Luttikhuizen; Leiden: Brill, 2003) 165-78

Knibb, Michael A. "Which Parts of *1 Enoch* Were Known to *Jubilees*? A Note on the Interpretation of *Jubilees* 4.16-25," in *Reading from Right to Left: Essays on the Hebrew Bible in Honour of David J. A. Clines* (ed. J. Cheryl Exum and Hugh G. M. Williamson; JSOTSup 373; London: Sheffield Academic Press, 2003) 254-62.

Koch, Klaus. "History as a Battlefield of Two Antagonistic Powers in the Apocalypse of Weeks and in the Rule of the Community," in *Enoch and*

Qumran Origins: New Light on a Forgotten Connection (ed. Gabriele
  Boccaccini; Grand Rapids: Eerdmans, 2005) 185-99
Kugel, James L. "The Story of Dinah in the Testament of Levi," *HTR* 85 (1992)
  1-34
Kugel, James L. "Reuben's Sin with Bilhah in the Testament of Reuben," in
  *Pomegranates and Golden Bells: Studies in Biblical, Jewish, and Near Eastern
  Ritual, Law, and Literature in Honor of Jacob Milgrom* (Winona Lake:
  Eisenbrauns, 1995) 525-54
Kugler, Robert A. *From Patriarch to Priest: The Levi-Priestly Tradition from*
  Aramaic Levi *to* Testament of Levi (SBLEJL 9; Atlanta: Scholars, 1996)
Kugler, Robert A. "Halakic Interpretive Strategies at Qumran: A Case Study," in
  *Legal Texts and Legal Issues: Proceedings of the Second Meeting of the
  International Organization for Qumran Studies, Cambridge, 1995: Published
  in Honour of Joseph M. Baumgarten* (ed. Moshe J. Bernstein, Florentino
  García Martínez, and John Kampen; STDJ 23; Leiden: Brill, 1997) 131-40
Kvanvig, Helge S. *Roots of Apocalyptic: The Mesopotamian Background of the
  Enoch Figure and the Son of Man* (WMANT 61; Neukirchen-Vluyn:
  Neukirchener Verlag, 1988)
Kvanvig, Helge S. "Origin and Identity of the Enoch Group," in *The Origins of
  Enochic Judaism: Proceedings of the First Enoch Seminar, University of
  Michigan, Sesto Fiorentino, Italy, June 19-23, 2001* (ed. G. Boccaccini;
  Henoch 24; Torino: Silvio Zamorani Editore, 2002) 207-12
Kvanvig, Helge S. "The Watchers Story, Genesis and *Atra-hasis*: A Triangular
  Reading," in *The Origins of Enochic Judaism: Proceedings of the First Enoch
  Seminar, University of Michigan, Sesto Fiorentino, Italy, June 19-23, 2001* (ed.
  G. Boccaccini; *Henoch* 24; Torino: Silvio Zamorani Editore, 2002) 17-21
Kvanvig, Helge S. "Gen 6,3 and the Watcher Story," *Henoch* 25 (2003) 277-300
Kvanvig, Helge S. "*Jubilees* – Between Enoch and Moses . A Narrative Reading,"
  JSJ 35 (2004) 243-61
Kvanvig, Helge S. "The Watcher Story and Genesis: An Intertextual Reading,"
  SJOT 18 (2004) 163-83
Kvanvig, Helge S. "Jubilees – Read as a Narrative," in *Enoch and Qumran
  Origins: New Light on a Forgotten Connection* (ed. Gabriele
  Boccaccini; Grand Rapids: Eerdmans, 2005) 75-83
Lambdin, Thomas O. *Introduction to Classical Ethiopic (Ge ʿez)* (HSS 24;
  Missoula: Scholars, 1978)
Lambert, David. "Last Testament in the Book of Jubilees," *DSD* 11 (2004) 82-107
Lange, Armin. "Dream Visions and Apocalyptic Milieu," in *Enoch and Qumran
  Origins: New Light on a Forgotten Connection* (ed. Gabriele
  Boccaccini; Grand Rapids: Eerdmans, 2005) 27-34

Larson, Erik W. "The LXX and Enoch: Influence and Interpretation in Early Jewish Literature," in *Enoch and Qumran Origins: New Light on a Forgotten Connection* (ed. Gabriele Boccaccini; Grand Rapids: Eerdmans, 2005) 84-89

Leslau, Wolf. *Comparative Dictionary of Ge'ez (Classical Ethiopic: Ge'ez-English / English- Ge'ez with an Index of the Semitic Roots* (Wiesbaden: Otto Harrassowitz, 1987)

Leuenberger, Martin. "Die 10-Siebent-Apokalypse im Henochbuch: ihre Stellung im material rekonstruierten Manuskript 4QEn(g) und Implikationen für die Redaktions- und Kompositionsgeschichte der Traumvisionen (83-91) und des paränetischen Briefs (92-105); Teil 1," *BN* 124 (2005) 57-102

Lichtenberger, Hermann. "Zu Vorkommen und Bedeutung von *yetser* im Jubilaenbuch," *JSJ* 14 (1983) 1-10

Loader, William. *The Septuagint, Sexuality, and the New Testament: Case Studies on the Impact of the LXX in Philo and the New Testament* (Grand Rapids: Eerdmans, 2004)

Loader, William. *Sexuality and the Jesus Tradition* (Grand Rapids: Eerdmans, 2005)

Mendels, Doron. *The Land of Israel as a Political Concept in Hasmonean Literature* (Tübingen: Mohr Siebeck, 1987)

Milgrom, Jacob. "The Concept of Impurity in *Jubilees* and the *Temple Scroll*," *RevQ* 16 (1993) 277-84

Milgrom, Jacob. *Leviticus: A New Translation with Introduction and Commentary* (3 vols; AB 3; New York: Doubleday, 1991, 2000, 2001)

Milik, Józef T. *The Books of Enoch: Aramaic Fragments of Qumran Cave 4* (Oxford: Clarendon, 1976)

Molenberg, Corrie. "A Study of the Roles of Shemihaza and Asael in 1 Enoch 6-11," *JJS* 35 (1984) 136-46

Morisada Rietz, Henry W. "Synchronizing Worship: Jubilees as a Tradition for the Qumran Community," in *Enoch and Qumran Origins: New Light on a Forgotten Connection* (ed. Gabriele Boccaccini; Grand Rapids: Eerdmans, 2005) 111-18

Müller, Karlheinz. "Die hebräische Sprache der Halacha als Textur der Schöpfung: Beobachtungen zum Verhältnis von Tora und Halacha in Buch der Jubiläen," in *Bibel in judischer und christlicher Tradition: Festschrift für Johan Maier zum 60. Geburtstag* (ed. Helmut Merklein, Karlheinz Müller and Günter Stemberger; Frankfurt am Main: Hain, 1993) 157-76

Müller, Karlheinz. "Die Halacha der Väter und das Gesetz des Mose: Beobachtungen zur Autorisierung der Halacha im Buch der Jubiläen," *BN* 116 (2003) 56-68

Najman, Hindy. *Seconding Sinai: The Development of Mosaic Discourse in Second Temple Judaism* (JSJSup 77; Leiden: Brill, 2003)

Newsom, Carol A. "The Development of 1 Enoch 6 – 19: Cosmology and
    Judgment," *CBQ* 42 (1980) 310-29

Nickelsburg, George W. E. "Apocalyptic and Myth in 1 Enoch 6-11," *JBL* 96
    (1977) 383-405

Nickelsburg, George W. E. "Riches, the Rich, and God's Judgment in 1 Enoch
    92-105 and the Gospel according to Luke," *NTS* 25 (1979) 324-44, reproduced
    in *George W.E. Nickelsburg in Perspective: An Ongoing Dialogue of Learning*
    (2 vols; ed. Jacob Neusner and Alan J. Avery-Peck; JSJSup 80; Leiden: Brill,
    2003) 2. 522-46

Nickelsburg, George W. E. "Enoch, Levi, and Peter: Recipients of Revelation in
    Upper Galilee," *JBL* 100 (1981) 575-600; reproduced in *George W.E.
    Nickelsburg in Perspective: An Ongoing Dialogue of Learning* (2 vols; ed.
    Jacob Neusner and Alan J. Avery-Peck; JSJSup 80; Leiden: Brill, 2003) 2.
    427-57

Nickelsburg, George W. E. "The Bible Rewritten and Expanded," in *Jewish
    Writings of the Second Temple Period: Apocrypha, Pseudepigrapha, Qumran
    Sectarian Writings, Philo, Josephus* (ed. Michael E. Stone; CRINT 2: The
    Literature of the Jewish People in the Period of the Second Temple and the
    Talmud; Assen, Netherlands: Van Gorcum; Philadelphia: Fortress, 1984)
    89-156

Nickelsburg, George W. E. "The Apocalyptic Construction of Reality in *1 Enoch*,"
    in *Mysteries and Revelation: Apocalyptic Studies since the Uppsala
    Colloquium* (ed. John J. Collins and James H. Charlesworth; JSPS 9; Sheffield:
    JSOT Press, 1991) 51-64; reproduced in *George W.E. Nickelsburg in
    Perspective: An Ongoing Dialogue of Learning* (2 vols; ed. Jacob Neusner and
    Alan J. Avery-Peck; JSJSup 80; Leiden: Brill, 2003) 1. 29-43

Nickelsburg, George W. E. "Patriarchs Who Worry about Their Wives: A
    Haggadic Tendency in the Genesis Apocryphon," in *Biblical Perspectives:
    Early Use and Interpretation of the Bible in Light of the Dead Sea Scrolls:
    Proceedings of the First International Symposium of the Orion Center for the
    Study of the Dead Sea Scrolls and Associated Literature, 12-14 May 1996* (ed.
    Michael E. Stone and Esther G. Chazon; STDJ 28; Leiden: Brill, 1998) 137-
    58; reproduced in *George W.E. Nickelsburg in Perspective: An Ongoing
    Dialogue of Learning* (2 vols; ed. Jacob Neusner and Alan J. Avery-Peck;
    JSJSup 80; Leiden: Brill, 2003) 1. 177-99.

Nickelsburg, George W. E. "Revisiting the Rich and the Poor in 1 Enoch 92-105
    and the Gospel according to Luke," SBLSP 37 (Atlanta: Scholars, 1998)
    2.579-605, reproduced in *George W.E. Nickelsburg in Perspective: An
    Ongoing Dialogue of Learning* (2 vols; ed. Jacob Neusner and Alan J. Avery-
    Peck; JSJSup 80; Leiden: Brill, 2003) 2. 547-71

Nickelsburg, George W. E. "The Nature and Function of Revelation in 1 Enoch, Jubilees, and Some Qumranic Documents," in *Pseudepigraphic Perspectives: The Apocrypha and Pseudepigrapha in Light of the Dead Sea Scrolls: Proceedings of the [Second] International Symposium of the Orion Center for the Study of the Dead Sea Scrolls and Associated Literature, 12-14 January 1997* (ed. Esther G. Chazon and Michael E. Stone; STDJ 31; Leiden: Brill, 1999) 91-119

Nickelsburg, George W. E. *1 Enoch 1: A Commentary on the Book of 1 Enoch Chapters 1-36, 81-108* (Hermeneia; Minneapolis: Fortress, 2001)

Nickelsburg, George W. E. "1 Enoch and Some Qumran Texts: Comparing Aspects of their Anthropology," in *Der Mensch vor Gott: Forschungen zum Menschenbild in Bibel, antikem Judentum und Koran. Festschrift für Hermann Lichtenberger zum 60. Geburtstag* (ed. Ulrike Mittmann-Richert, Friedrich Avemarie, and Gerbern S. Oegema; Neukirchen: Neukirchener-Verlag, 2003) 75-87

Nickelsburg, George W. E. "Response to Hanen Eshel and Esther Eshel," in *George W.E. Nickelsburg in Perspective: An Ongoing Dialogue of Learning* (2 vols; ed. Jacob Neusner and Alan J. Avery-Peck; JSJSup 80; Leiden: Brill, 2003) 2. 469-71

Nickelsburg, George W. E. "The Greek Fragments of 1 Enoch from Qumran Cave 7: An Unproven Identification," *RevQ* 21 (2004) 631-34.

Nickelsburg, George W. E. "Where is the Place of Eschatological Blessing?" in *Things Revealed: Studies in Early Jewish and Christian Literature in Honor of Michael E. Stone* (ed. Esther G. Chazon, David Satran, and Ruth A. Clements; JSJSup 89; Leiden: Brill, 2004) 53-71

Nickelsburg, George W. E. *Jewish Literature between the Bible and the Mishnah* (2d ed.; Minneapolis: Fortress, 2005)

Nickelsburg, George W. E. "Response: Context, Text, and Social Setting of the Apocalypse of Weeks," in *Enoch and Qumran Origins: New Light on a Forgotten Connection* (ed. Gabriele Boccaccini; Grand Rapids: Eerdmans, 2005) 234-41

Nickelsburg, George W. E. and James C. VanderKam, *1 Enoch: A New Translation* (Minneapolis: Fortress, 2004)

Olson, Daniel C. "'Those Who Have Not Defiled Themselves with Women': Revelation 14:4 and the Book of Enoch," *CBQ* 59/3 (1997) 492-510.

Olson, Daniel C., in consultation with Melkesedek Workeneh, *Enoch: A New Translation; The Ethiopic Book of Enoch, or 1 Enoch, Translated with Annotations and Cross-References* (North Richland Hills: BIBAL Press, 2004)

Olson, Daniel C. "Historical Chronology after the Exile according to 1 Enoch 89-90," *JSP* 15 (2005) 63-74

Pomykala, K. F. "A Scripture Profile of the Book of Watchers", *The Quest for Context and Meaning* (ed. C. A. Evans and S. Talmon; Leiden: Brill, 1997) 263-84

Puech, Émile. "Les songes des fils de Semihazah dans *le Livre des Géants* de Qumrân," *Comptes Rendus de l'Académie des Inscriptions et Belles Lettres* janvier-mars (2000) 7-26

Puech, Émile. "Le Testament de Lévi en araméen de la geniza du Caire," *RevQ* 20 (2002) 511-56

Ravid, Liora. "Purity and Impurity in the Book of Jubilees," *JSP* 13 (2002) 61-86

Reed, Annette Yoshiko. "Heavenly Ascent, Angelic Descent, and the Transmission of Knowledge in *1 Enoch* 6–16," in *Heavenly Realms and Earthly Realities in Late Antique Religions* (ed. Ra'anan S. Boustan and Annette Yoshiko Reed; New York: Cambridge University Press, 2004) 47-66

Reed, Annette Yoshiko. *Fallen Angels and the History of Judaism and Christianity: The Reception of Enochic Literature* (New York: Cambridge University Press, 2005)

Reed, Annette Yoshiko. "'Revealed Literature' in the Second Century B.C.E.: Jubilees, 1 Enoch, Qumran, and the Prehistory of the Biblical Canon," in *Enoch and Qumran Origins: New Light on a Forgotten Connection* (ed. Gabriele Boccaccini; Grand Rapids: Eerdmans, 2005) 94-98

Regev, Eyal. "Moral Impurity and the Temple in Early Christianity in Light of Ancient Greek Practice and Qumranic Ideology," *HTR* 97 (2004) 383-411

Reid, Stephen Breck. *Enoch and Daniel: A Form Critical and Sociological Study of the Historical Apocalypses* (2d ed.; BIBAL Monograph Series 2; North Richland Hills: BIBAL Press, 2004)

Rönsch, Hermann. *Das Buch der Jubiläen oder der kleine Genesis* (Amsterdam: Rodopi, 1970; Leipzig: Pues's Verlag, 1874)

Rook, John. "The Names of the Wives from Adam to Abraham in the Book of Jubilees," *JSP* 7 (1990) 105-17

Rothstein, David. "Sexual Union and Sexual Offences in Jubilees," *JSJ* 35 (2004) 363-84

Rothstein, David. "Joseph as Pedagogue: Biblical Precedents for the Depiction of Joseph in Aramaic Levi (4Q213)," *JSP* 14 (2005) 223-29

Ruiten, Jacques T. A. G. M. van. "The Garden of Eden and Jubilees 3:1-31," *Bijdragen, tijdschrift voor filosofie en theologie* 57 (1996) 305-17

Ruiten, Jacques T. A. G. M. van. "The Interpretation of Genesis 6:1-12 in Jubilees 5:1-19," in *Studies in the Book of Jubilees* (ed. Matthias Albani, Jörg Frey, and Armin Lange; TSAJ 65; Tübingen: Mohr Siebeck, 1997) 59-75

Ruiten, Jacques T. A. G. M. van. "The Interpretation of the Flood Story in *The Book of Jubilees*," in *Interpretations of the Flood* (ed. Florentino García

Martínez and Gerard P. Luttikhuizen; Themes in Biblical Narrative 1; Leiden: Brill, 1998) 66-85

Ruiten, Jacques T. A. G. M. van. "Eden and the Temple: The Rewriting of Genesis 2:4 – 3:24 in *The Book of Jubilees*," in *Paradise Interpreted: Representations of Biblical Paradise in Judaism and Christianity* (ed. G. P. Luttikhuizen; Themes in Biblical Narrative: Jewish and Christian Traditions 2; Leiden: Brill, 1999) 63-94

Ruiten, Jacques T. A. G. M. van. "Visions of the Temple in the Book of Jubilees," in *Gemeinde ohne Tempel/Community without Temple: Zur Substituierung und Transformation des Jerusalemer Tempels und seines Kults im Alten Testament, antiken Judentum und frühen Christentum* (ed. Beate Ego, Armin Lange, and Peter Pilhofer; WUNT 118; Tübingen: Mohr Siebeck, 1999) 215-27

Ruiten, Jacques T. A. G. M. van. *Primaeval History Interpreted: The Rewriting of Genesis 1-11 in the Book of Jubilees* (JSJSup 66; Leiden: Brill, 2000)

Ruiten, Jacques T. A. G. M. van. "Abraham, Job and the Book of *Jubilees*: The Intertextual Relationship of Genesis 22:1-19, Job 1:1 – 2:13 and *Jubilees* 17:15 – 18:19," in *The Sacrifice of Isaac: The Aqedah (Gen 22) and its Interpretations* (ed. Edward Noort and Eibert Tigchelaar; Themes in Biblical Narrative 4; Leiden: Brill, 2002) 58-85

Ruiten, Jacques T. A. G. M. van. "Eve's Pain in Childbearing? Interpretations of Gen 3:16a in Biblical and Early Jewish Texts," in *Eve's Children: The Biblical Stories Retold and Interpreted in Jewish and Christian Traditions* (ed. Gerard P. Luttikhuizen; Biblical Narrative 5; Leiden: Brill, 2003) 3-26

Ruiten, Jacques T. A. G. M. van. "The Covenant of Noah in *Jubilees* 6.1-38," in *The Concept of the Covenant in the Second Temple Period* (ed. Stanley E. Porter and Jacqueline C. R. de Roo; Leiden: Brill, 2003) 167-90

Ruiten, Jacques T. A. G. M. van. "A Literary Dependency of Jubilees on 1 Enoch," A Reassessment of a Thesis of J. C. VanderKam," *Henoch* 26 (2004) 205-209

Ruiten, Jacques T. A. G. M. van. "A Literary Dependency of Jubilees on 1 Enoch," in *Enoch and Qumran Origins: New Light on a Forgotten Connection* (ed. Gabriele Boccaccini; Grand Rapids: Eerdmans, 2005) 90-93

Ruiten, Jacques T. A. G. M. van. "The Birth of Moses in Egypt according to *The Book of Jubilees (Jub 47.1-9)*," in *The Wisdom of Egypt: Jewish, Early Christian, and Gnostic Essays in Honour of Gerard P. Luttikhuizen* (ed. Anthony Hilhorst and George H. van Kooten; AJEC 59; Leiden: Brill, 2005) 43-65

Sanders, Jack T. "When Sacred Canopies Collide: The Reception of the Torah of Moses in the Wisdom Literature of the Second-Temple Period," *JSJ* 32 (2001) 121-36

Satlow, Michael L. "Jewish Constructions of Nakedness in Late Antiquity," *JBL* 116 (1997) 429-54

Satlow, Michael L. *Jewish Marriage in Antiquity* (Princeton: Princeton University Press, 2001)

Schiffman, Lawrence H. "3 Enoch and the Enoch Tradition," in *Enoch and Qumran Origins: New Light on a Forgotten Connection* (ed. Gabriele Boccaccini; Grand Rapids: Eerdmans, 2005) 152-61

Schiffman, Lawrence H. "Sacrificial Halakhah in the Fragments of the *Aramaic Levi Document* from Qumran, the Cairo Genizah, and Mt. Athos Monastery," in *Reworking the Bible: Apocryphal and Related Texts at Qumran: Proceedings of a Joint Symposium by the Orion Center for the Study of the Dead Sea Scrolls and Associated Literature and the Hebrew University Institute for Advanced Studies Research Group on Qumran, 15-17 January, 2002* (ed. Esther G. Chazon, Devorah Dimant, and Ruth A. Clements; STDJ 58; Leiden: Brill, 2005) 177-202

Schmidt, B. "The Origins of Enoch Traditions: The View from the Outside," in *The Origins of Enochic Judaism: Proceedings of the First Enoch Seminar, University of Michigan, Sesto Fiorentino, Italy, June 19-23, 2001* (ed. G. Boccaccini; *Henoch* 24; Torino: Silvio Zamorani Editore, 2002) 49-53

Schofield, Alison, and James C. VanderKam, "Were the Hasmoneans Zadokites?" *JBL* 124 (2005) 73-87

Schuller, Eileen. "Response to 'Patriarchs Who Worry about their Wives: A Haggadic Tendency in the Genesis Apocryphon," in *George W.E. Nickelsburg in Perspective: An Ongoing Dialogue of Learning* (2 vols; ed. Jacob Neusner and Alan J. Avery-Peck; JSJSup 80; Leiden: Brill, 2003) 1. 200-12.

Schwarz, Eberhard. *Identität durch Abgrenzung: Abgrenzungsprozesse in Israel im 2. vorchristlichen Jahrhundert und ihre traditionsgeschichtlichen Voraussetzungen: Zugleich ein Beitrag zur Erforschung des Jubiläenbuches* (Europäische Hochschulschriften 162; Frankfurt: Peter Lang, 1982)

Scott, James M. "The Division of the Earth in Jubilees 8:11–9:15 and Early Christian Chronography," in *Studies in the Book of Jubilees* (ed. Matthias Albani, Jörg Frey, and Armin Lange; TSAJ 65; Tübingen: Mohr Siebeck, 1997) 295-323

Scott, James M. *On Earth as in Heaven: The Restoration of Sacred Time and Sacred Space in the Book of Jubilees* (JSJSup 99; Leiden: Brill, 2005)

Segal, Michael. "The Relationship between the Legal and Narrative Passages in Jubilees," in *Reworking the Bible: Apocryphal and Related Texts at Qumran: Proceedings of a Joint Symposium by the Orion Center for the Study of the Dead Sea Scrolls and Associated Literature and the Hebrew University Institute for Advanced Studies Research Group on Qumran, 15-17 January,*

2002 (ed. Esther G. Chazon, Devorah Dimant, and Ruth A. Clements; STDJ 58; Leiden: Brill, 2005) 203-28

Shimoff, Sandra R. "Banquets: The Limits of Hellenization," *JSJ* 27 (1996) 440-52.

Smith, Mark Stratton. "Reading, Writing and Interpretation: Two Notes on Jubilees and Pseudo-Jubilees," in *Hamlet on a Hill: Semitic and Greek Studies Presented to Professor T. Muraoka on the Occasion of His Sixty-Fifth Birthday* (ed. M. F. J. Baasten and W. Th. van Peursen; Leuven: Peeters, 2003) 441-47

Steck, Odil H. "Die Aufnahme von Genesis 1 in Jubiläen 2 und 4 Esra 6," *JSJ* 8 (1977) 154-82

Steudel, Annette. "Ehelosigkeit bei den Essenern," in *Qumran Kontrovers: Beiträge zu den Textfunden vom Toten Meer* (ed. Jörg Frey and Hartmut Stegemann with the collaboration of Michael Becker and Alexander Maurer; Einblicke 6, Paderborn: Bonifatius, 2003) 115-24

Stone, Michael E. "The Axis of History at Qumran," in *Pseudepigraphic Perspectives: The Apocrypha and Pseudepigrapha in Light of the Dead Sea Scrolls: Proceedings of the [Second] International Symposium of the Orion Center for the Study of the Dead Sea Scrolls and Associated Literature, 12-14 January 1997* (ed. Esther G. Chazon and Michael E. Stone; STDJ 31; Leiden: Brill, 1999) 133-49

Stone, Michael E. "Aramaic Levi in its Contexts," *JSQ* 9 (2002) 307-26

Stone, Michael E. "'Levi Aramaic' Document and the Greek Testament of Levi," in *Emanuel: Studies in Hebrew Bible, Septuagint and Dead Sea Scrolls in Honor of Emanuel Tov* (ed. Shalom M. Paul, Robert A. Kraft, Lawrence H. Schiffman and Weston W. Fields; Leiden: Brill, 2003) 429-37

Stone, Michael E. "The Book(s) Attributed to Noah," *DSD* 13 (2006) 4-23

Stuckenbruck, Loren T. *The Book of Giants from Qumran: Text, Translation, and Commentary* (TSAJ 63; Tübingen: Mohr Siebeck, 1997)

Stuckenbruck, Loren T. "4QEnoch Giants[a] ar (Pls. I-II)," in *Qumran Cave 4. XXVI Cryptic Texts and Miscellanea Part I* (ed. Stephen J. Pfann et al.; DJD 36; Oxford: Clarendon, 2000) 8-41

Stuckenbruck, Loren T. "4QInstruction and the Possible Influence of Early Enochic Traditions: An Evaluation," in *The Wisdom Texts from Qumran and the Development of Sapiential Thought: Studies in Wisdom at Qumran and its Relationship to Sapiential Thought in the Ancient Near East, the Hebrew Bible, Ancient Judaism, and the New Testament* (ed. Charlotte Hempel, Armin Lange, and Hermann Lichtenberger; BETL 159; Leuven: Peeters; Leuven University Press, 2002) 245-61

Stuckenbruck, Loren T. "Genesis 6:1-4 as Basis for Divergent Readings During the Second Temple Period," in *The Origins of Enochic Judaism: Proceedings of the First Enoch Seminar, University of Michigan, Sesto Fiorentino, Italy,*

June 19-23, 2001 (ed. G. Boccaccini; *Henoch* 24; Torino: Silvio Zamorani
Editore, 2002) 99-106

Stuckenbruck, Loren T. "Giant Mythology and Demonology: From the Ancient
Near East to the Dead Sea Scrolls," in *Die Dämonen / Demons: The
Demonology of Israelite-Jewish and Early Christian Literature in Context of
their Environment* (ed. Armin Lange, Hermann Lichtenberger, and K. F.
Diethard Romheld; Tübingen: Mohr Siebeck, 2003) 318-38

Stuckenbruck, Loren T. "'Angels' and 'God': Exploring the Limits of Early
Jewish Monotheism," in *Early Jewish and Christian Monotheism* (ed. Loren T.
Stuckenbruck and Wendy E. S. North; London: T&T Clark, 2004) 45-70

Stuckenbruck, Loren T. "The Origins of Evil in Jewish Apocalyptic Tradition: The
Interpretation of Gen 6:1-4 in the Second and Third Centuries B.C.E.," in *The
Fall of the Angels* (ed. Christoph Auffarth and Loren T. Stuckenbruck; Themes
in Biblical Narrative 6; Leiden: Brill, 2004) 87-118

Stuckenbruck, Loren T. "'Reading the Present' in the Animal Apocalypse (1
Enoch 85-90)," in *Reading the Present in the Qumran Library: The Perception
of the Contemporary by Means of Scriptural Interpretations* (ed. Kristin De
Troyer and Armin Lange; SBLSymS 30; Atlanta: Scholars, 2005) 91-102

Suter, David Winston. "Fallen Angel, Fallen Priest: The Problem of Family Purity
in 1 Enoch," *HUCA* 50 (1979) 115-35

Suter, David Winston. "Revisiting 'Fallen Angel, Fallen Priest'," in *The Origins of
Enochic Judaism: Proceedings of the First Enoch Seminar, University of
Michigan, Sesto Fiorentino, Italy, June 19-23, 2001* (ed. G. Boccaccini;
Henoch 24; Torino: Silvio Zamorani Editore, 2002) 137-42

Suter, David Winston. "Mapping the First Book of Enoch: Geographical Issues in
George Nickelsburg's Commentary," in *George W.E. Nickelsburg in
Perspective: An Ongoing Dialogue of Learning* (2 vols; ed. Jacob Neusner and
Alan J. Avery-Peck; JSJSup 80; Leiden: Brill, 2003) 2. 387-94

Testuz, M. *Les idées religieuses du Livre des Jubilés* (Geneva: Droz; Paris:
Midard, 1960)

Tigchelaar, Eibert J. C. *Prophets of Old and the Day of the End: Zechariah, the
Book of Watchers and Apocalyptic* (OTS 35; Leiden: Brill, 1996)

Tigchelaar, Eibert J. C. "Eden and Paradise: The Garden Motif in Some Early
Jewish Texts (1 Enoch and Other Texts Found at Qumran)," in *Paradise
Interpreted: Representations of Biblical Paradise in Judaism and Christianity*
(Themes in Biblical Narrative 2; ed. Gerard P. Luttikhuizen; Leiden: Brill,
1999) 37-62

Tigchelaar, Eibert J. C. "Some Remarks on the Book of Watchers: The Priests,
Enoch, Genesis, and 4Q208," in *The Origins of Enochic Judaism: Proceedings
of the First Enoch Seminar, University of Michigan, Sesto Fiorentino, Italy,*

June 19-23, 2001 (ed. G. Boccaccini; *Henoch* 24; Torino: Silvio Zamorani Editore, 2002) 143-145

Tigchelaar, Eibert J. C. "A Cave 4 Fragment of Divre Mosheh (4QDM) and the Text of 1Q22 1:7-10 and Jubilees 1:9, 14," *DSD* 12 (2005) 303-12

Tigchelaar, Eibert J. C. "Jubilees *and* 1 Enoch and the Issue of Transmission of Knowledge," in *Enoch and Qumran Origins: New Light on a Forgotten Connection* (ed. Gabriele Boccaccini; Grand Rapids: Eerdmans, 2005) 99-101

Tiller, Patrick A. *A Commentary on the Animal Apocalypse of 1 Enoch* (SBLEJL 4; Atlanta: Scholars, 1993)

Tiller, Patrick A. "Israel at the Mercy of Demonic Powers: An Enochic Interpretation of Postexilic Imperialism," in *Conflicted Boundaries in Wisdom and Apocalypticism* (ed. Benjamin G. Wright III and Lawrence M. Wills; SBLSymS 30; Atlanta: SBL, 2005) 113-21

Ubigli, Liliana Rossa. "The Historical-Cultural Background of the Book of Jubilees," in *Enoch and Qumran Origins: New Light on a Forgotten Connection* (ed. Gabriele Boccaccini; Grand Rapids: Eerdmans, 2005) 137-40

Uhlig, Siegbert. *Das äthiopische Henochbuch* (JSHRZ 5/6; Gütersloh: Mohn, 1984)

VanderKam, James C. *Textual and Historical Studies in the Book of Jubilees* (HMS 14; Missoula, Mont.: Scholars Press, 1977)

VanderKam, James C. *Enoch and the Growth of an Apocalyptic Tradition* (CBQMS 16; Washington: CBA, 1984)

VanderKam, James C. *The Book of Jubilees* (2 vols.; CSCO 510-511; Louvain: Peeters, 1989)

VanderKam, James C. "The Jubilees Fragments from Qumran Cave 4," in *The Madrid Qumran Congress: Proceedings of the International Congress on the Dead Sea Scrolls, Madrid 18-21 March, 1991* (2 vols; ed. J. Trebolle Barrera and L. Vegas Montaner; Leiden: Brill, 1991) 2. 635-48

VanderKam, James C. "The Granddaughters and Grandsons of Noah," *RevQ* 16 (1994) 457-61

VanderKam, James C. *Enoch: A Man for All Generations* (Columbia: University of South Carolina Press, 1995)

VanderKam, James C. "The *Aqedah, Jubilees*, and PseudoJubilees," in *The Quest for Context and Meaning: Studies in Biblical Intertextuality in Honor of James A. Sanders* (ed. Craig A. Evans and Shemaryahu Talmon; BIS 28; Leiden: Brill, 1997) 241-61

VanderKam, James C. "The Origins and Purposes of the Book of Jubilees," in *Studies in the Book of Jubilees* (ed. Matthias Albani, Jörg Frey, and Armin Lange; TSAJ 65; Tübingen: Mohr Siebeck, 1997) 3-24

VanderKam, James C. "Isaac's Blessing of Levi and His Descendants in *Jubilees* 31," in *The Provo International Conference on the Dead Sea Scrolls:*

Technological Innovations, New Texts, and Reformulated Issues (ed. Donald W. Parry and Eugene C. Ulrich; STDJ 30; Leiden: Brill, 1999) 497-519

VanderKam, James C. "The Angel Story in the Book of Jubilees," in *Pseudepigraphic Perspectives: The Apocrypha and Pseudepigrapha in Light of the Dead Sea Scrolls: Proceedings of the [Second] International Symposium of the Orion Center for the Study of the Dead Sea Scrolls and Associated Literature, 12-14 January 1997* (ed. Esther G. Chazon and Michael E. Stone; STDJ 31; Leiden: Brill, 1999) 151-70

VanderKam, James C. "Biblical Interpretation in 1 Enoch and Jubilees," in *From Revelation to Canon: Studies in Hebrew Bible and Second Temple Literature* (JSJSup 62; Leiden: Brill, 2000) 276-304

VanderKam, James C. "Enoch Traditions in Jubilees and Other Second-Century Sources," in *From Revelation to Canon: Studies in Hebrew Bible and Second Temple Literature* (JSJSup 62; Leiden: Brill, 2000) 305-31

VanderKam, James C. "Genesis 1 in Jubilees 2," in *From Revelation to Canon: Studies in Hebrew Bible and Second Temple Literature* (JSJSup 62; Leiden: Brill, 2000) 500-21

VanderKam, James C. "Jubilees and Hebrew Texts of Genesis-Exodus," in *From Revelation to Canon: Studies in Hebrew Bible and Second Temple Literature* (JSJSup 62; Leiden: Brill, 2000) 448-61

VanderKam, James C. "Jubilees and the Priestly Messiah of Qumran," in *From Revelation to Canon: Studies in Hebrew Bible and Second Temple Literature* (JSJSup 62; Leiden: Brill, 2000) 462-75

VanderKam, James C. "Jubilees, the Book of," in *Encyclopedia of the Dead Sea Scrolls* (2 vols; ed. Lawrence H. Schiffman and James C. VanderKam; Oxford: Oxford University Press, 2000) 1. 434-38

VanderKam, James C. "*Jubilees*' Exegetical Creation of Levi the Priest," in *From Revelation to Canon: Studies in Hebrew Bible and Second Temple Literature* (JSJSup 62; Leiden: Brill, 2000) 545-62

VanderKam, James C. "Studies in the Chronology of the Book of Jubilees," in *From Revelation to Canon: Studies in Hebrew Bible and Second Temple Literature* (JSJSup 62; Leiden: Brill, 2000) 522-44

VanderKam, James. "Studies on the Prologue and Jubilees 1," in *For a Later Generation: The Transformation of Tradition in Israel, Early Judaism, and Early Christianity* (ed. Randal A. Argall, Beverly A. Bow, and Rodney A. Werline; Harrisburg, Pa.: Trinity Press International, 2000) 266-79

VanderKam, James C. "The Angel of the Presence in the *Book of Jubilees*," *DSD* 7 (2000) 378-93

VanderKam, James C. "The Putative Author of the Book of Jubilees," in *From Revelation to Canon: Studies in Hebrew Bible and Second Temple Literature* (JSJSup 62; Leiden: Brill, 2000) 439-47

VanderKam, James C. *The Book of Jubilees* (Sheffield: Sheffield Academic Press, 2001)

VanderKam, James C. "The Interpretation of Genesis in 1 Enoch," in *The Bible at Qumran: Text, Shape, and Interpretation* (ed. Peter W. Flint with the assistance of Tae-Hun Kim; Studies in the Dead Sea Scrolls and Related Literature; Grand Rapids: Eerdmans, 2001) 129-48

VanderKam, James C. "The Wording of Biblical Citations in Some Rewritten Scriptural Works," in *The Bible as a Book: The Hebrew Bible and the Judaean Desert Discoveries* (ed. Edward D. Herbert and Emanuel Tov; London: The British Library and Oak Knoll Press in association with The Scriptorium: Center for Christian Antiquities, 2002) 41-56

VanderKam, James C. "Anthropological Gleanings from the Book of Jubilees," in *Der Mensch vor Gott: Forschungen zum Menschenbild in Bibel, antikem Judentum und Koran: Festschrift für Hermann Lichtenberger zum 60. Geburtstag* (ed. Ulrike Mittmann-Richert, Friedrich Avemarie, and Gerbern S. Oegema, Neukirchen: Neukirchener Verlag, 2003) 117-31

VanderKam, James C. "Response to George Nickelsburg, '1 Enoch: A Commentary on the Book of 1 Enoch: Chapters 1-36; 81-108'," in *George W.E. Nickelsburg in Perspective: An Ongoing Dialogue of Learning* (2 vols; ed. Jacob Neusner and Alan J. Avery-Peck; JSJSup 80; Leiden: Brill, 2003) 2. 379-86

VanderKam, James C. "The Demons in the *Book of Jubilees*," in *Die Dämonen / Demons. The Demonology of Israelite-Jewish and Early Christian Literature in Context of their Environment* (ed. Armin Lange, Hermann Lichtenberger, and K. F. Diethard Romheld; Tübingen: Mohr Siebeck, 2003) 339-64

VanderKam, James C. *From Joshua to Caiaphas: High Priests after the Exile* (Minneapolis: Fortress, 2004)

VanderKam, James C. "Open and Closed Eyes in the Animal Apocalypse (1 Enoch 85-90)," in *The Idea of Biblical Interpretation: Essays in Honor of James L. Kugel* (ed. Hindy Najman and Judith H. Newman; JSJSup 83; Leiden: Brill, 2004) 279-92

VanderKam, James C. "Scripture in the Astronomical Book of Enoch," in *Things Revealed: Studies in Early Jewish and Christian Literature in Honor of Michael E. Stone* (ed. Esther Chazon, David Satran and Ruth Clements; JSJSupp 89; Leiden: Brill, 2004) 89-104

VanderKam, James C. "Reflection on Ideology and Date of the Apocalypse of Weeks," in *Enoch and Qumran Origins: New Light on a Forgotten Connection* (ed. Gabriele Boccaccini; Grand Rapids: Eerdmans, 2005) 162-70

VanderKam, James C. "Response: Jubilees and Enoch," in *Enoch and Qumran Origins: New Light on a Forgotten Connection* (ed. Gabriele Boccaccini; Grand Rapids: Eerdmans, 2005) 162-71

VanderKam, James C. "Sinai Revisited," in *Biblical Interpretation at Qumran* (ed. Matthias Henze; Studies in the Dead Sea Scrolls and Related Literature; Grand Rapids: Eerdmans, 2005) 44-60

VanderKam, James C. and J. Milik, "Jubilees," in *Qumran Cave 4.VIII Parabiblical Texts Part I* (ed. Harold Attridge et al.; DJD 13; Oxford: Clarendon, 1994) 1-185

Venter, Pieter M. "Spatiality in Enoch's Journeys (1 Enoch 12-36)," in *Wisdom and Apocalypticism in the Dead Sea Scrolls and in the Biblical Tradition* (ed. Florentino García Martínez; BETL 168; Leuven: Leuven University Press and Peeters, 2003) 211-30

Vermes, Geza. "Leviticus 18:21 in Ancient Jewish Bible Exegesis," in *Studies in Aggadah: Targum and Jewish Liturgy in Memory of Joseph Heinemann* (ed. J. J. Petuchowski and E. Fleischer; Jerusalem: Magnes Pr. and Hebrew Union College, 1981) 108-24

Vermes, Geza. "Genesis 1-3 in post-biblical Hebrew and Aramaic Literature before the Mishnah," *JJS* 43 (1992) 221-25

Wacholder, Ben Zion. "*Jubilees* as the Super Canon: Torah-Admonition versus Torah-Commandment," in *Legal Texts and Legal Issues: Proceedings of the Second Meeting of the International Organization for Qumran Studies, Cambridge, 1995: Published in Honour of Joseph M. Baumgarten* (ed. Moshe J. Bernstein, Florentino García Martínez, and John Kampen; STDJ 23; Leiden: Brill, 1997) 195-211

Wacker, Marie-Theres. "'Rettendes Wissen' im äthiopischen Henochbuch," in *Rettendes Wissen* (ed. Karl Löning; AOAT 300; Münster: Ugarit-Verlag, 2002) 115-54

Wassen, Cecilia. "The Story of Judah and Tamar in the Eyes of the Earliest Interpreters," *Literature and Theology* 8 (1994) 354-66

Werman, Cana. "*Jubilees* 30: Building a Paradigm for the Ban on Intermarriage," *HTR* 90 (1997) 1-22

Werman, Cana. "Qumran and the book of Noah," in *Pseudepigraphic Perspectives: The Apocrypha and Pseudepigrapha in Light of the Dead Sea Scrolls: Proceedings of the [Second] International Symposium of the Orion Center for the Study of the Dead Sea Scrolls and Associated Literature, 12-14 January 1997* (ed. Esther G. Chazon and Michael E. Stone; STDJ 31; Leiden: Brill, 1999) 171-81

Werman, Cana. "The Concept of Holiness and the Requirements of Purity in Second Temple and Tannaitic Literature," in *Purity and Holiness: The Heritage of Leviticus* (ed. M. J. H. M. Poorthuis and J. Schwartz; Jewish and Christian Perspectives Series 2; Leiden: Brill, 2000) 163-79

Wevers, John William. *Septuaginta: Vetus Testamentum Graecum I: Genesis* (Göttingen: Vandenhoeck und Ruprecht, 1974)

Wevers, John William. *Notes on the Greek Text of Genesis* (SBLSCS 35; Atlanta: Scholars, 1993)

Wintermute, O. S. "Jubilees," in *The Old Testament Pseudepigrapha* (2 vols; ed. James H. Charlesworth; New York: Doubleday, 1983, 1985) 2. 35-142

Wise, Michael O. "4QFlorilegium and the Temple of Adam," *RevQ* 15 (1991) 123-32

Wright, Archie T. *The Origin of Evil Spirits: The Reception of Genesis 6.1-4 in Early Jewish Literature* (WUNT 2.198; Tübingen: Mohr Siebeck, 2005)

Wright, Benjamin G., ed. *A Multiform Heritage: Studies on Early Judaism and Christianity in Honor of Robert A. Kraft* (Homage Series 24; Atlanta: Scholars, 1999)

Wright, Benjamin G. "Sirach and *1 Enoch*: Some Further Considerations," in *The Origins of Enochic Judaism: Proceedings of the First Enoch Seminar, University of Michigan, Sesto Fiorentino, Italy, June 19-23, 2001* (ed. G. Boccaccini; *Henoch* 24; Torino: Silvio Zamorani Editore, 2002) 179-87

Wright, Benjamin G. "Wisdom, Instruction, and Social Location in Sirach and *1 Enoch*," in *Things Revealed: Studies in Early Jewish and Christian Literature in Honor of Michael E. Stone* (JSJSupp 89; ed. Esther Chazon, David Satran and Ruth Clements; Leiden: Brill, 2004) 105-22

Wright, Benjamin G. "Ben Sira and the *Book of the Watchers* on the Legitimate Priesthood," in *Intertextual Studies in Ben Sira and Tobit* (ed. Jeremy Corley and Vincent Skemp; CBQMS 38; Washington, D.C.: Catholic Biblical Association, 2005) 241-54

Yarbro Collins, Adela. "The Theology of Early Enoch Literature," in *The Origins of Enochic Judaism: Proceedings of the First Enoch Seminar, University of Michigan, Sesto Fiorentino, Italy, June 19-23, 2001* (ed. G. Boccaccini; *Henoch* 24; Torino: Silvio Zamorani Editore, 2002) 107-12

Index of Modern Authors

Index of Ancient Sources

(reference to individual verses occurring in sequence in major discussions of chapters indicated in bold are not included)